INDIANS AND EUROPE

An Interdisciplinary Collection of Essays

INDIANS AND EUROPE

An Interdisciplinary Collection of Essays

Edited by Christian F. Feest

UNIVERSITY OF NEBRASKA PRESS
LINCOLN AND LONDON

© 1989 by Alsno Verlag/edition herodot
All rights reserved
Manufactured in the United States of America

⊗

First Nebraska paperback printing: 1999
Most recent printing indicated by the last digit below:
10   9   8   7   6   5   4   3   2   1

Library of Congress Cataloging-in-Publication Data
Indians and Europe: an interdisciplinary collection of essays / edited by Christian F. Feest.
p.   cm.
Originally published: Aachen, Germany: Edition Herodot, 1987.
Includes bibliographical references and index.
ISBN 0-8032-6897-1 (pbk.: alk. paper)
1. Indians of North America—Public opinion.   2. Public opinion—Europe.   3. Indians
of North America—Historiography.   4. Indians of North America—Pictorial works—
History.   I. Feest, Christian F.
E98.P99I53   1999
970′.00497—dc21
98-48153   CIP

Reprinted from the original 1989 edition by Alano Verlag/edition herodot, Aachen,
Germany.

CONTENTS

PREFACE

"Are there many Indians in Europe?"
(Ohio gas station attendant, filling up the car of European anthropologist who had mentioned his research interest in American Indians)

Americans (scholars and non-scholars alike) tend to be impressed by the substantial amount of popular interest in everything relating to North American Indians prevailing in many parts of Europe. Asked about the reasons for this strange fact, Europeans (scholars and non-scholars alike) tend to be a little puzzled themselves. The interest dates back to the time when Europe discovered to its own surprise that a "New World" blocked the direct westerly access to India, and the surprise has not much diminished since then. It is an interest that has found its expression in literature, in the visual arts, in music, and in politics, but perhaps most importantly in various aspects of popular culture.

On a scholarly level, the European fascination with American Indians has led to the existence of various traditions of related research often separated by boundaries of language and academic administration. In a sense, the present book is the outgrowth of an attempt to overcome these divisions. It was during the 1980 meeting of the European Association of American Studies in Amsterdam that a number of European students of the Indianist field first discovered their mutual existence and decided to keep in touch. It seems significant that an American, Wilcomb E. Washburn, was responsible for this truly Columbian event, because up to this point most contacts of the European scholars had been with their American colleagues rather than within Europe. Since 1980, this informal American Indian Workshop has held annual meetings usually organized around a single theme; it has published an equally informal *Newsletter* attempting to cover the European Indianist scene; and it is now beginning to publish its own journal, the *European Review of Native American Studies*. At about the same time, parallel efforts led to the publication of a collection of papers by Europeans in the North American Indian Studies field (Hovens 1981), to be followed later by a second volume (Hovens 1984). When late in 1981 I was asked by Edition Herodot, the publisher of the Hovens volumes, to submit plans for a follow-up volume to the series, I suggested "Indians and Europe" as a suitable theme for such a project. Not only would such a book contribute to an explanation of the European preoccupation with Native Americans/Indians, but it would also help to outline that vast field of research ideally suited for European students with Native American-related research interests. All too often, it seemed, time and effort was wasted on studies for which sources were only insufficiently available in Europe - more often than not because the potential for research on sources that were available was not fully appreciated. Who else but European scholars should be qualified to assess the importance of and finally make available the many important pieces of information on North

1

American Indians/Native Americans hidden from general view in European repositories? Who if not the Europeans would be able to read and recognize the importance of records written in odd and exotic languages (which for the majority of North American Indianists still includes everything that is not just English).

As soon as the idea had been accepted by the publisher, it was suggested to the American Indian Workshop during its 1982 Paris meeting that the 1984 Rome workshop should be devoted to "Indians and Europe." Versions of just over a third of the papers included in the present volume were consequently read and discussed not far from the Colosseum in which the Indians of Buffalo Bill's show had pitched their tipis almost a hundred years ago. Most of the papers prepared for Rome and all of the other ones now published were specifically commissioned for this book.

In planning Indians and Europe, efforts were made to achieve several balances at once: it seemed desirable to have as many countries as possible represented by at least one author, to cover all periods from the 16th to the 20th centuries, to include approaches from many different branches of the academic enterprise, and to deal more or less evenly with the major aspects of the question. It was also clear from the outset that the focus on European scholarship could not mean a total avoidance of American colleagues. The number of authors actually asked to contribute (but also of papers promised by prospective contributors) was substantially bigger than the one now included. Some of the ultimate imbalances (such as the lack of any Scandinavian contribution) are the result of the inevitable reduction of plans to reality. Still, the final selection is varied enough, and if many contributions reflect something of the emotional relationship typical of the popular European interest in American Indians, it becomes in itself a document of it.

The absence of contributions by Native American authors to this book may require a brief explanation. Despite the fact that many of them would have been able to discuss their views of or experiences in Europe, "Indians and Europe" is dealing more specifically with European views of this relationship, with images that are part of the Old World's cultural heritage. In those instances in which Native American visitors seem to offer their opinions on Europe and the Europeans (especially some of Catlin's and Buffalo Bill's Indians as described in this volume), there is reason to believe that either they themselves or those who wrote or spoke for them, stood firmly in a European tradition. A quick glance in the other direction is afforded by R.D.Theisz's essay dealing with references to foreigners in Lakota war songs, from which it may be gleaned that Native American views of Europeans also follow stereotypic, howbeit different, patterns.

No untertaking of the proportions of this book would be conceivable without the energy, dedication, and patience of many people. First and foremost praise must be heaped on the authors of the papers that follow, most of whom met

2

all the deadlines set by the editor only to find out that the project was ultimately delayed by almost two years. While some of the authors were involved with the project from its very beginning, others joined at various stages of progress. Those of the first hour deserve credit for their patience, those who came later for their extra effort to catch up with the rest. Thanks are also due to the authors who are not represented in this volume. Some of them spent much time in researching and drafting papers that were either not what the editor had been looking for, or that were never written. In most cases, however, their work though unpublished and sometimes unwritten will in some ways be reflected in the book.

No book could exist without a publisher. The present book has even two publishers. As mentioned above, it was through the active interest of Edition Herodot, represented by M.K.Ramaswamy, that the project was moved from the dreaming to the planning stage. At a critical juncture for the volume, Edition Herodot entered into an agreement of cooperation with Rader Verlag, and moved its operations from Göttingen to Aachen. It was Wendelin Rader who finally revived the initial enthusiasm and thereby helped to produce a book that will hopefully please both its readers and its authors.

This is not the first book to be written on this general subject matter, and it does not claim to be the one that will obliterate the necessity for further books on "Indians and Europe." Quite to the contrary, the editor will consider the book a success if it contributes to the stimulation of the additional work that is so obviously needed.

C.F.Feest

REFERENCES CITED

Hovens, Pieter (ed.)
  1981   North American Indian Studies. European Contributions. Göttingen: Edition Herodot.
  1984   North American Indian Studies 2. European Contributions. Society and Art. Göttingen: Edition Herodot.

THE WILD MAN AND THE INDIAN IN
EARLY 16TH CENTURY BOOK ILLUSTRATION

Susi Colin

Soon after Columbus' letter containing the news of the discovery of new islands reached Gabriel Sanchez, treasurer to the Spanish king, copies were sent to Europe's important centers of learning and trade. The news was passed on to printers, who busied themselves with the task of informing a larger reading public of the sensational findings across the Atlantic Ocean. These earliest printed reports of the New World, the 17 editions of Columbus' letters, the numerous editions of Vespucci's accounts and more voluminous works by a variety of travelers[1] did not only verbally inform the reader of the magnificent new lands and their savage inhabitants, but were also illustrated. Astoundingly, many accounts depicted the natives of these remote regions, whom only a handful of Europeans had actually seen.[2]

One might wonder what these early images were like, considering they were rendered at a time when European artists hardly had the chance to study American Indians in person. For the most part, they were largely ethnographically incorrect as the only source of information of any kind for the illustrators in the years following the Discovery were the very texts they were illustrating themselves.[3] William C. Sturtevant has pointed out that the nature of the source material available to a contemporary artist portraying what has not yet previously been known, determines the degree of accuracy in the images he produces. In this case, personal visual observation of life models is most meaningful, followed by depictions derived from first hand visual observation, and lastly items brought over to Europe from America such as costumes, decorations, and weapons led to some accuracy in certain detail. The sources that are more misleading, which might generate inaccurate depictions are verbal sources, written or oral, and hearsay, which formed the most significant complex of source material for the contemporary illustrator in this early period (Sturtevant 1976:417ff).

The predicament of the sixteenth century illustrator facing the task of visualizing peoples he had never seen or even heard of before, is in a way analogous to that of a twentieth century colleague asked to portray living beings that may be found in outer space. Assume that such a modern day illustrator had never seen a photograph of the alien beings but was only provided with a description, in all likelihood our space age contemporary artist would probably look for inspiration in the imaginary world of space-movies and cartoons. From all the available fantastic images he would probably select that particular type of space creature or Mars monster that would - with some alterations - best fit the image evoked by the verbal description. The Renaissance artist confronted with much the same problem attempts an analogous

5

solution, seeking models in the pictorial tradition of strange races and monsters and selecting the one that he associates most with the image evoked by the descriptions. However, the early explorers themselves could hardly see the peoples who inhabited the new lands across the Atlantic through a lens unclouded by European cultural prejudice and the values of Christian dogma. If the eye-witnesses of the New World themselves were unable to report their experiences in an objective way (cp., e.g., Quinn 1976:635ff), what could illustrators lacking direct visual information, who drew from these first hand accounts replete with preconceptions and misinterpretations do, but make associations with images anchored in their own tradition, images that the discoverers themselves seemed to call for.

Nevertheless we should refrain from dismissing these early portrayals of American Indians, however inaccurate, as mere fantasy products.[4] To do so would imply the application of twentieth century scientific standards to a time, when science based on "pure" objective observation was slowly being developed, from which the precepts of modern ethnology and ethnography were not to evolve for centuries (see Rowe 1964). A twentieth century artist borrowing from popular images of space men is aware of the fact that he is dealing with products of the imagination. However, an illustrator in the sixteenth century, who drew upon traditional visual material pertaining to strange peoples and even monstrous races often was not. He most probably believed in the existence of giants, of pygmies, cynocephali, and skiapods. After all, they were cited by authoritative classical sources, ancient Greek and Roman authors, and were incorporated in the hierarchy of creatures by none other than the early Church Fathers and Christian philosophers, such as Augustinus and Isidore of Seville.[5] Even after more than fifty years of exploration in the New World, and increasing contacts with foreign peoples in various parts of the globe, monsters and creatures half human, half animal still haunted serious scientific works of the time. François Descerpz claimed that his *Recueil de la diuersité des habits*, printed in 1562 and reprinted with closely copied woodcuts by Sluiperius in 1572, was "worked after nature." It provides us with a quite accurate depiction of Brazilian Tupinamba Indians; however, it also includes various monsters.

But what were the iconographic traditions used by the illustrators of the early sixteenth century to depict the exotic inhabitants of the new lands in the West? Surprisingly enough, they mainly did not draw upon previously established visual forms of extra-European exotic peoples. Instead they focused on a more familiar creature, one who had become extremely popular in the art and literature of the preceding century, the Wild Man.[6]

Wild Men have long been a traditional motif in European art and folklore. Their history reaches well back to fauns, centaurs, satyrs, and the gods Silenus and Silvanus of Antiquity, the lower strata of gods and demi-gods of the Graeco-Roman pantheon, creatures, who roamed the woods and gardens, also the fertility gods and the patrons of plants and animals.

Inhabiting the vague zone between the world of man and the animal kingdom, the Wild Man reveals his bestiality by a shaggy growth of hair covering his entire human body, excepting only his face, hands, knees and elbows. His female counterpart is described as having breasts, that are so misshapen that she carries them over her shoulders while running - although her hideousness is ignored for the most part by the artists, who preferred to depict her as a beautiful but hairy maiden (Bernheimer 1952:93-98). Wild Folk are depicted as going about unclothed, although at times their nakedness is mediated by some sparse foliage wound around their loins. The Wild Man often carries a tree trunk or a club used either as walking stick or weapon. He is of enormous physical strength and sometimes is portrayed as giant in size. However, he is also shown as a dwarf and is said to be able to alter his size at will. Hairiness, nakedness, and the tree trunk or club are the attributes of the Wild Man and may serve as a means of iconographic identification, although any of these attributes may be absent (Husband 1980:1f, Bernheimer 1952:1-15).

Shying away from human contact like a wild animal despite his enormous physical strength, chosing his abode in the remotest and wildest part of the forest to lead a life as a hunter and gatherer without the knowledge of agriculture and even the crudest form of technology, the Wild Man stands apart from civilized human society. His unabated aggressiveness, his unreasonable outbursts of anger, expressed often in the uprooting of trees, and his violence directed against animals and trespassers of his territory (in fact, when Wild Men gathered a fierce battle was inevitable) in combination with his inability to communicate through speech, brought him in close relation to the spiritual stature of animals and lunatics, both of whom were believed to be devoid of reason. Throughout the Middle Ages and well into the eighteenth century wildness and insanity were interchangeable concepts. Madness was not understood as a psychological or mental disease or disorder, but rather as a social condition - as a fall from grace. Insanity as well as wildness were regarded as the result of the liberation of the animal forces in all of us, however tamed, i.e. repressed by the norms and necessities as determined by the Christian ethos (Husband 1980:4ff, Bernheimer 1952:9ff; cf.Foucault 1973:71-79). The Wild Man becomes wild, not because he is created that way, but rather because of his hostile environment, his being raised in the wilderness, the hardness of his life, and his lack of reason.

The condition of wildness, however, is curable by acculturation. At this point it is interesting to consider the argument presented in the struggle for the abolition of Indian slavery in the first half of the sixteenth century in Spain. This controversy centered basically on whether or not the American Indians were in the Aristotelian sense, slaves by nature. If they were, then, as Sepulveda believed, they were above all, devoid of reason and consequently inferior to their European masters. If they were not, as Las Casas was convinced, their state of wildness was reversible by a slow process of acculturation, with particular emphasis on being initiated into the mysteries of the True Religion (Hanke 1949:esp.ch.VIII, 1959; O'Gorman 1941, Gómez Canedo 1966). Although the traditional Wild Man played no role in this discussion, the similarity of the preconceived image of the Indian and the Wild Man leads to a self evident analogy. However, in the case of the traditional Wild Man, the process of acculturation was not performed by patient friars bringing the word of God into the wilderness, but rather with the help of a metaphorical image, a beautiful maiden, who tames the Wild Man by the power of love (Bernheimer 1952:125f, Husband 1980:9).

The theme of the taming of the Wild Man was very popular throughout the century preceding the Discovery, treated in many literary works and depicted as a moralizing theme on the love chests and wedding coffrets of the time (Bernheimer 1952:123f, Husband 1980:114). Nevertheless, curing both wildness and insanity was impossible without the grace of God and the knowledge and acceptance of the True Faith, which inevitably leads the Wild Man back to a civilized way of life. In some cases he could even attain the stature of a holy man, as in the legend of Saint Chrysostomos. Chrysostomos, a pope, who frustrated about his inability to save the soul of a child wailing in purgatory, flees into the wilderness to lead an ascetic life. There he slowly changes into a Wild Man. Although resistant at the outset, he is overwhelmed by sensual desire, and rapes a princess, who seeks shelter at his rock. Overcome with guilt and dread, he kills the girl. Fortunately God performs a miracle, the girl and her child are saved miraculously, he finds his way back to a civilized life and eventually becomes a Saint (Husband 1980:107ff; on the legend cp.Williams 1925,1935).

The legend of Chrysostomos reveals yet another aspect of the Wild Man's brutish qualities, his untamed and uncontrolled sexual appetite. The Wild Man is pureported to frequently abduct beautiful maidens, whom he holds captive in the wilderness, until a fearless knight arrives to rescue her. Sexual lust is also found in his female counterpart. Disguised as a pretty maiden, the Wild Woman tries to seduce any man who crosses her path. Her ugliness, however, is only revealed during sexual intercourse (Bernheimer 1952:34f). Uncontrolled desire also typifies the culinary habits of the Wild Man. He is always hungry, consuming in bulk wild berries, roots, and uncooked meat - a custom closely associated with bestiality (Bernheimer 1952:9, Lévi-Strauss 1975:285ff). He eats at all times of the day and the night, and if the opportunity arises he will devour humans with great relish, although he prefers young infants who are not yet baptised (Bernheimer 1952:23).

Thus the Wild Man embodies the antithesis of the values of Christian civilization. If Christian man could not define what he meant by civilization in positive terms, he could point at the Wild Man and describe what it was not.

8

In his ungodliness, his animality, his inability to control his desires and to civilize his lust in marriage, his lack of speech and reason, he reifies the subconscious fears of civilized European society itself. He stands as a warning of what might happen once the ways of Christianity are abandoned (Bernheimer 1952:3f, Husband 1980:4f), he played just the role the American Indian as Ignoble Savage was to play in seventeenth century colonial America (Sheehan 1980:esp.ch.2,3).

The American Indian described in the earliest published reports following the discovery of the New World shares quite a number of qualities characteristic of the Wild Man of European literary and pictorial tradition. The relationship of the Wild Man of the paradisaic islands across the Atlantic, so enthusiastically described by Columbus, to the Wild Man roaming the forests in Europe, becomes obvious in the more prosaic descriptions of Vespucci.

Vespucci's letters were exceedingly popular all over Europe; printed in numerous translations and included in big literary compilations as well as reproduced in broadsheets. Although Vespucci reveals a remarkable matter of fact attitude in his reportage of the unfamiliar customs of the Indians and often is astoundingly cautious in terms of moralizing compared to some of his contemporaries,[7] he somehow still evokes in his readers just the prejudices and preconceptions he wishes to avoid.

Vespucci's "subconscious" prejudice becomes obvious in the *Mundus Novus*, in his description of the physical appearance of the natives. He repeatedly reports their nakedness while trying to emphasize their similarity to the European body type:

"They have indeed large square built bodies, well formed and proportioned, and in color verging upon reddish" (Levillier 1951:302), "... and I believe that if they went clothed, they would be like ourselves" (Levillier 1951:311).

A description, that certainly leaves no doubt that the Indians did not bear the monstrous features of the Wild Man. The Indian women, although as libidinous as the Wild Woman, do not share her ugliness:

"They have bodies which are tolerably beautiful and cleanly. Nor are they so unsightly as one perchance might imagine; for as much they are plump, their ugliness is the less apparent, which indeed is for the most part concealed by the excellence of their bodily structure. It was to us a matter of astonishment that none was to be seen among them who had flabby breasts" (Levillier 1951:303).

This was certainly a noteworthy observation, considering the preconceived Wild Woman image would have pictured her as a truly horrifying creature with her shrivelled body and long flabby breasts. New World women were observed

Fig. 1. "De flore pulchro." Engraving by Israel van Meckenem (1500-1503), Washington, DC, National Gallery of Art.

Fig. 2. Title page of the Rostock edition of the *Mundus Novus* printed by Hermann Barkhusen (1505). London, British Museum.

to be distinctively beautiful and Vespucci also noted with bewilderment that they even kept their fine bodies after childbirth. It was only in the seventeenth century that a depiction of the American woman appeared that represents her as the witch-like creature of the European imagination.[8]

In his *Lettera* sent to Piero Soderini in 1504 Vespucci becomes even more precise in his attempt to make clear, that the Indians were not Wild Men, as he stresses their hairlessness, and even their disgust for body hair:

"They have no hair at all on the body, except long and black hair on the head, especially the woman, which renders them beautiful. ... They do not let any hair [grow] on the eyebrows [nor] in the eyelashes, nor in any other place [whatsoever], exception made for the hair of the head, for they hold hair to be something ugly" (Levillier 1951:311).

Nevertheless hairiness is not necessarily a primary physical attribute of the Wild Man. In fact in the Middle Ages and the Renaissance artists had at times given up portraying this feature. An engraving by Israel van Meckenem executed between 1500 and 1503 shows eight Wild Folk tussling among the leaves of a floral ornament; all of them are hairless (Fig. 1). Two members of

10

the lower group are armed with crude, knotty clubs made from tree trunks. Another Wild Man sits astride a rather long branch at the bottom of the picture, aiming an arrow at the buttocks of another Wild Man trying to escape. The weapons depicted in this engraving appear in numerous other Wild Man scenes. Their weapons and also the fact that they do battle without the protection of body armor agrees with Vespucci's description of the Indians:

"Their weapons are bows and arrows, and when they advance to war they cover no part of their bodies for the sake of protection, so like beasts they are in this matter" (Levillier 1951:303).

In the *Lettera* he describes these weapons in more detail, explaining, that although they are well wrought, they are still primitive because of the natives' lack of iron for cutting edges, for which the Indians have fashioned sharpened fish-bones or fire hardened wooden points. He also makes note of another weapon, the war clubs, which have knobs, "of most excellent workmanship" (Levillier 1951:311), an advanced form of the European Wild Man's tree trunk.

Fig. 3. Diagram depicting the geographic position of the Indians in regard to that of the Europeans from Jan van Doesborch, *Van der niewer werelt* (1506-1510). Courtesy of the John Carter Brown Library at Brown University, Providence, RI.

11

The *Rostock* edition of Vespucci's *Mundus Novus* printed by Hermann Barkhusen in 1505 has a woodcut on the title page which depicts a naked couple (Fig. 2) clearly identifiable as Wild Folk, but meant to represent the inhabitants of the New World.[9] The hairlessness of the figures and the long flowing hair of the woman fit Vespucci's description perfectly, nevertheless, the illustration still retains the iconographic tradition of the Wild Man theme. Hairiness, this prominent feature of the traditional Wild Man, was only incorporated twice in sixteenth century illustrations of the American Indian. In some of the woodcuts accompanying Hans Staden of Homburg's narrative of his captivity by the Tupinamba in Brazil, printed in Marburg in 1557, some Indians are depicted with body hair, although they were designed after Staden's own drawings or under his supervision (Staden 1557, Sturtevant 1976:433). Staden, who does not mention in his text that his captors were hairy, may have been ignored by the designer of the woodcuts, although most probably, the lines were meant to indicate body paint. Nevertheless, in Theodor de Bry's edition of Hans Staden's narrative in the third part of his *Great Voyages* of 1592, these lines were interpreted as hair (de Bry 1592).

Fig. 4. Two Wild Couples representing Indians from Jan van Doesborch, *Van der nieuwer werelt* (1506-1510). Woodcut, Courtesy of the John Carter Brown Library at Brown University, Providence, RI.

12

Fig. 5. Fighting Wild Men respresenting Indians from Jan van Doesborch, *Van der nieuwer werelt* (1506-1510). Woodcut, Courtesy of the John Carter Brown Library at Brown University, Providence, RI.

A comparison of the figures in the Meckenem engraving to those of the *Rostock* title page reveals that the bow and the arrow that the Wild Man shakes at the woman, are by no means a deviation from traditional Wild Man iconography (as erroneously assumed by Quinn 1976:642), nor are they unlike the Indian weapons as described in the text.

The erotic contents of the scene on the *Rostock* title page, in which the woman holds the nipple of her breast between her fingers, a gesture common to erotic depictions, and the depiction of the man wielding bow and arrow, an allusion to the love god Cupid, also common to Wild Man imagery (Gloria Gilmore-House in Husband 1980:142), indicates that the woodcut might have previously been used in another context. The eroticism of the scene does not contradict the supposition that the figures were meant to represent American Indians. The liberal sexual behavior of the natives, their promiscuity, the lasciviousness of the women, who even applied venomenous insects to enlarge the sexual organs of their partners (which sometimes proved fatal; Vespucci after Levillier 1951:302), was noted with a mixture of disgust and envy by the European observers. Vespucci writes:

"They marry as many wives as they please: and son cohabits with mother,

Fig. 6. Scene from Grüninger, *Diß büchlin saget,* Strassburg (1509) depicting the clubbing of a young member of Vespucci's crew. Woodcut, New York Public Library, Rare Book Division.

Fig. 7. Wolfdietrich meets Rauhe Else, from *Das Heldenbuch mit synen figuren* printed by Johann Knoblouch in Strassburg (1509). New York Public Library, Print Division.

brother with sister, male cousin with female, and any man with the first woman he meets. They dissolve marriages as often as they please. ... The women as I have said are very libidinous... When they had the opportunity of copulating with Christians, urged by excessive lust, they defiled and promiscuted themselves" (Levillier 1951:303).

Two woodcuts showing a similar scene appear in the Dutch translation of the *Mundus Novus* published by Jan van Doesborch in Antwerp between 1506 and 1510. On the title page, repeated on fol. 6 verso is a triangular diagram depicting the geographical position of New World inhabitants in relation to Europe following Vespucci's description precisely[10] (Fig. 3). The Europeans, identifiable by their dress, occupy the segment at the top, while the Indians, in the vertical rectangle at the left are represented as a Wild Couple.

The iconographical meaning of this scene, in which a woman reaches out for a bow that her companion is offering her is of minor importance, and is probably a refined and altered version of a diagram after Vespucci, which appears in a booklet containing miscellaneous news, printed in 1505 or 1506 (Anonymous c.1505-1506). What is significant is that it was especially designed

14

for the *Mundus Novus* clearly demonstrating the identification of the American Indian with the Wild Man.

More evidence can be found in the two text illustrations of the *Mundus Novus* that van Doesborch certainly used the Wild Man imagery to depict Indians. The first, on fol. 3 recto, shows two Wild Couples (Fig. 4). The group in the center consists of a man and a woman in exactly the same pose as in the diagram, except that the wild man presents his bow and hides his arrow behind his back. It seems most likely that the same model was used for this group as well as the one in the diagram. However, in the text-illustration, the woman is flanked by another man carrying a knotty club, who points at her as if to offer his mate to the man on the right, who is flanked by yet another woman who looks on. This scene might have been chosen for its erotic allusion. The text that appears below the woodcut discusses the lecherousness of Indian women and the propensity of Indian men to have sexual intercourse with any woman regardless whether she is a close relative or not.

The second woodcut in this work shows two groups of naked Wild Men aiming their arrows at each other (Fig. 5). The aggressive character of this scene fits well with the description that appears below the illustration. Here, Vespucci explicates the technique of Indian warfare, a technique, which because of the lack of any recognizable battle plan and leaders, must have appeared similar to the aimless and chaotic battling of the Wild Man:

Fig. 8. Wild Woman fighting a dragon abducting a child from a German antiphonary. Manuscript illumination (about 1500). The Pierpont Morgan Library, New York.

15

"The nations wage war upon one another without art or order" (Levillier 1951:303).

Barkhusen's and Doesborch's woodcuts were certainly inspired by Wild Man imagery, although it is possible, that the blocks themselves were recycled from some other context related to the traditional Wild Man theme, excepting the diagram, which was especially designed for the edition. The German translation of Vespucci's *Lettera, Diß büchlin saget...* (Vespucci 1509), published by Johannes Grüninger in Strassburg in 1509, contains three illustrations in the text that were especially designed for the edition - a standard practise in Grüninger's workshop (Kristeller 1888:7f).[11] They depict various episodes from Vespucci's narrative. Although it cannot be denied that Grüninger's illustrations do not count among the ethnographically correct portrayals of American Indians, they were certainly designed to closely follow Vespucci's descriptions in the text.

Two of the woodcuts contained in this booklet deal with a rather sensational and gruesome aspect of Indian life (repeatedly remarked on by Vespucci and

Fig. 9. Woodcut depicting the customs of the Indians from Grüninger, *Diß büchlin saget*, Strassburg (1509). Woodcut, New York Public Library, Rare Book Division.

Fig. 10. Woodcut of a cynocephalus, believed to inhabit South America from *Aggivnta alla qvarta parte* printed by Alessandro Vecchio in Venice (1623). New York Public Library, Print Division.

16

Fig. 11. Woodcut of a cynocephalus butcher shop from Lorenz Fries, *Uslegung der Carta Marina* printed by Grüninger in Strassburg (1527). Woodcut, New York Public Library, Rare Book Division.

other eye witnesses with great shock) namely their cannibalism, a custom shared also by the traditional Wild Man. The illustration that appears on fol. E 4 verso (Fig. 6) depicts the tragic death of a young crew member during the third voyage. Vespucci narrates that in an attempt to establish contact with a group of Indians, who previously had been quite shy, a young man was sent out to meet a group of women who had appeared on the shore. As he came nearer to them, the women encircled him. They gazed at him with awe and even touched him with astonishment. However, the unwary sailor was being ambushed, attacked from behind by a woman wielding a club, who felled him with one stroke. Their mates, who had been in hiding rushed onto the beach and fired a shower af arrows at the landing party. The sailors fled to the safety of their ships, from where they observed their comrade's body being dragged into a cave in the rocks. In the following days his shipmates could only observe the natives roasting and feasting on their friend. Frustrated in their inability to respond to this gruesome act, the shocked Europeans aboard the ships were further taunted by the flagrant exhibition of pieces of human flesh that the Indians gnawed on.

In the foreground, Grüninger's woodcut shows the man being met by the women and then lured into the trap; and also the woman swinging her club. In the background another group of natives is shown in joyful anticipation of the

17

expectant meal while the corpse disappears into the cave. This woodcut as a whole is not based upon traditional Wild Man imagery, although the figures of the natives themselves seem to indicate such an allusion. However, in an edition of *Das Heldenbuch mit synen figuren* published in the same year in Strassburg by Johann Knoblouch there appears a woodcut in the *Epic of Wolfdietrich* that bears a certain compositional resemblance of the group of Indian women surrounding the unlucky crewman.

In this woodcut (Fig. 7) the native woman touching the young sailor is replaced by a hairy wild woman, Rauhe Else, who reaches out for Wolfdietrich with whom she has fallen in love. He offers her his hand, although taking the precaution of keeping his other hand in easy reach of his sword. The Wolf-dietrich story ultimately ends on a happy note, although in the course of the tale he is temporarily changed into a wild man, who is reduced to crawling on all fours under the influence of Else. But as so often is the case in fantastic and allegorical literature, a miracle occurs: Wolfdietrich's human status is restored and Else, after having bathed in the Fountain of Youth is turned into a beautiful princess.[12]

It would be difficult to find a model in Wild Women pictorial tradition for the Indian woman who clubs the European to death. Wild Women were generally portrayed as rather docile, domestically oriented figures (Bernheimer 1952:39). Nevertheless she was sometimes depicted attacking wild animals and monsters, as is the case in a marginal illumination of a German antiphonary dating from about 1500 (Fig. 8). Here she wields her club in an attack on a dragon, whom she also holds by the tail. However, her fierce behavior comes in the defense of a child, whom the monster tries to carry away.

In Grüninger's *Diß büchlin saget* the woodcut illustrating the chapter captioned *von irē leben und sitten* ('of their lives and customs') is a visual synopsis of the brutish and strange customs of the natives described in the following pages (Fig. 9). In the foreground we see a group of natives, two men and a woman holding a child on her lap, engaged in conversation. Another native standing to the right is shown emptying his bladder. "They are a people neat and clean of person owing to the constant washing they practice," writes Vespucci. "When, begging your pardon, they evacuate the bowels, they do everything to avoid being seen; and just in this they are clean and modest, the more dirty and shameless they are in making water (both men and women). Because even while talking to us, they let fly such filth, without turning around or showing shame, that in this they have no modesty" (Levillier 1951:312).

In the background of the same cut an Indian woman stands in front of two rather European looking huts. She is waiting for a native butcher to finish the gruesome job of chopping up a human arm. In addition a human hand and leg are shown on his butcher block. This scene is directly derived from Vespucci, who evokes the impression that human flesh is a common part of their diet:

"... for they eat one another, the victor the vanquished, and among other kinds of meat human flesh is a common article of their diet with them.

"... I knew a man whom I also spoke to, who was reputed to have eaten more than three hundred human bodies... I say further, they themselves wonder why we do not eat our enemies and do not use as food their flesh, which they say is most savory" (Levillier 1951:303).

The scene of a cannibal butchershop is of some interest in that a similar scene appears in Lorenz Fries's *Uslegung der Carta Marina*, also from Grüninger's press, published in 1525 and reissued in 1527 and 1530. Fries's book is a compilation of descriptive essays arranged in alphabetical order on remote, unfamiliar places and peoples as well as those close to home.

The chapter on cannibals in the 1525 and 1527 edition is illustrated with a woodcut that shows cynocephali (Fig. 10), a race of dog-headed monsters, originally believed to inhabit some part of India. In a kind of open air butchershop a cynocephalus is depicted cutting up a human leg on a crude table made from rough hewn wooden beams. A female, overwhelmed by hunger reaches out for the raw flesh. Another cynocephalus nearby looks on gnawing at an arm, while a fourth approches from the left with a camel laden with another victim. From an overhead rack hang human arms and legs, a sight which Vespucci also reports in his *Mundus Novus*:

"... And I likewise remained twenty-seven days in a certain city where I saw salted human flesh suspended from beams between the houses, just as with us it is the custom to hang pork" (Levillier 1951:303).

The image of human body parts hanging in the smoke, suspended to dry, or roasting on a grill must have been dramatically emblazoned on the European imagination: for this image was to become one of the major iconographical attributes of the American Indian in the sixteenth century.

However, the similiarity of the two woodcuts and the analogy of American man-eaters and cynocephali goes beyond compositional similiarities and the mere sharing of attributes, because in the *Uslegung* the oriental monsters represent the occidental cannibals:

"The cannibals are a ferocious and loathsome people, dog-headed, so that one shudders looking at them. And they inhabit an island, which Christoffel Dauber [Christopher Columbus (S.C.)] of Jamia [Genoa (S.C.)] discovered some years ago. ... The cannibals go about naked, except that they adorn themselves with parrot feathers of many colors... This people likes nothing better to eat than human flesh, and therefore they go to the surrounding islands frequently during the year to catch people."[13]

Although astonishing, the choice of cynocephali for this illustration makes sense, because it adheres closely to the text as do the scenes in Grüninger's *Diß büchlin saget*.

However, Fries was not the only printer in the early sixteenth century, who relocated cynocephali in the New World. Another woodcut in a German book containing descriptions of the nations of the world also identified the dog-headed people with New World cannibals. The book only survives in a reprint in Italian translation of 1623 entitled *Aggivnta alla quarta parte delle Indie de Sig.Giovanni Botero*. However, the German original was convincingly dated by Oakeshott (1960) about one hundred years earlier. On fol. A 2 verso it shows a cynocephalus depicted with horse-like legs (Fig. 10). According to the text on the opposing page, this creature was mentioned by Pliny in his *Historia Naturalis* and, as later verified in reports of the discoveries, inhabits the region of Santa Cruz in the New World. These monsters, the text continues, make their living from theft and eat human flesh like the people in Brazil, who despite their human skins are similar to these animals in all their attitudes.[14]

These are the only two instances in the sixteenth century which I have come across, in which occidental Indian tribes were actually identified with the

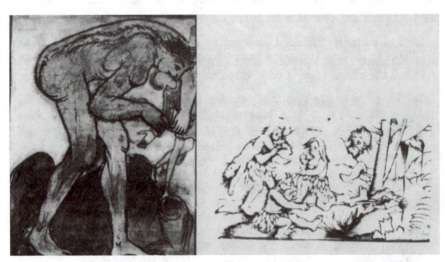

Fig. 12. Man-eating giant. Manuscript illumination. Eleventh century. London, British Library. Cotton Ms. Tiberius B.V.vil i.

Fig. 13. Cannibals in feathered dress from a woodcut map in Lorenz Fries, *Ptolemy* printed by Grüninger in Strassburg (1522). New York Public Library, Rare Book Division.

20

Fig. 14. Woodcut of Brazilians from Lorenz Fries, *Uslegung der Carta Marina* printed by Grüninger in Strassburg (1527). New York Public Library, Rare Book Division.

traditional oriental cynocephali. The existence of these images demonstrates, that reports of man-eaters in America could lead to such far flung association. In any event, for a contemporary of the sixteenth century there was no doubt that the new found peoples, whether entirely human or dog-headed, were indeed monstrous in their habits, although not necessarily in physical appearance.

In many works in the tradition of the oriental wonders, the *Alexander Romance* and the *Marvels of the East*, the image of the Wild Man serves an unique iconographic function in that the descriptive contents of the text do not always match up with the accompanying illustrations. For instance, these texts do not report the existence of a hairy creature in the remote Orient. Nevertheless, an eleventh century English manuscript containing the *Marvels of the East* depicts a man-eating giant, who exhibits this physical trait (Fig. 12).[15] In disregard to the descriptive caption below the illumination, the monster is depicted as hairy, indicated by a mane of hair growing along his spine and arms. In all likelihood it was amended by the illuminator, who, probably wishing to emphasize the brutish character of the otherwise human looking monster, added hairiness as a physical attribute (Husband 1980: 40f). In fact, this illumination is an early example of what was to become common practice later on. Wild Men were often interpolated in the illustrations of

21

these texts, although they were often totally inconsistent with the narrative contents.

Hairiness, which by the twelfth century becomes a visual indicator of a savage and unruly nature was often associated with exotic but otherwise human races: however clearly to be distinguished from truly physically aberrant creatures. In the century preceding the Discovery the substitution of the figure of the Wild Man for the savage and exotic races in illustrated travel literature simply reflected the medieval civilized Christian's view of native barbaric' people (Husband 1980:52).

By the end of the fifteenth century this view, so clearly reflected in Doesborch's and Barkhusen's illustrations of the *Mundus Novus*, as well as the *Uslegung* and the *Aggivnta* was slowly changing. The increasing interest during the Renaissance in natural phenomena sparked an increasing degree of attention to natural detail in the visual arts. The invention of the study of the perspective, and the study of human and animal anatomy and plants, also resulted in a more thorough examination of the sources available for a more accurate depiction of exotic peoples (Pochat 1970:97; for a survey of the periods, see chapters V, VI, and VII). Consequently hairiness as well as dog-headedness, which was never reported as existing in the New World by eyewitnesses, ceased to be or was never again utilized in depictions of exotic races in America.[16] However, we should not forget that even relatively enlightened travelers like the friar André Thevet, who visited the New World in the middle of the century expressed astonishment that Indians were not as hairy as he had previously imagined (Joppien 1978). Lorenz Fries's *Ptolemy* of 1522 printed by Grüninger might serve as a symptomatic example of this change. It depicts American cannibals on a map of South America more precisely as a group of people in feather dresses feasting on a roasted human body (Fig. 13).

Nevertheless the Wild Man continued to influence the image of the American Indian; however in an entirely different context. The Brazilians in Fries's *Uslegung* of 1525 and 1527, for example, are shown as two naked warriors armed with shield, spear and bow. They appear, faithful to the Wild Man tradition, with a pair of unicorns, animals always closely associated with the Wild Man (Fig. 14) (Einhorn 1976:139-144). This particular image, however, seems to have been a depiction of the savage on a more general level, as the 1530 edition of the work reveals, where they represent the savage inhabitants of Ormuz.

The peaceful harmony of the seated group in the Grüninger cut in *Diß büchlin saget* in sharp contrast to the dreadful scene of butchery (Fig. 9), is paralleled by a variety of portrayals of Wild Folk. In fact, the designer of the block seems to have derived his inspiration for the figure of the woman with the infant on her lap from an engraving by Martin Schongauer (Fig. 15) executed somewhat earlier, between 1480 and 1490. This engraving shows a Wild

Fig. 15. Wild Woman supporting a shield with an infant on her lap. Engraving by Martin Schongauer (1480-1490). New York, Metropolitan Museum of Art, Harris Brisbane Dick Fund, 28.26.9.

Fig. 16. Wild Family. Engraving by Master bxg (1470-1490). Vienna, Albertina.

Woman seated on a rock, an infant at her breast. Although the woman in the engraving plays a strictly heraldic role, she is linked with the idyllic existence of Wild Folk (Husband 1980: 185ff), also expressed in a similarly harmonious scene dating from about the same time (Fig. 16). This engraving by Master bxg shows a Wild Family frolicing with their two children in an almost paradisaic landscape. Idyllic scenes like this earmark the development of a rather different perception of the Wild Man - a romanticized interpretation which inverts the negative concepts which had previously embodied this figure.

After the Crusades the localization of power within the feudal system gradually lost significance and eventually collapsed. Economic and political powers shifted to the growing middle classes composed of craftsmen and merchants living in the emerging cities which were becoming the vital economical, political and cultural centers. However, some feudal social and political institutions persisted, religious dogma in particular proved particularly restistant to change. Ultimately the conflict between old and new social order became intractable and led to a series of religious and social wars especially in Germany. Therefore it is not surprising that the Wild Man, the very embodiment of the negation of the concepts and institutions which had themselves fallen into disfavor, was reconsidered. Wasn't he, after all, free from the burdens and injustices of civilization; able to lead a freer, simpler and more harmonious life? Couldn't he, free of the arbitrary dictates of a corrupt religious institution, live in accordance to the will of God? Was he, in his closeness to nature not in the end more innocent and more in touch with the ideal state of society? Although maintained as a symbol for original sin, his closeness to nature somehow immunized him to the corrupting influence of civilization. As a result, the Wild Man was now pictured as belonging to the paradisaic society, which had been lost to humankind (Bernheimer 1952:143ff, Husband 1980:13ff; on primitivism see Boas and Lovejoy 1935).

Despite the barbarity and cruelty reported by the eye-witnesses, there was no doubt that the American Indians in their wild state bore remarkable similarities to the primitivism of European Wild Men in this new idealized incarnation. In fact, in Columbus' *Letter to Gabriel Sanchez* the idyllic condition of New World savagism is duly reported. Columbus stresses the state of innocence of the American savage, emphasizing his peaceful nature. He suggests that in reality he practices the essential, the true principles of Christianity. The true concept of Christian Love, which had been turned upside down in the Old World is seen in part as embodied in the peoples of the New World:

> "... they are of simple manners and trustworthy, and very liberal with
> everything they have, refusing no one, who asks for anything they may
> posses, and even themselves inviting to ask for things. They show greater
> love for all other than for themselves..." (Eames 1892:5).

This was indeed an observation also made by Vespucci:

> "The wealth which we affect in this our Europe and elsewhere, such as gold,
> jewels, pearls, and other riches, they hold of no value at all; and although
> they have them in their lands they do not work to get them, nor do they
> care for them" (Levillier 1951:313f).

The disregard for worldly riches - due to their ignorance of trade, "they neither buy nor sell" (Levillier 1951:313f) - common ownership of the little material wealth they possess (feathers and colorful stones and some "rosaries" made from shells) and particularly land, certainly evoked in the European mind the image of an ideal state of society, the image of a people still living in the Golden Age. The idea that civilization itself was an error, was expressed very early by the Church Fathers themselves. Augustinus (*Civitas Dei*, book 13, ch. 14) explained that following the fall from grace in the Garden of Eden mankind was doomed to live an existence outside of paradise, a life in sin. The ideal state man enjoyed in prehistoric times, i.e. in paradise, was later on shifted from remoteness in time to remoteness in geographical location. The

24

Fig. 17. Title page of the Low German Vespucci *Van den nygje Insulen vnd landen* printed by Jacob Winter in Magdeburg (1506). Braunschweig, Stadtbibliothek, C 57 4°.

terrestrial paradise was believed to exist as a real place in the East. In addition it was believed that savage tribes, who like the Brahmans of India, who lead a holy life although ignorant of God, also enjoyed living in an ideal social state (Baudet 1965:10ff).

The association of the New World with terrestrial paradise - or at least the expectation of it being located somewhere in the New World - dates back as far as Columbus and Vespucci, who concludes in his *Mundus Novus* "That surely if the terrestrial paradise be in any part of this earth, I esteem it is not far distant from these parts" (Levillier 1951:304). Generally it was believed that the natives inhabiting these paradisic regions, were certainly marked by sin. Nevertheless, it was felt that they were also destined in some way to establish an ideal society. This was a possibility that Las Casas, perhaps the most outspoken advocate of humane treatment of Indians in the early period of Spanish colonization propagated. He thought that the ideal society would emerge almost automatically once the word of God and civilization was brought to the Indians in a gentle way (Hanke 1949:ch.V).

The association of the New World and its inhabitants with mankind in the prelapsarian condition may possibly be the theme of the title illustration in the LowGerman translation of Vespucci's *Lettera* printed by Jacob Winter in Magdeburg in 1506 (Vespucci 1506) (Fig. 17). Winter combined two segmented woodcuts which had previously been used by Martin Brandis in his *Van der clage on ansprake de Belyal* (for reproduction see Schramm, vol.12). The naked couple on the left now representing the people discovered in the New World, was taken from a scene depicting Adam and Eva's expulsion from Paradise

25

Fig. 18. Woodcut depicting South American Indians. Broadsheet probably printed in Augsburg by Johann Froschauer (1505-1506). New York Public Library, Print Divisions.

(fol.2 verso; Schramm,12:413), while the figure of the Portuguese king receiving a letter on the right, was recycled from the image of King Solomon (fol. 9 verso; Schramm,12:422). The recycling of disparate older woodblocks in new combinations to provide new meanings was widely practised in the early period of printed book illustration and was particularly favored by the printers of Magdeburg (see Schramm,12).[17] Although Winter might have selected the image of Adam and Eve, because he needed a naked couple, it is also justified to assume, that he chose this scene, emblematic and widely known to the contemporary reader, because he wanted to indicate that the contents of the book related to the discovery of the terrestrial paradise and its inhabitants.

Whether or not Winter's use of this image was to make a definite allusion to terrestrial paradise may never be decided with certainty. What is clear though, is that the image of the Noble Savage also associated with the Wild Man was incorporated in the earliest depictions and descriptions of the American Indian. A large woodcut illustrating a broadsheet printed in 1505 or 1506 probably by Johann Froschauer in Augsburg, depicts eleven exotically dressed savages on a shore engaged in a variety of activities. In the background two European vessels approach from the open sea (Fig. 18).[18] The inscription below the

Fig. 19. Woodcut depicting a cannibalistic Indian family from Jan van Doesborch, *Of the newe landes* (1510-1515). London, British Museum.

Fig. 20. Wild Family in a cave. Manuscript illumination in pen and ink from the "Ballad of a Wild Man," France (about 1500). Paris, Bibliotheque Nationale, Ms.fr.2374, fol.3 verso.

picture, an extract from Vespucci, may be regarded as a short synopsis of wildness in its American form: This woodcut is the earliest known printed visual representation of American natives that reveals some ethnographical accuracy, in the details of precious stones used as decoration, feather head-dresses, and other ornaments (Schuller 1930:484f).

The illustration is also meant to give some indication of Indian customs: their cannibalism and their loose morals. Of main importance, however, is the group in the center of the composition consisting of a seated woman holding an infant at her breast. Another child reaches out to his mother. A third, yet larger child stands a little apart with his father, who in turn face the woman and children.

This scene of savage family harmony, which served as a model for van Doesborch's illustration of his English extract of Vespucci and a Latin broad-sheet, whose contents mainly focusses on Balthasar Springer's journey to Oriental India (Fig. 19) (Doesborch 1515-1520, c.1520)[19] closely corresponds, except for some minor detail, to a scene depicting a Wild Family in a cave that illustrates a fragmentary manuscript dating from about 1500 (Fig. 20).[20] The composition of the group on the German broadsheet appears reversed be-cause of the process of copying directly on printing blocks. The illustration

27

from the manuscript, a pen and ink drawing, is one of a set of four illuminating the theme of the *Four Conditions of Society*: the poor man, the craftsman, the rich man, and the savage man, which were accompanied by ballads. This manuscript is linked to a satirical work by Henri Baude preserved in manuscript entitled *Les Trois Etats*, contained in a compendium bearing the opening inscription "Dits pour metter en tapisserie," i.e. possible subjects for tapestry design. Therefore it has been speculated that the illustrations and ballads of the *Four Conditions of Society* were originally meant as a tapestry design. Whether or not this is the case is of minor interest here, however, it is probable that a copy of the drawings in the French manuscript may have reached Froschauer's workshop in Augsburg, probably as a part of a design-book of a traveling journey-man. Froschauer most likely utilized it as the model for the group on the broadsheet.

Aside from compositional similarities, there are analogies in the meaning of the Wild Man scene expressed in the ballad and the primitivistic view of the Indian group on the broadsheet. Unlike the poor man, portrayed as a bandaged man, wasting away in a filthy bed in his miserable hovel, Wild Man as well as Indian lead a healthy life in harmony with nature. Unlike the rich man, both reject the vane material goals of civilized life, the amassing of great fortune by heaping riches upon riches. Both are better off than the craftsman, who exemplifies the "golden" mean between wealth and poverty, but who is not quite satisfied with the day to day struggle to eke out a decent existence. In fact, both, the Wild Man and the New World Savage, lead a life superior to any social class in the civilized world, because of their closeness to nature (Husband 1980:128-131).

The close relation of the idealizing portrayals of the Wild Man and the Indian were meant as a critical commentary on the unsatisfactory social structure of Renaissance civilization. In this regard the primitivism of the American Indian is presented as untouched by the corruption of a degenerated society. This was a concept inherent in the earliest visual interpretations of Native American life, as well as the earliest descriptions by the eyewitnesses. However, the concept of the Noble Savage, superior in his rudimentary social organization, conforming to the laws of nature, only came to full bloom much later in the writings of the French Enlightenment. In the early sixteenth century, Europeans, in particular in Spain, were still preoccupied with the question whether Indians were true men or animals, or perhaps humans of inferior quality meant only for service to the Whites as slaves.

The early images of the American Indian, as we have seen, reveal a dualistic concept of the natives of the New World: on one hand as inferior beings in direct oppostion to the ideals of civilized Christian society engaging in cannibalism and sexual licentiousness, and on the other, as a critical counter to society which had gone awry. These concepts were also embodied in the Wild Man, who, in the end was merely a product of fantasy. However, to the illustrators at the beginning of the sixteenth century, who could not verify the descriptions of the New World travelers nor rely on their own personal observation, the image of the Wild Man, who shared many qualities with the American Savage, was the one which fitted best. The Wild Man himself, however, disappeared from the visual arts and literature by the end of the century. The replacement of this fantasy figure by the Noble and Ignoble Savage of America, a real figure which embodied the main concepts of his European counterpart, was finally inevitable in a world that gradually was more attuned to reality.

NOTES

1. For a quantitative analysis of early printed reports on the Discovery spanning the period from 1493 to 1532, translations and conclusions on the reception by the readership, see Hirsch 1976.

2. Eight of the seventeen verifiable editions of the Columbus letter contain visual information. Six of them show figures representing American Indians. Of the 30 issued of the Vespucci letters printed before 1516 (including extracts) 18 were illustrated, 12 of which show Indians; many of them are discussed in the text.

3. Although there are some artists in the period discussed, who actually did see and portray Indians (Christoph Weiditz, who saw them in the entourage of Cortés at the Spanish Court in 1528), some who saw Indian artifacts (Dürer and probably Hans Burgkmair), and some who either might have seen artifacts or were supervised in their depiction of Indians by someone who had some knowledge of them (the artist of the Munich woodcut, Froschauer?), it is safe to assume that the majority of the illustrators in that early period did not.

4. This is particularly true for most of the illustrations of this early period. However, even rather fastidious illustrators like Theodor de Bry who started publishing his series of books on America in 1590, have been accused by some scholars of producing fantasy images.

5. Ancient travel literature of curious and monstrous races was very abundant. In the early Middle Ages Augustinus dedicated chapter 8 of book XVI of his *City of God* to monstrous creatures. For a good short overview see H.W.Janson (1952:73ff).

6. William C. Sturtevant suggested to me that he also believes that early European depictions of American Indians are derived from Wild Man imagery. In this regard D.B. Quinn (1976:642f) also mentions that the illustrations in the Rostock edition of Vespucci's letter and van Doesborch's *Mundus Novus* were derived from Wild Man imagery. However, he does not go so far as to assume a direct association of Indian and Wild Man for these illustrations. See also Carter Ratcliff (1981:104) who expresses the belief that the Wild Man imagery that was gradually vanishing in the arts by the end of the 16th century and during the first half of the 17th century reappeared, transformed to the image of the Noble Savage.

7. Dr. Chanca, who accompanied Columbus on his second voyage, as well as Michele da Cuneo treated the Indians with condescension in their accounts. For a survey of the earliest accounts on America see Gerbi (1976).

8. The association of the Wild Woman with witches has been pointed out by Bernheimer (1952:35). The Indian woman depicted in the ornamental architecture in the thirteenth part of the *Great Voyages* printed by Matthias Merian in 1627 is clearly depicted as a witch.

30

9. Sabin describes this woodcut in his *Dictionary* no. 99,334 as depicting "two naked Indians, a man and a woman... with large bow and arrow..." vol. 26, p. 446.

David Beers Quinn (1976:642) also believes that the couple was meant to represent Indians though he is convinced that the image was inspired by traditional Wild Man imagery.

Epistola Albericij. De nouo mundo, Rostock, Hermann Barkhusen 1505. There are two copies. One is in the British Museum, the other one in the Stadtbibliothek Frankfurt.

10. See Levillier (1951:306) for the description of how to draw the diagram.

11. In contrast to the common practise of that time, Grüninger even refused to lend or borrow printing clichés as well as his woodcuts. In a letter, Pirckheimer complains that he must have Grüninger print his *Ptolemaeus* because the printer was not willing to lend his original cuts for any price.

12. After the Discovery the location of the Fountain of Youth was believed by some to be in the New World. In 1513 Ponce de Leon set out from Puerto Rico on an expediton to find it in the southeast of North America (Florida).

13. "Die Canibali seind ein grimmes schützliches volck/ sehe hunds köpfen gleich dz eine grauset & sy ansicht. Vnd habend ein Insul innen welche Christoffel Dauber von Janua bey kurtzen jaren erfunden hat. ... Die Canibali gond alle nackend on allein das sie sich zieren mit Papagallen federn mancherley farb/... Diß volck isset nichts lieber dan menschen fleisch/ vñ darumb so faren sye offt im iar vß in andere vmbliegende Insulen lewt zu fahen/ vnd so sie fahen junge knab/ hauwen sie vonn stunden an vß wie wir den hämmelen thund/ vff das sye feißt vn dester besser zu essen werde/ die alten ertödten sye vñ essen ir ingeweid/ das ander fleisch hencken sye vff wie wir den schweinen thund. So sye aber frawen fahent/ seind die selbigen jung/ so behalten sy die/ das sy vil kinder machenn gleich als wir die hennen vmb der eyer willen..." (Fries 1527:fol.C2 recto).

14. Following is the full text that appears in the *Aggivnta* on New World cynocephali:
"Plinio secondo nella sua Istoria Naturale, nel sesto Libro, Capitulo primo, racconta che visono alcuni huomini, i hanno el capi di canne, il che si è verificato nei scoprimenti dell'indie, imperoche nella Prouincia die Santa Croce si sono ritrouati mostri con la testa canina, e in vea di fauellare hanno vn certo suono, o genito appunto latrato da cane, la braccia simuli a quelle de Gl'huomini, le gambe, ei piedi come quelli del cauallo; vestono di pelli di animali, viuono di rapnia mangiono carne humana, come quelli del Brasil, che dalle membra humane in poi sono quest'animali simiglianti in tutte loro attiono." fol. A 3 recto.

15. The British Library, Cotton Ms. Tiberius B.v. vol i. The manuscript is a

compilation of texts containing the 'Marvels of the East'.

16. This is certainly true for cynocephali. Monsters like the headless people, giants etc., however, still haunted the maps of the New World even in the 17th century.

17. See Schramm, vol.12. The volume contains the early illustrations of the Magdeburg printers in their entirety.

18. *Dise figur anzaigt uns...* probably by Froschauer in Augsburg about 1505-1506. There are only two copies surviving, one of which is in the Staatsbibliothek Munich, the other, in the New York Public Library, Spencer Collection.

19. The only surviving copy known of the broadsheet is at the Universitäts-bibliothek Rostock.

20. The Four Conditions of Society, France, about 1500, Paris, Bibliothèque Nationale, Ms. fr. 2374, fol. 3 verso.

REFERENCES CITED

Anonymous
c.1505-1506 Geschichte kürzlich... [Probably printed by Johann Weissenberger, Nuremberg.]

Baudet, Henri
1965 Paradise on Earth: Some Thoughts on European Images of Non-European Man. New Haven-London.

Bernheimer, Richard
1952 Wild Men in the Middle Ages: A Study in Art Sentiment and Demonology. Cambridge, MA.

Boas, George and Arthur D.Lovejoy
1935 A Documentary History of Primitivism and Related Ideas. Baltimore.

Botero, Giovanni
1623 Aggivnta alla gvarta parte dell'Indie, del Sig. Giovanni Botero Benese. Di Mostri & Vsanze di quelle Parti, e di quei Re con le Figure al Naturale, Raccolte nouamente da Allessandro de Vecchi. Venetia.

Chiapelli, Fredi (ed.)
1976 First Images of America: The Impact of the New World on the Old. Berkeley, CA.

de Bry, Theodor
1592 Americae tertia pars memorabilem provinciae Brasiliae Historiam continens, Germanico primum sermone scriptum a Ioanne Stadio Homburgensi Heso... Frankfurt:T.de Bry.

Descerpz, François
1562 Recueil de la diuersité des habits qui sont de present en vsiage tant es pays d'Europe, Asie, Affrique et Illes sauuages. Le tout fait apres le naturel. Paris:Richard Breton.

Doesborch, Jan van
c.1506-1510 Van der nieuwer werelt oft landtscap nieuwelicx gheuonden vanden dooluchtighen coninc. van Portugael door den alder besten pyloet ofe zee kender der werelt. Antwerp.
c.1515-1520 Of the newe landes and of ye people founde by the messengers of the kynge of portygale named Emanuel Antwerp.
c.1520 De nove mondo. Antwerp.

Eames, Wilberforce
1892 The Letters of Columbus on the Discovery of America: A Facsimile of the Pictorial Edition. New York.

Einhorn, Jürgen W.
1976 Spiritualis Unicornis. Das Einhorn als Bedeutungsträger in Literatur und Kunst des Mittelalters. München.

Foucault, Michel
1973   Madness and Civilization. A History of Insanity in the Age of
        Reason. New York-Toronto.
Fries, Lorenz
1525   Uslegung der Mercarten oder Cartha Marina. Darin man sehen mag
        wa einer in der welt sey und wa ein ietlich land Wasser und Stat
        gelege ist. Das als in de büchlin zefind e. Strassburg: Grüninger
        (reprinted 1527,1530).
Gerbi, Antonello
1976   The Earliest Accounts of the New World. In: Chiapelli 1976,1:37-43.
Gómez Canedo, Lino
1966   ¿Hombres ó bestias? Nuevo examen critico de un viejo tópico.
        Estudios de Historia Novohispania 1:29-51.
Hanke, Lewis
1949   The Spanish Struggle for Justice in the Conquest of America.
        Philadelphia.
1959   Aristotle and the American Indian. A Study in Race Prejudice in the
        Modern World. Chicago.
Hirsch, Rudolf
1976   Printed Reports on the Early Discovery and Their Reception. In:
        Chiapelli 1976,2:538-562.
Husband, Timothy
1980   The Wild Man: Medieval Myth and Symbolism. Catalog of an
        exhibition held at the Cloisters. New York.
Janson, H.W.
1952   Apes and Ape Lore in the Middle Ages and the Renaissance. Studies
        of the Warburg Institute 20. London.
Joppien, Rüdiger
1978   Étude de quelques Pourtraits ethnologiques dans l'Oeuvre d'André
        Thevet. Gazette des Beaux-Arts,ser.6, 91:125-136.
Kristeller, Paul
1888   Die Strassburger Bücherillustration im XV. und im Anfang des XVI.
        Jahrhunderts. Leipzig.
Levillier, Roberto
1951   The First Voyages of Amerigo Vespucci. Buenos Aires.
Lévi-Strauss, Claude
1975   The Raw and the Cooked. Introduction into the Science of Mytholo-
        gy. New York-Hagerstown-San Francisco-London.
Oakeshott, Walter F.
1960   Some Woodcuts by Hans Burgkmair. Oxford.
O'Gorman, Edmundo
1941   Sobre la Naturalezza Bestial del Indio Americano. Humanismo y
        Humanidad. Indagación en torno una polemica del siglo XVI.

Filosofia y lettras 1:141-156.

Pochat, Götz
1970   Der Exotismus während des Mittelalters und der Renaissance. Voraussetzungen, Entwicklungen und Wandel eines bildnerischen Vokabulars. Uppsala.

Quinn, David Beers
1976   New Geographical Horizons: Literature. In: Chiapelli 1976,2:635-658.

Ratcliff, Carter
1981   Odd Men Out. Art in America (Summer 1981): 104.

Rowe, Johan Howland
1964   Ethnography and Ethnology in the Sixteenth Century. Kroeber Anthropological Society Papers 30:1-19.

Schramm, Albert
Der Bilderschmuck der Frühdrucke.

Schuller, Rudolf
1930   The Oldest Known Illustration of South American Indians. Indian Notes 7:484-497.

Sheehan, Bernard
1980   Savagism and Civility. Indians and Englishmen in Colonial Virginia. Cambridge.

Sluiperius, Johann
1972   Omnia fere gentivm nostraeq: aetatis Nationum Habitus & Effigies. In eosdem Joannis Sluiperij Herzelensis Epigrammata. Adiecta ad singulas Icones Gallica tetrasica. Antwerp: Joannes Bellerus.

Staden, Hans
1557   Warhafftige beschreibung eyner Landschafft der wilden/ nacketen/ grimmigen menschfresser leuthen/ in der newen welt America gelegen... Marburg: Andreas Kolbe.

Sturtevant, William C.
1976   The First Visual Images of Native America. In: Chiapelli 1976: 1,417-454.

Vespucci, Amerigo
1506   Van den nygen Insulen vnd landen so ytz undt kortliken befunden sindt dorch den koninkg van Portugal. Magdeburg: Jacob Winter.

1509   Diß büchlin saget, wie die zwē durchleüchtigstē herrē her Fernandus K. zu Castilien und herr Emanuel K. zu Portugal haben das weyte mōr ersuchet und findet vil Insuln, vnnd eine Nüve welt von wilden nacketen Leüten vormals vnbekant. Strassburg: Johannes Grüninger.

Williams, Charles Allyne
1925   Oriental Affinities of the Legend of the Hairy Anchorite: The Theme of the Hairy Solitairy in its Early Forms with Reference to "Die Lügend von Sanct Johanne Chrysostomo". University of Illinois Studies in Language and Literature 11:427-509.

35

1935   The German Legends of the Hairy Anchorite. University of Illinois
        Studies in Language and Literature 18:5-140.

THE MYTH OF THE INDIAN MONARCHY: AN ASPECT OF THE CONTROVERSY BETWEEN THEVET AND LERY (1575-1585)

Frank Lestringant

For explorers, the question of Indian chieftainship was a basic one. Before anything else, they had to find out whom to speak to. Isolated individuals, encountered by chance while coasting along unknown river banks offered no guarantee if they didn't express themselves in the name of authority, in other words, if they hadn't been delegated by some chief or king. One can therefore understand the confusion and even indignation André Thevet felt when facing the anarchy seemingly governing the destinies of certain peoples such as the Patagonians of whom he wrote: "There are no men so beastly, wild and cruel as these men are, who have never savored another obedience than that which they impose one upon another, without any royalty or principality existing among them; when going to war, however, they choose one amongst themselves, to whom the others pay their respect and whom they obey" (Thevet 1575,2: f.905 r.).

The absence of authority relations in a people makes its members similar to those of a savage horde. Lack of government is synonymous with lack of humanity - and in this case Thevet placed himself in the school of Aristotle for whom man is, of course, above all a political animal. The Patagonians escape the state of pure beastliness only by war: Then a dispersed and anarchic peace-time society is regrouped and structured around one pole. Interpersonal relations like *respect* and *obedience* emerge at the moment in which a chief appears, even if only temporarily. In the feudal view still adhered to by Thevet (1516?-1592) and many of his contemporaries, the relationship between vassal and liege-lord governs the hierarchy inscribed into the core of the social structure. Its function is essentially military in origin, and it only comes fully into play on the occasion of conflicts in which fidelity and gratitude between the partners are validated by an exchange of reciprocal obligations.

At the top of this traditional construction stands the king who is first of all commander-in-chief of the armies and then dispenser of equitable justice. Montaigne himself cannot conceive of another image of royalty when, in his essay *Des Cannibales* of 1580, he makes his Tupinamba Indian speak, whom he had met eight years earlier at Rouen. The principal prerogative claimed for himself by this eminent person ("This was a Captain, and our sailors called him King," explains Montaigne) is "to lead into war" (Montaigne 1965:214 = *Essais*, I,31 - "Des Coches"). In times of peace, a privilege somewhat analogous to the ceremony of royal entries in medieval and modern Europe remained of his authority: whenever he was visiting the villages of his realm, the path in front of him was cleared and the "hagues of their woods" were cut down. In other words, like towns of France opening themselves generously to their royal "infants" such as described by Agrippa d'Aubigné in the first book of the *Tragiques* (d'Aubigné 1969:34),[1] the villages of Brazil removed their palisades and all other obstacles upon the approach of a savage king. This peaceable and "gentle" rite is in fact related both in the Christian occident as well as in Brazil to seizure by force. The manifestations of the power of the chief or king thus appear characterized even in peace by war-like symbolism.

Doubtlessly, monarchy did in fact represent in the eyes of the majority of the observers the perfect form of social organization. The Norman sailors of whom Montaigne speaks, spontaneously apply the model to Brazilian society. More prudently, the author of the *Essais* cannot avoid in the same chapter to compare the heroic virtues of these naked and anthropophagic athletes to those of the grand captains of antiquity known to him through Plutarch. But the image of the king shines through each of them in filigree: for proof see the unobliging and deceitfully naive parallel - indeed attributed to the loose language of the cannibal captain - between the pitiful appearance of the infant-king Charles IX surrounded by his stout Swiss guard, and the Apollinian and valorous royalty of the Brazilian chiefs (Montaigne 1965:213 = *Essais*, I,31).[2]

What did the Patagonians lack then, if not the essential: That monarchic principle which assures the coherence and stability of the social group, and which in times of peace perpetuates the ties sealed or confirmed during war by transforming them now into a splendid demonstration? Sporadic and little ostentative, the Patagonian royalty is moreover elective - and that is a trait of undeniable weakness for Thevet, a true servant of the Valois-Angoulême dynasty for four consecutive governments, or for his friend Guillaume Postel, the visionary author of *De Orbis Terrarum Concordia* (cp. Mesnard 1951). In the eyes of the legalistic theoreticians - among whom particularly the name of Jean Bodin has to be remembered - and despite the contradiction brought forward at the time of the religious wars by their anti-royalist adversaries, true monarchy is that which is founded on blood rather than on choice by an aristocratic assembly. The legitimacy of the elected monarch is purely human and random; that of the hereditary monarch emanates from divine law. Ultimately, the best form of government which could be recognized among the Indians, that is in the final analysis the greatest good which one could wish them, is indubitably hereditary monarchy. If the anarchistic Patagonians, geographically and morally situated on the borders of humanity, have therefore nothing but an episodic and caricatured relationship to royalty, it is in turn the political system of other nations in America, apparently more cultured and keeping better company, which will be able to conform itself to the state of monarchy at the price of some distortion.

One can see that the problem is at the same time an epistemological and a political one: on one hand it is clear that one could understand others only if they somehow resemble oneself; hence the mirror-image of royalty, the image of the Noble Savage is flashing back to Renaissance Europeans. On the other hand, the domination of someone else is only possible under the condition that he belongs to a socially structured entity. No domination can be imagined that is not human, or in other words social. It is known, moreover, how quickly the Conquista had seized the vast empires of Mexico and Peru with their quite developed systems of government; and with what difficulties on the other hand it had progressed in less densely populated regions where the political organization was also more lax and intermittent, such as in New Mexico or in Araucania. With a mind sharpened for his time of geopolitical exigencies, André Thevet, the cosmographer, ultimately recognized the Patagonians as a strategic limit. Their withdrawal to the extremities of the known world and even more their chronic lack of social organization made them a people that "would not let itself be handled without mittens" (Thevet 1575,2:f.905r.). It was consequently up to the colonizer to look for another field of exercise, and to the legislator for a people easier to subjugate. The model of that dreamed-of monarchy, ideally projected on another society, paradoxically was encountered where it was least expected: among the anthropophagical Tupinamba of the Brazilian coast. But it was with them the French of the Renaissance had the most extensive acquaintance since the beginning of the great discoveries.

The naked king of Brazil

The naked king of Brazil is a figure which takes an increasingly defined shape in the course of the successive versions of Thevet's Brazilian report (*Singularitez* of 1557, *Cosmographie Universelle* of 1575, *Vrais Pourtraits et Vies des Hommes illustres* of 1584, *Histoire de deux voyages* and *Grand Insulaire* of around 1584-1590): It is that of the "half-giant" Quoniambec, a Tamoio chief in the neighborhood of Rio, whose imposing stature could only have been equal to the extent of the territories under his jurisdiction. The historical existence of this person appears to be well attested - and doubtlessly he may be identified with Konyan Bebe whose prisoner the Hessian harquebusier and mercenary Hans Staden had been for ten months (cp.Luchesi 1982). According to the respective eyewitness accounts of the German and the Frenchman, he had combined a voracious appetite - hadn't he claimed to have eaten five Portugese? - with a somewhat exhibitionistic vaingloriousness. In the *Wahrhafftige Historia* as well as in the *Cosmographie Universelle* (Staden 1979:88-89; cp.Thevet 1575,2:f.924r.-v. and Lussagnet 1953:88-89,n.3) he is represented in the same posture: proudly parading in front of an audience of fearful subjects assembled in the confines of a *maloca*, and declaiming with long steps the deeds of his warlike exploits. This "ambulant oration" of the Tamoio chief has nonetheless opposite meanings in the two cases. For Hans

Staden, the prisoner, destined to serve as food for the Indians who looked upon him as one of their Portuguese enemies, Konyan Bebe is that intransigent henchman who will abandon him to the jests and sadistic plays of his men, in front of which he would have to jump with feet bound, accompanied by the blows and derision of the assistants.

On the other hand, the portrait drawn by Thevet who has to be counted among the French allies of this valiant "king," despite being also appalling, is destined to raise sympathy. This is achieved by two apparently contradictory means: The comicality of the situation, and epic aggrandisement. A figure painted in strong colors, Thevet's Quoniambec has indisputably Rabelaisian manners: after having drunk vinegar added to water, the only alcoholic drink still available to Villegagnon's colonists, he belches noisily and breaks into laughter about these digestive manifestations as eloquent as they were unexpected. In addition, he beats his breast, "shoulders and thighs" (Thevet 1575,2:f.924r.; Lussagnet 1953:89) while making known to the public his ogre-like desires which would instantly reduce the strongest and nimblest of the "Margageats," his enemies, to minced meat - if he could only lay his hands on him. This buffooning truculence finds its symbolic key in the nudity of the person. Adorned in fact only by the feathers of his diadem and the strands of beads of his necklace, the king is "totally naked," and in the nude parades himself in front of Villegagnon and his retinue. The paradisian simplicity of his dress does not keep him in the least from narrating the heroic litany of his prowesses with a lot of gestures and with a voice so terrible, Thevet assures us, "that one almost would not have heard the thunder" (Thevet 1575,2:f.924v.; Lussagnet 1953:92).[3] The "audience" granted by the French captain to the most "venerable" of his indigenous political partners almost slips into outright comedy. But the elementary rules of diplomacy preclude making fun of the counterpart, as much as the wrath of the savages could be deadly or at the very least disastrous for the small band of colonists whose fate and survival depend to a large extent on the supply of provisions by the natives. The terror experienced by Staden when facing the naked and tyrranic ogre is not far from being shared by the French who at the same time feel some desire to deride the Adamite monarch. Thus, the contrast epitomized by the bared and menacing body of the indigenous king is perfect: simultaneously, he invites laughter and inspires very real fear. This oscillation which makes the scene conjured up by Thevet a model of diplomatic ambiguity, translates the relationship between European and Indian with singular precision. The other one who ignores the established usages (such as how to dress properly) is the object of implicit contempt. From this derives the derision which is invariably attached to the gesticulating and drollingly demonstrative nakedness of Quoniambec. But as the relationship to the partner appears to be a necessity of a strategic kind, there is the danger that the other party takes note of the disdain in which it is being held and hence refuses any peaceful exchange.

This is the reason for the symbolic compensation by which Thevet elevates Quoniambec to the mythic rank of a king of outstanding qualities. Physical qualities in the first place: "Big and of strong build, standing some eight feet tall," the Tamoio chief possessed such strength that "he could have carried a bushel of wine in his arms" (Thevet 1575,2:f.924r.; Lussagnet 1953:89). Emphasizing the exaggeration, Thevet does not hesitate a little further on to focus on the shoulders loaded with two culverines both of which he fires at his enemies at the same time. In inventing this Herculean prowess to glorify the Tamoio chief (Thevet 1575,2:f.952v.; Lussagnet 1953: 232. Cp. Fig.1 of this paper), the cosmographer manifestly behaves himself as the perfect courtier of the unlikely monarch whom his pen is about to create. And by virtue of a style sometimes inclined towards eulogistic discourse, he in fact gradually converts the Brazil of the cannibals into another Europe. The lodge - or *maloca* - festooned on its outside by heads of enemies taken in war and ritually devoured is ennobled by the title "palace" from the moment the "king" dwells there (Thevet 1575,2:f.924r.; Lussagnet 1953:92).[4] For such a sovereign by an epidemic rudely ravished from the affection of his people, the funerary

Fig. 1. "Quoniambec's ruse" from Thevet's *Cosmographie Universelle* (1575), 2:f.952v.

41

panegyric reserved for the braves is recited: "S'il eust vescu, il eust faict de grandes choses, estant secouru des nostres" ("If he had lived, he would have done great deeds, having stood by our people" - Thevet 1575,2:f.924r.; Lussagnet 1953:92). The physical excellence of the hero has its corollary in a moral elevation in which the appetite for vengeance fades in front of an absolute contempt for death, and in which vainglory is transformed into true glory. To complete the fiction, Thevet against all likelihood offers a devotion fit for the Tridentine Reform: "He took such great pleasure to watch us as we were making our prayers, that he fell on his knees and raised his hands to heaven, just as he had seen us doing ..." (Thevet 1575,2:f.924v.; Lussagnet 1953:93).

Evidently, this series of commonplaces which define the perfect gentleman and reveal Quoniambec to be an accomplished prince serves a protocolary function. Quoniambec is the model of the Good Savage, susceptible to be converted to Christianity and consequently to become a reliable wheel in the machinery of the colonial enterprise which was just taking place under the administration of Admiral de Coligny. The exaggeration of the panegyric concentrating on the single figure of the chief permits him to be viewed at the same time as a *model* and as a *medium*: A model of a partner whose virtues conform to the chivalresque and feudal ideal of the European leaders: a medium between the civilized world and the savage world which miraculously embodies that composite node in which the noisy and ridiculous nudity allies itself to the majesty of an able body and a noble soul.

This remarkable and complex portrait whose ideological and political implications we have tried to analyze, was taken by Thevet's enemies as a particularly telling example of his presumption and foolishness. In his *Histoire d'un voyage faict en la terre du Bresil* which twenty years after the events presents his eyewitness account of the adventure of Antarctic France in the years 1555-1560, the Calvinist pastor Jean de Léry uses the "funny" Quoniambec as his favorite target in a polemic principally directed against the cosmographer of the king (Léry 1585:146-147). Insisting, for example, on the plain unlikelihood of placing on the shoulders of a naked man two pieces of artillery discharged simultaneously without causing the least scratch to their human support, Léry for good measure makes fun of the "delusions" and "old women's tittle-tattle" emanating from the prolific pen of "the cosmographer by royal decree" (Léry 1580: f.B7v., "Preface"). This violent attack would be rebutted in that chapter of the *Vrais Pourtraits et Vies des Hommes illustres* of 1584 devoted to the memory of the valorous Tamoio chief. Forced by the charge of his adversary to surpass his previous declarations, Thevet accentuates the hyperbolic character of what now becomes a panegyric of proper form. Placed in his gallery of illustrous men on the same level as the Cesars and the Tamerlans (Thevet 1584,2:Liv.VIII, ch.135, "Julius Cesar, Premier Empereur"; 2:VIII,138: "Tamerlan, Empereur des Tartares"), Quoniambec appears as the prototype of that new humanity discovered beyond the oceans, which "in several particulars" surpasses that of the Old World (Thevet 1584,2:VIII,149,f.661v.). The lately manifest barbarity of the cannibal king is at least mellowed, as throughout this chapter neither the question of his anthropophagy nor of his elementary dress is raised. Cannibalism and nudity, in other words, the two aspects most evidently shocking to Europeans - and which at the same time are the significant feature in an ethnocentric definition of the "Savage" - are simply omitted in this portrait now conforming to the prosopographic genre where Thevet can place it without difficulty. Later on, we will return to the value of the emblem which for the New World and through the bias of a generalizing synecdoche clothes the solitary figure of the Tamoio chief. Let us take up for the moment an idealization which borrows the double dragoman from the style of the period and from a flourishing of unexpected metaphors. The "terrible" Quoniambec, "adorned with the most exquisite rarities, belonging both to the body and the mind" (Thevet 1584,2:VIII,149, f.661v.), also appears "shining of several virtues" which, for example, make him predisposed to religious matters. The Latinisms of a lexicon characterized by a certain pedantry make out of the "gigantic procerity" of the beneficiary the tangible incarnation of the "absolute superiority" in his place. In doing so, Thevet agrees with a mode of traditional thought which recognizes in the body a reflection of the mind. A king worthy of his title would never have a common or weak stature. As we have seen at the beginning of this paper, Montaigne does not offer any different way of reasoning with regard to the cannibal captain encountered in Rouen. The latter was surprised to see that the infant-king Charles IX, despite his fragile constitution, was commanding over a detachment of strong Swiss. Moreover, it seems that Thevet returns here to an old hypothesis concerning the origin of monarchy, of which the cleric Jean de Meung in a famous passage of his *Roman de la Rose* had made himself the interpreter. In the analogous context of a comparative ethnographic description of the peoples of America, the lawyer Marc Lescarbot would be citing this verse again at the beginning of the 17th century:

"Un grand villain entre eux eleurent
Le plus corsu de quants qu'ilz furent
Le plus ossu, et le grigneur,
Et le firent Prince et Seigneur."
("A great villain they chose among themselves
The strongest one they had
The most bony one and biggest
And made him Prince and Lord.")
(Meung 1970,2:42, verses 9579-9582, cited by Lescarbot 1617:944).

At the dawn of feudal society and the monarchic principle of the crown, the necessity of common protection had entailed the election of the strongest, soon aided in his defensive task by an escort of sergeants. In effect, Thevet's Quoniambec is indeed the "strongest," ("plus corsu") of the Tamoios, whose "eight feet" of height assure him of the incontestable superiority over the members of the group: Supreme king, because "half-giant." Or more exactly - and inversely - it is because Thevet has made a European-style monarch out of the war chief that he has to confer upon him an exceptional stature. In the absence of written laws and a fixed code of justice defining as well the modes of accession to power and the prerogatives of the sovereign, the only criteria to determine the royalty of the Indian chief are of a physical kind: athletic frame and impressive muscles bulging, contrary to all racial accuracy, on the arms and shoulders of Quoniambec in *Hommes Illustres*. Thus, the gigantism appears in this sense as a sign of supreme dignity, at the same time that it is the indispensable attribute of the nude monarch. In the absence of this "gigantic procerity," how could one distinguish him from the thousands of his equally nude and able subjects?

It is true that Thevet invests even the least of the few ornaments found on the powerful anatomy of the chief with royal meaning - and this is particularly noticable in the iconography. The feather diadem is thus interpreted as a crown in the two engraved portraits of the Brazilian king - the woodcut in the *Cosmographie Universelle* and the copper plate of *Hommes Illustres* (Thevet 1575,2:f.924r., 1584,2:VIII,149,f.661r.; Lussagnet 1953:90-91). Equally, the row of feathers arranged over the hip, the bead necklaces, the crescent breast ornament of bone, and the ear ornaments which one could amuse oneself in comparing to those worn by King Henri III at the beginning of the prosopographic collection - enter the composition to define the pomp and magnificence of a truly royal "habit." Now we know by the testimony of the ethnologists that such attributes were not only the exclusive privilege of the chiefs, but in all likelihood were shared by all the warriors. The only object which perhaps may have had the function of insignia pertaining to princely dignity was the staff ending in a bouquet of feathers. However, as Alfred Métraux (1928:266 - "Insignes de commandement") has pointed out, this was less a mark of authority than a dance accessory indispensable for the celebration of certain feasts - if in both cases it is not simply the famous Tupinamba club, extremely schematized and ornamented with a collar of fine down, which was used in combat and above all in the ritual slaying of prisoners. Whatever its form and exact definition may be, it is obvious that in the eyes of Thevet and his illustrator this instrument takes the function of a scepter and as such is placed in the right hand of the "half-giant." The simple proximity in the gallery of illustrous men prepared by the cosmographer, of this exotic figure to Julius Caesar, the "First Emperor" (VIII,135), Soliman the Magnificent (VIII,146), or Charlemagne (IV,3), indicates the most remarkable adaptation of the "ethnographic panoply" of Brazil to the universal and timeless status of representation of a prince. By redefining the otherwise so correctly reproduced ornaments, King Quoniambec is turned into a kind of eternal monarch.

A myth contested

In his recourse to Jean de Meung, Marc Lescarbot noted certain distinctions between the regions and the periods, and defined the narrow and exact limits of the prerogatives of the American king, which according to him did not extend beyond the duration of war or of an expediton. Moreover, similarly to the ancient kings of Germania cited by Tacitus, he governs "more by example than by command" (Lescarbot 1617:944).[5] Far from heeding this prudence of the historian or the scruples of the comparativist, Thevet is inclined to perennialize and to some extent institutionalize the status of the Indian monarchy. Thus, during the "summit meetings" to which Quoniambec is periodically invited by Villegagnon, the two sovereigns - the viceroy of Antarctic France and the Tamoio King - debate their ambitious plans of conquest in the presence of their counselors: "Time and again he was summoned by our Chief to discover in conferring with him that which would be to take or to find" (Thevet 1584,2:VIII,149, f.661v.). One of the principal reasons for the metamorphosis of chief Quoniambec into an "illustrous man" is indisputably the necessity to adapt the figure of the terrible barbarian to the protocol of the diplomatic exchange.

Undoubtedly it would be appropriate to take into account the personal enthusiasm of Thevet and his legendary propensity for aggravating his most outrageous assertions from one work to the next, just to contradict his critics. But it is at least significant to observe how the myth of Quoniambec gains progressively in precision and coherence. Now nothing is ridiculous about him anymore: he merits to figure totally in the rank of *proceres*. Moreover, since, contrary to what happens in Léry and de Bry, for Thevet there exists no unique, homogenous and transparent vision of the American savage, dislocated in the opposition between insult (his laziness, stupidity, and perpetual thievery) and praise' (his valor and hospitality), the image of the chief serves to fill this obvious lack of symbolic cohesion. In the extensive work of the cosmographer, Quoniambec appears in fact as one of the rare examples in which the American achieves a veritable individuality and thus escapes the odd litany of discordant adjectives with which he is usually shrouded. In other words, attention is given by Thevet to the relationship to the other side only on the political level of leadership. The "king" of Brazil rather than the common Indian is considered by him to be the only acceptable interlocutor, and this at the price of the little "fiction" which the American monarchy represents. So, even if no general type of "Good Savage" analogous to the one outlined in Léry's *Histoire* or Montaigne's *Essais* (see Lestringant 1978) is found in the writings of the

Fig. 2. Portrait of Quoniambec from Thevet's *Cosmographie Universelle* (1575), 2:f.924r.

Fig. 3. "Roy du Promontoire des Cannibales" from Thevet's *Cosmographie Universelle* (1575), 2:f.955v.

cosmographer of four kings, there exists instead a political paradigm named Quoniambec.

One can imagine the misunderstandings to which the adulator of some chief of the Tamoio confederation could expose himself. Léry would reply in the year following the publication of *Hommes illustres* in the third edition of his Brazilian *Histoire* (1585) by ridiculing the "scientific Quoniambec" (Léry 1585:f. qq5, "Preface"), adorned with rare and improbable virtues like a bed of flowers. Declining to use the horticultural or pictorial metaphor and taxing as vain "hyperbole" (Léry 1585:f.qq7v.) the exaggerated eulogies addressed by Thevet to the memory of the deceased King of Ubatuba, Léry moreover experienced a malicious pleasure in bringing low the pretended dignity of the indigenous chief. His "palace" would in fact reduce itself to a "pig sty," and the vast "territory of his command" to some acres of brush and forest (Léry 1585:f.qqq5). From a strictly ethnographic point of view, there can be no doubt that Léry may have been right. We know today that the authority of the Tupinamba chief did not have the extent erroneously supposed by Thevet. Being first of all a war chief, following the already correct interpretation of Marc Lescarbot (1617:644; cp. our note 5), he was chosen with regard to his valor and the number of prisoners taken by him and offered at the communal

46

banquet. Thus his power was rarely hereditary. Outside the war path where his authority appears to have been effective, the "king's" power was blurred in times of peace within the framework of a much looser social organization: the warrior returned to his *maloca* and his extended family dominated by the authority of a venerable old man. It would even be easy to confront Thevet with his own assertions found elsewhere, as in his *Histoire de deux voyages aux Indes Australes et Occidentales* where the rights of the chief are seen to amount, however temporarily, to as many duties. According to a scheme recently proposed by the anthropologist Pierre Clastres in his somewhat ideal model of the "society against the state," based on the neighboring case of the Guayaki of Paraguay (Clastres 1974:ch.2, "Echange et pouvoir, philosophie de la chefferie indienne") the chief is defined by his ability to "guarantee food supplies" to serve the needs of the group. He thus would appear to be tributary towards the whole of his community. The exchange is to his disadvantage whereas he is in command during the brief periods of seasonal warfare (that is, in August), at the moment of the catch of a certain species of fish, and in November when the corn is ready for the manufacture of corn-beer, he must in return assure the provisioning of his men and sacrifice for them his reserves: "The rest of these poor people go to their villages to be fed sometimes at the expense of the enterprising gentlemen" (Thevet c.1585: f.32v.-33r.).[6]

The chieftainship - and this applies particularly to the Tupinamba - thus appears as an intermittent phenomenon which, moreover, is expressed much more by obligations of an economic and military nature - haranguing and feeding the troop, marching first into combat - than by real and durable prerogatives (Métraux 1948:113-114; cp. Lussagnet 1953:252,n.2). In this respect, Pierre Clastres has shown that the triple privilege of the chief, also recognized by Staden, Thevet and Léry - speechmaking, abundance of food, polygyny - practically forces him into continual linguistic, economic, and sexual expenditure, attempting to prove at each moment by this constant diminution of his forces the "innocence" of his power.[7] In this respect, Léry was a better ethnographer than the cosmographer of the French king. And yet he may have missed the essential point in the argument of his adversary. To place despite all likelihood a value on the person and function of the king of America, made it possible in turn to propose a colonial project of vast dimensions. The homology of social structures on both sides, the neighboring concepts of seigneurial dignity and of the "eminence" accorded to the "principal" of the savages are conducive to facilitate the taking of peaceful possession. The Indian monarchy represents the myth indispensable for the establishment of alliances with the new peoples and further for the installation of jurisdiction over their territories. The isolation of a unique figure which marvellously realizes the monarchic principle transposed into Indian chieftainship considerably simplifies the transactions because the key to domination rests in a single individual, easy to convert and to corrupt.

The "myth of Quoniambec" has not been understood any more by the modern interpreters of Thevet than by Jean de Léry who held rather pessimistic views regarding the conversion of the savages and was scarcely inclined towards audacious colonial schemes. Adhering without restriction and without the least check to the theses of the unfortunate cosmographer already in disrepute after centuries of suspicious criticism, Arthur Heulhard celebrates in turn the political intelligence of the good Quoniambec, which he opposes to the beastly indifference of his men: "His subjects were of a shameful stupidity," quietly declares Chevalier de Villegagnon's biographer (Heulhard 1897:114).[8] Hardly less literal and naive is the reading of that anonymous Brazilian writer reviewed by Herbert Baldus, who on the contrary indignantly refers to the ferocity of that "despotic lord," master over a territory extending from Bahia to Santos, and excuses himself for having to show to the "civilized" reader Thevet's portrait of an anthropophagic brute only governed by his instincts. The little monarchic fiction of the cosmographer thus remains plainly operative three centuries later. But whereas the letter of the myth continued to act in the direction of admiring sympathy for Heulhard, or of real or simulated horror for the anonymous commentator of the *Jornal do Instituto Historico e Geographico Brasileiro* (Anonymous 1850 cited by Herbert Baldus 1954: no.64),[9] the underlying political meaning remained without appreciation to the same degree to which it implicitly persisted to structure the dominant colonialistic thinking of the period. The sympathetic eulogy and the outright rejection were in fact based on the same lack of comprehension, and further on the refusal to take into account the relationship between the observer and the observed, the powerful colonizer and the colonized to be.

The two faces of the giant

It seems, however, that in its symbolic implications the myth of the Indian monarchy surpasses the strict usefulness in a colonial context. In Thevet, for example, the political use of the fiction in no way excludes much wider connotations by which it contributes to a global and rounded vision of the history of mankind. One may recall that the chapter dealing with Quoniambec in *Hommes illustres* is opened by a comparison of the Old and New Worlds, which turns to the advantage of the latter. If America might appear by some indications less cultured than her European and Asian sisters, she in turn surpasses them as much by "the beauty and fertility of the country" as by the "gracefulness" of her inhabitants. In other words, as Montaigne would say a little later, this infant-world was lacking nothing but a good teacher to bring out all the qualities still only potential, which if developed would make the student his teacher's rival. Thevet thus augurs that the newly discovered people, while being "removed from the true sun of justice," had nonetheless received some obscure foreboding of the Revelation. They would be all the easier to convert as this trace preexists in them of the Christian truth which they had not managed to retain the first time. Thevet whose expansionistic optimism would conform well to the vision of the conquistadors, would also approve of their opponent Michel de Montaigne's prediction: "This other world will only enter into the light when ours will depart from it. The universe will fall into paralysis; one member will be lame, the other vigorous" (Montaigne 1965:909 = *Essais* III,6 - "Des Coches"; cp.especially Bataillon 1959). The "incomparable amazement" (Thevet 1584,2:VIII,149, f.661r.) seizing the cosmographer at the sight of new horizons is actually inseparable from the perspective of a world crisis and renewal. According to the thesis of *translatio imperii* whose course was fulfilling itself from East to West by following the daily path of the sun, America represents the future of Christianity, divided and moribund in Europe. In this context, the gigantism attests to the almost intact youth of a continent for whom the slow process of decay has scarcely begun. Whereas the giants of the Old World belong to the antediluvian age and now exist only in the form of scattered bones - witness the skeleton exhumed in Saint-Germain-des-Prés (Thevet 1575,2:f.906v.)[10] - those of the New World are still quite alive.

One sees from this that a figure like that of Quoniambec could be charged with assuring a profound change of history. And the contrast is even more impressive in Montaigne's exchange set in Rouen between the vigorous Brazilian captain and the fragile crowned child reigning over France. The movement which saw the transfer of the Empire (political power and natural vitality) from one bank of the ocean to the other appears irreversible.

Yet it is necessary to modify this perspective to some extent: The American gigantism is afflicted with a fundamental ambiguity. If in fact its present appearance is a survival of a previous stage of humanity, this survival can be interpreted in two absolutely antithetical ways. One can well stress - and this is Montaigne's view - the future possibilities this infant-world is promising. One can as well place the accent on the archaic (and thus monstrous) character of these people who have even escaped the common evolution and whose excessive stature clearly contradicts the universal "ageing" to which the meaning of history amounts. In a theocentric vision of the world, these giants represent indeed a diabolic anomaly. And how could anyone from Pigafetta to Thevet explain the survival of the titanic Patagonians other than as an obvious exception from the Flood (Thevet c.1586:f.269r.)?[11] There could, in fact, be little doubt that the athletes encountered by Magellan on those southern shores were the parents of the criminal generation which preceded and by its excesses caused the "universal inundation." At this point, gigantism becomes a negative sign by which a superabundance of sin and a blasphemous haughtiness acquire a very concrete dimension. Following Thevet's reasoning, it is because they had given proof of an exaggerated confidence in their physical strength and in their abundance of substance that these giants of the antipodes "are despisers of heavenly spirits, eat and devour men, and altogether indulge in all those vices in which those had wallowed who had lived before the flood" (Thevet c.1586:f.269r.). How are these two myths to be reconciled, which coexist, for example, in the cosmographer's work, where one finds almost face to face the laudatory portrait of the "great king" Quoniambec and the outright pejorative depiction of the Patagonian "giantry" (Thevet 1575,2:f.906v.)?[12] In fact, the different treatment accorded here and there to the equally imaginary figures of the Brazilian and Patagonian giants seems to depend to a large extent on the communicative relations in their respective places. The giantlike Patagonian only exists by having no contact with others - that is, particularly with the conquerors coming from Europe. Negative gigantism characterizes those born in an exile maintained by a durable separation. The "half-giant" Quoniambec, on the contrary, results from a contamination of the ethnographic reality of Brazil with the values of the feudal prince imported directly from the Old World. Just as the Patagonian such as we come to see him, is the exaggerated result of a restriction, the Brazilian appears as the result of a conjunction. His lesser degree of "procerity" - he is at most a "half"-Patagonian - indicates well the hybrid character of this mythic composition. As an intermediary between the demonic titans escaped from the Flood and the miserable mankind of a world in its decline, Quoniambec represents the ideal middle ground to resolve the division of the universe and to reestablish man's necessary unity and continuity between his future and his past. The dichotomy set up between the Patagonian anarchist and the Brazilian monarch thus explains itself in terms of spatial relations. The withdrawal of these monsters of corruption to the extreme borders of the inhabited world accounts for the very survival of the Patagonians at the threshold of our modern age. Or, to repeat the immanentistic hypothesis formulated by Girolamo Cardano in his tract *De rerum varietate* of 1557, the gigantism of these faraway people could be seen as the result of autonomy and autarchy: "If one would live in the same country, with the same customs, without traveling nor receiving travelers, it follows that all the qualities, good or bad, will develop to the extremes" (Cardano 1557:22, cited after Céard 1977:232). The cold climate of Patagonia favored the inclination of its inhabitants to grow big, the absence of an opening to the rest of the world added to this natural disposition. The great discoveries, on the other hand, which once again initiated circuits of exchange and which on a beautiful winter day of 1519-20 removed the isolation from the Patagonian plains, would necessarily bring about a progressive reduction of the disparities having originated in autarchy. The voyage of the seas endangered the gigantism of the Americans in all possible manners: From a strictly genetic point of view the danger is caused by sexual, alimentary, and microbic exchange. And on the linguistic level the gigantism, as a legend linked to the distance and the difference of languages, is simply abolished, once a truly communicative relationship appears.

Significantly, Magellan's successive versions of the "invention" of the Patagonians all stress the impossibility or at least failure of exchange attempted by the navigators. At the end of a brief and ominous encounter mutually concluded by the shooting of arrows and the firing of cannons, the gigantism of the barbarians was preserved in their state of isolation. The Spanish embarked again and left these decidely inhospitable banks overshadowed by the silhouette of the terrible and titanic Patagonian hardly seen in the mists of dream (for an evocation of different scenarios of Magellan's encounter, see Lestringant 1987).

With singular foresight, Girolamo Cardano has thus discovered in the generalized exchange over the whole surface of the world the principle of a triumphant *entropy* - the same of which deleterious and harmful effects Claude Lévi-Strauss (1955:478)[13] would deplore four centuries later. But even though the author of *Tristes Tropiques* discovered an inescapable impoverishment of the field of research promised to anthropology - now reduced to the little enviable role of *entro*pology -, Renaissance men like Cardano could not but rejoice over the reduction of profusion and the associated simplification of the world. While waiting for the slow work of the erosion of the extremes to be accomplished - and the fabulous "procerity" of the Patagonian would continue to be perceived for the next 300 years -, the generation of the doctor from Bologna was in a position to contemplate the finally visible entire order of the universe in its profuse diversity.

Quite differently fared the myth of the "half-giant" Quoniambec, on the contrary a son and not a victim of the growing entropy. Being both symbol and result of an encounter, he took the place of a collaborator - in the economic and political sense of the word - since he delivers unhesitatingly to the conquerors the strategic keys of his vast kingdom. "It was he himself," declares Thevet, "who advised us to seize the neighboring rivers and islands and there to build the forts for our defense" (Thevet 1575,2:f.924r.). The active role which he plays in the reunion of the two halves of the world needs not be further demonstrated. The prestige which he gets from the dialogue with the men of the West adds to his tall stature, and it is precisely for this reason that Thevet has selected him from among all the savages.

From monarchy to family

In conclusion, it remains to be shown why the myth of Quoniambec was unique in this respect, whereas the Patagonian giantry from Pigafetta to Dom Pernetty was still popular during the very age of Enlightenment. First of all one should remember André Thevet's function in the course of his long carreer. Cosmographer of four successive kings (Henri II, François II, Charles IX, and

Henri III), he wrote the major part of his works in the shadow of the sovereign and thanks to financial support from him or his bankers such as the Florentine Bencivenni.[14] From this vantage point it is understandable that for him the monarchic principle would have to be a constant point of reference. Having to attempt a universal description of the world and being placed as he was in the position of a courtier offering to the king the innumerable riches of the creation, Thevet thought of the political relations between nations in terms of interpersonal exchanges between monarchs. Hence the "invention" of Quoniambec who brought to the Prince of Europe the travesty of his image as an American Hercules in the form of a plausible anamorphosis. Between those mirror-images, the logic of gift and reciprocal gift could fully come into play, in the direction of an expansion of the power of the French monarch sooner or later destined to amalgamate with his trans-Oceanic reflection.

But the triumphant myth would be rapidly spoiled by the unmerciful polemic against the cosmographer of the four kings, nourished by the pastor Jean de Léry, and soon taken up by the diligent pens of historians like Urbain Chauveton, Jacques-Auguste de Thou, or Lancelot Voisin de la Popelinière.[15] The context in which Jean de Léry must be seen is fundamentally different from the Parisian and courtly universe of the royal cosmographer. Since the time of his Swiss exile in Geneva and later in the country of Vaud, he published the six consecutive editions (1578-1611) of his Brazilian relation, long before matured in the France of the persecutions and civil wars. One can imagine him, based on his personal situation, being less respectful than Thevet towards a monarchy which, during a hot night in August of 1572, had taken the true and final face of tyranny. Without having perhaps been himself an advocate of tyrannicide, as recommended after the massacres of Saint Bartholomew's night by certain others of his denomination, there can be no doubt that Léry had nourished a durable resentment towards whatever emanation of an authoritarian power necessarily incarnated by a single person. Witness the long debates reported in chapter VI of the *Histoire d'un voyage faict en la terre du Brésil*, whose stake appears to have been as much political as theological. Opposed to the tyrant Villegagnon, a much more lukewarm Catholic than usually represented, but desirous of being the sole master on board, and who would end up sending three of the recalcitrant Huguenots to the bottom of the bay of Rio de Janeiro, are the fourteen members of the "Geneva" party who formed a directorial college for the colony of Refuge. In the face of a monarchy declared to be illegitimate since it had parted ways with the scriptures, the formula of a consistory took shape (cp.Reverdin 1957). The quarrel quickly took a deadly turn: Refusing to be "subjects" of the king of Antarctic France (Léry 1580:80), Léry and his companions proceded to open rebellion, rejoicing at the prospect of seeing the flesh and the "broad shoulders" of the Chevalier de Malte "serving as food for the fish" (Léry 1580:82).

That hate for the tyrannic monarchy is also found in the persistent caricature of Thevet's Quoniambec. By all accounts, it is not just capricious of Léry to take the "half-giant" of Ubatuba as his favorite target of ridicule, the dignified counterpart of the athletic Villegagnon whose privileged interlocutor he had been as we have seen. In Léry's eyes, Quoniambec epitomized an inacceptable notion of this indigenous society and which despite the ever present delusions of Satan represented to him a last outpost of Eden. In the Brazilian utopia of the *Histoire d'un voyage* there is no place for the Indian monarch.

On several occasions, Léry insists, for example, on the role of the old men who in endless speeches exhort their people to take vengeance (Léry 1580:196-197), and who conduct their tribe in their migrations to new fields or against enemy territory (Léry 1580:202). In doing so, he deliberately mixed up two positions which Thevet had taken care to distinguish: The military chief who, according to the cosmographer, is a man in the full vigor of manhood, and the "old man" who plays somewhat the role of a sage whose extended family, assembled in the *maloca*, listens to his bellicose speeches.

This confusion permits Jean de Léry to remove not only the most hampering person of Quoniambec, but also the specific function which he filled in the Tamoio microcosm as originally described by Thevet. And Léry does not miss any occasion to remind of the basic lack of leadership positions. In connection with the long march which took all of the group "without order, however without confusion" towards the battlefield, the men armed with bows and clubs, the women bent under the weight of the carrying basket, as well as the children, Léry could see neither "field marshal" nor "anyone who draws up the quarters for the rest" (Léry 1580:202). In this way, a social and military utopia is portrayed, in which the community, though deprived of leaders and orders, displays an admirable cohesion and executes its tasks in perfect harmony. Only the subtle would be able to translate this miraculous state as a "non-anarchic anarchy." If one believes Léry, the "Toüoupinambaoult" society is based on an egalitarian principle, such that there are "amongst them neither kings nor princes," and that all the warriors are "almost equally great lords amongst themselves" (Léry 1580:196). One could not attempt a more flagrant denial of Thevet's fiction of the "great king" Quoniambec.

According to Jean de Léry's hypothesis, the myth of the Indian monarchy definitely proceeds from a misunderstanding. It is a simple error of translation which initially had brought forth the phantastic notion of an Indian monarch. An exchange in the famous *Colloque de l'entrée ou arrivée en la terre du Brésil ... en langage sauvage et François* (Léry 1580:314) in fact proposes to substitute for the "frustrating" term of "kings" that of "fathers of families." And it is that same expression that one finds in Léry in the contexts of welcome and hospitality, in which "the old one" opens his house to the stranger, offers him food and drink, and sometimes even his daughter (Léry

1580:283,285).[16] The *moussacat* in his functions of generous and attentive host - and obviously this figure has a long posterity, at least up to Diderot's Tahitian - replaces the terrible *morbichat* so dear to Thevet, whose thundering authority, like that of a cannibal Jupiter, far from limiting itself to his little family, extends over all the people.

If from Thevet to Léry the "father of the family" has ultimately replaced the chief, the cell of the family has effaced the state. For the monarchic system, as incarnated and magnified in the person of the giant-like king Quoniambec, the intimate and domestic circle is substituted, in which the mother and her children are grouped around the father. A telling image of this spatial and sociological restriction is offered by one of the first engravings found when leafing through the *Histoire d'un voyage* and whose title could be: "Brazilian family with pineapple" (Léry 1580:107; see our Fig.4). Tenderly embracing the naked warrior armed with bow and arrows, the Tupinamba woman slightly in his rear holds a round and chubby child in the traditional carrying band. The pineapple in the foreground and the fruit of the "choine" tree in a dish, as well as the hammock in the background of the composition, just give the indispensable touch of exotism to this idyllic genre scene.

The paradisiac image of the woodcut, which is as fictive as the *terribilita* of the cannibal King, attests to a certainly more modern vision of the American Indian, whose aftermath has not yet stopped to enliven the realm of dreams, which has installed itself alongside the field of contemporary anthropological investigation. If proof is desired for the favor in which the *Histoire d'un voyage* is held today more than ever, it is found in Lévi-Strauss's grateful recognition of it as the "breviary of the ethnologist." Isn't it possible to see a direct continuation of Léry's iconography in that extraordinary photo entitled "Intimity" by the author of *Tristes Tropiques*, which shows us the Nambikwara family grouped into a happy and smiling plot?

Léry has thus eclipsed Thevet, just as the Brazilian family has undermined the prestige the cosmographer had wanted to give to the improbable "half-giant." However, in the related eclipse of politics, already noticable in Léry and later restored by the modern ethnologists (cp.Delpech 1980), it would be appropriate to recognize the stigmata of an unhappy perception of a world which since the years 1555-1565 and after the repeated setbacks of France in America was no longer to be conquered, at least temporarily, but to be dreamed about in the ineffable way of nostalgia (cp.Julien 1948: 163-263).

NOTES

1. Verses 563-580 of book I of *Les Tragiques* read in full:
    "Jadis nos Rois anciens, vrais peres et vrais Rois,
    Nourrissons de la France, en faisant quelquesfois
    Le tour de leur païs en diverses contrees,

Faisoyent par les citez de superbes entrees.

....

.... à leurs Rois triomphans,
Triomphans par la paix, ces villes nourricieres
Prodiguoyent leur substance, et en toutes manieres
Monstroyent au ciel serein leurs tresors enfermez,
Et leur laict et leur joye à leurs Rois bien-aimez."

2. "The king spoke to them for a long time ... They said that they found it very strange in the first place that so many big men, bearded, strong and armed who were around the king (it is probable that they spoke of his Swiss guard), submitted themselves to obey to a child and that they would not rather choose one amongst themselves as a commander..."

3. This scene had already been presented in an embryonic state in his *Singularitez* (Thevet 1557:f.103v.-104r.). But Quoniambec, "the most esteemed and renowned king of all the country," is still a pale figure when compared with his later renditions in Thevet 1575 and 1584.

4. "You also should have seen his palace which is a lodge as rich as that of others, all adorned and decorated on the outside with heads of his massacred and eaten enemies." The hyperbolic term "palace" ('palais') appears already in Thevet 1557:f.103v.

5. Lescarbot is citing Tacitus, *Germania*, chapter VII: "Reges ex nobilitate, duces ex virtute sumunt. Nec regibus infinita ac libera potestas, et duces exemplo potius quam imperio, si prompti, si conspicui, si ante aciem agant, admiratione praesunt." Lescarbot, however, points out the following distinctions: "In Virginia and in Florida they are more honored than among the Souriquois (or Micmac). But in Brazil he who has taken most prisoners and killed most enemies is taken for their captain, whose children are not able to inherit this rank."

6. It is true that the universal cosmographer and "insuliste" speaks in this page "about the island and river of St. Dominique" on the height of "Fernambourg" (Pernambuco), and not about the riverine tribes of the coast of Rio de Janeiro.

7. Regarding the privilege of the chief to make speeches, for example, Clastres (1974:136) writes: "The chief's obligation to make speeches, that constant flow of empty speech which he *owes* to the tribe, is his infinite debt, the warranty which prohibits the man of speech to become the man of power." By all evidence, André Thevet can only supply a diametrically opposed interpretation of Quoniambec's display of loquacity. In his eyes, it is on the contrary the effective and terrifying speech of a monarch, whose power is not only political and military but is exercised magically over persons and events.

8. As even the title of Heulhard (1897) implies, the author has enthusiastically

Fig. 4. Untitled woodcut of Tupinamba family from Léry's *Histoire d'un voyage* (1580), 107.

subscribed to the Thevetian myth of the dialogue of monarchs between Villegagnon and Quoniambec.

9. Herbert Baldus is understandably surprised at the troubled horror which towards the middle of the last century inspired the portrait of a Renaissance Indian "de aspecto mais sonolento do que feroz."

10. In Thevet (c.1586:f.269r.) the author amplifies the digression relating to giants from his previous work: "And because several are reluctant to believe what they cannot find at their own doorstep, I am quite content to make a statement here on some giants who have been seen and recognized in our France, so that by these means I could recover those poor disbelievers from the pit of incredulity, who have scruples to listen to talk about the existence of giants today. At the Jacobine monastry of Valence one can still see the portrait of a giant called Buard who measured eight ells in height, together with the bones of the monstrous man. In Loches, Captain Pontbriant and some others found in an underground chamber a sitting man of marvellous stature, who, judging from the proportion of his bones, must have stood some eight grand feet high. To avoid prolixity, I will desist from mentioning the giant of Saint-Germain-des-Prés in Paris, as also the one said to have been brought down by King Arthus of the

Albionic Britons on the Isle Notre Dame of this city of Paris, as well as others." For a recent summary of this question, see Céard 1978.

11. "Those who hold that the great flood had completely destroyed the brood of the Earthborn, will find by the account I shall give how they mistake ..." (Thevet c.1586:f. 269 r.).

12. This chapter of the *Cosmographie* entitled "About an Island where the men are from ten to twelve feet high" (ff.903-906) is the redundant and exaggerated transformation of the sober account of Antonio Pigafetta, the companion of Magellan's voyage.

13. "Every verbal exchange, every line printed establishes a communication between interlocutors, thus creating an evenness of level where before there was an information gap and consequently a greater degree of organization."

14. On the financial support given by Jean-Baptiste Bencivenni, "abbé de Bellebranche" and librarian of Catherina Medici, and notably on his contribution to the financing of the *Vrais Pourtraits et Vies des Hommes illustres*, see Balmas 1965.

15. On the composition of this network of convergent writings which Marcel Bataillon has called "the Huguenot corpus relating to America," see Bataillon 1974. Some additions on this question will be found in Lestringant 1984.

16. The *moussacat* is alternately defined as the "good father of the family who feeds those passing by" and as the "old master of the house."

17. In the same vein, see also Lévi-Strauss 1982. As the title indicates this is less a critical reading of Léry than a "retrospective confession," using Léry as a medium.

REFERENCES CITED

Anonymous
1850 O chefe indio Quoniambebe. Revista trimesal de Historia e Geografia ou Jornal do Instituto Historico e Geografico Brasileiro 13 (segunde ediçâo, 1872): 517. Rio de Janeiro.

Baldus, Herbert
1954 Bibliografia Critica da Etnologia Brasileira, vol.I. Sâo Paulo.

Balmas, Enea
1965 Documenti inediti su André Thevet. Melanges Bruno Revel, 33-66. Firenze.

Bataillon, Marcel
1959 Montaigne et les conquérants de l'or. Studi Francesi 2(3): 353-367.
1974 L'Amiral et les "Nouveaux Horizons." Actes du Colloque L'Amiral de Coligny et son temps, 41-52. Paris: Societé de l'Histoire du Protestantisme Français.

Cardano, Girolamo
1557 De rerum varietate libri XVII. Basilae: H.Petri.

Céard, Jean
1977 La Nature et les Prodiges. L'Insolite au XVIème siècle, en France. Genève: Droz.
1978 La querelle des géants et la jeunesse du monde. The Journal of Medieval and Renaissance Studies 8(1):37-76.

Clastres, Pierre
1974 La Société contre l'Etat. Paris: Editions de Minuit.

d'Aubigné, Agrippa
1969 Les Tragiques. Henri Weber, ed. Paris: Gallimard.

Delpech, Sophie
1980 Introduction. In: Jean de Léry, Histoire d'un voyage. Paris: Plasma.

Heulhard, Arthur
1897 Villegagnon roi d'Amérique. Un homme de mer au XVIème siècle. Paris: Ernest Leroux.

Julien, Charles-André
1948 Les voyages de découverte et les premiers établissements. Paris: P.U.F.

Kohl, Karl-Heinz (ed.)
1982 Mythen der Neuen Welt. Zur Entdeckungsgeschichte Lateinamerikas. Berlin: Frölich und Kaufmann.

Léry, Jean de
1580 Histoire d'un voyage faict en la terre du Bresil. 2nde édition. Genève: Antoine Chuppin (cited after reprint edition, Genève 1975: Droz).
1585 Histoire d'un voyage faict en la terre du Brésil. 3ème édition.

Genève: Antoine Chuppin.

Lescarbot, Marc
1617   Histoire de la Nouvelle France. 3ème édition. Paris: Adrian Périer.

Lestringant, Frank
1978   Les représentations du sauvage dans l'iconographie relative aux ouvrages du cosmographe André Thevet. Bibliothèque d'Humanisme et Renaissance 40:583-595.
1984   L'Excursion brésilienne: note sur les trois premières éditions de L'Histoire d'un voyage de Jean de Léry (1578- 1585). Mélanges sur la littérature de la Renaissance, à la mémoire de Verdun-L. Saulnier, 53-72. Genève: Droz.
1987   La flèche du Patagon ou la preuve des lointains. Actes du Colloque Voyager à la Renaissance. Paris: Maisonneuve et Larose.

Lévi-Strauss, Claude
1955   Tristes Tropiques. Paris: Plon.
1982   Eine Idylle bei den Indianern. Über Jean de Léry. In Kohl 1982:68-70.

Luchesi, Elisabeth
1982   Von den "Wilden/Nacketen/Grimmigen Menschfresser Leuthen/in der Newenwelt America gelegen." Hans Staden und die Popularität der "Kannibalen" im 16. Jahrhundert. In Kohl 1982: 71-74.

Lussagnet, Suzanne (ed.)
1953   Le Brésil et les Brésiliens. Paris: P.U.F.

Mesnard, Pierre
1951   L'Essor de la philosophie politique au XVIème siècle. Paris: J.Vrin.

Métraux, Alfred
1928   La civilisation matérielle des tribus tupi-guarani. Paris: Librairie orientaliste Paul Geuthner.
1948   The Tupinamba. Handbook of South American Indians 3: 95-133. Bulletin of the Bureau of American Ethnology 143/3. Washington: G.P.O.

Meung, Jean de
1970   Le Roman de la Rose. Félix Lecoy, ed. Paris: Honoré Champion.

Montaigne, Michel de
1965   Essais. Villey-Saulnier, ed. Paris: P.U.F.

Reverdin, Olivier
1957   Quatorze calvinistes chez les Topinambous: Histoire d'une mission genevoise au Brésil (1556-1558). Genève: Droz.

Staden, Hans
1979   Wahrhaftige Historia. Henri Ternaux-Compans, trsl. Paris: A.-M.Metailié.

Thevet, André
1557   Singularitez de la France Antarctique. Paris: Les héritiers de

Maurice de la Porte.

1575   La Cosmographie Universelle. 2 vols. Paris: L'Huillier et G.Chaudière.

1584   Les Vrais Pourtraits et Vies des Hommes illustres, Grecz, Latins et Payens. 2 vols. Paris: veuve J.Kerver et G.Chaudière.

c.1586   Le Grand Insulaire et Pilotage. Paris, Bibliothèque Nationale, Ms.fr. 15452.

c.1588   Histoire de deux voyages aux Indes Australes et Occidentale. Paris, Bibliothèque Nationale, Ms.fr.15454.

THIS NEW PREY:
ESKIMOS IN EUROPE IN 1567, 1576, AND 1577

William C. Sturtevant and David Beers Quinn

The first Eskimos in Europe seem to have landed in the Netherlands. However, the earliest was probably not Zierik, who came ashore in Zeeland in A.D. 849, according to a local tradition, and founded the town named after him. In the town hall of Zierikzee is preserved what is claimed to be his boat, along with some of his gear. It is a West Greenlandic kayak, but it cannot be traced back earlier than the eighteenth century and no doubt was collected when Dutch whalers began frequenting Greenland waters after 1600 (Nooter 1971:63-70).[1]

1566 captives

The first Eskimos who can be securely documented in Europe were brought to Zeeland in 1567: a woman and child kidnapped some months earlier by French sailors, evidently in Labrador. Only two sources of information on these unfortunate people have been found so far. In the Hague in 1577 and 1578 Adriaen Coenen kept a book into which he copied pictures of Eskimos brought to England in 1576-1577 by Frobisher. Next to one sketch of them he wrote that he had seen other such people at the time of the Calvinist rising of 1566-1567 when the owners of the Mill inn in the Hague had charged admission to see a woman and child who were dressed in sealskins (the hairy side out). Although Coenen remarked that the woman did not speak much, she had evidently learned some appropriate European behavior since Coenen saw how she shook her head and joined her hands when she was shown some Catholic images (see Appendix 2). The rest of our knowledge of these captives comes from three versions of a broadside containing a woodcut showing an Eskimo woman and little girl surrounded by a typeset descriptive text. The text is in German, but contains two spellings indicating that the unknown original model was in Dutch: Zeeland rather than German Seeland, and Zeehonts for German Seehunds. One version was printed by Matthäus Franck in Augsburg (Fig. 1c), and survives in two copies, one in the Zentralbibliothek, Zurich (PAS II 7:4) and one in the Graphische Sammlung, Staatsgalerie Stuttgart (Inv. 10593). Only one copy survives of each of the other two versions: one printed by Hans Wolf Glaser in Nuremberg (Fig. 1a) (British Library, 1750.c.2.4) and one dated 1567 printed by Anthony Corthoys the Younger in Frankfurt am Main (Fig. 1b) Herzog Anton Ulrich-Museum, Braunschweig, KK 744).

All three were probably printed in 1567: The text says that the woman and child were captured in August, 1566, and arrived in Antwerp at least eight months later "in this year 1566" (in the Julian calendar 1567 began on March 25, some seven months after the capture). Detailed comparison of the very similar texts and woodcuts indicates that there must have been a Dutch original (presumably published in Antwerp) from which was derived a German version (now unknown) which served as the model for the Augsburg version on the one hand, and for the more similar Nuremberg and Frankfurt versions on the other hand; the latter two may in fact both be derived from another lost version itself copied from the model for the Augsburg version.[2] One translation (Appendix 1) will serve for all three texts - no additional information appears in the other versions, which differ only in spellings and in minor ways in syntax.

All three broadsides seem to have been news reports of the exhibition of the two Eskimos in Antwerp. The texts all state that they were to be seen there, and do not say they were exhibited in the cities of publication.

According to the broadside texts, the woman, aged 20, and her seven year old daughter were captured by French sailors in "Nova Terra" (also "Terra Nova") (Appendix 1). In eight months the woman had learned to speak some French (or Basque?) - enough to be misunderstood as confirming European preconceptions about the cannibalism of savages. Although it was reasonable for the broadsides to compare her complexion to that of "the half Moors," since the eastern Arctic was thought by many to be part of Asia, the claim that the text says that her captors tried to "talk with her through two Moors" (Quinn 1981a) is a mistranslation based on misreading the black-letters for *oder auch mit jr durch Wort reden* ("nor also talk with her through words") as an impossible *oder auch mit ji durch More reden*.

The identification of the "wild woman" (*wilde Fraw*) "with her little daughter" as Eskimos depends on the pictures. The clothing and the facial tattooing plainly agree with what is known of later Eskimos all across the eastern Arctic, and in the eighteenth and nineteenth centuries one of the major differences between Eskimos and their Indian neighbors was precisely in clothing.

Then where within the Eskimo region was "Terra noua which is a new district a few years ago first discovered by the French and Portuguese"? Greenland Eskimos were apparently not met by Europeans, after the Norse, until 1585 (although on his third voyage in 1578 Frobisher saw some, without making direct contact, and found in an Eskimo tent a box of nails that perhaps indicates an unrecorded earlier European contact - Stefánsson 1938,1:cxv, 2:36). Documents relating to Basque whaling from the early 1540's to the mid 1580's - mostly Spanish, but some French - consistently refer to the region of their activities on the north coast of the mouth of the St. Lawrence in the Strait of Belle Isle (between modern Labrador and Newfoundland) as Terra Nova, occasionally Tierra Nova or Tierra Nueva, and the form Terra Nova also occurs in Portuguese sources on the same region. French Terre Neufve (and similar

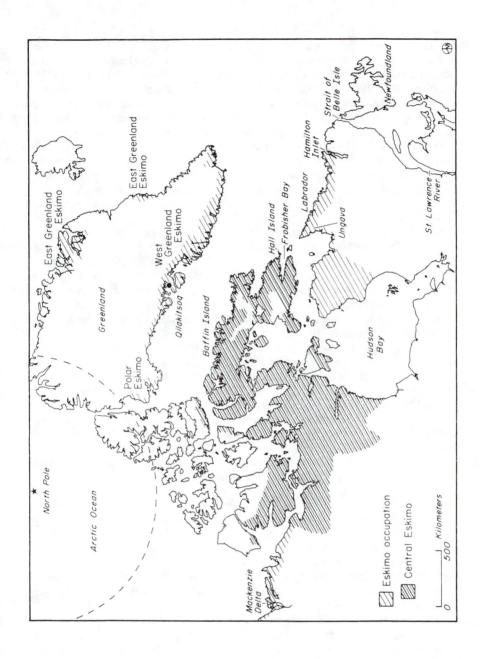

forms) was used from about 1514 into and beyond the 1560's for this region and especially for the south shore of the Strait and for modern Newfoundland, both frequented by Breton fishermen (Quinn 1979:87-94,100-102,107,183-186; Barkham 1977, 1978, 1980:52). "Nova Terra" shifts the Spanish and Portuguese name to Germanic word order. By the 1560's there were each year more than 1000 Basques in 15 to 20 ships spending at least six months on this coast, yet there are no unambiguous references to contacts with Eskimos and very few references to natives of any kind (Barkham 1980).

Archaeological evidence indicates that the southern Labrador coast in the sixteenth century was occupied by Indians, bearers of the Point Revenge culture (ancestors of the Montagnais, Micmac, or Beothuk?). About A.D. 1400 Thule Eskimos from Baffin Island or perhaps the Ungava area began spreading down the Labrador coast. As they moved further along the coast they displaced both earlier Dorset Eskimos (although evidence for contact with them is slight) and also Indians. On present evidence it was not until the late sixteenth century (a precise date cannot yet be suggested) that they reached Hamilton Inlet. The oldest Thule archaeological site excavated there contains European materials, including some Basque tiles; the presence of such goods may have drawn Eskimo settlers this far south and perhaps temporary trading parties even farther (Kaplan 1983,1:21,105-106,154-155,160-169,234-235, 2:6-7; Jordan and Kaplan 1980; Fitzhugh 1978).

Hamilton Inlet is some 450 km up the coast from the limits of the area visited by Basque fishermen before the 1560's, according to the documents on their activities that have been located thus far. However, what seems to be Hamilton Inlet is indicated on several Norman charts prepared before 1560 (Quinn 1981c:49-51), showing that some French and probably Portuguese vessels had reached areas where Eskimos might have been found. But the two Eskimo captives seen in Antwerp provide evidence that by 1566 Europeans had reached farther up the Labrador coast, or Eskimos farther down it, or both, than is otherwise well documented. Future archaeological work on the Labrador coast south of Hamilton Inlet, and future archival discoveries, can be expected to extend this evidence.

The ethnographic accuracy of the pictures is much greater than that of the text of the broadsides. We are shown readily recognizable quite ordinary Eskimos, accompanied by a text emphasizing cannibalism, gigantism, paganism, and promiscuity. Perhaps the oddly-shaped sealskin clothing and the tattooing were so exotic that no sensational distortions of the picture were necessary to attract curious Europeans at that date. Even so, the portraits are skillfully done, especially considering that they are woodcuts on broadsides for a popular audience.

The depictions can be compared with later eastern Eskimo clothing and tattooing, and with evidence from eight mummies (six adult women, and boys about six months and four years old) dating from about A.D. 1475 recently

Fig. 1. The 1566 captives, woodcuts. a (top), Nuremberg broadside (By permission of the British Library). b (bottom left), Frankfurt broadside (Herzog Anton Ulrich-Museum Braunschweig, Museumsfoto B.P.Kaiser). c (bottom right), Augsburg broadside (Staatsgalerie Stuttgart).

65

discovered at Qilakitsoq, just north of Disko Island, West Greenland (Hart Hansen et al. 1985). The clothing of the coastal Labrador Eskimos is not known until the eighteenth century, when the forms and materials had undergone European influence. The clothing shown in the woodcuts in some respects more resembles that of nineteenth century Baffin Island and Greenland than it does eighteenth century Labrador clothing. However, styles probably changed in all regions in the two to three centuries following 1566, and the dress of all eastern Eskimo women and children was quite similar. Comparison of the pictures with the available ethnographic evidence does permit some judgements on the accuracy of details shown in the different versions of the woodcuts.

The facial features in the Nuremberg and Frankfurt versions may be more accurate than those in the Augsburg version (Quinn 1981a), although the clear difference in the artists' skills makes it difficult to be certain. The Augsburg artist followed Mannerist conventions in unrealistically showing the contours of the woman's body under her heavy skin clothing. The straight hair of the other two versions is also more correct than the wavy hair in the Augsburg woodcut. The hair is uncolored in the Nuremberg copy, whereas in the Augsburg version the woman's hair is wrongly tan and the child's grey. In all three versions, the skin areas are painted brown (in the Frankfurt version crudely so, overlapping onto the hair).

The woman's facial tattooing is of the widespread Eskimo female type. The Augsburg and Frankfurt versions but not the Nuremberg one have greyish blue color painted between some of the pairs of dotted lines on her chin. This probably followed the specification in the accompanying text that the marks were "sky blue," for in reality only the pricked (or sewn) lines were themselves blue. The layout of the lines on the chin, cheeks, and forehead is quite closely paralleled in a skillful 1768-1769 oil portrait of a woman from the Labrador coast (Taylor 1984:511 fig. 3; Plischke 1954:Taf. 9; cf. Savours 1963) as well as in patterns from Baffin Island (Boas 1888:561, 1901:108) and nearby areas (Hawkes 1916:106; Mathiassen 1928:200; Birket-Smith 1929a:228), and from fifteenth century West Greenland (Hart Hansen et al. 1985:116-132). The curved V-shape on the forehead in the Nuremberg and Frankfurt versions is more like the documented patterns than is the straighter forehead line in the Augsburg version, and the spacing of the lines on the chin may also be more accurate in the other two versions.

The woman's hooded parka is well depicted. The tall hood with central seam has parallels in northern Labrador 300 years later (Boas 1901:51), although it was probably wider at the base, and the parka shoulders were probably looser (both typical of all women's parkas, so an infant can be carried inside) (Driscoll 1980:14-15). Long, rather pointed hoods of approximately this form are also documented for later times for various Central Eskimo groups, and for West Greenland (Boas 1888:163; Driscoll 1980; Damas 1984:411,452,611), as well

66

as for West Greenland in 1475 (Hart Hansen et al. 1985:147-154,206-210). The slit below the head opening, implied more by the Augsburg version, is probably an error. The bottom edge of the parka should be bilaterally symmetrical - all three woodcuts seemingly have an error on the woman's right hip, but the Augsburg and Frankfurt versions are more accurate over her left hip. The rounded apron-like extension in front is correct, but there was surely a tail extension in the back (Taylor 1984:515; Driscoll 1980:14-16; Boas 1888:555, 1901:51; Mathiassen 1928:172-177,186; Hart Hansen et al. 1985) which appears only in the Nuremberg and Franfurt versions and even there shorter than comparative evidence implies. In this respect the parka is closer to West Greenland types, which have shorter tails than the extra-long ones of eighteenth century Labrador women's parkas.

The woman wears short summer trousers, typical of Baffin Island (Boas 1901:52,54) and elsewhere (Mathiassen 1928:177-178), with an interesting decorative band around the bottoms. In all three pictures there is a gap between the tops of the boots and the trousers. In the late seventeenth and the eighteenth century (but not later) women's boots on the Labrador coast were much higher and flared out widely at the tops (Taylor 1984:515; Driscoll 1983:20,30; Jefferys 1772:pl. 195). Evidently we have here an earlier style, resembling other eastern Eskimo ones. The construction of the boots was misunderstood by all the artists, although they may have intended also to show short leggings worn above the boot tops, as was later typical of Baffin Eskimos (Boas 1888:556; Mathiassen 1928:185-186; cf. Hawkes 1916:40-41,167,171 for knee-length boots without leggings). In that case the Nuremberg and Frankfurt woodcuts are more accurate. None of the three shows the typical crimped seam where Eskimo boot soles are attached to the uppers; the Augsburg version misleadingly hints at heels.

Comparative data on small girls' clothing are scarcer, but there seems no reason to question seriously the depictions here, except for the slit in the left cuff which is shown in the Nuremberg and Frankfurt versions. The child may be wearing a separate cap (Hawkes 1916:173; Mathiassen 1928:187,189) or more likely an attached hood. Her parka is of the appropriate shape for a little girl, except for the ragged edges and the short neck opening (Boas 1888:557, 1901:53-54; Mathiassen 1928:193). She holds an unrecognizable object in her left hand in the Nuremberg and Frankfurt versions.

The coloring applied to the clothing is better in the Augsburg version than in the other two. It is tan except for decorative grey bands around all openings of the woman's parka and around the bottoms of her trousers, and grey flaps at the tops of both pairs of boots (or leggings). In the Frankfurt version both parkas and hoods are tan, except for the woman's grey cuffs, her trousers are also tan except for grey decorative bands around the bottoms, and both have dark grey boots. The Nuremberg version is carelessly colored in a non-significant manner.

The clothing of Labrador Eskimo women and girls is not sufficiently distinct from that of other eastern Eskimos (or is not known to have been so in the sixteenth century) to permit the positive identification on this basis alone of the provenience of the people shown in the woodcuts. But any hypothesis of origin elsewhere than the Labrador coast, for example Baffin Island, the Ungava area, or Greenland, involves much more unlikely assumptions about undocumented voyages.

It is possible that French Basques transferred the captives to one of the Dutch or Flemish ships to which they often sold salt cod and whale oil in the Bay of Biscay, or they may have fallen into French hands from a Spanish Basque ship victualling at La Rochelle. Landed in Zeeland, they were sent to be exhibited in the Hague and Antwerp (where first is uncertain). Their ultimate fate is unknown, but they cannot have survived long and certainly never saw their homeland again.

It is striking how isolated the 1567 broadsides are. Their source is entirely unknown and they left no descendants, in sharp contrast with the written and especially the pictorial evidence on the next Eskimos in Europe, those brought from Baffin Island to England by Martin Frobisher in 1576 and 1577. No doubt this is because the first captives were incidental to local and secretive, although well established, commercial exploitation of the maritime resources of the Labrador region, whereas the later captives were evidence collected during Arctic explorations supported by the English crown and by risk-taking merchant entrepreneurs at high levels. These were voyages searching for commercial opportunities in new lands to be claimed for England, and attempting to locate the supposed Northwest Passage leading to the riches of China - Frobisher's backers called themselves the Cathay Company. Informations about the captives became part of the publicity and propaganda of colonial expansion, and therefore also part of the new geographical, scientific, historical, and artistic knowledge of the world beyond Europe.

Frobisher's captives

In the 1570's the country explored by Frobisher was an "unknown boundary," *Meta Incognita* as it was called, between Europe, Greenland, America, and Asia. Symptomatic is the uncertainty on what to call the natives. The English vacillated between people of Cathay, Tartars, Tartar Indians, country people, strange people, and even Moors, but not of course Eskimos. Contemporary English authors do not call them wild, and only rarely savage. George Best refers to them as "savages" occasionally, usually in contexts alluding to violent conflict; more often he calls them "country people," although twice he does refer to them as "the Caniballes" (Stefánsson 1938,1:114,115). However, French sources usually call Frobisher's captives *sauvages*, and Dutch and German call them *wild*.[3]

However, there is absolutely no doubt as to where Frobisher's Eskimo captives were taken (in contrast to the 1566 captives). He met Eskimos only on Baffin Island, in the same region on both his 1576 and 1577 expeditions, and he saw no other American natives. The site of his main activities in Frobisher Bay is well identified, from nineteenth and twentieth century archaeological explorations (Stefánsson 1938,1:cvi,cxiv, 2:240-247; W. Fitzhugh in Damas 1984:379 fig. 2; Sayre et al. 1982).

For Frobisher's four captives there is important written evidence, both on the circumstances of the captures and on their fates. Once again, however, some of the best evidence is pictorial. It is remarkable how many pictures of them are known to have been made. Many of the images have not survived; some lost originals can be deduced from derivative copies that were preserved. Sometimes they are found in collections of depictions of dress - conceived as habits in both senses of that word, as both costumes and customs (Defert 1984) - or in miscellanies with drawings of monsters, exotic animals, and unusual occurrences. Pictures were an important response of European curiosity about the larger world then being explored, paralleling the very miscellaneous objects in cabinets of curiosities (*Kunstkammern*) and the compilations and summaries of written accounts.

Living people were also collected as evidence, trophies, and objects of curiosity. George Best in 1578 described the conclusion of Frobisher's first voyage in these words (Stefánsson 1938,1:49):

"Now with this new prey (which was a sufficient witness of the captain's far and tedious travel towards the unknown parts of the world, as did well appear by this strange infidel, whose like was never seen, read, nor heard of before, and whose language was neither known nor understood of any) the said Captain Frobisher returned homeward, and arrived in England."

On 11 August 1576, Frobisher's ship arrived in the supposed strait given his name (now Frobisher Bay in southeastern Baffin Island).[4] On 19 August a party went ashore on "Burchers Island," probably on the south shore of the bay, and first saw Eskimos - a group of 19. The Englishmen seemed more frightened than the Eskimos, for they escaped to their ship and quickly prepared it for defense. Then, putting an English hostage ashore, they took an Eskimo hostage on board, where he tasted (and disliked) English food and drink and received some "trifles" before being returned and the English hostage recovered. Frobisher thought he perceived "these strange people to be of countenance and conversation proceeding of a nature given to fierceness and rapine" (Lok in Stefánsson 1938,1:161), so sailed off. A day or so later the English returned to another or the same island and again went ashore, where they saw both abandoned winter houses and occupied summer tents, and soon an umiak with apparently friendly people. The Eskimos exchanged garments of sealskin and of polar bear skin, and raw meat and fish (including salmon) for English bells, looking-glasses, "and other toys." Visiting the settlement, Frobisher thought that he was about to be attacked, so held the point of his weapon (a partisan) at the throat of an Eskimo man while he finished his investigation, and then returned to his ship. Another Eskimo then "went willingly" aboard, received "many trifles of haberdash," and was understood to agree to lead the ship in his kayak "through the straits to the West Sea" which would require only "two days rowing" (at least some of the communication by signs failed, for they were in an enclosed bay). Perhaps it was this man, rather than the one captured later (as John Dee thought) who was understood in an interview largely via signs to indicate that while there were no gold, siver, or cloth in his own country - the name for which was recalled by Frobisher's men interviewed by Dee in England as Pycknemay, Pycknea, Pygmenai, or Pyckenay - he was willing to guide them to "Mania" (the mythical straits of Anian?) a month's sailing away, where such riches did occur (Taylor 1930:276).

Five Englishmen took him ashore in the ship's only boat, thinking he went for his kayak and equipment. Frobisher, still mistrustful, ordered that he be set ashore apart from the other Eskimos and within sight of the ship. This was done, but the boat then rowed around a point of land out of sight of the ship, evidently to trade with the Eskimos. Three of its crew went ashore, the two remaining in the boat rowed it into sight again, then, disobeying calls from the ship, rowed back out of sight. Neither the boat nor the five men were ever seen again by the English.

According to local "oral history" collected in 1861 and 1862 by Charles Francis Hall, after one or more winters with the Eskimos the five men left in a boat they built, but were blocked by ice and froze to death. Hall did find remains left by Frobisher's activities, but the reported Eskimo traditions about his three expeditions are suspiciously precise, given the time elapsed and the numerous intervening contacts with Europeans in the region. Both the details and Hall's interpretation of their significance may have been influenced by his familiarity with the accounts published by Hakluyt and by his use, during his main interview, of a book containing a summary of the voyages (Hall 1864,1:271-272,300-304; 2:151-153,284-286,344-347; on his interpreter, 1:162-169; on his use of a reference book, 1:303).

Frobisher spent a couple of days in the neighborhood, searching for his men or for hostages to take to force their return. Having "lost his boat and five of his best men" (the remaining crew amounting to only 13), he realized that he would have to terminate his explorations. Furthermore, as Lok wrote, he "most of all other was oppressed with sorrow that he should return back again to his country bringing [not] any evidence or token of any place whereby to certify the world where he had been." Best phrased it that "the Captain (not withstanding) desirous to bring some token from thence, of his being there, was greatly discontented, that he had not before apprehended some of them." So he needed captives, to exchange for his lost men and boat and to take home as trophies.

Returning to the spot where he had lost his boat, he was met by "a number of the boats and men of that country coming towards the ship," including one umiak containing 20 men (although only 19 had been counted a few days earlier). Making his ship ready for defense, he prepared to capture some of them. The Eskimos reasonably refused to approach the clearly hostile ship. However, the man who had first come aboard before was more trusting.

Frobisher stood alone at the ship's side, "having at his feet in secret his weapons," tossing clothing into the sea to attract him. He was frightened off by a sailor reaching for his kayak with a boathook, but then approached again. Tinkling small bells and throwing them into the sea Frobisher "enticed" him closer, until finally as he reached for a bell Frobisher siezed his hand, grabbed his wrist with his other hand, and heaved him bodily aboard with his kayak (Fig. 12a). "Whereupon when he found himself in captivity, for very choler and disdain he bit his tongue in twain within his mouth." His companions watching the capture from "within an arrow shot of the ship," pulled off. Waiting two more days in hope of exchanging his captive for his lost crewmen, Frobisher finally gave up and sailed for England on 25 August, arriving in London in early October.

Hall's laconic journal of the voyage includes cultural data on the Eskimos from his observations in Baffinland, and probably also from the captive - a 17-item vocabulary, and the following passage:

"They be like to Tartars, with long black hair, broad faces, and flat noses, and tawney in color, wearing seal skins, and so do the women, not differing in the fashion, but the women are marked in the face with blue streaks down the cheeks, and round about the eyes. Their boats are made all of seal skins, with a keel of wood within the skin: the proportion of them is like a Spanish shallop, save only they be flat in the bottom, and sharp at both ends" (Stefánsson 1938,1:153).

Michael Lok ended his account of Frobisher's voyage with a description of the captive and his reception (here we transcribe from the original damaged manuscript, Lok 1577:f.53v.):

"And so came to London with their Ship Gabriel the ixth day of October & there were ioyfully received with the great Admiration of the People, bringing with them their stran*n*ge man & his Bote, which was such a wonder vnto th[e] whole City, & to the rest of the Realm that heard of yt, as seemed neuer to have happened the like great matter to any mans knowledge....And because that I haue heard Report of many strange Tales &

fayned fables touching the personage & manners of this strange man: I haue thought good therfore to declare the very Truthe therof, to satisfy the world & allso to express his Picture as well as may be done with Ink & Paper [the illustration is now lacking in the manuscript]. He was very [ ] good sh[ape]...he...[fay]re & [s]strongly pight & made,...his Neck, his Brest,...very brode face, & very fat & fu[lle] [about] his Body. But his Legs shorter & smaller [then the] [pr]oportion of his Body requyred. And his hands...[H]is heare cole Blak, & long hanging & tyed [vp a]boue his fore head. His Eyes little and a ... blak Beard. His Culler of Skyn all ouer his Bo[dy & fa]ce, was of a dark Sallow, much like to the tawny Mores; [or ra]ther to the Tartar Nation, whereof I think he was. [His] Countenance sullen or churlish and sharp withall."

Responding to auditors investigating the financial failure of Frobisher's voyages, Lok on 26 January 1578 still thought the captive worth mentioning as a positive result:

"Now, when Martin Frobisher was returned home again, in October 1576, with his strange man of Cathay, and his great rumor of the passage to Cathay, he was called to the Court and greatly embraced and liked of the best" (Stefánsson 1938,2:185).[4a]

The bills for the costs of the expedition (Lok 1576-1583) indicate that Frobisher and Lok did what they could to care for their captive in England. There are entries of £1/1O/6 "for household charge, [a]potticarye, in his sicknes & folke highered to tende him, & wynd him"; of 16s. "for beddinge for him spoyled in his siknes"; of £5 "to mr. crowe the surgyon, for openynge of the Indian man, & [em]balmyng him dead, preservid to have him bin sent backe againe in to his countrye" (why this was not done is unspecified); of 11s. 4d. "for a coffyne, bran, to pack him, & other" (all on p.15v.); and finally "for buryinge the tartar Indian man In Saint Olaves churchyarde" (63v). The parish records for this church in Hart Street, London, survive but the individuals listed as buried there in 1576 cannot possibly include the Eskimo man (Cheshire et al. 1980:25,38; originals also examined 8 June 1985 by W.C.S.). Coenen (Appendix 2) implies that he died about fifteen days after arriving in London. According to Best (Stefánsson 1938,1:50) he died "of a cold which he had taken at sea." One can guess that, like most other American natives taken to Europe in the first centuries after Columbus, he succumbed to some European disease to which he lacked resistance.

Lok's comment, quoted above, is not the only indication that pictures were prepared of the man and his kayak. George Best reported that the Eskimo man captured on the second expedition in 1577 was shown on board Frobisher's ship "the picture of his countryman, which the last year was brought into England (whose counterfeit we had drawn, with his boat, and other furniture, both as he was in his own, and also in English apparel)" (Stefánsson 1938,1:65). A somewhat ambiguous entry in the catalogue of John Tradescant's museum at Lambeth near London indicates that in 1656 he preserved at least a picture of the man, and perhaps also his actual kayak and less likely his bow and dart as well: "A Canow & Picture of an Indian with his Bow and Dart, taken 10 leagues at Sea. *An.*° - 76" (Tradescant 1656:42; MacGregor 1983:94; the wrong information about where he was captured seems a typical collector's exaggeration).

The bills for Frobisher's first voyage show in two places entries for payments to Cornelis Ketel, a Flemish painter then living in London, for making pictures of the man. He charged £5 for full-lengths - the same price for the Eskimo and for portraits of Frobisher and Lok (but £6 for a painting of their ship *Gabriell*). These are called simply "great pictures," except for one explanation (Lok 1576-1583:15v.): "a great picture of the whole bodye of the strainge man in his garments." The portrait of Frobisher is the only one known to survive - in the Bodleian Library, Oxford (Lane Poole 1912:20-21). It is on canvas, full-length, 81 1/2" x 37" (about 207 x 94 cm), and is inscribed over the subject's right shoulder: "A[n]o D[omi]ni 1577 / Aetatis suae 39 / C[ornelis] K[etel] F[ecit]"; there is a one-year discrepancy in the date, and the subject's name is given only in a later inscription lower down which reads "Martin Frobisher miles / ex dono / Gvalteri Charleton. M.D." The bust section is reproduced as the frontispiece in Stefánsson 1938,1; the whole painting is reproduced in black and white by Morison (1971:499) and in color in a postcard and a slide issued by the Bodleian Library (both published by Woodmansterne Ltd., Watford). This painting shows Ketel to have been a highly skilled portraitist who paid particular attention to details of clothing. Ketel charged £1 each for "small pictures" - both of the Eskimo and of Master Christopher Hall. These were evidently busts, for in one case (Lok 1576-1583:15v.) they are described as "small pictures of his head." Of the Eskimo man, five "great pictures" are listed: one "in Englishe ap[par]ell" (63v.) - and Frobisher claimed reimbursement for the large amount of £1/10/0 "for apparrell for the strainge man of Cathay or new land India" (14v.) - and four "in his [native] apparell" (63v.) or "in his garments" (15v.). Of the latter, one is specified as for the Queen and one for the Cathay Company which backed the voyage. There were in addition three "small pictures" (15v., 63v.). The bills also include charges for frames, although the numbers and descriptions do not quite match. Seven "great frames" were billed (at 8s. each) (15v., 63v.) for only five great pictures of the Eskimo (all frames seem to be specified as for pictures of the "strainge man" or the "tartar man"; and adding the "great" pictures of Frobisher, Lok, and the *Gabriell* makes a total of eight). Two of the great frames were "for the strainge mans pictures to send over seas" (63r.). On the other hand, only one "small frame" (at 2s.) was billed (63v.).

Fig. 2. The 1576 captive. a (top), Drawing by Lucas de Heere, Table 1:8 (Rijksuniversiteit te Gent). b (bottom), Drawing by Adriaen Coenen, Table 1:9 (Koninklijke Bibliotheek, The Hague).

74

The bills also include payments for making what seems to have been a wax cast, perhaps of his head alone: £1/13/4 to "wm. Cure duchemane [i.e., Dutchman] graver, for making a moulde of hard earthe of the tartar man ymage to be caste in waxe," 10s. "for wax to make his mold in picture" (both on f.15v.), 5s. "for moldinge stufe to Jonas Chentege [sp.?]" (63r.), and £1 to Ketel "for his picture naked, or waxe molde" (63v.).

Neither the wax cast nor any of Ketel's eight pictures of this man has survived. Only one picture positively identified as depicting him is known: a watercolor drawing by Lucas de Heere, which is inscribed "Wild man brought from the northern lands by M. Frobisher the year 1576" (*Homme sauuage ammene des païs Septentrionaux par M. Furbisher L'an 1576*) (Heere 1568-1576:f.124).

Lucas de Heere (b. 1534, d. 1584) was a skilled costume artist and tapestry designer, a native of Ghent where he worked most of his life except for the periods from 1566 until 1577 when he was a Protestant refugee in London. While there he was in contact with other Flemish refugee artists and publishers, including Philipp Galle and Abraham Ortelius; Cornelis Ketel was then in London, and in the same circles, although there is no evidence that de Heere knew him there (Chotzen and Draak 1937:xiv; Yates 1975:27,134n.16; Hodnett 1971:18). By 20 April 1577 de Heere had returned to Ghent (Busscher 1866:208; Chotzen and Draak 1937:xii). His Eskimo drawing may have been done from life in London, or more likely was derived from a now-lost depiction by Ketel or another. It appears at the end of a manuscript now in Ghent that contains 190 costumed figures in 97 watercolor drawings, mostly European types of his own times and before but including a few Turks, (North) Africans, Egyptians, Persians, and Ethiopians (Heere 1568-1576; Busscher 1866:189-191; Yates 1975:20-22). This volume was evidently begun in London in 1568, and may have been completed there with the dated Eskimo drawing. Another de Heere manuscript, in the British Library (Add. MSS. 28,330), contains a written text and 22 costume figures (on eight sheets) relating entirely to the British Isles. This manuscript was prepared in 1573-1574 but at least the text was revised considerably later. The costume figures are entirely of British subjects, and all of them have equivalents in the Ghent manuscript (Chotzen and Draak 1937:lxxii-lxxv). Most of the costume studies in these two manuscripts were based on published and manuscript sources, often considerably improved, but some of the contemporary British figures may have been done from life. The pose and the slim body of the Eskimo man agree with de Heere's other costume studies; here as elsewhere he used a standard mannikin-like figure to display the carefully-depicted costume details. The body build disagrees with Lok's description of this man, although he does have the black beard mentioned by Lok. Chotzen and Draak (1937:lxxvi) suggest that the details of the costume as opposed to the body build indicate that this Eskimo figure was copied from someone else's depiction. The same deduction may be made from the fact that the Eskimo figure includes a background, in contrast to all the other costume studies in the two manuscripts (at least those in the London manuscript, fully reproduced in Chotzen and Draak (1937), and the several dozen in the Ghent manuscript reproduced by them and by Yates (1975); most of the Ghent figures have never been published and we have not seen the manuscript). Behind the Eskimo appear a man in a kayak and a European ship. The latter closely resembles a ship in a siren device that de Heere inscribed as drawn in London in August, 1576 (Yates 1975:28, pl. 18b). Ethnographic evaluation of this drawing is best done in conjunction with the depictions of the 1577 captives, which are very similar and include some representations derived from the 1576 voyage.

In 1577 Frobisher returned to Baffin Island with a larger expedition in search of ore - they loaded some 200 tons, all of which turned out to be absolutely worthless - and also with some hope of recovering the men lost the previous year.[5] On 19 July on Hall Island at the northern opening of Frobisher Bay, contact was warily negotiated with a party of Eskimos (Stefánsson 1938,1:58-60, 2:14). Each side suspiciously refused invitations by signs to visit, and then two representatives of each engaged in classic silent trade: English knives, pins, "points" (i.e. laces for clothing), "and such trifles" for two Eskimo bow cases "and such things as they had." After the trade broke off Frobisher and Christopher Hall, unarmed, approached two Eskimo men, "meaning, if they could lay sure hold upon them, forcibly to bring them aboard, with intent, to bestow certain toys and apparel upon the one, and so to dismiss him with all arguments of courtesy, and retain the other for an interpreter." A few items were exchanged, one Eskimo even cutting off the tail of his parka and giving it to Frobisher. Then the two Englishmen suddenly seized the Eskimos. They scuffled and the two Eskimos broke loose, retrieved their bows and arrows, and chased the Englishmen towards their boat, wounding Frobisher in his buttock with an arrow. The other Englishmen coming to the rescue fired a "caliver" and the Eskimos ran off. But Nicholas Conger, a fast runner "and a good wrestler," caught one and "showed his companion such a Cornish trick, that he made his sides ache against the ground for a month after" (and no doubt gave him the injury from which he later died in England).

Ten days later, in a grave on a small nearby island, various implements were found including a sled and harness the use of which the captive demonstrated with an English dog (Stefánsson 1938,1:64) - probably the source of the detail in one illustration, for sleds drawn by (many) dogs were not used in summer.

On July 31 in York Sound, on the south shore of the bay, some possessions of the men lost in 1576 ("about 50 leagues" - 150 nautical miles?! - further up the bay) were found in temporarily unoccupied Eskimo summer tents. On 1 and 2 August the 16-18 Eskimo owners were encountered nearby and attacked in an effort to take captives. They fled in an umiak and a kayak, chased in two pinnaces by a party of 30-40 Englishmen firing "calivers" who forced them ashore where the Eskimos broke their paddles to prevent capture of their boats. In a sharp fight with bows and arrows used on each side, one Englishman was wounded and five or six Eskimos killed, three by drowning when they leaped off a cliff to avoid capture after being wounded. (Churchyarde 1578: B1v.-B2r. gives the numbers as 13 Eskimos vs. 30 Englishmen, and mentions the suicides.) The rest escaped, except for two women, "one being old and ugly... the other being young and encumbered with a sucking child at her back." "The old wretch, whom divers of our sailors supposed to be either a devil, or a witch, had her buskins plucked off, to see if she were cloven footed, and for her ugly hue and deformity, we let her go: the young woman and the child, we brought away" (Settle 1577 [2nd. ed.]:Bvir; Stefánsson 1938,2:17, 1:68). The child had been shot in the arm by an English arrow(?). Frobisher's surgeon applied salves, but the mother cured the wound "by continual licking with her own tongue."

The abandoned Eskimo tents were looted of "poor stuff" and "trifles, more to be wondered at for their strangeness, than for any other commodity needful for our use." It is not stated whether these souvenirs included the kayak, paddle, bow and arrow, throwing board, and bird darts that were demonstrated and drawn later in England (Stefánsson 1938,2:17, 1:69).

The English observed with great curiosity the behavior of the captive man and woman. When they were first brought together they acted in such a way that they were taken not to be acquainted - which seems unlikely, for the places where they were captured were not distant in terms of Eskimo movements, the land was thinly populated, and the woman was from a group that had evidently captured the Englishmen in 1576 while the man let it be understood that he knew about that affair. Although they soon became very solicitous of each other, "for so much as we could perceive, albeit they lived continually together, yet did they never use as man and wife" while "the man would never shift himself, except he had first caused the woman to depart out of his cabin, and they both were most shamefast, lest any of their privy parts should be discovered, either of themselves, or any other body" (Best in Stefánsson 1938,1:69-70, and similar remarks on p. 125).

In subsequent brief and mostly hostile meetings with Eskimos in several places in Frobisher Bay - once with a group estimated at about 100 people (large for the area) - Frobisher tried without success to use his captives as intermediaries, interpreters, and hostages in order to gain news of his lost men and recover them. At least once the captives tried and failed to escape. Probably a good deal of Best's and Settle's perceptive remarks about details of Eskimo appearances, behavior, and artifacts (Stefánsson 1938,1:123-127, 2:19-23) derived from observing them.[6]

As the Englishmen completed their fruitless mining, they gave up hope of recovering the lost crew members, whom they decided had probably been eaten by the Eskimos. European preconceptions of savages as cannibals turn up

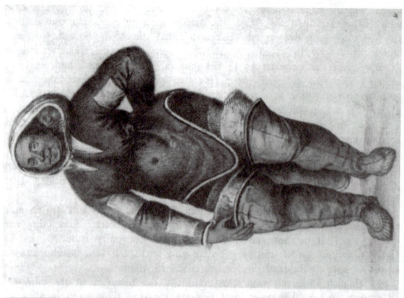

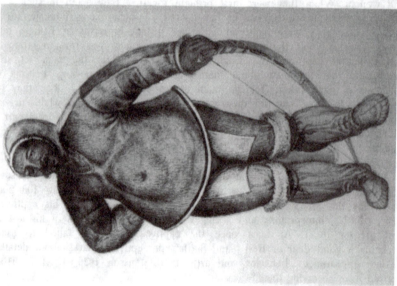

Fig. 3. The 1577 captives. Original drawings by John White. a (left), Kalicho, Table 1:17 (British Museum). b (right), Arnaq and Nutaaq, Table 1:27 (Both: Permission of the Truster of the British Museum).

78

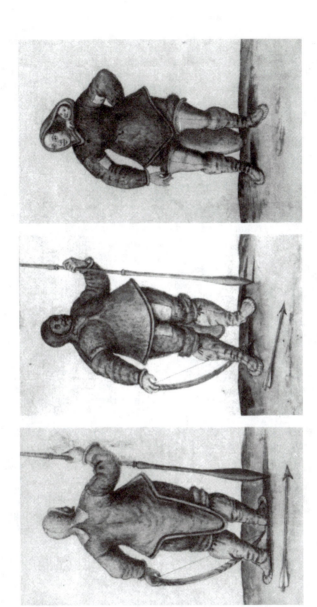

Fig. 4. The 1577 captives. Copies after drawings by John White. a (left), Kalicho, front view, Table 1:18 (British Museum). b (center), Kalicho, back view, Table 1:19 (British Museum). c (right), Arnaq and Nutaaq, Table 1:28 (All: Permission of the Trustees of the British Museum).

repeatedly in the accounts of these Eskimos, and seem to have been taken as confirmed by observations that their cuisine included dogs, entrails, "raw" meat (actually probably merely less cooked than the English habit), and "carrion" (meat and fish hung longer than the English would eat).[7] Soon after their capture, native food for the man, woman, and child was accepted from other Eskimos "for that as yet, they could not digest our meat" (Stefánsson 1938,2:19).

Frobisher's three ships departed on 23 August reaching England about a month later. The captives arrived in Bristol aboard the *Ayde* in early October, with Best and Settle (Frobisher having left the ship at Milford Haven in Wales, to ride to London to report).

The captives immediately attracted considerable interest. What were thought to be their names were recorded in England in various spellings. That of the man can be standardized as *Kalicho*. The woman's is modern Eskimo *Arnaq*, and the baby's probably *Nutaaq*.[8] He was described soon after his capture on 2 August as a nursing boy 12 months old; when the adults died in November he was said to be about 14 or 15 months old (Best and the French edition of Settle, in Stefánsson 1938,1:34, 2:238).

Within a few days of his arrival in Bristol, Kalicho was on display. On October 9, "before the maior and many others," he paddled up and down the river Avon at high tide, killing two ducks with his "dart" before landing in the Marsh and carrying his kayak "through the Cittie vppon his backe." He also demonstrated "at the weare and other places, where many beheld them, he would hit a ducke a good distance of[f] and not misse" (Adams 1639, 1910:115; Bristol Calendar 1690). The captives' food preferences were noted in the same accounts: they were said to eat nothing but raw meat. According to Coenen and the 1578 broadside (Appendices 2, 3) while they ate raw meat und fish and bad-smelling flesh and drank water, in England they also ate roasted and boiled meat, in large quantities. The supplementary passages in the French edition of Settle, wrongly saying that Kalicho was presented to the Queen who allowed him to kill her swans on the Thames, add that "they once killed a fowl[9] and ate all the entrails including the dung" (Stefánsson 1938,2:237). The way that Arnaq nursed her child carried on her back inside her parka was noted (Bristol Calendar 1690) - she "gave suck casting her breasts over her shoulders," a detail that may sound improbable, but two anthropologists who have studied in topless societies have told us it is possible for some women and has been seen.

According to Coenen (Appendix 2), the odor of the captives was unpleasant to the English. Perhaps their single sets of garments began to stink in the warmer English climate.

The account in Settle states that they showed no amazement at what they saw, except that, "wild people that they are, they bowed deeply on seeing people" (surely a comment based on contemporary European prejudices rather than an accurate report). It also says that Kalicho, after watching Frobisher's trumpeter mount a horse, tried the same but "got on exactly backwards, with his face towards the tail, and was very diverted to see the horse caper." This seems an unlikely story, given the broken ribs from which he was sufferung greatly at the time.

Frobisher claimed the very large sum of £17/8/5 for expenses at Bristol "for Apparell, and Charges, for the strainge man and strainge woman, there, who dyed there" (Lok 1576-1583:74r.). A nice detail provided in Coenen's manuscript (Appendix 2) is that they had learned to use two polite expressions of Elizabethan English, "God give you good morrow" and "farewell."

The most touching information on the captives was recorded in Latin by Dr. Edward Dodding (1577) on November 8, the day after he had performed an autopsy on Kalicho. Dodding was a well-trained medical man of his day, whose report is that of a sympathetic physician more than an anatomist or scientist, although he does say that he "was bitterly grieved and saddened, not so much by the death of the man himself as because the great hope of seeing him which our most gracious Queen had entertained had now slipped through her fingers, as it were, for a second time" (thus implying that she did not see the 1576 captive either).

The doctor was called in to examine Kalicho "while his strength was still unimpaired." He detected "an 'Anglophobia' [*Anglium diceres metum*], which he had from when he first arrived, even though his fairly cheerful features and appearance concealed it and gave a false impression with considerable skill. His own actions, however, either betrayed it openly and exposed it... or else they betokened an incipient fatal illness." He suffered continually from "deafness and intense head-pains," and then or later from shortness of breath. The physician thought he was over-fed, considering his condition, remarking that his "unhealthy voraciousness" was satisfied through "misguided kindness." He recommended blood-letting, but Kalicho refused and was supported in this by those taking care of him. He evidently treated himself in an Eskimo mode, for "he made an incantation for every time his pain abated."

Dr. Dodding was called again an hour before Kalicho died, and found him semi-conscious, without appetite, and with speech impaired. "He summoned up to a certain extent all the energies and faculties which he had abandoned, came back to himself as if from a deep sleep and recognised us as people he knew. But I turned my attention to medication, and he spoke those words of ours which he had learned, the few that he could, and in turn replied quite relevantly to questions. And he sang clearly that same tune with which the companions from his region and rank had either mourned or ceremonially marked his final departure when they were standing on the shore (according to those who heard them both)." It is doubtful that Englishmen could distinguish one Eskimo tune from another - but here is evidence for a death song. Kalicho's last words were in English: "God be with you."

The physician performed an autopsy, finding that two ribs had been badly

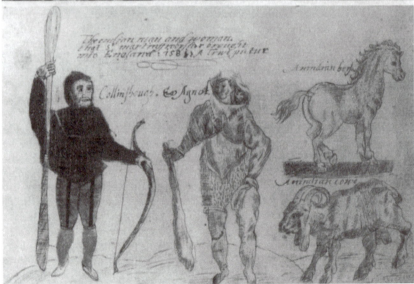

Fig. 5. The 1577 captives. a (top), Lower section of engraving by Philipp Galle, Table 1:30 (Rijksmuseum, Amsterdam). b (bottom), Drawing by William Burch, Table 1:31 (Permission: Dean and Chapter of Canterbury).

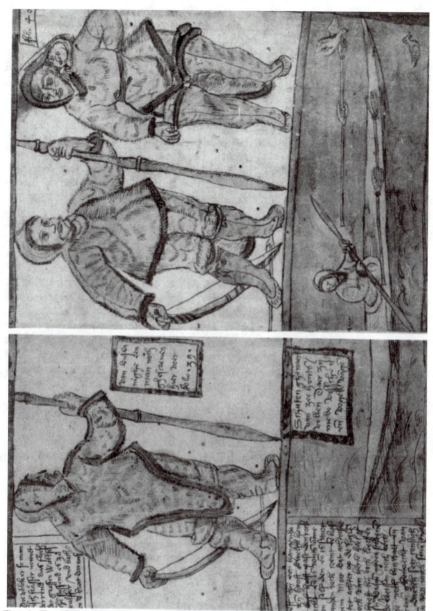

Fig. 6. The 1577 captives: Kalicho, Arnaq and Nutaaq, kayaker. Drawings by Adriaen Coenen, Table 1:40 (Koninklijke Bibliotheek, The Hague).

broken in a fall "and were still gaping apart without having knit together." He assumed the injury had been neglected aboard ship (so implying that the fall had occurred more than a month before). The left lung was found to be infected, filled with fluid, and evidently collapsed. Thus presumably the broken ribs were on his left side, which helps to explain how he could accurately throw his bird dart on the Avon, although any movement must have been very painful. A head injury, inadequately described, was also discovered.

After Kalicho died, Dr. Dodding showed his body to Arnaq and took her unwillingly to observe the burial. He insisted that she do so, that the burial be "without ceremony," showed her human bones dug up in the graveyard, and kept her there until Kalicho's "body had been completely covered over with earth," all in order to demonstrate that the English did not practice human sacrifice or cannibalism as he was convinced the Eskimos did - "so that she might learn to put aside the fear henceforward."

Dr. Dodding reported that Arnaq was troubled with boils on 7 November, "which broke out very densely on her skin next day," but he did not comment otherwise on her health. Perhaps it was for Arnaq that 5s. was paid to "doctor gilbarte for fyssyke for sours" (Lok 1576-1583:74r). But she soon died, for Kalicho was buried on 8 November and Arnaq on 12 November, both at St. Stephen's church in Bristol - in consecrated soil although each is characterized as "heathen" in the parish register (Cheshire et al. 1980:37; Quinn 1979:218).

Nutaaq, the baby, survived only a short time. Frobisher hired a nurse to take him from Bristol to London, where they stayed eight days at the Three Swans inn. John Gymblet, surgeon, was paid 5s. to treat him, but Nutaaq died and Frobisher sent the nurse back to Bristol. The sum of £2/11/6 was claimed as the costs for the nurse, the inn, and for "buriall of the childe in parish of saint olaves in harte streate" (Lok 1576-1583:74r.,75v.). It is surely no coincidence - but the reason is not clear - that this is the church where the 1576 captive was also buried. The parish register does not record the two burials, and not because they are hidden behind Christian names (Cheshire et al. 1980:37-38): all those buried in 1576 and 1577 are so characterized as to preclude any being Eskimo, and none of those named as christened at this church in these years can possibly be an Eskimo.

The news of Frobisher's expeditions spread rapidly. By January, 1579 it reached Moscow by a rather indirect route, probably beginning with the publication of Best's book in London in 1578. In the class "State Papers, Foreign, Russia" in the Public Record Office, London, there is an unsigned document (SP 91/1,13) endorsed "Advertisementes owt of Russia Towchyn *Master* Furbishers viage to the Northwest" and headed "the 26 Ianuarie 1578 [=1579] in Musco" that reads as follows:

"As touching *Master* Furbyshers voyage / We haue hard of a Russe, that was the Princes [Ivan IV's] Rentgatherer in Iugorie that the place whervnto he

84

comethe, is not farre beyond the Ryver Ob. And the people which dothe inhabite thear, are called the Pakij Samwedeij, And are those that kyllethe the Sealles / Also he told me that they complayned greatlye of the takyng awaye of a man, a woman & a chylde / and of Leavyng of hys men thear / This Country is a goodlye Countrye / And bordereth on the one syde to Cattaij [Cathay], and on the other syde to Ciberes"

The Eskimos had become Piakeï Samoyeds of western Siberia, beyond the Yugor Straits southeast of Novaya Zemlya and north of Sibir, which latter name in the sixteenth century referred to Isker, a Tatar khanate near present Tobol'sk, taken by the Cossacks in 1579.[10]

The financial accounts for Frobisher's second voyage indicate that Cornelis Ketel was again engaged as a painter. He must have been called to Bristol from London in October or early November, 1577. The bills are only for paintings of the woman (presumably with her baby in her parka), not the man. Ketel made two "great pictures" at £4 each and two "small pictures" at £1 each. One of each was for a present to the Queen "at new yeares daye," and there is an entry for the cost of transporting them to Hampton Court. The other two were for the Cathay Company. Charges are listed for three frames, those for the Queen's pictures and one for the Company's "great" picture (Lok 1576-1583:74r,75r.).

There is independent evidence that Ketel's paintings given to the Queen - one of the 1576 man and one of Arnaq - survived for a time in the royal collections. In 1592 Jacob Rathgeb, secretary to the Duke of Württemberg, on a visit to Hampton Court saw "life-like portraits of the wild man and woman whom Martin Frobisher the English captain, took in his voyage to the New World, and brought alive to England" (Rye 1865:18). These must be the pictures of "A Cataia, or Island Man" and "A Cataia Woman" listed as sold from Hampton Court after the execution of Charles I, but brought back after the Restoration and catalogued among the pictures of James II (1685-1688) at Hampton Court (Rye 1865:205; Cheshire et al. 1980:34).

No later record of any of Ketel's portraits of Eskimos has been found. However, two paintings of Frobisher's captives, probably either by Ketel or derivatives of Ketel paintings, survived as late as 1776 in the armory of the Duke of Bavaria. An inventory of 1689 clearly described them:

"2 raised [überhöchste, perhaps 'framed'] panels painted on cloth on one a man on the other his wife together with a child of a wild kind, the man was named Calitgoch, the woman Egnocth, the child Nutiocth, these people are from Greenland, belonging to the king in Denmark or Sweden, in 1577 thrown out of the sea by a lucky and unforeseen gale in Holland, which Count Morice, erstwhile general of the Dutch in other words, received as they are here pictured before the eyes together with two of their little

Fig. 7. a (left), Frobisher's 1577 fight with Eskimos. Drawing by or after John White, Table 1:35 (Permission of the Trustees of the British Museum). b (right), "Portrait of three wild people brought to England, their clothing, weapons, tents, and boats," engraving published with French edition of Settle's account, Table 1:37 (By permission of the Houghton Library, Harvard University).

86

Fig. 8. a (left), Engraving published with Latin and German editions of Settle's account, Table 1:38 (Settle 1580 Latin, Library of Congress). b (right), Engraving published with Italian edition of Settle's account, Table 1:39 (Courtesy James Ford Bell Library, University of Minnesota).

skin boats, of which he kept one, but the other little boat together with the oar and these pictures he made a present of to a Count of Hanau, who afterwards presented it to His Princely Majesty Duke William of Bavaria remembered in Christ, as is to be seen here before the eyes, and to observe moreover, that there is no rivet of iron at all in this little boat, but it is pieced together only with sea fish bones [i.e. baleen] and kept in good condition" (Stöcklein 1911; reprinted in Plischke 1921).[11]

The paintings, which could not be located in 1921 (Plischke 1921), and the kayaks were presumably separately collected but merged in the inventory.[12] The names and date for the Eskimos correspond precisely to Frobisher's captives. Perhaps they were copied into the inventory from inscriptions on the canvases (compare the inscription on the surviving Ketel portrait of Frobisher), while the erroneous information on their provenience was confused with local tradition on the history of the kayaks and paddle.

Surviving illustrations

There are 18 surviving depictions that are potential primary sources on the appearance and clothing of Frobisher's captives and on their equipment. Comparison suggests stemmata implying that about 13 additional depictions once existed and served as models for those now known, in addition to the 19 lost paintings or drawings mentioned in written records (Table 1).

The de Heere watercolor of the 1576 captive (Fig. 2a; number 8 in Table 1) is realistically colored. (The drawing has evidently never been published in color; the following notes were made from a colored 35 mm transparency.) The parka is light grey, except for the white edging around the hood opening and the bottom, the darker grey of the triangle below the throat (the "hood yoke"), and the tan of the inner surface of the tail. The trousers are tan, with the patches slightly lighter in color and the edgings around the bottoms light grey with a faint indication of a horizontal zigzag line across them. The boots are tan. A narrow strip of the man's skin, reddish brown like his hands and face, shows between his trousers and boots. He has a moustache and a small beard on the point of his chin, both black. The arrow has a black point, and seems to lack fletching. The paddle, including the drip rings, is tan.

There are two watercolors by John White, a front view of a standing man with a bow, presumably Kalicho (Fig. 3a; Table 1:17), and a front view of a standing woman with a baby in her parka, Arnaq and Nutaaq (Fig. 3b; Table 1:27). Although unsigned and unlabelled, these are certainly by John White because they are by the same hand as the paintings of "Virginia" Indians and natural history subjects which they accompanied in a volume first mentioned as sold by a London bookseller in 1788, and the Virginia ones are identified by

Table 1. Depictions of 1576 - 1577 Eskimos.

Items within square brackets are deduced from surviving images. The rest are known from textual references or surviving examples. Entries for the latter are starred, and their catalogue or inventory numbers are given.

1576 captive:
1. Full-length in oils, in native dress, by Ketel, October, 1576. For the Cathay Co.
2. Full-length in oils, in native dress, by Ketel, October, 1576. For the Queen. Last seen in 1688.
3. Two full-lengths in oils, in native dress, by Ketel, October, 1576. To send overseas.
4. Full-length in oils, in English dress, by Ketel, October 1576.
5. Three busts in oils, by Ketel, October, 1576.
6. Life-cast in wax, by Cure and Ketel, October, 1576.
7. [Full-length, with paddle, bow and arrows, kayaks and ship in background.] Same as 1, 2, or 3?
*8. Full-length with paddle, bow and arrows, kayak and ship in background, in watercolors, by de Heere, 1576. Rijksuniversiteit te Gent, Centrale Bibliotheek (Mas. 2466, f.124). After 7. (Fig. 2a).
*9. Full-length with paddle, bow and arrows, kayaks and ship (capture scene) in background, in ink by Coenen, December 1577. Koninklijke Bibliotheek, The Hague (78 E 54, f.48 v.). After 7. (Fig. 2b).
10. Drawing mentioned by Lok in 1577. After 1 or 2?
11. Drawing in native dress, with kayak and gear, carried aboard 1577 voyage according to Best. After 1, 2, or 7?
12. Drawing in English dress, carried aboard 1577 voyage according to Best. After 4?
13. Portrait, probably with bow and dart, perhaps with kayak. Owned by Tradescant in 1656. After 1, 2, or 7? Same as 1, 7 or 11?
1577 captives:
14. [Kalicho, full-length with bow and arrow and paddle.] Same as 1, 3, or 7?
15. Kalicho, in oils on canvas, with name inscribed. Last seen in Munich in 1776. After 14?
16. [Kalicho, full-length with paddle and bow and arrow, watercolor by White.] Same as 14?
*17. Kalicho, full-length with bow, watercolor by White about 1588. Dept. of Prints and Drawings, British Museum (L.B. 1[30] with offset L.B.2[30]). After 16. (Fig. 3a).
18. [Kalicho, full length front and back views, with bow and arrows and paddle, by White.] After 16?

Table 1. Depictions of 1576 - 1577 Eskimos.

---

*19. Kalicho, full-length front and back views, with bow and arrows and paddle. Watercolor copied between 1593 and 1614. Dept. of Prints and Drawings, British Museum (L.B. 3[11] and 3[10]). After 18. (Fig. 5a,b).

20. Arnaq with Nutaaq, full-length in oils by Ketel, October-November 1577. For the Queen. Last seen in 1688.

21. Arnaq with Nutaaq, full-length in oils by Ketel, October-November 1577. For the Cathay Co.

22. Arnaq with Nutaaq, bust in oils by Ketel, October-November 1577. For the Queen.

23. Arnaq with Nutaaq, bust in oils by Ketel, October-November 1577. For the Cathay Co.

24. Arnaq with Nutaaq, in oils on canvas, with names inscribed. Last seen in Munich in 1776. Same as or after 21?

25. [Arnaq with Nutaaq, with double hood roots, full-length, watercolor by White.] After 20 or 21?

26. [Arnaq with Nutaaq, with single hood root, watercolor by White.] After 20 or 21?

*27. Arnaq with Nutaaq, with double hood roots, full-length, watercolor by White, about 1588. Dept. of Prints and Drawings, British Museum (L.B. 1[30], with offset L.B. 2[31]). After 25. (Fig. 3b).

*28. Arnaq with Nutaaq, with single hood root, full-length, watercolor copied between 1593 and 1614. Dept. of Prints and Drawings, British Museum (L.B. 3[12]). After 26. (Fig. 4c).

29. [Arnaq with Nutaaq, and Kalicho, full-lengths by Gheeraerts.] After 20, 21, or 25, and 14 or 16.

*30. Arnaq with Nutaaq, and Kalicho, full-lengths, engraved by Galle, probably 1578-1582. Examples in Rijksmuseum-Stichting, Amsterdam; Metropolitan Museum of Art, New York; Musée des Beaux-Arts, Rennes; and elsewhere. After 29. (Fig. 5a).

*31. Arnaq with Nutaaq, and Kalicho, full-lengths, ink drawings by Burch, 1590-1591. Canterbury Cathedral Archives (Literary MSS. A14, f.10r). After 30. (Fig. 5b).

32. [Fight between Frobisher and Eskimos, watercolor (?) perhaps by White in Baffinland.]

33. [Kayaker with bird spear.] Same as or after 11?

34. [Kayaker with bird spear, by White.] After 33? Part of 32?

*35. Fight between Frobisher and Eskimos, with kayaker, watercolor by or after White. Dept. of Prints and Drawings, British Museum (L.B. 3[13]). After 32. (Fig. 7a).

Table 1. Depictions of 1576 - 1577 Eskimos.

36. [Arnaq with Nutaaq, with single hood root, and Kalicho (front and back) with paddle and bow and arrow, with kayaker with paddle and bird spear. Several now-unknown woodcuts published by John Aldee, 1578.] After 20, 21, or 25; 14 or 16; 32 or 35.

*37. Kayaker with bird spear, Arnaq with Nutaaq and Kalicho in background. Woodcut published 1578 with French translation of Settle. Many examples known. After 33 or 34; 14 or 16; and 20, 21, 25, or 26. (Fig. 7b).

*38. Kayaker with bird spear, Arnaq with Nutaaq and Kalicho in background. Woodcut published 1580 with Latin and German translations of Settle. Many examples known. After 37. (Fig. 8a).

*39. Kayaker with bird spear, Arnaq with Nutaaq and Kalicho in background. Woodcut published 1582 with Italian translation of Settle. Several examples known. After 37. (Fig. 8b).

*40. Arnaq with Nutaaq, front and back views of Kalicho with paddle and bow and arrow; kayaker with paddle and bird spear. Ink drawings by Coenen, 1578. Koninklijke Bibliotheek, The Hague (78 E 54, ff.410v.-411v.). After 36. (Fig. 6).

*41. Arnaq with Nutaaq and Kalicho with paddle and bow and arrow, kayaker with paddle and bird spear, with text in German. Woodcut published by Jobin, Strasbourg, 1578. Zentralbibliothek, Zurich (PAS II 15/32). After 36. (Fig. 9).

*42. Arnaq with Nutaaq and Kalicho with paddle and bow and arrow, kayaker with paddle and bird spear, with text in German. Woodcut published by Manger, Augsburg, 1578. Kupferstichkabinett, Staatliche Museen Preussi-scher Kulturbesitz, Berlin (361-10). After 41. (Fig. 10a).

*43. Arnaq with Nutaaq and Kalicho with paddle and bow and arrow, kayaker with paddle and bird spear, with text in German. Woodcut published by Heussler, Nuremberg, 1578. Germanisches Nationalmuseum, Nuremberg (HB 24 415). After 42. (Fig. 10b).

engravings derived from very similar drawings that were published in 1590 by Theodor de Bry who credited his originals to White. De Bry did not copy the Eskimo drawings. The surviving set of drawings was evidently prepared as a presentation volume by John White about 1588; the other pictures in the set, and thus these Eskimo ones also, are not original field sketches (nor are they exactly the drawings copied for de Bry) (Hulton and Quinn 1964,1:24-25; Hulton 1984:28-29). Both these drawings are now accompanied by offsets made on blank intervening leaves when the volume was damaged by water in 1865 (Fig. 11) (Hulton and Quinn 1964,1:11,28).

The man's parka and trousers are light silvery grey, except for narrow white edging around the hood opening, the triangular neck insert (hood yoke), the left cuff, and the parka bottom (including the tail); a narrower black stripe is shown above the white at the cuff, the parka bottom, and perhaps the hood yoke. The patches on the thighs are white. Above the boots are broad bands of white fur; to judge by the de Heere drawing, these are attached to the trousers rather than the boots. The boots are tan, tied in place by a black cord around the tops. His moustache and beard appear to be sandy, but the offset shows that originally they were both strongly over-painted in black (Fig. 11a).

The woman's parka and trousers are tan, except: the hood is edged with a broad band of white fur, there are two triangular insets of white at the neck (double hood root), square white decorative patches on the arm, and narrow white edging around the cuff, tail, and parka bottom (with a thin black stripe inside the white on cuff and parka bottom); a broad grey band is around the trouser bottoms; there is a bluish button-like toggle at the base of the hood opening. Her boots are somewhat lighter tan, with a thin black stripe at the tops below a broad band of bluish grey fur (somewhat lighter in color than the adjacent trouser bottoms). The cord around her waist and up her front is black; in the offset (Fig. 11c) it seems to be joined with a knot or perhaps a small toggle between her breasts. Her facial tattooing is in small blue spots. The pattern shows much more clearly in the offset (Fig. 11b,c): a horizontal row of 5 or 6 dots across her chin; one dot at the right corner (left in the offset) of her mouth and a crescent of 7 dots down from the left corner of her mouth; goggle-like circles of dots around the eye sockets and above the eyebrows, with Y-like forks on each cheek; a V-like line of dots paralleling the two arcs over her eyebrows, and a line of dots running inside the far right loop of the goggles.

There are three watercolor drawings, a front and back view of a man, presumably Kalicho, with a bow, arrow, and paddle (Fig. 4a,b; Table 1:19), and a front view of Arnaq with Nutaaq (Fig. 4c; Table 1:28). These were in a volume of copies made between 1593 and 1614 by a member of John White's family, based on his original sketches (from which the two described above were probably worked up earlier, by White himself). The volume was acquired by

Sir Hans Sloane from White's family after 1709 (Hulton and Quinn 1964, 1:27; Hulton 1984:21). The colors of these copies are not significantly different from the two White originals.[13]

An uncolored engraving titled "America," one of a set of four, 20 x 13.6 cm, representing the Four Continents (reproduced in Parent 1984:146-147)was engraved by Philipp Galle (b.1537, d.1612) after a now-unknown drawing by Marcus Gheeraerts the Elder, and printed in Antwerp. The center and top of the plate display figures of South American Indians, long conventionalized as symbols of America, along with four parrots (Honour 1975a:item 91; Hulton and Quinn 1964,2:pl. 146b). On the bottom of the sheet appear a South American opossum (ultimately from Waldseemüller's 1516 woodcut map [George 1969:63]), a goat, and standing figures of an Eskimo man and woman with baby (Fig. 5a; Table 1:30), clearly part of the complex here considered. The plate is undated and has no text except for the title and the names of the artist and engraver. Gheeraerts (b. ca.1520, d. ca.1590), a painter from Bruges, was in England from 1568 through January 1577 but had gone to Antwerp by September 1577 (Honour 1975a:118; Hodnett 1971:12,16), before Frobisher's second expedition had returned to England. Galle was also in England during this period, in the same circle of Dutch and Flemish refugees as de Heere and Gheeraerts (Yates 1975:27). The Four Continents engravings have not been precisely dated, although others based on Gheeraerts drawings were published by Galle in 1578 and 1582 in Antwerp (Hodnett 1971:16,71).

There is a drawing, very closely related to the engraving after Gheeraerts, of the standing man and woman together with Gheeraerts's goat (labelled "An indian cowe") just to the right of the figures, beneath an ordinary horse (labelled "An indian hors") (Fig. 5b; Table 1:31). The woman's clothing is uncolored, but the man's is very imaginatively painted: green boots, red trousers with yellow spots and black stripes, dark blue parka spotted in red and yellow with the hood edged in yellow and with a yoke of red and yellow stripes and yellow dots, edged in yellow and with a yellow and red fringes. These drawings are in a practice-book of ink drawings and miscellaneous notes now in Canterbury Cathedral library (but bought in the nineteenth century and lacking previous associations with Canterbury).[14] The book was prepared between 1590 and 1593 by William Burch "alias Ellis alias Vicar of the Kings-benche in Southwarke" near London. He was an apprentice bound on a twelve-year term to one John Nettleton, gent., so far unidentified but perhaps a court or prison official, for whom he prepared the book. Burch was evidently about 17 or 18 years old when he made the Eskimo drawing on folio 10r.; it is undated, but 9r. is dated 29 September 1590 and 10v. is dated both "25 october /William Burch" and also 30 July 1591.

The page cannot have been based solely on the Gheeraerts-Galle engraving, since the drawing is accompanied by information not on the engraving: the names of the Eskimos are given as "Collinshough & Arnot," and the drawing is

Fig. 9. The 1577 captives. Woodcut published in Strasbourg, 1578, Table 1:41 (Zentralbibliothek, Graphische Sammlung, Zurich).

captioned "The indian man and woman / that sir martin Frobysher brought / into England:158   A True picture." The date is incomplete, a blot replacing the last digit; Frobisher was knighted in 1588. Perhaps this information came from oral sources, although the relative accuracy of the Eskimo names implies a written source at least for them.

The notebook contains English and Latin verses and tags, handwriting practice, and a huge variety of drawings, of coats of arms, of Nettleton's large coin collection, of mythological and religious allegories, of a great many domestic and foreign animals, birds, and fishes, a few monsters, but no foreign human types except for the Eskimos, a woman milking a reindeer, and men leading a camel and a giraffe. Most, perhaps all except the coins, must have been copied from published or manuscript sources, among them probably Conrad Gessner's *Historiae animalium* (1551-1558) and one of André Thevet's volumes.

Drawings with accompanying text in Dutch (Appendix 2), in a manuscript now in the Koninklijke Bibliotheek, The Hague, were prepared in 1577- 1578 by Adrian Coenen of Scheveningen.[15] The Eskimo drawings, discovered in 1964 by Gert Nooter, consist of (a) on folio 48v. (called folio 39 by Coenen) a standing man with bow, arrows, and paddle in a landscape with a European ship and two kayaks in the background, which Coenen says he copied in December, 1577 (Fig. 2b; Table 1:9); and (b) on folios 410v.-411r. (Coenen's 409), the last two

94

Fig. 10. The 1577 captives. a (top), Woodcut publishes in Augsburg, 1578, Table 1:42 (Staatliche Museen Preussischer Kulturbesitz, Kupferstichkabinett, Berlin). b (bottom), Woodcut published in Nuremberg, 1578 (Germanisches Nationalmuseum).

pictures in the volume, within a frame labelled '1578 in England,' a front and back view of a standing man adjoining a front view of a woman with baby, said by the accompanying text to be Kalicho, Arnaq, and Nutaaq, and a man in a kayak (Fig. 6; Table 1:40). Within the picture on 410v and apparently planned as part of the layout is a cross-reference to the other picture on "folio 39," whereas on the latter there is a cross- reference to "folio 409" in a box written over the watercolor after the picture was completed. As Wenger (1975:222) points out, the original copied for the first drawing seems to have been by a different hand than those copied for the second set, despite the great similarity in the pose and details of the man's figure. The colors of these drawings imply that they were copied from uncolored originals. The man on f.48v. has grey clothing and a black beard, and holds a pink paddle and bow. The standing man on 410v. wears a violet parka edged in yellow and tan trousers and boots, and has a pink paddle and bow; the man in a tan kayak with a pink paddle and pink and grey bird spear wears a tan to pink parka with yellow trim around his face. The man on 411r. again has a violet parka trimmed in yellow, tan trousers, pink boots, violet paddle and bow, violet arrow with grey point; the woman's parka and trousers are tan and her boots violet, all with yellow trim.

Adrian Coenen (b. 1514 or 1515, d. 1593) - he also wrote his surname as Coenenzoon and Coenensoen - is not known to have visited England. He is mentioned about 1573 as the representative in the Hague of his nearby native town, was *strandvonder* of Holland (with personal rights to lagan on the beaches), and was later appointed by William of Orange as the Scheveningen *vischafslager* "fish auctioneer" (Wenger 1975:219). His "Fish Book" shows him to have been an educated man with wide-ranging interests, literate in German as well as Dutch, able to translate into Dutch from at least English, Latin, and French, and familiar with contemporary publications by Olaus Magnus, André Thevet, and (according to Wenger) Guillaume Rondelet and Belon du Mans. His manuscript in the Hague contains a miscellany of drawings with accompanying descriptive texts (in Dutch and occasionally German), of fish, shellfish, whales, and fishing and whaling, of exotic animals (elephant, camel, great anteater, turkey, reptiles, amphibians, birds, insects - but no plants), striking natural phenomena (volcanoes, comets, aurora borealis), mythical monsters (unicorn, dragon, mermaids, and various humanoids with Classical and Medieval pedigrees such as pygmies warring with cranes, uniped, acephal), and exotic people: Lapps (from Olaus Magnus), an African, a Tupinamba man, and South American cannibals (related to woodcuts after Hans Holbein, for example on maps of the Münster Ptolemy series). The order is quite random, and the Eskimos drawings seem entirely unrelated to other drawings nearby or elsewhere in the volume.

A watercolor of a fight between Eskimos and Englishmen (Fig. 7a; Table 1:35) was in the volume of copies after White. However, it is stylistically more like the White originals and may well be by White himself, although if so probably done on a different occasion, perhaps earlier, than the two originals described above. The depiction seems to be a representation, by someone who was present, of Frobisher's 1577 skirmish with Eskimos, and this provides the only evidence that White was a member of the expedition (Hulton and Quinn 1964,1:13; Hulton 1984:8, 29). White's biography is extremely poorly documented apart from his role in Ralegh's Roanoke colony in the 1580's.

A woodcut, titled "*Le Portraict des trois Sauuages admenez en Angleterre, leurs habits, armes, tentes & bateaux*", was added as a tailpiece to the French translation of Settle published in Geneva in 1578 (Fig. 8b; Table 1:37). There was no illustration in the 1577 English editions of this book. The German and Latin translations (made from the French) published in 1580 by Katharina Gerlachin and Johannes vom Berg in Nuremberg contained a woodcut that was based on the Geneva one; the same woodblock, with different typeset titles, was used to print the plate on the verso of the German title page and for a double-page tipped-in following the Latin title page (Fig. 8a; Table 1:38). The Italian translation also made from the French and published in Naples in 1582 used a new woodcut copied from the Geneva one but with the background laterally reversed (Fig. 8b; Table 1:39).[16]

There are three versions of a hand-colored woodcut printed in 1578 on a broadside with a typeset German text across the bottom, nearly identical in all three (Appendix 3). Comparison of the details of the woodcuts and the printed texts makes it certain that the first version is one that ends "Printed in Strasbourg Anno 1578," which was discovered and reproduced by Weber (1976: 270,272,289) who identified the printer as Bernhard Jobin, and suggested that the text was translated by Johann Fischart, who worked with Jobin, from a now-unknown English original. The sole known copy is in the Zentralbibliothek, Zurich (PAS II 15/32) (Fig. 9; Table 1:41). From Jobin's handbill was derived one "Printed in Augsburg by Michael Manger, Anno M.D.LXXVIII" (reproduced in Strauss 1975,2:667), of which the only known copy is in the Kupferstichkabi-nett, Staatliche Museen Preussischer Kulturbesitz, Berlin (361-10). From this in turn was derived the third version, "Printed in Nuremberg by Leonhard Heussler, 1578" (reproduced in Strauss 1975,1:423), which is known to survive only in a slightly damaged copy in the Germanisches Nationalmuseum, Nurem-berg (HB 24 415) (Fig. 10; Table 1:42,43). The colors are apparently significant. In the first, Strasbourg, version, the parkas and trousers are dark brown except for light brown edging of the hoods and (in the two standing figures) black bands at the cuffs, over the shoulder seams of the sleeves, around the bottoms of the parkas (including the tails), and around the bottoms of the trousers; the triangular areas at the throats (hood yokes) and the edge of the man's right cuff are uncolored. The boots are light brown. The man has a black beard and moustache. In the Augsburg version all the clothes are light reddish brown except that the edgings of the hood openings and of the man's cuffs are uncolored, and all have black decorative bands as in the Strasbourg

97

version. The hood yokes are again distinguished: black for the woman, and for the man black below a tan rim. In the Nuremberg version the clothes are light brown, with dark decorative bands.

One key to the puzzling interrelationships of the pictorial and textual descriptions of Frobisher's captives is provided by an entry which the London printer John Aldee made in the Stationers' Register on 30 January 1578, for a projected publication entitled "A discription of the purtrayture and Shape of those strange kinde of people whiche the worthie master Martin Fourbosier brought into England in Anno 1576. and 1577" (Arber 1875:145). No copy of this publication has yet been located. Since the fee charged Aldee, 4d., was the normal one for "ballads" and other evidently short items (whereas Henry Bynnyman paid 10d. on 22 November 1578, when he entered Best 1578 [Arber 1875:154b]), one can surmise that this was a pamphlet or a single sheet. But that it was in fact published - and indeed known not only in England but very quickly in continental Europe - is strongly implied by several of the surviving descriptions of Frobisher's Eskimos.

The descriptions of Eskimo artifacts and behavior accompanying the second set of drawings in the Coenen manuscript (folios 410v.-411v., Appendix 2) and on the 1578 woodcut (Appendix 3) are very similar, clearly derived from the same source. The order of major topics is somewhat different: both begin with the hair and follow with details of men's clothing; Coenen then moves to boats followed by weapons, then to women's clothing followed by food; the woodcut moves first to women's clothing followed by food, then to boats followed by weapons. But within each of these categories, the details given and their ordering are nearly identical. However, Coenen's introductory sentence in German about making "bread" from whale meat does not appear on the German woodcut, nor do his concluding remarks which give the captives' names. Probably both Coenen and the 1578 woodcut drew on the text of Aldee's publication.

The data they give are close to those published in 1577 by Settle in a brief ethnographic sketch (Stefánsson 1938,2:19-23). Many details correspond, and occasionally the order of sentences also. But the relation is not direct, and there is considerable accurate detail in Settle which is not in the other two accounts, as well as vice versa. On the other hand, the agreement is closer than with the ethnographic sketch published by Best in 1578 (Stefánsson 1938,1:123-128). It appears that Settle in 1577, the lost account of 1578, and Best in 1578, all drew on primary data from participants in the expeditions, and in addition the lost account drew on Settle or else shared with Settle a written source not seen by Best. The brief addition to the French translation of Settle, published in 1578 (Stefánsson 1938,2:237-238), does not contain anything that can otherwise be reconstructed for the lost 1578 publication except for the names of the 1577 captives (but these spelled quite differently from Coenen's versions).

Ethnographic evaluation

The similarities and differences between the illustrations of Frobisher's captives can be assessed by comparing recurring visual complexes, each of which is a recognizable composition of artifacts and figures. Some complexes recur in different contexts in more than one picture. The artifacts in them can be evaluated as to accuracy by comparison with modern anthropological evidence from field and museum studies. These latter describe Eskimo societies more than 300 years after Frobisher or some distance away from Baffin Island, or both. Thus there are possibilities, indeed probabilities, that the comparative data reflect formal or stylistic differences due to both temporal changes in Baffinland Eskimo culture and the effects of diffusion (or migration). Eskimo cultures did not change radically during this period, so that extrapolation to the sixteenth century does not risk serious anachronisms, provided reasonable care is taken to eliminate nineteenth century elements. The culture of the Baffinland Eskimos, in the southeast part of Baffin Island where Frobisher landed, closely resembles that of the other Central Eskimo groups: the Iglulik on northwestern Baffin Island and the Melville Peninsula, and the Netsilik, Copper, and Caribou Eskimos to the west and south. It was also similar to the adjacent Ungava region of the northern Quebec-Labrador peninsula, and to that of the Polar Eskimos in far northwestern Greenland (Damas 1984:391-395). West Greenland Eskimo culture was also similar, especially before the major effects of Danish-Norwegian colonization began in the mid eighteenth century. Central Eskimos, Quebec-Labrador, and Greenlandic artifact types (and Western Eskimo ones as well) were generally similar and have forms that are intimately interrelated. They must resemble late sixteenth century Baffinland Eskimo artifacts much more closely than do other possible models for the European artists who depicted Frobisher's Eskimos - most notably, sixteenth century western European artifacts. Ethnographic comparisons thus provide a measure for seriating the depictions that is independent of the more narrowly artistic characteristics of the pictures themselves. The argument is inevitably somewhat circular, but once the probable accuracy of the whole pictures, of the complexes within them, and of the artifactual elements of these complexes have been gauged, then the illustrations can serve as ethnohistorical sources on the types and form of artifacts present among the Baffinland Eskimos of 1576-1577.

Six complexes can be distinguished in the surviving illustrations of Frobisher's Eskimos. The patterning of their shared elements and the manner in which the complexes co-occur in the different illustrations demonstrate that this is a single group of depictions going back to perhaps three or four lost originals. The principal doubt is whether the de Heere picture, labelled as of the 1576 captive, belongs to this group: although it shares very similar artifacts with the other illustrations (and adds no new ones), the composition

Table 2. Occurrence of complexes.

Illustrations (Numbers as in Table 1)	Complexes					
	Man, bow	Arnaq, Nutaaq	Kayaker	Fight	Capture	Tent, sled
de Heere (8; Fig. 2a)	x		?			
White original, man (17, Fig.3a)	x					
White original, woman (27;Fig.3b)		x				
White copy, man (19; Fig. 4ab)	x					
White copy, woman (28; Fig. 4c)		x				
Galle and Burch (30, 31; Fig. 5)	x	x				
Coenen f. 48v (9; Fig. 2b)	x		?		x	
Coenen ff. 410v-411r (40; Fig.6)	x	x	x			
White, fight (35; Fig. 7a)			x	x		
Settle (37, 38, 39; Figs. 7b, 8)	x	x	x			x
1578 broadside (41, 42, 43; Figs. 9, 10)	x	x	x			

is strikingly different and in a few instances the forms of the artifacts differ slightly and are probably more accurate. The situation is complicated by the lack of good contemporary written evidence that the man captured in 1577 was painted or drawn from life by Ketel or anyone else, while the 1576 captive is well-documented as having been. Yet there are several instances of derivative illustrations claiming to show Kalicho, the 1577 captive, along with Arnaq and Nutaaq. Coenen's distinction between the two men is thus important, but difficult to explain: he dates the two illustrations differently, they are widely separated in his book, evidently were copied from different originals, and are accompanied by separate descriptive texts - yet the poses as well as the artifacts shown are essentially the same.

Of the six complexes, two illustrate the captives themselves (Man with bow; Arnaq and Nutaaq), one shows the most prominent activity of the captives in England (Kayaker), and three depict central incidents in Frobisher's contacts with the Eskimos in Baffin Island (Fight scene, Capture scene, Tent and sled).

The following discussion is organized by complexes, with the illustrations identified by the numbers assigned in Table 1.

Man with bow. This occurs in two versions, differentiated by the posture and composition of the figure. The one by de Heere (8, fig. 2a), labelled as showing the man captured in 1576, differs from all the others. Yet one of the

100

latter (9, Fig. 2b), by Coenen, also shows the earlier captive according to the accompanying text and other details, although the composition is the same as in depictions supposedly of Kalicho, the 1577 captive (including one, 40, also by Coenen). All variants, including de Heere's, show very similar artifacts: always a bow, usually one or two arrows, and often a kayak paddle.

All depictions of the 1576 and 1577 men show a black moustache and small beard. This is particularly evident in what is probably the best portrait, that by White (17, Fig. 3a); although they are brown or sandy in the surviving original, the black overpainting in this area was lifted off by water damage and shows clearly on the offset (Fig. 11). Michael Lok described the physical features of the 1576 captive in some detail, and these seem unexceptionably Eskimo and probably applied equally to Kalicho, with one important exception: Lok's damaged manuscript says "and a [   ] blak Beard" (read by Collinson as "and a little [cole] blak beard" - Stefánsson 1938,1:166). This was the only Eskimo Lok had seen, so his implicit standards were the features of Caucasoid Englishmen. That the beard was worth mentioning means that it was extraordinarily prominent for an Eskimo. Among the Central Eskimo, according to Birket-Smith (1940:60), "the *beard* is decidedly much less prolific than that of the Europide race-group... thus a comparatively well grown beard is always... much thinner... than what Europeans would understand by a well-grown beard." Of 96 adult men he observed, 19 had no beard and only six a "fairly full" beard (presumably by Eskimo standards). So it is very likely that Kalicho did not have as noticeable a beard as the 1576 captive, and this is one of the features carried over into pictures said to represent him.

The form, construction, and decoration of the man's parka show good agreement in all versions, and corresponds very well with nineteenth century men's summer sealskin parkas from Baffinland and other Central Eskimos. The symmetrical patches on the arms probably represent a rather distinctive local style, as they seem not to be closely parallelled elsewhere but recur on Arnaq's parka. Surely they are decorative rather than repairs. The attachment of the hood to the body of the parka both in front and in back is unusual. The triangular hood yoke in front shown by White (17) is probably correct. According to Birket-Smith (1959:8) this form occurred in recent times in Greenland but not Baffin Island, but it does persist in Central Eskimo women's sealskin parkas (Driscoll 1983:10,14). It appears in de Heere (8) and elsewhere among our pictures (sometimes with the inverted Y-shaped highlights shown by White below it misinterpreted as part of the construction). Gheeraerts (30, Fig. 5a) or his model got it wrong, although one of Coenen's drawings (9, Fig. 2b) does show a more believable rectangular yoke. However, this last seems likely to have been a misinterpretation by Coenen or his source, given the agreement between the other pictures, even though a similar form of yoke is documented for West Greenland (Hatt 1916:Tav. 6,1).

The back views (19, 40 - Figs. 4b, 9) contain an error. Birket-Smith

(1959:14, and in Hulton and Quinn 1964,1:142) pointed out that the split hood root at the rear is without parallel in any Eskimo parkas; "moreover, there is a median seam on the crown of the head but never on the nape." Clearly White (or his model) developed the back view from the front view rather than from life, and did not even trouble to reverse the bow and paddle to opposite sides. The rest of the back view was readily deduced from the front view, but not these details. Two of the small figures in the right background of 35 seem more correct, as they appear to have no hood roots or a single triangular one.

The trousers and boots are like modern Central Eskimo ones (except for the copyist's misunderstandings in 30 and 37), although square decorative patches on the inner thighs seem to have been a local style of the time.

The bow held by the man is very well shown, especially in 8 and 17 but with confirmatory details in 9, 40, and 41. The slight distortion due to difficulties with perspective is clarified by the modern comparative evidence. The bow agrees with Settle's description of Baffinland Eskimo bows as made of wood, with sinews lashed on the back and a sinew bowstring (Stefánsson 1938,2:21). It is a modified composite bow, with a wooden belly and a strengthening sinew cable lashed to the back by a narrow band at the center and in broader spaced diagonal or chevron bands on each limb near the ends. There may also have been a reinforcing piece of wood or whalebone attached to the belly. The lashing seems to conform to the "secondary Arctic type" defined by Birket-Smith (1918:16) and Murdoch (1885:310-313), which was not known to Birket-Smith for the Central or Greenland Eskimos, although a similar form from Southampton Island was described and illustrated by Boas (1901:64-66). Settle gave the length of Baffinland bows as about 90 cm and Coenen (Appendix 2) as 114 cm, whereas some recent Central Eskimo bows ranged from 120 to 130 cm (Boas 1901:64) and Birket-Smith (1918:14) says the length was about half the owner's arm span or some 75-80 cm. The lengths indicated by the depictions are as follows, with the more accurate ones first:[17] 8: 77-84 cm; 17 and 19: 90-106 cm; 9: 100-110 cm; 40: 91-99 cm; 41: 86-84 cm; 37: 116 cm; 30: 107-127 cm.

Far the best arrow is shown by de Heere (8, Fig. 2a). The shape and attachment of the point conform closely to those of metal points illustrated by Boas (1888:504-506), Mathiassen (1928:57), and Taylor (1974:64-70). Best and Settle both mention arrow points of iron; Settle distinguished three types of arrowhead, said those of iron or stone were heart-shaped and not barbed, and described the arrows as of wood with foreshafts and nock ends of bone (Stefánsson 1938,1:126, 2:21). The parts of the shafts were not distinguished by any of the artists, although modern comparative evidence confirms that bone foreshafts were certainly present. All the arrows except de Heere's are merely conventionalized representations of European-type arrows, without evidentiary value. The others are shown fletched, but in the wrong manner. Settle (Stefánsson 1938,2:21) very clearly described fletching with two tangential feathers lashed on, which is precisely the expected form (Birket-Smith 1929b:63,245-246). The absence of fletching on de Heere's otherwise quite accurate arrow probably reflects another type brought to England, for Birket-Smith (*ibid.*) records occasional arrows without feathers. According to Settle (Stefánsson 1938,2:21) the arrows "pass not in length half a yard or a little more" while Coenen (Appendix 2) also says half a yard (i.e. 46 cm). The one shown by de Heere is about 50-48 cm long, while the others can be estimated at from 53 to 88 cm. Modern Central Eskimo arrows measure about 50 to 95 cm (Boas 1901:63; Taylor 1974:61).

The double-bladed kayak paddle is very well shown in this and other complexes, always with the drip rings which kept water from running over the kayaker's hands. These are typical of Central and Greenland Eskimo paddles (Birket-Smith 1929b:79,263; Rousselot 1983:195), and those shown seem quite clearly to have been separate bone rings as on an early paddle in Copenhagen (Meldgaard 1980:10) rather than being bands of leather or simply shoulders carved on the wood shaft (Rousselot 1983:195; Boas 1901:79; Taylor 1974:120). Two shapes of blade are shown, one with more or less parallel sides by de Heere (8), typical of later Central Eskimo paddles (Rousselot 1983:195), and the others "lancet-shaped," which is thought to have been the more ancient form in Greenland (Meldgaard 1980:10; Rousselot 1983:195). This seems good evidence that both types existed in Baffin Island in the 1570s, and perhaps indicates that de Heere's drawing shows the 1576 captive while the others depict Kalicho (or at least Kalicho's paddle). Coenen (Appendix 2) says the paddles were about 180 cm long, while modern evidence indicates a range of about 200 to 350 cm. All the paddles depicted are from 190 cm (no. 37) to 275-307 cm (no. 9) long.

Arnaq and Nutaaq. Far the best depiction of the woman and baby captured in 1577 is John White's drawing (27, Fig. 3b). If his original that White closely followed here was not itself painted from life or based on his own sketches from life, it was much closer to a model done from life than are the other depictions of the woman and baby, all of which must trace back either to a version of this one by White or to White's model. It is difficult to fault any details drawn by White, while all the other pictures of Arnaq and Nutaaq contain inaccurate deviations and none contains anything accurate that is not shown by White. Both this and White's picture of Kalicho (17) give an impression of immediacy and careful observation, not only in the forms of the artifacts but in the physical features and expressions of the subjects, their skin and hair color, and the meticulous rendering of the appearance of the fur on their garments. They are better in this regard than are the excellent pictures of a Timucua Indian man and woman that White copied from now- lost originals by Jacques Le Moyne, or his copies of Turkish, Tartar, Pictish and Ancient British figures by other artists (illustrated in Hulton and Quinn 1964,2). The only distorted element in White's Eskimo figures is the indication of both individuals' navels. Birket-Smith (1959:10), who was well acquainted with the texture of Eskimo garments and their appearance when worn, singled out this feature as "most absurd". However, Paul Hulton identified it as one of a few stylistic conventions of the Mannerist school of northern Europe evident also in some of White's "Virginia" drawings (Hulton and Quinn 1964,1:10; Hulton 1985:38,184). Probably the navels were not shown in White's original drawings, and they do not appear in 28 and 19, copied from other White originals.

The color of the fur garments seems to indicate that they were of sealskin, which modern evidence shows to be summer wear (Birket-Smith 1959:10; Driscoll 1983:14,23), although to some they seem to be of caribou skin (Hart Hansen et al. 1985:160) which would be more appropriate for winter garments. John Aldee's text evidently said that Frobisher's captives wore garments of both sealskin and deerskin (Appendixes 2, 3). Perhaps the closest parallels to the forms of Arnaq's garments are those of the six women dated about A.D. 1475 found preserved in West Greenland (Hart Hansen et al. 1985). These agree very well, except that the Greenland hoods are somewhat taller and less full, the apron-like front flaps are a bit longer, and they lack the decorative symmetrical arm patches and double hood roots. The latter are not known from recent Baffinland, but ones very similar in shape are common to the west, where they are decorative white "false hood-yokes" said to represent walrus tusks (Birket-Smith 1929b:84; Driscoll 1980:16, 1983:14,225-227). The thigh-high boots with center seam worn over stockings or inner boots which have a broad fur border at the top are not now found in Baffinland but are typical of recent Greenland as well as Southampton Island (Driscoll 1983:14; Birket-Smith 1959:10). Above the stockings is a decorative fur band around the bottoms of the short trousers; this cannot be the top of a second pair of stockings, which would be without Eskimo parallels (Birket-Smith in Hulton and Quinn 1964,1:143n.)

The parka in 27 (Fig. 3b) lacks the seams joining the sleeves to the body, which are a fundamental feature of all Eskimo women's parkas. White must have failed to copy them from his original drawing or sketches, for he did show the seams in the model for 28 (Fig. 4c) and they appear in most other illustrations of Arnaq (30, 40, 41). On the other hand, the single hood yoke of the others must be a feature carried over from the portraits of Kalicho; it is common on Central Eskimo women's parkas (Birket-Smith 1929b:84), but the distinctive double false hood-yokes of 27 must be correct, Arnaq cannot have had two parkas, and the two styles would not be expected contemporaneously in any small Eskimo population.

In White's drawing (27) Arnaq has the thong needed to support her baby in the back of her parka. The form is typical, and shows even more clearly in the offset of this drawing. It runs from just below her neck down between her breasts, where it is knotted to the apex of an inverted V, the bottoms of which are attached to a belt cord (for photographs of such cords see Damas 1984:423,483,586; James 1985:v,22,42,44,45). The cord is attached to a round bluish button-like toggle at the neck. This harness was misinterpreted in all the other depictions of Arnaq. In the copies (28, 37, 40, 41) it has become simply a belt, and the toggle has moved down to become an impossible brooch (it is missing in 30). Strangely, the variant after Gheeraerts (30, Fig. 5a) is different, preserving the inverted V but without the line down from the neck or the one across the base of the V. And the double false hood-yokes have also left a trace here, although they were misinterpreted. This implies a variant original model. But the club held by Gheeraert's Arnaq was borrowed from some depiction of a European wild person (compare Colin's chapter in this volume).

Arnaq's facial tattoo pattern can be reconstructed from several variants.[18] All the lines seem to be dotted. The curved V on the forehead shows in all versions (except 37, which omits the tattoo; this is the only tattoo line in 30). The curved lines from the bridge of the nose across the cheeks are clear on the White original (27) and its offset, and probable in 40, possible in 41. The other lines show plainly only on the offset of 27: goggle-like circles around each eye, a downward curve from the right corner of the mouth (and probably also from the left corner), and a horizontal row of five dots across the chin. This pattern corresponds very well with those documented for the Central Eskimos and for West Greenland (e.g. in Hart Hansen 1985:121; Boas 1888:561, 1901:108, 1907:472; Hawkes 1916:106). The only features that seem a little unusual are the horizontal row of dots on the chin (rather than a series of vertical lines) and perhaps the goggles around the eyes.

Kayaker. The kayaker in White's fight scene (35, Fig. 7a) strikingly resembles the one in 40 and 41 (Figs. 6,9) in the position of the paddle and in the rather awkward posture of his head. The one in the Settle engraving (37, Fig. 7b) differs in these respects (and has been laterally reversed in copying), but is clearly related to the one in 40 and 41 by the bird darts, one of them striking a bird in flight. One original must be the ultimate source of all; probably it was based on observing the demonstrations by the captives in England.

Baffinland kayaks preserved in museums range from 525 to 670 cm long, averaging 596 cm (six examples; data for four from J.-L. Rousselot, personal communication 1985, and for two from Chapelle 1964:175,205), while Boas (1888:486) gave a range of about 760 to 820 cm. Coenen's length for the kayak brought by Frobisher (Appendix 2) translates to 640 cm. Those in our pictures can be estimated as follows (the first ones being certainly too short): 37: 448-327; 8: 398; 9:465, 480, 652, 41: 745-549; 40: 773-633; 35: 800-652. The general profile of the kayaks is apparently poorly shown in all the pictures - the bow should be higher than the stern, and the angle of the underside of the bow is wrong (Rousselot 1983:317). Perhaps the best depiction in this regard is 9 (Fig. 2b); 37 (Fig. 7b) is better except for the erroneous angle of the deck near the bow. The profile in 35, 40, and 41 seems wrong, but it curiously resembles Mackenzie delta kayaks of 1826 pictured by Franklin (1828:pls. 7-9). Most kayaks, and especially those from Baffin Island and Labrador, have a bow longer than the stern. Boas (1888:486) gives the ratio of 4 to 3 (1.75), while the data in Chapelle (1964:175,205) and Rousselot (1983:305-306,317, and personal communication 1985) on six kayaks from this region show a range from 1.72 to 2.05. All the pictured kayaks agree; the foredeck is longer than the afterdeck except in 35 and 37 where they are of equal length. Central Eskimo and West Greenlandic kayaks have a coaming around the cockpit, rising higher before than aft (Rousselot 1983:317). This is well shown in 8 and 9, poorly in 37, but the coaming seems to have been misinterpreted as a flat band in 35, 40, and 41. The odd projection behind the kayaker in 37 (Fig. 7b) perhaps is based on the back part of a European saddle. However, kayaks from Baffin Island and Labrador (only) sometimes have a pair of cord loops somewhat aft of this position (Boas 1888:487; Haberland 1975:Taf. 6 [this is B2057, reattributed by Rousselot 1983:305] which may have been better depicted by the original model for this engraving (the European and Eskimo parallels for this detail were suggested to us by Rousselot in 1985).

Bird darts thrown from a kayak with a throwing board are universal among the Eskimos. Normally they have several barbed bone points at the end, or else they have a single end point but several barbed bone points attached to the middle of the shaft. The type depicted, with multiple barbed prongs both at the tip and at the middle is unusual but is documented for the Central Eskimo (Rousselot 1983:116-120,315; Damas 1984:435). For the Baffinland Eskimos specifically, the only evidence for this type is apparently these illustrations and Settle's description of a long dart "with many forks of bone on the fore end, and likewise in the midst" (Stefánsson 1938,2:21). The pictures seem to show three prongs at the tip and three in the middle. The shapes of the prongs are best shown by the dart on the kayak deck in 40 and 41 (Figs. 6,9). Modern bird darts are about 150 cm long; those shown were evidently somewhat exaggerated, for they seem to measure 290-240 (40), 228-158 cm (41), or 206-148 cm (37).

A throwing board appears only in the engraving (37, Fig. 7b) published by Settle, who also refers to bird darts being "cast out of an instrument of wood, very readily" (Stefánsson 1938,2:21). The manner of use is quite well shown, and it is doubtful that an artist could be this accurate depending only on a verbal description. Yet the form of the implement is very poorly indicated, not corresponding to any Eskimo types (the Hudson's Bay Company rumor quoted in Hulton and Quinn 1964,1:44n. to the contrary notwithstanding). This engraving once again reflects elements no doubt more correctly shown in its ultimate model, but with details here misinterpreted and distorted.

The kayaker's clothing does not differ significantly from that shown in the "man with bow" complex, and the paddle is also discussed under that heading.

Fight scene. The drawing by or after John White (35, Fig. 7a) almost cer-

Fig. 11. a (top) Kalicho. Detail of the offset from White's drawing in Fig. 3a (British Museum).
b (bottom left), Arnaq, detail of White's drawing in Fig. 3b. c (bottom right), Detail of
offset of the same (here laterally reversed). (All: Permission of the Trustees of the
British Museum).

tainly depicts the fight between Frobisher's men and the Eskimos in which the woman and child were captured in 1577. It agrees in part with the written descriptions of that incident. The ship's boat, however, is clearly not one of the rowing pinnaces described in Settle's account. She is strongly built in clinker fashion with her keelson clearly shown. The boat would seem to be somewhat curved from stem to stern, but the extent of the curvature may be exaggerated in the drawing. The man standing in the stern holds a steering oar, and only one oarsman is seen. Two men, evidently without helmets, are firing calivers at Eskimos on the cliff, while another man, perhaps an officer, threatens them with his sword while protected by his target. Three or four other men are vaguely seen crouching behind targets at the port side. The boat may be some 4.5 m long and is comparatively broad, allowing four men to sit or stand across her width.

The kayaker in the foreground belongs to the complex previously discussed, but the other elements of the scene seem to be unique. The landscapes shown by Coenen (9, Fig. 2b, supposedly of the 1576 voyage) and the Settle engraving (37, Fig. 7b) are evidently unrelated. The hypothesis that White was on Frobisher's 1577 voyage depends entirely on the accuracy of this scene. According to Birket-Smith (1959:12) "this picture can hardly have been made by a person who has not actually been on the spot", and Hulton and Quinn agree: "the details are convincingly drawn and strongly suggest that the drawing was made from direct experience" (Hulton and Quinn 1964,1:13); "it would have been impossible for anyone to reconstruct this Arctic scene... in such convincing detail if he had not himself witnessed it and recorded it on the spot. As the drawing is a copy, the original would have been still more convincing" (Hulton 1985:8). There is no other evidence that White was a member of this expedition, and the five voyages to America that he said in 1593 he had made are all better accounted for otherwise (Hulton and Quinn 1964,1:13), Hulton (1985:8) thinking it "is perhaps unlikely" that White counted the Frobisher voyage as his first (because Baffin Island was not recognized as part of America?). Hulton (1985:8) adds that if White did not draw the original, "this would suppose the existence [on the voyage] of another English artist, of at least White's calibre, of which there is no evidence whatever."

But perhaps the accurate details of most of the artifacts can be explained by observations of the 1576 and 1577 captives in England, by White or by another artist whose work he could have copied. The activities shown would then have been based on verbal descriptions by members of the expedition. The cliff and the treeless landscape could have been sufficiently well described, although the rotting ice pans are remarkably well shown. The five tents on the hill at the left (Fig. 12b) agree well with Baffin Island forms according to Birket-Smith (1959:12; and cf. the early photographs in Mary-Rousselière 1984 and James 1985:23,34,35). However the rectangular plan is much less likely than one with a D-shaped end (or ends) (William W. Fitzhugh, personal communication 1985; Boas 1888:551-553). The slight indications of low walls may be influenced by European tent forms, or perhaps they derive from rows of stone tent weights which were better shown in the original drawing. Another detail is the five long weapons carried by men in the background (four on the point and one by the tents). While these are vaguely shown, two or three appear to have separate long points or foreshafts, or perhaps are harpoons with indications of the line attached to the head. Settle (Stefánsson 1938,2:21) described long lances with separate long bone points, sharp on both sides "not much unlike a rapier, which I take to be their most effective weapon." Central Eskimo lances in recent times had bone foreshafts but with stone or metal points (Rousselot 1983:11,312). On balance, the evidence seems slightly to favor the presence of White on the scene, although he need not have observed the fight close up.

Capture scene. Coenen's first drawing (9, Fig. 2b) is described by him (Appendix 2) as an illustration of Frobisher's 1576 voyage. The ship shown is consistent with the *Gabriell*, a 30 ton ship with four masts and two tops that was constructed in 1576 (Lok's financial accounts printed in Quinn 1979:193-194). The sails are furled, the bow anchor run out, and the spars and rigging clearly shown. She has a moderately high forecastle and a somewhat higher rear castle, with a deep well, and carried a broadside of four guns. Frobisher employed the *Gabriell* in 1577 also, but there appears to be nothing in the narratives of that voyage corresponding with this scene. The setting is a small bay, with apparently sandy shores. Six Eskimos are vaguely shown on hills at the left, while one man on the beach carries his paddle as he is about to enter his well-depicted kayak. Another kayak is being paddled near the ship. A man in a kayak alongside the ship reaches out with his right arm (Fig. 12a). This must be intended to show the moment of his capture - Frobisher even grasps the man by his wrist, as described by Lok (Stefánsson 1938,1:164). These details, striking as they are, do not seem to require the presence of an artist among the *Gabriell*'s small company; the original drawing could have been done in England on the basis of verbal descriptions and from observation there of the captive and his kayak (the kayaks and the man in the foreground are described above).

Tent and sled. The engraving published by Settle (37, Fig. 7b) contains at least four complexes, the first three having been discussed above: the man with bow (here given a kayak also), Arnaq with Nutaaq, the kayaker, and one more. The last complex is unique and so cannot be divided (as it might be if some of the lost illustrations are found). It consists of three elements, none of them ethnographically accurate. In the center is a walled tent, with a seated figure inside and a man with a bow outside. The tent is European and not at all Eskimo in form, and thus is either based on the textual references to Eskimo tents (e.g. Settle in Stefánsson 1938,2:22) or is much distorted from one in a better original. Next to the tent is a dog pulling a sled. Again the

Fig. 12. a (top), Detail of the capture scene in Fig. 2b. b (bottom), Detail of the tents in fig. 7a (Enlargements drawn by Jo Ann Moore, from photographs).

110

forms are European, not Eskimo: the sled resembles a small boat which seems to have two shafts attached to a collar on the dog (Eskimo dog harnesses being very different). This was probably invented to illustrate Kalicho's demonstration of a dog sled found in a burial, an incident described by Best (Stefánsson 1938,1:64). In the center background are three very small crudely conventionalized figures: a man holding a bow in his left hand while offering a dead bird in his right hand to a seated woman who is playing with a child.

Conclusion

We hope this discussion may encourage the discovery of additional evidence to resolve some of the remaining problems. New archaeological or documentary findings may well strengthen the hypothesis that the 1566 captives were kidnapped from Labrador by Basque (or possibly Breton) sailors. It may be that there are documents that will tell us more about what happened to them in Europe. But it is difficult to imagine likely evidence that might show they were captured not in Labrador but in Greenland - as is the initial impression of most Eskimologists from the style of the woman's clothing. Even if European contacts with Greenland in the 1560s are eventually proven, it is unlikely that this kidnapping will be mentioned in any documents that certainly refer to Greenland, which at that period might well have been included in "Terra Nova", and it is extremely unlikely that the captive woman's clothing style can be shown not to have occurred in Labrador.

Additional evidence, especially pictorial, can perhaps be found to add details on Frobisher's captives and to elucidate some of the remaining historical and ethnographic questions about them. Especially to be hoped for is the discovery of a copy of John Aldee's lost 1578 publication, which would illustrate ethnographic details more accurately than its derivatives (40, 41, perhaps 9, 30, and 37), might clarify the relationships between the drawings by John White and the other illustrations, and would contain the English text lying behind the descriptions in Dutch and German (Appendixes 2, 3). It is probably too much to hope for the survival of any of Cornelis Ketel's Eskimo portraits, so that certainty on the seriation of the surviving depictions is unlikely to be achieved. But we may anticipate learning more about the model for White's scene of the fight between Frobisher and the Eskimos (35), and for the unique elements in Settle's engraving (37) and in Coenen's depiction (9) of the capture. Was Kalicho painted or drawn from life, or were all pictures purporting to show him derived from Ketel's or another's portraits of the 1576 captive? New pictures might improve knowledge of sixteenth century Baffinland Eskimo artifacts, including several details of the form of kayaks, the shapes of the hood yokes and hood roots of men's parkas, and the construction of arrows and lances.

However, the ethographic details in the surviving depictions are confirmed

111

to a remarkable degree by modern anthropological evidence, especially in comparison to the few other European depictions of American natives in the sixteenth century (cf. Sturtevant 1976). The textual evidence on Baffinland Eskimo culture that is in the accounts of Frobisher's expeditions and of the captives in England (including the written material accompanying several of the illustrations) is also quite extensive and, while rather elementary, is reasonably objective and accurate as compared to nearly all other sixteenth century evidence on North American natives (and much seventeenth and eighteenth century evidence). Several reasons for this situation may be suggested. Frobisher and his men were not particularly self-confident and over-weaning in their contacts with the Eskimos. The technological and numerical balance between the two sides was more equal than usual, and the Europeans clearly recognized and admired (as they did repeatedly over the next 300-350 years) the cultural adaptations achieved by the Eskimos in order to survive in their extreme environment. To European eyes the region was barren and relatively devoid of interest except for its human occupants. Perhaps also the Eskimos were thought of as Asians, outliers of the rich and complex civilizations sought by the Muscovy Company and other Europeans (and already contacted by their enterprises reaching eastward). For these and perhaps other reasons, the captives in England aroused a remarkable amount of scientific and popular interest, including that of reputable painters whose work rapidly diffused in Europe, along with written accounts of Frobisher's search for the Northwest Passage and of the new prey he brought back as evidence of his supposed success.

NOTES

1. A barely possible early visit of Eskimos to Europe can be deduced from manuscripts and maps based on the work of the Danish geographer Claudius Claussøn Swart (Claudius Clavus) who wrote that some time between 1425 and about 1430 he had himself seen both pagan Karelians (*Kareli infideles*) in Greenland and pygmies (*Pygmei*) of the far west captured at sea in a small skin boat (*in parua naui de coreo*; a kayak or a non-Eskimo coracle?) which in his day was hung in Trondheim cathedral along with a long skin boat (*longa nauis de coreo*; an umiak or a kayak?) in which other such pygmies had previously been captured (Bjørnbo and Petersen 1904:136[178]-137[179]). This passage may imply, although it does not specifically state, that the "pygmies" as well as their boats were taken to Norway. The boats did not survive, and there are problems with Swart's reliability (Nansen 1911,2:269-272; Gad 1971:173-175; Bjørnbo 1911:110-114; Kejlbo 1971:79-81), among them that his maps showing Greenland were based on earlier sources rather than his own observations, his assertion that the pygmies he saw were a cubit tall (no doubt because Greek *pygmea* is 'cubit') and that there were more than one in a kayak (if such it was), and the fact that documented Scandinavian contacts with Greenland ceased by 1410. For other early instances of Eskimos or their kayaks said to have arrived in Europe - all dubious at best - see the sources cited by Rousselot 1983:211-212,227-228, plus Plischke 1916 (the last pointed out to us by Rousselot).

2. These conclusions are based mainly on detailed comparisons of the texts and enumerations of shared innovations made by Christian F. Feest. We are also indebted to him for discovering Strauss 1975, which reproduces all three versions (vol. 1:135,201,376). Good large color reproductions of the Zurich copy of the Augsburg version are in Zerries and Rousselot 1978:54 and Sturtevant 1980. Only the copy in Stuttgart (evidently first mentioned in Sturtevant 1976:452n.51) was missed by Strauss.

3. The semantics of these terms even now disagree as between languages. We have translated Dutch, German, and French consistently as 'wild', recognizing that no modern equivalent can be accurate. Variants of the word Eskimo are first recorded as the name for Indian groups near the mouth of the St. Lawrence - in English in 1584, in French in 1611 - perhaps borrowed from the oral usage of sixteenth century Basque whalers. The modern Eskimo were named this in European languages only from the mid seventeenth century, and not exclusively so until the early eighteenth century (Goddard 1984).

4. For the 1576 capture the most detailed description is by Michael Lok, one of the principal backers of the voyage, who evidently got most of his information by interviewing Frobisher. Another account is by George Best, who was not on this voyage although he did accompany Frobisher in 1577 and 1578. A third, far the briefest, is by Christopher Hall, master of the *Gabriell* on the 1576 voyage. These three descriptions are nowhere significantly contradictory. Lok's, in a damaged manuscript (British Library, Cotton MS. Otho E VIII), was first printed by Collinson (1867:79-87; reprinted by Stefánsson 1938,1:151-161). Best's is known only from its 1578 published version (reprinted by Stefánsson 1938,1:1-129). Hall's is known only as printed by Hakluyt (1589:615-622; 1600:57-60; Quinn 1979:201-207 reprinted the former and Stefánsson 1938,1:147-154 the latter). Where these are quoted from Stefánsson, we have modernized the spelling.

4a. After the above was written, D.B.Q. found a passage of similar import in a newsletter written by Thomas Wood to Richard Bagot "From London 28 of October" reporting for "10 October 1576":

> Certayne of our marchant*es* in Iune last sent one Captayne Furbusher with 2 shypes and a pinesse to syke the Land of Cathay where ye Portingalles also trade but be an other way clene contrary for the Portingales make the then coorrse rond a bote affryca and ar iij yeeres on a viage / but o*u*r men say the haue brought a ma*n*n of the Country with them and a bote the toke him be Force / he eateth raw Fleshe / o*u*r men haue lost a bote and v me*n* / .... (L.a. 987, Bagot Papers, Folger Shakespeare Library, Washington).

In modern spelling this is:

> Certain of our merchants in June last sent one Captain Frobisher with two ships and a pinnace to seek the land of Cathay where the Portuguese make they their course round about Africa and are three years on a voyage, but our men say they have brought a man of the country with them and a boat. They took him by force. He eats raw flesh. Our men made their course north by Greenland but our men have lost a boat and five men.

5. The principal sources on this expedition are two accounts by participants. Dionyse Settle published a small book printed twice in London in 1577, from which it was copied for Hakluyt's collections (1589:622-630; 1600:32-39). The first printing or edition of 1577 was reprinted by Stefánsson (1938,2:1-25) and by Quinn (1979:207-216). A French translation, with a little added material on the Eskimo captives in England (the latter reprinted in Stefánsson 1938,2:237-238), appeared in 1578, and from

114

this French version were made translations in German and Latin, both 1580, and Italian, 1582. One of us (W.C.S.) has examined and compared copies of both English Settles and the French, German, Latin, and Italian translations. George Best's account was published separately in London in 1578 (reprinted in Stefánsson 1938,1:1-129); this was also used by Hakluyt (1600:47-96). Modernizing the spellings, we cite Stefánsson's printings except in a couple of cases where the second English edition of Settle is better (cf. Parks 1939).

6. The cultural data in most of the sources on the Frobisher voyages and on the captives in England have been indexed by Quinn (1981b:37-42). We do not repeat this material except as it is relevant to the depictions of the captives, which Quinn did not analyze in detail. A fairly well rounded and accurate ethnographic sketch of Baffin Island Eskimos in the 1570s could be written from these sources. The effort should be made, because this European-Native contact was very unusual: literate observes here interacted with a society almost certainly not affected at all by prior direct or even indirect influences from Europe or any other state system or indeed by contacts with any sedentary society. Even influences from Indians far to be south must have been minimal.

7. Ideas about the Eskimos and observations of them may have been influenced by a passage in a famous book of travel lies that was evidently carried by Frobisher's expedition as a sort of guide book. The financial accounts for the outfitting of the 1576 voyage record the purchase of a few useful maps and books, including a copy of "Sir John mandevylle, englishe" (Lok 1576-1583:9r.). This must have been the 1568 edition of the Travels, which describes "a great yle" off the east coast of Asia near the country of Prester John, "wherin dwell people as great as giants of xxviii or xxx fote of length....& they haue no clothinge but beasts skyns that hang on them, & they eat no bread but flesh raw, and they drink milke, & they haue no houses, & they eat gladiyer fleshe of men then other" (Mandeville 1568:ch. 92, p. Mi v.). A similar passage appears on sig. Hvi v. of the edition of Mandeville's Travels published in London in 1496.

8. We are indebted to Louis-Jacques Dorais (personal communication 27 August 1984) for suggesting interpretations of the variant spellings. He comments that since Eskimo personal names are derived from common words and expressions, the man's name cannot be identified. Among possibilities are *Kalisuuq* 'who has the habit of hauling something,' *Qarliksaq* 'which may be used as trousers,' and *Kallisuuq* 'which habitually thunders.' What were supposed to be the personal names of the woman and baby probably were not. Rather, the woman was called *Arnaq* 'woman'

115

and the baby *Nutaaq* 'something (or someone) new' or *Nutaraq* 'baby (i.e. young new thing)' (as also suggested by Stefánsson 1938,2:235-236, using an older orthography and less precise translations). We have adopted the last two, in the modern Eastern Canadian Inuktitut orthography, but for the man's name we have simply standardized a spelling to represent a probable English pronunciation (the Eskimo pronunciation being unrecoverable).

The original spellings are as follows. (1) In the new material added to the 1578 French translation of Settle's account (Stefánsson 1938,2:237): Calichoe, Egnoge, Nutioc. (2) In a series of interrelated manuscripts in Bristol: Callichogh, Ignorth (Adams 1639); Callicho, Ignorth (Adams 1910:115, in a manuscript written between 1623 and 1648); Callychough (Bristol Calendar, ca. 1690); Callicho or Callichog or Cully Cla, Ignorth (Seyer, Annals of Bristol, 1790, cited in Stefánsson 1938,2:238); Callicho or Cally Chough, Ignorth (Seyer, Memoirs, 1821-1823, cited in Stefánsson 1938,2:239). (3) In the burial records for 1577 in the Parish Register of St. Stephen's church, Bristol: Collichaug, Egnock. Printed Collichang in Cheshire et al. 1980:37 and Quinn 1979:218, but the letter can equally well be "u" which agrees better with other spellings. (4) In Dr. Dodding's 1577 autopsy report (the Latin original, printed in Stefánsson 1938,2:136): Calichoughe. (5) In Coenen 1577-1578, in Dutch after an unknown English original: Caliohosh, Egnorth, Nutenocth. (6) In a 1689 inventory record of now-lost paintings once in Munich (Stöcklein 1911), in German after unknown English(?) originals: Calitgoch, Egnocth, Nutiocth. (7) In Burch 1590-1593:10r. from an unknown source on a drawing copied in 1590-1591: Collinshough, Agnot.

A very curious parallel to some of the spellings of the name Kalicho appears in versions of Mandeville's *Travels*: the names of two angels among a people of the far east of Asia are given in the earliest manuscript, in French, dated 1371, as "Caco et Calo. Mais Caco est mauuais et Calo est bon," while an English manuscript of ca. 1410-1420 says "there are two manner of angels, that is at [sic] say one good another ill, as men of Greece say, Chaco and Calo. Chaco is the ill angel and Calo is the good" (Letts 1953,1:221). The Greek is *kakos* 'bad' and *kalos* 'good'. But this manuscript was first (badly) printed in 1725. All English editions of Mandeville printed before 1576 were based on another, "defective" manuscript which evidently lacked this passage - at least it is not in the 1496 or 1568 editions (we have not checked the 1499, [1501?], 1503, or [1510?] editions printed by Wynkyn de Worde or attributed to him).

9. The French says *un dain*, which Cheshire et al. 1980:46 interpret as *une daine*, translating 'a doe.' But a 1720 edited version of this passage (Stefánsson 1938,2:238) changes the word to *une poule* ('a fowl'), evidently

taking the original to represent *une dinde* (literally 'a turkey-hen'). An allusion to one of the ducks seems more likely than to a doe (or to a buck, *un daim*, evidently rare in modern French although Littre gives *un dain, dame* 'bête fauve plus petit que le cerf' for the sixteenth century, as well as *un dinde* 'coq d'Inde, dindon').

10.   This is presumably the "formal protest [that] came from Moscow [in January 1579] to the effect that Frobisher was unlawfully carrying off Russian subjects" which is mentioned, without a reference, by Taylor (1930:120), taken from her (again without a citation) by Kirwan (1959:24), and cited from the latter by Saladin d'Anglure (1979:121; 1980:201). The document was quoted, with its archival reference, in French translation by Quinn (1981a:313). It is, however, unknown to specialists on the Samoyeds, although its mention of the Piak (Nenets for 'forest'; plural Piakeï) Samoyeds seems to predate the earliest known occurrence of this name by about a century (V.I. Vasiliev, personal communication 12 December 1984). That Best 1578 was the source of the news is indicated by his discussion of the location of Frobisher's discoveries in relation to "Moscovia" and the river "Obby" or "Obij" (Stefánsson 1938,1:21,23), and especially by a passage in which he described the natives met by Frobisher: "These people I judge to be a kind of Tartar, or rather a kind of Samowey, of the same sort and condition of life that the Samoweides be to the northeastwards, beyond Moscovy, who are called Samoweydes, which is as much to say in the Moscovy tongue, as eaters of themselves, and so the Russians their borderers do name them. And by late conference with a friend of mine (with whom I did sometime travel in the parts of Moscovy) who hath great experience of those Somoweides and people of the northeast, I find, that in all their manner of living, those people of the northeast, and these of the northwest, are like" (*ibid.* p. 123). Best also mentions the loss of Frobisher's men in 1576 and his kidnapping of natives in 1576 and 1577 (pp.49,50,60,68). A less likely source is Settle's book, published in English in 1577 and French in 1578, which does not refer to Samoyeds or the river Ob but mentions the loss of Frobisher's men and his taking of captives.

11.   We are indebted to Christian F. Feest for bringing Plischke 1921 to our attention and for assisting with the translations here, and to Jean-Loup Rousselot for providing a copy of Stöcklein 1911.

12.   Unless the kayaks accompanied the paintings from England, which seems highly unlikely, they were a separate accession. The one that was in Munich in 1689 and 1776 survives with two paddles in the Staatliches Museum für Völkerkunde, Munich (Zerries and Rousselot 1978:22, Abb. 58;

Rousselot 1983:228). If the inventories can be trusted, they had already arrived in Europe between 1588 and 1597, and thus are the oldest documented surviving Eskimo kayak and paddles: Maurice of Nassau (1567-1625) became captain and admiral-general of the United Netherlands in 1588, while William V was duke of Bavaria from 1579 until he abdicated in 1597 (dying in 1626). The kayak is southwest Greenlandic in type, but is only 3.36 m long, evidently made for a boy; the lashings of its wooden frame are baleen (Rousselot 1981). Of the two double-bladed paddles now with the kayak, one is a well-made example with the "lancet-shaped blades" typical of the earliest known West Greenland paddles (Meldgaard 1980:10, Zerries and Rousselot 1978:22; Rousselot 1981, 1983:228). The other paddle, however, was constructed by fastening together with iron nails and lashing two single-bladed paddles or oars (of European or perhaps American Indian origin) (Rousselot 1981). This one was presumably added to the kayak between 1689 and 1776.

A kayak voyage from Greenland to Holland is impossible (and in any case a woman and baby would not have been in a kayak) (Nooter 1971:8-9; Zerries and Rousselot 1978:22; Rousselot 1983:209-212). Kayaks which came ashore in Holland and Scotland in the seventeenth and eighteenth centuries were probably set overboard as Dutch ships that had captured them in Greenland neared the European coasts (Nooter 1971:10-11), or some at least may not have been kayaks, but rather small leather-sheathed coracles or boats from Ireland or even from Western Siberia or Scandinavia. But 1597 is before the earliest known Dutch whaling voyages to Greenland. Sixteenth century kayak forms are too poorly known to rule out, on purely typological grounds, Baffin Island, Labrador, or East Greenland as the provenience of the one surviving in Munich.

13. The White drawings and the early copies of them are in the Department of Prints and Drawings, British Museum. They were described in detail in Hulton and Quinn 1964. The catalog numbers are as follows: A, the man by White: 1906.5.9.1(29), E.C.M. 63, L.B. 1(30); B, the offset of this: 199.a.2., L.B. 2(30); C, the woman by White: 1906.5.9.1(30), L.B. 1(31); D, the offset of this: 199.a.2, L.B. 2(31); E, the fight: 199.a.3.f.12v., E.C.M. 78, L.B. 3(13); F, the copy of the man, front view: 199.a.3.f.11r., L.B. 3(11); G, back view: 199.a.3.f.5v., L.B. 3(10); H, the copy of the woman: E.C.M. 64, L.B. 3(12). Color reproductions are as follows (coded by the arbitrary letters just mentioned): Hulton and Quinn 1964,2 (A: pl. 62; B: pl. 63); Hulton 1984 (A: pl. 63; B: pl. 64); less good, Cumming, Skelton, and Quinn 1971 (A: fig. 285; B: fig. 286; F: fig. 287; G: fig. 288); Croft-Murray and Hulton 1960 (E: frontisp. to *Plates*); Josephy 1961 (E: p. 285); less good, Honour 1975b (E: p. 17) and Morison 1971 (E: frontisp.). A black and white reproduction of the offset of the woman (D) is in Hulton and Quinn

1962,2:pl. 78a; the offset of the man (E) has not previously been published.

14. These drawings were first noticed by David Sturdy in the 1970s. We thank him for bringing them to our attention, and for providing some information on Burch, Nettleton, and the acquisition of the manuscript. W.C.S. studied the manuscript in Canterbury in 1984.

15. The manuscript, a bound volume of 412 folios, about 32 x 22 cm, has never been published nor described in any detail. The only publication of any of the illustrations seems to be Wenger's 1975 reproductions of the Eskimo drawings. W.C.S. examined the original briefly in 1982 and obtained photographs of a few pages. According to Gert Nooter (personal communication 1982) there is another Coenen manuscript with drawings of whales and other subjects, but none of people, in the Koninklijke Maatschappij voor Dierkunde van Antwerp/Societé Royale de Zoologie d'Anvers, while a third volume, mentioned by Coenen, has been lost.

16. Kalicho, Arnaq, and Nutaaq must be almost unique as known, named individuals whose portraits ended as typifying whole populations. By way of the woodcut in the French version of Settle they entered the set of costume types of exotic peoples, almost endlessly copied. This career began in pictures on both manuscript maps and maps printed in the Netherlands, especially associated with Greenland (where Frobisher's landfalls of 1576-1577 were long supposed to lie, even as late as by Gad 1971, 1984:556). Among these derivatives are two standing figures, a tent, a dog-drawn sled, and a kayaker on a manuscript map of the north Atlantic prepared in 1605 by Hans Poulson Resen, bishop of Zealand (Cumming, Skelton, and Quinn 1971:226-227; Gad 1971:222,241); and the standing man holding a kayak with the rectangular tent nearby, taken directly from the Settle engraving, plus two kayakers and four standing figures varied from that engraving, on a small manuscript chart of a bay in west Greenland prepared by James Hall to illustrate his account of the Danish expedition he accompanied in 1605 (Cumming, Skelton, and Quinn 1971:210). These and the series beginning about 1598 on maps printed by Hondius, the Blaeus, the Visschers, Ortelius, and others, will be described elsewhere by W.C.S.

17. Two scales have been used to estimate the lengths of the paddles, bows, arrows, bird darts, and kayaks shown in the illustrations. One assumes the man's stature to be 160 cm (a reasonable average for an Eskimo; cf. Stewart 1973:49,138), and uses the paddle length thus determined as a scale for the length of the kayak and bird dart (which do not appear

119

adjacent to a standing man). The other scale assumes the man's lower arm length (which can be read directly in all the illustrations) to be 42 cm. This figure is based on the average length of 20 Eskimos ulnae in the Smithsonian collections (measured for us by Stephanie Damadio) plus the average hand length for seven living Eskimo men given by Hrdlička (1930:252). When the estimated lengths for the depicted objects are given in the text as a range between two figures the first figure is scaled from stature, and the second one from lower arm length; where only one figure is given, it is based on lower arm length.

18. Sturtevant (1965:62) criticized the barely-distinguishable details of the pattern in the White original as reproduced in at least some copies of Hulton and Quinn 1964, but it was not until 1985 that he examined the offset which clarifies the pattern.

REFERENCES CITED

Adams, William
  1639   A Summary of pettie Chronicle of the first Inhabitants of this
         famous Iland. Manuscript in Bristol Archives Office, BAO 13748(4).
  1910   Adams's Chronicle of Bristol. Francis F. Fox, ed. Bristol: J.W.
         Arrowsmith.
Arber, Edward (ed.)
  1875   A Transcript of the Registers of the Company of Stationers of
         London; 1554-1640 A.D. Volume II. - Text. London: Privately printed.
Barkham, Selma
  1977   The Identification of Labrador Ports in Spanish 16th-Century
         Documents. Canadian Geographer 14 (1):1-9.
  1978   The Basques: Filling a Gap in our History Between Jacques Cartier
         and Champlain. Canadian Geographical Journal 96(1):8-19.
  1980   A Note on the Strait of Belle Isle during the Period of Basque
         Contact with Indians and Inuit. Études/Inuit/Studies 4(1-2):51-58.
Best, George
  1578   A True Discourse of the late voyages of discouerie, for the finding
         of a passage to Cathaya, by the Northweast, vnder the conduct of
         Martin Frobisher Generall: Deuided into three Bookes... London:
         Henry Bynnyman. [Entered by the printer in the Stationers'
         Register on 22 November 1578, without naming the author, under the
         title "A true discourse of the voiages of master Captaine Frobissher
         for a discovery to Cataia by the Northwest nowe Called Meta
         incognita. Divided into iij bookes Conferred and sett out by the
         consent of the generall and all the Captaines of the whole cumpany"
         - Arber 1875:154b.]
Birket-Smith, Kaj
  1918   The Greenland bow. Meddelelser om Grønland 56:1.
  1929a The Caribou Eskimos, Material and Social Life and Their Cultural
         Position. I, Descriptive Part. Reports of the Fifth Thule Expedition,
         vol. V. Copenhagen.
  1929b The Caribou Eskimos: Their cultural position. Copenhagen: Gylden-
         dalske Boghandel, Nordisk Forlag.
  1940   Anthropological observations on the Central Eskimos. Reports of the
         Fifth Thule Expedition, vol. III, No. 2.
  1959   The Earliest Eskimo Portraits. Folk 1:5-14.
Bjørnbo, Axel Anthon
  1911   Cartographia Groenlandica. Meddelelser on Grønland 48.
Bjørnbo, Axel Anthon, and Carl S. Petersen
  1904   Fyenboen Claudius Claussøn Swart (Claudius Clavus), Nordens ældste
         Kartograf. En Monografi. Det Kongelige Danske Videnskabernes

Selskabs Skrifter, 6. Række, Historisk og Filosofisk Afdeling 6(2):8(43)-260(302). Copenhagen.

Boas, Franz
1888   The Central Eskimo. Smithsonian Institution, Bureau of [American] Ethnology Annual Report 6:399-675.
1901   The Eskimo of Baffin Land and Hudson Bay, from Notes Collected by Capt. George Comer, Capt. James S. Mutch, and Rev. E.J. Peck. American Museum of Natural History Bulletin 15(1).
1907   Second Report on the Eskimo of Baffin Land and Hudson Bay... American Museum of Natural History Bulletin 15(2).

Bristol Calendar
[ca.1690] [Manuscript.]
        Bristol Public Library, MS.B.10163(3).

Burch, William
1590-1593 A boke of drawing, of the shapes and formes of diverse beasts, fouls, & birds, Fishes, monsters, and serpents, trees, herbes, plantes, and flowres wch diverse ar idents [?] of antiquoties. Manuscript, 163 leaves, 33.3 x 22 cm, in Canterbury Cathedral Archives, Literary MSS. A14.

Busscher, Edmond de
1866   Recherches sur les peintres et sculpteurs à Gand, aux XVIe, XVIIe et XVIIIe siècles. XVIe siècle. Ghent: E. de Busscher et fils.

Chapelle, Howard I.
1964   Arctic Skin Boats. Pp. 174-211 in The Bark Canoes and Skin Boats of North America, by Edwin Tappan Adney and Howard I. Chapelle. United States National Museum, Smithsonian Institution, Bulletin 230.

Cheshire, Neil, Tony Waldron, Alison Quinn, and David Quinn
1980   Frobisher's Eskimos in England. Archivaria 10:23-50.

Chotzen, Th.M., and A.M.E. Draak
1937   Beschrijving der Britsche Eilanden door Lucas de Heere, een Geillustreerd Geschrift uit zijn Engelsche Ballingschap. Antwerp: De Sikkel.

Churchyarde, Thomas
1578   A Prayse, and Reporte of Maister Martyne Forboishers Voyage to Meta Incognita. London: Andrew Maunsell.

Coenen (Coenenzoon, Coenensoen), Adriaen
1577-1578 Een visboock. Manuscript, 412 folios, in Koninklijke Bibliotheek, The Hague, 78E54.

Collinson, Richard (ed.)
1867   The three voyages of Martin Frobisher, in search of a passage to Cathaia and India by the north-west, A.D. 1576-8... Works Issued by the Hakluyt Society, [1st series, no. 38].

Croft-Murray, Edward, and Paul Hulton
  1960   Catalogue of British Drawings. Vol. I. XVI and XVII centuries. 2 pts.
          [Text; Plates]. London: British Museum.
Cumming, W.P., R.A. Skelton, and D.B. Quinn
  1971   The Discovery of North America. London: Elek.
Damas, David (volume editor)
  1984.   Arctic. Vol. 5 of Handbook of North American Indians (William C.
          Sturtevant, general editor). Washington: Smithsonian Institution.
Defert, Daniel
  1984   Un genre ethnographique profane au XVIe: Les livres d'habits (Essai
          d'ethno-iconographie). Pp. 25-41 in Histoires de l'anthropologie
          (XVIe-XIXe siècles), presente par Britta Rupp-Eisenreich. Paris:
          Klincksieck.
Dodding, Edward
  1577   Doctor Doddyngs Reporte of the Sicknesse and Death of the Man at
          Bristol which Capt. Furbisher brought from the North-west: and of
          the Nature of the Woman of that Contrie yet livynge. Manuscript in
          Public Record Office, London SP12/118. [Dated 8 November; in Latin,
          printed in Stefánsson 1938,2:135-137; English translation by N.
          Cheshire and T. Waldron in Quinn 1979:216-218, revised and with
          commentary in Cheshire et al. 1980:40-50.]
Driscoll, Bernadette
  1980   The Inuit Parka. Pp. 11-20 in The Inuit Amautik: I Like My Hood
          to be Full [Exhibition catalog]. [Winnipeg:] Winnipeg Art Gallery.
  1983   The Inuit Parka: A Preliminary Study. Unpublished MA thesis in
          Canadian Studies, Carleton University, Ottawa.
Fitzhugh, William W.
  1978   Winter Cove 4 and the Point Revenge Occupation of the Central
          Labrador Coast. Arctic Anthropology 15(2):146-174.
Franklin, John
  1828   Narrative of a second expedition to the shores of the Polar Sea, in
          the years 1825, 1826 and 1827. London: John Murray.
Gad, Finn
  1971   The History of Greenland, I: Earliest Times to 1700. Translated from
          Danish by Ernst Dupont. Montreal: McGill-Queen's University Press.
  1984   History of colonial Greenland. In Damas 1984:556-576.
George, Wilma
  1969   Animals and Maps. Berkeley and Los Angeles: University of
          California Press.
Goddard, Ives
  1984   Synonymy [of the name Eskimo]. In Damas 1984: 5-7.
Haberland, Wolfgang
  1975   Das gaben sie uns: Indianer und Eskimo als Erfinder und Entdecker.

Wegweiser zur Völkerkunde, Heft 17, Museum für Völkerkunde, Hamburg.

Hakluyt, Richard (ed.)
1589   The Principall Navigations, Voiages and Discoveries of the English Nation... London: George Bishop and Ralph Newberie.
1600   The Third and Last Volume of the Voyages, Navigations, Traffiques, and Discoueries of the English Nation... London: George Bishop, Ralfe Newberie, and Robert Barker.

Hall, Charles Francis
1864   Life with the Esquimaux... 2 vols. London: Sampson Low, Son, and Marston.

Hart Hansen, Jens Peder, Jørgen Meldgaard, and Jørgen Nordqvist (eds.)
1985   Qilakitsoq: De grønlandske mumier fra 1400-tallet. Nuuk: Grønlands Landsmuseum, [and] Copenhagen: Christian Ejlers Forlag.

Hatt, Gudmund
1914   Arktiske skinddragter i Eurasien og Amerika, en etnografisk studie. Copenhagen: J.H. Schultz

Hawkes, E.W.
1916   The Labrador Eskimos. Canada Department of Mines, Geological Survey Memoir 91, Anthropological Series 14.

Heere, Lucas de
1568-1576 Theatre De Tous Les Peuples et nations de la terre auec leurs habits, et ornemens diuers, tant anciens que modernes. Manuscript of 129 leaves with 195 watercolor drawings, in Rijksuniversiteit te Gent, Bibliotheek, MS. 2466.

Hodnett, Edward
1971   Marcus Gheeraerts the Elder, of Bruges, London, and Antwerp. Utrecht: Haentjens Dekker & Gumbert.

Honour, Hugh
1975a   The European Vision of America. [Exhibition catalogue.] [Cleveland:] Cleveland Museum of Art. [Also as: L'Amérique vue par l'Europe Paris: Éditions des musées nationaux, 1976.]
1975b   The New Golden Land: European Images of America from the Discoveries to the Present Time. New York: Pantheon.

Hrdlicka, Aleš
1930   Anthropological survey in Alaska. Bureau of American Ethnology Annual Report 46:19-374.

Hulton, Paul
1984   America 1585: The Complete Drawings of John White. [Chapel Hill:] University of North Carolina Press, and [London:] British Museum Publications.

Hulton, Paul, and David Beers Quinn
1964   The American Drawings of John White, 1577-1590, with drawings of

European and Oriental subjects. 2 vols. London: British Museum, and Chapel Hill: University of North Carolina Press.

James, William C.
1985   A Fur Trader's Photographs: A. A. Chesterfield in the District of Ungava, 1901-4. Kingston and Montreal: McGill-Queen's University Press.

[Jefferys, Thomas]
1772   A Collection of the Dresses of Different Nations. Ancient and Modern....Vol. IV. London: Thomas Jefferys.

Jordan, R.H., and S.A. Kaplan
1980   An Archaeological View of the Inuit/European Contact Period in Central Labrador. Études/Inuit/Studies 4(1-2):35-45.

Josephy, Alvin M. (ed.)
1961   The American Heritage Book of Indians. New York: American Heritage [and] Simon & Schuster.

Kaplan, Susan A.
1983   Economic and Social Change in Labrador Neo-Eskimo Culture. 2 vols. Unpublished Ph.D. dissertation in anthropology, Bryn Mawr College.

Kejlbo, Ib Rønne
1971   Claudius Clavus and the Sources of the Vinland Map. Pp. 77-83 in Proceedings of the Vinland Map Conference, ed. by Wilcomb E. Washburn. Chicago: University of Chicago Press for The Newberry Library.

Kirwan, L.P.
1959   The White Road: A Survey of Polar Exploration. London: Hollis & Carter.

Lane Poole, Rachel (Mrs. Reginald)
1912   Catalogue of portraits in the possession of the University, Colleges, City, and County of Oxford. Vol. I. The portraits in the University collections and in the town and county halls. Oxford Historical Society vol. 57. Oxford: Clarendon Press.

Letts, Malcolm (ed.)
1953   Mandeville's Travels; Texts and Translations. Works Issued by the Hakluyt Society, Series II, vols. 101-102.

Lok, Michael
1576-1583   [Financial Records of the Cathay Company.] Manuscripts, 2 vols., in Public Record Office, London, E.164.35.

1577   [Account of Frobisher's first voyage.] Manuscript in British Library, London, Cotton MS. Otho EVIII.

MacGregor, Arthur
1983   Collectors and collections of rarities in the sixteenth and seventeenth centuries. Pp. 70-97 in Tradescant's Rarities...., ed. by A. MacGregor. Oxford: Clarendon Press.

Mandeville, John
[1496] [No title. End:] Here endeth the boke of Iohn Maunduyle, knyght....London: Rychard Pynson. [Copy seen: British Library G.6713].
1568 The Voiage and trauayle, of syr John Maundeuile knight, which treateth of the way toward Hierusalem, and of maruayles of Inde with other Ilands and Countryes. London: Thomas East.

Mary-Rousselière, Guy
1984 Les Tununirusirmiut retrouvés. Eskimo 27:9-10.

Mathiassen, Therkel
1928 Material Culture of the Iglulik Eskimos. Reports of the Fifth Thule Expedition, vol. VI, No. 1.

Meldgaard, Jørgen
1980 Grønland/Greenland. Pp. 1-6 in Etnografiske genstande i Det kongelige danske Kunstkammer 1650-1800/Ethnographic Objects in The Royal Danish Kunstkammer 1650-1800. Edited by Bente Dam-Mikkelsen and Torben Lundbæk. Nationalmuseets skrifter, Etnografisk række, vol. 17. Copenhagen.

Morison, Samuel Eliot
1971 The European Discovery of America: The Northern Voyages, A.D. 500- 1600. New York: Oxford University Press.

Murdoch, John
1885 A study of the Eskimo bows in the U.S. National Museum. Report of the U.S. National Museum for 1884 (Annual Report of the Smithsonian Institution for 1884, pt. 2):307-316 + 12 pls.

Nansen, Fridtjof
1911 In Northern Mists: Arctic Exploration in Early Times. 2 vols. New York: Frederick A. Stokes Co.

Nooter, Gert
1971 Old Kayaks in the Netherlands. Mededelingen van het Rijksmuseum voor Volkenkunde, Leiden, Nr. 17.

Parent, Alain (ed.)
1984 La Renaissance et le Nouveau Monde. [Exhibition catalogue.] Québec: Musée du Québec.

Parks, George B.
1939 The Two Versions of Settle's Frobisher Narrative. Huntington Library Quarterly 2:59-66. [Followed on pp. 67-68 by "Variant Editions of Settle's Account of Frobisher," by Roland Baughman.]

Plischke, Hans
1916 Verschlagungen von Bewohnern Amerikas nach Europa in Altertum und Mittelalter. Petermanns Mitteilungen 1916:93-95.
1921 Eine Verschlagung von Eskimo nach Holland aus dem Jahre 1577. Petermanns Mitteilungen 67:125.

1954   Die Kulturen der außereuropäischen Erdteile in Übersicht. Führer durch die Schausammlungen des Instituts für Völkerkunde Universität Göttingen. Göttingen: Kommission Deuerlichsche Buchhandlung.

Quinn, David B. (ed.)
1979   New American World: A Documentary History of North America to 1612. Volume IV: Newfoundland from Fishery to Colony. Northwest Passage Searches. New York: Arno Press and Hector Bye, Inc.

Quinn, David Beers
1981a   La femme et l'enfant Inuit de Nuremberg, 1566. Recherches Amérindiennes au Québec 11(4):311-313.

1981b   Sources for the Ethnography of Northeastern North America to 1611. National Museum of Man, Mercury Series, Canadian Ethnology Service Paper No. 76. Ottawa.

1981c   The Americas. Pp. 47-58 in The maps and text of the Boke of Idrography presented by Jean Rotz to Henry VIII now in the British Library, edited by Helen Wallis. Oxford: Roxburghe Club.

Rousselot, Jean-Loup
1981   [Description of kayak, 732, and two paddles, 733 and no number, in Staatliche Museum für Völkerkunde, Munich.] Manuscript; copy in possession of W.C.S.

1983   Die Ausrüstung zur Seejagd der westlichen Eskimo, untersucht in ihrem kulturellen Kontext. Münchner Beiträge zur Amerikanistik 11.

Rye, William Brenchley
1865   England as Seen by Foreigners in the Days of Elizabeth and James the First... London: John Russell Smith.

Saladin d'Anglure, Bernard
1979   Le Quarte monde nordique de Mercator (1595). Études/Inuit/Studies 3(2):119-122.

1980   Le "Syndrome chinois" de l'Europe nordique, ou la demesure de l'Amerasie entre le temps de l'astrolabe (1480) et l'espace du chronomètre (1780). L'Ethnographie 1980(1):175-211.

Savours, Ann
1963   Early Eskimo Visitors to Britain. Geographical Magazine 36(6):336-343.

Sayre, Edward V., Garman Harbottle, Raymond W. Stoenner, Wilcomb Washburn, Jacqueline S. Olin, and William Fitzhugh
1982   The Carbon-14 Dating of an Iron Bloom Associated with the Voyages of Sir Martin Frobisher. Pp. 441-451 in Nuclear and Chemical Dating Techniques: Interpreting the Environmental Record, ed. by Lloyd A. Currie. American Chemical Society Symposium Series, No. 176.

Settle, Dionyse
1577   A true reporte of the laste voyage into the West and Northwest

regions, &c. 1577 worthily atchieued by Capteine Frobisher of the sayde voyage the first finder and Generall. With a description of the people there inhabiting, and other circumstances notable... London: Henrie Middleton. [First edition; second edition identical title, imprint, and year.]

1578   La navigation dv capitaine Martin Frobisher anglois, és regions de west & nordwest, en l'année M.D.LXXVII. Contenant les moeurs & façons de viure des peuples, & habitäs d'icelles, auec le portraict de leurs habits & armes, & autres choses memorables & singulieres, du tout incognues par deça. [Translated by Nicolas Pithou.] [Geneva?:] Anthoine Chuppin.

1580   Beschreibung Der schiffart des Haubtmans Martini Forbissher auss Engelland, in die Lender gegen West vnd Nordtwest, im Jar 1577. Darinnen diser Lender Inwohner sitten vnd weiss zu leben, sampt jren Trachten vnd Waffen Abcontrefeiung, auch andern, zuuor vnbekandten vnd sonderlichen sachen, angezeigt wirdt. Auss dem Frantzoesischen auffs trewlichste in das Teutsche gebracht. Nuremberg: Durch Katharinam Gerlachin und Johanns vom Berg Erben.

1580   De Martini Forbisseri Angli Navigatione in regiones occidentis et septentrionis Narratio historica, Ex Gallico sermone in Latinum translata per D. Joan. Tho. Freigivm. Nuremberg: In officina Catharina Gerlachin, & Hæredum Iohannis Montani.

1582   Lo scoprimento delle Stretto Artico et di Meta Incognita ritrovato nel'anno MDLXXVII & 1578 dal Capitano Martino Forbisero Inglese. Posto nvovamente in Ivce nel nostra idioma Italiano dal Sig. Gio. Lorenzo Anania done si contengono le maniere i costumi e gli habiti di quei popoli con le tante minere d'oro, e gioie che ui sono state scoperte: & altre cose memorabili degne di sapersi infino ad hora occolte. Naples: Gio. Battista Cappelli.

Stefánsson, Vilhjalmur (ed., with Eloise McCaskill)

1938   The Three Voyages of Martin Frobisher, In search of a passage to Cathay and India by the North-West, A.D. 1576-8... 2 vols. London: Argonaut Press.

Stewart, T.D.

1973   The People of America. New York: Scribner's.

Stöcklein, H.

1911   Naturgeschichtl. Raritäten d. 16. Jahrhdts. in d. Münchener Staats-Sammlgn. Das Bayerland 22. Jahrgang, Nr. 32:513-514. Munich [Clipping, with added notes from A. Jacobi, 1930, and K. Birket-Smith, 1931, in museum catalogue, Staatliches Museum für Völkerkunde, Munich.]

Strauss, Walter L.
1975   The German Single-Leaf Woodcut 1550-1600. A Pictorial Catalogue. 3 vols. New York: Abaris Books, Inc.

Sturtevant, William C.
1965   Ethnographic details in the American drawings of John White, 1577-1590. Ethnohistory 12(1):54-63.
1976   First visual images of Native America. Pp. 417-454 in First Images of America. The Impact of the New World on the Old, ed. by Fredi Chiapelli, Berkeley, Los Angeles, London: University of California Press.
1980   The First Inuit Depiction by Europeans. Études/Inuit/Studies 4(1-2):47-49.

Taylor, E.G.R.
1930   Tudor Geography, 1485-1583. London: Methuen & Co.

Taylor, J. Garth
1974   Netsilik Eskimo Material Culture: The Roald Amundsen Collection from King William Island. Oslo, Bergen, Tromsø: Universitetsforlaget.
1984   Historical Ethnography of the Labrador Coast. In Damas 1984:508-521.

Tradescant, John
1656   Musæum Tradescantianum: Or, A Collection of Rarities Preserved at South-Lambeth neer London. London: John Grismond. [Facsmile: Old Ashmolean Reprints I, Oxford, 1925.]

Weber, Bruno
1976   "Die Welt begeret Allezeit Wunder": Versuch einer Bibliographie der Einblattdrucke von Bernhard Jobin in Strassburg. Gutenberg-Jahrbuch 1976:270-290. Mainz.

Wenger, Béatrice
1975   Esquimaux en visite en Hollande au XVIe siécle: Représentation et dessins. Inter-Nord 13-14:217-222.

Yates, Frances A.
1975   The Valois Tapestries. 2nd ed. London: Routledge & Kegan Paul.

Zerries, Otto, and J.L. Rousselot
1978   Die Eskimo. Katalog zur Ausstellung. Munich: Staatliches Museum für Völkerkunde.

Appendix 1. Translation of the text of the 1567 handbill

[For the original German, legibly reproduced, see Strauss 1975,1:135,201,376. The translation below follows the Nuremberg version most closely. Significant differences are indicated by F for the version printed in Frankfurt am Main and by A for the version printed in Augsburg. This translation revises and replaces that in Sturtevant 1980.]

True portrait of a wild woman, with her little daughter, found in the district called Noua terra, and brought to Antwerp, and publicly seen by everyone there, and still to be seen. In this year 1566 there arrived at Antwerp by ship from Zeeland [F: Zeland; A: Zeelandt], a wild woman, a small person, together with her little daughter, and was shaped and clothed as this picture shows, and was found in Terra noua, which is a new district a few years ago first discovered by the French and Portuguese, and this woman with her child and her husband [A: with her husband and her little child] was met by the French (who had voyaged to this district, and come ashore, and sought strange adventures), and the man was shot with an arrow through his body. However he would not surrender, but bravely took his stand to defend himself, and in this skirmish he was severely wounded in the side by another Frenchman with a broadsword, then he took his own blood from his side in his hand, and licked it out of his hand, and took his stand to defend himself still more fiercely than before. Finally he was struck and wounded in his throat so much that he fell to the ground, and also died from this wounding. This man was 12 feet tall and had in 12 days killed 12 people with his own hands, Frenchmen and Portuguese, in order to eat them, for they like to eat no flesh better than human flesh. And as they seized the woman, she took her stand as though she were completely raving and mad, because of her child that she would have to leave behind, because the sailors wanted to bring her away to the ship, for she so loved the child, that she would rather lose her life than lose her child. Since she was now so mad, they let her alone a bit, then she went to the place where she had hidden her child, and then she was calmer than before, then they took the woman with her child, and brought her away, and none of the Frenchmen could understand a single word of hers, nor also talk with her through words. But she was taught enough in 8 months, that she confessed that she had eaten many men. Her clothes are made of seal's [Zeehonts] skins, in the manner that this picture shows. The paint marks that she has on her face are completely blue, like sky blue, and these her husband makes on her, when they take them for wife, so they can recognize their wives [A: and these the husbands make on their wives, so they can recognize them], for otherwise they run among one another like the beasts, and the marks cannot be taken off again with any substance. And these marks they make with the juice of a kind of plant, which grows there in the country. Her body is yellow,

130

brown, like the half Moors. The woman was 20 years old when she was captured, in the year 66 in August, the child 7 years. Let us thank God the Almighty for his blessings, that he has enlightened us with his word, so that we are not such completely wild people and man-eaters as are in this district, that this woman was captured and brought out, since she knows nothing at all of the true God, but lives almost more wickedly than the beasts. God grant that she also be converted to acknowledge him, Amen. Printed at Nuremberg, by Hans Wolf Glaser [F: Printed in Frankfurt am Main 1567; A: Printed in Augsburg, by Matheus Franck].

Appendix 2. Description of Eskimos by Adriaen Coenen

[The Dutch text below was transcribed from photographs of the original manuscript by Charles T. Gehring, translator and editor of the New York State Library's New Netherland Project (and slightly revised by W.C.S.). Abbreviations have been expanded in italics; "y" is written "ij" except where modern Dutch writes "i"; "u" is written either "u" or "v" according to the pronunciation; elided "t" has not been changed to modern "'t"; the original capitalization has been preserved; word breaks at line ends are indicated by hyphens. Rolf Loeber kindly provided us with a preliminary transcription of the Dutch. The English translation printed here is also by Gehring. Earlier we used a manuscript draft English translation made about 1964 by Gert Nooter (some of which was abstracted in Quinn 1981b). For a somewhat too free French translation see Wenger 1975.]

[f.48v. (Coenen's folio 39):]
[Title in frame at top of cartouche:] Een Wonderlijcke gheschiedenisse van eene wilden Man hoe / dat hi is ghevanghen gheworden en*de* tot londen gebracht inde maent va*n* November /
[Over picture, within cartouche, upper left:] folio 409. / noch va*n* dusda- /nige wilde luyden / ghescreven /
[f. 49r.:]
[Above upper cartouche:] fo 40. /
[Within upper cartouche:] Hier heb dij beminde leser de ghelijckenisse en*de* bescrivinghe van een / sekeren wilden persoon de welcke ontrent de maent van Julius lest leden / bij Capiteyn Fourbasher en*de* zijne compagnie, zeylende naer tlant van / kattay, in een zeeker onbekent Eylant daer noyt niemandt van te voren / (ymmers soo binne*n* menschen gheduncke*n* aenghearriveert is) en*de* sij hebben / eene*n* ghevanghen met sijn Schuyte daer inne hij was, ghemaeckt va*n* seeckere / vellen van zeehonden oft zeelden lanck 22 voet en*de* onderhalfve voet breet / op het alder breetste vande welcke vellen ghemaeckt sijn alle zijne cledere*n* / wel constelijcke met zenuwe*n* ghenayt en*de* tsame*n* ghevoecht den welcke*n* de*n* / voorseyden Capiteyn allyceerde door tgheluyt van seekere Bellen daer / toe hij seere groote affectie droech en*de* meenende deselve te nemen, / en*de* ontfanghen wt de handen van de voorschreve*n* Capiteyn is bij de selve*n* / met de hant ghevat en*de* door hulpe van de*n* Schipmeester en*de* seeckere an-/dere*n* persoene*n* men haelde hem met sijn Boot in des voorseyden Capiteyn*s* / Schip ghetrocken en*de* tot binne*n* deser staet van londe*n* leve*n*de ghebracht / hij ontrent vijftien dagen gheleeft ende niet anders eetende dan rau vleesch /
  Ende nu is de selfde Capiteyn Fairbasher weder wut ghevare*n* / met drij Schepen met veel volck ende victaily en munyti God wil hem / goede aventuer verleenen Dit figuer met dit ghescrift is / mij*n* Adriaen Coenen*zoon* gedaen

132

ende gegeven om dit vremt ende wonder-/baer vis boock mede te setten bij
ander vremde monsteren Inden Jare / ons heeren 1577 in december /
[Within lower cartouche:] In den tijden Als men alhier In hollant die beelde
stormighe dede door /die Goesen soe hebbe ic Adriaen Coenenzoon ghesien een
Wilt Wijf met / een kint ende men sagh se om gelt dese vrouwe was mede
gecleet aldus da-/nich faetsoen van cleedighe als desen wilde man met zeehonts
vellen of / robbe vellen dat Ruych buten ende dat kint was mede aldusdanigh
gecleet zij en /hadde geen sprake over haer oft en wolde niet spreken. Item
van dese vrouwe / hebbe ic gesien in scravenhage in de herbergh van den
molen daer dese vrouwe / haer meesters die se liet besien tuis lagen   Te
weten al dit dat die waerdinne / genaemt Anna pouwels Tot dat wilde wijf
sprac ende wees haer op een deel / beelden die somige vergult waren somighe
geverwet (alsoe haer man hooft man was / van sint Antonis Outaer daer om
die beelde daer gevlucht waren ende gebercht)   En Anna pouwels wees ende
seyde siet lecht u hande samen dit is u heer / u godt ende soe wijsende op de
beelde Waer op die wilde vrouwe haer hooft / scudde ende slooch haer hooft
om hoge ende leyde aldaer haer hant te / samen   Aldus dat daer wel an haer
scheen dat zij kennis hadde van / Godt van hemelrijcke Als ic an dit wel an
haer bemerckte   Aldus / kent Godt almachtich wel den zijnen ende den zijnen
hem hem zij loft / Amen /
[410v.-411r.:]
[Within upper border of frame at top of cartouche, 411r.:] 1578 In engelant /
[In frames at top of cartouches:] [410v.:] DIT SIJN LUYDEN [411r.:] DIE RAWE
VISCHEN EETEN /
[In box, upper right corner of cartouche, 411r.:] folio 409 /
[In box, upper left corner of cartouche, 410v.:] Die voelcker so man /fisch
fraesser nennet / derrend das fleisch / der grossen Wallfis-/schen stossend es
zu / pulffer, und back-/end broot daraus /
[In box on 410v., in cartouche between the two views of the man:] Van dusda-
/nighe een / man noch / ghescreven / hier voer / folio 39 /
[In box on 410v., within lower cartouche:] Schuten ghemaect / van zee honts-
/vellen Daer zij / mede visschen / ende vogele vangen /
[Along left side and bottom of 410v.:] hier na volcht de / beschrijvinghe van
den / kathayschen luyden / also ghenaemt eerst / siet ghij wat / voor lieden
zijn / ende oock hoe dat se / ghecleet gaen / De persoonen / en zijn niet
seer / hooch maer dick en / sterck ende men-/merckt aen haer / lieden wel
dat / sij vroom ende / cloeck zijn ende / naer dat men haer / can aen sien
bij som-/mighe teeckenen / dat sij oock wat / verstants hebben / heurlieder
haer / is seer swart ende / het han[gh]t hen seer / lanck gelijck de / wilde
Irische so / sij dat plegen te / draghen zijn ha-/bijt is eenen lijf-/rock van
harten / vellen dat haa-/rich is ofte van / zee honden vellen / de haricheyt
doen / sij binnen inden / winter ende tso-/mers doen se de / haricheyt buyten
/ aen sijn lijfrock heeft hij een hangende / kap dat is voor zijn hooft dwelck

133

hem / gheheel glat ant hooft past den rock / is seer wel ghemaeckt en*de* is
ronts *om*me / gheboort men den selfden en*de* is swart / En*de* het voorste van
den rock coemt ee*n* luts-/ken over den riem Maer dat achterste / deel coemt
hem tot achter op de hiele*n* / zij*n* coussen zijn oock van herte*n* heel af /
comende daer af heeft hij oock leerssen / die seer wijt zij*n* sij en drage*n*
gheen schoene*n* / dan alleenlijck de leerssen noch oock / gheen wollen lake*n*
noch lijnwaet en*de* / sij hebbe*n* schuytkens ghemaeckt zee honde*n* vollen
dwelck seer constigh / is gemaeckt en*de* sij zijn lanck seve*n* Engel-/sche
gaerden en*de* ee*n* halve gaert breet en*de* boven ist toeghemaeckt [411r.] lue*n*
Int middel [(crossed out:) en*de* sijzijn lan(ck)] heeft het een ront gat gelijck
hier gheteykent staet zijn / [410v.] Roye*n* daer hij met Royet zij*n* twee
engelsche gaerden lanck en*de* hij hout se in den m(iddel) [411r.]) (m)et beyde
de handen en*de* Roeyt also stijff voort dat hem geenen/
[Within lower right border of frame:] schuitenaer naer /
[411v.:]
[Upper left, above upper cartouche:] folio 409 /
[Within upper cartouche:] schuitenaer naervolghen en can nogh hem gelijck zijn
Zijn gheweer / ende wape*n* zij*n* booghen ende pijlen en*de* [(crossed out:) dan]
den boghe is ee*n* En-/gelsche elle lanck en*de* den pijl ee*n* halve Engelsche
gaert. Ende/ also heeft hij een langhe pijlen so ghij hier sien moecht en*de*
noch /veel ander vremde pijllen die noyt niet ghesien en sijn daer / mede
willen zij die voeghelen dooden die op de zee sijn Sij van-/ghen oock veel
diversche vremde visschen die sij rou en*de* ongheso-/den eeten, en*de* oock zee
honden daer sij haer mette [(crossed out:) vallen] vellen va*n* / cleeden en*de*
noch meer ander die te lanck soude*n* zijn /om al int particuliere te varhalen/
[At left outside cartouche, opposite preceding 7 lines:] Diver-/sche vre*m*- /de
vissce*n* / die zij / ongesoo-/den / eeten /
[Framed title for following cartouche:] Hier volcht oock het ghestalt der /
vrouwen. /
[Within lower cartouche:] Eerstelick Tvrouwe*n* haer is oock seer swert en*de*
wast so lanck / alst haer van ander vrouwe*n* sij en vlechten noch en bindent
niet op / maer latent hanghen. haer aenschijn is seer vremt ghespickelt met /
blau ghelijck ghij hier siet haer cleedere*n* zij*n* van sulcken herten vel- /len als
des mans lijf rocken en*de* oock so ghefaettioneert dan alleen-/lick op de arme*n*
hebben sij twee viercante stucken wit voecsel seer / costelick daer op geset
tachterste van hun cleedt is veel langer dan / des mans en*de* haer hoije*n* zijn
dieper ende wijder. Sij draghe*n* haer / kindere*n* altijts In hare*n* hoet op den
rugghe en*de* sij hebbe*n* cousens an ghelijck / de mans en*de* oeck twee paer
leerssen ee*n* paer met lanck haer naest hun been / en*de* ee*n* ander paer sonder
haer en*de* seer fraij gheboort sij sijn oock seer wijt / over die knie*n* dan me*n*
haer beene*n* sien can. haer handen zij*n* seer saecht / en*de* sij hebbe*n* zeer
corte voete*n* voorts zijn se wel gheproportioneert ghelijck / ander vrouwe*n*
behoeren. Haer ionck kint is haer seer gelijck behalve*n* dat / het noch so niet

134

en is ghespickelt int aensicht heur eten is rau oft onghe-/soden vleysch dwelck seer vuyl stinckt en*de* sij en hebben ghee*n* broot Maer in / Engelant hebben .sijt ee*n* lutsche*n* werm late*n* werde*n* hare*n* dranck is water,/ daer In dat het vleis warm is ghemaeckt gheweest. En*de* ee*n* van dese / persoene*n* eet meer dan twee ander en*de* sij stincke*n* oock so seer, dattet nie-/mant bij dueren en can En*de* van de gene die in Engelant gebracht zij*n* hebbe*n* / luttel [(crossed out:) tijt] engels conne*n* leere*n* spreke*n*. Dan, God geve yo goud marroe. Ende / farewel. Maer hadden sij der eenigen tijt gheweest, sonder twijvel sij / soudent wel geleert hebben. Den eersten Man die deerste reyse in En-/gelant gebracht wert is tot londen ghestorve*n*. Ende op dese ander reyse / bracht me*n* eene*n* man met een vrouwe ende een kint Den eerste*n* mans / naem is onbekent geweest en*de* den laetsten mans naem was CALIOHOGH/ der vrouwe*n* name EGNORTH en*de* het kindts name NUTENOCTH./ den lesten man met de vrouwe zij*n* tot Bristoo gestorve*n* en*de* het kint In / londen /
[At left, outside cartouche, opposite preceding 8 lines:] Van de-/sen eerste*n* / ma*n* is / noch hier voor af / gescreven / folio 39 /

[f. 48v. (Coenen's folio 39):]
[Title:] An amazing story of a wild man, how he was captured and taken to London in the month of November.
[Over picture:] Folio 409 describes other wild people of this sort.
[f.49r.:]
[Above cartouche:] folio 40.
[Within cartouche:] Here you have, dear reader, the picture and description of a certain wild person who was taken captive about July last by Captain Fourbasher and his company on their way to Kattay, who had come to a certain unknown island which no one had ever visited before (as far as people can remember). He was taken captive with his boat which he was in. It was made of skins of seals and was 22 feet [6.7m] long and one and a half [45.7 cm] wide at its widest. All his clothes were skillfully made of such skins, sewn with sinews and thus joined together. The aforesaid Captain enticed him by the sounds of some bells, which pleased him very much, and which he thought he could have by taking them from the hands of the above mentioned Captain, who grabbed him by the hand with the help of the ship's master and certain other persons. They pulled him with his boat into the ship of the aforesaid Captain and was brought alive to within this city of London, where he lived about fifteen days, eating nothing but raw meat.

And now the same Captain Fairbasher has sailed out again with three ships with many people, provisions, and munitions. May God grant him a good journey. This picture with this description has been made by me, Adriaen Coenenzoon, and submitted in order to place it in this strange and amazing fish book with other strange monsters. In this year of our Lord 1577 in December.

[Within lower cartouche:] During the time of the image-breaking by the Gueux here in Holland, I, Adriaen Coenenzoon, saw a wild woman with a child, and one could see them for money. This woman was dressed in the same manner of clothing as this wild man, with seal skins with the hair on the outside and that child was dressed in the same way. She had no language or did not want to speak. Also, I saw this woman in The Hague at the inn of the Mill where this woman's masters lived and had her on display. And I heard all that the landlady, called Anna Pouwels, said to that wild woman while showing her some statues, of which some were gilded and some were painted (because her husband was reponsible for the St. Antonis altar, that is why those statues had escaped and were kept there). And Anna Pouwels pointed and said, "Look, put your hands together, this is your Lord, your God," and while she was pointing to the statue, the wild woman shook her head and raised her head up and put her hands together. From this it seemed that she had some knowledge of God in heaven. Thus it seemed to me in any case by watching her. Thus God the Almighty knows his own and they know him. Let us praise him. Amen.
[410r.-411r.:]
[Within upper frame, 411r.:] 1578 in England.
[In frames above, 410r.-411r.:] THESE ARE PEOPLE WHO EAT RAW FISH.
[In box, upper right, 411r.:] folio 409.
[In box, upper left, 410v.; in German:] The people who are called fish eaters, they dry the flesh of the great whale fish, beat it into powder, and bake bread from it.
[In box on 410v., between two views of the man:] A man of this sort one may see in the earlier folio 39.
[In box on 410v., lower cartouche:] Boat made of seal skin, used for catching fish and birds.
[Text along left side and bottom of 410v.:] Here follows the description of the Kathay people as they are called. First you see what kind of people they are and also how they are dressed. These people are not very tall but stout and strong, and one sees that they are pious and brave. And they also have some intelligence, as one can see from certain signs. Their hair is very black and it hangs very long, as the wild Irish are accustomed to wear it. Their dress is a coat made of deer skins which are hairy or of seal skins. They have the hairy side inside in the winter and outside in the summer. Their coat has a hanging hood which is for their head and which fits them smoothly around the head. The coat is very well made and edged all around with the same and it is black. And the front of the coat hangs a little below the belt, but the back reaches their heels. His trousers are also made completely of deer skins. He also wears boots that are very wide. They do not wear shoes, only boots. They [wear] neither wool cloth nor linen. And they have boats made of seal skins, which are ingeniously made, and they are seven English yards [6.4 m] long and a half yard [45.7 cm] wide, and they are covered above. In the middle it has a

round hole just as drawn here. The oars with which he rows are two English yards [1.53 m] long and he holds them in the middle with both hands and rows so vigorously that no oarsman can follow him or keep up with him.

[Above cartouche, 411v. upper left:] folio 409. [411 v.:] Their weapons are bows and arrows and the bow is one English ell [1.10 m] long and the arrow half an English yard [45.7 cm]. And he also has a long arrow as you can see here and many other strange arrows that have never been seen before. With them these people kill the birds that are at sea. They also catch many strange and different fish, which they eat raw and uncooked, and also seals with the skins of which they clothe themselves, and many other things too many to tell about in detail.

[Outside cartouche, opposite preceding lines:] Different strange fish that they eat uncooked.

[Framed title:] Here follows also the description of the women.

[Within lower cartouche:] First of all, the women's hair is also very black and it grows as long as the hair of other women. They do not wear it in braids and they do not tie it up but let it hang loose. Their faces have very strange blue speckles as you see here. Their clothes are of the same deer skins as those of the man's coat and are made the same way, except on the arms they have two square white patches very skillfully stitched on. The back of their clothes is much longer than those of the men and their hoods are deeper and wider. They always carry their children in their hoods on their backs. They have trousers of the same kind as those of the men and they also have two pairs of boots, one pair with the long hair against their legs and another pair without hair, and very handsomely edged. They are also very wide over their knees so that their legs can be seen. Their hands are very soft and they have very short feet. Furthermore they are well proportioned as is the case with other women. Her young child resembles her very much except that its face is not speckled as much. Their food is raw or uncooked meat which smells very bad, and they do not have any bread but in England they cooked meat a bit. Their beverage is the water in which the meat has been heated. And one of these people eats more than two others and they smell so bad that no one can bear it near them. Those who have been brought to England have been able to learn to speak little English except for "God geve yo goud marroe" and "farewel." However, if they had been there for some time, they would no doubt have learned it well. The first man who was brought to England on the first voyage died in London. On the other voyage they brought with them a man with a woman and a child. The name of the first man is not known and the name of the second man was CALIOHOGH. The woman was called EGNORTH and the child NUTENOCTH. This man and this woman died in Bristol and the child in London.

[At left, opposite preceding lines:] This first man has been described on folio 39.

Appendix 3. Translation of text accompanying 1578 woodcut

[The translation here is of the text of the earliest version, printed in Strasbourg; the infelicities and awkward constructions reflect those of the original. The texts (and pictures) of the versions printed in Augsburg and Nuremberg are derivatives of this one, recut and reset with some different spellings but without useful additions or clarifications - except as the hand-coloring of the Strasbourg version obscures some details in the reproductions.]

Notable description, together with a proper picture of a strange unknown people, of a newly discovered district or island, in recent time explored by Master Martin Frobiser, by an extraordinary and never dared voyage out of England towards the vernal occident, for the consolation and delight of all Christendom. The world always demands miracles, and can hardly be satisfied with miraculous signs: Now however God the Lord also accedes thereto, and daily shows them the most miraculous miracles, and the best most certain signs of his future coming: Which is namely, according to his own prophecizing word, that as a testimony his kingdom, which is the Christian belief, will extend over all peoples in the entire world from one sea to the other. Such he shows today, in that he has allowed the Christians out of Europe, and not the Turks out of Asia, to find, discover, edify, instruct, and bring to discipline and order the most distant, most unknown, wildest ends of the world, where one would scarcely have looked for habitations of animals, let alone humans.

So that I presently be silent about the Spanish, Portuguese, and Floridian sea voyages which are now sufficiently known and notorious: So I will here only remember the thoroughly newest, and still wholly unheard of voyage of the English into strange islands, and briefly describe them together with the people found therein.

Last 77th year, Master Martin Frobisher, native of England, a man very able in the art of Cosmography or investigation regarding the world and in the experience of the sea, has from computation discovered that much, that far on the side of and behind the Kingdom of Ireland must lie islands or land, which are either inhabited or could well be inhabited. Has therefore as the very first undertaken to investigate such through the unknown sea: In the hope, if he be successful, to gain through commerce a good profit, together with his [people]. Thus he sailed from England with a ship, and set his course for the southern part of Ireland, straight towards the sunset. Then after he had sailed across many seas, after the fourteenth day he had seen the land he had so longed for. But as he looked for a suitable harbor or port, to enter so that he could disembark some of his [people] on the land: He met several ship of fishermen or birders, who pursued both fish and birds with such kind of ships as here depicted, and caught them with such instruments the like of which are also here indicated. Who, when they perceived the miraculous (as it appeared to them) form of the English ship, were as terrified by the strangeness as if they saw a sea-monster, and they also fled away immediately, as soon as the ship began to approach them: Master Frobiser pursued them, so that he could catch some of them for informants, but they were much too swift for him with their kind of ship. Nevertheless one was so bold, who dared to wait for the ship to arrive: This one Master Frobiser entices to him with good words and friendly gestures and also shows him from a distance various beautiful delicious things, so long, until he brought him hither into the ship.

As soon as he was in the ship, Frobiser ordered him bound, so that he would not jump into the water and swim away. Subsequently he also took into the ship the man's little ship and his gear wherewith he shot at the birds. Laden with such goods, he went straight again for England: When he had landed there, he immediately has shown the queen and the nobles this strange man, together with the ship and his missile, as testimony of everything, otherwise so unbelievable, that he related extensively of the situation and suitability of the strange land, and how one could so easily sail there from England. Briefly to conclude, with his account Frobiser aroused in many a desire to explore this new land likewise. So that soon thereafter a number of ships were fitted out, in which Frobiser sailed with many young nobles for the aforesaid island, landed there, and most industriously discovered the situation. But because we do not here have the intention to put forth a history of scarcely believable things that they discovered, we will satisfy ourselves on this paper with describing the appearance and clothing of the strange men who were brought from the distant island to England.

They are in appearance equal to ours: Of medium color, although more pale: entirely black hair, which extends in the men to the shoulders, in the woman to the hips: it is also on the crown not unshaped, also without distinct ribbons and cords. They color the face in various ways: the eyebrows are surrounded with separate blue stripes, as also the chin. The man's clothing is a deerskin pulled over the bare skin, of which in wintertime they turn the fur inwards, in summertime outwards. To this skin a hood is sewn, also from the same skin, which he uses for a hat. The border of the coat is beautifully edged with black furs: the front part of the coat hangs scarcely below the navel, but the back part to the heels: They have breeches and stockings of the same animal skin: which are also their shoes. The women's clothing is almost not unlike the men's, except for the sleeves, which along with the deerskin they decorate with other white furs: their coats are somewhat longer, and the hood much more ample, wherewith they carry their child within. They use two pairs of stockings over each other, of which the inner is of deer's fur, the upper is smooth: They have soft hands and rather short legs. In their country they eat raw meat and fish without bread: but in England they eat a little roasted. Their drink is water and meat broth: They eat much, and double more than an Englishman: What is repugnant to the English, tastes good to them. The ship is made of sea calves' skin, twenty-one Strasbourg ells long, one and a half wide. Inside are two long poles, which spread it apart, with thwarts tied on in the middle, which stretch it apart at the sides. In the middle on top is a hole, that the man inside can stand upright in, and use the paddle, which paddle is six ells long, and he manages it when he navigates, in the middle with both hands from one side one after the other: and travel with it so quickly, that in London, when it was discovered, no one could approach him on the water. Their arms are bows and arrow. He also has a missile with which he brings down birds, and this so certain that it never fails him. They are not so completely awkward that they cannot learn and comprehend something: therefore it is hoped this new land will be well suitable to the kingdom. &c. Printed in Strasbourg Anno 1578.

EARLIEST EXTANT PAINTING OF GREENLANDERS

P.J.P. Whitehead

Introduction

The iconography of exotic peoples - their physical appearance as much as their artifacts - is always important to ethnology and never more so than when it has derived from those past ages where the verbal dictionary, in breadth, depth and accuracy, lagged far behind the visual one. For example, the Latin descriptions of Tupinamba bows and arrows given by Marcgrave (1648:278), based perhaps on actual handling of the objects in northeastern Brazil, are useful inasmuch as they specify materials and describe uses, but they simply cannot rival the wealth of data to be extracted from the superb picture of a Tupinamba Indian holding perhaps even the same bow and arrows and painted by Marcgrave's colleague Albert Eckhout in 1643 (Etnografisk Samling, Nationalmuseet, Copenhagen, EN 38A 3; Due 1980:35 - color plate). At that time the gap between the verbal and the visual modes of description was considerable. Gradually, however, as ethnology developed into a science in its own right and adopted descriptive precision from other disciplines, the gap has dwindled, to the extent that nowadays a visual representation may seem merely an adjunct that epitomizes some lengthy text. That the gap does still exist, however, is clear when one considers the continuing value of portraiture in its power to express individual variation, as much in complex artifacts as in people. Of course, ethnology has not neglected iconography, but it is still possible to find novel or underexploited iconographic sources that with patience can yield a great deal of data, as for example Eckhout's Tupinamba portrait in Copenhagen (Whitehead 1985).

Another important picture in the Nationalmuseet, Copenhagen, is one that can be claimed as the earliest extant oil painting of Eskimos, being four Greenlanders painted by an unknown artist in about 1654 (Fig. 1). It is not a wholly neglected source, having been commented upon (e.g. by Birket-Smith 1916:17-18, and by Bobé 1927) and reproduced with a general description and history by Meldgaard (1980:5, color plate). However, its ethnographic data can still usefully add to what is known from other visual, verbal or material sources, and it seems worthwhile to bring together and discuss the rather scattered and incomplete references to the production of the painting and also its relationship to contemporary engravings and to a now lost painting formerly at Schwedt on the Oder (and by some attributed to Albert Eckhout). In claiming a significant place for the Copenhagen painting in the chronology of early Eskimo iconography, one must bear in mind how few representations were actually made before 1654 and what a small proportion of such original drawings or oil paintings have survived. An excellent review of the sixteenth century iconography of Eskimos has been given in the previous paper by Sturtevant and Quinn (1987), but a brief summary is given here in order to emphasize what a landmark the Copenhagen painting was in terms both of renewed interest in Eskimos and of the amount of ethnographic detail that artists now included.

European contact with Eskimos presumably dates back to the early Viking explorations, but it is striking that the first serious attempts to depict these native *skrælings* came in the second half of the sixteenth century and long after the first visual images of Indians from the more southern parts of the New World. Possibly there were climatic reasons why Europeans were slower to draw or paint Eskimos and it is indeed the case that all the early pictures, right up to the mid-seventeenth century, were based on Eskimos that had been kidnapped, first by the French in Labrador in 1566, then by Martin Frobisher on Baffin Island in 1576 and 1577, and finally by David Dannel in western Greenland in 1654 (the Copenhagen painting). Altogether, there is evidence of at least 21 drawings or paintings of Eskimos made partly or wholly from life prior to 1600, of which only three originals survive, the rest being known from copies, from prints or from references in the literature. If any originals exist from the period 1600 to the Copenhagen painting of 1654, then they seem to have been missed by all previous workers.

The following are the recorded life studies of Eskimos made prior to the Copenhagen painting:

A. *Labrador Eskimos, 1566*
 1. Woman and child. Unknown artist, lost, known only from handbills
B. *Frobisher's Eskimos, 1576*
 2. Man with bow, man in *kayak* behind. Lukas de Heere (1534-1584), water-color, *EXTANT*, Universiteitsbibliotheek, Ghent (but perhaps based on 3,4, or 5 below)
3-10. Man. Cornelis Ketel (1548-1616), eight pictures in oils, all lost, known only from documents (Public Record Office, London, PRO E 164/35, f.15v.; see also Rye 1865:205)
 11. Man (presumably the same as above). John White (fl. 1577-1593), presumed a watercolor, lost, suspected from literature reference (Best 1578) and a copy by Adriaen Coenensz (1514-ca.1583)
C. *Frobisher's Eskimos, 1577*
12-16. Woman and child. Ketel (see 3 above), lost
 17. Man. White (see 7 above), watercolor, *EXTANT*, British Museum, Dept. Prints & Drawings. At least eight subsequent copies or versions are known
 18. Man from rear. White (see 7 above), watercolor, lost, known from three later copies or versions
 19. Woman and baby. White (see 7 above), watercolor, *EXTANT*, British Museum, Dept. Prints & Drawings. At least eight subsequent copies or ver-

sions are known
20. Skirmish with Eskimos. White (see 7 above), presumed a watercolor, known from two later copies or versions
21. Man in kayak. White (see 7 above), presumed a watercolor, lost, known from five later copies or versions.

Thus, only 21 more or less "on the spot" or "from life" pictures of Eskimos are known prior to the Copenhagen painting, and only three of them are actually extant and can be consulted for ethnographic information. All other known representations in this period are derivative and their detail at least potentially suspect. The Copenhagen painting, as one of only four extant pictures and the only surviving oil painting, is therefore of considerable ethnographic interest.

The Copenhagen painting

This painting, showing four Greenlanders of around 1654 in traditional costume, is in the Etnografisk Samling of the Nationalmuseet (oils on canvas, 171.5 by 121.5 cm, EN 38C1). After the John White drawings of over seventy years earlier, it would appear to be the next life study of Eskimos, as well as the first of Greenlanders. It is also, with the loss of the Ketel paintings, the earliest extant oil painting of Eskimos. Such claims, fully supported here by the literature (but in no way fully explored in the many hundreds of possible repositories that might contain unrecorded or overlooked pictorial representations of Eskimos), such claims are rash; but perhaps they will stimulate contradiction. It is certainly curious that no original pictures of Eskimos seem to be recorded from the fourteen or so expeditions sent out after those of Frobisher in the search for the Northwest Passage, concluding with the Thomas James voyage of 1631-32 (after which the quest remained dormant for more than a century).

The Copenhagen painting stems not from the great exploratory expeditions, but from the period of renewed interest by the Dano-Norwegian monarchy in asserting rights over its territories in the North Atlantic, most particularly over Greenland. Three expeditions were mounted by Christian IV, in 1605, 1606 and 1607, on each of which James Hall was the chief pilot. Accounts of these three voyages were reviewed and some reproduced by Gosch (1897a), who included Hall's map of King Christian's Fjord, on which are drawn five very crude Eskimos (one holding an upright kayak, one supporting a bow with his left hand, also a tent, thus strongly reminiscent of the woodcut in Dionyse Settle's *True report* of Frobisher's second voyage - Settle 1578, 1580a, 1580b). The first two expeditions brought back Eskimos whose public exhibition, as well as private study by the chronicler Arild Huitfeldt (1546-1609) might well have led to drawings which are now lost; some of their artifacts were given by Christian IV to the Elector of Saxony in Dresden (where an adze and a knife are now in the Staatliches Museum für Völkerkunde - Israel 1965), while a kayak was deposited in the Schiffergesellschaft in Lübeck with a reference to the 1606 voyage (Meldgaard 1980:3). One can note that the account of the third voyage was written by another English participant, Josias Hubert, who according to Purchas (1625,3:827) included "representations of Landsights curiously delineated" by himself (or copied from Hall); Purchas had the manuscript and drawings, but did not publish them, and he was perhaps unaware that the voyage had already been given by Lyschander in his *Den Grønlandske chronica* of 1608 (which was mined by Isaac de la Peyrère for his *Relation dv Groenland* of 1647; his plate (opp. p. 145) shows a Greenland man, woman and child, possibly based on sketches of those brought back from the 1605/06 expeditions). Meanwhile, James Hall undertook a fourth and final voyage, in 1612, but was slain by Greenlanders; the accounts of the voyage by John Gatonbe and William Baffin (Gosch 1897a) did not have illustrations.

Equally disappointing from the iconographic point of view was Jens Munk's voyage to Hudson's Bay in 1619-20. Eskimos were encountered along the northern shore of Hudson's Strait and in his manuscript journal, as well as in his published *Navigatio septentrionalis* (Munk 1624), he claimed that the appearance of the people and their artifacts were shown in the accompanying picture; unfortunately, the journal has a blank space, while the woodcut in the *Navigatio* shows Eskimos, but entirely naked (see Gosch 1897b; also Hansen 1970:239, Fig.).

With the accession of Frederik III in 1648 came another wave of Danish interest in the northern territories, initiated by Henrik Müller, head of the Customs Department, who applied for privileges of navigation and trade in Greenland and was granted a thirty year monopoly in April 1652 (Gad 1970:237). A month later Müller sent off the first of three summer expeditions, all commanded by a Dutchman, David Urbanus Dannel in the ship *St. Jacob*. It was on the third voyage, in 1654 and in the Fjord of Godthaab, that the four Eskimos of the painting were induced to come aboard and to make the voyage to Europe, bringing with them artifacts (harpoons, bladder darts, bird darts) which came to Frederik III's *Kunstkammer* and are perhaps among those existing now (Meldgaard 1980:6). A short summary of Dannel's third voyage (and logbooks of the first two voyages) was printed by Bobé (1916).

The four Greenlanders were landed at Bergen, apparently staying long enough to be drawn and perhaps painted, before being sent to Copenhagen; unfortunately the man of the party died *en route*. From Copenhagen the three women were dispatched to Flensburg, where Frederik III had earlier lived as governor of Schleswig-Holstein (and had just retreated there because of plague), and from thence to Schloss Gottorp in Schleswig where Frederik's cousin Friedrich, third Duke of Holstein-Gottorp, held court and showed an equally great interest in the new and the curious. Five years earlier, Friedrich had appointed Adam Ölschläger or Olearius (1603-1671) as Keeper of the Ducal

144

Library and *Kunstkammer*, one of the foremost scholars of the time. Olearius eagerly seized the chance to study the three Greenland women and to compile a detailed description of them (Olearius 1656 - see below). He noted that Frederik III wanted the three women returned to their homeland once they had learnt Danish and adopted Christian ways, but no more Danish ships sailed for Greenland and the women merely returned to Copenhagen and survived until around the siege of 1659, when they died of *sprinkler* (spotted fever) according to Arni Magnússon (MS. A. 228, 8v. - relevant excerpts in Anonymous 1930:223-224; see also Bobé 1927).

It was to be another sixty years before Danish interest in Greenland was revived, this time by the foundation of Håbets Koloni (Colony of Hope) by the Lutheran missionary Hans Egede, leading to the formation of the Bergen Grønlandske Compagnie and, as a promotional ploy, the exhibition in Copenhagen of the two Greenlanders Poq and Qiperoq (whose life-size portrait is yet another of the pictorial treasures of the Nationalmuseet - Meldgaard 1980:15 - color plate).

The painting

The four West Greenlanders in the painting (Fig. 1) are identified (in red, from left to right above their heads) as the man Thiob and the women Cabelou, Gunelle and Sigjo. They appear to be a little under life size.

Thiob:

Facing half to his left and about 152 cm in height, wearing a short-sleeved jacket without a flap at the front, the hood over his head, dark trousers and calf-length boots. He wears a white bone or shell bracelet on his right wrist and in that hand holds the top of a kayak harpoon or bladder-dart (143 cm total length), the head rather similar to that of an early *Kunstkammer* specimen EL c 26 (Meldgaard 1980:7,8 - 158 cm total length). In his left hand he holds a wooden bow (88 cm), possibly of a single piece of wood, and a single arrow, the two resembling but not identical with the *Kunstkammer* specimens EL b 1 and EL c 32b (Meldgaard 1980:9,10). The sinew backing of the bow, very carefully depicted, runs as a longitudinal bundle from one end to the other, with an outer layer of herring-bone binding about 30 cm down from the nock and running continuously to presumably 30 cm from the other nock (hidden); the binding shows some affinities with the Arctic type (e.g. specimen 2506 of Murdoch 1885:Fig. 24), but is presumably a secondary development of West Greenland (see Birket-Smith 1916:17-18; also 1924:185 *et seq.*, the painting reproduced and various artifacts discussed). Sandwiched between the sinew backing and the bow stave is a shiny black strip.

Fig. 1. Painting by an unknown artist of four Greenlanders. Nationalmuseet, Etnografiske Samling, Copenhagen.

146

Cabelou:

About 133 cm in height, peering between Thiob and Gunelle, with a hand on the latter's shoulder, thus mostly hidden, but with a short black skirt, apparently bare legs, and calf-length boots. The hood of her jacket is thrown back and her hair is in a double coil or bun on top of her head; her face is tattooed with nine vertical blue lines around her chin and two thin arched blue lines rising up and then following the curve of her eyebrows (carefully described by Olearius 1656:170, who gave her age as 25).

Gunelle:

About 137 cm in height, body turned a quarter to her left, wearing a long-sleeved jacket open in a "V" at the neck and with a tall hood, the front of the jacket with a long "tail" to her knees; she appears to have an apron of lighter color across her front, but the painting is not very explicit. She wears a short dark skirt and calf-length boots, the legs being otherwise bare. There is a hint of tattooing below her mouth (see also Olearius 1656) and she wears a brown neck-lace. In her left hand she holds a rather well depicted herring (*Clupea harengus*). The high hood, the rather wide shoulders of the jacket and the long flaps hanging down at front and back represent a style that had disappeared by colonial Greenland times (Meldgaard 1980:6). According to Olearius (1656:170) she was 45, with two children left in Greenland.

Sigjo:

The smallest of the group, only 117 cm in height and much the youngest in appearance (aged 13 *fide* Olearius), partly hidden by Gunelle and partly cut off by the edge of the picture. Her hood is thrown back and the long frontal flap of the jacket can be seen, as well as calf-length boots. In her right hand she holds a sea bird (probably a gannet, *Sula bassensis*). Her face is not tattooed and her hair is not piled on her head.

The background to the painting is plain, without any attempt to provide a landscape setting (presumably because the artist had no experience of Greenland). In the top left corner is a small wooden plaque suspended by a nail in *trompe l'oeil* style which reads:

mit Ledern SchiffLein aüff
dem Meer. degron Lein der
zein hein undt her• von:
Theiren undt Vögelen ha
ben see Ire tracht das
kalte Landt von Mitter nacht
:Bergen:• den 28 September
Anno 1654

The rhymes *Meer/her* and *tracht/nacht* show that the text is actually a four-line verse. Misspelt words (*Theiren*, *see* and *zein*, *hein*) as well as the extraordinary rendering of "the Greenlanders" as *degron Lein der*, shows that the painter knew little German, and would indicate that he was merely given a text to copy. The lines can be translated as:

> With small leather boats on the sea
> The Greenlanders go hither and thither
> From animals and birds they get their garb
> [In] the cold land of midnight
> > Bergen   28 September 1654

The painting has no recorded history prior to its appearance in the 1673/4 inventory of Frederik III's *Kunstkammer*, where it is given (f.161) as *Et Skilderie af fire Grønlændere* (Meldgaard 1980:6).

Olearius engravings

The first appearance of these Greenlanders in literature, somewhat *in locis absconditis* one might say, was in the *Vermehrte Muscowitische und Persianische Reisebeschreibung* of Olearius (1656:163-179, book 3, ch.4). Olearius embellished his account with two engravings (p.172 and on the page opposite). The first (Fig. 2) generally follows the painting, but is partly reversed. Thiob (on the right) shows only minor differences from the painting, as also Cabelou, who is similarly positioned, but does not hold a fish. Gunnelle, on the other hand, no longer peers over their shoulders, but stands separately. The fourth figure is totally different, however. She stands sideways, right shoulder to the viewer, right arm extended and index finger pointing, also her high hood is drawn up over her head. Presumably this is Sigjo, although she has now grown almost as tall as the others and has been given the hint of a beard. The second engraving (Fig. 3) shows the four Greenlanders in shoulder-length portrait, their heads grouped as in the painting (but reversed). They are similarly labelled over their heads, but with some variant spellings (Thiob, Kabelaŭ, Kŭneling, Sigoko). The major difference from the painting is that Sigjo now has her hood up, as in the first engraving. The composition of this plate is curious, the figures very low down and the whole of the upper half devoted to stylized clouds (the picture seems to evoke mournful wastelands).

Ten years later Olearius published a catalogue of the Gottorp *Kunstkammer*, in which he included a brief note about the Greenlanders (with a reference to his earlier book) and provided yet another engraving (Olearius 1666:4-5, pl.3). In this engraving (Fig. 4) Thiob has been omitted and the remaining three figures (full length, numbered 1, 2, 3) are redrawn and reversed from the 1656

148

Fig. 2. Engraving of four Greenlanders from the *Vermehrte Muscowit. Persian. Reisebeschreibung.* of Olearius (1656:172).

Fig. 3. Engraving of four Greenlanders from the *Vermehrte Muscowit. Persian. Reisebeschreibung.* of Olearius (1656: opp.172).

plate, with Sigjo graced by an even more pronounced beard and the other two women acquiring some whiskers also. Suspended in the background is a kayak (with a man inside wielding a double-paddle), which suggests a more permanent gift from Frederik III than just the loan of the three women.

Possible sources for the Olearius engravings are discussed below.

Schwedt painting

Thomsen (1938:110-125), in what still remains the best study of the Dutch painter Albert Eckhout (c. 1610-65), drew attention to ten curious paintings of exotic peoples at that time hung in the hall of the Schloss at Schwedt on the Oder, which he attributed to Eckhout. He noted that in one of the paintings (see Fig. 5) there was the figure of a Greenlander which exactly matched the tall-hooded versions of Sigjo in the Olearius engravings of 1656 and 1666. Until 1928 these paintings were at the Schloss at Pretsch on the Elbe, when they were transferred to Berlin before going to Schwedt, but they are unsigned and nothing is recorded of their early history. At the end of the war they were destroyed by fire (Eckhart 1978:194-196) and are now known only from Thomsen's photographs. That they were indeed painted by Eckhout is perhaps doubtful (Whitehead and Boeseman 1987). They have been commented upon by van Luttervelt (1942:67-68), Börsch-Supan (1973:75), Döry (1974:col.1499, and 1975:205-206) and Joppien (1979:344-345), all of whom noted possible sources for the figures, including the Olearius engraving for the Greenlander, which would date the Schwedt painting as not before 1656. Some of the other Schwedt paintings received an even later *terminus post quem* (as late as 1680) on the assumption that their figures also derived from specific published models. In the case of the Schwedt Greenlander, which is not reversed from the first Olearius engraving, it is difficult to see that the engraving and the painting had the same source, i.e. a sketch. The painting seems more likely to be a departure from the engraving, with costume details further misunderstood.

Prior sketches

The Olearius engravings are sufficiently like the painting that they must have a common source. It is highly unlikely that they were derived solely from the painting, since there seems no reason to give two versions (full figure and also shoulder-length) or to have made any changes (Sigjo with her hood up, Cabelou separated from Thiob and Gunelle, and a totally new version of Sigjo standing sideways). The source of the engravings must surely have been sketches and the existence of more than one, as well as the differences from the painting, show that these were independent of the painting and not drawn from it. The often considerable similarity of detail between the engravings and the painting, however, shows that these were prior sketches which were

150

Fig. 4. Engraving of Greenlanders from the catalogue of the Gottorp *Kunstkammer* by Olearius (1666: pl.3)

Fig. 5. Detail from a painting once in the Schloss at Schwedt on the Oder (see text at p.150).

explicit and could well have been good enough to have served for the painting itself in the absence of the subjects themselves.

The minimum number of sketches would be four:

i.   Thiob and the three women in shoulder-length portrait, with Sigjo wearing her hood up (Olearius 1656: opp. 172)

ii.   Thiob and Gunnelle, full figure, standing beside each other, Thiob holding bladder dart, bow and arrow (left half of painting and reversed for Olearius 1656:172, Fig.)

iii. Cabelou, full figure (presumably reversed for Olearius 1656:172, Fig.)

iv.   Sigjo facing sideways, hood up, finger pointing (Olearius 1656:172, Fig. and the Schwedt painting).

It is assumed that the 1666 engravings for Olearius's account of the *Kunstkammer* were merely redrawn from the earlier engravings (once more reversed). It is very possible, however, that more than four sketches were made, although Olearius may not have seen more than those listed here. He might in turn have passed the sketches on, at least one of them coming eventually to the artist of the Schwedt picture. Alternatively, they might have accompanied gifts to another *Kunstkammer*, for example that of Johann Georg II, Elector of Saxony; a search through the treasures of the Sächsische Landesbibliothek or the Kupferstich-Kabinett in Dresden might be rewarding. In 1751 the Gottorp *Kunstkammer* was transferred to Copenhagen to join the Royal *Kunstkammer*, but no hint of any sketches emerged during the very thorough preparations for the exhibition of surviving *Kunstkammer* objects (*Det Indianske Kammer*, 1979) and the compiling of a fully illustrated account (Dam-Mikkelsen and Lundbæk 1980). If the Greenlander sketches still exist, most likely they are not in Copenhagen.

The painter

The almost certain existence of sketches before the actual painting was made now liberates the latter from certain constraints of time and place. It need not have been painted in Bergen and thus need not have been painted before Thiob's death on the journey to Copenhagen. Furthermore, the painting need not have travelled from Bergen to Copenhagen and then from Copenhagen to Flensburg and on to Gottorp, nor need its fate have anything to do with the Schwedt painting. In turn, this makes it even more difficult to hazard an artist, since he would have worked almost anywhere and used the presumably colored sketches. Most likely it was painted in Bergen or Copenhagen.

Mr. Puccio Speroni, conservator of pictures for the Nationalmuseet, has noted strong stylistic similarities between the Greenland painting and the large ethnographic paintings by Eckhout that hang in the same institution, some of which he has personally restored and thus, over a period of many weeks, observed extremely closely. My own opinion, after careful but much briefer study, is that the treatment of the faces is different; the artifacts, although depicted with care, lack the crispness of Eckhouts detail; and the clothes do not show sufficient understanding of texture and form. However, there also seems clear circumstantial evidence to rule out Eckhout, since in September 1654 he had already been over a year in Dresden at the court of the Elector of Saxony and would remain there until 1663 (Thomsen 1938:56). Thus there is no way that Eckhout could have drawn sketches which included Thiob, unless he was rushed to the spot by the Elector or on the orders of Frederik III. To bring Eckhout to Copenhagen (or Flensburg or Gottorp) to paint the picture from another man's sketches, or to send the sketches to Dresden and then return the finished painting to Gottorp or Copenhagen, is to go too far beyond the evidence. One can note also that Eckhout signed and dated all but one of the large ethnographic paintings now in Copenhagen, even adding a signature and date over an overpainted area in the Tarairiu man. However, he did not sign the painting of a Tarairiu dance, nor the twelve still-lifes also in the Copenhagen collection, so the lack of a signature on the Greenlander painting is persuasive, but not conclusive.

A perhaps more likely artist is Salomon Haven (d.1670), originally from Stralsund, but settled in Bergen from about 1625. His reputation, chiefly as a portraitist, was such that Christian IV when visiting Bergen in 1641 urged him to come to Copenhagen, but Haven refused, apparently on grounds of age, and he remained in Bergen until at least 1657 (Schnitler 1923:160). Thus, Haven was resident in Bergen when the Greenlanders arrived, he was a portrait artist, and he was known to the King. Birket-Smith (1924:6), in a passing remark and without any explanation, suggested Haven as artist, but also mooted his son Lambert. The latter can be excluded, however, since in 1653 or a year before the Greenlanders arrived, he and his brother Michael went to study art abroad, mainly in Italy (Schnitler 1923:160). What is significant is that the Haven brothers were sent on their tour by none other than Frederik III, which shows that Salomon Haven was still very much favored at court. Even if there was no time to commission a complete painting while Thiob and his compatriots were in Bergen, Frederik III could well have requested such a painting had he heard that Haven had made sketches. All this would explain the presence of the picture in Frederik III's *Kunstkammer* and would avoid the problem of bringing Eckhout to Bergen or the sketches to Dresden and the painting then back to Copenhagen. As noted by Schnitler (1925), Haven does not seem to have left any signed paintings, but a series of panels commemorating Catherina Janiche (d.1628) in the Mariakirken, Bergen, are attributed to him; in the panel depicting the raising of Lazarus, one of the figures is believed to be a self-portrait. Examination of these panels may help to confirm the otherwise purely circumstantial evidence that Haven painted the Greenlanders.

The patron

No hint has ever been found to suggest who might have commissioned the Greenlander painting. Two patrons seem possible, the King (with a strong interest in *exotica*) or the merchants (with a view to its use for promotional purposes).

It is perhaps significant that the same year and almost at the same time that the Greenlanders arrived in Bergen, Frederik III received from his cousin Johan Maurits of Nassau-Siegen (1604-79) none other than the Eckhout paintings now in the Nationalmuseet. The 1673/4 and later inventories of the *Kunstkammer* specify the gift as eight full-length portraits of Amerindians and Negroes, the Amerindian dance, two portraits of Johan Maurits (lost in the Christianborg castle fire of 1794) and three portraits of Africans (perhaps by Jasper Becx and not by Eckhout). The choice of paintings (rather than artifacts) for this gift was probably made by Johan Maurits, but the paintings in any age are extremely impressive and could very easily have inspired Frederik III to collect or commission others that showed exotic people. The fact that the Greenlander painting was already in the *Kunstkammer* by at least 1673, together with artifacts that must surely have come from the same voyage, seems to reinforce Frederik III's involvement with the picture.

For the merchants, one can only point to the painting of Poq and Qiperoq, made in 1724 when they were fêted in Copenhagen, and argue that much the same motives operated in 1654, that is to say a need to produce some tangible focus for whatever financial or other negotiations required it (much like a scale model in the boardroom of a steamship company). Alternatively, the intention may have been to present the painting to the King.

Whether painted for the merchants or for the King, it is perhaps worth noting that the family Lindenov may in some way have been connected with the painting. In 1654 the initiative for negotiating the gift of paintings from Johan Maurits to Frederik III appears to have been taken by Admiral Christoffer Lindenov, who had apparently reassured Johan Maurits that such a gift would be acceptable to the King (letter Johan Maurits to Frederik III, 13 July 1654; cited in Bobé 1900:381 and Thomsen 1938:11). Lindenov had served as a captain under Johan Maurits in Brazil (Algemeen Rijksarchief, The Hague, O.W.I.C., *Dagelijkse Notulen*, 68: 8 March 1642) and moreover knew Albert Eckhout so well that he borrowed from him in 1645 the large sum of 3,000 guilders on behalf of the Danish East Indies Company (van Gelder 1960:16). If Lindenov was already negotiating the acquisition of paintings for Frederik III in 1654, did he also negotiate the Greenlander painting? Is it merely coincidence that the man who accompanied James Hall on the 1605 and 1606 Danish Greenland expeditions was none other than Lindenov's father, Admiral Godske Lindenov? The connection deserves to be probed.

154

Conclusions

The 1654 painting of Greenlanders in the Nationalmuseet is the 22nd recorded picture of Eskimos made from life (or the 26th if its four prior sketches are counted). More important, it ranks as the 4th earliest extant original picture. As an ethnohistorical source, therefore, it is of prime importance. It is probably a reliable (but not always fully explicit) source for the following:

a. Jackets and hoods (male versus female styles; 17th century versus later styles; Greenland versus other styles)
b. Trousers (rather little detail, however)
c. Skirts (Gunelle's the best depicted)
d. Boots (rather more explicit in the engravings, however)
e. Harpoon, bow and arrow (especially impressive is the detail showing attachment of the bladder and also the herring-bone backing to the bow)
f. Body ornaments (bracelet on Thiob, necklace on Gunelle)
g. Body decoration (tattooing on Cabelou's chin and forehead, also perhaps on Gunells's chin; Cabelou's hair style versus Sigjo's or Gunelle's)
h. Physiognomy (whether constructed from sketches or painted absolutely from life, there is a strong feeling of "personality" in the four faces, which suggests that they are not merely stylized exotics, but real people).

The value of an iconographic source, such as this painting, depends greatly on our confidence in the artist. When the artist is unknown, then the circumstances of the painting must be evaluated instead. In this case, there is no doubt that the subjects were actual people, that they were named, that they travelled in northern Europe, and that sketches of them were made on the spot by someone sufficiently competent as to merit modern comparison with such a master as Eckhout. It would seem, therefore, that this painting can be trusted and should be placed, together with the John White drawings and the Albert Eckhout paintings, in the very highest ethnohistorical category by those exploring the original people of the New World.

Acknowledgements

The Greenlander painting is reproduced here by kind permission of the Nationalmuseet, Copenhagen, and I record also my sincere thanks to Mag. sc. Berete Due and Dr. J. Meldgaard of the Etnografisk Samling for their generous help and suggestions; Mr. Puccio Speroni discussed technical aspects of the painting and argued the case for Albert Eckhout as the artist. I am also indebted to Mr. Jonathan King of the Museum of Mankind, London, for commenting on this paper and drawing my attention to literature that I might otherwise have missed. Finally, Prof. Hans-Hubert Schönzeler helped to decipher the inscription on the painting and arrived at what seems the most plausible interpretation.

155

REFERENCES CITED

Anonymous
1930 Árni Magnússons levned og skrifter, 2. Kommissionen for det Arnamagnænske Legat. Copenhagen: Gyldenalske Boghandel.

Best, G.
1578 A true discourse of the late voyages of discouerie, for finding of a passage to Cathaya, by the Northwest, vnder the conduct of Martin Frobisher Generall: divided into three bookes... London: Henry Bynnyman.

Birket-Smith, K.
1916 The Greenland bow. Meddelelser om Grønland 56:1-28.
1924 Ethnography of the Egedesminde District with aspects of the general culture of West Greenland. Meddelelser om Grønland 66:1-484.

Bobé, L.
1900 Museografiske meddelelsen II. Danske Magasin (5) 6:379- 381.
1916 Christian Lunds relation til Kong Frederik III om David Danels tre rejser til Grønland 1652-54. Danske Magasin (6) 2:202-232.
1927 Grønlændere i Danmark. Det Grønlandske Selskabs Aarsskrift 1926-27:5-28. Copenhagen.

Börsch-Supan, E.
1973 Die Chinamode in der Malerei des 17. und 18. Jahrhunderts. In: China und Europa [exhibition catalogue, Schloss Charlottenburg, Berlin], 61-75.

Dam-Mikkelsen, B., and T. Lundbæk
1980 Etnografiske genstande i det Kongelige Danske Kunstkammer 1650-1800. Nationalmuseets Skrifter, Etnografisk række 17. Copenhagen: Nationalmuseet.

Döry, L.
1974 Exoten. In: Reallexikon Deutscher Kunstgeschichte 6: 1491- 1511.
1975 Zur Entstehung der Chinoiserie. In: Festschrift für Peter Wilhelm Meister zum 65. Geburtstag (Hamburg: A. Ohm), 201-208.

Due, B.
1980 America. In: Dam-Mikkelsen and Lundbæk 1980:17-39.

Eckhart, G.
1978 Schicksale deutscher Baudenkmale im 2. Weltkrieg. Eine Dokumentation der Schäden und Totalverluste auf dem Gebiet der Deutschen Demokratischen Republik, 1. Munich: C.H. Beck.

Gad, F.
1970 The history of Greenland, 1. Earliest times to 1700. [English translation by E. Dupont]. London: C. Hurst (1st. ed. 1967).

Gosch, C.C.A.
1897a   Danish Arctic expeditions, 1605 to 1620. Book 1. - The Danish
         expeditions to Greenland in 1605, 1606, and 1607; to which is added
         Captain James Hall's voyage to Greenland in 1612. London: Hakluyt
         Society.
1897b   Danish Arctic expeditions, 1605 to 1620. Book 2. - The expedition of
         Captain Jens Munk to Hudson's Bay in search of a North-West
         Passage in 1619-20. London: Hakluyt Society.

Hansen, T.
1970   North west to Hudson Bay. The life and times of Jens Munk.
         [English translation by J. McFarlane and J. Lynch]. London: Collins
         (1st ed. 1965).

Israel, H.
1965   Alte eskimoische Werkzeuge mit eisernen Klingen. Abhandlungen und
         Berichte des Staatlichen Museums für Völkerkunde Dresden 24:5-30.
         Berlin.

Joppien, R.
1979   The Dutch vision of Brazil. Johan Maurits and his artists. In: E.
         van den Boogaart, H. Hoetink and P.J.P. Whitehead, Johan Maurits
         van Nassau-Siegen, 1604-1679. A humanist prince in Europe and
         Brazil. Essays on the occasion of the tercentenary of his death
         (The Hague: Johan Maurits van Nassau Stichting), 297-376.

Luttervelt, R. van
1942   West-Indië en het Verre Oosten in den Euopeesche visie der 17de
         eeuw. Historia... Schrift Geschiedenis en Kunstgeschiedenis 8:65-73.

Marcgrave, G.
1648   Historiae rerum naturalium Brasiliae, [8 books]. In: G. Piso and G.
         Marcgrave, Historia naturalis Brasiliae, auspicio et beneficio
         illustriss. I. Mavritii Com. Nassav illius provinciae et maris summi
         praefecti adornata. In qua non tantum plantae at animalia, sed et
         indigenarum morbi, ingenia et mores describuntur et iconibus supra
         quingentas illustrantur. Leiden: F.H. Haak, L. Elzevier.

Meldgaard, J.
1980   Greenland. In: Dam-Mikkelsen and Lundbæk 1980:1-16.

Munk, J.
1624   Navigatio, septentrionalis. Det er: Relation eller bescriffuelse, om
         seiglads oc reyse, paa denne nordvestiske passagie, som nu kaldis
         Nova Dania: igjennem Fretum Christian at opsöge, huilcken reyse,
         voris allernaadigste herre, Konning Christian den Fierde, vdi det
         aar 1619... Copenhagen: Henrich Waldkirch. (2nd ed. in 1723, with
         biography of Munk, pp.1-24.)

Olearius, A.
1656   Vermehrte newe Beschreibung der Muscowitischen und Persischen

157

Reyse so durch gelegenheit einer Holsteinischen Gesandschafft an den Russischen Zaar und König in Persien geschehen. Schleswig: Fürstl. Druckerei (facsimile ed. 1971, Tübingen: Max Niemeyer Verlag).

1666   Gottorfische Kunst-Kammer, Worinnen Allerhand ungemeine Sachen, So theils die Natur, theils künstliche Hände hervor gebracht und bereitet. Vor diesem aus allen vier Theilen der Welt zusammen getragen. Schleswig: Johann Holmein.

Purchas, S.

1625   Hakluytus posthumus or Purchas his pilgrimes. Contayning a history of the world, in sea voyages and lande-travells, by Englishmen and others... In fower parts, each contayning five books. 4th ed. vols. London: Henry Fetherstone.

Rye, W.B.

1865   England as seen by foreigners in the days of Elizabeth and James the First. Comprising translations of the journals of the Dukes of Wirtemburg in 1592 and 1610; both illustrative of Shakespeare. With extracts of the travels of foreign princes and others, copious notes, and an introduction, and etchings. London: John Russell Smith.

Schnitler, C.W.

1923   Haven, Salomon. In: U. Thieme und F. Becker (eds.), Allgemeines Lexikon der Bildenden Künstler (Leipzig), 160.

1925   Skulptur og malerkunst i 16. og 17. aarhundre. Norsk kunsthistorie, 1:364-365. Oslo.

[Settle, D.]

1578   La navigation du capitaine Martin Forbisher anglois, és region de west & nordwest, en l'année M.D. LXXVII. La Rochelle: Anthoine Chuppin.

1580a   De Martini Forbisseri Angli Navigatione in regiones occidentis et septentrionis Narratio historica, Ex Gallico sermone in Latinum translata per D. Joan. Tho. Freigivm. Nuremberg: Catharina Gerlach.

1580b   Beschreibung Der schiffart des Haubtmans Martini Forbissher auss Engelland, in die Lender gegen West und Nordtwest, im Jar 1577. Nuremberg: Katharina Gerlachin.

Sturtevant, W.C., and D.B. Quinn

1987   This New Prey: Eskimos in Europe in 1567, 1576, and 1577. In: C.F. Feest (ed.), Indians and Europe (Aachen: Rader Verlag), 61-140.

Thomsen, T.

1938   Albert Eckhout, ein niederländischer Meister und sein Gönner Johan Maurits der Brasilianer. Ein Kulturbild aus dem 17. Jahrhundert. Copenhagen: Ejnar Munksgaard.

158

van Gelder, H.E.
  1960   Twee Braziliaanse schildpadden doer Albert Eckhout. Oud Holland
          75:5-30.
Whitehead, P.J.P.
  1985   Pictorial record of a 17th century Tupinamba bow and arrows.
          Zeitschrift für Ethnologie 110(1): 111-125.
Whitehead, P.J.P., and M. Boeseman
  1987   A portrait of Dutch 17th century Brazil. Animals, plants and people
          by the artists of Johan Maurits of Nassau. Amsterdam: Koninklijke
          Nederlandse Akademie van Wetenschappen and North Holland
          Publishing Company.

ESKIMOS IN SCOTLAND: c.1682-1924

Dale Idiens

The aim of this paper is to draw together the available information concerning Eskimos who arrived in Scotland between about 1682 and 1924, and to test the evidence for believing that certain kayaks in Scottish collections relate to particular Eskimos and therefore to particular dates.

The earliest references to Eskimos in a Scottish context appear in the late 17th century and concern Orkney, a group of islands off the north coast of Scotland. The Rev. James Wallace, minister of Kirkwall on Orkney, writing in about 1688, said:

"Sometimes about this country are seen these men they call *Finnmen*. In the year 1682, one was seen in his little Boat, at the South end of the Isle of *Eda*, most of the people of the Isle flocked to see him, and when they adventur'd to put out a Boat with Men to see if they could apprehend him, he presently fled away most swiftly. And in the year 1684, another was seen from *Westra*, and for a while after they got few or no Fishes for they have this Remark here, that these *Finnmen* drive away the fishes from the place to which they come. These *Finnmen* seem to be some of those people that dwell about the *Fretum Davis* a full account of whom may be seen in the natural and moral History of the *Antilles* Chap. 18. One of their boats sent from *Orkney* to *Edinburgh* is to be seen in the Physitians hall, with the Oar and Art he makes use of for killing Fish" (Wallace 1693:28).

This account was not published in the author's lifetime but issued in 1693, five years after his death, by his son Dr. James Wallace who dedicated the work to Sir Robert Sibbald. The first edition was very popular, and in 1700 Dr. Wallace published it again in London, this time with some alterations. To the above paragraph by his father Dr. Wallace added the following note:

"I must acknowledge it seems a little unaccountable how these Finn-men should come on this coast, but they most probably be driven by Storms from home, and cannot tell when they are any way at Sea, how to make their way home again; they have this advantage, that be the Seas never so boisterous their Boat being made of Fish Skins are so contrived that it can never sink, but is like a Sea-gull, swimming on the top of the Water. His shirt he has so fastened to the Boat, that no Water can come into his Boat to do him damage, except when he pleases to untye it, which he never does but to ease nature or when he comes ashore."

Dr. Wallace also remarked that: "There is another of their Boats in the Church of *Burra* in *Orkney*" (Wallace 1700:60-61).

A similar description, published a year later in 1701 by the Rev. John Brand, adds some further information:

"There are frequently *Finnmen* seen here upon the Coasts, as one about a year ago on *Stronsa* and another within these few months on *Westra*, a Gentleman with many others in the Isle looking on him nigh to the shore, but when any endeavour to apprehend them they flee away most swiftly; which is very strange, that one Man sitting in his little Boat, should come some hundred of leagues, from their own Coasts, as they reckon *Finland* to be from *Orkney*; it may be thought wonderful how they live all that time, and are able to keep the sea so long. His boat is made of Seal skins, or some kind of leather, he also hath a coat of Leather upon him, and he fitteth in the middle of his Boat, with a little Oar in his hand and Fishing with his lines: And when in a storm he seeth the high surge of a wave approaching, he hath a way of sinking his Boat, till the wave pass over, least thereby he should be overturned. The Fishers here observe that these *Finland* or *Finland-Men*, by their coming drive away the Fishes from the Coasts. One of their Boats is kept as a Rarity in the *Physians Hall at Edinburgh*" (Brand 1701:50- 51).

Orkney and Shetland folklore is rich in traditional stories of both Finnmen and Selkie-folk, or seal people, and for some time the strange visitors to Orkney waters were interpreted in terms of that tradition. However, the descriptions of their clothing and boats leaves no doubt that the visitors were Eskimos, and although Wallace, who recorded them first, calls them Finnmen, both he and his son believed them to be Eskimos from the Davis Straits, and refer directly to a French source (Poincy 1658), which describes Eskimo dress, kayaks and equipment from the Davis Straits area, and is based upon an account by Captain Nicolas Tunes who took a ship from Flushing to the Davis Straits in 1656.

Despite this, speculations that the Orkney visitors might have come from Finland, Lapland, or some other part of Europe, continued to recur in later discussions. Since they had evidently appeared of their own volition, by means of small and fragile craft, it was easier to credit the relatively short journey from northwest Europe to Orkney, rather than the greater distance from Greenland or the Davis Straits.

"What can these Finnmen have been? Is it possible Eskimos can have been driven over from Greenland? Or can there have been a substantial basis of actual fact for the traditional Shetland Finns that 'came ow'r fra Norraway'? The Burray and Stronsay instances all point to the *kayaks*, or whatever they were, being driven from the east, and the ones seen off Eday and Westray may, with equal probability, have come from that quarter. Besides, Cape Farewell, the nearest point of Greenland to the Orkneys, is 1,180 nautical miles from the Noup Head of Westray, whilst the Norwegian Coast, at the southern end of Finmarken, is 750, and at the nearest point only 240 miles" (Tudor 1883:341-342).

However, it was generally agreed that skin-covered boats of the type described by Wallace and Brand did not occur in Europe, and "it is at once obvious to anyone acquainted with the Eskimo kayak that the skiffs described by Brand and Wallace were nothing else than kayaks" (MacRitchie 1890:358).

Another factor which has served to keep alive the argument for a European source is uncertainty over how long a kayak can stay afloat before the skin cover becomes waterlogged and useless. Opinions on this point differ greatly: forty-eight hours is the period which has frequently been referred to (Whitaker 1954:99), although some commentators with first-hand knowledge of Eskimo technical practices aver that a well-greased kayak might, under ideal conditions, function for up to two weeks in the sea (Aberdeen Press and Journal 1976). Nonetheless, a voyage of over 1,000 miles by kayak, whether deliberately or accidentally undertaken, does not seem to be the most promising explanation for the appearance of the Orkney visitors, although it cannot be entirely ruled out.

A more likely explanation may be connected with kidnapped Eskimos who escaped or were put off homeward-bound European vessels in the North Sea. From the earliest days of European discovery in the Arctic it was common practice for Eskimos to be abducted for examination as "scientific curiosities." Frobisher's two expeditions of 1576 and 1577 returned to England with captive Eskimos (cp. Sturtevant and Quinn, this volume), as did the ships of John David in 1586. In 1605 a Danish expedition took a number of Eskimos, five of whom were exhibited in Denmark. Several prisoners tried to escape and were recaptured, and others jumped overboard, but their curiosity value was such that altogether about thirty Eskimos were kidnapped by Danish, Norwegian and Dutch ships in the first half of the seventeenth century. European intentions, officially at least, were benign, for the charter granted in 1636 to the Greenland Company of Denmark by Christian IV required "that they annually provide us with a pair of young persons, born in this country, about 16,18 or 20, whom one could here teach the fear of God, language and literary skills to the salvation and welfare of the said land for all time" (Mikkelsen 1954:58).

The Dutch government became so concerned at the high level of abductions that in 1720 a Decree was passed by the *Staten Generaal* prohibiting the murder or kidnapping of Eskimos by Dutch whalers, and more than one scholar has argued that this may well have frightened transgressors, when nearing their home port, into putting their prisoner over the side in order to avoid prosecution by the authorities (Nooter 1971:10). A well-meaning crew, conniving in such an escape, could have ensured that an Eskimos took his kayak with him, thus having a chance of survival.

This argument may go some way towards explaining not only the Orkney visitors, but also the curious case of the Eskimo who is said to have paddled his kayak into the mouth of the River Don near Aberdeen in about 1700.

The Rev. Francis Gastrell, making a tour of the east of Scotland in 1760 remarked in his diary for 12 October 1760,[1] that in King's College Chapel in Aberdeen he saw

> "a canoe about seven yards long by two feet wide, which about thirty-two years since was driven into the Don with a man in it who was all over hairy, and spoke a language which no person there could interpret. He lived but three days, although all possible care was taken to recover him."

Some twenty years later Francis Douglas saw among the natural and artificial curiosities in the Marischal College in Aberdeen a kayak which is believed to be the same one described in 1760 by Gastrell.

> "A CANOE, taken at sea, with an Indian man in it, about the beginning of this century. He was brought alive to Aberdeen, but died soon after his arrival, and could give no account of himself. He is supposed to have come from the Labrador Coast, and to have lost his way at sea. The canoe is covered with fish skins, curiously stretched upon slight timbers, very securely joined together. The upper part of it is about twenty inches broad at the centre, and runs off gradually to a point at both ends. Where broadest, there is a circular hole, just large enough for the man to fit in, round which there is a kind of girth, about a foot high, to which he fixed himself, probably, when he did not use his oar, or paddle; which when he chose it, he stuck into some lists of skin, tied around the canoe, but slack enough, to let in the padle, and some other awkward utensils which were found stuck there. THE canoe is about eighteen feet long, and slopes on both sides, but the bottom is flat for three or four inches in the middle, and gradually sharpens as it approaches the extremities till it ends in a point" (Douglas 1782:114-115).

The information given by Douglas about the Eskimo differs from Gastrell's as he says the canoe was taken at sea, otherwise his account is in accordance with Gastrell although he goes into greater detail in his description of the canoe. Unfortunately the 18th century records of the University of Aberdeen give no further information about the acquisition of the kayak, but in the 19th century catalogue of antiquities there is a reference to an "Esquimaux Canoe, in which a native of that country was driven ashore near Belhelvie about the

164

beginning of the eighteenth century and died soon after landing"[2] (Belhelvie is a coastal village just north of the mouth of the River Don). This catalogue also lists another kayak "new, with darts, paddles etc presented by Captain William Gibbon, Aberdeen, in 1800." These two kayaks are very probably the same two now in the University of Aberdeen Anthropological Museum, Marischal College.

Aberdeen also provides one of the best documented, and possibly the happiest case of an Eskimo visitor to Scotland in Eenoolooapik (Fig. 1), an Eskimo about 18 years old, who came to Aberdeen in 1839 with Captain Penny of the *Neptune*. By the early 19th century European whalers were beginning to find their known fishing grounds less abundant. The Dutch had virtually ceased whaling by 1800 for that reason, although Scottish ships continued whaling until well into the 20th century. Penny acquired the services of Eenoolooapik to obtain expert advice on the expected seasonal movements of the whales, and also to assist in mapping areas only partially known to the Europeans. It appears Eenoo agreed willingly to make the journey to Aberdeen and he co-operated fully with Penny and his crew.

EENOOLOOAPIK.

Fig. 1. Eenoolooapik, in Aberdeen 1839-40. (Engraving by James Henderson. Frontispiece to A. McDonald, *A Narrative of some passages in the History of Eenoolooapik*, Edinburgh, 1841).

165

Interestingly, the Treasury made a grant of £20 to Eenoo while he was in Aberdeen for the purchase of "whatever might be necessary to establish him in his native country in more comfortable circumstances" (McDonald 1841:39), but refused any financial assistance to Captain Penny in his proposal to investigate the accuracy of Eenoo's map and the existence of a fresh whale fishery. In the event, Eenoo's map turned out to be completely accurate, but the *Bon Accord*, Penny's new ship, was late in arriving at the new fishing ground, and the promised whales had left. Despite this lack of success for the whalers, Eenoo was put off the ship to join his relatives "admidst the cheers of the crew, with all of whom he was a great favourite" (McDonald 1841:105), taking with him a small skiff to carry the immense quantity of European articles he had acquired.

This instance of contact between Eskimo and Scot appears to have been of benefit to both sides. Although Eenoo suffered a severe illness in Aberdeen he fortunately recovered, and was returned safely to his own people, as promised.

Another well-known example of an Eskimo who enjoyed a co-operative relationship with Scots is John Sakeouse (Fig. 2), official interpreter on Captain John Ross's expedition to the Arctic in 1818. Sakeouse, from Jacob Sound in the Davis Straits, arrived in Leith, the port of Edinburgh, in 1816 on the *Thomas & Ann*, a Greenland whaler commanded by Captain Newton. Some accounts say that he stowed away, and that he wanted to become a missionary and to study the art of drawing. Sakeouse was made much of in Leith, and gave kayak demonstrations in Leith Harbour which were reported at length in the Edinburgh press:

"We do not recollect ever to have seen so vast an assemblage of persons of all ranks at Leith to witness any public exhibition, as were collected there on Thursday, to see the contest between the Esquimaux youth and the six-oared whale-boat. Not a part of the pier, the windows and roofs of houses, but were crowded; the latter at the imminent risk of many lives. The exhibition commenced at a little before two o'clock, and lasted till half past three. His dexterity in managing his canoe was admirable, and he evidently showed his ability to overcome his opponents in point of speed, by the advantages he often gave them, and which he as often redeemed. He was very expert in diving, which he did several times, and also in throwing his darts. When at a considerable distance from the beacon, he threw one of his darts, and stuck the bulb of the beacon with the greatest certainty. He was so fastened into his seat, that he could not fall out, as a drawing, like the mouth of a purse, girds him about the loins, so that, in an instant, he was seen to dive under the water, head down and keel uppermost; again in the twinkling of an eye, he raised himself erect out of the water, and scudded along as if nothing had happened. A raft of wood impeded his progress down the harbour after starting, when, to the astonishment of the spectators he crossed the raft with his canoe, and again launched into the water. His canoe is a very great curiosity, weighing in all

Fig. 2. John Sakeouse, in Edinburgh 1816-19. (Contemporary engraving after Amelia Anderson. Below the portrait is Sakeouse in his kayak followed by a description of his kayak demonstration in Leith Harbour. Scottish National Portrait Gallery).

Fig. 3. John Sakeouse, in Edinburgh 1816-19.(Oil painting by Alexander Nasmyth. Scottish National Portrait Gallery).

Fig. 4. First communication with the Natives of Prince Regents Bay, as Drawn by John Sakeouse and presented to Capt Ross August 10 1818. (J.Ross, *Narrative of a Voyage of Discovery* ..., London, 1819, facing page 88.Original watercolor in the British Museum).

167

Fig. 5. Ock-o-kok, in Dundee ca. 1873-74 (Dundee Central Library).

16lbs. He rows it by one oar or paddle, and he is so very dexterous in managing it, that he out-sails any boat with six oars. The harbour was crowded with boats, filled with elegantly dressed females. Previous to the exhibition the public had an opportunity of inspecting the canoe and the following curiosities, at a ware-room at the West Dock, viz. - Two sea unicorn's horns, the skulls of a sea horse and a bear, the ear of a whale, and the preserved skin of a black eagle. The Esquimaux was dressed in the fashion of his country, from the waist downwards, in undressed sealskin, his jacket of the same, only the undressed side inwards. He is a good looking healthy young man, and apparently very docile. He understands a little English and when he overcomes the method of talking common to his country (a species of whispe-ring), there is little doubt that he may soon become proficient in our language. We were astonished to hear expressions made use of to him on Thursday, by some of the crew of the ship which brought him here, exactly the same as we have heard in conversations between natives of the interior of Africa. Happily

168

Fig. 6. Uno-Atwango, in Dundee ca. 1873-74 (Dundee Central Library).

Fig. 7. Shoodlue, in Dundee 1895-6 (Dundee Central Library).

the whole passed off without any serious accident, though several people fell into the harbour, but were got out safely, completely ducked" (Edinburgh Evening Courant 1816). In 1817 Sakeouse went back to the Davis Straits with Captain Newton to discover that his only surviving relative, a sister, had died during his absence, and so he chose to return to Leith with the whaling fleet at the end of the season. Early in 1818 he met Alexander Nasmyth, the Scottish landscape painter, who gave Sakeouse drawing lessons and also painted his portrait (Fig. 3).

Through the good offices of Nasmyth's friends Sir James Hall, President of the Royal Society of Edinburgh, and Captain Basil Hall, Sakeouse was brought to the attention of the Admiralty, and engaged on Captain John Ross's arctic expedition of 1818 as an interpreter. Ross's narrative of the voyage is peppered with references to Sakeouse who clearly was a most valuable member of the expedition and even provided an illustration of his own for the published account (Fig. 4). When the expedition returned Sakeouse was sent back to Edinburgh for further instructions, and would doubtless have usefully accompanied subsequent expeditions to the Arctic, but he unfortunately caught typhoid and died in Leith on 14 February 1819. According to the very long obituary in *Blackwood's Magazine* (1819) which Sakeouse merited, he died a Christian, but the whereabouts of his grave is not known, although it is likely to be in Leith.

Eskimos continued to visit Scotland on whaling vessels throughout the nineteenth century and even later. In Dundee there are records of seven or eight separate visits by Greenland Eskimos between 1873 and 1924 (People's

Journal 1925). They were Ock-o-kok (Fig. 5), and Uno-Atwango (Fig. 6) brought by Captain Adams in about 1873; an Eskimo (name not known) brought by Captain Allen of the *Ravenscraig* in 1875; Olnik brought in 1885 or 1886; Shoodlue (Fig. 7) brought by Captain Milne in 1895; Billy the Yak, brought by Captain Murray of the *Active*, in 1905; Kinnewatchee-me-Uttuk, also brought by Captain Murray in 1907; and Nowyabek, brought by Captain John Pearson in 1924.

It is unlikely that any of these Eskimos were coerced into leaving their homes and their motive for visiting Scotland seems to have been sheer curiosity, although Kinnewatchee-me-Uttuk came to learn the art of cutting mica. They each stayed for a short time - the period of one winter season - until the whaling ship that brought them returned to Greenland (Ock-o-kok was to have returned, but unfortunately died). Most of them lived in local boarding houses and were exhibited in Dundee music halls to raise money to pay for their keep. The best known and most popular of them all was Shoodlue, who was a priest or medicine man from Black Lead Island, Cumberland Sound. He and Captain Milne had known each other for many years and Shoodlue asked if he could visit Scotland for a season. Because of his long contact with whalers he understood English fairly well and could speak a little. He lived in the Sailor's Home while in Dundee, "and Mr Ritchie made some money by exhibiting him all over the country. He gave an exhibition on his canoe at the tidal basin of Dundee Harbour and also gave an entertainment with his melodeon at a social meeting in the Hillbank Hall. Baillie Forwell and Rev. John Macpherson were present at that memorable entertainment, the latter gentleman - I remember well - scowling the whole time, as he could not stand instrumental music. It was Captain Milne who brought Shoodlue from his home on Cumberland Gulf " (People's Journal 1925). Shoodlue was still well-remembered in Dundee some thirty years later as the champion marmalade-eater of all time (Dundee used to be famous for the making of marmalade jam).

The written evidence for Eskimos in Scotland spans some 240 years, but the material evidence is harder to identify and assess. The question is, can any of the surviving kayaks in Scotland be associated with known Eskimos? It appears that many Eskimos arrived in Scotland with their own dress, kayaks and hunting equipment. The kayaks especially excited much interest among Scots, themselves a sea-going people, so one would expect some of the early examples to be retained in Scottish collections. However, Scots whalers and explorers also brought back kayaks from expeditions to the Arctic and now, with only a very few exceptions, it is no longer possible to distinguish between these two categories. The current state of information regarding kayaks in Scotland is as follows.

In 1933 W. C. Souter listed eighteen kayaks in Scotland (out of a total of thirty-three in Great Britain). There were three in Dundee (one a frame only); six in Edinburgh (four in the Royal Scottish Museum, one in the Royal College of Surgeons, and one in Dreghorn School, Colinton); three in the Hunterian Museum, Glasgow; three in Aberdeen (one in the Marischal College, one in the Medico-Chirurgical Society, one brought back in 1932 by Captain Watson of the *Lord Talbot*); and one each in the museums of Inverness, Montrose and Peterhead (Souter 1934:13). Today there are sixteen kayaks in Scotland. Losses in the past fifty years have been the "Lord Talbot" kayak which was disposed of in 1939 from the church in which it was stored, the Inverness kayak which was written off about twenty years ago, the kayak listed for Dreghorn School, Colinton (Souter gave no data for this kayak, and the Dreghorn School no longer exists), and two kayaks (one a frame only) from Dundee. The museum in Dundee still has two kayaks but one was transferred from Montrose in 1958. Additional kayaks are one in Marischal College, Aberdeen, (presented by Captain Gibbon in 1800 but not known to Souter), a Greenland example (1984.277) in the National Museums of Scotland (transferred from the University of St. Andrews and unknown to Souter), and a kayak with paddle and hunting equipment (A.804 a-m) recently added to the collections of the City Art Gallery and Museum, Glasgow, which was made in 1959 by Eskimos at Igdlorssuit, West Greenland, for a Scottish student in anthropology, Kenneth Taylor.

All sixteen kayaks can be attributed, on the basis of either surviving documentation or formal characteristics, to the region of Greenland and the Davis Straits. Dating them is more difficult, and much effort has been devoted to the task of trying to link particular kayaks to particular Eskimos, especially in the case of the early visitors to Scotland. Unfortunately, there is no real proof in a single instance to justify such a relationship. The most acceptable case for an early kayak is the example (576) believed to be from East Greenland in the Anthropological Museum of the University of Aberdeen. The weight of evidence linking this kayak to the Eskimo who arrived either in the mouth of the River Don or on the coast nearby in about 1700, although circumstantial, is strong. Souter suggested that the kayak belonging to the Medico-Chirurgical Society in Aberdeen (and now hanging in their modern rooms in the Medical School at Foresterhill, Aberdeen), might have been the one Eenoolooapik had with him in Aberdeen in 1839 (Souter 1934:19). However Eenoo took his kayak with him when he returned to the Arctic on the *Bon Accord* in 1840 (McDonald 1841:78) and it seems unlikely that he would have arrived in Scotland with two kayaks.

The kayak that Dr. James Wallace said was in the church at Burray in Orkney about 1700, disappeared long ago, and certainly by 1883 (Tudor 1883:341). The search for the Orkney kayak which was sent to Edinburgh in the late 17th century for exhibition in the College of Physicians is also a lost cause, although it has occupied many. According to Wallace the kayak was sent to Edinburgh "with the Oar and the Dart he makes use of for killing fish" in about 1688. It seems that the kayak was obtained for the College of Physicians through the good offices of Sir Robert Sibbald, to whom Dr. James Wallace

171

dedicated the second edition of his father's book *Description of the Isles of Orkney* in 1700 stating that the materials were collected by his father at Sir Robert Sibbald's request. Sibbald was a noted physician and naturalist, first President of the Royal College of Physicians, and Geographer to Charles II. Both Sibbald and his friend and fellow-physician Sir Andrew Balfour were keen collectors of natural and scientific curiosities. When Balfour died in 1694 his collection was sold for £400 to the Town Council of Edinburgh for exhibition in the College of Edinburgh (later to become the University of Edinburgh) as the *Museum Balfoureanum*. The catalogue of this collection as listed in the Minutes of the Town Council for 10 May 1695 includes, beneath a heading "Without the Presses," the entry "A Fin-Man's Boat from Orkney. Vid. Nat:et Mor Hist:des Antilles." Two years later Sibbald presented his own collection to the College, and the *Museum Sibbaldiano* joined the *Museum Balfoureanum*, although clearly there had been some interchange between the collections of the two colleagues before.

For some reason the Fin-Man's Boat was not transferred immediately to the College of Edinburgh despite being catalogued in 1695, for the Minute Book of the College of Physicians for 24 September 1696 reads "The qlk day ye colledge considering yt dr Balfours curiosities are all in ye Colledge of Edr. and amongst them ye boat belonging to ye College of Physicians and yt the same boat is likely to be lost they having no convenient place to keep it doe give the sd boat to ye Colledge of Edr. ther to be preserved and yt be insert there yt its gifted by ye royall Colledge." Unfortunately, as MacRitchie (1890:361) notes, no trace of any acknowledgement of this transfer can be found in the records of the Town Council, which managed the University at this period, or in the records of the University itself, and although there are several published references in the eighteenth century to the importance of the museum collections of the University, no specific mention is made of the kayak. For example, Daniel Defoe, writing anonymously:

"a curious and noble Museum ... It contains a vast treasure of curiosities of Art and Nature, domestic and foreign from almost all parts of the world ... that are not to be found either in those of the Royal Society at London or the Ashmolean at Oxford" (Gentleman 1748:79).

But despite its importance the museum suffered considerable neglect during this period and much of the great collections of Balfour and Sibbald were lost (Pennant 1790:247). The Town Council apparently suspected some Keepers of the museum collections of having sold off specimens for their own profit, and on electing Dr. John Walker, Professor of Natural History, as Keeper in 1779, the Council required him "within three months after the date of his Commission make up and deliver in to the Clerks hands a full list or Inventory of all the curiosities or rarities belonging to the said University."[3] This inventory,

172

delivered to the Town Council on 22 March 1780,[4] is the first known catalogue of the Museum since those of Balfour and Sibbald almost a century earlier, and although a number of ethnological items are listed there is no mention of the Fin-Man's Boat, which must have been lost or destroyed either before transfer to the University (as the College of Physicians feared it might be), or subsequently, and certainly prior to 1780. The Greenland kayak in the collection of the Royal College of Surgeons in Edinburgh, sister-institution to the College of Physicians, has been put forward as an alternative candidate for the Fin-Man's Boat. But there is no documentary evidence to support such a theory, and the kayak itself appears to be a 19th century example.

When the University Museum collection was finally transferred to the Museum of Science and Art (now the National Museum of Scotland) in 1865 there were three kayaks in the collection. Only two of these kayaks, U.C.764 and U.C.765, survive, the third, U.C.763, having been written off soon after transfer. Regrettably, no information from the University accompanied the kayaks to the Museum of Science and Art and nothing is known about them. These kayaks must have come into the University collection after 1780 and may therefore be associated with later Eskimo visitors to Scotland, such as John Sakeouse for example, who is likely to have had his kayak with him in Edinburgh when he died in 1819.

With the exception of the 18th century River Don kayak in Aberdeen, and a kayak in the Hunterian Museum, Glasgow, which was brought back on a whaling ship in 1787,[5] there is no evidence that the majority of kayaks in Scottish collections are not 19th century examples, unless future research on materials and construction can suggest otherwise. As Nooter (1971:72) emphasises in his study of early kayaks in Dutch museums, there is insufficient data available concerning the technical development of kayaks. The limited documentary evidence, which has been extensively overhauled by numerous writers, cannot take us further than the level of assumption.

NOTES

1. Unpublished diary in The Shakespeare Museum, Stratford-upon-Avon, England.
2. Manuscript Catalogue of Antiquities and Principal Curiosities in the Museum and Library of Marischal College compiled by Professor William Knight *ante* 1844. MSM.106. University of Aberdeen Library.
3. Edinburgh Town Council Minutes, 3 November 1779, p.139.
4. Edinburgh Town Council Minutes, 22 March 1780, p.316.
5. Personal communication from Dr. Euan MacKie, Hunterian Museum. It is not clear which kayak of the three in the Hunterian is the earliest.

REFERENCES CITED

Aberdeen Press and Journal
  1976   26 November, reported interview with a Greenlander, Ulrik Lennert
          (Administrator to Qanaq Eskimos near the American Thule Airbase).
Brand, Rev. John
  1701   A Brief Description of Orkney, Zetland, Pightland-Firth and
          Caithness. Edinburgh.
Douglas, Francis
  1782   A General Description of the East Coast of Scotland. Paisley.
Edinburgh Evening Courant
  1816   Saturday, 7 September.
A Gentleman
  1748   A Tour through the Whole Island of Great Britain. Vol. IV. 4th ed.
          London.
McDonald, A.
  1841   A Narrative of some passages in the History of Eenoolooapik.
          Edinburgh.
Macritchie, David
  1890   Notes on a Finnish Boat Preserved in Edinburgh. Proceedings of the
          Society of Antiquaries of Scotland 24. Edinburgh.
Mikkelsen, E.
  1954   Kajakmandan fra Aberdeen. Grønland, Copenhagen.
Nooter, G.
  1971   Old Kayaks in the Netherlands. Mededelingen van het Rijksmuseum
          voor Volkenkunde 17. Leiden.
Pennant, T.
  1790   A Tour in Scotland (Part II), Vol. III. London.
Peoples Journal
  1925   9 May. Dundee.
Poincy, Louis D. P. De
  1658   Histoire naturelle et morale des Iles Antilles de l'Amerique ...
          Rotterdam.
Souter, W.C.
  1934   The Story of Our Kayak and Some Others. Being the Presidential
          Address to the Aberdeen Medico-Chirurgical Society. Aberdeen.
Tudor, J. R.
  1883   The Orkneys and Shetland: Their Past and Present State. London.
Wallace, Rev. James
  1693   Description of the Isles of Orkney. Edinburgh.
  1700   An Account of the Islands of Orkney. London.
Whitaker, Ian
  1954   The Scottish Kayaks and the 'Finn-Men.' Antiquity 28.

MOHAWKS ABROAD:
THE 1764 AMSTERDAM ETCHING OF SYCHNECTA

George R. Hamell

In 1982 an exhibition titled *The Birth of New York: Nieuw Amsterdam 1624-1664* was shown at the New York Historical Society. This temporary exhibition had been jointly researched and organized by the *Gemeentearchief* Amsterdam and by the *Amsterdam Historisch Museum*, to which the exhibition traveled the following year. An English-version catalogue of the same title was published, which like the exhibition focused upon the Dutch experience in *Nieuw Amsterdam*, from its founding in 1624 to the English succession in 1664.

Among the catalogue's essays is one which describes the favorable and even glowing perceptions of *Nieuw Amsterdam*, which found material expression in contemporary Dutch maps, prints, and pamphlets, and in the visual and literary arts generally. *Nieuw Amsterdam* was a "richly blessèd land where milk and honey flowed" (Jacob Steendam in van Gelder 1982:26,39). *Nieuw Amsterdam*, like the New World generally at the time of its discovery and colonization, was a place where Old World mythical realities and historical metaphors had converged (cf. Sahlins 1981; cf. Honour 1975). Nowhere were the Old World's preconceptions of the New World and its inhabitants more apparent, than in the Old World's contemporary visual arts.

The boundless fruits, metaphorical or otherwise, of the Netherlands' far-flung colonies and trading partners were brought to the wharves and warehouses of Amsterdam and other European ports. Among the riches from the *new* world across the Atlantic, were *naturalia* and *artificialia*, the wondrous expressions of nature and the marvellous artifices of exotic people - "curiosities" which found avid reception among royal and scholarly collectors of such things. The cultural efficacy or impact upon Western Europe of exotic stones, plants, animals, artifacts, and even humans, was largely a function of their perceived and ascribed new-worldliness or other-worldliness. This intellectual phenomenon was occuring throughout Western Europe and had been since the late Renaissance. The same phenomenon underlay the initial positive New World Indian response to both the Europeans and *their* artifices (cf. Hamell 1983). After all, culture contact had ideological implications for the philosophically-minded of both the Old and the New Worlds.

In late 17th century Amsterdam, one of the common and truly popular institutions to which East Indies and West Indies exotica gravitated was the *Blauw Jan* Inn. At the *Blauw Jan*, which doubled as a zoo or menagerie, one could not only see a New Netherland's beaver, but exotic people also, such as giants and dwarves (cf. van Gelder 1982:38). It was in response to questions concerning the *Blauw Jan* and its menagerie that Margriet B. de Roever, an associate of the *Gemeentearchief Amsterdam* brought the 1764 Amsterdam etching of Sychnecta to my attention.[1] The etching (Fig. 1) is in the collection of the Prints and Drawings Department, *Gemeentearchief Amsterdam*. In the latter's collection, as well, is an associated notarial document (NA 13604/1237), dated 19 December 1764, which provides information about the circumstances of Sychnecta's exhibition at the *Blauw Jan*. Neither the etching, nor the document, had been included or mentioned in *The Birth of New York* exhibition and catalogue, since they post-dated the period of interest by 100 years.

With the cooperation of Boudewijn Bakker, Chief Curator of the Department of Prints and Drawings, a photograph of the etching and a photocopy of the associated notarial document, *Summons Served Upon the Widow of Anthony Bergmeyer on Behalf of Hyam Meyers*, were obtained. A translation of the latter document was arranged through the courtesy of Charles Gehring, Translator and Editor of The New Netherland Project, New York State Library, Albany. This document also mentions Sychnecta by name and the names of two other principals in the circumstances of his involuntary exhibition at the *Blauw Jan*. These were Hyam Meyers, complainant and New York City merchant, whose surname is variously spelled in other documents as Miers, Mejors, or Myers; and one Lorentz Blessius (Lawrence Blasius), who had accompanied Meyers and Sychnecta from New York to England, and who then fled to Amsterdam, taking Sychnecta with him.

Since neither the etching, nor the circumstances of Sychnecta's exhibition in Amsterdam had been previously reported in the ethnohistorical literature on the Iroquois, further research was warranted, but postponed. However, as so often is the case in such matters, the catalyst to more prompt research was fortuitously discovered - an oblique reference to Sychnecta in Carolyn Thomas Foreman's *Indians Abroad: 1493-1938* (1943), which was then being consulted for other information.[2]

Foreman notes the feud over financial arrangements which arose in 1843 between George Catlin and Arthur Rankin in regard to the public exhibition of a party of Ojibwa in the Egyptian Hall on Picadilly, London. Apparently because the circumstances and the exhibitor's motivations were so similar, *The (London) Times* published "A Hint to Messrs. Catlin and Rankin," in which reference was made to the occasion 78 years earlier when "John Schuppe and Hyam Miers were called to order by His Majesty's government for exhibiting two Mohawk warriors at the Sun Tavern" (Foreman 1943:171). *The Times* had published an extract from the *Proceedings in the Lords on a Complaint of advertising Two Indian Warriors to be shown, 5 March 1765* (Cobbett and Wright 1813,16: 50-51). The latter document provides the most complete, contemporary account of the purported circumstances underlying Sychnecta's exhibition at the *Blauw Jan* in Amsterdam in 1764 and subsequently in 1765 in London at the Sun Tavern. However, this document continues the story only until the intervention of the Lords of Trade in March 1765 and their directive that Sychnecta and his Mohawk companion be immediately returned to America.

In review the etching purportedly depicts a young Mohawk warrior, named Sychnecta, who in 1764 was being shown at the *Blauw Jan* in Amsterdam. The associated December 1764 Amsterdam notarial document also mentions Sychnecta by name, stating that he was one of *three* "Indians" brought over from New York by Hyam Meyers and who (Sychnecta) upon landing in England had been carried off to Amsterdam by one Lorentz Blessius, who had arrived with them. The March 1765 *Proceedings...* quotes part of Hyam Meyers's (Myers) deposition that *two* Mohawks, neither mentioned by name, had been brought over from New York (City) and that subsequent to their landing at Bristol, England, one of the Mohawks had been carried off to Amsterdam by their interpreter. The interpreter was undoubtedly Lorentz Blessius, and the Mohawk, Sychnecta, who had been allegedly sold by Blessius to the widow of Anthony Bergmeyer, proprietess of the *Blauw Jan* Inn.

The internal evidence of the etching, the *Summons...*, and the *Proceedings...* suggested that further documentation might be found among the administrative papers of Sir William Johnson (cf. Sullivan et al. 1921-1965). At the time Johnson was the British Superintendent of Indian Affairs for the Northern District in North America, a resident of the Mohawk Valley downriver from the Mohawks' Lower and Upper "Castles", and a relative by marriage of the Upper Castle or Canajoharie Mohawk, Joseph Brant - himself a celebrated visitor to London in 1775. A check of the Johnson papers' index volume for the names of Sychnecta, Lorentz Blessius (Lawrence Blasius), and Hyam Meyers (Miers, Mejors, or Myers) was immediately rewarding. Information in the Johnson papers complements that of the preceding primary documents. The Johnson papers not only identify Sychnecta as a young Canajoharie Mohawk, but also Lorentz Blessius (Lawrence Blasius) as a "german Taylor" of the same place. In addition these papers introduce two other principals in this affair - Trosoghroga, Sychnecta's Canajoharie Mohawk companion in exhibition abroad, and the apparent instigator of this affair, George (Ury) Klock Sr., a Palatine German settler and neighbor of the Canajoharie Mohawks. Further discussion with citations will be found below. We turn now from a review of the discovery process to successive discussions of the Sychnecta etching's authenticity, historicity, and reliability.

Authenticity

The etching (Fig. 1), titled *Een Wilde, SYCHNECTA genaamt, van de MOHAWK uyt NOORD-AMERICA te zien geweest in Blaauw Jan 1764*, is in the Dreesman Collection (Dr.pr.1436, negative number D6839), Department of Prints and Drawings, *Gemeentearchief*, Amsterdam, Netherlands. Its dimensions are given as 26 cm by 19.5 cm. The etching is an original impression, dating to 1764.

The name of the artist, who drew the original image from life and from which the etching was prepared, appears at lower left - "*P. Barbiers adv[ivum] delin.*" - and that of the person who prepared the etching at lower right - "*A. Smit fecit.*" The etching purportedly depicts a young Mohawk warrior, Sychnecta, in contemporary traditional dress, as he appeared in his exhibition at the *Blauw Jan* Inn, Amsterdam in 1764. The etching is marked by the conceptual incongruity of the representations of a pair of snowshoes in the foreground at Sychnecta's feet and what appears to be a palm tree, sketchily drawn in the background to the right of Sychnecta. Note should be made also of the pipe tomahawk held in Sychnecta's right hand, and the bow and two arrows in his left hand. We will return to the probable significance of the palm tree, the pipe tomahawk, and the bow and arrows in the concluding discussion of the etching.

The etching was prepared by A. Smit, an etcher, drawer, and portrait painter, active in Amsterdam from 1764 to 1792 (Scheen 1969; de Roever, personal communication). Thus the *Sychnecta* etching dates to his earliest period of activity in Amsterdam. The etching was based upon an original drawing - taken from life (*adv[ivum] delin.*) - by Pieter Barbiers, who was born in Amsterdam in 1717 and died there in 1780 (Scheen 1969:49; de Roever, personal communication). Except for his first lessons from his father, Anthonie Barbiers, Pieter was self-taught - a designer of carpet patterns, a decorator of fans and wallpapers, and later, a stage or scene decorator for theaters. It is to Barbiers's latter vocation and Sychnecta's public exhibition in the *Blauw Jan* that we can ascribe the etching's theatrical composition - Sychnecta's pose and the exotic landscape in which he has been placed.

Historicity

There exist sufficient independent documentary sources to confirm beyond a reasonable doubt the factual basis of the etching's subject matter - Sychnecta and his exhibition at the *Blauw Jan*, Amsterdam in 1764. To date three independent primary sources have been identified - the *Summons...* (NA 13604/1237), dated 19 December 1764 and in the *Gemeentearchief* Amsterdam; the *Proceedings...*, dated 5 March 1765 (cf. Cobbett and Wright 1813,16: 50-51); and miscellaneous correspondence, papers, etc., dating 1764-1765, which have been published in *The Papers of Sir William Johnson* (Sullivan et al. 1921-1965). A few of these pertinent Papers had been previously published within other historical series (cf. New-York Historical Society 1878:3-4; 1923:23; O'Callaghan 1849-1851,2: 1004-1007; 1853-1887,7: 708-709).

When read in conjunction, the December 1764 Amsterdam *Summons...* and the March 1765 London *Proceedings...* provide a sufficiently complete narrative of the purported motivations and circumstances of Sychnecta's departure from New York City in early 1764 through his imminent return to America by order

Fig. 1. Een Wilde, SYCHNECTA genaamt, van de MOHAWK uyt NOORD-AMERICA, te zien geweest in Blaauw Jan 1764. Drawn by P(ieter) Barbiers; etching by A.Smit. (Courtesy, *Gemeentearchief* Amsterdam.)

179

of the Lords of Trade in March 1765. In turn, documents among the Johnson papers provide valuable information concerning the period immediately prior to his departure from London to America.

We begin with a discussion of the Mohawk name Sychnecta, whose nominative root, -neht- (pine tree), perhaps only fortuitously associates him with a present day Mohawk Valley community and long-established Mohawk Valley place-name. This is the Mohawk's old name for Albany, New York - Skahnéehtati, meaning "On the Other Side of the Pines, or Beyond the Pines" (Lounsbury 1960:26). Since the 17th century, this place-name had also been applied to an Euroamerican settlement on the Mohawk River about 14 miles northwest of Albany and which was also literally beyond or on the other side of the pine barrens, which survive today - the present day city of Schenectady, New York.

However, Sychnecta's home was in neither of these mid-18th century Euroamerican communities on New York Colony's western frontier. Rather it was in the Upper Mohawk Castle (i.e. village) of Canajoharie (Sullivan et al. 1921-1965,4: 316-317; 11: 36-37). While the December 1764 Amsterdam Summons... states that Sychnecta was one of three Indians brought to England by the New York (City) merchant, Hyam Meyers, all the other documentary sources consistenty mention or describe only two. Sychnecta's Mohawk companion was named Trosoghroga and was also from the Upper Mohawk Castle of Canajoharie (Sullivan et al. 1921-1965,4: 342). Both Sychnecta and Trosoghroga were described as young men, whose Anglicized names were Hermanus and Joseph, but not necessarily respectively (Sullivan et al. 1921-1965,4: 316-317, 753-754; 7: 708-709; 11: 36-37, 754-755, 766-772).

While there is a present-day, Mohawk Valley, Euroamerican community of Canajoharie, the mid-18th century Upper Mohawk Castle of the same name was not at this location. Rather, Kana'tsyóhare, or "Washed Kettle... after a kettle-like basin worn in rocks of a creek..." (Lounsbury 1960:25), was then located near present day Indian Castle, New York, about 40 miles upriver from Schenectady.

Although the middle reaches of the Mohawk Valley had been the homeland of the Mohawks, by the mid-18th century most Mohawks had out-migrated to settlements in northern New York and Canada, a process which had begun nearly a century earlier (cf. Fenton and Tooker 1978:470-476; Guldenzopf 1984). By the mid-18th century there were more Mohawks living in settlements to the north than in the Mohawk Valley. Those Mohawks who remained in the Valley occupied two relatively small and highly acculturated communities - the Lower Mohawk Castle at Fort Hunter, New York, and the Upper Castle of Canajoharie. Both communities were bounded by royal and colonial land patents and surrounded by increasing numbers of Euroamerican settlers. Notable among these were the Palatine Germans with whom Sychnecta's and Trosoghroga's interpreter, Lorentz Blessius (Lawrence Blasius) can probably be identified - a "german Taylor" and inhabitant . of Canajoharie (Sullivan et al. 1921-1965,4:

316-317).

In 1750 Canajoharie had about 214 residents and 20 years later it was reported to have a population of 180 men, women, and children in 38 houses (Guldenzopf 1984:83, 87). During the American Revolution (1777), both the Canajoharie and Fort Hunter Mohawk settlements were attacked and plundered by a group of Americans and some allied Oneida Iroquois (Fenton and Tooker 1978:475). By the end of the war and the Treaty of Paris (1783) virtually all of the Mohawks and in-migrated refugee Indian groups had abandoned the Valley. The Mohawks of Canajoharie under the leadership of Captain Joseph Brant resettled upon lands along the Grand River in Ontario, Canada - the present day Six Nations Reserve - granted to them in compensation by the British government (Fenton and Tooker 1978:476).

Throughout the 18th century and especially during the period of the Seven Years War, 1756-1763, the British government through the New York colonial administration attempted to maintain peaceful relations with the Valley Mohawks and mediated numerous land-related disputes arising from encroaching Euroamerican settlement in the Valley. While British diplomatic policy towards the Mohawk and other Great Lakes Indians was ethically premised, as so often in diplomacy, it was most frequently implemented for more pragmatic reasons.

British policy towards and its implementation in regard to the Mohawks of Canajoharie and Fort Hunter had potentially far-reaching implications and consequences. While the total population and warrior strength of the Valley Mohawks were relatively low during the third quarter of the 18th century, they retained socio-political ties with their far more numerous brethren to the north on the St. Lawrence River and within French Canada, and with the Upper Iroquois - the Onondaga, Cayuga, and Seneca - to the west. These groups were a potential threat to British colonial interests in northeastern North America *vis-à-vis* the French. Ethics and pragmatics were both catalysts in the British government's intervention in Sychnecta's public exhibition in Amsterdam and subsequently in London.

New York's colonial administration and even the Canajoharie Mohawks were suspicious of the motivation behind Sychnecta's and Trosoghroga's imminent trip abroad, especially since they perceived George Klock Sr. as its instigator. In a letter dated 3 February 1764 to the New York's Lieutenant-Governor Cadwalader Colden, Sir William Johnson wrote that

"Two or three days ago I received information that Lawrence Blasius a german Taylor an inhabitant of Canajoharie, has inveigled two young Indians of that place to accompany him to England, these Indians being of George Klocks party one of them always living at his house, there is great Reason to think that he is principally concerned in sending them on some of his customary Fraudulencies. The Canajoharies on hearing of their Departure sent to me, desiring their journey should be stopped, as they were ignorant of the Cause of it, and justly apprehend they go on no good Design" (Sullivan et al. 1921-1965,4: 316-317).

On the same day Johnson sent a letter of similar content to General Thomas Gage at New York City (Sullivan et al. 1921-1965,11: 36). Blessius, Trosoghroga, and Sychnecta were already reported to be in the city at this date. In Gage's reply, dated 13 February 1764, he noted that Blessius (Blasius) hat approached him to request an "order to embark on the Transports" and that he (Gage) refused, since Blessius did not have "a pass from you (Johnson) for the savages to leave the Country" (Sullivan et al. 1921-1965,4: 325). Gage emphatically stated to Johnson that "No private Grants of Land whatever will be allowed of, and we must take every Measure necessary to prevent it" (Sullivan et al. 1921-1965,4: 325; cf. 353).

While Johnson's suspicions of Klock's and Blessius's motive for taking Sychnecta and Trosoghroga to England - to secure or confirm a private land grant - was reasonable, later documents suggest that this was not their actual or at least their only motive, which was to make money through the public exhibition of the two young Mohawks. For within the year of Sychnecta's and Trosoghroga's departure for England, Johnson, Colden, and Gage successfully prevented George Klock *Jr.* and his associate, Martah Nestel (Martin Nestle) from taking two other Canajoharie Mohawks abroad to England, Holland, and Germany "in order to Shew, and make money by them" (Sullivan et al. 1921-1965,11: 473-474; cf. 523). Ten years later, in the winter of 1773-1774 George Klock *Sr.* allegedly seduced another "foolish" young Canajoharie Mohawk to England "where he exposed him for a Shew" and defrauded the young Mohawk of his money on the return passage (O'Callaghan 1849-1851,2: 1004-1007).

One has reason then to suspect that this too was the motive for Sychnecta's and Trosoghroga's earlier trip abroad. It was perhaps because Blessius could not secure a pass to take the two Mohawks out of the colony and secure (free) passage to England on a military transport vessel, that a suspected partnership was formed between Klock Sr., Blessius, and Hyam Meyers. It had been reported that Blessius had a "Choyce of Partners at New York to engage with him" in some unnamed endeavor (Sullivan et al. 1921-1965,4: 353). Like Blessius, Meyers also tried unsuccessfully to secure "a proper certificate for the Indians" from Johnson through an intermediary at Albany (Sullivan et al. 1921-1965,4: 342, 353). Hyam Meyers is described in the pertinent sources as a New York (City) merchant (Amsterdam *Summons...*) and as having "suffered by the Indian trade" (Sullivan et al. 1921-1965,4: 342). Regardless of what responsibilities George Klock Sr. and Lawrence Blessius had in Sychnecta's und Trosoghroga's exhibition abroad, the documentary sources are unanimous in ascribing sole responsibility to Hyam Meyers and in obliquely condemning his mercenary motives (cf. O'Callaghan 1853-1887,7: 708; Sullivan et al. 1921-1965,4:

1921-1965,4: 687; 11: 772).

However, there is some suggestion that Sychnecta and Trosoghroga were not quite "innocents abroad" and that they were informed and willing associates in this affair. In his testimony to the House of Lords Meyer (Myers) asserted that his association with Sychnecta ans Trosoghroga had been at their initiative and had been a reciprocally-beneficial one. Meyers stated that while at New York and

> "...being about to come to England, the two Mohawks that are now with him came down to New York, and desired him to bring them to England to see their father [King George III?], but, having no money to pay their passage, he first consulted his friends about it, who advised him to bring them over, as he might reimbuse himself the expence of their passage by shewing them..." (Cobbett and Wright 1813,16: 51).

It appears that Meyers had indeed made some arrangements with Sychnecta and Trosoghroga whereby in return for the latters' public showing, he would not only pay the expenses of their passage to and from England and probably their expenses while there, but also pay them a flat fee or a share of the net proceeds of their exhibition. For upon their return to New York City Sychnecta and Trosoghroga unsuccessfully tried to collect "a Demand of 100 Dollars Each on Myers" (Sullivan et al. 1921-1965,4: 753). A similar arrangement had apparently been agreed upon about 10 years later between George Klock Sr. and the Canajoharie Mohawk he had taken to England and exhibited "for a Shew" (O'Callaghan 1849-1851,2: 1004-1007). It seems that all the principals - Klock, Blessius, and Meyers, and Trosoghroga and Sychnecta - share at least some responsibility in this affair.

British intervention in this affair was of course a pragmatic, but ethically-premised political response to the concerns of the Canajoharie Mohawks themselves. The latter had voiced their concerns to Sir William Johnson, who in turn in the letter cited above, expressed them to Lieutenant-Governor Colden and to General Gage (cf. Sullivan et al. 1921-1965,4: 316-317; 11: 36). However, the specific reason for the Canajoharie Mohawks' concern is not given, only Johnson's extrapolations.

As noted above, within the year of Sychnecta and Trosoghroga's departure from New York City to England, George Klock Jr. and Martah Nestel (Martin Nestle) unsuccessfully attempted to take two other Canajoharie Mohawks abroad - to England, Holland, and Germany - "in order to Shew, and make money by them" (Sullivan et al. 1921-1965,11: 473-474, cf. 523). In this instance the concern of the Canajoharie Mohawks was explicitly expressed in Johnson's letter of 20 November 1764 to General Thomas Gage. In regard to Klock Jr. and Nestle's plan, Johnson writes that

"The Indians are all much offended at it, and begged they [Klock Jr. and Nestle] might not be allowed to carry away their people but have them sent back, there were two of y^e. same Nation taken away in the same manner last Year [sic] & never heard of, wh. has done a good deal of Harm" (Sullivan et al. 1921-1965,11: 473-474).

Johnson had earlier noted that unless prevented, this act "will give the utmost Dissatisfaction to the Indians in General, & to the Mohawks in particular" (Sullivan et al. 1921-1965,11: 473).

When in March 1765 the British House of Lords became aware of Sychnecta's and Trosoghroga's public exhibition at the Sun Tavern on the Strand, London, they intervened for the same ethically-premised, but pragmatically-motivated reasons, and passed two resolutions.

"Resolved, 1. That the bringing from America of any of the Indians who are under his Majesty's protection, without proper authority for so doing may tend to give great dissatisfaction to the Indian nations, and be of dangerous consequence to his Majesty's subjects residing in the colonies. 2. That the making a public shew of Indians, ignorant of such proceedings is unbecoming and inhuman" (Cobbett and Wright 1813,16: 51).

Copies of these resolutions and notices of the imminent return of Sychnecta and Trosoghroga (Hermanus and Joseph) to New York at public expense, along with further instructions upon their arrival, were sent by the Lords of Trade directly to Lieutenant-Governor Colden (cf. New-York Historical Society 1878:3-4; O'Callaghan 1853-1887,7: 708) and to Sir William Johnson (cf. New-York Historical Society 1923:23; O'Callaghan 1853-1887,7: 709; Sullivan et al. 1921-1965,4: 687).

In a letter to Johnson, dated 27 May 1765, Colden acknowledged the receipt of the communications from the Lords of Trade and noted that Sychnecta and Trosoghroga had already returned. Similar to the recommendations received from the Lords of Trade, Colden advised Johnson that in the governement's intervention in this affair was demonstrated the strong regard which King George III and the House of Lords had for the Mohawks, such that the King and the Lords

"...would not suffer any of them to have the disgrace of being exhibited as a public shew. At the same time the Mohawks may learn to guard against the Delusions of mean base spirited pretending friends" (Sullivan et al. 1921-1965,11: 754).

Having identified the principals involved and discussed the circumstances,

184

motives, and implications of Sychnecta's exhibition abroad, there remains in the review of the historicity or historical authenticity of the 1764 Amsterdam etching only to provide a chronological sketch of this affair. While in his March 1765 testimony Hyam Meyers implies that he, Lorentz Blessius, Trosoghroga, and Sychnecta left New York City in April 1764 - "about 11 months ago" - eyewitness statements bracket the date of their departure between 16 February and 27 February 1764 (Sullivan et al. 1921-1965,4: 342, 353). Meyers's statements in the Amsterdam *Summons...* and in his testimony in the *Proceedings...* imply that he, Blessius, and the two Mohawks sailed directly to the port of Bristol on the west coast of England. Neither the date of their landing in Bristol, nor the elapsed time between the date of their departure from New York City and that of their arrival in Bristol is given.

In his testimony to the Lords of Trade Hyam Meyers asserted that sometime after their arrival at Bristol, he proceeded to London, leaving Lorentz Blessius, the interpreter, in charge of Sychnecta and Trosoghroga (Cobbett and Wright 1813,16: 50-51). In this testimony and in the Amsterdam *Summons...* Meyers further stated that in his absence Blessius "with stealth and without the knowledge or consent, much less agreement of this complainant [Meyers]" carried Sychnecta off to Amsterdam, where Blessius purportedly sold Sychnecta to the widow of Anthony Bergmeyer, proprietess of the *Blauw Jan* Inn. Meyers further testified that "upon the first knowledge of this transaction" he immediately went to Amsterdam in order to recover Sychnecta, taking the other Mohawk with him, "but notwithstanding all his endeavors, he could not get him again, being cast in a cause which he instituted there for that purpose..." (Cobbett and Wright 1813,16: 51). Since there is no other record in the *Gemeentearchief* Amsterdam of legal proceedings taken by Meyers on behalf of Sychnecta (de Roever, personal communication), we may assume that Meyers's "cause which he instituted there for that purpose" was the *Summons Served Upon the Widow of Anthony Bergmeyer*, dated 19 December 1764.

We must now pause to question the creditibility of Meyers's statements and testimony in regard to the completeness, sequence, and timing of the events related so far. For while Meyers's statements imply a relatively rapid order of events, the dates of his departure from New York City, 16-27 February 1764, and of his Amsterdam *Summons...*, 19 December 1764, show an elapsed time of nine months for these events. Either Meyers' passage to England was uncommonly slow or circuitous, or Meyers did not act as quickly as he stated in going to Amsterdam to petition Sychnecta's release from the *Blauw Jan* - which is suggestive of his collusion with Blessius in this episode. However, it is more probable that Meyers deliberately failed to mention that he and Blessius had also exhibited the two Mohawks in Bristol for some unstated period of time subsequent to their arrival there, and/or in Ireland as one of the pertinent document states (cf. Sullivan et al. 1921-1965,11: 772).

Unsuccessful in his attempt to secure the release of Sychnecta from the

Blauw Jan Inn, Hyam Meyers then went to the Hague, where he applied for assistance to Sir Joseph Yorke, the British ambassador to Holland (Cobbett and Wright 1813,16: 51). Sir Joseph Yorke instructed Meyers to return to Amsterdam and that he (Yorke) would have Sychnecta delivered to Meyers. Yorke further stated that he desired that Sychnecta and Trosoghroga be carried back to their own country, by way of England, and that he (Yorke) would write to the British Secretary of State, to whom he directed Meyers to apply upon his arrival in England (Cobbett and Wright 1813,16: 51). The implication was that the British government was prepared to be of logistical and financial assistance to Meyers in the return of the two Mohawks to New York.

Hyam Meyers's credibility is most seriously damaged when we learn by his own admission that upon returning to London, he neither applied to the Secretary of State, nor to the Board of Trade. Rather, claiming that he was only attempting to reimburse himself for past expenses, as well as to earn money to enable him to return Sychnecta and Trosoghroga to New York, he rented a room for eight days from John Schuppe, proprietor of the Sun Tavern. *The Gazetteer and New Daily Advertiser* of 4 March 1765 carried the following notice.

"That there is to be seen, at the Sun Tavern, facing York Building in the Strand, two Indian Warriors of the Mohawk nation, from ten in the morning till six in the evening; each person to pay one shilling" (Cobbett and Wright 1813,16: 50).

Notice and complaint being made on the following day of this activity, the House of Lords intervened, summoning John Schuppe and Hyam Meyers to testify before them. Their suspicions of Meyers's credibility and motives in this affair were no doubt supported by the letter they had received from Sir Joseph Yorke, acquainting them with what happened in Amsterdam and with his instructions to Meyers, which the latter had obviously chosen to ignore.

Meyers and Schuppe were ordered not "to shew the said Indians from this time," but to take proper care of Sychnecta and Trosoghroga until the Lords of Trade could arrange their return to America (Cobbett and Wright 1813,16: 51). On 16 March 1765 Sychnecta and Trosoghroga set sail for New York at public expense on board the "Friendship Captain Frost" *(sic)* and on 1 June 1765 they were said to have "Just Landed" at New York City (O'Callaghan 1851-1887,7: 709). Placed under the charge of Lieutenant Archilles Preston, an "Indian Officer" in Johnson's service, Sychnecta and Trosoghroga subsequently traveled by sloop up the Hudson River to Albany (Sullivan et al. 1921-1965,4: 753; 11: 754). In the *Journal of Indian Affairs*, Johnson Hall, for 4 June 1765, Guy Johnson recorded that the

"Same time Joseph, & Hermanus two Canajoharie Indians who has been

186

Seduced to England, Ireland &c by one Myer. - arrived from London, via N York, & brought Sir Wm. Johnson a Letter from the Lords of Trade, & the following Resolutions of the House of Lords relative to the Inveigling the Indians" (Sullivan et al. 1921-1965,11: 772).

In conclusion the historicity or historical authenticity of the subject matter of the Amsterdam etching, *Een Wilde, SYCHNECTA genaamt, van de MOHAWK, uyt NOORD-AMERICA, te zien geweest in Blaauw Jan 1764*, is beyond question. In regard to pre-American Revolution iconography of the Iroqois the etching is among the best documented, and one suspects that additional documentation could be found, particularly in contemporary newspapers of New York City, Bristol, London, and Amsterdam. In term of the accompanying documentation of the subject matter the Sychnecta etching has few other equals which predate 1775 - equalled or surpassed only by Jan Verelst's portraits of the three Mohawk "kings" from Canajoharie and Fort Hunter, who visited Queen Anne in England in 1710 (cf. Bond 1952). In terms of its historicity *and* its ethnographical reliability the Sychnecta etching has even fewer pre-1775 equals - surpassing in my opinion even the Verelst portraits. It is equaled only by the ten watercolor and ink drawings by the Jesuit Father Claude Chauchetière which illustrate significant events in the history of the nominally Mohawk Mission du Sault (Caughnawaga), 1667-1687, in French-Canada (cf. Gagnon 1975:83-87; Gagnon and Cloutier 1976:29-54).

Reliability

In evaluating the ethnographical reliability of the Sychnecta etching we are principally concerned with demonstrating that the image is not a copy *in pars* or *in toto* of some earlier image, regardless of the latter's authenticity, reliability, and ethnographical appropriateness.

Additionally, we are concerned that the image is not only an original one, but also taken from life, as the Sychnecta etching was, and therefore accurate in its ethnographical details. Finally, we should note that the presence of ethnographically valid details within the image is not itself proof that the image was actually taken from life. Probably more frequently than we are aware, such details, more or less appropriate, were "curiosities" acquired by the artist for use as studio props - for example, Rembrandt van Rijn (Strauss and van der Meulen 1979:363-365) or Benjamin West (Garvan 1976; Sellers 1976).

Unlike an image's authenticity and historicity, one can not in the same sense prove its ethnographical reliability. One can only corroborate it through a complex feedback process of comparison and contrast with other demonstrably reliable ethnological and historical materials, including other images.

Space prohibits the detailed evaluation of the ethnographical reliability of the Sychnecta etching here. I can only assert it. The etching was based upon an original image, by Pieter Barbiers, taken from life (*ad vivum*), and was not to be a composition *in pars* or *in toto* from an earlier original and/or mechanically-reproduced image. However, there are the expected resonances both in style and details with some of these.

The reliability of the Sychnecta etching is corroborated with documented contemporaneouns, archaeological and ethnological collections. These ethnological details include Sychnecta's head decorations - including nose and ear pendants, possible head painting or tattooing, and the decoration of the scalplock; details of traditional dress of the period - including shirt, robe or blanket (here shown rolled down to the waist), and beneath which there is indication of a breechcloth, and below, leggings and moccasins; details of ornaments - including probable silver or brass (King George II or III) medals, gorgets, and armbands; and other artifactual accessories - the pipe tomahawk whose handle was apparently wrapped at intervals with brass or copper wire, the bow and arrows (the blunt and expanded tip arrow used to hunt birds and squirrels; the other, anomalous), and the pair of snowshoes.

Corroboratory ethnological specimens can be found in the collections of the National Museum of Man, Ottawa, Canada (cf. Brasser 1976), the National Museum of Ireland, Dublin (cf. Phillips 1984), the Museum of Mankind, London (cf. King 1982), the Musée de l'Homme, Paris (cf. Fardoulis 1979), and elsewhere on the continent (cf. Krickeberg 1954; Linné 1958). Many of these specimens comprise collections made by military officers who were stationed in the lower Great Lakes region. Sir William Johnson had a collection of such "Indian finery" himself, and acquired such "curiousities" for others upon request (cf. Elmer 1848:116; Linné 1958:35-36; Sullivan et al. 1921-1965,1: 182, 183, 323-324; 12: 80). This activity appears to be an under-appreciated adjunct of the "Indian Trade."

Conclusion

Potential objections to the concluded, ethnographical reliability of the Sychnecta etching might be raised upon the basis of the sketchily drawn palm tree in the background and the apparent anachronistic presence of the bow and arrows. Both potential objections are reasonably countered. By 1764 the flintlock musket had been in use among the Iroquois for well over a century. As a weapon of war the musket did not replace the ball-headed club or the tomahawk, although it had largely eclipsed this function of the bow and arrow. By the etching's date, the bow and arrow was principally the plaything of boys, or used by Iroquois men to hunt birds and small game. It is probable that the inclusion of the bow and arrow in the Sychnecta etching served a purpose other than ethnographical reportage. Like the tomahawk and the palm tree in the background, they were rather long-standing European visual symbols or metaphors for Sychnecta's other-worldliness - his exotism, as *Een*

Wilde - a curiosity sufficient to amuse the curious of Amsterdam.

Sychnecta was neither the first, nor the last Iroquois abroad, nor the first Indian from New York to be exhibited in Amsterdam - in 1644 two former soldiers of the *Westindische Compagnie* and a certain Hermanus Meyer formed a partnership to display a "wild Indian named Jaques" from the colony (van Gelder 1982:38). By 1644 the practice of exhibiting New World Indians in Europe was already over a century old (cf. Foreman 1943). Iroquoians from along the St. Lawrence River had been among the earliest to be taken back.

So neither the event, circumstance, and motive, nor the ethical and pragmatic concerns of Sychnecta's exhibition in Amsterdam in 1764 and during the following year in London, were unique. Rather, they conform to, and therein confirm a common cultural pattern (cf. Bond 1952; Foreman 1943). So much so, that in the public feud between George Catlin and his partner Arthur Rankin, in regard to the London exhibition of a party of Ojibwa in 1843, *The (London) Times* reminded the two of the instance of Sychnecta's and Trosoghro-ga's exhibition in that city 78 years earlier (Foreman 1943:171).

From the historical sources, one suspects that (Canajoharie) Mohawks were frequent visitors or were frequently exhibited abroad during the 18th century - particularly in London - where they were popularly perceived as exotic "wildmen." It is perhaps from such practices and popular preconceptions that the term "Mohock" (Mohawk) came to be applied in that century to "a class of aristocratic ruffians who infested the streets of London at night" - an usage which first appeared in 1711-1712 (Jonathan Swift in Oxford 1933,6: 582) - and perhaps only coincidentally after the visit there of the three Mohawk "kings" in 1710. Certainly this preconception or perception survives in the mystique of the "Mohawk" - a hairstyle worn by today's urban "ruffians."

The exhibition of North American Indians in Britain and in Europe continued through the 18th century and well into the present century - as continuing popular symbols or metaphors of the "wild west" (cf. Honour 1975). The ethical concerns raised since the 16th century by the public exhibition of Indians have been more recently transferred to museum exhibition contexts - especially the propriety of the traditional museum exhibition and interpretation of Indians as another feature of the continent's natural history - the *native* American as the "natural man."

Finally, the experience of Sychnecta raises an extremely important, but ultimately unanswerable question. What were the subsequent transculturative roles played by such individuals, who like Sychnecta, had journeyed to not only colonial capitals but to the capitals of Britain and Europe, and returned to their homelands? What preconceptions or perceptions did they have of Europeans and European culture, and how did these structure and orient their subsequent behavior within the two culture contexts of their colonial home-lands?

189

NOTES

1. I wish to thank Margriet B. de Roever, research associate, *Gemeentearchief Amsterdam*, who brought the Sychnecta etching and its associated notarial document to my attention, and Boudewijn Bakker, Chief Curator, Department of Prints and Drawings of the same institution, who provided me with a photograph of the former and a photocopy of the latter. I also wish to thank Charles Gehring, Translator and Editor, New Netherland Project, New York State Library, Albany, who translated the notarial document for my reference, as well as other reference materials.

   An earlier and expanded verson of this paper had been prepared and circulated to colleagues for comment. I wish to thank David Guldenzopf, State University of New York - Albany, Graduate Anthropology Program, who upon reading the earlier draft, called my attention to the reference to George Klock Sr.'s exhibition of a Canajoharie Mohawk in England in the winter of 1773-1774.

2. Since this paper was written, the author has also dicovered Bond's (1952:107) note on this subject with references to two other primary documents not cited here.

REFERENCES CITED

Bond, Richmond P.
1952   Queen Anne's American Kings. Oxford: Clarend London Press.

Brasser, T.J.C.
1976   "Bo'jou, Neejee!" Profiles of Canadian Indian Art [exhibition catalogue]. Ottawa: National Museum of Man.

Cobbett, William and J. Wright (eds.)
1813   The Parliamentary History of England, from the Earliest Period to the Year 1803 ... Volume 16, A.D. 1765-1771. (36 vols., 1806- 1820). London: T.C. Hansard.

Elmer, Ebenezer
1848   Journal Kept During An Expedition to Canada in 1776. Proceedings of the New Jersey Historical Society. (3): 95-146, (4):150-194.

Fardoulis, Anne Vitart
1979   Le Cabinet du Roi et les anciens Cabinets de Curiosités dans les collections du Musée de l'Homme. Microfilm, Service photographique - centre de documentation, Centre national de la recherche scientifique. Paris.

Fenton, William N. and Elisabeth Tooker
1978   Mohawk. In Bruce G. Trigger (ed.), Northeast. Vol. 15 of Handbook of North American Indians, 466-480. Washington: Smithsonian Institution.

Foreman, Carolyn Thomas
1943   Indians Abroad: 1493-1938. Norman: University of Oklahoma Press.

Gagnon, François-Marc
1975   La Conversion par L'Image: Un Aspect de la Mission des Jésuites auprès des Indiens du Canada au XVIIe Siècle. Montreal: Éditions Bellarmin.

Gagnon, François-Marc and Nicole Cloutier
1976   Premiers Peintres de la Nouvelle-France. Tome 1. Série Arts et Metiers. Ottawa: Ministère des affairs culturelles.

Garvan, Anthony N.B.
1976   The Consequence: The Social Impact of Benjamin West's Painting. In: Symbols of Peace: William Penn's Treaty with the Indians [exhibition catalogue]. Philadelphia: Pennsylvania Academy of Fine Arts.

Guldenzopf, David
1984   Frontier Demography and Settlement Patterns of the Mohawk Iroquois. Man in the Northeast 27 (Spring 1984): 79-94.

Hamell, George R.
1983   Trading in Metaphors: The Magic of Beads. In: Charles F. Hayes, III et al. (eds.), Proceedings of the 1982 Glass Trade Bead Conference.

Research Records 16, Research Division, Rochester Museum and
Science Center, 5-28. Rochester.

Honour, Hugh
1975   The New Golden Land: European Images of America from the
Discoveries to the Present Time. New York: Pantheon Books.

King, J.C.H.
1982   Thunderbird and Lightning: Indian Life in Northeastern North
America 1600-1900 [exhibition catalogue]. London: British Museum
Publications Limited.

Krickeberg, Walter
1954   Ältere Ethnographica aus Nordamerika im Berliner Museum für
Völkerkunde. Baessler-Archiv, Neue Folge 2. Berlin.

Linné, Sigvald
1958   Three North American Indian Weapons in the Ethnographical
Museum of Sweden. Connoisseur 141 (567): 34-36.

Lounsbury, Floyd G.
1960   Iroquois Place-names in the Champlain Valley. Report of the New
York-Vermont Interstate Commission on the Lake Champlain Basin
(1960), Legislative Document (1960), Number 9: 23-66. Albany:
University of the State of New York/State Education Department.

New-York Historical Society
1878   The Colden Letter Books, Volume 7, 1765-1775. Collections of the
New-York Historical Society for the Year 1877. Publication Fund
Series 10. New York.

1923   The Letters and Papers of Cadwallader Colden, Volume 7, 1765-
1775. Collections of the New-York Historical Society for the Year
1923. John Watts DePeyster Publication Fund Series56. New York.

O'Callaghan, Edmund B. (ed.)
1849-1851 The Documentary History of New York. 4 volumes. Albany: Weed,
Parsons and Company.

1853-1887 Documents Relative to the Colonial History of the State of New
York. 15 volumes. Albany: Weed, Parsons and Company.
Oxford

1933   The Oxford English Dictionary... A New English Dictionary on
Historical Principles... Volume 6, L-M. (12 volumes). Oxford:
Clarendon Press.

Phillips, Ruth B.
1984   Patterns of Power: The Jasper Grant Collection and Great Lakes
Indian Art of the Early Nineteenth Century. Kleinburg: McMichael
Canadiana Collection.

Sahlins, Marshall
1981   Historical Metaphors and Mystical Realities: Structure in the Early
History of the Sandwich Islands Kingdom. Association for Social

Anthropology in Oceania, Special Publications Number 1. Ann Arbor: University of Michigan Press.

Scheen, Pieter A.
1969   Lexicon Nederlandse beeldende kunstenaars, 1750-1950. 's-Gravenhage: P.A. Scheen.

Sellers, Charles Coleman
1976   The Beginning: A Monument to Probity, Candor and Peace. In: Symbols of Peace: William Penn's Treaty with the Indians [exhibition catalogue]. Philadelphia: Pennsylvania Academy of Fine Arts.

Strauss, Walter L. and Marjon van der Meulen
1979   The Rembrandt Documents. New York: Abaris Books.

Sullivan, James et al. (eds.)
1921   The Papers of Sir William Johnson. 14 volumes. Albany: University of the State of New York.

van Gelder, Roelof
1982   "A Richly Blessèd Land Where Milk and Honey Flow": New Netherlands Seen by Dutch Eyes. In: The Birth of New York: Nieuw Amsterdam 1624-1664 [exhibition catalogue]. Amsterdam: Gementelijke Archiefdienst.

UNTIL THEY ARE CONTAMINATED BY THEIR MORE REFINED NEIGHBORS:
The Images of the Native American in Carver's *Travels Through the Interior* and Its Influence on the Euro-American Imagination

Daniel E. Williams

During the summer of 1797 Friedrich von Schiller, the German poet and dramatist, read and then re-read with great interest a curious travel book which described the people and places of the North American wilderness of the upper Mississippi. The book, Jonathan Carver's *Travels Through the Interior Parts of North America in the Years 1766, 1767, and 1768* (London, 1778), deeply touched Schiller's imagination, particularly the descriptions of the Indians, for no sooner had he finished reading it than he began to consider ways to make use of its subjects in his own poetry. Within a short period of time, one or two days in fact, he completed what he believed was one of his most successful poems: "Nadowessiers Totenlied" (Nadowessier's Death Song). He immediately sent the poem to several friends for their comments, and within one day of receiving it Goethe wrote back, praising the poem for its savage realism and commending Schiller for introducing such exotic subjects as an Indian funeral speech into neo-classical poetry. Goethe wrote:

> "Das Totenlied... hat seinen echten realistisch humoristischen Charakter, der wilden Naturen, in solchen Fällen, so wohl ansteht. Es ist ein großes Verdienst der Poesie, uns auch in diese Stimmungen zu versetzen, so wie es verdienstlich ist, den Kreis der poetischen Gegenstände immer zu erweitern."

> ("The Deathsong... has a genuine, realistic, humorous character, which in such cases fits so well the wildness of Nature. It is a great merit of poetry to also place us in these moods as it is a merit to always widen the boundaries of poetic subjects") (Stapf s.a.:318).

What Schiller experienced in reading Carver's narrative and what Goethe experienced in reading Schiller's poem was what each believed was a true sense of the native inhabitants of North America - the Indians in their "original purity." Each was fascinated with Carver's Indians, and each shaped his image of the American wilderness according to Carver's descriptions. On the whole, their feelings for both were entirely positive.

This was exactly what Carver had intended in writing his narrative. Although ironically he died before he could enjoy the literary success which he had struggled so hard to achieve, he was one of the most popular and successful American writers in the eighteenth century. His narrative, based on his actual journeys, became an almost immediate bestseller and was published nearly sixty times in various forms during the next one hundred years, including translations in French, German, Dutch, Swedish, and Greek (cp. Parker 1976:222-231). Its influence was even greater than its popularity. Not only was it the first book written by a colonial American to have a large international following, but for the next three quarters of a century it was cited as a standard authority on the native peoples and places of the upper Mississippi. Without a doubt, the book touched the imaginations of countless people on both sides of the Atlantic, shaping their images of both the Indians and the wilderness. At a time when the idea of a separate American national identity was being formed, the book's highly favorable descriptions of the land and its people appealed to thousands and was disseminated to tens of thousands.

Today, however, Carver's *Travels* is one of the least popular of all early narratives of exploration. Despite the fact that for nearly a century it was one of the most popular of all books describing the Indians of North America, it is rarely read today as either literature or history. And despite the fact that recently several historians have proven the general accuracy of most of Carver's statements concerning the Dakota, his reputation remains quite low (cp. Blegen 1963, Medeiros 1977, Parker 1976, Savage 1979). The reason for this decline involves Carver's use of borrowed material. Both Carver and the authenticity of his book came under increasing attack throughout the nineteenth century, until finally by the beginning of the twentieth century he was accused of being an illiterate shoemaker incapable of writing the narrative which appeared under his name (cp. Bourne 1906). As certain literary historians have proved, parts of the book, including several passages pertaining to the Indians, were taken from other previous sources, particularly from the narratives of Hennepin, Lahontan, Charlevoix, du Pratz, and Adair. As a result, Carver's *Travels* was thoroughly discredited, believed to be merely a kind of literary hoax perpetrated by a London hack writer who knew little about America and less about Indians. Embarrassed by the charges of plagiarism, both intellectual and literary historians ceased to consider the narrative as a significant work.

This view, however, although still prevalent today, is false. The discovery and publication of Carver's manuscript journals prove beyond a doubt that he was literate, that he did make a three year journey into the wilderness, and that he was responsible for at least three quarters of the material included in the published version of his journey. Moreover, the question of what is and what is not Carver is entirely irrelevant. While it is true that, in order to make the book more marketable, both Carver and his London editor expanded his original narrative by adding passages from previous writers, this was nothing unusual. Throughout the seventeenth and eighteenth centuries unacknowledged compilations were common, especially in New World narratives. More importantly, Carver was far more popular than any of his sources, and consequently it was his glowing vision of the wilderness and its native inhabitants that touched the European imagination so deeply. Since Carver's *Travels* was one of the most popular of all American wilderness narratives published in Europe, and in view of the many stereotypes and clichés in Europe today concerning the people and places he wrote about, it is necessary to examine Carver's perceptions and his influences.

Gathering information about the Indians was one of Carver's primary intentions in his journey into the American interior. After the Treaty of Paris had been signed in 1763, concluding the Seven Years War (known also as the French and Indian War), Carver set out to explore the regions of the upper Mississippi and Great Lakes which France had been forced to surrender to England. He saw both tremendous possibilities in these regions and a tremendous ignorance about them. In 1766 he left Fort Michilimackinac, the most western British post, in order to "... make that vast acquisition of territory, gained by Great Britain in North America, advantageous to it" (Carver 1778:17). It was his grand intention not only to acquire information concerning "... the manners, customs, languages, soil and natural productions of the different nations that inhabit the back of the Mississippi," but also to "... ascertain the breadth of that vast Continent, which extends from the Atlantic to the Pacific Ocean..." (Carver 1778:18). Ultimately, Carver was disappointed in his attempt to cross the continent. He did, however, spend nearly two years exploring the head-waters of the Mississippi, and during this time he had continual opportunity to observe the several Indian nations who lived in these regions, particularly Dakota, Chippewa, Winnebago, Ottawa, Sauk, and Fox. In fact, with the Dakota, or "Naudowessee" as he called them, Carver resided for five months during the winter while waiting for the rivers to thaw. He returned from his experiences with a generally favorable view of the Indians and a decidedly favorable view of their land.

In a chapter describing Indian "Manners," Carver wrote that "[i]t may with truth be said of them, that they are the worst enemies, and the best of friends, of any people in the whole world" (Carver 1778:141). Such a striking juxtaposition of opposites was by no means a contradiction; rather, to Carver it was an appropriate indication of the many extremes he believed made up the Indian character and which made the Native American so difficult for Europeans to understand. The Indian, as Carver described him, was both violent and gentle, corrupt and innocent, cruel and kind, ignorant and intelligent, industrious and lazy, indifferent and loving, calm and passionate, deceitful and trustworthy, ultimately even both savage and civilized. The constant use of such contrasts, which are found throughout the narrative, was not meant to depict the Indians as either inconstant or unstable but to describe them as belonging to an entirely different and complex world, the wilderness, which demanded an entirely different set of responses. Consequently, both Indians and wilderness resist oversimplification. Although he made the same mistake as so many others in minimizing Indians diversity and generalizing about "the Indian," he nevertheless described Native Americans neither strictly in terms of the "Noble Savage" nor of the "Savage Brute," but as having elements of both. Only by understanding the harsh realities of wilderness life could Europeans appreciate the wide range of responses required by Indians to survive. According to Carver,

> "[t]he character of the Indians... is composed of a mixture of ferocity and gentleness. They are at once guided by passions and appetites, which they hold, in common with the fiercest beasts that inhabit the woods, and are [as well] possessed of virtues which do honor to human nature" (Carver 1778:224).

Of the virtues Carver admired the most were the generosity, hospitality, loyalty, strength, courage, and intelligence of the Indians. Perhaps in order to lessen fear of the Indians and to encourage western settlement, Carver continually mentioned the kind and friendly receptions he received from the Indians throughout his travels. In one passage he stated that "[n]o people are more hospitable, kind, and free than the Indians" (Carver 1778:151). Elsewhere he wrote that

> "... notwithstanding [that] the inhabitants of Europe are apt to entertain horrid ideas of the ferocity of these savages, as they are termed, I received from every tribe of them in the interior parts, the most hospitable and courteous treatment" (Carver 1778:29).

Here Carver was specifically attempting to refute the commonly accepted notion of Indian savagery (cp. Berkhofer 1978). Because of the hostilities between Indians and whites which followed the Seven Years War, generally known as Pontiac's War, negative accounts of Indian brutality and treachery were spread throughout the colonies and England (cp. Parkman 1851). But Carver, by stressing the hospitable receptions he encountered, described the Indians as anything but wild, frenzied, and furious. Not only were a majority of the Indians he met quite friendly, but they also displayed an unusual level of self-control. Instead of unrestrained hostility, he described the Indians as being "... extremely circumspect and deliberate in every word and action" (Carver 1778:138). Such a refinement of manners cast the Indians as rational - and not savage - beings.

Throughout the narrative Carver continued to undermine the common assumptions supporting the idea of Indian savagery. Although he affirmed the notion of Indian stoicism, stating that they refused "to betray on any account whatever their emotions," he nevertheless was impressed by the intensity of their loves and loyalties (Carver 1778:139). In another passage confuting Indian

198

savagery, he wrote that "for notwithstanding they are esteemed savages, I never saw among any other people greater proofs of parental or filial tenderness" (Carver 1778:139). Deep attachments characterized social relations throughout Indian society, from the familial to the tribal level. Concerning tribal unity, Carver wrote that "they possess an attachment for that band to which they belong, unknown to the inhabitants of any other country" (Carver 1778:226). Far from being savage, the Indians exhibited certain qualities that, when compared with Euro-American cultures, made them seem quite civilized.

Partly because of his own indigence, Carver was most impressed with the lack of either selfishness or self-interest in the Indian villages he visited. Finding little jealousy or greed, he often remarked upon Indian generosity and their nonmaterilistic way of life. He stated that "[t]he Indians in their common state are strangers to all distinction of property, except in the articles of domestic use, which every one considers as his own, and supply the deficiency of their friends with any superfluity of their own" (Carver 1778:142). Both directly and indirectly, Carver used this liberal spirit of sharing to attack the concept of profit in European societies. In part reaffirming the well-worn notion of the Indians living in the mythical Golden Age, he wrote that

"The Indians, except those who live adjoining to European colonies, can form to themselves no idea of the value of money; they consider it when they are made acquainted with the uses to which it is applied by other nations, as the source of innumerable evils. To it they attribute all the mischiefs that are prevalent among Europeans, such as treachery, plundering, devastations, and murder" (Carver 1778:142).

Building on this theme of communal sharing and emphasizing the absence of unequal distribution, Carver then attacked the practice of imprisoning debtors.

"They esteem it irrational that one man should be possessed of a greater quantity than another, and are amazed that any honor should be annexed to the possession of it. But that the want of this useless metal should be the cause of depriving persons of their liberty, and that on account of this partial distribution of it, great numbers should be immured within the dreary walls of a prison, cut off from that society which they constitute a part, exceeds their belief. Nor do they fail on hearing this part of the European system of government related, to charge the institutors with a total want of humanity, and to brand them with the names of savages and brutes" (Carver 1778:142-3).

In having the Indians accuse the Europeans of savagery, Carver has, of course, intentionally reversed the usual cultural stereotypes, but his reasons for this reversal have less to do with his experiences in America than with his

199

experiences in Europe. As with writers of the New World before and after him, he manipulated aspects of Indian life in order to criticize what he found distasteful in his own.[1] As he severely suffered from poverty in London during the last ten years of his life, he was particularly interested in stressing the nonmaterial aspects of Indian culture so that he could ridicule European materialism.

Carver often favorably compared Indians with Europeans. In addition to praising Indian strength, courage, and endurance, he extolled their natural intelligence, thus refuting claims of Indian degeneracy:

"The Indians discover an amazing sagacity, and acquire with the greatest readiness any thing that depends upon the attention of the mind. By experience and an acute observation, they attain many perfections to which Europeans are strangers" (Carver 1778:140).

As examples of these "perfections," Carver mentioned a variety of wilderness skills which impressed him, including the Indians' uncanny sense of direction and their ability to track animals. Moreover, he was also impressed with Indian medicines and cures. While he was skeptical of their mixing religion with medicine, he noted that the Indian "priests" (as he called them) "frequently are successful... in administering the salubrious herbs they have acquired a knowledge of " (Carver 1778:212). Not only could these "priests" lower fevers and heal wounds, but - according to Carver - they could even miraculously cure venereal disease.

But the most favorable comparison Carver offered was between Indian innocence and European corruption. In order to make another criticism of European practice, he employed some equally well-worn conventions of the Noble Savage. When describing a young "Winnebage prince" making an offering to the Falls of St. Anthony, he wrote:

"I was greatly surprised at beholding an instance of such elevated devotion in so young an Indian, and instead of ridiculing the Ceremonies attending it, as I observed my servant tacitly did, I looked on the prince with a greater degree of respect for these sincere proofs he gave of his piety; and I doubt not but that his offerings and prayers were as acceptable to the universal Parent of mankind as if they had been made with greater pomp, or in a consecrated place... Whilst I beheld the artless, yet engaging manners of this unpolished savage, I could not help drawing a comparison between him and some of the more refined inhabitants of civilized countries, not such, I own, in the favor of the latter" (Carver 1778:50-51).

In another passage Carver stated that the Indians "worship the great creator with a degree of purity unknown to nations who have greater opportunities of improvement" (Carver 1778:107).

According to Carver, such innocent manners could be found in all aspects of Indian life - in their dress, government, dances, feasts, and rituals. His remarks concerning Indian sexuality, for example, emphasized the theme of innocence, and thus indirectly challenged European morality. Exhibiting the typical white man's fascination with Indian women, he favorably described what he called their "amorous temperature" and the lack of guilt or shame attached to premarital sex (Carver 1778:191). Carver, a New Englander, was understandably impressed with this as he was with the practice of polygamy, which, considering that he had wives and children on both sides of the Atlantic, is not surprising. Here again, his own problems and perspective gave impetus to his description of the Indians.

Like so many writers of his age, Carver was influenced by the cult of the Noble Savage, and in many of his descriptions the Indians displayed those qualities usually attributed to the primitive noblemen who gained such popularity in the works of such writers as Montaigne and Rousseau. Strength, wisdom, friendliness - all were a part of this portrayal. Innocence, of course, made up a large part of it, but with innocence both happiness and simplicity were also included. The wilderness around the upper Great Lakes was by no means Paradise; nevertheless, according to Carver, the Indians were essentially happy. Speaking in general of the Indians he encountered, he wrote that "[t]hey never suffer themselves to be overburdened with care, but live in a state of perfect tranquility and contentment" (Carver 1778:141). In one of his manuscripts he made his longing for the natural harmony of the Indians even clearer: "These people," he wrote, "pass their life without prisons [and] almost without trouble in a state of sweetness and tranquility and I believe [that they] enjoy a happiness that the more refined are strangers to, living quietly under the laws of instinct that wise nature has imprinted upon their minds from the cradle" (Parker 1976:112).

Yet neither innocence nor happiness was complete, and Carver did not hesitate to depart from the Noble Savage tradition in order to criticize what he considered the less appealing aspects of Indian life. In fact, he often balanced the European view of the Noble Savage with the frontier American view of the bloodthirsty savage. Not all details of Indian experience were admired. For instance, when describing a Chippewa village, Carver could not help but express his disgust concerning one particular practice:

"But the inhabitants, in general seemed to be the nastiest people I had ever been among. I observed that the woman and children indulged themselves in a custom, which though common, in some degree, throughout every Indian nation, appears to our ideas, of the most nauseous and indelicate nature; that of searching each other's heads [for lice], and eating the prey caught therein" (Carver 1778:69).

Obviously, Carver could not escape his own system of values, and, although he was sometimes aware of his prejudices, he could not but express his distaste when his values were offended. For example, when commenting on sex roles and the division of labor, his distaste was evident. Although he admired the "leisure time" of men when in camp, he was critical of their complete lack of industry. Indian women, he felt, were treated as little more than slaves. They performed "every kind of drudgery" while the men were "remarkably indolent." Carver's own work ethic was apparent when he stated that

"[Indian men b]eing naturally indolent, if provisions just sufficient for their subsistence can be procured with little trouble, and near at hand, they will not go far, or take any extraordinary pains for it, though by so doing they might acquire greater plenty, and a more estimable kind" (Carver 1778:136).

An even greater indication of Carver's affronted values was his reaction to what he considered "many ridiculous stories of enchantment and magical tricks." Although he admired the quality of devotion he observed in Indian religious practice, he felt that the Indians were far too superstitious and often allowed their fear of evil spirits to control their lives. Several incidents were mentioned in which a band or village had abandoned a particular area because of evil spirits. Once he told the story of a large town which had been abandoned because of the appearance of an evil spirit. According to Carver, who believed that men were more evil than spirits, this was merely "... a stratagem of the French or Spaniards" to trick the Indians out of their land (Carver 1778:41). Another time he related the story of an island in Lake Superior which the Chippewas refused to approach, despite its pleasing appearance and location, because several generations earlier an evil spirit had been seen there. This Carver found particularly ridiculous, since the island was supposedly covered with "a heavy shining, yellow sand" which he assumed was gold (Carver 1778:84). He was also quite skeptical of the trusting of "Manitous" for protection against attack. As a cautious veteran of the Seven Years War, Carver thought it unwise not to post guards when hunting or raiding in distant territories. Referring to Indians in general, he stated that

"They place great confidence in their Manitous, or household gods, which they carry with them; and being persuaded that they take upon them the office of centinels, they sleep very securely under their protection. These Manitous... are nothing more than the otter or martin skins... for which, however, they have great veneration" (Carver 1778:210).

Carver respected the Indian worship of the "Supreme Being, or Giver of Life," a belief he felt consistent with Christianity, but he felt that the Indians spent more time worshipping the evil spirit, "to whom they ascribe great power, and suppose that through his means all evils which befall mankind are inflicted" (Carver 1778:210). Indian religious practice, he concluded, was motivated more out of a fear of evil than a love of good. In summarizing Indian religion, he wrote that

"The human mind in its uncultivated state is apt to ascribe the extraordinary occurences of nature, such as earthquakes, thunder, and hurricanes, to the interposition of unseen beings; the troubles and disasters also that are annexed to a savage life, the apprehensions attendant on a precarious subsistence, and those numberless inconveniences which man in his improved state has found means to remedy, are supposed to proceed from the interposition of evil spirits; the savage consequently lives in continual apprehensions of their unkind attacks... Fear has of course a greater share in his devotions than gratitude, and he pays more attention to deprecating the wrath of the evil than to securing the favor of the good beings" (Carver 1778:214).

Carver's strongest condemnation of the Indians, however, concerned their incessant warfare and the unrestrained cruelty their wars encouraged. In his view, the Indians believed that "... war ought to be the chief business of their lives, that there is nothing more desirous than the reputation of being a great warrior, and that the scalps of their enemies, or a number of prisoners are alone esteemed valuable" (Carver 1778:168). As a result, Indians were easily aroused to take to the warpath and, once aroused, were "totally insensible to the controls of reason or humanity" (Carver 1778:226). In war, Carver believed, the Indians displayed their worst characteristics, including cruelty and treachery. "They know not how to keep their fury within any bounds, and consequently that courage and resolution, which would otherwise do them honor, degenerates into a savage ferocity" (Carver 1778:226). Without any restraints, this ferocity led to inhumane levels of both torture and revenge, practices which Carver believed kept the Indians locked into their primitive state.

According to Carver, the Indians' "greatest pride is to surprise and destroy" (Carver 1778:174). Although he acknowledged the "destructive efficacy" of their tactics, he condemned the manner in which the Indians surprised their enemies (Carver 1778:174). Accustomed to European styles of warfare, Carver often equated surprise attacks with treachery, such as Pontiac's successful assaults on frontier garrisons. At Michilimackinac, for example, Pontiac's followers peacefully traded at the fort for several weeks while they plotted their attack. Then, using a game of lacrosse to divert the attention of the soldiers, they attacked without warning. But the cruelest and most sensational - and ultimately the most influential - of all Indian attacks described in the narrative was

203

the Fort William Henry Massacre, which took place in 1757 and in which Carver was personally involved.

There is no doubt that Carver exaggerated both the number of those massacred and the French complicity, but what actually happened is less important than how Carver perceived and described what happened.[2] And according to the narrative, the British garrison at William Henry under Colonel Munro, a total force of two thousand three hundered, was forced to surrender the fort to General Montcalm, whose army of French and Indians totalled thirteen thousand. By the terms of the surrender agreement, signed by both commanders, Munro's entire command and all family members would be allowed to peacefully leave the fort and proceed unmolested on their way. Although they were allowed to keep their arms and personal possessions, all ammunition was left behind. But as soon as the British were outside the walls of the fort, they were attacked and plundered by the Indians. According to Carver, a colonial militia officer stationed at William Henry, the Indians massacred more than half of the men, woman, and children while the French soldiers stood by and watched. Carver wrote that

"the Indians began to murder those that were nearest to them without distinction. It is not in the power of words to give any tolerable idea of the horrid scene that now ensued; men, women, and children were dispatched in the most wanton and cruel manner, and immediately scalped. Many of the savages drank the blood of their victims as it flowed warm from the fatal wound" (Carver 1778:178).[3]

For several pages Carver narrated sensational scenes of the massacre which supposedly either happened to him or near him. Although wounded, he escaped by running into the forest, where he climbed a small hill and watched as the "bloody storm" continued to rage (Carver 1778:181).

In this and other passages, including lurid descriptions of scalping and torturing of captives, Carver described the Indians as having "no idea of moderating the ravages of war" (Carver 1778:191). And he believed that these cruel excesses resulted from the Indians' exaggerated fondness for revenge, which at times dominated their thoughts and actions. In fact, when discussing Indian warfare, he stated that "[t]he passion of revenge, which is the distinguishing characteristic of these people, is the most general motive [for their wars]. Injuries are felt by them with exquisite sensibility, and vengeance pursued with unremitted ardor" (Carver 1778:168). Once motivated by the desire for revenge, the Indians became obsessed, unable to continue the normal routine of their lives until their rage had been satisfied. Elsewhere Carver wrote that the "diabolical lust of revenge... is the predominant passion in the breast of every individual of every tribe" (Carver 1778:189).

As Carver described them, the Indians did not live in perfect harmony with either themselves or their environment, but through what he called the "sanction of immemorial custom" they had achieved a rough balance between needs and sufficiency (Carver 1778:29). Yet with the arrival of the Europeans the Indians began to lose not only their land but as well this balance. Nowhere in the narrative did Carver come closer to approaching an idealized romantic primitivism than in his descriptions of the harmful effects resulting from contact with Europeans. Clearly he preferred "those tribes who have had little intercourse with the Eurpeans" (Carver 1778:25). Throughout the narrative examples were given of the different ways the Indians had been corrupted; everything from economic competition to venereal disease had been acquired from the Europeans.[4] The most frequently cited causes of corruption were the greed of fur traders, French intrigue, and in particular alcohol. When commenting on the natural hospitality of the Indians, Carver stated that he was "convinced, that till they are contaminated by the example, and spirituous liquors of their more refined neighbors, they [would] retain this friendly and inoffensive conduct towards all strangers" (Carver 1778:29). Overall, he believed that the Indians had lost "their original purity." For example, he wrote that

> "The southern tribes, and those that have held a constant intercourse with the French or English, cannot have preserved their manners or their customs in their original purity. They could not avoid acquiring the vices with the language of those they conversed with; and the frequent intoxications they experienced through the baneful juices, introduced among them by the Europeans, have completed a total alteration in their characters" (Carver 1778:129).

Carver, in fact, nearly attributed all the misery he saw among the Indians to alcohol. Concerning the Winnebagos, he stated in his journal that "[t]his people, was it not for their excessive fondness of spirituous liquors, which they purchase of traders at a most extravagant price with their provisions, would live with that ease and plenty which would be almost admired by many white people among us" (Parker 1976:79). Not only were provisions, possessions, and furs traded for alcohol, but also captives. According to Carver, the trading of captives, or "slaves" as he called them, had originally been encouraged by French Jesuits. In order to save captives from torture, they had urged "the traders to purchase such slaves as they met with." But, because of the corrupting influence of alcohol, this plan had backfired.

> "Instead of being the means of preventing cruelty and bloodshed, it only caused dissensions between Indian nations to be carried on with a greater degree of violence, and unremitted ardor. The prize they sought for being no longer revenge or fame, but the acquirement of spirituous liquors, for which their captives were to be exchanged, and for which almost every

nation is immoderately fond, they sought for their enemies with unwonted alacrity, and were constantly on the watch to surprise and carry them off " (Carver 1778:192).

Carver consistently condemned "the little benefit too many of the Indian nations have hitherto received from their intercourse with those who denominate themselves Christians." He felt that the Indians had already acquired too many of the "errors and vices" from Europeans and that these corruptions were responsible for most of the serious problems which confronted the Indians. As a result, he thought that these problems could be resolved if the Indians inherited more positive aspects of European culture. Not surprisingly, Carver advocated greater efforts be taken to Christianize the Indians, which he believed would not only amend Indian superstition but likewise Indian savagery.

"So that the doctrines of genuine and vital christianity be introduced among them... it would clear away the superstitious or idolatrous dross by which the rationality of their religious tenets are obscured. Its mild and beneficent precept would likewise conduce [them] to soften their implacable dispositions, and to refine their savage manners" (Carver 1778:107).

Carver's belief that Christianity would provide a cure-all for all Indian problems and corruptions was indeed simplistic, but it was not pointless. On the contrary, he intended to reduce both the complexity and the severity of problems connected with the Indians specifically to lessen European apprehension of them. Above all else, Carver was a New World advocate, and his narrative was a continual celebration of the American wilderness and its immense potential. According to Carver, who carefully shaped his descriptions to attract interest and to arouse sympathy, it was inevitable that "at some future period, mighty kingdoms will emerge from these wildernesses" (Carver 1778:19). The primary promise described was material prosperity, which seemed almost assured. Not only did the wilderness offer a richness of natural resources but also gold. As Carver described it, somewhere west of the Shining Mountains there was an Indian tribe whose most common utensils were made of gold. Concerning the Shining Mountains (the Rocky Mountains), he stated that "[p]robably in future ages they may be found to contain more riches in their bowels" than all other gold mines known to man (Carver 1778:78). Moreover, the American wilderness not only promised wealth, but also freedom - an idea increasingly popular by the end of the eighteenth century.[5] In the interior, wrote Carver, "future generations may find asylum, whether driven from their country by the ravages of lawless tyrants, or by religious persecutions" (Carver 1778:78). Consequently, in this context Carver's favorable view of the Indians and his simplistic approach to their problems become understandable. So that others would share his enthusiasm and his dreams, he reduced and sometimes ignored the difficulties posed by both wilderness life and Indian-White contact.

Carver's Indians were not irrevocably hostile, only corrupted. They were actually friendly, kind, and generous. The hostilities of the past, including the recent Pontiac's War, resulted from the harmful effects of greedy traders, French intrigue, and alcohol. When these were removed, replaced by more rational English policies and Christianity, then the Indians would exhibit their true hospitable nature. Those things Carver was most critical of (their constant warfare, their curelty, their irrational desire for revenge) would be mollified by the supervision and influence of the English. Inevitably civilized life would replace primitive life, and the Indians, instead of resisting this process, would actually aid it if guided by benevolent policies and humane examples. Just as Carver neglected to mention the severity of the winters in the northern Great Lakes region, he failed to mention exactly where or how the Indians would live in the "mighty kingdoms" of the future. Carver did not intend that this question concern his readers.

There is another factor which influenced Carver as he shaped his image of the Indians - his desire to write a bestseller. When he set out on his journey, he carried with him a commission from Robert Rogers, then commander at Fort Michilimackinac, promising him eight shillings a day for his services. When he returned, he discovered that Rogers had been arrested for treason and that his commission was worthless. With no prospects in America, Carver, then fifty-eight years old, sailed for England, where he hoped to improve his poor financial state by petitioning the government for his money and by selling his narrative. For the next ten years, however, he suffered continual difficulties and disappointments, resulting in poverty and hardship. But throughout this period Carver maintained the hope of ending his financial problems through the publication of his journals, and it was this force of determination which eventually brought about publication in 1778. Yet publication alone was not enough. During the latter half of the eighteenth century the London book market was glutted with travel narratives. Tales from around the world, such as Captain Cook's, were published, pirated, and republished, and in nearly all of them some account of the Noble Savage was evident. Carver's journals, dealing with the little known upper Mississippi, faced steep competition. Without any great discoveries, without any history-making events, Carver was forced to find something in his experiences that would appeal to his readers, and what he discovered and emphasized were the Indians.

As his manuscript journals indicate, Carver carefully rewrote his basic narrative three times, expanding some sections, rearranging others, accentuating the dramatic and the exotic. After he was finished he turned the manuscript over to an editor with the instructions to "embellish or give better sence [sic] to the journal" (Parker 1976:29).[6] The editor responded by nearly doubling the size of the book and by reorganizing its entire structure. Rewriting Carver's description and borrowing passages from previous travel narratives, he specifically expanded the Indian sections in order to capture reader interest and to set Carver up as a kind of Indian authority. He was highly successful in both. As it was finally published, Carver's *Travels* was a collaborative effort between two men who knew what readers wanted in travel narratives and how to satisfy their expectations.

By the late eighteenth century the European imagination was highly responsive to the Noble Savage tradition. According to one literary historian, it was during this period that the Indian emerged as a sympathetic literary character on a widespread popular level (Bissel 1925:213). Both Carver and his editor were aware of this tradition and its appeal, and, in the words of another literary historian, "furnished much support to the Noble Savage idea" (Fairchild 1928:100). Although Carver's Indians departed from the tradition in several ways, their departures could be attributed to either corruptions resulting from European contact or acquired responses to the harsh demands of their wilderness environment. Without a doubt Carver shaped his Indians to appeal to the imagination of his readers. In many ways - intellectually, emotionally, culturally and sociologically - Europeans of the late eighteenth century needed the Noble Savage, and Carver responded to their imaginative needs.

Just how successful he was in reaching his goal of a bestseller is quite clear. The narrative's numerous editions and translations "made Carver a familiar name to explorers, geographers, literary figures, speculators, teachers, students, and others who became interested in the American West in the century following its publication" (Parker 1976:38). Despite the objections raised by some that the book was a mere compilation of previous narratives, Carver's *Travels* remained popular throughout the nineteenth century, making it one of the most popular of all American wilderness narratives. But more important than its popularity was its influence. In its abridged version, originally edited by the German educator and writer, Joachim Heinrich Campe, the narrative reached thousands of young readers, providing many with their first glimpse of America and of the Indians. This abridgment, specifically intended as an educational text for young people, was published in various translations throughout Europe. No other book of its kind reached as many European readers of the nineteenth century, young and old, as did Carver's *Travels* (cp. Parker 1976:229-231).

Tracing the distribution of ideas is never easy, but in the case of Carver a number of direct literary influences can be seen, such as the example of Schiller's poem. In America, for instance, James Fenimore Cooper extensively used the narrative for one of his most famous novels, *The Last of the Mohicans* (1826). As several literary historians have pointed out, Cooper relied on the narrative for information concerning the novel's central scene, the massacre at Fort William Henry, and also for a variety of details concerning Indian manners and habits (cp. French 1960, Philbrick 1964). The correspondences between Carver and Cooper are so great in the massacre scene that at least six "major features" of action are shared (Philbrick 1964:211). An even more striking influence of Carver in America was the word "Oregon," which appeared in print for the first time in Carver's *Travels* (cp. Elliott 1921, 1922, Parker 1976). As described in the narrative, the Oregon was one of the four great rivers in the North American continent and, once discovered somewhere in the west, would establish the mythical northwest passage. This notion was not new, but Carver popularized it. There was, of course, no great Oregon River, but with Carver's help the name became attached to the general area in which the river was thought to be.

In Europe the influence were even greater. Some of the most famous writers in the late eighteenth and early nineteenth centuries read, admired, and used Carver's *Travels*. Schiller's "Totenlied" and the funeral oration in the narrative upon which it is based share not only thoughts and structure but actually words and expression (cp. Augustin 1982, Jantz 1959, Stapf s.a.). In addition to Schiller, two of the most influential of Carver's admirers were William Wordsworth and François-René de Chateaubriand. Not only were both romantic writers known to have read Carver's *Travels* but also to have borrowed details, ideas, and descriptions from it. The three subjects which touched their imaginations the most were Carver's descriptions of wilderness beauty, of Indian religion, and of Indian attitudes towards death. Specifically, Carver's young Winnebago prince devoutly worshipping by the Falls of St. Anthony and the two eloquent funeral speeches inspired both writers.

Wordsworth, for example, once stated that "[t]he only modern books that I read are those of travels..." (Cooper 1915:112). While he was referring to the vast genre of travel narratives, the frequent echoes of Carver in his poetry make it clear that he knew this particular travel narrative fairly well (cp. Bissel 1925, Cooper 1905,1915, Fairchild 1928). Although he alluded to Samuel Hearne's *Journey from Hudson's Bay to the Northern Ocean* as the source for his poem, "The Complaint of a Forsaken Indian Woman," there is as much Carver as Hearne in the poem. In his "Descriptive Sketches," Wordsworth described a rustic peasant praying in the woods by a waterfall in exactly the same manner as Carver's prince. Like the prince, the peasant "holds with God himself communion high, /There where the peal of swelling torrents fills /The skyroofed temple of the eternal hills" (Wordsworth 1888:15). Clearly, what Wordsworth admired in Carver was the natural religion of the Indians, which in many ways reinforced his romantic notions of communion with nature. But in "Book Three" of *The Excursion* Wordsworth expressed his disillusionment with the more savage aspects of Indian life. Using imagery directly out of Carver, he described the disappointing discoveries of the Solitary, a traveler recently returned from America. Having set out to discover "Primeval Nature's child," the Solitary found little to please or inspire him except Carver's "Muccawiss" (his name for the whippoorwill).

209

"So, westward, tow'rd the unviolated woods
I bent my way; and roaming far and wide,
Failed not to greet the merry Mocking-bird;
And, while the melancholy Muccawiss
(The sportive bird's companion in the grove)
Repeated o're and o're his plaintive cry,
I sympathized at leisure with the sound;
But that pure archetype of human greatness,
I found him not. There, in his stead, appeared
A creature, squalid, vengeful, and impure;
Remorseless, and submissive to no law
But superstitious fear, and abject sloth"
(Wordsworth 1888:439).

Such disillusionment with primitive life is not evident in the writings of Chateaubriand, who used Carver's narrative in creating his own Indian characters. As several literary historians have pointed out, Chateaubriand was not only influenced by Carver but actually borrowed passages from him (cp. Berkhofer 1978, Chinard 1918, Gautier 1949, Slotkin 1973). In his travel narrative, *Voyage en Amérique* (1827), for example, Chateaubriand showed obvious influences in his descriptions of Indian ferocity (he also mentioned the drinking of blood), of Indian indolence, and of Indian superstition and fear. The treatment of adultery, of prisoners, and of death also exhibited more than a passing knowledge of Carver. His descriptions of Dakota language, moreover, can be traced directly to *Travels*. Significantly, he also shared with Carver the view that the Indians had been thoroughly spoiled by contact with Euro-Americans. Civilization, he believed, by introducing commercial trade and alcohol among the Indians, had brutalized them. Instead of being the Noble Savages of the forest, he referred to acculturated Indians as beggars at the doors of trading posts. In his novels, *Atala* (1801) and *René* (1805), however, his Indian characters remained quite noble. Chactas, for example, had much the same natural nobility as Carver's Winnebago prince. The most famous scene in *Atala*, the climactic burial of Atala in the forest by a mountain waterfall, echoed Carver's funeral speech as well as his prince's devotions.

Carver's motivations - to promote and to entertain - are literary rather than historical impulses. Interested more in acquiring readers than in presenting facts, he carefully selected and arranged detail in order to create a particular image of the Indians - an image intended to manipulate reader response on imaginative and emotional levels. As Berkhofer stated so well,

"The Indian of imagination and ideology has been real, perhaps more real, than the Native American of actual experience and contact... Although each succeeding generation presumed its imagery based more upon the Native Americans of observation and report, the Indians of imagination and ideology continued to be derived as much from the polemical and creative needs of whites as from what they heard and read of actual Native Americans" (Berkhofer 1978:71).

Carver's Indians reveal much about the "polemical and creative needs" of his culture. Despite accuracy of detail, they are literary characters - imaginative representations created to satisfy European preconceptions of primitive life in the North American wilderness. Carver gave his Indians exactly those virtues he felt his culture lacked, but at the same time he gave them those sensational characteristics which met the requirements of the European definiton of "savagery."

What Carver actually observed among the Indians and what were already Indian stereotypes are difficult to separate. Certainly he mixed the two together. Before he even began writing, the Noble Savage tradition was already well established and much admired. In fact, two of Carver's sources, Lahontan (cp. Chinard 1935) and Adair (cp. Washburn 1973) specifically praised the Noble Savage in order to criticize the European (Berkhofer 1978). Yet, ultimately, the question of what he observed among the Indians and what he imposed upon them, like the question of what is and what is not Carver, is irrelevant. Carver is significant as a popular writer, as one who touched the imaginations of an astonishing number of people. Writing during a time of great intellectual turbulence, he popularized ideas which directly influenced the attitudes of his readers and indirectly through the works of other writers.

Not an original thinker, Carver was locked into the intellectual climate of his time, unable to escape preconceptions and prejudices. When he went into the wilderness, he carried with him standard Euro-American conceptions of what civilization and savagery were. When he wrote his narrative, he described the Indians according to these concepts, and these notions were in turn distributed to all those he influenced. His Indians were noble, but they were also savage. Although he expressed admiration for the Indians, he never for a moment doubted that "stately palaces and solemn temples... [would] supplant the Indian huts" (Carver 1778:19-20). Such - he believed - was progress, the course of civilization.

NOTES

1. For two examples of this, see the essays "On Cannibals" and "On Coaches" by Montaigne (1595), and Lahontan (1705).
2. There is without a doubt an anti-French bias in Carver's *Travels*. Published in London in 1778, the same year France entered the American Revolution against the British, the narrative appeals to traditional British prejudices, which had been aroused by the recent political events.
3. Elsewhere Carver described the Indians as devouring the hearts of their victims. Although he specifically stated that they were not cannibals, he believed that their uncontrolled rage led them to acts of atrocity. Such descriptions contributed to the myth of the "bloodthirsty savage."
4. Carver specifically stated: "I think I may venture to pronounce that it [venereal disease] had not its origin in North America" (Carver 1778:213).
5. Carver is ambiguous about the American Revolution. In the introduction he referred to the "unhappy divisions that at present subsist between Great-Britain and America," but he did not make any reference to either future British or American empires in the New World. Cautiously, he stated only that the country "promises, in some future period, to be an inexhaustible source of riches to that people who shall be so fortunate as to possess it" (Carver 1778:19,23).
6. Carver's editor is believed to have been Alexander Bicknell. For information concerning Bicknell's role, see (Parker 1976:31-33).

Adair, James
1775   The History of the American Indians: Particularly those Nations adjoining to the Mississippi, East and West Florida, Georgia, South and North Carolina, and Virginia. London: Edward and Charles Dilly.

Augustin, Siegfried
1982   Nadowessiers Totenlied. Der Indianer im Gedicht. München: Ronacher-Verlag.

Berkhofer, Robert F. Jr.
1978   The White Man's Indian. New York: Alfred A. Knopf.

Bissel, Benjamin
1925   The American Indian in English Literature of the Eighteenth Century. New Haven: Yale University Press.

Blegen, Theodore C.
1963   Minnesota: A History of the State. St. Paul: University of Minnesota Press.

Bourne, E. G.
1906   The Travels of Jonathan Carver. American Historical Review 2:287-302.

Carver, Jonathan
1778   Travels through the Interior Parts of North America in the Years 1766, 1767, 1768. London: J. Walter (Edition cited in text is Walpole, NH: Isaiah Thomas, 1813).

Chinard, Gilbert
1918   L'exotisme américain dans l'oeuvre de Chateaubriand. Paris: Hachette.
1935   L'Amérique et le réve exotique dans la littérature française au XVIIᵉ et au XVIIIᵉ siècle. Paris: Droze.

Cooper, Lane
1905   Wordsworth's Sources. Athenaeum, p. 498.
1915   A Glance at Wordsworth's Reading. In: Methods and Aims in the Study of Literature. (New York: Ginn and Company), 96-132.

Elliot, T. C.
1921   The Origin of the Name Oregon. Quarterly of the Oregon Historical Society 22:91-115.
1922   Jonathan Carver's Source for the Name Oregon. Quarterly of the Oregon Historical Society 23: 53-69.

Fairchild, Hoxie Neal
1928   The Noble Savage, A Study in Romantic Naturalism. New York: Columbia University Press.

French, David P.
1960   James Fenimore Cooper and the Fort William Henry. American Literature 32: 28-38.

Gautier, J. M.
    1949   Un Inspirateur Anglais de Chateaubriand et de Schiller: Jonathan
            Carver. Revue de Littérature Comparée 33: 416-422.
Jantz, Harold
    1959   Schiller's Indian Threnody. In: John R. Frey (ed.), Schiller 1759/1959,
            Commemorative American Studies (Urbana: University of Illinois
            Press), 58-75.
Lahontan, Baron de
    1705   Dialogues curiex entre l'auteur et un sauvage de bon sens qui a
            voyagé et mémoires de l'Amérique Septentrionale. La Haye.
Medeiros, Patricia M.
    1977   Three Travelers. In: Everett Emerson (ed.), American Literature
            1764-1789. The Revolutionary Years, (Madison: University of
            Wisconsin Press), 195-201.
Montaigne, Michel Eyquem de
    1595   Essais. Paris.
Parker, John
    1976   The Journals of Jonathan Carver. St. Paul: Minnesota Historical
            Society Press.
Parkman, Francis
    1851   History of the Conspiracy of Pontiac. New York.
Philbrick, Thomas
    1964   The Sources of Cooper's Knowledge of Fort William Henry. American
            Literature 36: 209-214.
Savage, Henry Jr.
    1979   Discovering America 1700-1875. New York: Harper & Row.
Slotkin, Richard
    1973   Regeneration Through Violence. The Mythology of the American
            Frontier. Middletown, Conn.: Wesleyan University Press.
Stapf, Paul
    s.a.   Der Briefwechsel zwischen Schiller und Goethe. München: Emil
            Vollmer Verlag.
Washburn, Wilcomb E.
    1973   James Adair's "Noble Savages." In: Lawrence H. Leder (ed.), The
            Colonial Legacy, III: Historians of Nature and Man's Nature, IV:
            Early Nationalist Historians (New York: Harper & Row), 91-120.
Wordsworth, William
    1888   The Complete Works of William Wordsworth. London.

THE TRAVELING EXHIBITION OF CAPTAIN SAMUEL HADLOCK, JR.: ESKIMOS IN EUROPE, 1822-1826

Robin K. Wright

Captain Samuel Hadlock, Jr. (1792-1829) was a 19th century entrepreneur who made and lost his fortune in Europe in the 1820's while exhibiting a traveling show of Eskimos. He is one of the earliest Americans known to have toured with Native Americans in Europe, having set out almost twenty years before the more famous George Catlin did with his Indian Gallery. Catlin became famous largely through his book, *Letters and Notes on the Manners, Customs and Condition of the North American Indians*, which was first published in London in 1841, and had appeared in ten editions by 1876. Hadlock lacked Catlin's literary talents, but he did keep a journal during the four years he was in Europe. This journal remained an obscure document in the hands of his descendants until 1934, when Rachel Field used it to write a book about Hadlock entitled *God's Pocket*. This book was not widely distributed, however, and Hadlock has remained a relatively unknown character. For this reason, an article about his life should be of value to those interested in the history of 19th century Indian exhibitions.

Late in 1821, Captain Hadlock set off for Europe from his home in the Cranberry Isles, Maine. He took with him an Eskimo couple, their two small children, and a large collection of artifacts. This included ten live sled dogs and a sled, a kayak, harpoons, bows and arrows and other hunting equipment, ivory carvings, native clothing from the Eastern Arctic as well as the Eastern Woodlands, and stuffed seals, bears, and birds. While exhibiting these "curiosities" throughout Europe during the next four years. Hadlock lost all four of the Eskimos and at least nine out of ten of the sled dogs through death, made and spent large amounts of money, and parted with most of the artifacts he had brought with him. He returned home in 1826 with what remained of his collection, a new wife whom he had married in Prussia, and a daughter born in Paris shortly before their departure. Hadlock fully intended to go back to Europe. He owned a house in Prussia and had promised his wife they would return there. He planned to kill and stuff a collection of seals and other arctic animals and sell them to European royalty for their collections of curiosities. His plans were cut short in 1829, however, when his ship, the *Minerva*, and all hands were lost at sea while on a voyage to the Arctic in pursuit of seals.

The primary source of information on Hadlock's four years in Europe is the two-volume, hand-written journal he kept during that time.[1] It is now preserved by the Islesford Historical Society Museum in Islesford, Maine. The journal is difficult to read with its flowing script and liberal phonetic spellings, but when it is deciphered, it reveals many descriptions of the sites he saw, with occasional asides for philosophical musings and poetry. Included are an account of the legend concerning the well of St. Winifred at the town of Holywell in the north of Wales; a poem about St. Winifred; a description of the Giants' Causeway in Ireland; an explanation of the solar system; a chronological list of important events from the creation of the world through the death of King George II in 1820; long lists of English words with German equivalents; a graphic account of prostitutes in Hamburg from which only one word has been deleted by a later reader; a three-page speculation on the works of nature versus the works of man; and a long version of the legend behind the Feast Day of St. John of Nepomuk celebrated in Prague. Rarely among these writings does one find a reference to the Eskimos. The brief descriptions of his exhibition are usually limited to a comment on his earnings. Several pages have been cut out or rearranged and resewn. Thus, we are forced to piece together Hadlock's story from what remains of the original document.

Rachel Field's romantic account of Hadlock's life, *God's Pocket*, was based primarily on Hadlock's journal, but also on the recollections of Hadlock's grandson, Samuel Sanford, who was in his eighties at the time she interviewed him in the 1930's. It is from this book that we have some information on Hadlock's life before and after the time documented by his journal.

Recently, several Vienna newspaper reviews, including one by the famous zoologist Leopold Fitzinger, and advertisements dating from the time of Hadlock's visit to Vienna have been located by Gerda Barth. These have added dramatically to the story and provided many fascinating and previously unknown details about the Eskimos and Hadlock's exhibition. It is only from these articles that we know the native names and ages of the Eskimos, how and where Hadlock recruited them, and the existence and death of a second Eskimo child. Hadlock's exhibition is described in far greater detail in these reviews than in either Hadlock's journal or Field's book, and through them we now know that in addition to a kayak performance, a re-enactment of an Eskimo marriage ceremony and a demonstration of sled dogs pulling a sledge were part of the show. In addition, for the first time we have learned that Hadlock's museum displayed some South Pacific artifacts including a preserved Maori head. Further material has been found by Christian Feest in Leipzig and Dresden and more research is being planned by him in the other European cities visited by Hadlock, which will be necessary to reconstruct the full story. What is known so far, however, is interesting enough.

Samuel Hadlock, Jr. was born on 11 March 1792 on Little Cranberry Isle, Maine, one of five sons and one daughter, whose father, Samuel Hadlock, Sr., built fishing boats and schooners, and participated in the West Indies and Atlantic Coast trade. His brothers continued in their father's line of work, but Samuel Jr. became fascinated with the Arctic waters and preferred sealing and whaling in the far north, bringing back many curiosities from that region. One Vienna newspaper account tells us that Hadlock spent a month with Capt. Parry

Fig. 1. Captain Samuel Hadlock, Jr.Cut-out silhouette by Edward Ward Foster, 1824. Courtesy Islesford Historical Society Museum, Islesford, Maine.

(probably Sir W. E. Parry the Arctic explorer) on "Malwille" (Melville?) Island. The same account reports that his whaling also took him to the south pole, which would explain the presence of South Pacific artifacts in his collection (Anonymous 1825a:634). American sealers and whalers were present in waters near New Zealand in the first decade of the 19th century (Owens 1981:31), but no mention of any trip there by Hadlock is made in his journal or Field's book. Hadlock married Amah Richardson of Bass Harbor in 1812, and they had three children, Samuel Taylor, Sally, and Smith Cobb. When Amah died in 1821, Hadlock left his three children in the care of his married sister, took his entire savings, his collection of curiosities, a family of Eskimos, and set off to make his fortune exhibiting his menagerie in Europe (Field 1936:8-13).

Hadlock gives us no information on where or how he met the family of Eskimos, but we know from Fitzinger's interview with Hadlock that he met them in "Baffins-Bay" while on a whaling expedition. Fitzinger tells us that Hadlock was so endeared to them that they voluntarily decided to come with him to Europe, and that they were baptized George and Marie in Hudsons Bay after Capt. Hadlock had instructed them in the Christian religion. George's native name was Niagungitok, and Marie's was Coonahnik, according to Fitzinger, and they were 27 and 25 years old (Fitzinger 1825:529; also Anonymous 1824c:519). A different Vienna reviewer gives their names as Neiangunitto and Kunahinok (Anonymous 1825a:635), whereas a lithograph published in

217

Dresden spells their names Niakungitok and Coonunnak. According to Field (1936:22), the woman was named Mary or Mamie Megunticook, probably derived from George's name, Niagungitok. Field's information was based on the recollections of Hadlock's descendants and is probably not as accurate as Fitzinger's first hand information from Hadlock. Hadlock never mentions the woman by name in his journal, and her husband is only referred to as George. He also never mentions the Eskimo children in his journal, but Rachel Field was told by her informants that there was indeed a "papoose" (Field 1936:21). Fitzinger tells us that they had two children. One died at eight month of age during the sea trip, and the other, three years old, died in England (Fitzinger 1825:529).

Hadlock exhibited his show in New York, Philadelphia, and Baltimore before leaving for Europe (Anonymous 1825a:634), and rather uncomplimentary news preceded him across the Atlantic: "One Hadlock," reported the London *Literary Gazette* for 21 May 1821, "brought back with him to New York an Esquimaux man a woman, and a child. Of these he made a show, and their exploits in a seal skin canoe, &c. were exhibited at so much per head to the natives of that city. Some rumours having got afloat, that he had kidnapped these poor Indians, he was indicted for a trespass and battery; but the mayor acquitted him" (Anonymous 1821:501). Hadlock probably sailed from the east coast to Liverpool late in 1821, as the first entry in the journal was made in Chester, just south of Liverpool, in January 1822. He may have had an agent at the beginning of his tour, as he mentions in his journal a Mr. Chidingdon who fell ill in Wales and was left behind. From Wales the entourage crossed to Ireland on the King's Steam Packet and spent five months in Dublin from January 1822 until early June, staying in lodgings at the corner of Sackville and Abbey streets. Hadlock went before the mayor of Dublin "to gitt permition to excibitt thare," and paid two pounds and ten shillings for his license. He says of his earnings for those months in Dublin, "Dun little good." He traveled from Dublin through Drogheda, Belfast, Limavady, and Coleraine. He exhibited at Donnybrook Fair in Ireland, and said of his earnings, "I dun torible wall, concidering I had bin exciberting at Dublin five munthes before." The fair lasted seven days, and after it closed he took passage on the steamboat *Mountaineer* and returned to Liverpool.

From Liverpool the troupe traveled by canal boat to Preston where the Preston Guild Fair was about to open. This fair was held only once every twenty years and lasted seven days. Hadlock was distressed to find lodgings scarce and expensive due to the popularity of the event: "lodinges was 20£. per weeke and I kood not git a room in the town to Excibit in, so I did not make mutch at that time." From Preston he went to Ormskirk to another fair, and from there to Wigan, Reading, Nottingham, Hull, and Lincoln. Somewhere during this period in the tour Marie became ill and died, yet no direct mention is made of it in the journal. The only clue to her death is Hadlock's account

218

of recruiting a gypsy woman to fill the vacancy in the show. This is first mentioned in his description of their stay at Hull when he refers to, "the Jipsey [gypsy] that I drest up in sealskin and excibited as an Indian Woomern [woman]." Field assumes that the baby had died by this time because no mention is made of either George or Hadlock having to care for it (Field 1936:38). We know from Fitzinger's account that the three year old child died in England (Fitzinger 1825:529).

From Hull they went to a fair in Lincoln, but here Hadlock states "the Madistrate found out that one was a Jipesey... the Magastrates found out that I was imposing on the Publick. Thay was determined to stop me and send us to prison for the efence commited on the publick... But I goot Knues [news] of the same and sot off that daye at another town and cleaned myself of them and laft [laughed] at thare under taking... Begun in another town at the same trade. Dun Wall." At Grantham the gypsy proved to be more trouble than she was worth, for Hadlock reports: "Dun middling wall, concidering that I had but wone [one] Indian. The Jipesey wass a Drunken Dissipated Cretour so I kood not depend upon hur. The other logers would tell that she want [wasn't] an Ingin which would git whispered about the town in a fue [few] owers [hours]. So it provented peple of kuming to see them which dun me mutch hurt at aney plase that I went." Rather than lose any more profits, he "turned the Jipsey out and took Cotch [coach] for London."

After three weeks in London he found another woman to replace the gypsy: "Gut another womern which ansored my purpes better then the first, she being the same kuller [color] and the same fetchers [features] which pases without Dispute. She conducks herself better then the Jipsey... I rote this in Pickidilly." This second replacement for Marie must have been well cast and considerably more convincing than the first gypsy, since she was apparently still with the show when it reached Vienna, and managed to fool the reviewers there completely. With his new recruit he set off for Reading, Abingdon, and Cheltenham. He stayed in Oxford for three weeks where he "Don Torable wall concidering the wether so bad." He next went to Bath where he spent another three weeks, but "Dun nothing," proceeding on to Frome and Bristol where he found a ship to carry letters home. At Bristol during the Spring Fair, George became ill and Hadlock decided to go on to London, where George recovered from his illness. On the road between Bristol and London, the troupe suffered another setback when a valuable bale of goods (worth £100) was stolen from the van. Hadlock must have been sorry indeed to lose it since "It contained the best of the curiosities that I had and all of the Indian dresses."

It was probably during the second of his two stays in London that Hadlock sat for a cut-out silhouette portrait (Fig. 1). It was done by one of the best of the silhouette artists of the time, Edward Ward Foster, who signed and dated the portrait 1824 (Field 1936:52-53). In London Hadlock had some competition, for a rival exhibit which featured "the Botokado Indian" had already been shown there (cp.King 1987). Another display of Botocudos (a coastal Brazilian tribe) also preceded the Eskimos in Vienna where they are mentioned as "those lately seen Indians called Botocudos" in an ad to promote Hadlock's show (*Allgemeines Intelligenzblatt zur Oesterreichisch-Kaiserlichen Wiener-Zeitung* no. 136, Vienna, 17 Juni 1825:p. 892). At this point Hadlock may have returned to Dublin and Londonderry, since he describes a horseace held near Londonderry, but this section of the journal has been resewn, and some pages are missing or out of place. His last entry in England was written in Hull in the early summer of 1824: "I took passage in the Brig Capt. Skarborough for Hamburg in Jerminey [Germany] on the continent to try my fortune thair."

Hadlock arrived in Hamburg on the 4th of July, 1824, where he hired an agent who is never mentioned by name in the journal. The first engagement he arranged was in the Simon Mansion Hotel. Hadlock's comment on the business there was "not dun much." He stayed in Hamburg until 11 September. He proceeded from there to Leipzig where he arrived on the 16th for the famous Michaelmas Fair held yearly in September. In Leipzig he had a booth built for the exhibit, and records that his receipts for the three week fair were $1500, at eight Groschen admission per person and half price for children and the serving class. The show was reviewed twice in the *Leipziger Tageblatt* (Anonymous 1824b,c) and advertised by handbills (Anonymous 1824a) and frequent newspaper ads. Here for the first time Hadlock describes George's performance in his kayak: "On Sunday in the after noon I put the Indian on the watter... for the last time in this town whare I took $600 in 2 owers [hours]. The croudes of spectaters ware great and mutch plesed to behold a native from the arctic regions Exploy [employ] his boat with such admirable dexteritey and kill his game so wall as he did."

It is difficult to trace Hadlock's exact route from Leipzig, as the journal has been reordered, but it is clear that he eventually made his way to Berlin, where he fell in love and got married. There is only one reference to his marriage in the journal, made in 1826 in Paris after the birth of their child. Thus, Field was forced to reconstruct the story from the recollections of Hadlock's grandson. According to Field, Hadlock had taken his exhibition to Charlottenburg, a suburb of Berlin. In order to get a license to exhibit in the town, he went to the house of the magistrate, Ludwig Russ, a wealthy and influential man who rose to an important position in the Royal Brass Foundry of Charlottenburg. His daughter, Dorothea Albertina Wilhelmina Celeste Russ, age 20, received Hadlock in her father's absence. According to the story, they fell instantly in love and Hadlock proposed marriage before the day was over. Her father is said to have opposed the marriage, and insisted that his daughter only marry an established housholder. For this reason Hadlock proceeded to liquidate most of his assets and purchase a house, said to have cost him no less than ten thousand dollars. He also acquired a coach and pair of horses in which to travel in style with his new wife (Field 1936:80-90).

Fig. 2. "The Eskimo in Moritzburg": George's water performance flanked by full-figures of "George Niakungitok" and "Marie Coonunnak." Above the only surviving sled dog in front of a tent. Lithograph by Rau after drawing by F.D.Reichel, Dresden 1825. Courtesy Museum der Geschichte der Stadt Dresden.

It must have been sometime during the period of his courtship, in late 1824, that some of Hadlock's collection of artifacts were acquired by the Kunstkammer of the Kings of Prussia. Twenty of these artifacts are now in the Museum für Völkerkunde in Berlin. It is tempting to speculate that he may have sold these artifacts in order to raise the money required to purchase a house. Or it may be that they were a gift to his father-in-law, who may have donated them to the Royal Museum in Hadlock's name. All of this must be speculation, however, since there is no documentation accompanying the Hadlock collection other than his name and the date, 1824.

The journal indicates that Hadlock went to Potsdam on 9 January 1825, where he visited the royal gardens and the palace. From there he went to Dresden, the capital of Saxony. He must have returned to Berlin in March, however, for the marriage certificate preserved by his grandson indicates that on 20 March 1825, the wedding took place. For some unknown reason Hadlock henceforth called his wife Hannah Caroline rather than her given names, perhaps because he had difficulty pronouncing them. They must have embarked immediately after their marriage for Dresden, since the journal states that four days later, on 24 March, the King of Saxony, Frederick Augustus I, presented him with a gold snuff box as a present. The king gave Hadlock the use of the palace gardens in Moritzburg for an extended run, and his journal records of his earnings here, "I exhibited on the watter in the great gardin whare I took $446 dollars in the furst day, the seckent day $200, the third day $150, the fourth $36 and finished with this town" (cp. Fig. 2).

Hadlock, his wife, and the company proceeded from Dresden to Prague where they arrived sometime in April and stayed until late May. It was here that Hadlock must have commissioned Antonio Sachetti, a theater painter in Prague, to paint a panorama of Baffin Bay and Copper Island, 30 feet by 12 feet, which replaced an earlier one, 40 feet long, but probably already worn out after many years of traveling (Anonymous 1824a). Fitzinger reviewed it favorably in Vienna, saying it was sufficiently well done to give an idea of a polar landscape (Fitzinger 1825:531). From Prague the company went to Vienna where they arrived 5 June and opened their exhibition on the 12th. The show received several reviews, and show times were advertised frequently in several newspapers from 17 June through 11 August. Admission was one guilder, with children and people from the serving classes admitted at half price (Reviews: *Wiener Zeitschrift* June 28, 1825; Fitzinger 1825 [July 5]; *Der Sammler* July 23 and August 23, 1825; *Allgemeine Theaterzeitung* August 11, 1825; Ads: *Allgemeines Intelligenzblatt* June 17, 1825; *Theaterzeitung* July 21 and August 2, 1825; *Wiener Zeitschrift* July 19, August 2, and August 11, 1825, *Wiener Zeitung* July 18, August 3, August 6, August 9, and August 13, 1825; *Der Sammler* August 2, 1825).

In addition to newspaper accounts, a large poster with images of both George and Marie (i.e. the second impostor) is preserved in the Vienna City Library (Fig. 3), based on "Mr. Schadow's very true drawing" (Anonymous 1825a:635; for a detailed discussion of the original drawings, see Israel 1987). Fitzinger describes Marie as having tattoos on cheeks and forehead, and wearing a fishbone nosestick, with typical features of the Mongolian race and hair like horse hair (Fitzinger 1825:529). In the poster she is shown wearing beaded nose ornaments and beaded hair pendants, but tattoos on the cheeks and forehead are not visible. The fact that everyone was fooled by her appearance indicates the total success that Hadlock had with the new Marie in concealing her true identity and avoiding another brush with the law. Whether Hadlock pierced her nose and tattooed her face or merely inked on her tattoos and simulated a pierced nose will never be known. Her principle role in the show was in the marriage ceremony which involved a dance and the eating of raw fish and "train" oil (oil rendered from whale, fish, or sea mammals), a ritual that she apparently performed quite convincingly.

Only a few clues that "Marie" was in fact an impostor are found in the reviews. Fitzinger tells us that the Eskimos spoke amongst themselves and with the Captain mostly by signs and some English, and what they said they said softly (Fitzinger 1825:529; but see Idiens 1987 for a similar observation on Eskimos displayed in Scotland). Thus no on heard Marie speaking the Eskimo

Mit hoher obrigkeitlicher Bewilligung.

Es wird einem hohen Adel und dem geehrten Publikum hierdurch ergebenst bekannt gemacht, daß

Zwey junge äußerst interessante und bewundernswürdige

Esquimaux = Indianer,

ein Mann und eine Frau (in ihrer aus Seehundsfellen künstlich mit Rennthier-Sehnen genähten Landestracht) von der Baffins-Bay am Nordpol, die vor kurzem durch den berühmten Kapitän Parry auf seiner Entdeckungsreise daselbst zuerst vorgefunden, und welche die ersten sind, die je nach Europa gekommen: Zugleich mit einer vortrefflichen und treu dargestellten

Panoramischen Ansicht der Baffins-Bay,

woselbst diese Esquimaux zuerst vorgefunden worden sind, nebst einer Ansicht der Land-Expedition vom Kapitain Franklin und der Kupfer-Insel. Zugleich ist auch ein

schöner Esquimaux-Schlittenhund,

nebst einem

Neu-Seeländischen Häuptling

eines kanibalischen Stammes am Südpol,

zu sehen, der in seiner mit bunten Vogelfedern verzierten Landestracht, ganz so, als wenn er lebte, dargestellt und dessen präservirter und schön tatowirter Kopf besonders merkwürdig ist. Ferner ein reichhaltiges

Museum

seltener und merkwürdiger Naturalien, Waffen und Kunstgegenstände aus den entferntesten Welttheilen, die zugleich belehrend und interessant und kürzlich erst von Amerika über England, Hamburg, Berlin und Dresden hieher gekommen sind.

Der Schauplatz ist im Saal zum Sperl in der Leopoldstadt, der Eintritt täglich des Vormittags von 10 bis 2 Uhr, Nachmittags von 4 bis 7 Uhr.
An Sonn-und Feyertagen wird erst um 4 Uhr geöffnet.

Der Preis ist 1 fl. W. W. Kinder unter 10 Jahren zahlen die Hälfte.

Fig. 3. Poster announcing display of the two "Esquimaux-Indians" and Hadlock's Museum in Vienna, 1825. Portraits of George and Marie after drawings by J.G.Schadow. Courtesy Stadtbibliothek Wien.

223

language. An anonymous reviewer tells us that the features of the man showed more "natural" characteristics than those of the woman, having small eyes and protruding cheek bones, while Marie is described as pretty, having more regular and common features (Anonymous 1825a:635,636).

According to Rachel Field, at one time there was a wood engraving of Marie which she saw hanging on Hadlock's grandson's wall. It had sustained smoke damage in a fire, but she was able to make out the image of a native woman wearing "a headdress of feathers and heavy ropes of beads," looking more like a Plains Indian than an Eskimo. The wood cut may have been one of the handbills used to advertise the show (Field 1936:21-22). Samuel Hadlock refers to the couple in his journal sometimes as "Esquimaux-Indians." There is no doubt that Hadlock was more interested in his profits than in any ethnographic accuracy, and would not have hesitated to use the more famous Plains Indians' appearance on his flier in order to attract a larger audience. It is possible that the wood engraving seen by Field was a stock image of a North American Indian rather than a portrait of Marie, but so far no such handbill has come to light: The Leipzig one carries no illustrations at all, whereas the Vienna poster is graced by the Schadow portraits.

George is described in greater detail than Marie in the reviews. He was an artist and sold his pen and pencil drawings of Arctic scenes of his family and dog. He was most remarkably skilled at paddling his kayak and spearing birds in flight, and could spear small coins in the center at 10 to 20 paces. He also demonstrated driving the dog sled, and though ten dogs were originally brought to Europe, only one remained by the time the group reached Leipzig. Nevertheless, the remaining dog was hitched to the sled and reportedly pulled George around with great vitality. The dog was described as a true breed, non-barking, harmless to humans but agressive against cats and other dogs, and lazy because of the warm climate. Both George and Marie are said to have adapted to the European climate and diet, liking roast beef, potatoes and coffee (Anonymous 1824c:519, 1825a:636), but in reality, the Eskimos must have fared little better than the dogs, and succumbed very quickly.

We are told that Mr. Karsten, a native Swede, was in charge of Hadlock's museum in Vienna, and answered the question of the visitors (Anonymous 1825b:352). There was also a printed description of the museum (Anonymous 1824a), several of whose descriptions were criticized by Fitzinger. Walrus tusks were described as shark teeth and one piece had the highly unlikely description of an Eskimo bed-spread made of kangaroo skin (Fitzinger 1825: 531). In addition to the Eskimo artifacts, the Vienna reviews tell us that Hadlock had a collection of artifacts from the South Pacific (or "south pole" as they refer to it). The star attraction of this display was the preserved head and simulated body of a Maori man dressed in a traditional costume. The display must have emphasized the cannibalism practiced by the Maori as well as the dramatic Maori tattoos, as one reviewer commented: "One can tell from his wild, boodthirsty face that he has tasted human flesh" (Anonymous 1825a:636).

Fitzinger tells us that Hadlock's Maori head was the well preserved head of "Rungitida Amas," head chief of "Coradica," who came to England with Capt. "Dicksen" to buy weapons, and, finding himself without money, he joined Hadlock's show in England. He died in Leeds, 20 April 1824, at age 22. Capt. Hadlock said he had a cast made of the body showing the deep incisions of the tattoo, and had the head prepared in the same way as that recently shown with van Aken's menagerie. The prepared head was set on the cast body and was dressed with Rungitida's own clothes (Fitzinger 1825:531).

The amount of detail in Hadlock's Maori story suggests that it might be true. He gives us the name Rungitida Amas. Rungitida could stand for Rangitira, the common Maori title for clan leaders or members of the aristocracy, but Maori words never end in a consonant or use the letters "s" as in Amas which may stand for Amahau. The town he is said to have come from, Coradica, probably refers to Kororareka, originally a Maori village, which became the largest whaling settlement in the Bay of Islands in New Zealand and was frequented by American and English sealers and whalers in the early 19th century (Owens 1981:33). The date and place of his death, the name of the captain with whom he came to England, and the method of preserving the head are also recorded. If this story is true, Capt. Hadlock shows himself to have been grimly devoted to his pursuit of profits, even to the extent of preserving and displaying his late Maori colleague.

Hadlock never mentions an encounter with a Maori chief in his journal, which seems odd, since it must have been a noteworthy experience if true, but Hadlock is known to have omitted other life and death details from his journal. It is tempting to speculate that Hadlock may have bought this preserved Maori head somewhere in his travels, either in England or New Zealand, and made this story up to go with it. Preserved Maori heads were produced in large numbers and sold as curiosities to visiting Euro-Americans by the Maori themselves. Maoris are known to have traveled from New Zealand to England, and exhibits of Maori curiosities such as van Aken's menagerie referred to by Fitzinger were likely shown throughout Europe during this time. It may well be that Rungitida came to England with Captain Dicksen,[2] met Hadlock there and joined his show, and died in Leeds just as Hadlock said. It is hard to believe, however, that Hadlock would have been capable of having Rungitida's head preserved using the complicated and time consuming Maori technique. Fitzinger doesn't tell us that Hadlock learned the technique from van Aken, just that the head is preserved in the same way (Fitzinger 1825:531). Hadlock may have had a cast of Rungitida's body made and then buried him after his death, appropriating his clothes and other artifacts which could have included a preserved head. Whether or not Hadlock preserved this Maori head himself, had it preserved, or merely acquired it along with his other South Pacific artifacts, this story is intriguing and worthy of further research.

In his journal, Hadlock says nothing of his South Pacific collection or the museum, and in fact says very little of Vienna itself: "This cittey is the Resedens of the Emper of Ostrey [Austria], allso the son [the young Duke of Reichstadt] of Boney [Bonaparte], as the emper is his Grandfather." He doesn't mention performing for the Emperor or Bonaparte's son, but he toured their palaces and grounds and writes of them: "A menagrey [menagerie] thair and plentey of fish in the pond of watter in the gardin." From Vienna he traveled to nearby towns such as Baden and Pressburg, in Hungary, where one of his horses died, and he was forced to purchase another pair.

On 24 September 1825, the Hadlock troupe set off from Vienna for Munich. Hadlock visited the King of Bavaria's summer palace outside Munich. In Munich he attended the theater when the Royal family was in attendance. Less than three days later, Hadlock had an audience with the king, Joseph Maximilian IV, in the palace gardens, where he presented his show complete with George's performance in his kayak: "On the 31st [sic!] of September I Exhibited for his Majesty at his pallis in Nimphingburg [Nymphenburg] with the Ingin on the watter in his Gardin, when the Quean of Swedland [Sweden] was thair and the royall famley of the King. Thay seemed to be mutch plesed to see the maney manuvers on the watters with the Esquimaux. The Gardin is splendid. Thair is 2 fountans as large round as my bodey and osends [ascends] 50 feate in the air. Thair the gratest founts in the world." On 4 October: "I preformed for the Rushish [Russian] imbasedor in the Inglish gardin of the King." At the same time, he established himself and the troupe in rooms at one of the best inns, where the show continued to do a thriving business. "On the 7th of October, the King and Royall famley visited my Exhibition in the black egle when the King seaid thatt he never saw sutch an Exibition in this town before. Allso the Quean of Swedland was in kumpaney with them."[3] He goes on to say: "On the 7th of October I shott [shut] my Exibition in Mintchin [Munich], and ast the Quean [Caroline Maria Therese] for permition to preform in hir gardin at hir sumer palis. She redley offerd for that puorpus as all the other Kinges had dun the same." On the 9th of October he exhibited there and took note of the "Menagerey of fowls... perttickler [particularly] from America." He made more money on this day than for any other single performance: "I preformed with the Indian on the watter in frunt of the Queans Pollis... the spectators amounted to about 6000... all seamed to be much pleased. The Indian turned himself bottom up severill times in his Canoe and with his dartes Dispatching sevrill geas [geese]." Two days later, back in Munich, Hadlock witnessed a celebration in honor of the King, who was being formally invested with the title of Joseph Maximilian IV. On 12 October the king died.

Hadlock and company set out for Stuttgart on 14 October arriving there on the 18th after a forced stop in Augsburg where the coach broke down. In Stuttgart, Hadlock performed for the King of Wurttemberg, William I. After this time Hadlock's luck took a turn for the worse, but unfortunately we can only speculate on the details of this change of fortune, since several of the notes on Stuttgart and much of the journal after this point are missing. Although not mentioned in the journal until several months later, it was during this period, when the troupe was in Strasbourg, that George died.

Field speculates that George met some violent death and/or lost his mind based on one paragraph which joins a missing page: "... This was dun the nite before I saw him. When he came to himself he opered to be sorey for the ofens and Crime thatt he haid comitted there. Maid [mad] people som times are as sensable as aney people in the world att times and at other times no Devils half so bad as them..." There is no way to connect this entry with George, however, and Hadlock may have been commenting on someone else entirely.

The journal continues on 1 December 1825: "This is the last day of my Exhibition in this town [Strasbourg?]. I close tonite and leave after tomorough for Pariss, distans 220 mildes, which will take me seven days jurney. My Museum goes in the post van and costes me 2 dollars per hundred wate [weight]. And I goe in my one [own] cotch and horses." Hadlock's bad luck continued, however, as he reports: "On my way one of my horses got sick and I wass oblige to leave him behind and take post horeses 50 mildes from Pariss."

When he finally arrived in Paris, Hadlock set up his exhibition in a large room he leased near the Palais Royal which cost him 600 francs per month or approximately $150. He remained in Paris from December, 1825, through April, 1826. He records both the birth of his daughter and his marriage in the same entry: "March 16th Pariss, 1826. May wife gott to bead [bed] with a fine Doutor [daughter] at 10 oclock in the evning in the Streat Rue De Croson, Hotel number 12, near the Streat Clerey, And wass marid on Sunday the 20th of March in Prushey [Prussia] one year sens [since]." He then adds: "I shoot [shut] up my Excibition on the 20th March and solt [sold] the same up to oxion [auction] and did not sell for aneything, so I kepp it myself after lusing 4000 dollars with the same, traveling from Stuckartt to this Cittey, and the Indian ding [dying] in Strassburg. Now this ends my excibiting indians."

The Hadlock family sailed to North America in the late spring of 1826. Back on the Cranberry Isles, Hadlock was reunited with his three children by his first wife, and built a house on Big Cranberry Island for his new family. Here Hadlock's wife settled in to what must have been a very foreign lifestyle in this isolated community. Called Hannah Caroline by her husband since their marriage, here she was called simply the "Prooshan Lady" by the Islanders, the name by which she has been known to the present day. A son, Epps, was born in September 1827. Hadlock busied himself shooting and stuffing seals. He also prepared for a voyage to the north to gather more seals which he planned to stuff and sell to the royalty of Europe when he returned there (Field 1936:130-137).

Hadlock fitted out the *Minerva*, a two-masted schooner a little over sixty feet long, for the voyage to the north. She had a crew of 17 in addition to

Hadlock and his son Samuel Taylor, age 14, who came along on his first and last sea voyage. They embarked in March of 1829. Their fate was unknown for over four years until Captain Stanley of neighboring Northeast Harbor returned from the northern waters with an account of the *Minerva* and her crew. According to Field's story, Captain Stanley had a chance encounter with some Eskimos in a remote part of Greenland where he had gone ashore to hunt seals. Several of them could speak a little English, and they had with them a gun which had Samuel Hadlock's name on the butt. When questioned about it they told him the *Minerva* had been frozen in the ice during the winter after its departure from the Cranberry Isles. Although he had a full shipload of skins, Captain Hadlock wanted more, and went out alone after a seal. He was caught in a snowstorm and never returned. As soon as it was light, the crew persuaded the Eskimos to help them search for their captain. He was found kneeling on one knee, his gun raised in the act of taking aim - frozen to death. The gun and a handkerchief that belonged to Hadlock were given to the Eskimos at the time. The ship was soon freed from the ice and set off without her captain, the last anyone ever saw of the *Minerva*.

Captain Stanley is said to have brought Hadlock's handkerchief, retrieved from the Eskimos, back to Hannah Caroline as proof of his death. The story continues that, on learning of her husband's death, Hannah Caroline immediately borrowed a horse and wagon. She loaded the stuffed seals previously preserved by her husband on the wagon, hauled them out to the dock and pushed them into the bay. A passing coasting packet from St. John is said to have fished up one of the cases containing a stuffed seal, and taken it to Boston where the seal was displayed in the old museum until fire destroyed it several years later (Field 1936:144-157).

Whether one believes this rather romantic account of the demise of Captain Hadlock or not, it must be admitted that his life was marked by a large degree of adventure and romance, from his earliest voyages to the Arctic until his final one in 1829. He exhibited his show of Eskimos and curiosities in the smallest to the largest of the country fairs of Europe, making and losing a fortune in the process. He didn't hesitate to defraud the public with two successive bogus "Eskimos" in the pursuit of his fortune, and managed to escape the law with no small amount of satisfaction. He progressed from these daring adventures to the romantic one of winning the hand of the daughter of the Magistrate of Charlottenburg, becoming a propertied member of the Prussian community who mingled with royalty and exhibited for Kings and Queens. Captain Hadlock's story slipped into obscurity after his death, little remembered by the rest of the world. Yet he remained a colorful character in the local history of the Cranberry Isles in Maine. His memory was preserved by his descendants and by the members of that small community. There, his Prussian wife lived out the remainder of her life, never to return to her native Prussia. In addition to raising Hadlock's children, she later remarried and had a second family. The Islesford Historical Society Museum in Islesford, Maine, proudly displays the few artifacts left to them by Hadlock's descendants. These include the cut-out silhouette portrait of Hadlock made while he was in London (Fig. 1), a photograph of his wife taken long after his death, their wedding certificate, and the gold snuff box which was a present to him from the King of Saxony.

While Hadlock's journal tells us very little of the Eskimos who mistakenly entrusted their lives to him, or of the content of his touring show, it does tell us something of the personality of one 19th century showman. The fact that Hadlock failed to mention such events as the deaths of his star performers, or any account of their lives, is in itself a statement. One would tend to assume that he relegated them to the same category as the rest of his "curiosities," which were important to him only as a means to greater profits. Hadlock mentioned his wife even more briefly than the Eskimos in his journal, and it is tempting to speculate that he may have used her in much the same way that he used the Eskimos, as a means to more profits. It is true that he began exhibiting for royalty only after his marriage, and his wife's social connections may have helped him gain entry into the more moneyed circles to which he had not previously had access. In any case, the story of Hadlock's life does shed some light on the values of one 19th century showman who sought his fortune by exhibiting Native Americans in Europe.

Final Note

The fascinating story of Captain Samuel Hadlock, Jr. came to my attention as an outgrowth of my research on Haida argillite pipes, a subject far removed from the Baffin Island Eskimos who were the stars of Hadlock's show. The Haida people live on the Queen Charlotte Islands, off the British Columbia coast, a continent away from Baffin Island and Hadlock's Maine home. During the 19th century, they carved tobacco pipes from a black carbonaceous shale for sale to the Euro-American fur traders who visted their islands in sailing ships. The specific argillite pipe which launched my efforts to track down information on Samuel Hadlock is now in the Museum für Völkerkunde in Berlin and is listed in the museum's catalog as being part of the Hadlock Collection (#IV B 62 - Fig. 4), acquired in 1824 by the Art Chamber of Prussian Kings. If the museum's records are correct, this pipe would be one of the earliest documented pieces of argillite in any museum collection. The pipe is carved in the form of a ship's billet head, a feature which decorated the prow of most Euro-American sailing ships in the 19th century. It is stylistically more closely related to pipes produced by the Haida people in the 1830's than those from the 1820's (see Wright 1979). For this reason the pipe has been something of an enigma, and the date of 1824 has been seriously questioned by scholars.

Fig. 4. Haida argillite ship pipe erroneously attributed to the collection of Captain Samuel Hadlock. Museum für Völkerkunde, Berlin, cat.no.IV B 62.

The Hadlock Collection was not cataloged until 1873 when it was incorporated into the newly established Museum für Völkerkunde in Berlin. Peter Macnair believes that it may have been mixed at that time with the Deppe Collection from New California, acquired by the museum in 1937. The original page from the 1873 catalog lists pipe #IV B 62 as being part of the Deppe Collection, but this entry is crossed out and "Hadlock" is written in. Since the Deppe Collection includes other Northwest Coast pieces, and the other Hadlock material includes only Eastern Woodlands and Eastern Arctic objects, the argillite pipe seems to fit more logically with the Deppe material. A pair of Eastern Woodlands moccasins listed with the Deppe material are equally out of place with the West Coast objects in this collection. Macnair has speculated that these moccasins and the argillite pipe may have been inadvertently switched in the record, and the moccasins may have come from the Hadlock collection rather than the argillite pipe (Peter Macnair, personal communication 1982; Macnair and Hoover 1984:203).

Captain Hadlock never visited the Northwest Coast in his short life, and his exhibition was focused on the Eastern Arctic. Thus, even though Hadlock was a sea captain, came from a family of shipwrights, and probably would have been fascinated with this pipe carved in the form of a ship's billet head, it seems unlikely that he would have had a Haida argillite pipe as part of his collection of artifacts. It is possible that he could have acquired the pipe from traders on the east coast of America or in England, in the same way that George Catlin probably acquired his argillite pipes twenty years later (see Wright 1977:49-51). Given the style of the pipe and the absence of any other

230

documented ship pipes from the 1820's, however, the Deppe accession date of 1837 is more believable than 1824.

Only after the above had been written, additional proof for this version came from the published list of Hadlock's collection (Anonymous 1824a). It lists apparently all the Hadlock pieces now in Berlin but significantly fails to mention any argillite item, even though it notes another Northwest Coast item, "a strange purse made of grass from Nootka Sound." While the question of the argillite pipe thus turned out to be based on a clerical error, the exercise of trying to resolve it has unearthed the interesting story of Captain Hadlock's touring exhibition of Eskimos.

NOTES

1. I would like to thank Louise Libby of the Islesford Historical Society Museum in Islesford, Maine, for making Hadlock's journal available to me; Peter Macnair, Curator of Ethnology at the British Columbia Provincial Museum in Victoria, for sharing his information on the Berlin Museum's accession records as they relate to the Hadlock pipe; and Christian F.Feest, editor of this volume, for his help in locating and translating the Vienna and Leipzig newspaper accounts of Hadlock's exhibition, which have greatly enhanced the scope of this article.
2. Captain "Dicksen" could have been either Francis or James Dixon. Francis Dixon left Sydney for London on the *Venerable* on 21 April 1823 carrying a mixed cargo, while James Dixon left for the same trip on the *Skelton* on 23 May 1823 with a cargo of colonial produce. Thanks to Erich Kolig and Gordon Parsonson for assistance on the Maori questions.
3. At least one item from Hadlock's collection must have been given to the Bavarian King. It is decribed as "An artificially made North American Indian porte-épée, decorated with porcupine quills" (Anonymous 1824a) and is indeed a unique item which in the meantime has passed through the collection of the Museum für Völkerkunde in Munich and a private German collection to the National Museum of Man in Ottawa. An attached Latin label associates it with Sir William Johnson, the British Superintendent of Indian Affairs before the American Revolution (Brasser 1976:143). How Hadlock came to acquire it in the first place is as yet unknown (Editor's note).

Anonymous
1821   Esquimaux. Literary Gazette 1821 (21 May): 501. London.
1824a   Verzeichnis der sich im Museum befindenden Naturalien, Waffen und Kunstsachen. Vom Nord- und Südpol, und aus anderen entfernten Weltgegenden. [Leipzig].
1824b   Sehenswürdigkeiten der Messe. Leipziger Tageblatt 90 (28 September):406-408. Leipzig.
1824c   Die indischen Esquimaux. Leipziger Tageblatt 99 (7 October):517-519. Leipzig.
1825a   Merkwürdigkeiten vom Nord- und Südpol. Wiener Zeitschrift für Kunst, Literatur, Theater und Mode 76 (28 June):634-636. Wien.
1825b   Die Esquimaux aus der Baffins-Bay am Nordpol. Der Sammler 88 (23 July):352. Wien.
1825c   Wasservorstellungen der Esquimaux. Allgemeine Theaterzeitung und Unterhaltungsblatt 96 (11 August):895. Wien.
1825d   Wasservorstellung des Esquimaux im k.k.Belvedere. Der Sammler 101 (23 August):404. Wien.

Brasser, Ted J.
1976   "Bo'jou, Neejee!". Profiles of Canadian Indian Art. Ottawa: National Museum of Man.

Field, Rachel
1934   God's Pocket. New York: The MacMillan Company.

Fitzinger, L.J.
1825   Die Esquimaux-Indianer und das Museum des Capitän Hadlock in Wien. Allgemeine Theaterzeitung und Unterhaltungsblatt 80 (5 July): 529-531. Wien.

Hadlock, Samuel Jr.
1822-1826 Unpublished Journal. Islesford Historical Society Museum, Islesford, Maine.

Idiens, Dale
1987   Eskimos in Scotland, c.1682-1924. In: C.F.Feest (ed.), Indians and Europe (Aachen: Rader Verlag), pp. 161-174.

Israel, Heinz
1987   Johann Gottfried Schadow and his Inuit Portraits. In: C.F.Feest (ed.), Indians and Europe (Aachen: Rader Verlag), pp. 235-241.

King, J.C.H.
1987   A Family of Botocudos Exhibited on Bond Street in 1822. In: C.F.Feest (ed.), Indians and Europe (Aachen: Rader Verlag), pp. 243-251.

Macnair, Peter L. and Alan L. Hoover
1984   The Magic Leaves: A History of Haida Argillite Carving. Victoria:

    B.C. Provincial Museum.

Owens, J.M.R.
    1981   New Zealand before Annexation. In: W.H. Oliver (ed.), The Oxford History of New Zealand (Oxford: Clarendon Press and Wellington: Oxford University Press).

Wright, Robin K.
    1977   Haida Argillite Pipes. Master's Thesis, University of Washington, Seattle.
    1979   Haida Argillite Ship Pipes. American Indian Art Magazine 5(1):40-47.

JOHANN GOTTFRIED SCHADOW AND HIS INUIT PORTRAITS

Heinz Israel

Johann Gottfried Schadow, born on 20 May 1764 in Berlin as the son of a poor tailor's family and died there on 27 January 1850 as an acknowledged authority in many artistic fields, may rightfully be considered as one of the major German sculptors of the classicist period. It is indeed his main works in this genre - such as the "Quadriga" crowning the Brandenburg Gate in Berlin - which keep his memory visibly alive in the public eye.

Apart from this, however, Schadow's talent for drawing, early recognized and lastingly encouraged by Tessaert, the Prussian court sculptor, has in the course of the decades resulted in a richly diversified oeuvre which its creator understood to combine with yet another of his inclinations, viz., theoretical studies on the physical stature of man.

In 1815 Schadow had been appointed Director of the Berlin Academy of Arts. In 1960 the present Academy of Arts of the GDR organized an exhibition of drawings including works by Schadow, some of which were identified as portraits of Inuits. It is this group of portraits which shall now be reconsidered in the context of European interest in Native Americans.[1] In the publication accompanying the exhibition noted above, A. Janda makes the following observations on Schadow: "During the last three decades of his life he finished the theoretical study of the proportions of the human body and the characteristic features in face and head formation of the peoples, which he had already started around the turn of the century and after 1815 continued with ever increasing intensity. The first results were being presented to the students of the Academy and later published in the voluminous plate books *Lehre von den Knochen und Muskeln* (1830), *Polyclet* (1834), and *National-Physionomien* (1835)" (Janda 1960:56). These publications as well as Schadow's late work *Kunst-Werke und Kunst-Ansichten* (1849) should be taken into account in any further study of his portraits.

According to the caption on one of the sheets, Schadow's Inuit portaits relate to "Esquimaux from Baffins Bay man and woman brought to Europe by Captain Hadlock 1824." More specifically, they consist of frontal representations, 19 by 27.5 cm (Fig. 1), and profile views, 21 by 28 cm (Fig. 2). Obviously the same woman is shown on yet another sheet, again from the front and also from the side (Fig. 3). These drawings, made in black chalk, were studies for lithographs (1824) as well as for the zinc etchings to be published in one of Schadow's major works, the *National-Physionomien* noted above (cp.Janda 1960:65; Mackowsky 1936:Taf.108,109).[2] On his use of zinc etchings, Schadow himself offered the following remarks with reference to the year 1828:

"One began to make use of printing from zinc plates. This printing process

Fig. 1. "Esquimaux from Baffins Bay," drawing by Johann Gottfried Schadow, 1824. Cp.Fig.2 of Wright's article in this volume. (By permission of the Academy of Art of the GDR.)

- even though otherwise being indeed of little cleanliness - offers the advantage that the writer or draughtsman did not have to work in reverse so that I have frequently made use of this method" (Schadow 1849:236).

It may not be without interest for the present purpose to inquire into the means of perception on which the creation of Schadow's drawings was based. Undoubtedly, drawing after nature was of prime importance for him. For 1823 Schadow noted:

"A certain Lasthausen, a Dutch wafer-baker, brought with him the two Chinese Haho and Assing who were later employed as royal servants. Both of them I drew after life, with exact measurement..." (Schadow 1849:204).

Looking back on the year 1825 Schadow remembered:

"During my work for *National-Physionomien* I was particularly aided by the fact that all of the personnel of the Turkish and Spanish embassies as well as a Spanish woman and her daughter were sitting for me" (Schadow 1849:218).

236

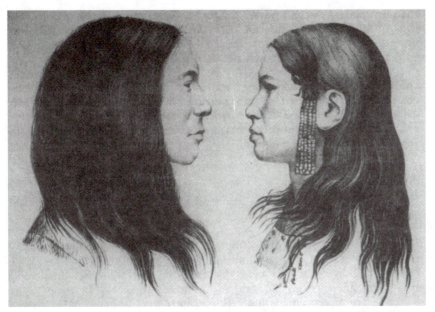

Fig. 2. Profile views of the "Esquimaux from Baffins Bay." Drawing by J.G.Schadow, 1824.(By permission of the Academy of Art of the GDR.)

On another basic source for his work as a draughtsman Schadow remarked:

"In addition to that... what living nature was offering me in foreign nations, I made use of the extensive collection of skulls of the university of this place. The portrait collection of Count Krasinski in the Royal Library, consisting of 24,000 portraits also helped me very much" (Schadow 1849:251).

And elsewhere, on the same question:

"In my researches I also had to consider Blumenbach's representations of skulls, called 'Decas.' These, drawn after measuring them with the eye, do give the national difference on first sight, but no measurements, therefore also no certain means for someone who wants to mold them plastically. I therefore spent several months to make the illustrations with compasses and callipers after the skulls in the museum of this place, all in half their natural size. As far as I know, only very few illustrations of similar accuracy exist. As is well known, the collection of the museum of our university[3] contains skulls from all parts of the earth" (Schadow 1849:205).

237

The quotations certainly reveal Schadow's consistent endeavor for scientific accuracy, for absolute faithfulness in details. And he certainly used every opportunity that offered itself to expand his knowledge. During a sojourn of several weeks in the Baltic Sea resort of Warnemünde in 1833, he had

"there unexpectedly enlightening reports on the condition of several tribes of peoples of America from two merchants who for several years had lived in Baltimore, Bahia and Rio de Janeiro.... compared their lively description with those of some learned travelers who remain in the biggest cities for only a few days"

and finally concludes:

"So suspicions arise regarding that which they relate to us, though with much spirit" (Schadow 1849:263).

This short review of Johann Gottfried Schadow's critical position vis-à-vis his subject was necessary before returning to his portraits of Inuits.

First of all it has to be stated that the viewer of Schadow's drawings of human types after looking through his published works has to come to the most likely correct conclusion that their creator was depicting anthropological realities, which in turn agrees completely with his theoretical position just noted. In the process, Schadow's mode of representation is free from idealization; he drew what he had seen and - even if only in part - had also measured with compasses and callipers. And this is what distinguishes his work from those of ethnographic illustrators of earlier times, such as the artists of the books of travel by Lafitau or Cook, who took the idealization of Greek art as their model.

Unfortunately, Schadow does not say anything (as far as I know) in his writings on the circumstances under which the Inuit portraits were made. What is known, is that in 1822 the American captain Samuel Hadlock had brought some Inuits to Europe for the purpose of display. Many had done so before and after him (cp., e.g., Bertelsen 1945, Bobé 1927, Bogen om Grønland 1978:89, Bugge 1965, Günther 1984, Israel 1965, Jannasch 1958, Plischke 1938), a kind of enterprise which later on notoriously flourished in a highly commercialized form under the German name of "Völkerschauen" (cp. Lehmann 1955).

Early in 1825 Hadlock's troupe also came to Dresden. According to a report in the local newspaper *Dresdner Anzeigen* (No.20 of 18 February 1825), among the travelers "passing into the city on 10 February 1825" and - fortunately for later researchers - mentioned by name, there were "Mr. Hadlock, American ship's captain, besides 2 Esquimaux and their interpreter, from Berlin." They took up lodging "in the g[olden or green] Crown." The public performance was announced by the expeditious manager-captain in number 25 of the same paper

238

Fig. 3. The second impostor of Mary Coonunnnak, thought to be an "Eskimo from Baffins Bay." Drawing by J.G.Schadow, 1824. (By permission of the Academy of Art of the GDR.)

on 25 February 1825 as follows:

"To a high nobility and to a most esteemed public I obediently beg to advertise that I have arrived here with two Esquimaux-Indians, man and woman, which together with my museum I will exhibit only for a short period of time in the hall of the restaurant of Mr. Kreutz on Altmarkt no.10, first floor, starting Monday, 28 February this year. The general approbation and the admiration which I have gained with these interesting humans in England, Hamburg, and most recently in Berlin, already affords me the flattering conviction that I will have to expect the same response and will find numerous callers here as well. Details may be taken from the bills posted. Hadlock, North American ship's captain."

This stay apparently lasted until early April. In the *Dresdner Anzeigen* No. 37 of 28 March (identically repeated in No.39 of 30 March 1825) Hadlock advertised as follows:

"To a high nobility and to a most esteemed public I most dutifully will not fail to announce that due to my imminent departure I will unfailingly close my museum on 6 April of this year. Even though there will be no reduction

239

in the price of admission, the undivided applause afforded to my rarities, nothing of which kind had ever been seen here before, more particularly to my Esquimaux-Indians, lets me nonetheless expect numerous callers during these last days, to which I herewith invite most devotedly. S.Hadlock, North American ship's captain."

Elsewhere in this volume, Robin K.Wright is dealing more fully with the story of Captain Hadlock's traveling display of Inuits. She is able to demonstrate that the original Inuit woman brought to Europe by Hadlock had died soon after her arrival in England. The captain replaced her at first by a gypsy and later probably by an English woman. Schadow's "mistrust" which we have quoted above in a different context, would thus also have been appropriate towards the models for his "Inuit" portraits. The modern viewer of the drawings will certainly accept the man without the least objection as a representative portrait of an Inuit. The woman, on the other hand, looks so little "typically Eskimoan" that - given Wright's article based on Hadlock's diary - there can now be little room for any doubt about the erroneous ethnic attribution of the woman on Schadow's drawings.

NOTES

1. Cat.nos Schadow 975-977. Permission to publish the material has kindly been supplied to the editor by the Academy of Arts of the GDR.
2. Regarding our Fig. 2, Mackowsky (1936:101) quotes from Schadow's manuscript log for 16 December 1824: "Thursday were printed Lyto in my big workshop, also the Eskimo."
3. Presently: Museum für Naturkunde der Humboldt-Universität zu Berlin.

REFERENCES CITED

Bertelsen, A.
1945   Grønlændere i Danmark. Meddelelser om Grønland 145(2). København.

Bobé, Louis
1927   Grønlændere i Danmark. Grønlandske Selskabs Aarsskrift 1926-27: 5-28. København.

Bogen om Grønland
1978   12.udg., 1.opl. København.

Bugge, Aage
1965   Kallihirua - polareskimoen i Canterbury. Journal "Grønland" 1965: 161-175. Charlottenlund.

Günther, Ernst
1984   Sarrasani wie er wirklich war. Berlin.

Israel, Heinz
1965   Grönland-Eskimo auf europäischen Gemälden aus dem 18. Jahrhundert. Abhandlungen und Berichte des Staatlichen Museums für Völkerkunde Dresden 25:35-62. Berlin.

Janda, A.
1960   Daniel Chodowiecki, Johann Gottfried Schadow, Karl Blechen. Ausstellung von Handzeichnungen aus dem Besitz der Deutschen Akademie der Künste zur Zehnjahresfeier der Akademie am 24. März 1960. Berlin.

Jannasch, Hans-Windekilde
1958   Reunion with Mikak. Canadian Geographical Journal 57:84-85. Ottawa.

Lehmann, Alfred
1955   Zeitgenössische Bilder der ersten Völkerschauen. In: Von fremden Völkern und Kulturen, Hans Plischke zum 65. Geburtstag (Düsseldorf), 31-38.

Mackowsky, Hans
1936   Schadows Graphik. Forschungen zur deutschen Kunstgeschichte 19. Berlin.

Plischke, Hans
1938   Die Entdeckung der Erde und die Philanthropie des 18. Jahrhunderts. Der Seewart 7:358-360. Hamburg.

Schadow, Johann Gottfried
1834   Polyclet oder von den Maassen der Menschen... Berlin.
1835   National-Physionomien... Berlin.
1849   Kunst-Werke und Kunst-Ansichten. Berlin.

FAMILY OF BOTOCUDOS
EXHIBITED ON BOND STREET IN 1822

J.C.H. King

> What have we here? a man or a fish? dead or alive? A fish: he
> smells like a fish... Were I in England... and had but this fish
> painted, not a holiday fool there but would give a piece of silver.
> There would this monster make a man; any strange beast there
> makes a man.
>
> (*Tempest*, Act 2, Scene 2)

The use of humans as freak shows attracts the public through a simple
structural opposition. On the one hand the person must be recognizably human
so that the audience can sympathize and identify with him or her; on the
other hand the human must be interesting - in this case repulsive, savage,
capable of performing great feats - or perhaps simply exotic. This type of
display is very ancient, but it is only in the 16th century that well documented
examples appear in any quantity in England. The most famous instance of the
display of non-Europeans at this time is that of the Inuit brought to England
by Martin Frobisher from his expedition of 1577 (Cheshire et al. 1980:23;
Sturtevant and Quinn 1987). It is thought that this may have provided the
basis for Shakespeare's comment from the *Tempest* (Altick 1978:45). In this he
clearly states the requirements for a human exhibit. It is necessary for a
"monster" or "any strange beast" to be made man, and yet at the same time he
must be curious. In this case the Canadian Eskimo is man-like but he is also
repulsive since he smells and is fish-like. The hey-day of these displays was in
the 19th century when innumberable parties of non-Europeans arrived in
Europe to be displayed in some form or other. Usually these people arrived with
their own costume and paraphernalia. People without clothing might pose a
problem. If they conformed to European physical stereotypes they might be
considered indecent, and at the same time might fail to conform to the image
of the savage with his or her exotic accoutrements. Sartje, the so-called
"Hottentot Venus," exhibited in London during the Napoleonic wars, seems to
have been exhibited naked. She was of interest to the public, and to science,
because of her steatopygia; this feature may have meant that she was not
considered sufficiently sexually offensive to have been clothed. A little more
than ten years later a family of Brazilian Indians was displayed with an exotic
variety of non-Brazilian costume; at home they would have worn nothing. This
note is intended to identify some of the contradictions inherent in this
exhibition.

In the early 19th century the Gê-speaking Botocudo lived between the Rio
Pardo and Rio Doce in the Brazilian province of Minas Gerais (Métraux

Fig. 1. Drawing of the Botocudo family in front of the backdrop derived from the Wied-Neuwied print of Puris in a shelter (cp.Fig.3). In this version, presumably by I.W. Gear and of an earlier date than the print, the child has been excluded, and Tono Maria is pointing out the monkey to her husband. 32.7 by 25.8 cms. Private collection. Photograph courtesy of the Trustees of the British Museum.

1944:531). They were primarily hunter-gatherers but by the beginning of the 19th century had taken up slash-and-burn agriculture, and particularly the cultivation of manioc. From the middle of the 16th century, when known as the Aimoré they first came into substantial contact with the Portuguese, they had a very war-like reputation (Hemming 1978:93-96). This reputation persisted into the 19th century and helped provide the savage stereotype for the display of "The Wild Indian Chief, Wife & Child" at 23 New Bond Street in 1822.

It is not clear exactly why the Botocudos came to London, but the showman X. Chabert published a leaflet designed (or so the title suggests) to educate the public: "A brief historical account of the life and adventures of the Botocudo chieftain, and family..." (Chabert 1822). This falls into two parts. The first describes the Botocudos and neighboring peoples in Brazil. This includes material on geographical location, subsistence, material culture, and physical appearance; it emphasizes religion and warfare (Chabert 1822:3-16). The second section describes the Botocudo woman, Tono Maria, her three husbands, Julio, Emmanuel, and Jochina, and the punishments endured by adulterers. She is said to have been an adulteress. With each act of adultery a scar was raised on her body. When 104 acts of adultery had been committed by a Botocudo the adulterer was killed. Tono Maria was said to have approximately 100 scars on her body. To the sexual interest was added that of slavery. Jochina, the third

244

Fig. 2. *The Wild Indian Chief, Wife & Child, as exhibited at 23, New Bond Street. /The Wild Indians, as in their Native Country. /Drawn & Engraved by I.W.Gear. /London Published by Zavier Shabert, 7 June 1822.* Chabert's print differs from the drawing in the addition of the child, two dead cats, and the second man on the backdrop. Many details are more definite in the print, particularly those of the costume, weapons, and vegetation. Tono Maria is now no longer pointing at the tree and it is not certain that Joachina's next move is intended to be the shooting of the monkey. 37 by 27 cms. Private collection. Photograph courtesy of the Trustees of the British Museum.

husband who came to England, and Tono Maria were slaves belonging to one Captain, later Colonel, Julian. They were brought to England by a French entrepreneur who bribed the owner's servants in order to extricate the family. We do not know why he did this. When they arrived in England, "the land of liberty," they were, so Chabert implies, set free. For a time they "lamented over their fate" and then decided to return to Brazil "where the Missionaries will instruct them and make them truly Christian," because the Portuguese owner had, in treating them "with every mark of kindness and parental affection" made them Christians. In the meantime they were exhibiting themselves of their own accord, of course, and naturally "for their own profit"[1] (Chabert 1822:16-20). Both this rather unlikely account and the prints of the display depend on the published account of the travels of Prince Maximilian zu Wied-Neuwied in Brazil in 1815-1817 (Wied-Neuwied 1820-1821).[2]

The two prints of the display emphasize the savagery of the family. The first one shows "The Wild Indians as in their Native Country," i.e. the family, captioned "as exhibited" in London, in front of a backdrop (Fig. 2; cp. Fig. 1). The backdrop is derived from a Wied-Neuwied (1820-1821:Taf. 3) print of a Puri family in their shelter (Fig. 3). This scene which has been described as one of the best known depictions of indigenous Brazilians, is romantic and even sentimental in its treatment of the family (Hartmann 1975:88). I.W. Gear,

245

Fig. 3. *Puris in ihrer Hütte* (Wied-Neuwied 1820-1821: Taf.3). 28.5 by 22.8 cms. Museum of Mankind library. Photograph courtesy of the Trustees of the British Museum.

the artist and engraver of this, the official print published by Chabert, shows a simplified version of the Wied-Neuwied illustration. The father is depicted lounging in his hammock, no longer gazing affectionately at his child who has disappeared: two additional men have been introduced into the backdrop; one is drawing a bow, the other dragging a dead cat, perhaps a jaguar. A second dead cat is included in place of the alert dog in the original print. The family, fully clothed in the Gear print, is looking towards a monkey in a tree, the idea being that Jochina is about to kill the monkey with his bow. Gear may also have taken the heads of Jochina and Tono Maria from a Wied-Neuwied (1820-1821:Taf. 10) illustration, that of the family of Botocudos on the move (Fig. 4).

The second print places the family sitting on English chairs (Fig. 5). The artist, R. Banks, uses the same faces from Gear and Wied-Neuwied. In both prints the clothing is extremely exotic and best treated with the third depiction of the family, in a cartoon. In this print, entitled "Curiosities and Monstrosities for 1822," the family is shown with William Bullock's Sami or Lapps who were exhibited in the same year at the Egyptian Hall round the corner from Chabert's display, and a host of absurdly fashionable Londoners (Fig. 6; Altick 1978:273-275). In all three representations Tono Maria and Jochina are wearing wooden lip and ear plugs, sometimes marks of status (Lowie 1944:384). There is nothing else of definite Brazilian origin. Tono Maria is wearing an enormous Hawaiian feather cloak over a demure white petticoat

246

Fig. 4. *Eine Familie der Botocudos auf der Reise* (Wied-Neuwied 1820- 1821: Taf.10), detail. This is one of the possible sources for the details of the adult heads, hair cuts, and wooden ornaments used by Gear and Banks. 29.2 by 22.9 cms. Museum of Mankind library. Photograph courtesy of the Trustees of the British Museum.

visible only in the cartoon. Round her shoulders in the Gear depiction she may also have a small Hawaiian feather cape while in the Banks print she has a necklace of blue feathers which may have been brought from Brazil. Her husband's basic costume appears to consist of a suit of pink ostrich feathers. In the Gear depiction this is covered with a skin shirt perhaps of North American Plains Indian origin with a porcupine quill rosette in the middle of the chest and a decorated hem; benath this rosette is an unidentified bag or ornament possibly of North American origin. On his shoulders Jochina too wears a Hawaiian cape and perhaps also a choker of jaguar fur. In the Banks print he is portrayed sitting on a belt, perhaps a finger-woven yarn belt of North American Woodlands Indian origin. The child has a similar feather costume perhaps including Hawaiian and Brazilian components of feather cape feather headdress which may be an authentic Brazilian tailfeather type or an allusion to the ancient stereotype of the Brazilian Indian with feather skirt and vertical tailfeather headdress. While this stereotype was often employed as a symbol of North American Indians, the clothing of the father seems to be a rare example of the usage of North American material in the depiction of a Brazilian. Finally the cartoon emphasizes the stereotype image further by giving all three people vertical tail-feather headdresses.

This exhibit crudely emphasized sex, savagery, exotism, and the blessings of Christianity. It is perhaps surprising that it aroused very much less interest.

247

Fig. 5. *Botocudo Chieftain Wife & Child.Exhibition at 23 new Bond Street Sketch'd from Life by R.Banks.* This, despite the inscription, seems to rely on the Gear print. Colors: general: lip and ear ornaments: white; shoes: black. Woman: cloak: yellow with red border; cape: black. Child: headdresses: yellow, red, blue, black; clothing: yellow, red. Man: costume: pink; sash: red, brown; chest ornament: white, yellow, red; cloak: black, with red collar. 24.5 by 24 cms. Private collection. Photograph courtesy of the Trustees of the British Museum.

than that of the Sami, which, instead of pandering to all that is worst in human nature, intended to educate. It was perhaps the educational aspect of Bullock's displays, and those of North American Indians which followed, that sets them apart from the simple racism of Chabert and which also made them so successful. The *Literary Gazette* for 1822 is very critical of the Botocudos display (Anonymous 1822:123-124) although they are said to be worth a visit. Significantly they are accorded one mention rather than the eleven given to the Lapps (Anonymous 1822:45,60,77,87,109,156,220,501-502,517-519,733,826); moreover on 9 March Bullock was boasting that 58,000 people had visited the Lapps. While the display of the Botocudos was more successful than that of Captain Hadlock's Inuit, it seems unlikely that they presented much competition for Bullock's Sami (Foreman 1943:127; Wright 1987); although racist attitudes were prevalent throughout society they were insufficient to make a display successful for this reason alone. Already by the 1820's for a display of people to be successful the public required something more then the simple contradiction appreciated by Shakespeare.

Fig. 6. CURIOSITIES and MONSTROSITIES for 1822. /Pub^d Feb^y, 1822 by S.W.Fores 41 Piccadil-ly. 33 by 22 cms. Private collection. Photograph courtesy of the Trustees of the British Museum.

NOTES

1. Profit-sharing between the entrepreneur and his Indians may have taken many different forms. In an advertisement in a Leipzig newspaper, Carl Ingermann (1825:629), the manager of another, Vienna-based Botocudo troupe of the 1820's, explains his principle: "As I am inclined to let my savage have the income from one performance in every city, I have appointed today's one for his benefit, and therefore request a respectable public to visit him in great numbers; he will also not fail to courteously thank each person visiting him" (Editor's note).
2. Maximilian zu Wied-Neuwied also took a Botocudo back to Germany. Rather than being displayed, Quäck the Botocudo lived for almost twenty years as a servant in Wied-Neuwied's household (Editor's note).

249

ASSEMBLY-ROOMS,
Cheltenham.

NOVEL & UNPRECEDENTED EXHIBITION

THE

Botocudo Chief
AND HIS WIFE,

May be Seen at the Assembly-Rooms,

On Tuesday next, July 2, 1822,

FOR A FEW DAYS ONLY

☞ *Doors to be open from One o'Clock (Sunday excepted) to Six.*

ADMITTANCE 1s. 6d.

This wild Indian Chief is the head of a Savage Tribe, inhabiting the interior of South America. They wander in the Forests, and feed on the various produce of the Chase. Their complexion is of a copper colour, their hair is a jet black, straight and stiff, and growing up from their foreheads. Their heads are of a very peculiar form, and the tip of their ears rests on their shoulders. To their ears and their lower lips they have a circular piece of wood most curiously attached. Though under the middle stature they are extremely well proportioned, and their feet particularly small. The Chief is about thirty years of age; and his Wife, who is about thirty-five, is considered a complete Venus in her native country.

During twelve months of their exhibition in London, they have been honoured with the patronage and approbation of the Royal Family, and the principal Nobility, and have been constantly visited by numberless crowds of every class of the Inhabitants of the British Metropolis, who have beheld them with unbounded approbation and wonder—whilst all the London Journals have been lavish in the most enthusiastic encomiums.

Previous to their return to their Native Woods, the Botocudo Chief and his Wife, the first of their tribe ever seen in Europe, will be exhibited at the Assembly-Rooms in Cheltenham for a few days only, having previously received numerous and urgent invitations from various parts of Great Britain—and they flatter themselves they will be viewed by the Inhabitants and Visitors of this fashionable Town with equal interest and gratification, as the Exhibition will likewise display a correct and faithful representation of the Scenery of the Country, their Huts, and the Furniture used by the Tribe in the Forests of South America.

Their full Costume, has been just received from America, and the elegant and costly Cloak worn by the Chieftain's Wife, will be found to correspond precisely with the dress now in the British Museum; in addition to which is a most curious Bed, composed of Plates of the Aloe Tree, and offered as a present to the Chief of the whole Tribe.

The Botocudo Chieftain is an Interpreter, who will readily answer any questions which may be desired.

THE FAMILY IS ACCOMPANIED BY

A young Indian Savage,
OF THE TRIBE CALLED PURIS.

This Puris Indian, now twenty-two years of age, was only ten years old when he was taken prisoner by a party of Portuguese, the Commander of whom had him educated, and kept him in his service up to the present time. Having been taken at a tender age, this Savage bears no external insignia like the Botocudos; but from his complexion, though not quite so dark as the others, the particular form of his head, his jet coloured and stiff hair, and especially from his eyes, his extraordinary origin will readily be discovered. Although below the middle size, he is remarkably well-proportioned. On account of his education his manners are quite gentle, and he can converse a little in three different languages.

To be seen and disposed of to Amateurs, on very reasonable terms, several Dress s, Implements of War, and other Curiosities used by the South American Savages.

Also for Sale at the Rooms, just published, an Historical Account of the Manners and Customs of the Savage Inhabitants of Brazil, by N. CHABERT.

Fig. 7. Bill advertising the display of Tono Maria and Jochina in Cheltenham. The most important difference between this display and the London one is the disappearance of the child and his apparent replacement by an adult Puri. They seem to have been displayed wearing different costume to that used in London; furthermore the display had the secondary characteristic of providing an opportunity for the sale of ethnographic material - which seems unlikely to have been entirely if at all of Puri or Botocudo origin. 16 by 25 cms. Second private collection. Photograph courtesy of the Trustees of the British Museum.

250

REFERENCES CITED

Altick, R.D.
1978   The Shows of London. Cambridge and London: Belknap Press.

Anonymous
1822   The London Literary Gazette; and journal of belles lettres, arts, sciences, &c. for the year 1822. London: B. Bensley.

Chabert, X.
1822   A Brief Historical Account of the Life and Adventures of the Botocudo Chieftain, and Family, now exhibiting at no.23, New Bond Street; together with, a faithful description of the manners and customs of the savage inhabitants of the country they come from. London: C. Baynes.

Cheshire, Neil, Tony Waldron, Alison Quinn, and David Quinn
1980   Frobisher's Eskimos in England. Archivaria 10.

Foreman, Carolyn
1943   Indians Abroad. Norman: University of Oklahoma Press.

Hartmann, Thekla
1975   A contribuição da iconografia para o conhecimento de Índios brasileiros do século XIX. Colleção Museu Paulista, Série de Etnologia 1.

Hemming, John
1978   Red Gold. The conquest of the Brazilian Indians. London: Macmillan.

Ingermann, Carl
1825   Öffentliche Schaugebung. Leipziger Tageblatt 123/1825 (3 May 1825):629. Leipzig.

Lowie, Robert H.
1944   Eastern Brazil: An introduction. In: J.H. Steward (ed.), Handbook of South American Indians (Bulletin of the Bureau of American Ethnology 143) I:381-397. Washington, DC: Government Printing Office.

Métraux, Alfred
1944   The Botocudo. In: J.H. Steward (ed.), Handbook of South American Indians (Bulletin of the Bureau of American Ethnology 143) I:531-540. Washington, DC: Government Printing Office.

Sturtevant, William C. and David B. Quinn
1987   This New Prey: Eskimos Kidnapped to Europe, 1566-1577. In: C.F. Feest (ed.), Indians and Europe (Aachen: Rader Verlag), 61-140.

Wied-Neuwied, Prinz Maximilian zu
1820-1821 Reise nach Brasilien in den Jahren 1815 bis 1817. Frankfurt: H.L. Bronner.

Wright, Robin K.
1987   The Traveling Exhibition of Captain Samuel Hadlock, Jr.: Eskimos in Europe, 1822-1826. In C.F. Feest (ed.), Indians and Europe (Aachen: Rader Verlag), 215-234.

AMONG THE SAG-A-NOSHES:
Ojibwa and Iowa Indians
with George Catlin in Europe,
1843-1848

Christopher Mulvey

> "We have long heard of the *Sag-a-noshes*, and we have been
> anxious to come and see them."
> (Ojibwa Chief to the English People)

On 25 November 1839, George Catlin left New York for Liverpool on the
steam packet-boat "Roscius." He took with him a collection of 507 portraits
and pictures of American Indians and American Indian life based on work done
with 48 tribes. In addition he had with him several hundred American artifacts
including a Crow Lodge that would "shelter 80 or more persons" (Catlin
1840:47). The collection was to be put on view for its first European public in
February 1840 at the Egyptian Hall, Piccadilly, London. George Catlin listed
eight dukes as attending the private showings, including in the number
Wellington himself. Where the upper classes led, the middle classes followed.
Indians were fashionable. So much so that George Catlin and the Honourable
C.A. Murray (a friend, a fellow prairie traveller, and a figure in London
society) went disguised as Indians to the Caledonian Ball of that year, one of
"the most brilliant and splendid affairs that can be seen in London." This was
not fancy dress but a carefully staged deception. Catlin dressed up as a
warrior of the Sac tribe; Murray dressed up as a "Bois Brulé" and in this role
acted as Catlin's interpreter (Catlin 1848,1:35,70).

Play acting as Indian was prelude to Catlin's including a theatrical dimension
into his Indian Exhibition by hiring 20 men and women to put on Indian
costume to make *tableaux vivants*. They staged eleven war scenes and eight
domestic scenes to illustrate the lectures that Catlin gave on Indian life. Much
rehearsed and practiced, they were a pronounced success. So enlivened, Catlin's
Indian Exhibition toured through the British Isles in the next two years
visiting Liverpool, Manchester, Sheffield, Leeds, York, Edinburgh, Glasgow,
Belfast, and Dublin (Catlin 1848,1:94-96,100). In the spring of 1843, Catlin
returned to Manchester for a third time and he obviously believed that he had
exhausted the potential interest of the English in the make-believe Indians. He
was planning to return to New York when, he said, nine Ojibwa Indians
appeared and they asked for his help. One of Catlin's descendants, Majorie
Catlin Roehm (1966:261), chronicling the story of George Catlin and her family
in the best light, says of this critical juncture: "He was decidedly against
exploiting the Indians abroad... but George, having seen the fine-looking
Ojibways, also saw a chance to fill his purse before going home."

Catlin's dilemma and ambivalence were displayed here in a way that typified the clash of compassion and opportunism in all his dealings with the American Indians. Catlin, among the first of America's ethnographers, was also one of her original showmen. He had no framework other than that of private enterprise with which to support himself and his projects. His research, his collection, his exhibition, and eventually his Museum of Mankind were undertaken on an entrepreneurial basis. He tried all his life to get the American Congress to buy his collection (he even tried to sell it to the British Museum), but he could get no support in the direction from American or English, public or private, sources (Truettner 1978:39,52; Plate 1962:200-203). Public and private action could and did pursue him as a debtor far more efficiently than it could help him as either scholar or artist.

So live Indians again entered the life of George Catlin and for the first time enter the book he was to call *Catlin's Notes of Eight Years' Travels and Residence in Europe, with his North American Indian Collection. With Anecdotes and Incidents of the Travels and Adventures of Three Different Parties of American Indians Whom he Introduced to the Courts of England, France, and Belgium.* This was issued as published by the author in London in 1848. The styling of the title was intended to make this book a match to his *Letters and Notes on the Manners, Customs, and Condition of the North American Indians. Written during eight years' travel amongst the wildest tribes of Indians in North America in 1832 to 1839* (Catlin 1841).

The American *Letters and Notes* had also been published in London, in 1841. It had been a critical and commercial success, a success that Catlin hoped to repeat. The second, the European, *Notes* were not then and have not been since received with the acclaim of the American *Letters and Notes*. In *Palette and Tomahawk* Robert Plate (1962:199) describes the second book as "harshly and carelessly written at a time of emotional depression... It failed in all respects." Plate's naive commentary is confirmed by William H. Truettner (1979:53), the most perceptive and well-versed of Catlin's biographers and critics. "*Travels in Europe*," he says, "is a careless and windy series of anecdotes, describing the bewildered reactions of Ojibwa and Iowa to European civilization." Judged alongside Catlin's other works as a piece of ethnology, *Travels in Europe* is not one of Catlin's successes but that is perhaps the wrong context for judging the book. It is in fact better read as an example of contemporary American travel books describing Europe, among which it is a very interesting text, with a distinctive quality attributable to the presence of the Indians.

The original party of nine Ojibwas of 1843 were succeeded in 1844 by a party of fourteen Iowa Indians; these in turn were succeeded in 1845 by a second party of Ojibwas, numbering eleven. From the first the appearance of Indians renewed English interest in Catlin's exhibition. He was immediately able to rent the Egyptian Hall again and crowds came in large numbers. Queen

Victoria herself sent the Ojibwas a £20 note and the promise of tartan blankets; eventually, Catlin arranged a royal audience at Windsor Castle. It was apparent that Catlin could not generate continuing interest in his Indian Exhibition unless he had Indians to exhibit. With the arrival of the Iowas, he was able to move the exhibition from the Egyptian Hall to the even more lucrative location of Vauxhall Gardens, where the Indians set up encampment in the open air. They added horses to the act and again they were a great fashionable, and a considerable financial, success. The Indians were able to save Catlin from commercial failure but as often as they were able to do so, they involved him in new commercial commitments (Catlin 1848,1:143-149; 2:117-119).

European commercialism (and disease) that were eventually to make this pattern of encounter of Indian and European as unhappy as those patterns established on the American continent were not the first problems that the Indians brought to Catlin. "George," says Majorie Roehm (1966:262), "was condemned by the press for exploiting the Indians for his own gain, although he made repeated denials." And this was an accusation made from the first arrival of the Ojibwas in 1843. Because of his involvement with the Indians and their agent, a man called Arthur Rankin, Catlin got the reputation as a mountebank. He began to lose the social reputation that had enabled him to meet with dukes.

Exploiting and preserving, conserving and commercializing, the simultaneous and conflicting impulses distinguished Catlin's special dedication to "his Indians" as he suggestively called them. The collection was inevitably a commercial property but, he claimed, the display of men and women as "wild Indians" was a means of saving them from the fate of London beggars. The publishing of his book about the Indians' experience of Europe was something that Catlin said in his Preface was "due to them." If the Indian in the wilderness was thought of "as a sort of wild beast," when he appeared before European courts and showed himself "the dignified, the undaunted (and even courteous) gentleman, he there gains his strongest admirers" (Catlin 1848,1:ix). Though the Ojibwas impressed the court at Windsor and the Iowas impressed the court at St. Cloud, it was nonetheless as wildmen that they pleased the peoples of London and Paris.

In the Preface to *Notes of Eight Years' Travels and Residence in Europe*, Catlin spoke of eight years of his life as having spent "amongst the wild Indians of the 'Far West' in the forests of America" and he offered his new work as "a brief summary of the scenes of eight years spent amidst the civilization and refinements of the 'Far East'" (Catlin 1848,1:v). The portions of his life were made antithetical and so were the perspectives. The book was to be a moral compensation to its subject, the Indians, as it was to be a financial compensation to its author, Catlin. The book would also state antithetically the difference between the Far West and the Far East; that is, between America and Europe. It was to be part of the moral compensation to the Indians that they would be shown to be finally superior in point of "civilization and refinements" to the Europeans. It is a curious fact that this truth was one that appealed alike to the Indians, Anglo-Americans, and the Europeans (and still does).

The interaction of values between Far West and Far East, between America and Europe, between Savage and Civilized, between Heathen and Christian made Catlin's book a classic statement of the Primitive in Society. The Indians, said Catlin, looked at London and Paris with a freshness and a clarity that the inhabitants could not achieve (Catlin 1848,2:307). At the same time the book was also a classic statement of the simple inhabitants of the New World's exposure to the corruption of the Old World. Viewed in this generic perspective, Catlin's *Notes of Eight Years' Travels* took its place alongside American travel literature of the period in which England and Europe were seen to be degenerate when judged against the republican purity of the United States. Catlin's simple Indian red men were made to sound like democratic American white men. The Indian became the "American" and spoke for the "best" American values in the face of the values represented by the European beggar, the European cleric, the European noble, the European sovereign.

This perspective that the Indian provided was exactly that of the common-sense observer of the ridiculous, a stock pattern of 18th century satire. *Gulliver's Travels* provides the classic model. Such a role for the American Indian within the European scene had been implicit from the beginning. But the role had been made most fully explicit in the 18th century, as Truettner (1979:70) observes: "By the end of the 18th century, [the Indian] emerged from the pristine wilds of America with a new role, designed to establish him as the model whom civilized man must never forget. As an innocent primitive untouched by the corrupt ritual of European society, he was proclaimed the chief exponent of natural law, the one splendid example who remained close to God's original image of mankind." In Manchester, Catlin represented the Ojibwa Indians as just such commentators on the European scene. They saw, he said, the mayor "'and his squaw, and many other beautiful squaws, all drinking; and they saw many people through the windows, and in the doors, as they passed along the streets who were quite drunk, and two or three lying down in the streets like pigs; and they thought the people of Manchester loved much to drink liquor'" (Catlin 1848,1:113). The mixture of naive and critical vision was well adjusted. Catlin's explanations only exposed further the perfidy of civilization's rationalizations. The Ojibwas looked across Manchester and, said Catlin, "'they saw a great deal of smoke and thought the prairies were on fire... They saw a great many large houses, which seemed as if nobody lived in. They saw a great many people in the streets, who appeared very poor, and looked as they had nothing to eat'" (Catlin 1848,1:114). George Catlin tried then to explain to the Indians that the empty factories and the starving people

256

were the result of a trade cycle and business recession.

The experience of Manchester and its filtering through the perception of the Indian and the presentation of the Yankee served as a good preparation for the yet more bizarre and distorted scene which was London. Here, they "'saw a great many fine houses, but nobody in the windows; saw many men with a large board on the back, and another on the breast, walking the street - supposed it was some kind of punishment; saw men carrying coal, their hats on wrong side before... a great many poor and ragged people on the sides of the roads; saw a great many men and women drinking in the shops...'" (Catlin 1848,1:129). This was to be the abiding impression not only of Manchester and of London but of England and of Europe. The great numbers of the poor and the great wealth of the nations. It impressed itself as a terrible fact upon every one of the Indians; but it is also the great impression that all Americans, red or white, took from England in the first half of the nineteenth century. The Indian traveler here is distinct only because his impression is not at all mitigated by a positive response to the English landscape. That was an effect that could override the appalling dismay generated by urban poverty in the American traveler. White Americans were highly susceptible to the seductive effects of a landscape deeply suggestive of a shared cultural heritage, one often re-enforced by pronounced racial and religious identifications.

The Indians were not so suggestible and for the most part passed over rural England without comment. Their sensitivity on the other hand to the human suffering (and degradation) within the English cities made them deeply distressed by an inexplicable scene that the Ojibwas reported to Catlin (1848,1:129-130) on their first tour about London. "They had passed two *Indians* in the streets with brooms, sweeping away the mud; they saw them hold out their hands to people going by, as if they were begging for money.'" The Ojibwa could not understand this since they argued that white men would not dress up as Indians nor would Indians beg. Catlin explained that these men were Lascars of the East Indies, unable for whatever reason to find berths as sailors. The Ojibwas determined to throw these pitiful crossing-sweeps money when next they met them.

It was curious that the Iowa Indians in the following year went through exactly the same pattern of reactions and experiences in London even down to the detail that "'they had passed *Indians*, with brooms in their hands sweeping the dust in the street!'" (Catlin 1848,2:9-10). The only new detail was the impression made upon the Iowas by the great quantities of fresh meat in butchers' windows. Catlin recorded an identical conversation with the Iowas explaining the condition of the Lascars (whom the Iowas called "Ojibbeways"). The generosity of the Indians to the London poor (and to the poor of Manchester, Glasgow, and Dublin) was something that Catlin constantly remarked on. In one day alone, they gave out 30 shillings in silver, "'which they thought would do a great deal of good and the Great Spirit would reward them for it'"

(Catlin 1848,2:114).

When the Iowas left England for Scotland, "the great numbers of poor and squalid-looking and barefooted creatures they saw walking in the snow had excited their deepest pity, they got in the daily habit of throwing pennies to them as they passed along. The numbers of the ragged poor that they saw there they represented as surpassing all they had seen in their whole travels" (Catlin 1848,2:174). The poverty of the poor of Glasgow matched the converting zeal of the clergy of Glasgow who crowded to the Indians' apartments to bring them the word of God, and to preach the need of a mission to the Iowa peoples and territory. An Indian called White Cloud, speaking for the Iowas, rebuked the Scottish clergymen, pointing to the poor of Glasgow and in his turn called for a mission and missionaries in Scotland. The clergy, taken aback, were not above learning a lesson themselves. Catlin (1848,2:177) reported that "one of them said to me that he never in his life heard truer remarks, or a lesson that more distinctly and forcibly pointed out the primary duties of his profession." It cannot be denied that there was a certain stylization in all these scenes even to the repeated details of parallel episodes involving different groups of Indians. The suspicion that Catlin was here working with a literary trope cannot be denied.

Benjamin Bissell's survey of the treatment of the Indian in eighteenth century English literature, a work first published in 1925, is suggestive. One of the commonest roles that the Indian was given to play was that of the rationalist commentator on European, Christian, or civilized behavior. Bissell (1968:71,74) points out that the law and various other professions were popular objects of these satirical pieces that presented imaginary Indian observations. "Religion," he writes, "is also a popular subject for these supposed criticisms of the savage. The Indian is pictured as listening gravely to the arguments of the missionaries, answering them with better ones of his own, and pointing out the inconsistency of the precepts with the practices of his would-be instructors in morals." In the case of George Catlin's nineteenth century versions of these scenes there was something more than literary trope. Catlin was no doubt presenting evidence based on some kind of real experience but the shaping forces of cultural convention were obviously strong. However, Bissell's (1968:77) conclusion gives pause for reflection: "The notion of the Indian cleverly ridiculing the follies of civilization and uttering high-sounding oratories in praise of natural goodness, is of course, purely fictitious, one of the many projections of the romantic imagination." But that assessment may understimate both Indian rhetoric and Indian analytical power.

Catlin had to encode according to imaginative patterns as well as pheno-menological ones. The complexity of judging the judgements of others on the question of Indian judgements on European values is well illustrated by this overlapping of perspectives. Prejudice and preconception are interlocked with reassessment and revision. Bissell (1968:214) points to a remarkable example of this process of reassessment: "The student of *belles lettres* cannot fail to be impressed by that singular product of the purely literary imagination, the transformation of the sinister and forbidding savage into the idealized embodiment of picturesqueness, pathos, fortitude, and heroic sentiment." These were the instinctive modes in which George Catlin responded to the Indian and his was one of the most powerful nineteenth century expressions of this idealization of the Indian. Catlin, says Truettner (1979:71), "wished to bolster the arguments in favor of nature and savage life that prevailed in the 18th century, to update them, in effect with more advanced scientific methods and on an abundance of personal testimony that spoke passionately of his high regard for the inhabitants of the Great Plains."

Eighteenth century conceptions had been reinforced by Romanticism; indeed reactions to the "Noble Savage" represent a continuity of thought between the eighteenth and the nineteenth century. Romantic conceptions of the Indian had themselves been reinforced by the realization that these primitive and noble cultures were actually threatened with extinction at the time when they were most to be appreciated. This nexus, of course, represents no paradox: it might be said to be consequential. Robert F. Berkhofer (1979:88) has made much of the connection in identifying early nineteenth century attitudes to the American Indian: "Most romantic of all was the impression of the Indian as rapidly passing away before the onslaught of civilization. The nostalgia and pity aroused by the dying race produced the best romantic sentiment... It made its mark on world literature through James Fenimore Cooper's *The Last of the Mohicans* (1826), and inspired George Catlin to do his famed portraits of noble Indians on the Plains and Prairies before it was too late to capture on canvas a dying race... they were in romantic eyes a poetical people whose activities took place in a sublime landscape and whose fate aroused sentiment." Despite Berkhofer's disdain for Romantic sentimentality on the subject of the Indians, it would be anachronistic to think that even he himself would have thought any more positively about the American Indian had he lived at the beginning of the nineteenth century.

While they were in Scotland, the Iowas received almost daily gifts of bibles, one for each. They had received several copies of the Good Book from English Christians; they were to receive still more in Ireland. Already in Scotland, Catlin (1848,2:174) said that along with the other gifts that the Indians were receiving, these bible were beginning to become a problem for a touring company. Jim, an Iowa brave, attempted several solutions to this. He first approached Catlin's assistant to see if he could effect an exchange of his collection of bibles for copies of *Punch*. "'I guess em swap!'" The assistant declined to negotiate this deal, saying that *Punch* would not accept the bibles, given by good people all over the United Kingdom (Catlin 1848,2:189). In Dublin, with yet more bibles on his hands, Jim came up with another solution. "The Bibles they had received," wrote Catlin, "and were daily receiving as 'the most valuable presents that could be made them,' he had supposed must of course have some considerable value." Jim therefore proposed to sell them at the Zoological Gardens Exhibition but no one would buy them. "'I guess em no good,'" said Jim, "' - I no sell em, but I get em a heap'" (Catlin 1848,2:194). There was no getting rid of these most valuable presents and Catlin (1848,2:307) made a final count for the Iowas when they left him: "Their Bibles had increased in their various boxes since the last census to more than a hundred and fifty; their *religious tracts*, which they could not read, to some thousands; their *dolls* [i.e. religious statues], in all, to fifty; and other useless toys to a great number." Catlin's exasperation with this indiscriminate, inconsiderate and counterproductive gift giving was evident.

Despite the dismal performance of Anglican, Methodist, and Catholic alike, despite the continuing exposure of European hypocrisy in preaching a gospel of brotherly love in cities like London, Glasgow, and Dublin, Catlin did not falter in his conviction that the Indians had much to learn from the Whites' civilization and the Whites' religion. In his own way, he could no more leave the Indians alone than could the ministers. Catlin's regret was that the Indians would return to the *"Far West"* of America having received such a bad impression of this civilization and religion in the *"Far East"* of Europe that they would have no cause to improve their lives or learn new ways.

At the same time, though, Indian dignity was emphasized by encounters with the British clergy and the British poor. Catlin preserved the stereotypes of a literature that used the "Noble Savage" to reinforce old role models but not to provide new ones. The Indian responded with amazement at the institutionalized and social brutality and this made the Indian appear the moral superior of the European. However, that same amazement provoked by the commonplaces of English life made the Indian appear the intellectual inferior of the European.

An incident that occurred on the Leeds to York railway exactly balanced in Catlin's telling the Indians' roles as naive and enlightened observers of the curiosities of the European scene. Looking out of the train window, the Iowas were astonished to see 40 to 50 fox hunters at full gallop across Yorkshire. "This," said Catlin, "was a subject entirely new to them and unthought of by the Indians; and knowing that English soldiers all wore red coats, they were alarmed, their first impression being that we had brought them on to hostile ground, and that this was a 'war-party' in pursuit of their enemy" (Catlin 1848,2:145). So far, the European view had the ascendency. The Indian perception was shown not so much to be wrong as amusingly misconceived; the reader could enjoy his expert knowledge and condescend to the naive Indian. At this point, Catlin explained to the Indians exactly what the Europeans were in fact doing. It was not a war party but was made up of noblemen and gentry who hunted without guns and who did not eat the fox. The Iowas amazed fear turned now to amazed contempt that "'chiefs'" should so risk their lives and horses for inedible meat and even destroy the pelt of the fox by pulling off the tail for a hatband trophy (Catlin 1848,2:145-146).

In this kind of scene and telling, Catlin's own posture was nicely poised. The opposition established here between Indian and European provided neither side with the upper hand. Iowa brave and English foxhunter were made both to seem faintly ludicrous. But Catlin as teller needed to identify with neither party. His position as White American offered a mediation of the extremes of *"Far West"* and *"Far East,"* combining merits of noble savage and nobility. This was almost an instinctive reflex (and defense) of the American in Europe. Catlin showed less anxiety in his social relationships in Europe than did, say, a traveler like James Fenimore Cooper, although Catlin's relationships with both London and Parisian Society were more equivocal than Cooper's relationships with either. Catlin, on the other hand, functioned less as the gentleman artist and more as the interpreter and purveyor of Indian culture for his gentlemen clients. At the same time, he played the reverse role since he was called upon to present European culture to the Indians. As he explained the one to the other, he was able to offset the claims of the one by the values of the other, appropriating an ideal middle out of the two real instances of social order.

The presence of the Indians guaranteed him some access to Society and at the same time secured him in some measure against the judgement of that Society. His accounts of the contacts between the Indians and nobles were all touched with this doubtful duality but made for amusing reading. The Iowas received several invitations to attend social occasions given by distinguished Londoners. "Amongst the first of these kind invitations," he wrote, "was one from Mr. Disraeli, M.P., for the whole party to partake breakfast at his house in Park Lane" (Catlin 1848,2:24). The highly stylized etiquette was a source of considerable anxiety to the Indians. One of these, known as the Doctor, painted his face three times over in preparation and they were all distressed that the invitation said that "Breakfast" would be at 12 Noon. They further prepared themselves for this Feast by starving themselves so as to eat hugely and please their host. They would not at first believe Catlin when he told them that at these late breakfasts in London, fashionable people distinguish themselves by eating fastidiously. The conflict between Iowan and London social custom was maximized by Catlin in his role as interpreter of cultures. Whatever misgivings that he might have had himself about going to breakfast with one of London's most dazzling hosts went unmentioned. In the event, the majority of the Indians decided to follow the custom of London and give themselves a solid meal before the Society Breakfast. The Doctor, the most enigmatic among Catlin's characterizations of the Indians, decided that he would neither compromise his own customs nor insult those of his hosts. He starved himself before the feast to observe Indian custom, and then he starved himself at the feast to observe English custom.

In his telling, Catlin mocked, gently, both the Doctor and Disraeli. Two

261

strange societies were brought into amusing as much as into illuminating contrast. The American reader could reinforce a sense that his own behavior represented a norm. The Society Breakfast engaged in by the upper classes of London was often commented upon by the American traveler. For Henry James (in 1869), it was the experience of a social custom that disconnected him from the United States, at the same time that it put him in touch with Byron, Sheridan, Scott, and Moore. It allowed him, and how he enjoyed it, to meet a social order "not obliged to go to an office or a store," for such meals were only given by those who had "a clear alternative to that passivity" (James 1956:561). Well into the second half of the nineteenth century Americans liked to comment upon the English custom which so flagrantly declared that the guests had no business to attend to and that they had no doubt not been to bed until two o'clock the previous morning. Catlin's attendance at Mr. Disraeli's breakfast party nicely combined his business, presenting Indians to Europe, with his pleasure, meeting distinguished Londoners.

The ambiguities of Catlin's participant-observer position and the opportunities for contrastive comment and comedy were even more accentuated when he moved beyond the upper classes to present the Indians to royalty. Again his own reactions to the scene were lost to his commentary since he reported not what he felt or thought but what the Indians did and said. The first encounter of this kind came when Queen Victoria invited the Ojibwas to Windsor Castle. Presentation at Court was one of the most sought after honors by visiting American dignitaries; ministers to the Court of St. James had their work cut out arranging meetings between sovereigns and the young ladies of the United States. The procedures were elaborately described for Americans in books such as Horace Greeley's *Glances at Europe* where he sardonically called it "Royal Sunshine" (Greeley 1851:96). It was a habit of much of this commentary to poke fun at the idea of monarchy at the same time as describing it in detail.

All of this republican interest and republican fun established an excellent framework for Catlin's presentation of Ojibwa and British dressing up when chief met queen. "Descending from the carriage," said Catlin of the Indians arrival at Windsor Castle, "the poor old chief, whose eyes were getting a bit dim with age, was completely nonplussed at beholding the magnificent figure (in scarlet and gold lace and powered wig) of (his apparent Majesty) Sykes, the well-known porter of the palace" (Catlin 1848,1:135). The Indian was only saved from a *faux pas* by the simultaneous arrival of several footmen, all of them dressed equally splendidly (and, it might be inferred, equally absurdly). The mistaking of Footman Sykes for Prince Albert reaffirmed the simplicities and the "naturalness" of the American Presidential pattern. Catlin's Indian made a point that other American commentators needed to make more explicitly.

There was considerably less of this mock-heroic tone in the next encounter between Indian and royalty that Catlin described. Since she had seen the Ojibwas, Queen Victoria did not think it necessary to see the Iowas; therefore

Fig. 1. Catlin's Iowa Indians dancing in front of King Louis-Philippe of France at the Tuileries, 21 April 1845. Oil painting by Karl Girardet, 1845 (Musée National du Château de Versailles, after A. Parent, *Une Autre Amérique* (La Rochelle 1982), pl.129)

they received no invitation to her court. Catlin reported them to be unhappy about leaving Europe without meeting a monarch; for which reason they agreed to accompany him to France, there to meet with King Louis-Philippe (Catlin 1848,2:198). For their part, when the Indians saw him they decided that he was a greater king than Victoria a queen since they saw less suffering among his subjects (Catlin 1848,2:217). The war chief gave Louis-Philippe a speech and a calumet. This was more satisfactory than the Ojibwa audience with Victoria when another clash between Indian and English protocol had arisen over the fact that the Indians had wanted to present a pipe of peace but could not give it to a woman; since it had to be given to the highest person present, it could be given to no one and the Ojibwa chief had returned with the pipe in his hand (Catlin 1848,1:138).

The tone of Catlin's account of the meeting at St. Cloud was more straight-forward than that of the account of the meeting at Windsor. There was no sense of distance here, no disdain nor amusement. Catlin spoke directly of his own feelings and did not disperse his response as he had done at Windsor or in London Society by way of the devices of the cultural interpreter or mediating American. For his part, Louis-Philippe spoke directly to Catlin in a

263

way that Victoria would not but also could not.

It is evident from the differing accounts of the two royal audiences that Catlin gave a highly personal coloring to the events that he described. This is to be expected; it is not very much more than any writer did then or does now. At the same time, it put at a distance the direct reaction of the American Indian to the European scene and it is only with difficulty that we can reach beyond Catlin to those Ojibwas and Iowas who traveled through the United Kingdom and through parts of Europe in the years from 1843 to 1848. However there are ways that can allow us to get a little closer to the Indian perception of Europe. Within the *Notes of Eight Years' Travels*, Catlin gave a fairly full account of the preparations and contents of a notebook compiled by Jim of the Iowas. At the same time there exists a document written and published in 1848 by one of the Indians themselves, the Ojibwa Maungwudaus, which gave some account of their travels with and without Catlin.

The Iowa Indian called Jim showed from Catlin's first meeting with the group that he had an unusual keenness not only to see as much as he could wherever he went but also to make a count of what he saw and eventually to make a written record. In London, he and the Doctor adopted white man's clothes so that they could extend their explorations without attracting attention. They visited churches and took note of gin-shops. At first the Iowas were reluctant to believe that English got drunk. This misapprehension was dispelled. "Jim said that he and the Doctor had counted two or three hundred [gin-shops] in one hour" (Catlin 1848,2:71). Some streets were so filled with miserable women and children that they did not wish to visit them again. Once more the Indians commented on the miserliness of the clergy's work: Jim "said he thought it was wrong to send missionaries from this country to the Indian country, when there were so many poor creatures here who want their help." The excess of gin-shops over churches continued to attract the Indians' attention and Jim set about a more systematic gathering of information. With a team of five, he counted the gin-shops between St. James Street and White-chapel and home again by Euston. The war chief kept score by notching a tally stick. They averaged a total of 450 gin-shops, or "chichobobboags" (Catlin 1848,2:99-101).

Jim continued his investigation of English social patterns to the point where he had Daniel, Catlin's man, help him to make a record book of all he saw. He kept statistics on poor houses, prisons, and breweries. He began to learn to write and to speak English in order to do this work more effectively. He was, said Catlin, so far successful that the Doctor became alarmed at the threat this posed to his "medicine" (Catlin 1848,2:154). In Dublin Jim got Daniel to give him statistics on the Queen's expenses so that these could be entered into the record book:

"£891,000 p. a. - Support of Royal Family

£60,000 p. a. - Queen's pin money (privy purse)
£12,550 p. a. - Footmen, coachmen, postillions
£5,854,851 p. a. - The Navy" (Catlin 1848,2:182).

When Jim learned that the Army cost yet more than the Navy, Catlin wrote that he "then conceived the idea of getting into his book the whole number of soldiers that were required in England, Scotland, and Ireland to keep the people at work in the factories, and to make them pay their taxes... [The Iowas] had discernment enough to see that such an enormous number of soldiers and police... would not be kept in pay if they were not necessary" (Catlin 1848,2:187). The great number and the high visibility of troops in Dublin had brought this fact of Victorian life to the Indians' attention. The link between the size of these armies in the three kingdoms, the general poverty, and the consumption of alcohol was made by Jim by way of a considerable body of evidence.

He recorded from *The Times* the facts that 29.000,000 gallons of ardent spirits were consumed in Great Britain and Ireland in the year 1844 at a cost of £24.000,000. He noted also that 50,000 died of drink, and that half the nation's cases of insanity, two thirds of the pauperism and three quarters of the crime were attributed to drink. "This, Jim said, was one of the best things he had got down in his book, because he said that the *black-coats* were always talking so much about the Indians getting drunk" (Catlin 1848,2:188). Obviously one of the Iowa's main motives in collecting his statistics were for the bearing that they had upon his own country and the activities of the white man there. At the same time, Jim's records constituted an indictment of the English social order, one that very plainly countered claims to "civilization and refinements." The presence of this statistical information and the consistent view point of the Indians, especially as it was expressed by Jim, made Catlin's *Notes of Eight Years' Travel* one of the most thorough-going condemnations of Victorian England that appeared in this genre of popular travel literature.

Many Americans commented upon the great poverty to be found in the great cities of the United Kingdom. Liverpool for instance, the landing place of the majority, shocked and dismayed them and reinforced convictions that the United States was indeed the great land that they had been led to believe it was. But even a Fourierian socialist like Horace Greeley thought it best to pass through Liverpool as rapidly a possible, to move on to London and to the landscape, and to see the things that were worth seeing. The superb railway system and the excellent hotels could rapidly shield the middle-class American from the brunt of urban squalor; after that he learned to shield himself from this reality as the did the British middle class. The Indians were not traveling first class; they were not staying in the best hotels; they did not participate in the special kind of selective seeing that shaped the travel books of the majority of the middle class, middle aged, middle of the century American travelers. It may be argued that the Indians saw what they wanted to see like any other traveler, but what they wanted to see was not so rigidly preselected into a positive passivity by the cultural, religious, and racial expectations of the group. The Indian walking through London identified with the Lascar crossing-sweep not with the Victorian pedestrian.

So it was that Jim of the Iowas took back to the Wilderness a record book filled with a statement "of the tens of thousands of civilized people who are in it," said Catlin, "recorded (to their amazement) as *blind*, as *deaf and dumb*, and *insane*; of *gallows* and *guillotines*, of *massacres* and *robberies*, the number of *grogshops*, ... of *coal pits*, of *treadmills*, ... of *rapes*, ... of *games laws*, of *Christianity*, of *drunkedness*, of *national debt* and *repudiation*" (Catlin 1848,2:308). In the absence of a copy of Jim's record book, we must rely on Catlin's account of its contents, but even the friendly White man used the Indian not for the Indian's purpose. The reference at the end of Jim's list to *"national debt* and *repudiation"* served the purpose of Catlin the American nationalist far more than it would appear to have served that of Jim the Iowa. At the same time, Catlin showed himself to be almost as willing as N.P. Willis himself - "the prince of American journalists in the middle years of the century" (Mowat 1935:121) - at hobnobbing with the English aristocracy. Nonetheless, Catlin was driven to go far beyond the normal white American in recording the destitution of the British population. While it must be argued that Catlin's account colored the Indians' impressions of Europe, it must also be argued that Jim's record book strongly influenced Catlin's *Notes*.

The report of Maungwudaus of the Ojibwa is a source that provides a more direct statement of Indian experience otherwise described in Catlin's book. Maungwudaus's piece is some nine pages long. It was published in the same year as Catlin's own text, 1848, and it was entitled *An Account of the Chippewa Indians, Who Have Been Travelling Among the Whites, in the United States, England, Ireland, Scotland, France and Belgium*.[1] Maungwudaus was one of the second party of Ojibwa (or Chippewa) that had joined Catlin in Paris in 1845. They had journeyed to him from London hoping that he could help them since they were having little success on their own (Catlin 1848,2:278). They did not return to America until 1848 though they left Catlin's Exhibition in 1846. Maungwudaus's account therefore overlaps with Catlin's for less than a year.

Maungwudaus's statement must not be presumed to have been entirely free of the white coloration that was for instance evident in Jim of the Iowas' record. Maungwudaus was working in a language foreign to him; he was dependent on Whites for publication; his document was authenticated (and it may be presumed approved) by the Canadian civil servant, William Heating, Esquire, Superintendent of Indian Affairs (Peyer 1982:66). The two records, Maungwudaus's and Catlin's, where they overlap or deal with similar subjects, confirm one another to a considerable degree.

Towards the end of the second volume of his *Notes*, Catlin introduced the second Ojibwa party and provided an illustration depicting the whole group.
266

Maungwudaus appeared as "1. Maun-gua-duas (a Great Hero) - Chief ... Age 41." Catlin provided further details in his text. "The chief of this party, Maun-gua-daus, was a remarkably fine man, both in his personal appearance and intellectual faculties. He was a half-caste, and speaking the English language tolerably well, acted as chief and interpreter of the party" (Catlin 1848,2:279). Maungwudaus attached to his own account a short statement entitled the "Pleasing Testimony of George Catlin, Esq." in which Catlin bore witness to the good faith and the good conduct of Maungwudaus and his companions. This was dated in London, April 20, 1848. Catlin said that the Indians had been constantly with him for a space of three years but there was some inconsistency here since Catlin's formal contacts with the second party of Ojibwas ended in 1846.

Maungwudaus's *Account* conformed to and confirmed the pattern of Indian descriptions of the European scene that were the standard of this genre. Following a brief statement about the journey across America and the Atlantic, Maungwudaus moved rapidly to the main topic of his opening pages, the city of London and its inhabitants.

"From Portsmouth, we went to London, and we remained a long time in this wonderful city; performed every day in the Egyptian Hall, in Piccadilly. This city is about ten miles broad, but some parts of it is about twenty miles long. Like musketoes in America in the summer season, so are the people in this city, in their numbers and biting one another to get a living. Many very rich, and many very poor; about 900 berths and about 1100 deaths every week in this city alone. There are many stone and iron bridges over the river Thames. The steamboats in this river are not so handsome as those in America. The St. Paul's Church and the Council House are very large buildings indeed. Most of the houses are rather dark in color on account of too much smoke" (Maungwudaus 1848:3-4).

At this point, the Indians were in the charge of a manager called Harris and he like Catlin introduced his party to Victoria. Maungwudaus's description combined naiveté and insight to generate the special quality of wisdom demanded for the reinterpretation or revision of common experience:

"Mr. Harris took us into the Queen's house. She is a small woman but handsome. There are many handsomer women than she. Prince Albert is a handsome and well built man. Her house is large, quiet country inside of it. We got tired before we went through all the rooms in it. Great many warriors with their swords and guns stands outside watching for the enemy. We have been told that she has three or four other houses in other places as large. The one we saw they say is much too small for her, and they are building a much larger one on one side of it" (Maungwudaus 1848:4).

267

Fig. 2. The second Ojibwa party dressed in Plains Indian style as portrayed and illustrated by Catlin (1848: Plate 18): 1. Maungwudaus (Great Hero), 2. Hail Storm, 3. Strong Rock, 4. King of the Loons, 5. Tempest Bird, 6. Bird of Thunder, 7. Elk, 8. Pelican, 9. Furious Storm, 10. Brave Warrior, 11. Woman of the Upper World, 12. unnamed child.

Like other American visitors to England in the 19th century, white as well as red, Maungwudaus was struck by the excesses of monarchical display, by the small stature and by the commonplace appearance of the great queen. He like other American travelers manifested his reaction to the sheer scale by way of boredom rather than by way of awe: "We got tired before we went through all the rooms." In 1851, Horace Greeley became angry when faced with this kind of thing; it affronted his republican code. Maungwudaus showed considerably more reserve than Catlin who was one of those Americans who enjoyed the act of homage making to the European monarch.

Maungwudaus's account of his meeting with King Louis-Philippe, Catlin's "wonderful man," was almost neutral:

"We went to France; stayed five months in Paris with Catlin's Indian Curiosities. Shook hands with Louis Philippe and all his family in the Palace called St. Cloud; gave them little war dance, shooting with bows and arrows at a target, ball play; also rowed our birch bark canoe in the artificial lake, amongst swans and geese. There were about four thousand French ladies and gentlemen with them. We dined with him in the afternoon in his Palace. He said many things concerning his having been in America when he was a young man. He gave us twelve gold and silver medals; he showed us all the rooms in his house" (Maungwudaus 1848:6).

Maungwudaus was quite willing to go beyond mere record particularly in the area of moral and social judgement though this may sometimes be a matter of inference on the part of the present-day reader. The Indian's comments on the

English male do not seem value free: "Many of the Englishmen have very big stomachs, caused by drinking too much ale and porter. Those who drink wine and brandy, their noses look like ripe strawberries" (Maungwudaus 1848:5). The grossness of the English physical appearance, in both men and women, was the subject of comment by numerous visitors from North America. Nathaniel Hawthorne in particular, when Liverpool Consul from 1853 to 1857, was given to making frequent comments in his notebooks about this fact of English life, one that he found disgusting in the extreme (see Hawthorne 1941:40-41,88, and elsewhere).

The behavior of English women was also the occasion of moral censure by Maungwudaus. Following a dinner given for the Indians by English army officers, the women present let it be known that they wanted to kiss the Ojibwas. Maungwudaus and his companions obliged.

"Then another officer said to us, 'Gentlemen, our pretty squaws are not yet satisfied; they want to be kissed on their mouths.' Then we kissed them on their mouths; then there was a great shout amongst the English warchiefs. Say-say-gon, our war-chief, then said in our language to the ladies: 'That is all you are good for; as for wives, you are good for nothing'" (Maungwudaus 1848:5-6).

Fig. 3. The second Ojibwa party dressed up in Micmac coats after their return, from left to right: Woman of the Upper World, Maungwudaus (The Great Hero), Bird of Thunder, The Elk, The Pelican, Furious Storm. After an anonymous daguerrotype, courtesy Smithsonian Institution, National Anthropological Archives, BAE collection.

The ladies wanted Maungwudaus to tell them what Say-say-gon had said, but the discreet Indian averted any insult in his translation. It was doubtful that the army officers had brought their wives to this function; the "pretty squaws" were very probably prostitutes. Had he been aware of this, it was not likely to have improved Maungwudaus's opinion of English women, or of army officers.

The Indians were sensitive to the insults implicit in these occasions and to the sense that they were not being treated as equals by many of those that they met. Towards the end of his *Account*, Maungwudaus recorded an incident in an English town when the Indians were jeered at by a group of young people who were watching a monkey performing in the street. It was the kind of scene which brought into sharp contrast an aggressive urban pattern of manners and the formal Indian pattern. But it did not go unremarked.

"A gentleman standing by, said to the audience, 'Look at the monkey take of his cap and make a bow in saluting these strangers; which of the two the strangers will think are most civilized, you or the monkey? You ought to be ashamed of yourselves. You may consider yourselves better and wiser than those strangers, but you are very much mistaken. Your treatment to them tells them that you are not, and you are so foolish and ignorant, you know nothing about it. I have been travelling five years among these people in their own country, and I never, not once, was insulted, but I was always kindly treated and respected by every one of them. Their little children have far better manners than you. Young men, the monkey pays you well for all the pennies you have given him; he is worthy to become your teacher.' We then threw some money to the monkey" (Maungwudaus 1848:9).

In this scene the gentleman traveler stepped forward opportunely. He offered the apology to the strangers for the brutality of European manners that many would like to offer to the American Indians. At the same time he gave expression to the exasperation and indignation of the Indians themselves. Maungwudaus, it could be inferred, was angry not only at the directness of the young men's insults but at their ludicrous injustice. The Indians were being mocked for being uncivilized by people who were themselves patently uncivilized. The Indian must have been the more angry because the *tu-quoque* argument must fail if delivered by the Indian himself. The satisfaction of having it delivered by the gentleman traveler was considerable. The role of the monkey in the scene must not be overlooked. The anthropomorphic and mimetic animal encoded all the contradictions of the scene and situation. The monkey represented animal nature, the brutal and the soulless, and at the same time the unspoilt, the innocent, the primitive. In the iconography of the hierarchical chain, the monkey stood close to man. Like man, but part of nature. With their technologically superior culture, white men had been from the first willing to identify the Indian with the monkey.

Maungwudaus presented in his scene in the English town an encapsulation of the debate and a dramatization of the issues. The cast was complete: the monkey, the lout, the Indian, the gentleman. In point of Europeanness, the gentleman and the lout were alike. In point of strangeness, the monkey and the Indian were alike. At issue was the point of civilization. The monkey was clearly not civilized since he was an animal; the gentleman clearly was civilized since he was a gentleman. He it was who accorded the greater civilization to the Indian. Further, the lout was shown to be lower than the animal since the lower being - the monkey - mimicked civilized behavior, while the higher being - the lout - mimicked brutal behavior.

Whether or not the scene enacted itself in actuality with quite such Aristotelian justness need not detract from its value as a record of the reactions of Maungwudaus. He showed by his representation of the scene the range of his reactions to European judgements on Indian nature and behavior.

A point on which the *Notes* of Catlin and the *Account* of Maungwudaus were very close was that of the unhappy ending of the relationship between American Indian and American White in Europe. Because of a death in the party of the Iowa Indians, they had decided to return to America. It was at that point that they were joined by the Ojibwas led by Maungwudaus. Catlin took the new party from Paris to Brussels at the invitation of the King of the Belgiums. In Brussels, two of the Indians died of smallpox. "The king of this country was very kind to us," wrote Maungwudaus. "The Belgians are like the French. Here poor Aunimuckwah-um and Mishimaung died with the small pox; and after we visited other towns on the borders of Germany, we returned to London again; and here our much respected war-chief, Say-say-on, died with the same dreadful disease that the others had died with" (Maungwudaus 1848:7). Catlin had not returned to London; he had returned to Paris, and he made a resolution not to show any more Indians, but like all previous decisions this was one dictated by the immediate economic chance as much as by anything else. His motives were as mixed at the end of his dealings with the Indians in Europe as they were at the beginning.

This tragic dimension provided a quality to Maungwudaus's *Account* that made a parallel to Catlin's own *Notes* and which distinguished both texts from the common pattern of nineteenth century travel books describing the American tour of Europe. It pointed to the fact that neither Maungwudaus nor Catlin were tourists; they were men making a living for themselves and their families, men failing to do so. "At Glasgow, two of my children died," wrote Maungwudaus, "another in Edinburgh; buried them in the burying ground of our friends the Quakers: and after we visited other towns at the North and the South, we went to England again; my wife died at Newark. The vicar of that church was very kind to us, in allowing us to bury her remains near the church" (Maungwudaus 1848:8-9). George Catlin had a similar story of personal tragedy to tell. In July 1845, his wife Clara had died in Paris just as they were planning to

271

return to New York. He had had to send Clara's body to America that she had longed to see and had himself stayed on alone in Europe (Catlin 1848,2:274-277; Roehm 1966:306). His wife had accompanied him for 13,000 miles of his journey through the Far West and following her death he took great consolation in the Far East that he had his children with him, especially his son George, aged three and a half. It was Catlin's tragedy, that like Maungwudaus, he had to commiserate the death of his son before very long. The child's body, like the wife's, was sent back to New York (Catlin 1848,2:311-325). With that Catlin left Paris and returned to London. Here he was to experience another kind of loss. In 1852, he went bankrupt and the whole of his Indian Collection fell into the hands of his creditors. Only then did he return to America as unhappy and as defeated as any of the Indians who had looked to Europe with promise.

These personal reflections filled the last chapter of his book about Europe. Reflections of a more general kind filled the penultimate chapter and there Catlin reiterated the points made in the Preface. The impression of the Indians upon the Europeans, he saw as almost entirely beneficial; the influence of the Europeans upon the Indians, he saw as almost wholly bad. He argued against letting Indians have too close a knowledge of the actualities of Christian civilization since they would use this to resist Christian doctrine. The ironies of this position were reinforced by the idealized role that Catlin ascribed to American pioneer civilization in mediating the extremes of pagan Indian territory and Christian Europe. "The Indians," he wrote, "should, with all their natural prejudices against civilized man, be held in ignorance of the actual crime, dissipation and poverty that belong to an enlightened world, until the honest pioneer, in his simple life, with his plough and his hoe can wile them into the mode of raising the necessaries of life" (Catlin 1848,2:310).

Catlin united the Indian and the pioneer in a ceremony of innocence and Robert Berkhofer has pointed to another way in which the Indian and the frontiersman held something in common in relation to civilization. "The white on the frontier," says Berkhofer (1979:94), "was as ill adapted for the coming of that civilization of which he was the vanguard as the last of the Indians trying to accomodate themselves to the new order. Both possessed too little 'Whiteness' and too much savagery to survive beyond a certain point in the history of the United States... [They exist in] that area between savagery and civilization... the still largely unsettled West to which Catlin and other artists rushed in their battle with time."

Catlin's conception of the frontier did not allow for such a complex definition of "whiteness," i.e. one in which many white men would not share. The result was Catlin's paradox that enlightenment was to be achieved by way of ignorance. This compounded the bitterness of the fact that these particular Iowa and Ojibwa Indians had come to Europe in the first place because the pressure of pioneers armed with plough and hoe had begun to drive them from their traditional ways. They had come to Europe not out of choice but because like Catlin's own, their way of life could not be supported in the United States.

In the spring of 1846, Catlin had returned to London to discover that another showman was exhibiting an American Indian. The war chief Say-say-gon had died, as reported by both Catlin and Maungwudaus, of smallpox. His skeleton had been purchased by an entrepreneur and put on display in Piccadilly, the street in which Catlin had staged his first European Indian Exhibition. Catlin was appalled by this demonstration of White greed. "I thought also," he wrote, "of the thousands of Indian graves I had seen on the frontier thrown open by sacrilegious hands for the skulls and trinkets they enclosed, to which the returning relatives were lurking back to take the last glance of, and to mingle the last tears over, with the horror of seeing the bones of their fathers and children strewed over the ground by hands too averse to labor and too ruthless to cover them again.

"I was here forcibly struck with the fitness of Jim's remarks about the hyaenas, of 'their resemblance to *Chemokimons*,' [white men] when I told him they lived by digging up and devouring bodies that had been consigned to the grave" (Catlin 1848,2:310-302).

There were in the three parties of Indians that had toured with Catlin, thirty-five in all; eleven lost their lives in the space of eighteen months. And as Maungwudaus recorded, more were to lose their lives after they had left Catlin. These mortal statistics reinforce the demonstrations of uncivilized behavior within a civilized society, which along with demonstrations of un-Christian behavior within a Christian society, were the very substance of any text which exposed the claims of European culture and religion by way of reference to "primitive" or to "unenlightened" man. The Indian's darkness might have been an absence of either the light of Rationalism or the light of Divine Revelation; his superior moral stance was measured by the disadvantages overcome in arriving at his position of higher judgement. While Catlin allowed "his Indians" to deliver these cultural and moral judgements, he did so in a way that was not finally subversive of either European culture or the Christian religion. The noble savage was called upon to deliver a conventional judgement upon the society that this literary type exposed. A radical critique might be inferred but it is not the message of the overt text.

NOTE

1. Thanks to Christian F. Feest for drawing my attention to this text which has recently been republished in an anthology of early prose by North American Indians (Peyer 1982). I have used the 1848 edition for quotations.

REFERENCES CITED

Austin, William
  1804   Letters from London. Boston.
Berkhofer, Robert F.
  1979   The White Man's Indian. New York.
Bissel, Benjamin
  1968   The American Indian in English Literature of the Eighteenth
          Century. New York.
Catlin, George
  1840   A Descriptive Catalogue of Catlin's Indian Gallery containing
          Portraits, Landscapes, Costumes, etc. London.
  1841   Letters and Notes on the Manners, Customs, and Condition of the
          North American Indians. Written during eight years's travel amongst
          the wildest tribes of Indians in North America in 1832 to 1839. 2
          vols. London.
  1844   Unparalleled Exhibition. The Fourteen Ioway Indians and their
          Interpreter, just arrived from the Upper Mississippi. London.
  1848   Notes of Eight Years' Travels and Residence in Europe, With His
          North American Indian Collection. With anecdotes and incidents of
          the travels and adventures of three different parties of American
          Indians whom he introduced to the Courts of England, France, and
          Belgium. 2 vols. London.
  1851   Museum of Mankind. London.
Cooper, James Fenimore
  1837   Gleanings in Europe: England. London
Greeley, Horace
  1851   Glances at Europe. New York.
Hawthorne, Nathaniel
  1941   The English Notebooks. Edited by Randell Stewart. New York.
Maungwudaus
  1848   An Account of the Chippewa Indians, who have been Travelling
          among the Whites, in the United States, England, Ireland, Scotland,
          France and Belgium; with very interesting Incidents in Relation to
          the General Characteristics of the English, Irish, Scotch, French,
          and Americans, with Regard to their Hospitality, Peculiarities, Etc.
          Boston.
Peyer, Bernd (ed.)
  1982   The Elders Wrote: An Anthology of Early Prose by North American
          Indians, 1768-1931. Berlin.
Plate, Robert
  1962   Palette and Tomahawk: The Story of George Catlin. New York.

Roehm, Majorie Catlin
    1962   The Letters of George Catlin and his Family: A chronicle of the American West. Berkeley.

Silliman, Benjamin
    1820   A Journal in England, Holland, and Scotland. New Haven.

Truettner, William H.
    1979   The Natural Man Observed: A Study of Catlin's Indian Gallery. Washington, D.C.

Willis, N.P.
    1835   Pencillings by the Way. London.

DICKENS ON THE INDIANS

Francesca Orestano

When Dickens, during his 1842 American tour, set out for the "Far West," Illinois and Ohio were still considered "western." From the letters Dickens wrote to his friends we know that he very much wished to meet some Indians, and with this purpose he traveled as far west as St. Louis - on the borders of the Indian territory - well equipped with letters that could help him to get in touch with the Indians (Dickens 1974:3-4).

But as far west as Baltimore, he had not succeeded in meeting a single Indian. Thus, while complaining that the "depths of the Far West" were but a dull, never changing scenery, he dressed up "imaginary tribes of Indians," scattering them "among the trees, as they used to be" (Dickens 1974:152, 154). A few days later, visiting the capitol of Harrisburg, he saw the very documents which accounted for the absence of Indians from these territories: the Pennsylvania Indian Deeds (surrenders made by the Delaware from 1682 to 1791; Dickens 1974:168, note), probably the Walking Purchase of 1737, which completed the sale of the Delaware lands, and the Iroquois Deed of 1736, with "a great turtle" as a signature (Dickens 1972:189-190). When he reached Upper Sandusky, a settlement of Wyandot Indians on the shore of Lake Erie, a treaty had just been concluded (Dickens 1974:207), and the Indians were already moving towards a reservation west of the Mississippi. The last of them to be seen looked like gypsies, "that wandering and restless people" (Dickens 1972:239). He also saw the Bloody Run valley (Dickens 1972:181) and several burial places such as Monks Mound (Dickens 1972:227) and the mound known as "Big Grave Creek" (Grave Creek Mound). The realistic representation of America consequently melts into an elegy:

"The very river [Ohio], as though it shared one's feeling of compassion for the extinct tribes who lived so pleasantly there, in their blessed ignorance of white existence, hundreds of years ago, steals out of its way to ripple near this mound ..." (Dickens 1972:205).

On the whole, in *American Notes*, Dickens' description of the Indians is conditioned by their absence, and by the compassion for their already lost cause. The passages on the Indians follow a descriptive pattern in which a subjective, emotional response finds an outlet in the already provided standard image of the Noble Savage (Zolla 1969: ch. V,113-137; D.H. Lawrence in Wilson 1956:927-938, on the influence of Hector St. John Crèvecoeur's *Letters from an American Farmer* on British romantic writers).

This image was heightened by the romantic rhetoric on the state of nature, as contrasted with the evils of civilization. Looking over the treaties at Harrisburg, for instance:

"Nor could I help bestowing many sorrowful thoughts upon the simple warriors whose hands and hearts were set there, in all truth and honesty; and who only learned... from white men how to break their faith, and quibble out of forms and bonds. I wondered, too, how many times credulous Big Turtle, or trusting Little Hatchet, had put his mark to treaties which were falsely read to him; and had signed away, he knew not what, until it went and cast him loose upon the new possessors of the land, a savage indeed" (Dickens 1972:189-190).

The savage not being part of the landscape, he is portrayed as a gentleman of nature - within a picturesque frame of primeval forest.

On the steamboat from Cincinnati to Louisville, Dickens met Peter Pitchlynn, a Choctaw chief. At last the lack of Indians had been thoroughly compensated for, as we may gather from the emphasis Dickens placed on the record of this meeting in *American Notes* (although there is no reference to it in Dickens's letters from America[1]). Not only is Pitchlynn an Indian chief (of one of the so-called Five Civilized Tribes; cp. Debo 1972) and "as stately and complete a gentleman of Nature's making as ever I beheld" (Dickens 1972:211); he is a white man in dress, in name, in the language he speaks, in culture and feelings. Some of his ancestors were English, and he had been educated at white man's institutions, such as the University of Nashville (Baird 1972: ch.I, and 20-21, 29-30). The conversation between Dickens and Pitchlynn is recorded with plenty of details, the subject being English literature, the poetry of Scott, the Indians portrayed by Cooper and their portraits painted by Catlin (which Dickens had seen at the Egyptian Hall, Piccadilly, in 1840; cp. Dickens 1974:201, note; Catlin's *Letters and Notes* (1841) and his *Notes of Eight Years' Travels* (1848) were in his library, see Stonehouse 1938). On the subject of politics they find open agreement in their criticism of American democracy, its government, its "well-skilled men of business"; Pitchlynn complains that

"A few of his brother chiefs had been obliged to become civilised, and to make themselves acquainted with what the whites knew, for it was their only chance of existence" (Dickens 1972:210, 211).

It is necessary to stress the fact that the Pitchlynn who gains Dickens's praise does not exactly fit in with the Noble Savage stereotype to which Dickens has hitherto resorted in his description of the Indians. Nevertheless, Dickens once more resorts to a familiar descriptive convention in order to draw Pitchlynn's portrait and he even regrets "not to see him in his own attire" (Dickens 1972:210). His beauty follows the aesthetic pattern of classical

278

statuary, his *humanitas* and behavior are those of a stoic philosopher (Zolla 1969:117). But, as is the case with J.F. Cooper's descriptions of the Indians, when defining Dickens's attitude towards them we must consider that on the one hand he deals with the personality of Peter Pitchlynn - probably in Dickens's eyes scarcely representative of the average Indian and rather a peculiar quintessence of Indian and white virtues - and that, on the other hand, the emptiness of the American landscape and the disappearance of the Indians allow him a great deal of imaginative and emotional freedom. Cooper settled his exotic utopia in the past of his historical novels; similarly Dickens's attitude is conditioned by the absence of the Indians and by the presence of Pitchlynn. When Dickens eventually faces what in his opinion is the "real" savage, in close comparison with English contemporary standards of civilization, we will find that the vein of his exoticism will dry up, together with the romantic tendency to idealization.

"Il passato indiano è lodato nella misura in cui è irrevocabile, buon pretesto per la polemica populista" (Zolla 1969:123) - "The Indian past is praised in so far as it is irretrievable, a convenient pretext for populist polemics"; see also Lawrence in Wilson 1956:939-940, and on Cooper's Leatherstocking novels, 949-966). We would maintain the same assumption for Dickens, but with the difference that the object of his polemic was the American government (cp. Orestano 1979).

In the years immediately following 1842, the Indian is not present in Dickens's fiction or writings, except for short casual references in which the Indians are seen "condescendingly or humorously, as barbarians" (Heilman 1946-1947,pt.1:40).

However it is worth recalling here that, still in America, and probably owing to the impossibility of a first-hand meeting with the Indians, Dickens wrote to Lea & Blanchard, booksellers in Philadelphia, asking for "a good copy" of Thomas McKenney and James Hall's *History of the Indian Tribes of North America* (McKenney and Hall 1836-1844) which he received (Dickens 1977:90, note)[2] and kept in his library together with many other books on America (Dickens 1977: Appendix "Inventory of Contents of 1, Devonshire Terrace, May 1854"; Stonehouse 1938:76; beside the books by Catlin and McKenney, there are J.F. Cooper's *Novels and Tales*, F. Marryat *Diary in America*, Harriet Martineau *Society in America* and *Retrospect of Western Travel*, and various American guide books). This book consists of a series of biographies on Indian chiefs, written by McKenney who was head of the Bureau of Indian Affairs. Besides description and anecdotes, the book mainly reports on the behavior of each chief in the negotiation with the American government as regards the conditions of their removal towards the western reservations. Ample room is given, therefore, to the speeches pronounced by the chiefs during those crucial years - the first decades of the 19th century - when most Indian leaders went to

Washington, on behalf of their tribes, had "a talk" with the president, received a medal and "other testimonials of respect," sat for official portrait, and were induced to sign the treaties which implied their removal beyond the white man's frontier. In the third volume of the book there is an attempt to give a scientific explanation of the problems connected with the presence of the Indians in America - a positive approach to matters such as their origin, race, progress, civilization. When Dickens in 1850 turned again to the subject of Indians, this book together with the increasing importance of science in Victorian culture and with the theories on evolution already in the air,[3] probably influenced his attitude towards them.

In *Some Account of an Extraordinary Traveller* (first published in *Household Words*, 20 April 1850, quoted from Dickens 1938a:261-271), a certain Mr. Booley, going upstream along the Mississippi, performs a journey *à-rébours* through various stages of civilization, until, at the very last, he meets an Indian settlement.

"He began to consider how, in the eternal current of progress, setting across this globe in one unchangeable direction" the Indians "... must be surely and inevitably swept from the earth."

Indians do not contribute to the advancement of science, art, letters.

"Savage nature was not... such a fine and noble spectacle as some delight to represent it... civilization, Mr. Booley concluded, was... with all its blemishes, a more imposing sight, and a far better thing to stand by" (Dickens 1938a:264).

Notwithstanding the fictional presence of Mr. Booley, here the actual Indians are met, and there is no need of imagination, of picturesque details, of pathetic elegy. There has been a shift towards a more realistic approach, in would-be scientific terms. "Progress" is the key-word in Dickens's new attitude, and it is related to the idea of civilization - science being one of its determining factors. The naturalistic utopia, and the myth of the Noble Savage, are regarded with scepticism.

This attitude has its antecedents in 18th century philosophy - with Voltaire (Bissell 1968:54), Saint-Simon (and Comte after him); and with Johnson and Burke in England (Bissell 1968:48, 53) - all thinkers who, although accepting the enlightened version of progress, and while recognizing the evils spreading out of civilization (for which political or religious harnessing was provided), were unwilling to accept redemption under the features of the Noble Savage, thus taking their distance from Rousseau, and from "... those visionaries who have attempted to persuade us of the superior vantages of a 'state of nature,'" as Johnson plainly stated (Bissell 1968:51).

On the other hand, when Dickens relates the idea of progress to science, the new scientific concept of evolution is foreshadowed - a belief already present in the trend of gradualism, opposed to the romantic idea of progress as revolution (Cosslett 1982:11). The evolutionary idea of progress, a central point in 19th century culture, was well accorded with the Victorian anti-revolutionary and conservative bias, for all its stress on the transmission of an inheritance accumulated through generations of mankind (Cosslett 1982:5).

Thus Dickens, both when echoing the ideas of Burke and Johnson, and when giving pre-eminence to the scientific, evolutionary idea of progress, shows, on the whole, a conservative standpoint (Nevins 1948:79-102, classes him under "Tory Condescension") of which the key is the rejection of the values connected with the state of nature. Whatever the conditions determining progress, the Indians stand at the bottom of its ascending stream - cut away from civilization, from science, their nobility as useless a tool as their stone-age weapons.

McKenney observed that "the intellectual acquirements of the Indians were as low as they are recorded to have been among any people on the face of earth. They had not letters and no learning. Not the slightest rudiments of a single science were known among them... Why they have advanced so little in all that constitutes the progress of society... Why was experience lost upon them?" And he concluded that "the experience of the past, and the aspiration of the future, were alike unheeded. Their existence was confined to the present... Their previous history and progress are utterly lost - lost in that long interval of darkness which precedes authentic history amongst all nations" (McKenney and Hall 1836-1844,3: 11-12).

In 1853 a group of Zulu Kaffirs were exhibited at the St. George Gallery, London, not a rare event at that time (Bushmen had also been on display, and, of course, George Catlin's Indians). This gave Dickens the opportunity of expressing, directly, his own ideas on the "savage."

In *The Noble Savage* (Dickens 1938b:133-138) the conviction of the very low position of the Indians in the human scale is heightened by a self-conscious feeling of superiority - the same which conditioned Victorian relationships with the rest of the world.[4] In this essay the first point made by Dickens is the utter rejection and confutation of the myth of the Noble Savage:

"I have not the least belief in the Noble Savage. I consider him a prodigious nuisance, and an enormous superstition ... He is a savage - cruel, false, thievish, murderous; addicted more or less to grease, entrails, and beastly customs; a wild animal with the questionable gift of boasting; a conceited, tiresome, bloodthirsty, monotonous humbug" (Dickens 1938b:133).
"He has no moral feelings of any kind, sort, or description; and his 'mission' may be summed up as simply diabolical" (Dickens 1938b:135).
"Here the very concepts of man's perfectibility, of innate moral sense, of

natural benevolence, are denied. Concepts as expounded in the 18th century by Shaftesbury, Butler, and then Godwin (against the Puritan ethics of man's natural bent to sinfulness and against Hobbes's rationalism) had been integrated by Dickens within his world view through the reading of the novels of Fielding, Sterne, Goldsmith, and Godwin - as if by osmosis (Palmer 1977). But the "savage" does not belong to the Dickensian world of universal benevolence. His is the role of the perfect villain, and in this essay Dickens makes a reference to Buffon, and to his theory of the inferiority of the American races of animals and men,[5] in order to stress the lack of humanity and morality in the natives. To account perhaps for this violent, visceral assault against the savage, it may be worth mentioning an observation made by the writer about his own attitude: "... is it idiosyncratic in me to abhor, detest, abominate and abjure him?" (Dickens 1938b:134).

The other point discussed in *The Noble Savage* is the position of those who will talk about the savage as they talk about "the good old times." In Dickens's opinion his disappearance is

"... a blessed relief and an indispensable preparation for the sowing of the very first seeds of any influence that can exalt humanity" (Dickens 1938b:133).
"It is not the miserable nature of the noble savage that is the new thing; it is the whimpering over him with maudlin admiration and the affecting to regret him, and the drawing of any comparison of advantage between the blemishes of civilisation and the tenor of his swinish life" (Dickens 1938b:134).

Among these "visionaries," and with tones of sharp derision, Dickens places George Catlin and his "Ojibbeway Indians" - "wretched creatures, very low in the scale" (Dickens 1938b:134).

Thus, besides the blow dealt at the Noble Savage, Dickens is in open polemic with those among his contemporaries who pour upon the savage their illusions, their humanitarianism, their fashionable philanthropism, their intellectual snobbery. Nothwithstanding this, civilization is still a good worth preserving carefully, as his conclusion makes clear:

"It is my opinion that if we retained in us anything of the noble savage, we could not get rid of it too soon ... If we have anything to learn from the noble savage, it is what to avoid. His virtues are a fable; his happiness is a delusion; his nobility, nonsense" (Dickens 1938b:138).

Many years later, in 1863, Dickens was to observe that

"it is curious to trace the savage in the civilised man, and to detect the hold of some savage customs on conditions of society rather boastful of being high above them" (Dickens 1938b:542-550, "Medicine Men of Civilisation," 542).

In the course of the years Dickens had found that it was impossible for him to keep the "Medicine Man" of the North American Indians out of his "Wigwam." The whole essay draws a comparison between the social customs of the savage and those of a civilized society. If there is any criticism in Dickens's new attitude, it is an overall irony whose aim is to suggest the existence of a fundamental identity at the core of different social contexts and races. Both parties under examination now stand on rather equal terms: there is no pre-eminence given to the superior values of British civilization, no talk of progress, no scale of evolution. We can notice, instead, a creeping vein of criticism against some highly civilized institutions, the "stupendous absurdities" of the House of Commons ceremonials - wigs, Windsor uniforms, Chancery petticoats - a "nonsense" which sets in a better light the odd proceedings of the Medicine Man of the Indians. In the conclusion of this essay a truly antagonistic note is struck:

"It is better that an Assembly should do its utmost to envelop itself in smoke, than that it should direct its endeavours to enveloping the public in smoke; and I would rather it buried half a hundred hatchets than buried one subject demanding attention" (Dickens 1938b:550).

At this time of his life Dickens seems to have found a definite place for the Indian: not within a romantic stereotype, nor as a living proof in the scientifically demonstrated course of progress; not as agent of the devil, capable of shaking Victorian moral battlements. The Indian has been integrated within a vision of anthropological relativism, *à la Montaigne* - while the real evils are those near at hand. This new attitude is confirmed by Dickens's choice of an Indian image in order to stress the negative effects of industrialism in England. As we may read in the description of Coketown:

"It was a town of unnatural red and black, like the painted face of a savage" (Dickens 1982:65).

NOTES

1. The only reference is in Dickens (1974:400), "To Miss Catherine Hutton, 23 Dec. 1842." Presumably Miss Hutton had asked Dickens to show her Pitchlynn's visiting card, and the portrait the chief had sent to the writer after their meeting. Dickens answered: "It gave me a great shock at the time, and I am very unwilling to tell you now, that my friend Pitch(lynn)'s card is *printed*. If it had been written, I would have sent it to you..." and "I have committed the offending picture (it *was* a bad one) to the flames ..." Here Dickens seems to contradict what he said in *American Notes*: "He sent me a lithographed portrait of himself... very like, though scarcely handsome enough; which I have carefully preserved in memory of our brief acquaintance" (Dickens 1972:211).

2. Thanks to Beatrice Cerruti who generously entrusted to me her copy of McKenney and Hall's *History*.

3. Charles Darwin's *Origin of Species* (1859) was in Dickens's library; cp. Stonehouse 1938.

4. Bédarida (1978:13) quotes from L. Faucher, *Etudes sur l'Angleterre* (1845): "L'Inglese sembra portato a credere che, eccettuato il popolo britannico, ormai giunto all'età adulta, tutti gli altri popoli siano ancora nell'età infantile" ("Englishmen seem inclined to believe that, except for their nation which has already reached maturity, all the other nations are still in their infancy").

5. G.-L. Leclerc de Buffon's *Natural History* (1797 ff) was in Dickens's library; cp. Stonehouse 1938. About the theories of Buffon and Corneille De Pauw on the North American Indians, see Cocchiara (1972:44-45).

REFERENCES CITED

Baird, W. David
 1972 Peter Pitchlynn, Chief of the Choctaws. Norman: University of Oklahoma Press.

Bédarida, François
 1978 L'età vittoriana (L'ére victorienne, 1974). Milano: Garzanti.

Bissell, Benjamin
 1968 The American Indian in English Literature of the Eighteenth Century [1925]. New York and Oxford: Archon Books.

Cocchiara, G.
 1972 L'eterno selvaggio. Palermo: Flaccovio.

Cosslett, Tess
 1982 The 'Scientific Movement' and Victorian Literature. Sussex and New York: The Harvester Press and St. Martin's Press.

Debo, Angie
 1972 The Rise and Fall of the Choctaw Republic. Norman: University of Oklahoma Press.

Dickens, Charles
 1938a Collected Papers. The Nonesuch Dickens. Bloomsbury: The Nonesuch Press.
 1938b Reprinted Pieces - The Uncommercial Traveller and Other Stories. The Nonesuch Dickens. Bloomsbury: The Nonesuch Press.
 1972 American Notes - For General Circulation (1842). J.S. Whitley and A. Goldman (eds.). Harmondsworth: Penguin Books.
 1974 The Letters of Charles Dickens, vol. III. M. House, G. Storey, K. Tillotson (eds.). Oxford: Clarendon Press.
 1977 The Letters of Charles Dickens, vol. IV. M. House, G. Storey, K. Tillotson (eds.). Oxford: Clarendon Press.
 1982 Hard Times - For These Times (1854). David Craig (ed.). Harmondsworth: Penguin Books.

Heilman, Robert B.
 1946-1947 The New World in Charles Dickens's Writings. The Trollopian 3:25-43, 4:11-26.

McKenney, Thomas L., and James Hall
 1836-1844 History of the Indian Tribes of North America, with Biographical Sketches and Anecdotes of the Principal Chiefs. Philadelphia: E.C. Biddle (1836-1838), F.W. Greenough (1838-1842), Rice & Clark (1842-1844).

Nevins, Allan (ed.)
 1948 America through British Eyes. New York: Oxford University Press.

Orestano, Francesca
 1979 Un cattivo sogno americano: le *American Notes* di Charles Dickens.

285

Quaderno II (Istituto di Lingue e Letterature Straniere, Università di Palermo), 25-65.

Palmer, William J.

1977   Dickens and the Eighteenth Century. Dickens Studies Annual 6:15-39.

Stonehouse, J.H. (ed.)

1938   Catalogue of the Library of Charles Dickens from Gadshill. London: Piccadilly Fountain Press.

Wilson, Edmund (ed.)

1956   The Shock of Recognition. London: W.H. Allen.

Zolla, Elèmire

1969   I letterati e lo sciamano. Milano: Bompiani.

AN EMERGING DUAL IMAGE OF NATIVE NORTH AMERICANS DURING THE 19TH CENTURY IN HUNGARY

László Borsányi

The effects of the discovery of the New World and of the changing economic conditions in western Europe, which gradually gave way to a new development, were to be felt considerably late in central Europe. Owing to her 150 years of Turkish occupation and nearly 400 years of Hapsburg dependency in the 16th to the 19th centuries, Hungary suffered especially enormous losses. In spite of these disadvantages a slowly increasing interest in the Americas, shown mainly by intellectuals and based upon secondary sources from western Europe, resulted in the adoption in Hungary of a classical European image of the western hemisphere's inhabitants during the 18th century.

In terms of the classical European conception, the image of Native Americans was to provide a contrast with everything that was considered to be highly ideal in the Old World. The first printed accounts on the American aborigines, which appeared in the Hungarian language mainly in geographical books after the mid-18th century, display a considerable influence of this guiding principle. The authors speak of "savages" of whom they know a lot but whom, at the same time, they despise and scorn because of their "primitive" system of beliefs, way of life, and customs (Bertalanffi 1757:985-93; Vetsei 1757:424-5). The word "primitive" applied to "Indians" in their texts simply conveys the old basic counterimage of what is "civilized," that is "European" and, of course, "good Christian" too.

It is interesting to see the way this image was enriched during the period of the Hungarian Enlightenment, when an anonymously published geographical book in 1796 devoted 42 of its 368 pages to America, including also a description of the "free Republic" where "commerce, crafts, and sciences flourish." The disdainful and superficial treatment of tribal peoples which can be observed in this work is obviously motivated by the comparison drawn with the value system of the enlightened man. Thus Native Americans become on its pages "witless guys living, like beasts, without laws, crafts, and sciences." Moreover they are dirty and lazy. "All they do is hunting, fishing, and smoking their pipe," they ramble and if they happen to capture someone who is a stranger they torture and eat him (Anonymous 1796:321-8).

A notable modification in this image is to be observed after the turn of the century when the spirit of independence comes to be ascribed not only to white settlers but also to savages in America. A book relying on a more expert and wider range of written materials than any of the previous publications introduces an expanding image of the "Land of Liberty" where even Natives could somehow be associated with freedom. The 1813 work by Zsigmond

Horváth, a Transdanubian Lutheran pastor, draws a fairly vivid and detailed picture of Indians. Horváth outlines their system of beliefs and customs, and praises their love of freedom and independence, their self-esteem and their ability to endure pain, but also describes at length the horrible cruelties they commit against captives (Horváth 1813:159-82, 282-91).

From the 1820's and 1830's onwards, however, from the period of the Hungarian Reform Age which laid a claim for bourgeois transformation, a remarkable new feature appeared in the accounts of those Hungarians who were ready to gain first-hand experiences in America. Their motivation derived from the fact that America became for Hungarian liberal progressive thought not only an exemplary political system but also a model as far as human behavior in the widest sense was concerned. And, at the same time, they could also rely on the multiplying articles on America, especially on the United States, published in Hungarian periodicals in the 1830's. These articles, though still adaptations or reviews of works by German, English, and French authors, put a special emphasis on the simplicity of human relations deriving from bourgeois equality, the liberal forms of contact and, as a basis of all these, on the extensive network of schooling and the gigantic press, with some 1200 organs in 1834 (Toldy 1834:136).

The long line of Hungarians who visited America for the purpose of studying her institutions, and who rendered an account of their experiences in books or at least in pamphlets, is headed by Sándor Bölöni Farkas, a Transylvanian nobleman. He arrived in the New World on 3 September 1831, in the company of Count Ferenc Béldy. In his book, first published in 1834 in Kolozsvár under the title *Journey in North America* he describes his thoughts on landing in New York as follows:

"Shall I find in this beautiful land the sanctuary of freedom, of supressed mankind and of rights? Is it the laws and institutions created by man himself that make man happier or are they happier who find their happiness in the loyal execution of the commands of despotism?" (Bölöni Farkas 1943:44).

Bölöni's answers to these questions are positive and his book, which can be read with interest and profit even today, exerted such a great influence on the growing anti-Hapsburg public opinion that its second edition in 1835 was banned by the Viennese Court. As an open-minded person he drew his ideas of Native Americans from his own experiences and was not biased by any prejudices. When, on his journey toward Niagara Falls, he learned in Kingston that the first settler had bought the site from an Indian for a bottle of brandy, and when he caught sight of a couple of Missisauga Indians canoeing on the Saint Lawrence river, he exclaimed:

"Poor Indians! You are already strangers in your own land and regarded merely as alien wanderers by the very people who had slain your ancestors" (Bölöni Farkas 1943:140).

Bölöni's most important message, meant for his contemporary fellow Hungarians of course, was that man and human societies, through their own consideration and by their own choice, are able to establish good governments which provide for the happiness of their people. His invaluable contribution to the image of a politically free America was soon completed with the image of a free economic development in the United States (cf. Bende 1837:196). This dynamic picture of American progress is certified by another Hungarian eyewitness, Ágoston Mokcsai Haraszthy.

Haraszthy was a wealthy landowner in Bácska, who visited the United States in 1840-41. He was so deeply impressed with what he saw that after his return to Hungary, he wrote a two-volume travel book and, even before his book's publication, converted his whole fortune into cash, and moved with his family to America. His work is far less politically conscious than that of Bölöni, but the traits of the American farmer, which are shaped by capitalist free competition and which are entirely unfamiliar for a Hungarian, emerge all the more clearly. During his sojourn, while making several trips in the western territories, especially in Wisconsin and Illinois, he spent some time with Winnebago and then with Sauk and Fox Indians and visited other tribes too. He is virtually the first Hungarian - with the earlier exception of mainly Jesuits from Hungary, in the Southwest - who gained firsthand experiences among tribal peoples in North America. He devoted detailed descriptions to his personal encounters with Native Americans (Haraszthy 1844,1: chapters 13-15) and these adventures were published later, in 1926, for juvenile readers in a separate volume under the title *Fifteen Weeks among Indians*.

Haraszthy's accounts are particularly interesting because they also reflect the familiar stereotype of "hostile and thievish savages" with its own contradictions. When, for example, his company arrives at the first Winnebago settlement, their guide

"... having exchanged a few words with them, got off his horse and directed us to follow him. So we also got off, unsaddled our horses, then according to his order, put all our luggage in a certain place, which, he said, he will guard lest they would be stolen" (Haraszthy 1844,1:161).

After this event he was haunted from time to time by the notion of the "thievish Indian" when they entered a native village. According to his personal experiences, however, when he leaves the Indian country he admits that they are

"... not so terrifying and savage as described by so many people. And anyone can sleep among them in greater security than in a herdman's camp in our country [i.e. in Hungary]. And he won't be killed or robbed of his gun - the most precious thing an Indian appreciates first and foremost - because they say, if a white man is robbed of his gun, he dies of hunger since he doesn't know how to use the bow. One cannot deny them the virtue that in case they become attached to someone, they take great care of him, and fulfil all his wishes. It is easy to win their love, and by showing them a stratagem or two one can earn respect among them" (Haraszthy 1844,1:211).

Apart from his four months' travel on the frontier, Haraszthy's main interest was not "the Indian" but the American customs and systems of government. Thus his book contains, first of all, a lot of practical information even on such particular problems as ways and modes of buying an estate. Following his instructions, a large number of political refugees emigrated to the United States in the wake of the social and political upheaval of 1848-49.

After the suppression of the 1848-49 Hungarian revolution and war of independence most Hungarian exiles turned their hopes toward America. Many had sought refuge in the New World and some, like Louis Kossuth, the tragic and solemn hero, and his followers went to mobilize the American public for intervention against Tsarist despotism, which had stamped out Hungary's fight for freedom and independence. Kossuth and his retinue were first greeted on their arrival in New York on 5 December 1851, by an Italian exile and an American Indian. Kossuth confirmed his reputation as a public speaker of irresistible rhetoric power and though there are only few scattered remarks of his concern for Native Americans, even these show his knowledge of the Indians's history and his interest in their culture. When he points out in his speech at the City Hall of Fall River, for instance, that nobody who is capable for self-government was born for oppression, his model comes from King Phillip's and Massasoit's examples:

"... when two hundred years ago your fathers landed here, they found the Indians under King Phillip and Massasoit capable to govern themselves" (Kossuth 1852).

There are also some unique pieces of Woodland Indian arts and crafts in Hungarian Museums from Kossuth's own collection (cf. Borsányi 1977). The story of one item is told in the book written by Mr. and Mrs. Pulszky who accompanied Kossuth in America. The report goes back to their visit at the Tuscarora Indian village near Niagara Falls on 25 May 1852:

"... [when] we entered, we perceived a squaw, embroidering cloth with beads. She took no notice of us; we endeavoured to make her understand that we wished to buy some of her needlework, but she remained silent, not as if she were indignant that we intruded, but altogether she seemed not to think us worthy of her attention in any way. Before the house stood a white carter... We asked the man whether he could not serve us as interpreter, but he said that the squaw understood and spoke English whenever she found it convenient" (Pulszky and Pulszky 1853,3:121-122).

"... when in the evening we came back to the hotel, we found some beadwork left here by the sullen Indian squaw, the first we had called at. When she had understood from the neighbours who had been her visitor, she brought as a present what she would not sell" (Pulszky and Pulszky 1853,3:124).

A few days later, while visiting the Onondaga reservation, Mr. and Mrs. Pulszky note in relation to the religious dances and sacrifices of the "pagan" Onondagas that

"one of them is certainly symbolic (probably they are all so, though the Americans do not understand them. On the whole they little trouble themselves with the rites of their red brethren)" (Pulszky and Pulszky 1853,2:142).

Besides their reminiscences, Mr. and Mrs. Pulszky devoted significant long discussions in their book to the history of Indians and came to the conclusion that the coexistence of the "hunter and the plowman" in the same country is "utterly impossible." Their next little story is intended to render the Native Americans' fate palpable.

"One of the western chiefs, in conversation with an American of note, who was his friend, explained their fate practically. Whilst speaking about his tribe and the proposals of the government, he requested permission to sit down on the bench on which the American was seated, as it was large enough to hold them both. Their talk became more animated, the Indian always drew nearer, the American yielded without perceiving it, until at length he was sitting at the edge of the bench; when the Indian gave him suddenly a slight push which threw him to the ground. The American was highly indignant at his behaviour; but the Indian rose and said, 'Be quiet, I did not do more than what you do with my nation. First, you require but a small place on the territory; the country (as you say) is large enough for you and for us; imperceptibly you advance and we recede, till at last a slight effort drives us away from our home. You are indignant, because you

do, for whom the inheritance of our fathers is to be lost for ever?'"
(Pulszky and Pulszky 1853,3:3).

According to their conception - with regard to the "extension of the tilled
soil" - the

"... red race in North America is doomed to extinction [because] the activity
of the Anglo-Saxons is fatal to every idle race; they are the great colonizers
of the modern age, but not the civilizers of savage nations" (Pulszky and
Pulszky 1853,2:2).

Apart from Haraszthy, another famous pioneer among those Hungarians who
found refuge in the New World was János Xántus, an outstanding naturalist of
his day. He arrived in America towards the end of 1851 and first earned his
living as a day laborer. In 1852 he was already topographer of the Pacific
Railroad Expedition. Between 1855 and 1857 he was member of a scientific
survey in Kansas Territory, then inhabited chiefly by Native Americans. In
1857 he went to Washington and obtained a commission in the U.S. Coast
Survey for southern California. Here he stayed at Fort Tejon, in the Tehachapi
Mountains, before moving to Baja California for two years in 1859.

Two books on his North American experiences were published during
Xántus's life-time. The first one, Xántus's letters (1858), deals with his travels
before arriving in California, and the second one (1860) is devoted to his
journey in California. Quite aware of the intense interest of his compatriots in
everything American, he undertook to interpret the Union - the land, the
peoples, the customs, and the life style. He was given to gross exaggerations
and certain oddities appear in his accounts, yet his vivid descriptions of his
encounters with the Indian tribes, of life in the pioneer settlements in the
Midwestern wilderness testify not only to his literary skill but also to his
open-minded approach to the aborigines as human beings. According to his
report on his August 1856 visit among the Wichitas, he doesn't even try to
hide his surprise.

"... In the center of the hut a perpetual fire is burning, and when members
of the two families come together, they lounge around the fire chatting. It
is a pleasing sight to a stranger, and it fills the visitor with the joy and
satisfaction of contemplating the blessings of domestic happiness. I confess
that I did not expect to find this among these people" (Xántus 1975:129-130).

And he ponders by what right the Choctaw Indians were allocated Wichita
lands, knowing nothing of the order, given by Andrew Jackson for the removal
of the Cherokees, a move which may have caused surprise even to U.S. Chief
Justice John Marshall whose decision in the Cherokee case the order had

292

ignored. Xántus's train of thoughts goes like this:

"The particular territory which embraces the Wichita mountain range belonged for many years to the Wichita Indians. By tradition, they have absolute and valid rights. According to their belief, they were born in these mountain ranges; the 'Great Spirit' bestowed the entire territory upon them and their descendants, and they have occupied it ever since. However, in spite of these claims, which are based on the possession, the entire territory down to the 100th western meridian was presented by Congress to the Choctaw Indians, provided they would move here from northern Texas, where they presently live. It is not easy to understand by what right this was done" (Xántus 1975:120).

Xántus portrayed the many Indian tribes he befriended with great sympathy and his sharp characterizations of the mid-19th century acquisitive American society probably have an enduring validity.

The new period of American history emerging immediately after the Civil War was not, however, conducive towards providing an unambiguously attractive political ideal for Hungarian liberalism which in many respects followed pre-1848 examples, since this period of American history shows signs of rapid political and economic development and relinquishment of former Puritan principles. But even so, Aurél Kecskeméthy (1877), the political writer inclined to conservatism, who evidently felt a malicious joy over negative phenomena and who toured a major part of the United States as an official representative sent to the Philadelphia World Exhibition in 1876, was forced to accept that all these changes indicated the direction of a new American self-knowledge.

Since he had not got much personal experience with Indians while on a constant move around the United States in 1876, Kecskeméthy searched for an answer to the question "Why do the Indians have to perish" only on a rather abstract level.

"The civilization of peoples requires time. A long time. That is why Indians are doomed to perish. They have not been allotted time enough to undergo this slow process. A human race attacked them and overrun them in a way that they had no chance to get close to it. The Europeans arrived with an accomplished civilization and gunpowder. The Indians were unable to accept this accomplished civilization, the religious and civil concepts and institutions at once, thus, by resisting them, these primitive peoples fought for their mere lives. And it was the gunpowder which won the battle. The American people, the American State could not wait, they are unable to wait, they have to advance irresistibly with the help of steam and electric power" (Kecskeméthy 1877:112).

293

As we have seen, Hungarians who had first-hand experiences among Native Americans intended to present the American Indian to other Hungarians as a human being and not just as an image, a symbol, or a convenient stereotype. However, since their generalizations of them as a people usually had to be rendered in terms of the old counterimage, their conceptualization of the "savages," whether "noble," "brutal," or "inferior," always shows an appreciative and emotive approach at the same time. Kecskeméthy's comment on the first news of the Little Big Horn battle of 1876 illuminates quite well this 19th century dual image:

"On hearing the news, horror and rage seized the whole of America. However, I did not come across any sense of shame anywhere, a feeling which, after all, would have been most reasonable. Isn't it outrageous! - not that a handful of miserable, savage people can defeat the American army but rather, - that a nation of 40 million people who consider themselves free and cultured, have no other means to deal with this miserable race but to destroy them and wipe them out on the pretense that they are incapable of civilization" (Kecskeméthy 1877:399).

REFERENCES CITED

Anonymous
1796   Rövid magyar geographia [A Short Hungarian Geography]. Pest: Trattner.

Bende, László Hodosi
1837   Le-irása az egész föld-kerekségnek [A Description of the Whole Wide World]. Pozsony: Schmidt Antal.

Bertalanffi, Pál S.I.
1757   Világnak két rend-béli rövid ismerete [Twofold Short Description of the World]. Nagyszombat: Academia.

Borsányi, László
1977   Megjegyzések a Magyar Nemzeti Múzeum Kossuth-gyüjteményének északamerikai indián hagyatékához [Notes on the North American Indian items in the Hungarian National Museum's Kossuth collection]. Folia Historica 5:107-120.

Bölöni Farkas, Sándor
1943   Utazás Északamerikában [Journey in North America]. Budapest: Officina.

Haraszthy, Ágoston Mokcsai
1844   Utazás Éjszakamerikában [Journey in North America]. Pest: Heckenast Gusztáv.

1926   Tizenöt hét az indiánok között [Fifteen Weeks among Indians]. Budapest: Pallas.

Horváth, Zsigmond
1813   Ámerikának haszonnal mutattató esmertetése, Vol.1. [A Beneficial Survey of America]. Györ: Streibig.

Kecskeméthy, Aurél
1877   Éjszak-Amerika 1876-ban [North America in 1876]. Budapest: Ráth Mór.

Kossuth, Louis
1852   Government Kossuth in Fall River. Fall River News, May 20.

Pulszky, Francis, and Theresa Pulszky
1853   White, Red, Black. Sketches of Society in the United States during the Visit of their Guest. 3 vols. London: Trübner and Paternoster.

Toldy, Ferenc
1834   A' szellemi és erkölcsi polgáriasodás' állapotja az Éjszakamerikai Egyesült-országokban. [Conditions of Spiritual and Moral Development and Bourgeois Civilization in the North American United States]. In: Ferencz Schedel (ed.), Tudománytár. Buda: Magyar Tudós Társaság.

Vetsei, István P.
1757   Magyar geografiája, az az: az egész világ négy részeinek ... rendes

és rövid le-irása ... [Vetsei's Hungarian Geography, or a Proper and Short Description of the Four Parts of the Whole World]. Nagy-Károly: Károlyi.

Xántus, János

1858   Levelei Éjszakamerikából [His Letters from North America]. Pest: Lauffer és Stolp.

1957   Letters from North America. Theodore Schoenman and Helen Benedek Schoenman (trsl. and ed.). Detroit: Wayne University Press.

1860   Utazás Kalifornia déli részeiben [Travels in Southern California]. Pest: Lauffer és Stolp.

INDIANS IN THE REPORTS OF POLISH TRAVELERS OF THE SECOND HALF OF THE 19TH CENTURY

Izabella Rusinowa

Among the variouns bits of information conveyed to Polish readers during the second half of the 19th century, North American Indians occupied much space in reports, letters, and books. As a result, a Pole from that period was enabled to form an opinion of his own about the history and traditions of the Indian tribes and to develop his own attitude about the contemporary events which resulted in a dramatic reduction of the native population in North America.

With the westward expansion of White settlements in the second half of the 19th century, Indian tribes were being restricted to reservations. This process was accompanied by the extermination of the bison and by the wars waged along the frontier between individual tribes and the U.S. Army (sometimes aided by local militia). Under the pressure of White colonists, the Federal Government did not adhere to treaties signed earlier with Indian tribes. The Indians resisted and fought against their oppressors. Thanks to the European press, the news about these events were reaching Poland quite quickly.

Polish readers could read about the Indians in the Polish papers appearing in all three sectors of the then partitioned Poland. In addition to reprints from foreign sources, letters were published that had been sent by Poles staying for various reasons and for various periods of time in the United States, including Jakób Gordon (Maksymilian Jatwot), Krystyna Narbuttówna, Kalikst Wolski, Roger Łubieński, Henryk Sienkiewicz, Sygurd Wiśniowski, and Emil Habdanek Dunikowski. In their reports from America they expressed in different ways their attitude towards the problem of the Red men. They often emphasized their moral superiority over the White settlers and deplored the physical and moral degradation - and ultimately the extermination - of the native popula- tions. They also criticized the attitude of the Americans who - bible in their hand - waged wars against the much weaker Indian tribes with the only goal of annexing their lands. Mostly fascinated with America and its dynamic development, the Polish travelers were, however, able to show more or less objectively the tragic fate of the Indian tribes, unwilling and unable to adapt themselves to the civilization of the Whites and to their constant pressure. Attitudes of the Polish travelers towards the annihilation of the aboriginal population of North America thus seems to be of interest in relation to the problem of one of the elements of the American myth developing in Poland in the 19th century, that is Indians vs. American colonization.

As early as by the 18th century much was known in Poland and in other European countries about the Indians living on the frontier of the newly established United States. The information came from Spanish and French

Catholic missions as well as from English sources. During the period of Enlightenment, Europe idealized the Indians as people who lived according to the laws of nature. The good, noble-minded, savage Indian, unblemished by the civilization of the White man, and more often than not represented by a member of the Iroquoian group of tribes, became popular thanks to the philosophers of the Enlightenment in the salons of both Paris and Poland. Warsaw had its additional information on the meeting of Polish national hero Kościuszko with Little Turtle, the Miami chief; even Little Turtle's appearance was known from a portrait painted by Kósciuszko (unfortunately now lost).

During the first half of the 19th century the translation of the popular novels by James Fenimore Cooper (1830, 1834a, b) increased the knowledge of Indian matters in Poland, even though they may not have helpful for a better understanding of the problems involved. This literature, mostly addressed to juvenile readers, as well as the extremely popular adventure books by Karl May published at the end of the century, in conjunction with the reports of Polish travelers, helped to shape the romantic stereotype of the North American Indian, his behavior and culture, his dress and religion, in the minds of Polish readers. Thanks to Cooper and, later, the weekly papers, Poles learnt the names of many Indian tribes, such as the Creek, Iroquois, Delaware, Apache, Comanche, Pawnee, Huron, Cheyenne, Cherokee, or Ottawa. They learned about their customs and methods of warfare, and words like wigwam, tipi, scalp, calumet, moccasin, bison, squaw, wampum, and tomahawk found their way into the Polish vocabulary.

Polish travelers arriving in the United States during the second half of the 19th century had to confront their notions about Indians with both the American reality and the Americans' stereotypes. This was a source of many shattered illusions and disappointments. The romantic vision of Indians brought by them from Poland very often - though not always - differed from what they saw on the spot. Henryk Sienkiewicz, for example, wrote about his disappointing meeting with Indians in a train station in 1876: "Unfortunately, instead of the noble qualities attributed to the heroes of Cooper's books, I have only found appearances" (Sienkiewicz 1877:127). During his trip through the United States in 1891, enraptured by the beauty of nature, Emil Dunikowski (1892:93) remembered the books read in his childhood: "... resting on the wooded slopes of the Adirondack Mountains, I can see the bewitching, melancholic lake down at my feet, Lake George which the Indians call Horican which means 'silver water.'"

Now and then, Polish travelers repeat in their reports sent to Poland the negative American opinions and attitudes concerning the Indian population: "There is no doubt that the Indian race morally ranks lower than the Black one; but the Americans from the South deny it in an effort to create another deplorable argument which would support slavery." The Indians whither away when confronted by the civilization which develops the Blacks; if civilization

298

gradually raises a Black to a level equal to that of White people, it is useless in the case of "the inert apathy of an Indian" (*Wędrowiec*, vol. 1873:172). Such opinions, however, were not expressed often. The journal *Wędrowiec*, for example, argued in the following way in 1873: "The Indians are often accused of idleness in thinking and of a lack of mental abilities. I think, however, that they would make excellent students if accustomed to another way of life. Remember that most of them speak three languages: their own, Spanish, and English" (*Wędrowiec*, vol. 1873:284). And Jakób Gordon (1867:142) who had been in direct contact with the Indians in the South wondered "... whether the Indians are really such savages as they are supposed to be. After all, their courage is commonly known."

Undoubtedly, many travelers writing for Polish newspapers often followed American opinion and divided the Indians into two classes: good ones, that is those submissive to the Americans and already living on reservations, and bad ones, that is those still defending their independence and territorial integrity. Krystyna Narbuttówna (1880:39), in her first Polish novel set in Texas in the middle of the 19th century with Indians among its heroes, follows American opinions in writing that: "... the Medocs[1] who had moved away from the blood-thirsty savagery of the Apaches... still were far away from the level of development attain by the Cherokees."

Most Polish authors of the 19th century seemed to realize that the negative opinions held by Americans regarding the behavior of the Indians, the inferiority of their civilization, and their social and moral degradation, were to somehow justify White attitudes towards the native populations, their physical liquidation, and the illegal occupation of their lands. Relating a discussion about the Apache he had heard in Arizona, Sienkiewicz quotes the words of his discussant "... who spoke with disregard and contempt about their courage. According to his views they were inferior to the White people in open battles; all their attacks took place at night and were by surprise, from an ambush. Besides, the present generations living near the settlement had to quiet down, being forced by their bloody experience" (Wiśniowski 1876:39-40).

Much space in articles and books is devoted to information about tribes living in the Midwest and sometimes also in California. According to reports about the physical appearance and other characteristics, an Indian "... with his haughty figure and savage look brought to mind a poorly tamed jaguar. His head reminds of an eagle's head, his face looks as if hewn in copper; and in this face the eyes - truly Indian eyes - glow coldly, quiet and apparently unconcerned, but ominous... The feathers move on his head, an axe and scalping knife behind his belt" (Wiśniowski 1880:142). The stereotypes of Indian behavior such as courage, boldness, uprightness, taciturnity, coolness, great respect for parents, knowledge of nature and animal customs, and the like were often emphasized and repeatedly quoted. As a result, the Polish reader learned the difference between a wigwam and a tipi, the ways of making peace with the enemies, the methods of painting the face and body, the construction of a bow, the role of women, the fighting techniques, as well as the games.

From the reports by Sienkiewicz and Wiśniowski one could learn about the great role of the bison in the life of the Plains Indians. According to Sienkiewicz the shortage of bisons was the cause of starvation and depopulation of Indian tribes, and of the wars between them. By the end of the 19th century one could read comments about the planned extermination of bisons by the fur-hunters. As a result, the still free-living tribes in the West had to seek the help of the U.S. Government and to accept life on the reservations (Sienkiewicz 1880:242, Wiśniowski 1876:198, 1879c:425).

Much information can be found about the use of horses by the Indians and their horse breeding and riding skills. Polish readers of that period felt a great attachment to the horse, and the many descriptions and illustrations of famous Indians sitting and fighting on horseback increased the sentiments of the Poles for the Indians rather than extending their understanding of the Indians' problems. As a matter of fact, the Indian warriors were obliquely identified with Polish *ulans*, or soldiers defending the sovereignty of their country. The horse added to the feeling of independence, enabling free movement from place to place.

In his notes from California, Hołyński (*Czas*, vol. 1871:421) writes about the poverty and the peculiar character of the tribes living there. "The wigwams made of bark and brushwood are plastered with mud... these dog-holes are the domain of deepest poverty: the thick, stuffy, animal-like air can make you vomit. Their basic food has been - and is until today - a sort of paste made of acorn flour and baked in the oven as bread is baked... they eat all kinds of meat, from horse meat to raw meat."

Apart from various pieces of information about behavior, clothing, and food, one could sometimes come across data concerning Indian cosmology, their sacred places, and their mythology and religion, as for example the sentimental story of Winiowa[2] quoted by Wiśniowski (1876:41). Much was written about the personal dignity and pride of the Indians. In 1890, a reporter writing about the visit of a circus to Warsaw, which included American Indians as one of the attractions, stated that "what is characteristic is the expression of their eyes: cold, with a touch of contempt" (*Wędrowiec*, vol. 1890:421).

Starting with the 1860's, Warsaw periodicals mention the names of Indian chiefs famous for their fights against the Whites, such as Red Cloud, Sitting Bull, Geronimo, Cochise, and write about war-dances, and the fights between the Indian tribes and the Americans for the preservation of independence. One also finds mention of the decline of the Indian population due to those fights, to epidemics, tuberculosis and alcoholism. The situation of the Indians was often taken into consideration at that time. Narbuttówna, Sienkiewicz, Wolski, and Łubieński believed that the low population of the Indians was a consequence of American policies towards them. "It is commonly known," writes Krystyna

Narbuttówna (1880:37), "that in an attempt to get rid of their innocent neighbors, the U.S. Government has allotted a vast territory to which - by force or by voluntary agreements - it has pushed all the Indian tribes formerly dispersed over all States." And in 1873 Lubieński wrote that "not always are the Indians the cause of war, and I am convinced that there would be no bloody clashes if they were treated in a humanitarian and just way" (*Wędrowiec*, vol. 1873:170).

Wiśniowski (1876:132) reported to his readers: "The newspapers are full of descriptions of the incidents in the Black Hills, these descriptions - often deliberately exaggerated - only fan the hatred of the Whites and instead of discouraging all the mutinous souls, only encourage them to seek bloody rows and revenge on the redskins."

The description of murder and violence by the Indians in the White border settlements were accompanied by numerous examples of violation of U.S. Indian policies by Whites. "According to the views prevailing in the borderlands, the White man has the same right to exterminate the Indians as to kill the rattlesnakes, grizzly bears, and other harmful creatures."

All Polish authors of the second half of the 19th century agreed that the American government not only did not adhere to its treaties with the Indians, but prior to sending military or scientific expeditions to areas still inhabited by sovereign Indian tribes often influenced public opinion with regard to the occupation of Indian lands by settlers. This was the case in 1874 when a group commanded by General Custer invaded Sioux territory in July and August. Wiśniowski who took part in this expedition as a journalist and chronicler published his letters in *Kłosy* and *Wędrowiec*, thus informing the Polish readers almost immediately about the events that were taking place. He wrote that "the aim of the government expedition was partly to show the redskins that our army is able to come even to the wildest corners of the country, and partly organized in the hope of making geographic and topographic discoveries." According to his report "... both the land around us and the Black Hills belong to the Sioux tribe, the most numerous among the Indian tribes in the North-west, capable of raising even ten thousand warriors. The ownership of their land has been guaranteed by the U.S. Government" (Wiśniowski 1876:18).

The discovery of gold and silver in the area of the Black Hills was responsible for the tremendous influx of seekers of fortune despite the government's guarantees. Fights became inevitable, and ultimately the Sioux were reduced in numbers, robbed of their land, and pushed onto the reservations.

Gordon (1866:152) in his letters from the United States mentions similar events taking place at an earlier time. The Americans had forced the Creek and Cherokee to abandon their land, in spite of the protests of the Indians. Due to the fact that Gordon hardly could have been a witness of events having occurred several decades previously, his account is somewhat distorted,

301

yet this is what Polish readers had to consider as historic facts. The President himself, it is said, had promised his care to the Five Civilized Tribes, who had their own written constitutions, newspapers, and printing presses, and he had guaranteed them their sovereign existence. Gordon informed Polish readers on this occasion, that many Indian chiefs had been invited to Washington to meet with the President and to receive various medals from the Americans; this, however, had not prevented the Americans from violating the Indians' independence and from committing them to federal prisons under the guard of the U.S. Army. Gordon also mentions that in some places special gangs had been organized for the purpose of getting into fights with the Indians to enable U.S. troops to intervene.

In Texas these gangs had contributed to the decline of the native population. According to reports by Holiński and Narbuttówna the natives of California had ben completely exterminated. Elsewhere, the continuous fights in the borderlands created an atmosphere of fear, mutual hatred, and uncertainty. Polish travelers understood that difficult situation, but they emphasized the numerical strength of the White settlers and predicted the inevitable end of the independence of the Indian tribes.

What fascinated the Poles was certainly the Indian way of fighting, their boldness and courage, their skills in marching and running, in throwing the lasso, and in using the bow, arrow, and gun. Writing about Indian skills, Sienkiewicz thought that the continual pressure exerted by the colonists on the Indians and their territories in search of riches and arable land had compelled the Sioux, Pawnee, and other tribes - unable to resist militarily - to rob and steal the property of the settlers and to attack them, or to put on fire their newly established farms. Pushing the Indians further and further to the west was accompanied by much cruelty and also by a deliberate distortion of the truth regarding their numbers, actions, and characters in order to add to the hatred of the endangered White settlers. As Wiśniowski wrote to his readers in Warsaw, "in the mouth of the natives [i.e. the Americans] an Indian thief stealing army horses usually is transformed into a whole gang of marauders" (Wiśniowski 1876:19).

While blaming the U.S. Government for its relentless attitude towards the Indians, smaller in number and poorly armed, the majority of Polish travelers clearly foresaw the doom of the tribes as early as the early 1860's. Krystyna Narbuttówna (1880:79) asked her readers the rhetoric question: "Will one day in the future the judgement of history not ask the Americans: What have you done to your younger brother?" and she added melancholically: "Soon the Americans will probably hoist by the dead body of the last Indian warrior the flag of victory - but not the flag of civilization." Sienkiewicz (1877) in his "Letters from America," on the other hand, wondered whether it had to be a law that the civilization of the White man ought to be as destructive as the example of the Indians had shown it.

302

Most correspondents realized that the Indian population pushed ever further and ever more fiercely to the West, could be classified into two groups: those who had much earlier accepted their defeat, who by virtue of treaties had agreed to remove to Indian Territory or to be placed on reservations (the remnants of tribes formerly living in the vicinity of the East coast); and those tribes still striving to retain some of their lands and independence. With the latter tribes wars were being waged during the second half of the 19th century, to subject them to the American reservation system and to confiscate their lands for the needs of the hundreds of thousands of European immigrants. After meeting some of the Western Indians, Polish travelers described to Polish readers their degeneration subsequent to their expulsion from their traditional lands.

Sienkiewicz (1880a:129) clearly indicates the true cause of their poverty and misery: American civilization which had robbed them of their land, giving them instead various diseases, alcoholism, and poverty, and which had failed to teach them how to use the knowledge and the abilities of the White man. "What one sees is only misery and despair: men are dirty and debased, women stretch their emaciated hands out of the wagons. You might ask: Why don't they work? They do not know how, and no one cares to teach them. They have stopped wars with the Whites, stopped robbery and hunting in exchange for blankets and ... for contempt."

Although the position of Secretary of the Interior had been filled between 1877 and 1881 by Carl Schurz, an honest German immigrant who fostered a more enlightened policy toward the Indians, R. Łubieński (1874:258) informed Polish readers that the Indian commission was "a gang of criminals and swindlers. They deliberately induce the Indians to drink heavily as to be more easily able to rob them of their land and to get the approval of the government." It is interesting that Polish correspondents were establishing a negative image of these agents in the minds of their readers. The merchants operating along the frontier were described as boarish individuals of bad character and low morality. This somehow suggested that contact with such individuals necessarily had to corrupt the Indians and to arouse hostile prejudiced against them among the Whites who wished them well. Wiśniowski (1876, 1880) sent to Warsaw a true description of a trading post and the trader on the frontier. The building was constructed of heavy wooden logs and had a sod roof. Its square yard was surrounded by a palisade with wooden watch towers in its four corners. Besides the trader, the personnel of the post consisted of outlaws whose work required neither effort, nor diligence, nor sobriety. In their dealings with the Indians, both the agent and his staff did their best to cheat the natives bringing furs to exchange them for commodities. Alcohol was sold in huge quantities and many Indians died during the ignominious drinking feasts. Wiśniowski himself, who was not prejudiced in favor of the Indians, saw all the harmful symptoms of the effect of the Whites on the life of the

Western tribes and on the disintegration of their families. The immoral conduct of the Whites whose cruel attitude towards the Indians was not prosecuted was accompanied by social degradation and alcoholism of the Indian tribes.

One can come across deliberations as to whether the tragic situation of the Indian nations might have been the consequence of the lack of any union between the tribes and of any joint action against the Whites. Or was it a result of the fact that the Indians were on a lower level of civilization? Or of the expansion and land hunger of the part of the European settlers? In one of the 1890 issues of *Wędrowiec* (vol. 1890:291) one could read the statement that the Indians "only knew how to die as heroes with weapon in their hand, quietly and with a smile of contempt for their conquerors."

Numerous American statistical data were also quoted to indicate the declining number of Indians in the United States. From the U.S. census as quoted by the correspondents, Polish readers could learn that compared with the distinct decrease in the number of Indians living under the formal care of the American Government, the number of Indians inhabiting the formally independent areas had dropped only slightly. The confinement of the native population to a number of reservations scattered all over the territory of the United States somehow protected the people who were now settling on the formerly Indian lands; but on the other hand, it also resulted in public criticism of the brutality and ruthlessness of the people who were putting the orders of the Federal Government into effect. This division of public opinion was not overlooked by Polish travelers. Thus, for example, it found an indirect reflection in Sienkiewicz's short story "Sachem" (Sienkiewicz 1880b) and in Narbuttówna's novel "In America" (Nabuttówna 1880), or in connection with the Warsaw performance of a circus in 1890 in which the former lords of the prairies were degraded to the role of clowns, presenting the past grandeur of their tribes and the skills of the once bold warriors. Press reports about examples of Indian begging caused great sadness for Dunikowski (1892:95) who had been reared on Cooper's books.

Not all reports sympathized with the life and customs of the Indians. Of a different opinion was, for example, Sygurd Wiśniowski (1875:280, 1879c:142), a naturalized American citizen and journalist who had had a few years' experience as a settler in Minnesota. From his own experience he knew very well the troubles connected with living near the Indian frontier. In his reports sent to the Warsaw press in the 1870's, he therefore presented views that differed from those of other Polish or European travelers. Fascinated with the rapid industrial and territorial development of the United States, Wiśniowski thought the Indians to be the only obstacle for the happy domination of the whole continent by the Americans. His farmer friends from Minnesota shared his views. In one of his articles he wrote: "I do not hesitate to count American Indians among the laziest creatures in the world, next to the Australasian Papuas." In another communication from 1875, one could read the following:

"The sloppy and treacherous Indian, demoralized to the backbone, should not be an obstacle to the advance of civilization. With iron will one must force him to work so as to enable him to make his living from a small farm (where he would live in a tidy little house) instead of making a poor living from hunting in thousands of square miles of land." Wiśniowski ends his lengthy reasoning with the suggestion that Indians might be forced into working in mines or in agriculture. He concludes: "Land belongs to mankind and not to its laziest portion: the four- and the two-legged panthers must retreat before the progress of civilization."

Wiśniowski seems to be the only Polish observer who wrote about the fate of the Indian tribes in the second part of th 19th century, who did so without sentimentalism. Both his mentality and his words were typical of the American frontier's man eager-to-get-rich-quick mentality irrespective of what it would cost him and others. Nevertheless, his views are interesting as an example of the propagation of a certain American stereotype adopted by the settlers. His opinion also reflects the effect of the American ideology of success which leaves no place for pity toward the losers. Only strong and relentless individuals could win in the struggle for wealth. For the weak, all that remained to be had in American life was the margin - the reservation in the case of the Indians.

This twofold opinion of Poles reporting about Indians in the second half of the 19th century seems to have been of interest to their compatriots at home, who watched with apprehension the fate of the tribes of the American West and who, at the same time, were fascinated with the rapid development of the United States. I have not come across any direct comparisons of the Indian problems with those of the Poles which were similarly difficult and complex. The information, however, contained in many books and periodicals of the period undoubtedly contributed to a wider knowledge and better understanding of Indian topics in Polish society, and to an important and component part of the American myth so common throughout Europe.

NOTES

1. No "Medoc" tribe exists or has ever existed. If "Modocs" are intended, they never lived close to the Apache, but at least some of them had been removed in 1873 from Oregon to Oklahoma, near the Cherokee reservation.

2. "Winona" is probably intended here.

REFERENCES CITED

Cooper, James Fenimore
 1830   Ostatni Mohikanin, opowieść historyczna z 1757 r. [The Last of the Mohicans]. Wilno (also Lwów and Warsaw 1884, Poznań 1890).
 1834a   Stepy [The Prairie]. Wilno (also Warsaw 1884, 1894).
 1834b   Pijonierowiealbo źródła Susheany [The Pioneers]. Wilno (also Warsaw 1878, 1894).
Dunikowski, Emil Habdanek
 1891   Listy z Ameryki. *Gazeta Lowowska*. Lwów.
 1892   Wrażenia z podróży do Ameryki. Lwów.
Gordon, Jakób
 1866   Przechadzki po Ameryce. Poznań, Berlin.
 1867   Podróż do Nowego Orleanu. Lipsk.
 1880   Wspomnienia Gordona. *Wędrowiec*. Warsaw.
Lubieński, Roger
 1874   Z Ameryki. *Kronika Rodzinna*.
 1900   Z Ameryki. Warsaw.
Narbuttówna, Krystyna
 1870-1 W Ameryce. *Kronika Rodzinna*.
 1880   W Ameryce. Warsaw (first 1875).
Sienkiewicz, Henryk
 1876   Listy z Ameryki. *Gazeta Polska*.
 1877-8 Listy z Ameryki. *Kłosy*.
 1880a   Listy z Ameryki. Warsaw.
 1880b   Sachem. Orso. Warsaw.
Wiśniowski, Sygurd
 1875   Szkice amerykańskie. *Kłosy*.
 1876   Obrazki z życia amerykańskiego. W kraju Czarnych stóp. *Kłosy*.
 1879a   Listy z Ameryki. *Kurier Warszawski*. Warsaw.
 1879b   Listy z Ameryki. *Gazeta Lowowska*. Lwów.
 1879c, 1880 Listy z Ameryki. *Wędrowiec*. Warsaw.
Wolski, Kalikst
 1872-3 Do Ameryki i z Ameryki. Podróże, szkice, obyczaje i obraski z życia mieszkańców Ameryki. *Kłosy*.
 1877   Do Ameryki i z Ameryki. Lwów (London 1878).

SOME RUSSIAN RESPONSES
TO NORTH AMERICAN INDIAN CULTURES

Alexander Vaschenko

Several significant historical and cultural circumstances determine to some extent the subject and the very character of the present essay. Even the slightest glance at the sum total of the material pertaining to the subject of "Indians and Russia/USSR" reveals many different but parallel levels of existence: scholarly activities, popular events, literature, history, museums and archives, art events, and an enormous number of apparently random facts and occurrences, each of which in itself proves to be significant and somewhat unique.

Every such level reflects at least a small measure of influence - sometimes quite profound - of North American Indian cultures on the social and cultural life of the Soviet Union, and should be studied separately and at length. Such kind of treatment, however, focussed on any one of the levels, would presently be rather difficult to undertake since nobody has as yet probed the bulk of the material under discussion. So, obviously, this task must wait for the future.

This is not to say, though, that the subject of "Indians and Russia" has never been analyzed in any form. Indeed, it has been touched upon more than once in relation to some other, more general problem. If we were looking, for example, at the history of Russian-American relations, the publications of documents and several recent attempts to write a history of Russian-Native American cultural contacts, we might find much interesting information. Thus, from N. Bolkhovitinov's book it appears that at the end of the 18th century Catherine the Great had asked (through Lafayette) George Washington and Benjamin Franklin for a favor: In order to edit a comparative dictionary she wanted a list of Indian words to be filled out for her - and quite soon a dictionary of Delaware and Shawnee words was sent to the Russian empress (Bolkhovitinov 1976:119-121).

Similarly, if we were looking at the literary aspect of the same question, we might discover that the Indians began to stir the imagination of the Russian writers and poets since the time of Lomonosov and Radischev (the 18th century, once again), and that the theme was reflected on and on through classic Russian literature up to Chekhov's time, and was ultimately inherited by Soviet writers of the 20th century. Again, much of this unique material enclosed in the framework of the general subject of early Russian-American literary connections may be found in print. This material, though, still remains to be looked at in view of the specific problem under consideration.

In folk tradition, the whole genre of the so-called *skaskas* (or tales) and of various "descriptions" written, dictated, or told by the Cossacks, the *pomors* (North Sea fisherman), and the like, reflects the long-standing general interest of Russians in the Northwest Coast of North America. To a small extent this body of information is documented in published texts, but remains to be studied and verified. Thus, e.g., Sergei Markov, the author of the novel *Yukon's Raven* and the documentary *Alaska Chronicle* attached to it, states in the latter narrative: "Somebody from the staff of the Russian-American Company had entered the mysterious cave on Atka island and had found mummies there, with their hands closed over their chests. In this way, the funerary customs of the Aleuts were first being discovered" (Markov 1970:282).

From these preliminary and somewhat random examples it becomes clear, perhaps, that what one might offer at present on the subject of "Russian responses" to Native American cultures, would be an initial and in many ways provisional essay, striving to be as objective as possible - and this is precisely what will be presented on the following pages.

At the outset, it would be necessary to make it clear that scholarly research as such in its historical perspective in the Soviet Union will remain largely outside the scope of the material presented. This is partly because it seems more exciting to dwell on general tendencies and the phenomena which in one way or another have attained national significance or recognition, and to try to interpret them. But it is also done on purpose, as a study of Soviet scholarly research on Native American cultures is currently being prepared on behalf of the Institute of Ethnography of the Academy of Sciences, Moscow.

It may be appropriate to start with some reflections on the nature of the general interest in American Indians both in Russia and the Soviet Union.

I remember N. Scott Momaday, the celebrated Kiowa writer, asking me just after arriving for his first visit to the Soviet Union: "Why is there such a great interest in American Indians in your country?" It remains a mystery for me to this day, how he had received this impression, but the question was quite appropriate, and it was rather difficult to answer it either immediately or quickly.

The basis of this general interest in American Indians was undoubtedly established during the 18th and 19th centuries as a result of the voyages of many eminent Russian explorers.

As far as we can judge from the documentary evidence, the meeting of Admiral Chirikov with the Aleuts happened to be the first direct contact betwen Russians and the native peoples of North America. The occurrence, rendered in the admiral's simple yet expressive words, has become widely known since: "... And somewhat after 10 o'clock there came to us several small skin boats, seven in number, each manned by one person, and stayed near the ship for a considerable time, and afterwards returned to the shore. Later, well after noon, there came fourteen boats of a similar kind, one man in each, and the only things we received from them were one hat made of the birch-tree, like the ones they had on their heads, and besides that four arrows" (Magido-vich 1962:220).

308

Of the experiences that followed later, much has been written by various Russian navy officers such as Lisiansky, Golovnin, Litke, Zagoskin, to name but a few. To these we can add the accounts of some of the members of the Russian-American trade company (Liapunova and Fiedorova 1979) as well as the descriptions of the aborigines made by the priests of the Russian church in the 19th and early 20th centuries.

From this vast array of material on the manner and customs, economy, trade relations, languages, and geographical distribution of the tribes, mostly of Alaska and California, including a significant number of paintings and drawings, one might easily compile a handsome anthology today. This rich and valuable heritage, however, still awaits critical scholarly analysis and synthesis, in order to define precisely what the Russian contribution to our present knowledge of North American aboriginal cultures might have been.

This period, covering roughly two centuries of first and early contacts, may be regarded as a beginning. It was characterized on one hand by the direct and manifest contacts between Russians and those specific areas of America, which for a time were in fact settled by Russian populations, and also by the accounts of the various Russian businessmen, scholars, officers, and travelers, who had been living in or passing through certain areas of the Atlantic states, or the interior of the country, in the 18th and 19th centuries.

On the other hand, within Russia the same period was characterized by the gradual formation of general and idealized concepts concerning North American Indians, well known to the literary or cultural historian of the periods of the Enlightenment and Romanticism.

These attitudes and concepts were being shaped primarily by the translation of the American classics and the reviews by the leading Russian critics of the time, as well as by attempts to emulate or elaborate upon some literary narratives and genres, involving Indians. These soon became the subject of the intense literary process of the 18th and 19th centuries and quickly achieved wide circulation (Nikolyukin 1981:26, 142).

One such celebrated case is the review by Alexander Pushkin of *A Narrative of the Captivity and Adventures of John Tanner*, published in 1836. The founder of classical Russian literature offered a very favorable evaluation of the narrative itself, adding some illuminating remarks as to the phenomenon of its realism in contrast to Cooper's and Irving's works, as well as some comments on the hypocritical policy of the American government towards the Indians. More than that, he translated a portion of the book and included it into the text of the review. To my knowledge this study by Pushkin is the first review of the "captivity narrative" in the history of literary criticism. Pushkin refers to the life of the aborigines as "full of labor, dangers, adventures unencountered and unexpressed." And this is how it happened that several decades before Longfellow's triumph in Russia, the Ojibwa first became known to the Russian public (Pushkin 1949:449).

Romanticism and realism went hand in hand for a time in the classical Russian literature of the 19th century, and several books in the romantic tradition have formed to a great extent the Russian perception of Native American cultures. The impact of these can be felt even today.

The most important of these sources was *The Last of the Mohicans* by James Fenimore Cooper, as well as some other volumes of the Leatherstocking saga. They were extensively and with admiration commented upon by Vissarion Belinsky, they were admired by Lermontov and many of his contemporaries. The reverberations of the influence caused by Cooper's novels are manifold, immediate as well as long-distance, even up to the 20th century, when between 1929 and 1940 Alexander Fadeev wrote a novel *The Last of the Udehes* (one of the small nationalities of the Far East of the USSR). Vladimir Lenin has also widely used in his writings the metaphor of "the last of the Mohicans."

Equally enthusiastic has been the reception of Longfellow's poem *The Song of Hiawatha* which was translated into Russian many times, especially by such important poets as K. Balmont and Ivan Bunin. When Chekhov in one of his short stories, "Malchiki," depicted the abortive attempt of two schoolboys to run away to the wild Indians (one of them, in fact, identifies himself with an Indian chief), he is already speaking about several generations of young people, who had been feeding themselves for a long time on this kind of literature. Even young Vladimir Lenin could not resist the temptation to write a playful "totemic letter" to one of his friends, which to this day remains undeciphered (Popov 1981).

This brief detour into literature only serves to stress the tremendous influence that the image of the Indian has had on the mind of the Russian public to whom the only thing that mattered was not "realism vs. romance," but the artistic truth of the subject. The general Russian reader came to love Uncas, Osceola, and Hiawatha, because in these characters he could recognize the universal human ideals of heroism, patriotism, the pathos and love of freedom, and the first glimpses of what the Indian's life with nature might have been like.

These ideas have obviously been taken very seriously not only because of the concrete political conditions of the Russian state in the 19th century, but because they appealed to the inner traits of the Russian character and therefore made such a perception possible. It is a well-known fact that the popularity of Cooper's, Longfellow's, or Jack London's Indians remains much greater in the USSR than in their own country.

The second period of Russian perception of North American aboriginal cultures covers approximately the time from the beginning of the 20th century to the late 1960s.

Since 1917, one of the principles of the cultural policy of the Soviet state has become: We must know how the other peoples of the world live. This is why, with this very assignment in view, a talented young scholar was sent in the early 1920's to do field work in the Pacific Coast area of North America - as it happened, under Franz Boas. The name of the scholar was Yulia P. Averkieva, who was a member of the Institute of Ethnography of the Academy of Sciences of the USSR, and who later became the leading historian and ethnologist, head of the American department, and editor-in-chief of *Sovietskaia Etnografiia*. Under her supervision, North American Indian and Eskimo studies began to develop in Moscow and Leningrad (the latter having a branch of the Institute as well as the Museum of Anthropology and Ethnography, containing some of the oldest and rarest North American Indian, Aleut, and Eskimo artifacts).

The articles and monographs by Averkieva as well as her always kind and understanding response to everyone who wished to consult or speak to her on the subject, both her authority and personal charisma have characterized an epoch in North American Studies in the Soviet Union. Her books *Slavery among the North American Indians* (1941), *The Nomadic Indian Society of the 18th and 19th Centuries* (1970) and *The North American Indians: From Clan to Class Society* (1974) have become for many decades the guides for the young scholar, and for still a larger audience the only reliable sources of information on the American Indians. They have achieved the status of a cultural factor of significant importance.

The subsequent works of other scholars from the same department - Zolotarevskaia, Zibert, Blomkvist, and others - have marked the maturing of scholarly Soviet "Indianistics" as a distinctive feature of the period.

The works of Lewis Henry Morgan, *Ancient Society* and *Houses and House Life of the American Aborigines* (both early translated into Russian), as well as their study by F. Engels in his work on *The Origin of Family, Private Property, and the State* have also fulfilled the same role, becoming highlights for both scholars and non-scholars alike. In other words, there has been no discrepancy between the scholarly and popular levels of perception regarding North American Indians since the very beginning of the century.

Generalizing upon the field of scholarly activities in the first half of the century, one can easily see that an emphasis has been placed on the ethnography of the native cultures of the Pacific Coast, especially the Tlingit and Kwakiutl, as well as the Far North (Eskimo and Aleut). The non-material culture (language, storytelling, and other forms of folk art) was as a rule not accorded attention at first, because of the geographic remoteness and sporadic accessibility of the necessary field material, as well as for related reasons.

One of the pronounced features of such studies in the Soviet Union has become the close link with the rich ethnographic data coming from the vast regions of the Far North, Siberia, or the Far East of the USSR and concerning the various native cultures. Each of the new discoveries of the ancient artifacts - whether they were Eskimo masks, winged objects, Chukchee "peliken" figurines, and even ceremonial complexes - has usually been at length reviewed in the press as well as in the scholarly periodicals, and immediately called for comparison with North American material, and has thus helped to keep the focus of interest on Native American cultures in general. Yu.P. Averkieva, being herself much interested in the institution of the potlatch, has pointed out its typological significance and has found many similar practices among the North American Indians (particularly in the Plains area) as well as among the folk cultures of the Soviet Union.

Because of their close similarity with the cultures of the Canadian North, the Chukchee and Eskimo of the Soviet North have been the most explored, written about, and in certain ways "popular." The only exhibition of Native North American cultures shown to date in the Soviet Union has been the "Sculpture Inuit" exposition of 1971, which was very successful and an event in the cultural life of the decade.

On the popular level, for several decades during the first half the 20th century North American Indians had become the domain of children's and juvenile literature. The bulk of what has been published about them was edited and interpreted accordingly - the manner oversimplified, the choice random, and too often based on secondary sources, adapted or retold, but understood to be "the real thing."

Several translations, however approximating the original, deserve notice. Two books by James Willard Schultz, especially *My Life as an Indian*, show that the tendency has been to look for original, native accounts, or for genuine Indian authors, although the choice was not always the best one. Adapted translations of Luther Standing Bear's *My People, the Sioux* and *Long Lance* by Sylvester Long stand in the same tradition.

The period, it seems, was marked by a certain measure of contrast between the well-established tradition of academic research on the Native Americans, and the lack of a tradition on the part of the translators-publishers of interpretation and aesthetic evaluation of the same phenomena. The approach of the translators up to the mid-60's was often limited by their individual taste - and so they felt they were the only authorities on the subject, willing to share their lucky findings with the reader.

When analyzing the literary activities and cultural processes of the time, one should bear in mind the grave historical circumstances which had not been favorable for the development of studies that seemed to be of second-rate importance. The damages of war, the necessity to restore the economy were some of these reasons both after 1919 and 1945.

One literary and cultural phenomenon, though, calls for special attention: The books by Grey Owl, the Canadian author. Two of these have been translated into Russian: *Sajo and Her Beaver People* (1940) and *Tales of an Empty Cabin* (1974). The general interest in nature-philosophical or naturalistic prose of this kind had been prepared by the tradition of classic Russian and Soviet prose - by the writings of V. Bianki, V. Arseniev, M. Prishvin, and others. Among the comparable Canadian/American authors of the time one can easily point at E. Thompson-Seton, largely translated and admired in the Soviet Union.

The call raised by Grey Owl in Canada for the preservation, not destruction, of the kingdom of the wilds was promptly heard by prominent Soviet writers. Some of them, moved by the personality of Grey Owl, thought that his works deserved greater attention. M. Prishvin, himself an ardent hunter and naturalist as well as an enthusiastic fighter for a reasonable and humane treatment of wildlife, has not only written an introduction to *Sajo*, but has actually retold yet another book by the same author, *Pilgrims of the Wild*. He explained his motives in a brief introduction: "Our Russian hunting has been for our writers not so much of a sport, as is the case with many foreign hunters. With us, hunting has sometimes been... the method of understanding nature. For the masses of people it is the love of nature or more exactly the poetry of life's joy, accessible to everybody. I strongly believe that in time our hunting will lead to the necessary action in defense of nature. I have decided to acquaint my readers with the works of the Indian writer Grey Owl..." (Prishvin 1971:9).

The humanistic, moral, as well as educational appeal of Grey Owl's prose has been fully perceived and many times underlined by Prishvin. Another prose-writer of the time, Andrei Platonov, has celebrated the phenomenon of Grey Owl in his essay "The New Rousseau," in which he remarks that "he is the man, who is constantly in need of the large organic relationship with the world - he could not learn to lead the... artificial life of the strange civilized European or American beings. He will die if the beneficial nourishment from the external forces will cease: the oxygen from the plants, and the pull from the blessed space, inhabited by the birds and beasts, where you can fulfill all the natural aspirations of man: freedom, deliberation, labor, and serenity... Such is this Rousseau," he concludes, "the philosopher, the writer, the naturalist, striving to save the Beaver People and Nature, in order to preserve the Indians and mankind" (Platonov 1976:369-370, 379).

The emergence of the next stage of the perception of Native North American cultures was determined by the many historical changes which had gradually taken place in the post-war world. As a result of the "Great Awakening" of the ethnic minorities within the United States during the 1960s, these groups came into the very midst of the social and cultural life. Politically the the well known process unfolded through the "fish-ins" of 1964 to the occupation of Alcatraz, and culminated in the revolt at Wounded Knee in 1973. Culturally, the consequences were even more varied and far-reaching, and so the inherently present interest in Indians has received new inspirations directly from the "New Indians," as journalist Stan Steiner has called them, and in time has reached the level of the United Nations.

The political and social activities of the Indians, widely reviewed in the press, have also attracted the close attention of Soviet scholars as well as of

313

the general public; articles, post-graduate works and Ph.D.s of the 1970's and 1980's clearly reflect this growing interest.

Within the USSR, on the other hand, the flowering of the multi-national cultures throughout the immense territory of the country has become one of the leading tendencies of the post-war reality. Contrary to the destiny of Native American cultures, the development of Soviet multinational cultures has been more or less steady, for they have never been denied their ancestral territory or their native language.

Bearing these differences in mind, we become immediately aware of the fact that the contemporary process of vigorous growth of the different national cultures, which for so long had been peripheral to world culture, is all-human by nature and has become the most important feature of our time. That is why, quite naturally, irrespective of geographical remoteness or cultural difference it everywhere receives "the shock of recognition," especially in the minds of the individuals concerned.

One good example of this may be the eager reception of the film *Dersu Usala* by Akiro Kurosawa, filmed after the book of the Soviet writer and explorer V. Arseniev. The central character of Dersu, the native Leatherstocking/Chingachgook of Siberia, has become the symbol of all traditionally nature-oriented peoples; the film has achieved tremendous success among North American Indians - that is, among those who have managed to see it. The movie goers around the world were deeply moved by the humane, pantheistic philosophy of Dersu who equates whatever passes him - be it beast, insect, Sun, or Moon - by one simple but profound truth: "Him very good people." (Besides, this is not a fictional character.)

Almost simultaneously, new films began to be made after the prose works of the contemporary Soviet writers of Siberia and the Far North, and these have opened, as it happened, new artistic and aesthetic vistas.

New trends have become apparent in the mid-1970's in the field of Native American Studies. After the untimely death of Yu.P. Averkieva something like a new generation of young "Indianist" scholars began to emerge, not only in Moscow and Leningrad, but also in several other cities. The field itself has begun to broaden in scope: The traditional ethnohistorical approach practiced at the Institute of Ethnography was intensified under Valery Tishkov, and has been adopted by the Department of Ethnography at Moscow State University. Besides, new aspects of the same subject have started to gain recognition: Literature und folklore (Institute of World Literature, Academy of Sciences of the USSR) and, somewhat later, languages (Institute of Linguistics of the Academy of Sciences).

From time to time, Native American guests have come to the Soviet Union to become part of this new development: such were the two visits by N. Scott Momaday (1974 and 1977), a visit of three Native American leaders (two Sioux and one Potawatomi), or the exposition by Creek artist Minisa Crumbo, to

314

mention but some of the most significant events. The mid-1970's turned out to be the time of bringing together all of the forces connected in some way with Native American Studies. This was also one of the aims and the main result of the scholarly symposium "American Indians in the Contemporary World" held by the Institute of Ethnography in 1982. The participants of the symposium became aware of the fact that "Indianist" research was being pursued in the national republics of the Soviet Union. Thus, a monograph on the Indian wars has recently been written in Pjarnu (Estonian SSR); from the same source comes also the Estonian translation of Dee Brown's *Bury My Heart at Wounded Knee*. This occurred before the 1984 publication of the Russian translation of the book - and it should be mentioned that its appearance in the Soviet Union had long been awaited and much anticipated since the publication of extracts in various Russian and Ukrainian periodicals.

This process of gathering the forces in the different branches of Native American Studies has just begun. It still has to include the museums all over the country and it still awaits registration of all private collections, however small they might be. At present, it is definitely known that collections of Native American artifacts exist in the museums of Leningrad, Moscow, Kasan', Vilnius, Tomsk, and possibly in some other cities. The creation of new regional museums reflecting the early Russian-American exploration is being debated in the press (Kuznetsov and Zaitsev 1985).

The late 1970's became characterized by a certain merging of scholarly and popular interests in Native Americans. The traditional popular interest in this subject existing in many of the Socialist countries of Europe, especially in Czechoslovakia, the GDR, Poland, and Hungary has appreciably contributed to this process. One might, in fact, state with a great deal of accuracy that much elementary and non-scholarly information about North American Indians has reached the general Soviet reader during the past two or three decades in the form of popular books and films produced in these countries. On the mass level, only a small part of the material has been absorbed directly from Anglo-American sources, translated or untranslated. The book by Miloslav Stingl, the Czech ethnographer, *Indians without Tomahawks*, covering the subjects of Indian culture, Indian wars, and the contemporary situation on a descriptive level, has been translated and even been re-issued before the publication of Dee Brown's book (Stingl 1971).

Another example to be given in this connection is particularly illustrative and even striking, especially as it has to do mainly with the "mass level." It involves the Polish writer of children's books, Stanislav Suplatovich, or Sat-Okh (Silver-Feather), as he chooses to call himself. He claims to be half Polish and half Shawnee by descent. The striking circumstances of his birth from a Polish revolutionary exile mother, who had come to North America to be adopted into the Shawnee tribe, has been told more than once both in Poland and in the USSR. From these data, as well as from Sat-Okh's books, it is assumed that later the young son of the Shawnee chief had gone through the Odyssey of removal and dispossession of the Shawnee tribe, one band of which, it is stated, "has fled to Canada." After that Sat-Okh did return to Poland to take part in the resistance struggle against Nazi occupation, and after the war settled in Gdansk dedicating his full time and energy to writing books on Indian subject matter. Of these, *The Land of the Salt Rocks* has become the most popular, telling the "Indian" part of his autobiography.

Among the younger generations of Soviet readers, the teenagers and people now in their twenties, the person and writings of Sat-Okh have acquired a tremendous popularity. It is maintained through constant contacts between him and some of his eager writer-publisher friends, mostly in Kiev, but also elsewhere. The wonderful story of Sat-Okh's life has been retold by children-book writer Nikolai Vnukov, the content of several of his books was used by other authors and journalists. One of the minor Moscow theater studios has made an attempt to stage *The Land of the Salt Rocks* in 1984. For all these people, and especially for a great number of young readers, Sat-Okh presently remains not a derivative, pan-Indian phenomenon of a "mass culture," but "the real thing."

From the beginning of the 1970's, the appearance of a huge quantity of mass-oriented popular Cowboy-and-Indian films, produced by the GDR DEFA Studio, became part of the cultural scene. Made after Fritz Steuben's Tecumseh novels or Liselotte Welskopf-Henrich's Dakota series and mostly lacking deep content or artistic quality, these films have nevertheless introduced to the young mass audience many general ideas and specific features of the daily life of Prairie or Southwestern Indians, such as traditional dress, cultural traits, etc.

These films together with the books of Sat-Okh became the two factors that triggered the development of the "Indian hobbyist" movement (or amateur Indianistics). It has begun to take shape during the late 1970's and the beginning of the 1980's, concentrating around Leningrad, but simultaneously developing in several other places. Attached to local clubs or branches of the Society of International Friendship, ot the Amateur Creative Activities Clubs, these groups of interested enthusiasts dedicate their time to promoting knowledge of the folk culture and contemporary condition of Native North Americans, to song-writing, to emulating the Indians' approach to nature, to the production of traditional Indian artifacts from headdresses to tipis, etc.

Since 1981 these groups have agreed to gather annually for their summer All-Union festivals or "Powwows," the event taking place in a camp comprising from seven (in 1982) to fourteen (in 1983) to twenty (in 1984) tipis. The festival combined the program events that had become traditional: dance shows, competitive exhibitions of self-made Indian costumes and artifacts, Indian tipi life, games, attempts to reproduce Indian cooking (partly by using substitutes provided by the local native cuisine), song competitions on Native American themes, and other activities. With each passing year the amateurish interests

316

of the participants gain in depth and shape. Special attachment seems to be demonstrated to Plains Indian cultures, especially those of the Dakota and Cheyenne, including the reconstruction of their dances and songs, dress, and sweatlodge (*inipi*); to the Apache, as manifested in their dress and horsemanship; and to the Ojibwa, only in the elements of dress and woodmanship. There are occasional Iroquois and Seminole motifs. The general interest in the Shawnee tribe is presently based exclusively on information derived from Sat-Okh. The marked socio-political compassion both in historical and contemporary terms with the American Indian Movement (AIM) and other prominent Indian leaders, such as Russell Means or Leonard Peltier, inspire all the rest.

In an attempt to formulate some general conclusions on the basis of what has been said above, it may be stated that several North American Indian culture areas, sometimes represented by one or two major tribes, have contributed to the traditional attention, or even keen interest, both in the Russian and Soviet general public and in scholarly circles. This influence has tended to concentrate on certain levels or on different spheres. Thus, the cultures of the Pacific Northwest, of Alaska, as well as of the Polar North, have traditionally become the domain of scholarly investigation; this was (and is) only natural, since the material, even the field data, have been most accessible from these areas and proved to be interesting from the point of view of typology, genesis of cultures in that area, and the like. Research dealing with these cultures to this day remains a strictly scholarly phenomenon, barely transcending the limits of academic activities.

An easily perceived traditional interest in several North American forest and hunting/fishing cultures, primarily represented by the Algonquians of the Great Lakes area, by contrast comes from literary sources: early Russian translations of James Fenimore Cooper's tremendously popular *Leatherstocking Tales* and Henry Longfellow's famous poem. To these one should add in the 20th century Thompson-Seton, especially his books about forest Indian life and lore, such as *Rolf in the Woods* (translated 1929) or *The Little Savages* (1960). All of these remain until today the most popular authors, "the contemporaries" of a great many of the Soviet readers of various ages. Their books are reissued, retranslated, and reinterpreted in view of the present understanding of such categories as "national writer," "ecology," "active humanism," "native culture," "realistic quality," etc. These writers appear to be of perennial importance to the Russian character as for the American, in these terms. Besides, they are understood in the context of classic Russian and Soviet literature, which is deeply concerned with the national heritage and the realm of nature - e.g., in the context of such works as Leonid Leonov's novel *The Russian Forest* (1953) or the authors of contemporary "village prose."

In this respect, the Ojibwa seem to be most widely known or, at least, heard of. And although one might say that the knowledge of Indian Woodland culture comes from a fictional tradition, it should be borne in mind that there were (and remain to be) some "factors of reality" which have always helped to hold the attention of the public on the subject. One of these is the fact that the geographical "middle belt" of Russia, stretching from the Belorussian SSR to the Ural Mountains and further on to Siberia, from the point of view of its natural conditions, the climate, and culture traits, is highly comparable to the respective surroundings of the Great Lakes area, or more broadly, to the Woodland region of North America, which is the traditional habitat of many Algonquian tribes. And so, when Russian readers come across Longfellow's line

"Give me of your bark, o birch-tree",

they identify themselves more easily with Hiawatha because of the sameness of the immediate surroundings which readily comes to their minds: the native birch, "the magic tree" both for the Algonquians and for the old Slavs, possesses great cultural importance, and from a very distant past has become the symbol of Russia.

The writer/naturalist tradition, the simultaneous interest in natural life and cultures, is a shared Russian-American trait: That is, perhaps, why Vitali Bianki has written the introductions to Thompson-Seton's books, Michael Prishvin to those of Grey Owl, and why this spiritual kinship has always been strongly felt. "As a Russian reader, I feel an especially close connection with the compassionate feeling on the part of the Indian hunter, this unrestricted longing to know, to experience what is there 'behind the mountains', as the Indian says, or, as we say, 'behind the blue seas,'" Prishvin wrote.

Last, but not least, the existence of the multitude of our domestic cultures, both Woodland and Desert, sedentary as well as traditionally nomadic, the many ways of living, the folklore traditions providing the reader with local versions of the Earth-Diver-Deluge mythological motifs, the Bear Mother and Trickster characters, has contributed and will no doubt contribute much more in the future to the growing knowledge of these matters (cp., e.g., V. Bianki's retelling of the "Tales of the Hunter," where the Munsee storyteller dwells on these folk-subjects.").

Speaking in terms of chronology, the more intimate attachment to Plains cultures is a much later phenomenon, and remains more general in character. This may be due to the stereotypic nature of the DEFA productions, whereas more authentic sources like J.W. Schultz or Dee Brown remain among the exceptions. The powwows of the young Soviet Indianists, however, much as those elsewhere, seem to be clearly oriented towards the Plains, being more especially inspired by Dakota elements. The appearance on Soviet screens of films such as *Mackenna's Gold* (USA) or *Ulsana* (GDR), on the other hand, has introduced the average cinema-goer to Apache culture.

In general it may be said that although spatial separation and the lack of frequent contacts with Native American cultures have slowed the process of the formation of concrete and stable perceptions or of a monumental image, this particular circumstance has also directed scholarly attention to more general or theoretical aspects, to comparative studies, the search for typological and genetic connections on the basis of archaeology, anthropology, folklore, etc.

This does not necessarily mean a lack of interest in the specific data. On the contrary, the next period of plunging into the unknown "known" seems to be at hand. The number of translations of contemporary American Indian authors such as N. Scott Momaday, H. Storm, Leslie Silko, Simon Ortiz, and others, as well as of Indian myths and legends is constantly growing.

New perspectives may be opened up with the realization of a recently adopted project, sponsored by the Goskomizdat (State Publishing Committee). It concerns the publication of a comparative series of books (documentaries, fiction, poetry, myths and legends, etc.). For each volume dealing with Native American (including Eskimo) cultures there will be a corresponding volume on one of the many national cultures of the Polar North or the Far East of the Soviet Union or Siberia. This experimental series, designed to assemble the many similarities as well as contrasts of the respective cultures, promises to be innovative in its editorial principles and at the same time will unify many of the traditionally existing tendencies in the field of the respective cross-cultural studies of both areas.

In conclusion, however approximate it has to remain, we may only state that the deep interest taken in Russia since an early period in Native American cultures has been an inherent tradition. At the present time, this tradition is steadily growing, and one of the most important reasons may be found in the fact that the Native American communities continue to show the characteristics of what is truly democratic in the culture of the United States, and because in all forms of its existence it is marked by strong folk elements. For that matter, it always has been regarded seriously, with love and deep, sincere concern, on any of the levels of attention in Russia as well as in the Soviet Union. And in this, it is hoped, there may be the main response that the Russians have made to Native American cultures. It is a strong conviction that because of their unique life-styles and dramatic history they have in many special ways become close relatives of our country as well as of the rest of mankind.

REFERENCES CITED

Bolkhovitinov, N.N.
   1976   Rossiia i voina SShA za nezavisimost' 1775-1783. Moskva: Nauka.
Kuznetsov, F., and S. Zaitsev
   1985   Vospitanyie istoriiei. Literaturnaya Gazeta, 16 janvaria 1985, p. 11.
           Moskva.
Liapunova, R.G., and S.G. Fiedorova (eds.)
   1979   Russkaya Amerika v neopublikovannykh zapiskakh K.T. Khlebnikova.
           Leningrad: Nauka.
Magidovich, I.P.
   1962   Istoriia otkrytiia i issledovaniia Severnoi Ameriki. Gosudarstvennoie
           Izdatelstvo geograficheskoi literaturi. Moskva.
Markov, S.
   1970   Yukonskii voron. Letopis' Aliaski. Moskva: Sovetskaia Rossiia.
Nikolyukin, A.N.
   1981   Literaturniie svazi Rossii i SShA. Moskva: Nauka.
Platonov, A.
   1976   Novii Russo. In: Velichiie prostykh serdets. Moskva: Moskovskii
           Rabochii.
Popov, I.
   1981   Indeiskaia tropa. Yunost' 7:91-96.
Prishvin, M.
   1971   Seraia Sova. Moskva: Detgiz.
Pushkin, A.S.
   1949   Sobraniie sochinenii v 10 tomakh, vol. 7. Moskva-Leningrad:
           Akademia Nauk.
Stingl, Miloslav
   1971   Indeitsi bez tomagavkov. Moskva: Progress.

WILLIAM BLACKMORE:
A 19TH CENTURY ENGLISHMAN'S CONTRIBUTION
TO AMERICAN INDIAN ETHNOLOGY[1]

Colin Taylor

William Blackmore (Fig. 1) was born in Salisbury, in August 1827. He trained as a solicitor and after qualifying in 1848 joined a firm of solicitors in Liverpool. It was here that he made contacts with a number of important Americans who were "getting rich quick" with land, mining, and railway developments in the American West. The resourceful Blackmore was soon involved in one scheme after another and thus became well-known in both British and American financial circles.

He made his first visit to the U.S.A. in 1863 and towards the end of that year heard of the archaeological collections from the mounds in the valley of the Mississippi. The largest collection was that of Squier and Davis then up for sale and in store at the New York Society. Outbidding competitors Blackmore purchased the entire collection for $10,000 and transferred it to England; it was the acquisition of this material that led to the founding of the Blackmore Museum in Salisbury which was opened to the public - with much ceremonial - in September 1867 (Fig. 2).

Although the business enterprises of Blackmore have been well documented in H.O. Brayer's 1949 case study of the economic development of the West, he frankly stated that it was impossible to elaborate upon the many scientific and philanthropic ventures which were as much a part of Blackmore's life as his complex business transactions. These ventures and interests were orientated towards American exploration, hunting, photography, anthropology, and Indian life and customs.

Blackmore's interest in the American Indian apparently began at an early age. Possibly the interest was initiated by the enterprises of George Catlin in Great Britain in the years 1839-45 when Catlin not only published his first edition of *Letters and Notes on the North American Indians* in London in 1841, but exhibited extensive collections of American Indian ethnographical material in Egyptian Hall, Piccadilly (cp. Mulvey, this volume). In later years, Blackmore was to become a firm friend of George Catlin and helped him financially when the latter fell on particularly hard times.

While Blackmore's frequent visits to the U.S.A. in the period 1863 to 1874 were primarily concerned with business affairs, his deep interest in the Indians, buffalos, and the development of the American West in general caused him to become increasingly involved in buffalo hunts, making exhibitions, and collecting photographs and data; during this period he gained an international

Fig. 1. William Blackmore (1827-1878).Founder of the Blackmore Museum, Salisbury, Wiltshire. Blackmore's great hobby was the pursuit of North American Indian studies and collecting.(Courtesy, Salisbury & South Wiltshire Museum).

reputation as a scholar of the American Indian. He built up a very extensive library of books on North American Indians which appear to have been housed at both his house in Carshalton and at the Museum in Salisbury. It was, however, generally to Salisbury that he would retreat after his strenous business trips, to study and catalogue his vast collection. The claim he made in 1876 - "during the last thirty years it has been my constant effort to collect and read all that has been written relative to these aborigines" - was no exaggeration; catalogues which were until recently housed in the library at the Blackmore Museum integral to the great exhibition hall, listed upwards of a thousand books on North American Indians, some of them extremely rare and early editions.

In addition, on display in the wall cases, were exhibits of a fine collection of ethnographical material from North American Indians such as feather headdresses, beaded and quilled pipe bags, and moccasins.

Blackmore's tragic death in April 1878, however, resulted in an equally tragic, inadequate recognition of his contribution to North American ethnology

322

except by a very limited number of scholars. Only in recent years has research begun to demonstrate that William Blackmore's 19th century interests and enthusiasm for American Indians and related studies had far reaching consequences which have both directly and indirectly influenced countless individuals, professionals and amateurs alike.

One fascinating facet of William Blackmore's activities in the American West which I can hardly detail here related to grandiose plans for development of the resources and wealth. In November 1871, for example, he wrote to his friend Dr. Ferdinand V. Hayden, the distinguished government geographer, regarding the founding of a "Grand Educational Institution of the West": "I want to commemorate your wedding," Blackmore wrote, "by founding jointly with you and others in the heart of the Rocky Mountains a college and museum devoted to the physical Sciences... there is a great want of such an institution in the country and I know of no one better or fitter to act as President as yourself... I shall like immensely to see you at the head of the leading Geological Institution of U.S. the Professor Huxley in fact of America..." (Brayer 1949:180).

Another project involved a program for establishing "English Settlements and Grand Educational Institute in the Great West." This program dated March 1872 outlined plans for acquiring the best parts of southern Colorado and northern New Mexico as sites for future English settlements. These were to be "composed of superior middle classes... men of intellect and position" and, with astounding

Fig. 2. Interior of the Blackmore Museum, Salisbury, founded in 1864 and opened to the public in September 1867.It housed an extensive collections of North American Indian material. (From an engraving, Illustrated London News, 14 September 1867).

arrogance, Blackmore stated that those parts of Colorado particularly selected for English colonization would "probably rule the destinies and shape the future policy of the United States." Further, from "its geographical position, vast mineral wealth, fertility, and, salubrity of climate" it would form one of the best sites "for the future Capital of North America" (HSNM0491).

Although such plans never reached fruition he correctly predicted that the mountain locked parks of southern Colorado would well adapt to agricultural products such as potatoes, turnips, cabbage, lettuce, wheat, barley and oats, and fine grass for livestock. Blackmore is also credited with suggesting the name "Manitou" for the town in southern Colorado where the explorer Dr. W. Bell built his home.

Photography and the American Indian

Blackmore early became interested in amassing an incomparable collection of photographs mostly of Indian subjects and, particularly after his 1863 visit, he began systematically collecting photographs and commissioning various photographers to capture the ethnology of the fast disappearing American aborigines, on photographic plates. That Blackmore has failed to get the recognition he deserves is well illustrated by the work of Robert Taft, an eminent researcher who had a particular interest in photographs of the American Indian. Taft makes no mention at all of Blackmore in his classic *Photography and the American Scene* (1938). This was a strange omission for Taft would surely have been familiar with W.H. Jackson's *Catalogue of Photographs of Indians* (1877) which identified negatives in the possession of the United States Geological Survey. In the introduction Jackson wrote: "The following series of Indian subjects is made up principally of the valuable additions which have been made to the original collections of this survey through the munificent liberality of William Blackmore Esquire of England who contributed them gratuitously for the advancement of ethnological studies." Jackson went on to say that "the contributions of Mr. Blackmore comprise first a collection of over four hundered negatives by Schindler (Shindler) of Washington, D.C., who had gathered them from various sources and which go back to the days of the daguerreotype twenty-five years ago; second a collection of about forty-five negatives made to his order, of the Pueblos, Apaches and Navajos in New Mexico in 1871; third a series of over three hundred very valuable negatives purchased from Alex Gardner Esquire of Washington, D.C., embracing all the prominent individuals who have visited their great father upon delegations during the last ten years."

Although Blackmore gave these negatives to the USGS archives he retained and added to his collection of photographic prints many of which were published on behalf of the "Trustees of the Blackmore Museum, Salisbury, England." Had Taft pursued any leads to the Blackmore collection he would

Fig. 3. Red Cloud and William Blackmore from a photograph taken by Alexander Gardner in Washington, May 1872.Gardner was commissioned by Blackmore to photograph a number of Indian delegations to Washington, these being published by the Trustees of the Blackmore Museum.(From a photograph in the Museum of Mankind, London).

Fig. 4. Little Raven, Arapaho Head Chief, photographed in Washington in 1871 for the Trustees of the Blackmore Museums, Salisbury.The New York Times for June 1871 reported that the Arapaho delegation was "astonished by our cities; such a gathering of men all in one place.... they do not understand our railways, telegraphs etc.They know such things are done, but they cannot understand by what power....they have no words in their language to comprehend all they see." (From a photograph in the Museum of Mankind, London).

have discovered a rich treasure of some 2000 photographs of American Indians taken between 1850-1875 which were not transferred to the British Museum or dispersed elsewhere until the 1930's. Some of these photographs would have been of considerable interest to Taft since there are scenes probably taken by J.D. Hutton on the Raynolds expedition to the head waters of the Missouri and Yellowstone rivers in 1859-1860. These field photographs of Northern Arapahos are undoubtedly amongst the earliest in existence of western Plains Indians taken in their native habitat. Of the expedition Taft wrote that no views of this and most other early exploring expeditions "are now accessible."

Delegations of Indians to Washington were photographed by Alexander Gardner at William Blackmore's expense (Fig. 4). One series - of many in a 41-volume collection - was of the Red Cloud delegation in May 1872.

A newspaper report written at the time of this visit refers to the fact that the Sioux were "deeply impressed with the interest taken in them by William Blackmore, an English capitalist engaged in developing the mining resources of Colorado and New Mexico, and grateful for the courtesies extended them by him" (HSNM0523).

Blackmore had earlier arranged for the entire Sioux delegation to be taken on a river tour down the Potomac. This must have been a memorable day for the delegation every courtesy being extended to them. They were picked up from their hotel in coaches while Red Cloud and Red Dog rode in a hackney carriage; in other carriages accompanying the party were the Blackmores and various dignitaries including Professor Joseph Henry. The day was highly successful and a contemporary report credited Blackmore with a "broad streak of humanity" and having the "welfare of the Indian race at heart." It was this, the report continued "that induced him to extend an invitation to the Indian delegation to take a trip down the river, which was as much a pleasure to him as to those who were the recipients of his courtesy."

Some days later, before leaving Washington, the Sioux called to bid farewell to the Blackmores. The delegation was received in one of the parlors of the Arlington Hotel and Blackmore addressed the chiefs through the interpreter. After complimenting them as "great chiefs" with "much power in your own country and with your own people" he generously presented each of them with the offer of a gun and "suitable ammunition" which they "could select in New York" at his expense. Mrs. Blackmore too arranged to send presents to both the wives and children of the chiefs. Concerned at the possible future developments Blackmore then offered the Sioux some sound advice. "I want again to impress upon you," he said "the necessity of educating your children and teaching them in the ways of the white men. We all of us, like old trees,are too fixed in our habits to change greatly. We can be broken, but not bent; but if you will take the young twigs - your children - you can train and bend them as you like, and when they have been taught and educated, although they will always remain red men at "heart," yet they will be wise in their heads as the white men and be able to do as much with their hands." Blackmore then concluded with some rather trenchant comments: "One word more and I have finished. It is that I urge you always to abstain from war with the whites, you have seen their numbers and their power, and you can not succeed. As Red Dog mentioned the other day, we are three nations - the Americans, the Red Men, and the English. It is my most earnest wish, and I pray that the great spirit will always keep us three nations in perpetual peace" (HSNM0520).

Although Red Cloud had visited Washington previously and Blackmore had tried to arrange photography at that time, the Sioux chief was reluctant to have his portrait made. Thus those taken in May 1872 were the first of this celebrated chief. It is of interest to note that Balckmore and Red Cloud clasp hands as a gesture of close friendship and also possibly as a reassurance to

326

the Sioux leader on his first experience before the mysterious "shadow catcher" (Fig.3).

Blackmore's collection was far ranging and represented work of many photographers - from a unique series of photographs taken by Orloff R. Westmann at the Taos Pueblos annual fiesta in September 1871 to those taken of Sioux, Crow, Arapaho, and Gros Ventre at the Fort Laramie Treaty in 1868. In all, to date, our notes list twenty eight photographers or studios covering the period 1847-1872.

Taos Pueblo 1871

Blackmore obviously enjoyed his meetings with the various delegations in Washington but he also met American Indians on their home ground.

One of his earliest contacts with Indians in their native habitat was at Taos, New Mexico, in late September 1871. In 1870 Blackmore had successfully negotiated the sale of land in Colorado and mortgage bonds on the Denver and Rio Grande Railway and realizing the considerable profits which could accrue from such transactions, towards the end of September 1871 he traveled to Elizabeth Town which was a gold mining town northeast of Taos. The object of the visit was to search the land office records there for titles to Spanish and Mexican land grants, he then traveled on to Taos arriving at the end of September. The Pueblo of Taos was built on the slopes of a high plateau at the base of a mountain sacred to the Taos people and even today its spectacular four and five story adobe buildings are a centre of attraction and interest. Inhabited for perhaps 900 years Taos was a trade centre for many western Indian tribes, such as the Comanche, Navajo, and Apache, and it was here, during the annual trade fairs that products of the chase and horticulture as well as arts and crafts were sold and traded.

For time immemorial the Annual San Geromino Fiesta has traditionally commenced on the evening of 29 September with Vespers at the San Jerome Chapel followed by the Sundown Dance. The following day of 30 September are the all-day trade fairs, relay races, dances, and pole climbing competitions.

Realizing the importance of the pictorial as well as written record of events Blackmore had hired the services of Orloff Westmann, a German immigrant, whose studios were in Elizabeth Town, and at the commencement of the main ceremonials on the 30th both were kept busy. Blackmore spent the day jotting detailed notes on his observations while Westmann made a series of a least fourteen photographs of groups and individuals who participated in the races, archery competitions, dances, and impressive cavalcades (Figs.5, 6).

In arranging his western sojourns he elicited the help of such notables as Joseph Henry, distinguished physicist and first Secretary of the Smithsonian Institution. On 17 April 1872, Henry wrote a personal letter to the Secretary

327

Fig. 5. Taos Pueblo, New Mexico.This was visited by William Blackmore in September 1871 when he commissioned Orloff Westmann, a photographer of Elizabeth Town, to take some fourteen photographs of the Annual San Geromino Fiesta and associated activities. Photograph by the author.

Fig. 6. Ute Indian buckskin and beaded ceremonial shirt probably collected by William Blackmore in Taos, New Mexico, September 1871.(From collections in the Museum of Mankind, London).

of War supporting Blackmore's application for a military escort, describing Blackmore as "an English gentleman of wealth and influence; a generous patron of science, both in his own and in our country" and he pointed out that his explorations would significantly advance the "knowledge of our western domain."

Thus on 8 June he said goodbye to Henry, who noted in his diary: "Mr. Blackmore called to take leave. He goes first to Colorado Springs, thence to Fort Ellis on the Yellowstone, then to Fort Benton, then down the Missouri to Omaha and then to Fort Garland in Colorado, from there to Pagosa Springs to Santa Fe and then back to New York and Washington at the end of October."

Although this was to be a journey of immense interest to Blackmore it also turned out to be one of deep tragedy. Blackmore had arranged to join the second Hayden expedition of exploration to the Yellowstone region towards the end of July. He left Washington the second week in June accompanied by his wife and they arrived at Salt Lake City on 22 June. After attending to business interests there, they traveled north to finally arriving in Bozeman in the middle of July. Mrs. Blackmore had been unwell during the journey and decided to rest with their hosts Mr. and Mrs. Lester Willson. Noting on 18 July that his wife appeared recovered Blackmore left her with their hosts and made for the Crow Agency some 35 miles distant. Late that day a messenger was sent to Blackmore informing him that his wife was again unwell and he hurried back to Bozeman. It was too late. Tersely he recorded in his diary: "Returned at 6.20 p.m. Mary had died at 5.55 p.m."

The Blackmores had previously made a pact before they left England "that burial would be made where death should find them." There were a few scattered graves dotted along the hill southeast of the city, where arrangements were made for Mary Blackmore's burial. Five acres of this area were purchased from the Rouse brothers and then deeded to the city by William Blackmore. "The deceased was buried on Friday evening according to the rites of the Episcopal Church, the Rev. W.S. Frackelton conducting the service..." Blackmore arranged for a stone monument to be made in Salt Lake City and on it was inscribed:

Mary Blackmore
Died July 18th 1872
Fide et Amore

To the south of the hill where Mary Blackmore was buried stands "a peak that patiently keeps an age long watch." On a clear day the peak is visible from the cemetery. Directing the expedition's topographer to map it carefully, Hayden then proposed that it be called Mount Blackmore in Mary Blackmore's honour.

The Crow Agency 1872

The untimely death of Mrs. Blackmore (probably from peritonitis) clearly marred the expedition. Blackmore, however, decided to continue with his plans and on 23 July 1872 he reached the Yellowstone River witnessing an encampment of "upwards of 100 lodges of Crows under Chief Long Horse" crossing the river, which at this point was about two hundred yards wide.

Another day's journey brought him to the Crow Agency on Mission Creek. Here Blackmore was introduced to the Mountain Crow chiefs whom he addressed at ssome length explaining that he was a friend of all the tribes, from the "Sioux to the Pueblo." Referring to the fact that the buffalo were decreasing in numbers, he urged that they learn to "cultivate the soil," build houses, keep stock, and he advocated the adoption of the white man's education.

Visiting the Sioux 1874

Two years later - in October 1874 - Blackmore was to again have cause for the development of a sympathetic attitude towards the Plains Indians when he traveled with his friend Colonel Irving Dodge through Kansas to a fork of the Platte River in search of buffalo.

On the second day out they came across a band of about 1,500 mixed Sioux and Cheyenne who were more than mildly alarmed by the escort of troops with Dodge. In the subsequent council, Two Lance - the principal chief present - told Dodge and Blackmore that they had been forced to leave the reservation in search of buffalo, as they were on the point of starvation. The previous day this small encampment of just one hundred and eighteen lodges had been successful in securing buffalo meat but they were in fear of the Ute Indians, soldiers, and buffalo hunters. Indeed, this fear was well justified as Two Lance's father, Whistler - formerly a chief of this band - had been murdered by white men south of the Platte some two years previously.

Blackmore evidently took a great interest in this visit to the village and writing about it extensively in his diary, and also did some collecting. In his file of "Indian Autobiographies" is a series of about thirty colored pictographs which Blackmore collected that day. This unique autobiography of "Mato Lanska," or Tall Bear, who was one of "the three head warriors of the Fox band of the Cut Off band of Ogallalla Dahcotahs", is identified in Blackmore's handwritting as follows: "Obtained from Tall Bear in the encampment of Two Lance's band (formerly Whistler's) of the Ogallalla Sioux on banks of Platte River about 30 miles south of Sidney Barracks in October 1874." One of these pictographs is shown (Fig. 7).

Blackmore, in company with other members of the party, walked through the village. He questioned the Indians on the meanings of sub-tribe names. Minniconjou, he was told, meant "those that plant close to the water".

Fig. 7. Oglala Sioux pictograph.Collected by William Blackmore from Two Lance's camp on the Platte River, Wyoming, October 1874.(From collections in the Museum of Mankind, London.Photograph by the author).

Ogallalla was "given at the time they had a fight amongst themselves and theythrew ashes into each other's eyes - and that is what it means". Brule, or Burnt, was given when "the prairie caught on fire and they got burnt."

George Catlin and William Blackmore

It was undoubtedly experiences like these which led Blackmore to consider the Indian problem in a more enlightened and sympathetic way. His notes indicate an increasing awareness of the destitute condition to which the once-proud lords of the plains were being reduced.

Thus by the time William Blackmore again made contact with the artist and explorer George Catlin he probably had more sympathy for that individual's romantic and generous view of the Plains Indians. George Catlin, as is well known, had traveled extensively among the Plains tribes some thirty years previously, publishing his classic "North American Indians" in London in 1841. Blackmore first involved himself with Catlin in a rather curious roundabout way. In 1864-1865 Catlin produced a series of fascinating water colors which depicted several episodes of the O-Kee-pa ceremonial of the Mandans. These were apparently based on his field notes and sketches made when he was in the Mandan villages in August 1832. A number clearly illustrated those parts of

331

the ceremonial which had sexual associations and which had been described in pseudo-Latin in his more popular works. These watercolors were subsequently deposited in the British Museum but prior to the transfer Blackmore appears to have had access to them. The result was the production of a unique pamphlet with the title "An Account of an Annual Religious Ceremonial practised by the Mandan Tribe of North American Indians" by George Catlin (1865). This pamphlet appears to have been ghosted from the watercolors and the detailed captions which accompanied it and, although Catlin vigorously denied direct authorship, the pamphlet does not appear to go beyond what Catlin intended to convey.

Whether Catlin ever knew that the pirated version was made at Blackmore's instigation is doubtful. The former's vigorous denial of authorship, and threat to prosecute "for any reprint or circulation of the same" (Fig. 8) undoubtedly suppressed any further publicity and the matter was quietly dropped. That Blackmore was deeply involved in the whole affair was known by at least one of his relatives. Some sixty years later, Mr. Frank Stevens - one time Director of the Salisbury Museum and a nephew of William Blackmore - informed L.J.P. Gaskin, then Librarian at the Horniman Museum, London, that Blackmore had "provided the cost of publication" and referred to both a manuscript copy and a watercolor drawing.

Late in 1871, George Catlin finally returned to New York after an absence of thirty-two years. He was now seventy-four years of age and his hearing seriously impaired. He still had, however, a remarkable enthusiasm for his lifelong dedication to perpetuating the Native Americans. By November 1871, he had formed an exhibition of paintings and sketches at the Sommerville Art Gallery at Fifth Avenue and Fourteenth Street. From there he wrote to William Blackmore inviting him to visit on Sunday, 27 November, "a dead day in New York," explaining that he would then be in his rooms above the gallery "when I should take infinite pleasure in showing and explaining to you my Indian paintings. There is no other man living to whom I am so anxious to make their abbildung fig 8

Fig. 8. George Catlin's spirited rejection of the pirated version of the O-kee-pa publication. This had been published in 1865 by William Blackmore at his own expense and seems to have been based on watercolors produced by Catlin, ca.1864-1865.

peculiar characteristics known, as to yourself." Catlin still continued with enthusiastic plans and outlined to Blackmore a "great work" on the North American Indian. This was to comprise two volumes, each containing one hundred plates and one hundred pages of text, at an estimated cost of about £10 per set. Unlike his previous highly successful volumes which were illustrated with line drawings, the new edition was to be illustrated with photographs. The original plates were to be produced in Antwerp (according to Catlin, at half the cost and to a better quality than those which could be produced in New York). In the course of their conversations, Blackmore apparently referred to his some two thousand photographs of the American Indian, which caused some concern on Catlin's part. "I did not understand," he wrote, "from our conversation, whether you intend publishing your 2000 photos, and if so I am at a loss to know how it may affect the 200 photos which I am anxious to put out."

Tragically the plans of both Catlin and Blackmore never reached fruition.

Catlin's health was failing and he was advised to move, to be with his daughters. By late October 1872, he had packed up all his paintings which had been on display at the National Museum (a project initiated by Blackmore through Joseph Henry) and arranged for them to be shipped to Jersey City. Shortly after, Joseph Henry told the Catlins of Mary Blackmore's death, but by then William Blackmore had returned to England and so the last communication between the two men was a letter written on Catlin's behalf by his daughter, Elizabeth, and dated 18 December 1872. In it she wrote that her father had several times attempted to write a letter of sympathy, "but his hand has long refused to hold either brush or pen." Elizabeth further paid high tribute to Blackmore in his association with her father: "My sisters and myself feel deeply sensible of the friendship and kindness you have shown to him... Before this reaches you he may have ceased suffering but I know that he will be glad to have been able through me to say a few last words to you."

George Catlin died on the morning of 23 December 1872. In the space of six months William Blackmore had lost two of his closest companions.

Blackmore's last visit to the U.S.A. was in 1874, however, his interest in American Indians appears to have continued unabated. In 1875 he entertained Colonel Henry B. Carrington (who commanded Fort Phil Kearney during the Red Cloud wars of the 1860's) both in London and Salisbury. Carrington later described Blackmore's Salisbury Museum as containing an "unsurpassed" collection of "Indian relics of war and the chase."

Blackmore also maintained correspondence with friends of earlier days in the U.S.A. such as Professor Joseph Henry and Colonel Dodge, the latter obtaining "Indian trunks or par-fleches filled with meat" for Blackmore, which were sent to Joseph Henry for conveyance to England.

He clearly followed the Custer campaign and massacre of 1876 with great interest, compiling an extensive file of newspaper cuttings and annotating them with personal observations or highlighting points of special interest.

The land speculations, and other business interests of Blackmore, however, began to go wrong and in the summer of 1877 "Blackmore's health began to show the cumulative effects of overwork, lack of rest, and general over indulgence." Land Trust Development programes in New Mexico had been placed in the hands of several "doubtful agents," and in letters to both his sister and his old friend Ferdinand Hayden, Blackmore spoke openly of "being gouged" and of "fraud and cheating." Desperately, Blackmore attempted to raise the necessary funds to travel to the U.S.A. and personally deal with the conflicting problems. It was not to be so.

A concussion due to a fall from an omnibus in London caused further depression to the promoter, and on the morning of 12 April 1878 "the quiet of the Belgrave Mansions apartment was suddenly shattered by the report of a pistol." His assistant found him slumped over his desk with a bullet in his head. "He died several hours later without regaining consciousness."

NOTE

This short paper is in part based on "Ho for the Great West: - The West of William Blackmore" which I published in the Silver Jubilee Publication of the English Westerners Society 1980, to which the interested reader is referred. There are also additional details on Blackmore - particularly referring to the Sioux delegation visit of May 1872 in my "Warriors of the Plains" (Hamlyn 1975). The "HSNM" references relate to material at the Historical Society of New Mexico, Santa Fe.

REFERENCES CITED

A more extensive bibliography is contained in the Silver Jubilee Publication referred to above.

Blackmore, W.
　　1868-9　The North American Indian. Journal of the Ethnological Society of London, New Series, 1.
　　1874　The North American Indian. London. Reprint of the introduction to Colonel Dodge's book; copy in the library of the Museum of Mankind.
Brayer, H.O.
　　1949　The Spanish Mexican Land Grants of New Mexico and Colorado, 1863-1878: A case study in the economic development of the West. Denver: Bradford-Robinson.
Catlin, G.
　　1871　Letter to William Blackmore, dated 16th April 1871. The publishers are unidentified. The arrangement for publishing the entire five-page letter, however, was made by William Blackmore (HSNM0245).
Dodge, R.I.
　　1976　Hunting Grounds of the Great West. London: Chatto & Windus. Introduction by William Blackmore.
Gaskin, L.J.P.
　　1939　A rare pamphlet on the Mandan Religious Ceremony in the library of the Horniman Museum. Man 1939: 141-142.
Hayden, F., et. al.
　　1863　Sixth Annual Report of the U.S. Geological Survey of the Territories. A report of progress of the explorations for the year 1872. Washington: Government Printing Office.
Raynolds, W.F.
　　1868　Report on the Exploration of the Yellowstone and the Country Drained by that River. Senate Executive Document 77, 40th Congress, 1st Session, Washington 1868.
Taft, R.
　　1938　Photography and the American Scene. New York: Macmillian.
Taylor, C.
　　1973　The O-kee-pa and Four Bears: An insight into Mandan ethnology. The English Westerners' Brand Book 15 (3).
　　1975　The Warriors of the Plains. London: Hamlyn.

NINE BELLA COOLAS IN GERMANY[1]

Wolfgang Haberland

When Johan Adrian Jacobsen, a 31 year-old Norwegian, returned to German soil on 15 August 1885, he had just completed a trip around the world. Sponsored by the Ethnological Support Committee, he had left on 31 May 1884 for Siberia to collect ethnographic objects for the Royal Museum of Ethnology in Berlin, especially in the Amur region, on Kamchatka Peninsula, and on Sakhalin. It was not his first trip undertaken on behalf of the Committee and the Museum. Already in 1881 to 1883 he had traveled so successfully to the Northwest Coast of North America and to Alaska (Woldt 1884) that he had been able to deliver to the museum more than 7,000 items from various Indian and Eskimoan groups. The trip to Siberia had likewise been a success and many boxes had reached Berlin directly from there.

Jacobsen, however, had continued his trip in an easterly direction to fulfill another request, this time for Carl Hagenbeck who then already owned a well-known animal shop and zoo in Hamburg. Jacobsen had been connected with Hagenbeck for some time before. Returning from a sojourn in South America, particularly Chile, to his older brother Johan Marten who was living in Hamburg, he had offered his services to Hagenbeck who was just looking for someone who could possibly assemble a collection of Eskimo artifacts and bring an Eskimo family to Europe. Adrian brought six Greenland Eskimos to Hamburg and traveled with them through Western Europe for eight months. This was the beginning of a new carreer for the former ship's captain.

In 1878, he fetched a group of Lapps (together with an ethnographic collection) to Germany, then accompanied three Patagonians on a tour for Hagenbeck, and in 1880 finally hired eight Labrador Eskimos. But this *Völkerschau* ended in disaster. The Inuit who had not been vaccinated contracted the smallpox and died in Darmstadt, Krefeld, and Paris (Taylor 1981). Both Jacobsen, who himself had been ill several times on this tour, as well as Hagenbeck were so shocked by this catastrophe that for the time being they refrained from any more displays of exotic peoples. This was also the reason why Adrian went on the collecting trip to northwestern America in 1881.

But when on his return he told Hagenbeck about the "Longheads" of Quatsino Inlet, i.e. artificial head deformation among the Kwakiutl, the interest in an Indian group was reawakened in view of the fact that Hagenbeck was already doing displays of peoples again. Hagenbeck would have preferred to send Adrian to the Northwest Coast right away, but Jacobsen had already signed the contract to go to Siberia. It was decided that his younger brother, Johan Fillip, who in the meantime had joined his brothers in Hamburg, was to go to the Northwest Coast to hire a group. Fillip did collect successfully but was unable to reach an agreement with a touring group. When Adrian learned

337

about this state of affairs in Siberia, he left Vladivostok on 20 April 1885 and after short visits to Korea and Japan reached San Francisco in the latter part of May, and Victoria, the capital of British Columbia, a few days later. According to his report, probably written as part of an autobiography in the 1930's, Adrian took a boat on 4 June from Vancouver Island to Kyuquot,[2] making purchases especially of cedar bark blankets and masks in various villages along the way. Leaving Kyuquot (and Nootka territory) with a new crew, he passed around Cape Cook to Koskimo. But neither here nor in Quatsino Inlet anybody was willing to go with him to Europe. So Jacobsen crossed the island (on foot?) and arrived on 15 June in Fort Rupert on the east coast of Vancouver Island, where he met his friend George Hunt with whose father he once again took up lodging. On 16 June Fillip also arrived there from the north, bringing with him an extensive ethnographic collection especially of Tsimshian and Tlingit material.

As to what follows, two different accounts exist. One is again from Adrian's memoirs: "We [i.e. Adrian and Fillip] consulted with George Hunt where there might be a chance to get an Indian troupe for Europe, but nowhere among the coastal tribes there seemed to be an inclination to undertake such a long journey. I was advised to go to Victoria and to look among the Indians who were coming there every year from the north to earn some money picking hops in Puget Sound. I heard from my brother that on the ship on which he had come to Fort Rupert, a number of Bella Coola Indians belonging to the Bella Bella tribe[3] had been traveling to Victoria. ... So we went to Victoria and caught up with the band of Bella Coola Indians who had been thinking about going to pick hops in the United States. ... We soon entered into an agreement with a little chief and nine[4] others and with the assistance of a government agent a contract was drawn up with every one of them,[5] and after about eight days by the end of June we were on our way home by Portland, Oregon, and the Northern Pacific Railroad."

The second version is contained in a booklet written or edited by F. von Schirp (a journalist and perhaps sometimes himself an agent of *Völkerschauen*), which was sold during the performances of the Bella Coolas in Germany: "By the end of June of that year [1885] the two bold explorers [i.e. Adrian and Fillip] met in Fort Rupert on the northwestern coast of Vancouver Island to induce several Kwakiutl Indians on behalf of Carl Hagenbeck... to make a trip to Europe. Initially their endeavors met with success. They managed to induce eleven Kwakiutl Indians to accompany them and a date for their departure had already been set. Shortly before their departure the Jacobsen brothers had gone into the neighborhood with one of their friends residing there, Mr. George Hunt, to complete their collections. This period of time was used by an English missionary living in Fort Rupert who represented to the Indians in glaring colors the dangers of a trip to Germany. Amongst other things he told them that Germany was twice as far away as England and that the travelers

338

Fig. 1. Last page of the contract of 25 July 1885 between Jacobsen and the Bella Coolas with their names and crosses, and the signature of Indian Superintendent I.W.Powell.

would not go by train across the continent but by boat around Cape Horn, which meant that for seven months they would be subjected to the dangers of sea sickness. As a result the Kwakiutl had fled by the time the Jacobsen brothers had returned.[6] Now the two decided to go to Victoria on the southern tip of Vancouver Island where most Indian tribes had assembled then to hold some major feasts. On the trip to Victoria they met nine Bella Coola Indians who also wanted to go to Victoria, and after long negotiations they succeeded to induce them to come on board of the steamship Boskowitz. In Victoria it furthermore took the power of persuasion of a resident Englishman, Mr. Max Dauel, and of a German, by the name of Karl Schößler to induce the redskins to sign a contract before the local Indian agent, Mr. Powel" (Schirp 1885:12-13).

It would be difficult to decide which of the two accounts[7] is the correct one, if there were no supplementary letters. Amongst others, Adrian wrote from Victoria on July 22 to his fiancée Hedwig Klopfer: "... and on the same day [in Fort Rupert] the Indians I had already hired came and declared that they did not want to travel with me... Imagine that it was a missionary who had alienated my first Indians from me by telling them all kinds of wild stories - the damned missionaries here do more evil than good." Thus the printed

Fig. 2. Ya Coutlas or Tom Henry, leader of the Bella Coolas in Germany in his gala outfit. Objects such as the Chilkat dress were certainly not his own property but were part of the collection assembled by Fillip Jacobsen.

Fig. 3. Ya Coutlas (Tom Henry) in European dress, the very model of a gentleman.

version of the hiring seems to be correct. In addition, Jacobsen cannot have left for Portland by the end of June as the contract with the Bella Coolas was signed only on 25 July 1885 in Victoria.

The contract was concluded in the office of Davie and Pooley in Victoria. It consists of a general section dealing with the duties of the Bella Coolas and four paragraphs dealing with Jacobsen's obligations. Moreover it specified that Jacobsen had to deposit $1,000 as security with Israel Wood Powell, the Indian Superintendent in Victoria. It was the latter point which was criticized by Hagenbeck who apparently had been informed in advance by Adrian. In a letter of 2 July 1885 he writes to Jacobsen: "I cannot understand why bond is being asked as the British government has never done this before and presently I still have here 52 Singhalese from Ceylon, now already in Europe for the third time, and never had to post bond." It is likely that bond was posted as it is also mentioned in the contract.

The contract was signed on the last page by nine Bella Coolas with their leader, the "little chief" of Jacobsen's account, on top. The signatures are crosses next to the type-written names which thus are easily legible (Fig. 1). The Indian names[8] by which the contract was signed are today no longer known

340

among the Bella Coola, wherefore it is impossible to determine to which families they may have belonged. It is known that the leader called Ya Coutlas in the contract was later called Tom Henry[9] (Figs. 2-3). In addition one or two European names of the group are known, whose identification with native names in the contract poses some problems. If Alex Davis was identical with Kimsquit Alex (Kopas 1870:236,143), and should the latter have been in Germany, it may have been Ham-chick (Fig. 4).[10] The last survivor of the Bella Coola troupe, Billy Jones (Kopas 1970:143), may be identical with Pooh-Pooh (Figs. 5-6) who became especially noted as the group's *hamatsa*. On a photograph acquired in 1978 in Bella Coola (Fig. 7), however, his Indian name is given as "Iklahuani" which would correspond to "Ick-lehoneh" on the list. As even older Bella Coolas could not agree in 1978 who was to be identified as Billy Jones (who had died in the 1940s) on the old photographs, none of the identifications rests of solid grounds. Like many others, the question will probably never be resolved.

After the treaty was signed, the group instantly went by boat to Portland (Oregon) where it must have arrived by 28 July. On this day letters of recommendation were given to Adrian and Fillip by A.D. Charlton, General

Fig. 4. Ham-chick in gala dress. His (later) English name was probably Alex Davis (also known as Kimsquit Alex).

Fig. 5. Pooh-Pooh, the *hamatsa* of the troupe, with scars from having been bitten.

341

Fig. 6. Pooh-Pooh in European dress.

Fig. 7. Billy Jones (Iklahuani = Ick-lehoneh?), ca.1940 in Bella Coola (after a photograph acquired in Bella Coola in 1978).

Fig. 8. Ick-lehoneh in gala dress during the trip through Germany. He may be Billy Jones, the last survivor of the Bella Coola troupe (Fig.7).

342

Manager Passenger Agent of the Northern Pacific Railroad Company in Portland. By train the party went via Minneapolis and Chicago to New York where they embarked on the steamship "Werra" of the Northern German Lloyd. They left on 5 August and arrived in Bremen ten days later.

Below, an account will be given of the trip through Germany undertaken by the nine Bella Coolas and the Jacobsen brothers. A reconstruction of their route will be followed by notes on their performances, the reactions of the German public, especially the press, and the life and reactions of the Bella Coolas inasmuch as they are known. Finally a few remarks will be offered on the (second) collection assembled by Fillip and Adrian, which accompanied the troupe as an exhibition.

The route

One could assume that by the time the Bella Coolas arrived in Bremen there had already been a firm schedule for their year in Europe. After all, this was not the first *Völkerschau* jointly organized by Jacobsen and Hagenbeck. But surprisingly there was practically no planning and only the first appearance in Leipzig had been firmly booked.[11] All other appearances were more or less improvised and arranged on short term. There exists an exchange of letters between Hagenbeck and Adrian Jacobsen[12] relating to possibilities and ideas, few of which, however, were ever put into effect. Many planned performances came to nothing as - at least initially - the fees asked by Hagenbeck and Jacobsen were too high and the offers too low. In any case, they constantly changed their plans. On 3 October, for example, Hagenbeck wrote: "If Scandinavia[13] does not come through we will take Berlin and be in Hamburg during the Cathedral Fair[14] where I believe good business could be made at Sagebiel's."[15] Already on the following day, Hagenbeck instructed Jacobsen to remain in Dresden until 8 November, afterwards perhaps to go to Magdeburg and to Hamburg for Cathedral Fair. By 26 October the plans had changed again: Halle was to be the next stop in case London (which had been mentioned as a possibility in the meantime) would not come through, afterwards Stuttgart, southern Germany, and Switzerland. But these ideas, too, had to be given up, and the same was true of trips to Prague, Vienna, and Budapest. What remained were towns in Saxony and Thuringia, Berlin, Breslau (the present Wrocław), Hamburg, and the Rhineland.

It proved to be very difficult to compile a list of places in which the Bella Coolas actually did perform (Table 1). It was mostly reconstructed from letters and postcards to Adrian Jacobsen as well as newspaper clippings. With few exceptions, no contracts are available, and Adrian never seems to have compiled an itinerary.

Table 1: Stops of the tour of the Bella Coola troupe in Germany, probably incomplete. Jena (no. 17) is not fully substantiated; there is a gap between Hamburg (no. 22) and Cologne (no. 23).

No.	Place	Location of performance	Start	Present	End
1	Bremen	Arrival from U.S.		15-08-85	
2	Hamburg				
3	Leipzig	Zoological Garden	11-09-85	14-10-85	
4	Dresden	Zoological Garden	15-10-85	02-11-85	
5	Chemnitz	Mosella-Saal	03-11-85	10-11-85	
6	Zwickau	Zum Goldenen Becher	10-11-85	16-11-85	
7	Halle	Salon zum Rosenthal	17-11-85	25-11-85	
8	Eisleben	Mansfelder Hof		28-11-85	
9	Sangershausen	Schweizerhütte	30-11-85	02-12-85	
10	Nordhausen	Zum goldenen Schiff	03-12-85	06-12-85	
11	Langensalza			11-12-85	
12	Mühlhausen	Weymars Festhalle		14/15-12-85	
13	Gotha	Thüringer Hof		17/21-12-85	
14	Erfurt			22-12-85	02-01-86
15	Weimar	Stadthaussaal?	02-01-86	06-01-86?	
16	Apolda		07-01-86?	11-01-86?	
17	Jena?				
18	Naumburg				18-01-86
19	Berlin	Kroll'sches Etablissement	19-01-86	07-02-86	
20	Breslau	Zoologischer Garten	11-02-86	27-02-86	
21	Berlin	Castan's Panoptikum	01-03-86	01-05-86	
22	Hamburg	Hagenbeck's Thierpark	08-05-86	23-05-86	
23	Cologne	Panoptikum	05-06-86	21-06-86	
24	Aachen	Restaurant Bavaria	21-06-86	01-07-86	
25	Elberfeld	Sommertheater Johannisberg	02-07-86	12-07-86	
26	Krefeld	Thiergarten	13-07-86	19-07-86	
27	Bremerhaven	Embarkment		21-07-86	

As he had married his fiancée Hedwig on 21 November 1885 in Dresden, and as she accompanied him all the way to Hamburg, he did not have to write to her and thus no letters, an otherwise important source, are available. The data especially on the brief visits to the smaller towns in Saxony and Thuringia are thus necessarily often quite vague.

Whether the Bella Coolas ever were in Jena, for example, cannot be decided at this point. The only indication that they may have been there is contained in a note from Hedwig to Adrian (who had gone to Berlin to negotiate) dated Weimar, January 1886: "... he [Bingusz, an agent/manager joined to Jacobsen in December 1885 by Hagenbeck] has brought the man [an unnamed inn-keeper in Jena] to the point where he offers us 100 marks per day and everything else free, the poor dunce will be well deceived, but for us it cannot be bad!" It is also questionable whether the Bella Coolas did briefly go to Lübeck between Hamburg and Cologne. It is likewise possible that other smaller places were visited as well, although there are no further leads.

The two visits to Berlin can be explained by the fact that in the beginning Castan, with whom Hagenbeck apparently would have liked to cooperate, had already booked "Sitting Bull Sioux Indians" (mostly Oglalas) under Frank Harvey. These probably promised a larger audience (and thus profit) than the rather "un-Indian" Bella Coolas. This competition certainly must have contributed to Jacobsen's decision to terminate the Bella Coolas' performances prematurely on 7 February, or two weeks ahead of schedule. When Castan became available later on and was in addition offering a rather good contract, Jacobsen and the Indians returned to Berlin.

It is also unknown on which ship or with which ship-owner the Bella Coolas accompanied by Fillip Jacobsen (who remained in British Columbia thereafter) had returned home. As usual between the brothers, a letter dated Victoria, 28 August 1886, is in Norwegian and thus is hard for me to understand. In any case, Fillip complained that the trip had gone through Baltimore and that this was a considerable detour. That the group had arrived in Victoria by 1 August 1886 as specified in the contract, is rather unlikely, as otherwise Fillip might certainly have written earlier.

The performances

Jacobsen was obviously attempting to show "original" dances, i.e. such dances and activities as were common among the Bella Coola or on the Northwest Coast. The booklet by Schirp (1885) sold in connection with the performances, lists a nine-part program on the last page. In addition, there is an "Explanation of the Feasts and Dances among the Indians" which may be regarded as a program, and which mentions eleven parts. The two lists match only in part. The performances had obviously been changed and expanded in

345

the course of time, perhaps also in an attempt to meet the expectations of the public. It may be assumed that the "Explanation" is the later version of the program. In addition to this, there were other changes. Thus, an article in the *Deutsches Tageblatt* (Berlin) of 15 March 1886 refers to an otherwise unrecorded Thunder Dance which became apparently part of the performance after 20 March 1886 (perhaps instead of another dance?). As the originality of the dances is stressed in this as well as in other articles and as this report also affords a view at the operation of the show, the following extract is herewith offered:

"First of all - and as far as we know this has never been sufficiently stressed before - their performances are having nothing artificial or fabricated. In whatever they do they behave perfectly original. This invaluable fact is to the credit of their guide, Captain Jacobsen, who indeed prevents his charges from making themselves interesting to the big crowds by changes in their productions. All Indians and particularly the Bella Coola possess a great gift for observation and a strong drive for imitation. They are born actors and always ready to adopt the habits, mainly however the bad habits of the civilized world. The authority of Captain Jacobsen has had the effect that the Bella Coolas here present are only showing their unadulterated, domestic customs in their presentations, but the ingenuous Indians have nonetheless been attempting on their own account to implement something new which would transcend the routine of the daily productions. Captain Jacobsen had been noticing for quite some time that they were busily engaging themselves in the carving of wooden works unknown to himself. Requesting an explanation as to the purpose of these masks, he was told about their intention of performing a new dance, the so-called Thunder Dance."

The article continues with a general account of the belief in thunderbirds on the Northwest Coast. "The Bella Coola, however, imagine the Thunder God as a quadruped without knowing his exact shape." He is said to dwell high in the mountains and in case of a thunderstorm, i.e. whenever the Thunder God is walking, one does not go on a hunt. One night, however, a hunting party had been surprised by a thunderstorm and one of them was able to see the Thunder God through a rent in his blanket. When everything was over, he got up. "He found his three companions benumbed and stiff - struck by lightning. Two of those killed on this occasion were the fathers of two of the Indians now in Berlin." It is then announced that the Thunder Dance would be added to the program "in the course of the following days."

From this certainly mostly correct report two things may be gleaned: The Bella Coolas became bored by the routine of doing the same dances over and over again (which is hardly surprising), and so decided to bring some variety into the program. As two of the Bella Coolas (the "sons" of those killed by lightning) apparently owned a right to this Thunder Dance, it could be performed. Unfortunately there is no further description of the dance and no

346

Fig. 9. The Bella Coola troupe: Scene from "Chief's Dance" (?). Front row from left to right: Isk-ka-lusta, Ya Coutlas, Que-noh; back row from left to right: Ham-chick, Pooh-Pooh, Kah-che-lis, Huck-mulshe, Ick-lehoneh, Elk-qut. Jacobsen's caption: "Indians dressed for feast.Mostly dressed in the Northern blankets, feathers in their hair, neck- and arm-rings, and dance aprons, leggins etc. Left the drummer and in the center the chief of the tribe - with speaker's or rather commander's baton in hand."

photograph of it, so we are ignorant of the appearance of the Thunder God as well as of other details.

Changes intended to satisfy the public are also indicated by the announcement in Breslau (and other places?) of a "Snowshoe race of the Indians."

The same advertisement in the *Breslauer Zeitung* of 21 February 1886 also mentions as a special attraction a "Voluntary incineration of a shaman (wizard)" not contained in the program. This part of the performance can also be documented in newspaper accounts from other cities as it caught the particular attention of the public (and the journalists). Initially, it may have been performed as an addition on special occasions or for big crowds, perhaps on the Bella Coolas' own initiative. Later on it was specifically advertised as an especially attractive number to help increase the rather poor profits. What was being shown may best be gleaned from a newspaper account which expresses well the fascination and helplessness of the public. Among the many accounts, the following one from the *Leipziger Nachrichten* of 29 September 1885 will be given here:

"The voluntary incineration of a shaman, which had been announced by the 'Zoological Garden' for Sunday afternoon, had drawn a rather numerous public which despite the copiously pouring rain was steadfastly expecting the interesting spectacle. Darkness was already setting in when the Bella Coola Indians got ready to enact the wizard's incineration subsequent to the preceding dance performances. That the event was of a serious and solemn nature to themselves could be seen from the vivid excitement and grave earnest with which they submerged themselves into the spectacle. It was the second performance of its kind. Others are unlikely to follow as the superstitious mind of the Indians is opposed to such performances mimicking the art of the true Indian wizards.[16] Whoever witnessed the performance received a clear idea of the nature of such shaman's sorcery. The pseudo-shaman emerged from the hut. A glaring glimmer of the fire fell on his face painted in a deep black. With slow and measured paces he went around the fire, uttering hollow broken sounds and shaking his head bedecked with flaring cedar bark ornaments as if seized by violent fever. In the meantime the other eight comrades were feeding the blazing fire while taking the preliminary steps for the awful act of the incineration by monotonous singing and deep-pitched beats of the drum. Now the shaman grew more and more excited, ever more strongly shaking his head in semi-frantic delirium.

Fig. 10. Healing ceremony during "Shaman's Dance"; being out of focus is typical for many of the particularly interesting "action"-photographs of the dances. Jacobsen's caption: "The curing of a sick by a medicine man. The doctor sings, accompanied by his rattle, dances, sucks blood from the skin of the sick person."

One more jump across the fire and the incineration was about to begin. A big wooden box was hauled up. Into this the shaman entered, dived down into it, reemerged with his hands extended, and then squatted in the box after having relinquished himself of his blanket and leggins. The box was closed with nails and carried by seven Indians into the fire where after a little while it went crackling up into flames under the red-hot pyres. But what strange sight! In the glowing embers a charred head and remains of a body! The illusion was striking. For a long time the band of Indians stared into the fire. Then suddenly loud calls were heard from the garden - and the shaman reappeared sound and unharmed in the circle of his comrades. How the trick of his incineration had been effected, even those standing closest to it were unable to figure out."

A second report published almost half a year later in the *Breslauer Zeitung* of 21 February 1886 closely parallels the first one. Besides documenting once more the surprise of both the public and the journalist it also illustrates how closely the Bella Coolas followed the same pattern. The major difference was that a piece of cloth was used instead of a carved box lid, but this may be due to the fact that the new box (which had, of course, to be carved for every incineration) may not have been ready. When I read one of the reports to the contemporary Bella Coolas it became the cause of great hilarity as the spectacle is based on an old and generally well known trick: Normally it is performed indoors with the help of a subterranean passage, here it just may have been done with the help of a pit and wet blankets.

Fig. 11. Mask dance of the Hamatsa Ceremony. Jacobsen's caption: "Indians performing a Winter Dance. The demons of the wood Päh Päh'Quallanusiva his brother Menis Hau Hau, the slave of the former and wife and son of the same."

Fig. 12. Scene from the "Cannibal's Dance," i.e. the Hamatsa Ceremony. In the background Ya Coutlas, apparently giving explanations, on the left Pooh-Pooh as *hamatsa*. Note the cedar bark ring with appended carved skulls. Jacobsen's comment: "Hamatsa in extasy."

Fig. 13. Bear Dance. Jacobsen's caption: "Nutlomatla (Fools) perform in a Bear Dance."

350

Fig. 14. "Game for nine persons." Standing in the background Ya Coutlas, next to him with drum probably Isk-ka-lusta, left foreground Pooh-Pooh. Jacobsen's caption: "Indians gambling for money. The game consists of 52 differently marked sticks which after some having been covered with cedar bark have to be guessed by each player."

Fig. 15. "2 Indians occupied with a guessing game" (Jacobsen).

In an attempt to draw more customers to the performances many rather strange ways were obviously taken. Thus on 5 January 1886 in Weimar the dances of the Bella Coolas were combined with a big military concert, so that, e.g., the "Princess Polka by Stör" was followed by the "Cannibal's Dance" of the Bella Coola. In other places, similar combinations may also have been made. But despite all of this, the financial success was far below the ex-

351

Fig. 16. Scene from a performance of the potlach. Jacobsen's caption: "The five standing Indians wear crowns which at Potlatches or Gift Feasts [?], and in addition expensive Northern blankets woven of mountain sheep and goat wool, and dyed with plants (mosses). The crowns and blankets represent a fortune and can only be worn by the very rich."

Fig. 17. Group from the Nutlomatla Dance. Jacobsen's caption: "Bella Coola Indians with dance masks of the Nutlomatla. First from left a spirit of the sea. Center: King of the salmon, right: King of the mountain goats. Seated left: the Nutlomatla (Fools or Jesters), seated right: the sea spirit Komoquwa." (This is not in Jacobsen's hand but was probably dictated.)

pectations of the promoters. Again and again the letters speak about the low profits. Early January 1886, e.g., Hedwig writes from Weimar to Adrian: "Evening business poor: only 7 marks, but in the afternoon many children, until 7 o'clock, therefore 73 marks." On 9 July 1886, Adrian from Elberfeld to Hedwig: "Yesterday 30 marks, today 6 marks." On the basis of an admission of 50 pfennigs for adults, 25 for children and 10 for students in groups this was truly not an overwhelming result.

In the Leipzig report about the incineration of the shaman mention is made of a house from which the "shaman" did emerge. It was a Northwest Coast house built perhaps on Hagenbeck's suggestion.[17] "Shortly after their arrival, the nine Indians built their hut corresponding exactly to the dwellings of their homes to serve them as their residence during the period of their stay. It is made of boards of cedar wood[18] and shows on its front the picture of a whale painted in garish colors, while on the sides are depicted a pair of bears which probably are fighting one another. In front of the hut rise man-high crest

352

Fig. 18. Scene from the Nutlomatla Dance. Jacobsen's caption: "The Nutlomatla of Fool's Dance with war-spears."

poles carved of cedar wood, also painted in several colors, which by their figures relate to the history of the respective house" (*Leipziger Intelligenzblatt*, 16 September 1885). As far as I know no photograph of this house exists, but it may be seen in the background of a drawing published in a Leipzig newspaper and less clearly in two drawings by Rudolf Cronau (1892:II, facing 388, Deckert 1904: facing 481; cp. Fig. 23). Whether such houses were also built in other places and what happened to the one in Leipzig is not known. The poles mentioned in the report can also be seen in the drawings. They had been carved by the Bella Coolas in Hamburg.[19] Their fate is also uncertain. Poles were likewise erected in other places, such as in Berlin[20] and Breslau, the latter one certainly coming from Vancouver Island.[21]

As can be seen from the numerous set photos (Figs. 9-21) taken by Carl Günther in Berlin[22] several masks and pieces of costume were used during the dances. Especially noticeable are the numerous Chilkat blankets and the Chilkat tunic worn by Ya Coutlas (Fig. 14), things hardly to be expected and never in such numbers among the Bella Coola. Most likely they were part of the collection assembled by Fillip among the Tsimshian and Tlingit. Most other parts of their costume were likewise hardly the property of the Bella Coolas, as Adrian wrote to Hedwig on 8 July 1885: "In the meantime I will go with a party of Indians to the West Coast of Vancouver Island to buy there the necessary clothing etc. for our Indian exhibition - it is a long and tedious

Fig. 19. Scene from the Winter Dance. Jacobsen's caption: "Bella Coola Indians in Winter Dance dress." "Bella Coola Indians in feast and dance costume. With neck and head rings which are badges of the various professions" (not in Jacobsen's hand, probably dictated).

work, but I hope to be ready with it in a month..." As to the masks and other implements, it is doubtful whether these (or at least most of them) had been brought along by the Bella Coolas. If they were in fact on their way to picking hops as reported in Adrian's late (and admittedly unreliable) account, they would hardly have carried masks with them, so that the ones used in Europe would have to come from the Jacobsens' collections. If they were on their way to a dance in Victoria (as indicated by Schirp 1885), they may have had some masks of their own, but certainly not to the extent and in the variety as shown in Germany. There is no proof for either version, but it may be assumed that the bulk of the masks used were not of the Bella Coola but a mixture from several groups on the Northwest Coast. It is therefore impossible to use the pictures to make inferences on the outfitting of the dances or on

354

Fig. 20. Scene from Winter or Society Dance. Jacobsen's caption: "Indians performing a Winter Dance, Bella Coola."

Fig. 21. Scene from Noalok Dance. Jacobsen's caption: "Left Father Sun, right his oldest son who keeps the soul of every dead in his house until the time has come to be born again with a relative. Father Sun and especially his sons have taught mankind the use of masks and dances."

355

Zoologischer Garten.

Heute Sonntag:

Im großen Saale: Capitän Jacobsen's

Bella-Coola-Indianer

von der Nordwestküste Nordamerikas (British Columbia).

9 Personen in ihren Original-Costümen,

nebst einer großen aus 1500 Nummern bestehenden

Sammlung ethnographischer Gegenstände.

Die Indianer bringen ihre Sitten und Gebräuche, Jagdspiele, Volks- und religiösen Tänze zur Darstellung.

Die Schaustellung findet täglich statt von 11 bis 1 Uhr und von 3 bis 7 Uhr, Sonntags und Mittwochs bis 9 Uhr Abends.

Heute Sonntag findet die Schaustellung theilweise im Freien, am Elephantenhause, statt.

Um 1/2 5 Uhr:

Schneeschuh-Wettlauf der Indianer.

Präcis 5 Uhr:

Freiwillige Verbrennung eines Schamanen (Zauberers).

Nach derselben Fortsetzung der Schaustellung im Saal

Eintrittspreis an Sonn- und Wochentagen 50 Pf.

Kinder unter 10 Jahren 10 Pf. [2669]

Actionäre und Abonnenten frei.

Auf dem großen Teich Eisbahn zu freier Benutzung.

Fig. 22. Advertisement from the *Breslauer Zeitung*, 21 February 1886, relating to "Voluntary Self-Incineration of a Shaman" and snow shoe race.

Bella Coola carving style. The fact that they were carving new masks in Germany has been noted above in connection with the Thunder Dance and will be further discussed below.

Reactions of the German public

As it is impossible to interview the contemporaneous visitors and as no testimonials survive, one has to try to infer them from other circumstances. One way is to look at attendance figures of the show. It has been mentioned in a different context that Carl Hagenbeck and Adrian Jacobsen were not satisfied with the results, and that their financial expectations were not fulfilled. The actual figures were in fact not very high, but on the other hand the even higher expectations have to be taken into account. But on some days and even for weeks at a time the income (and thus the attendance) may have been satisfactory. Despite this probability, Adrian seems to be constantly complaining in his letters. Very early during the show, on 16 September 1885

Fig. 23. Drawing of dances of the Bella Coolas from a Leipzig newspaper. In the background the house built by the Bella Coolas and the two crest poles.

he wrote from Leipzig to Hedwig: "Sunday it was stormy and rain was threatening, and thus the receipts (971 marks). Monday it was the most lovely weather but no visitors - only 306 marks. Yesterday perhaps even more beautiful, but only 265 marks." On 12 October 1885 from the same place: "Sunday the weather was fine but unfortunately the receipts were not in consonant with the weather - only about 820 marks." From Cologne Adrian wrote in June of 1886 to Hedwig: "Business here is quite good and Castan has nothing to complain about. Last Sunday had 4,000 persons, today we may well have almost the same..."; and on 15 June from the same place: "Over the two Whitsuntide holidays we had receipts of over 3,000 marks." Whole school classes to whom special invitations were often sent helped to increase the attendance.[23] For Berlin we have some figures since part(?) of the cards announcing the classes are available. According to these cards, e.g., 225 students came to the performance of 21 January 1886, 75 to the one of 22 January, and 834 to the show on 25 January. For the ten days between 21 and 30 January 1886 (and excluding Sunday) the probably incomplete evidence totals 2,019 students visiting the performances. This also does not include a group guided by Aurel Krause, the well-known Northwest Coast traveler, who did not

357

give any figures on his card. Kopas' (1970:236) assertion that one performance was attended by 3,000 children is certainly an exaggeration. Although the cards represent all types of schools of the time, the high percentage of grade schools is especially noticable, an interesting phenomenon that contrasts with the present situation of schools visiting German museums.

The number of visitors is only indirect evidence for the reactions of German audiences since we do not know whether the public's expectations were fulfilled by the show. In addition, no precise figures exist. Another source for the reactions are Adrian's memoirs repeatedly noted above. With regard to the audiences he wrote: "... but by and large the public remained rather cool with respect to our performances. Only the scholars thought that this was the most magnificent ever to be shown in this field." These remarks are, of course, highly subjective and come from the reminiscences of an almost 90-year old man, which as we have seen are not always to be relied upon. But the assessment of the audiences is supported by earlier statements in Adrian's surviving letters.

Our major source on the reactions of the public are undoubtedly the numerous newspaper reports fortunately preserved by Adrian Jacobsen. Most of them are friendly and show interest, remarkably fair to the Bella Coolas (even if sometimes lacking in understanding) and relatively free of discrimination. The latter point is especially notable: Never or very rarely are the Bella Coolas called savages, subhumans, or primitives, an attitude later and even today frequently encountered. As an example, an account published in the *Zwickauer Tageblatt* of 11 November 1885 may be reproduced: "Carl Hagenbeck's Bella Coola Indians began their performances yesterday, Tuesday, afternoon in the rather well suited hall of the hotel 'Golden Cup.' The members of the troupe are exclusively men in their twenties and thirties of muscular build and interesting facial features. Of the dances performed yesterday with indefatigable perseverance the 'Winter Dance' as well as the 'Potlash or Gift Feast' were especially interesting. In performing the first dance in the home country of the strangers on special festive occasions, the dancers have to take special care not to fall down, because as soon as one touches the ground in falling, he is killed without mercy.[24] The 'Gift Feast' is held whenever one wants to become chief or distinguish himself as a famous man, on which occasion he invites all of his relatives and friends and presents them with furs, jewellry etc. On this occasion one can also observe the remarkable eloquence with which the Indians cry up their presents."

On 9 November the same journal had already reported extensively on the Bella Coola: "Today a troupe of nine Indians is to arrive at the 'Golden Cup' hotel, which will be displayed there starting Tuesday, 10 November. Originating from the far northwest of America and belonging to the tribe of Bella Coolas, they represent an extraordinarily interesting and ethnologically highly valuable expedition from a region of whose cultural history in general there is as yet

358

little knowledge... For today, only something about the Indians themselves... The Bella Coola, whose tribe is reckoned among the Koloshes-Indians have been reduced by wars with their neighboring tribes and by epidemic diseases to around 400 heads. They are distributed over around 10 villages. According to their external appearance they are middle-sized people, broad-shouldered with strong breast and nervous arms as they result from constant life in the canoes. The color of their skin varies from yellowish-red to yellowish-white, the bristly hair now cut short according to European fashion varies from deep black to black-brown. Their hands are of middle size, the feet plump and fleshy, while the facial expression with strong cheek bones reminds strongly of the inhabitants of Polynesia. Their dress which in their home country is the most conceivably primitive, had to be adapted according to European patterns; it consists in the main of a piece of blanket of cedar bark and raccoon furs. On festive occasions they wear an apron decorated with shells, birds' beaks, and pieces of copper, phantastic board-like caps, and in their stead especially during dances masks carved of wood, decorated with hair and feathers and painted in several colors representing monsters of the sea and land or animals considered sacred. For jewellry the Bella Coola wear earrings made of shell, bone, sharks' teeth. In their quite singular language consisting almost only of palatal and guttural sounds, their language is called 'Sequevanisti.' In their character these Indians are peaceful and obliging, but cling with a certain tenacity to their old traditions." Given the many details and the fact that the Bella Coola had not even arrived in Zwickau, it seems clear that this information was not based on actual observation, but probably on a press release. If it did not reflect the public's perceptions, it may nonetheless have helped to shape them.

In a report of the *Breslauer Zeitung* of 16 February 1886, one can read amongst other observations: "The Bella Coola Indians inhabiting on British territory in northwestern North America bear hardly any resemblance to the redskins from the territory of the United States which are also known in Breslau from previous displays. - Professor Virchow who has used the opportunity of their presence in Berlin for making these people the object of extensive anthropological researches writes about them in the following words: 'The Bella Coola Indians brought from British Columbia to Europe by Mr. Jacobsen are different from all American savages so far presented here. By virtue of the deformation of their heads, the special formation of their faces, their quite singular language, their highly developed artisanship they are instantly, on first acquaintance rendered conspicuous among the multitude of American native peoples. Thus they afford one of the most interesting objects for the observation of every thinking human being.' - ... After the lecture, the latter [Bella Coolas] perform in unbroken sequence their manifold dances, incantations, mask plays, shooting exercises, and hunting scenes which they accompany by means of very simple instruments with a regular, noisy, and for our

359

understanding not quite symphonic music. The majority of their dances stands in relation to the religious beliefs of the Bella Coola; it caused much trouble to Mr. Jacobsen to persuade the people to the profanation caused in their own and their tribesmen's eyes by the public performance of, e.g., the Hamatsa Dance or the incantation of the shaman. After the performance of the dances and games, the Indians come down into the hall and move through the audience; before whose eyes they give examples of their artisanship, and especially of woodcarving, by the production of new house crests, masks, etc., also on occasion they go outside to the areas of the garden covered with snow to represent snowshoe races with their domestic snowshoes."

An extraordinary amount of space in the reports is taken up by the Hamatsa Dance including the parts of the ceremony not shown. Almost all newspapers report about it more or less extensively and more or less correctly. In the *Leipziger Zeitung* of 18 September 1885, for example, one can read the following about the Hamatsa Ceremony: "Of all their dances the so-called Hamatsa or Cannibal's Dance is the most interesting. In this dance, the custom of cannibalism has been preserved at least symbolically. The Hamatsas or cannibals, who belong to the most respectable of the tribe and in a sense are regarded as sacred, play the leading role in it. Although it is now forbidden to them to slaughter slaves or prisoners of war and to devour them, today - as Captain Jacobsen reports - they eat at their great festivals human corpses and more especially - unbelievably as it is - not perhaps the corpses of those recently deceased, but of those people who have already been dead for one or two years and now are mummified. Any time a Hamatsa has participated in such an awful meal, he receives as a badge a skull artificially carved of wood, which he wears as an ornament on a wreath of cedar bark (Figs. 11-12). ... Among the Bella Coolas presently staying here there is also a genuine Hamatsa by the name of Hamchick[25] who judging from the number of skulls he wears and which may correspond to our price medals, must have participated in eight of the above-mentioned appetizing meals. The eating of human flesh is presently also symbolized by winning over an inhabitant of the village who lets himself be bitten by the Hamatsa who sucks a few drops of blood, which always costs the Hamatsa much money, because he has to pay much for the fun which in this case is identical with the honor. Even if the Hamatsa performs this act properly, so that his victim suffers only little pain and that the wound will soon heal, the wound marks will always remain, which one can observe on the breast and arms of several of the Indians brought over; if the bite is in the first place, a higher amount has to be paid. The Hamatsa Dance which serves as an entertainment is performed in most phantastic costumes and is accompanied by a peculiar, nothing less than aesthetic music... Most interesting are the grotesque masks covering the head, commonly representing a sea or land monster" (Fig. 11). Many similar descriptions could be added here.

But not only such "sensational" and exciting aspects of Bella Coola life and of their performances were extensively dealt with by the press (and presumably discussed by the public). As an example of another kind of report may serve the following quotation from the *Leipziger Intelligenzblatt* of 13 October 1885 dealing with Bella Coola dances in wider perspective: "By expressing joy over sociability the dance is in a way the first step, the mediating link to culture. How it can be developed in this direction is shown by the choreographic productions of the Bella Coola Indians who use to take their material from the 'program of movements' consisting of more than 50 dances. As a rule they dance usually eight main numbers: The Chief, Shaman, Mask, Hamatsa or Cannibal, Bear, Fool, Winter, and Society Dance. Drum beat marks the performances. According to the meaning of the dance and its relation to the life of the people, the participating Indians appear in appropriate costume. Dance masks, neck and head rings of cedar bark, long-fringed blankets, and the apron hung with rattling and rustling pieces of metal form the decorative element. An outright striking impression is created whenever the Bella Coolas perform their dances in the evening, at a time used in their own homes for the most part for this entertainment. The dark of the night is calculated to heighten the imaginative in the appearance of the Indians; the blazing fire around which they move in circles with vivacious jumps and accompanied by loud singing and drum beats throws peculiar lights on the savagely embellished figures with their faces painted in many colors, and outlines them as stark silhouettes in front of a light surrounding. Travelers who have witnessed those dances assert that the performances of the Bella Coolas agree in this respect fully with the truth of nature, and that it is in fact a pleasure to be able to observe a whole sequence of them and in particular the most characteristic ones on one occasion, something which is rare in the Indian territories, or at least has to be gained by special offerings."

The reports often notice that the Bella Coolas did not at all look like "Indians." On one hand they were compared to Polynesians, on the other hand to Japanese and this not only by journalists but by respectable scholars of the time. "The resemblance of these Indians with the Japanese is such a remarkably big one that Professor Virchow is completely right in claiming that the Columbians are descended from the Japanese" (*Breslauer Zeitung*, 12 February 1886). At the opening performance in Berlin, lectures were delivered by Virchow, Bastian, and Aurel Krause: "Virchow in his explanations pointed to the great resemblance of these Bella Coola Indians in unpainted state to the Japanese - by the way, the Japanese embassy was in a body present in the hall - and added moreover that their head formation was an artificial, forcibly modeled one" (*Berliner Börsencourier*, 20 January 1886).

The "Japanese appearance" is also touched upon in Jacobsen's memoirs when he writes: "My Indians were all dressed in European clothes, and did not look very strange. As soon as we came into the Rocky Mountains where the people do not know the coastal race, I always only heard one question: 'Where do the

Japanese travel to, where do the Japanese want to go?'" Whether this really happened as related or whether this observation goes back to Virchow's remarks can today no longer be ascertained.

This "un-Indian appearance" may also have been the reason for (a few) articles in which (sometimes in a rather hateful way) the genuineness of the Bella Coolas is placed in doubt (e.g., the "Humoristic supplement" of the *Breslauer Gerichtszeitung*, February 1886; *Cölner Sonntags-Anzeiger*, 6 June 1886). The latter source is referred to by Adrian in letter of 8 June 1886 to Hedwig: "... it is the old story, one local paper has represented our Indians as not genuine or at least the readers get this impression - so we have to force the good man to retract his statement - which he can never do..." In Aachen he apparently had the same problem, witness his remark of 1 July 1886: "... and there as everywhere else there were the old stories relating to the genuineness..."

So much on the German press reaction. How far it was representative of the general public is hard to tell. Certainly the reports do not cover all moods and voices, but it may be assumed that the generally not unsympathetic attitude towards the Bella Coolas may have been correct.

Reactions and life of the Bella Coolas in Germany

Unfortunately no testimonials by the Bella Coolas themselves are known with the exception of the (alleged) remarks published by Kopas (1970:236). According to these, our Bella Coolas were great ladies' men.[26] On the occasion of my own visit in Bella Coola in 1978 there was likewise repeatedly mention made of their German girl friends. It was the only detail still known to the present villagers.[27] I then took these accounts to be the usual exaggerations of men returning home, until I found among the photographs taken in Berlin one showing Isk-ka-luska with his German girl friend (Fig. 24). So some truth has to be behind the rumors.

The Bella Coolas certainly did not have much leisure time in Germany, because they had to appear in two performances per day. According to the agreement they were bound to hold performances between 8 a.m. and 12 noon and from 1:30 p.m. to 6 p.m. The net working hours per day thus amounted to eight and a half, seven days a week. This limit was obviously only partly heeded by the organizers. In a surviving agreement relating to their appearances in "Kroll's Etablissement" in Berlin, the working hours are given as from 10 a.m. to 1 p.m. and from 3 p.m. to 10 p.m., which adds up to a daily net workload of 10 hours. In the contract for Elberfeld it is said: "The Indian troupe has the obligation to produce itself from 10 in the morning until the beginning of darkness," which in July certainly amounted to from 10 to 12 hours. How often the program was repeated during such a time period cannot

362

be said for sure, but it may be assumed that the dances were at least produced three or four times per day.

It is little wonder that the Bella Coolas in time became tired of doing the same dances over and over again. Even the greatest enthusiasm cannot be maintained under the pressure of such a burden. This may have been one reason why they (and Jacobsen?) tried to introduce changes into the program as illustrated by the story about the Thunder Dance. Nevertheless the spirit was sagging towards the end of the trip as Adrian reported to Hedwig. On 18 June 1886 he writes from Aachen: "The Indians don't want to travel anymore - and we have already had problems to talk the people into coming with us this far." And on 14 July from Krefeld: "... and the Indians are morose, they believe that we will keep them here."[28] On 16 July: "... the chief has been ill for three days or at least complains about being ill - I am convinced there is nothing wrong with him and they are all rather morose..." And on 18 July: "Today is the last day with the people and I am not sorry for it - because it is a miserable business - and never will be anything else - the people also now make no more effort, they don't want to work anymore - Tom had been in bed until today because of being homesick."

Yet the Bella Coolas had been enthusiastic during the first months and even after half a year were still at their job with fervor. On 16 September 1885, Adrian had written: "... they dance very well and make rather beautiful things - so far they are very obedient - if they remain this way, I don't ask for more." Proof for the fact that these were not only Adrian's perhaps prejudiced impressions comes from newpaper accounts. Thus, the *Breslauer Morgen* of 13 February 1886 says: "In all their productions, the Indians in their savage finery displayed a certain enthusiasm; they appeared to be proud of their achievements."

According to their contract the salary of the Bella Coolas consisted of 20 dollars per month plus lodging and board. Kopas (1970:235) also notes that Ya Coutlas received an additional $250 for his job as interpreter. While this cannot be substantiated by documentary evidence, it is certainly possible and also may be connected with his role in persuading the others to join him. The Bella Coolas seem to have sent some money home,[29] but were also making purchases, especially of clothing.[30] As the Berlin photos show they placed great stress on being dressed according to the best fashion of the time (Fig. 3,6,25). Seven surviving bills totaling the substantial amount of more than a thousand marks were written out by J. Marten Jacobsen for payment by Hagenbeck.

The money for these and other expenses they certainly must have incurred did not come from their salaries but from the sale of carvings which were apparently made in great numbers. Already on 10 September 1885 Hagenbeck had written to Jacobsen: "Also see to it that the people get good soft wood from which to carve little things such as canoes etc., because this is good advertisement for us if such things are being sold and so get among the public; the profit should, of course, be kept by the Indians so the guys will take more pleasure in their work." Such admonitions are often repeated in the correspondence with Jacobsen. In a letter dated only 1885, Hagenbeck writes: "I would like to ask you that you have carved by the Indians two house crest poles approximately 7 to 8 feet high and painted, as I intend to sell the same to a private museum for a good price. I will then also need some straw basketry and perhaps a small boat model and two masks (also may be newly carved) and 4 to 6 pieces of fishhooks or something else." According to these letters and the newspaper reports we have to assume that there are presently many objects in collections that have been carved by the Bella Coolas during their stay in Germany. So far, only an Eagle mask and a Nulmal mask, both carved in Leipzig, can safely be documented in the Museum für Völkerkunde, Berlin (Haberland 1979:B-6, H-19), and a Hamatsa mask of the Crooked Beak of Heaven-type in the Etnografisk Museum of the University of Oslo (Haberland 1979:K-32), which was made in Hamburg.[31] It would be an interesting and rewarding task to try to assemble the pieces produced by the Bella Coolas in Germany, or to attempt to identify them (which should not be much of a problem as they or Jacobsen certainly had not brought enough cedar wood from back home).[32]

During their tour the Bella Coolas were generally[33] living in one big room together with Fillip Jacobsen. Their diet was European, and they seem to have liked beefsteak and fruits most of all. Two accounts dealing with the "private life" of the Bella Coolas can be quoted from newspaper clippings.

The first account is part of a longer essay titled "A visit with the Bella Coola Indians in the Breslau Zoological Garden" and published on 12 February 1886 in the *Breslauer Zeitung*: "[Afterwards] the younger Jacobsen [Fillip] took me to the Bella Coolas who had made their domicile in the rooms situated on the first floor of the new building. There it looked a little pell-mell: bows, arrows, masks, blankets, everything over and under one another. The wild sons of the West partly sat on the floor, partly on chairs and were occupied with the carving and repair of masks and with the mending of stockings... The most cheerful one of the company is young Ishle-Quanu who was just repairing a giant animal mask as I was entering and who with a jovial smile was clapping with its beak. When I asked how these people of nature were passing their time, the young Jacobsen replied that his charges were very peaceful and industrious. Most of the time they were occupied with woodcarving. Sometimes they were performing a dance for their private entertainment. He had also given them playing cards which they used to play with according to a method devised by themselves,[34] which he was unable to comprehend. I now offered cigars to the strangers which they partly accepted with a friendly grin, partly with a clearly discernible 'Danke Ihnen' - which is the extent to which they have learned to speak German. They also gladly accept beer, but they are not

Fig. 24. Isk-ka-lusta and his German girl friend.

allowed to drink more than one glass of it. Otherwise they become intoxicated and then are supposed to be very dangerous.[35] Besides their own language they can speak 'Chinook' in which idiom they communicate with their guides. They also understand a little English. ... When I departed, the strangers intoned a soft song which did not at all sound unharmonious, but was confined to the lower ranges."

Whereas this may have been their everyday life, the other report tells us about a social gathering attended by the Bella Coolas.[36] The author of this account published in the *Leipziger Tages-Anzeiger* of 11 October 1885 was Maria Cronau, the wife of Rudolf Cronau who both wrote about and drew the Bella Coolas himself: "In your last article you write that the Indians should soon be introduced to our own habits and customs. I think that this has already been done in every respect. They have, for example, a predilection for European dress, they are accustomed to the use of knife and fork in a way which can only have been acquired through long practice, yet we know that Captain Jacobsen has only a few months ago acquainted these people with our civilized customs when he took them away from their savage homes. Even though their food is quite different from ours (consisting mostly of fish put

365

Fig. 25. Huck-mulshe in European dress.

Fig. 26. Elk-qut (Alcius) with cape of strips of rabbit fur.

into a box filled with water and brought to boil by means of red hot stones), they nonetheless relish our cuisine. They also like beer very much, but rarely get more than one or two glasses per day. They live peacefully with one another, are faithfully obedient to their chief and quietly obey his orders. They do not seem to know envy or jealousy, as I have never noticed that they ever envied one another in case the chief (whose English name is Tom) had not evenly distributed the fruits which I brought them on occasion and which they passionately love. In the evenings after the performances they sit together in their common room around a long table and talk about the events of the day. They are always happy if there had been a large audience and are also sorry if the circle of spectators had not been as big, as it recently had unfortunately happened more often due to the bad weather. They also busy themselves with drawing, painting, or woodcarving in which they are artists as witness the many masks and house crest poles. An agreeable change from these different activities is provided by their evening meals consisting as a rule of tea, bread, and cold meat. The chief who presides at the head of the table helps himself first, the others follw him, and everyone takes an equal amount, and thus no quarrels arise. They have also already become real gourmets, as 'dancing-master' Chazley (so-called by us because he always leads the dances

366

with tambourine in hand) said a couple of days ago when offered a German beefsteak, that it had 'no taste.' ... I am almost afraid that I am overly trying your patience and yet I want to relate of the visit the Bella Coolas made with us last Tuesday. I had invited them for dinner and they punctually appeared at the given time, with joyfully smiling faces. At the table they behaved most mannerly and did perfect justice to the food. Parenthetically, they can eat unusually large quantities and you can get an approximate idea of this if I tell you that six pecks just of fruit were devoured by them. After dinner I had arranged a little game, which as a rule is only played by children. Rewards were attached to a dial, which were given to the fortunate winner whose number came up. Prices included, e.g., children's musical clocks, small pianos, trumpets, color-boxes, glass mirrors, chains, earrings, etc. But the devotion is indescribable with which every one turned the dial and watched the pointer, and the rejoicing if he won, or the laughter of the others if he lost. When the game was over, another one was played, and finally they performed their domestic dances in which a tray served instead of the drum. It was late in the evening when these rare guests left us after having thanked us and asked us to visit them at a later date in their home country so that they could show us their hospitality. You will see from this that the 'savages' can be also good-natured and that they have already fully accustomed themselves to our customs and usages. Where they will go from here is as yet uncertain, but it certainly will happen soon, which is a reason to make good use of the short period of time remaining. The impresarios, Messrs. Jacobsen and Pinkert,[37] are especially deserving the support of the public in that the whole enterprise is associated with high costs. I am convinced that no visitor of the zoological garden, which does offer so much else that is educating and beautiful, will leave the same dissatisfied."

So much for this interesting account. It is unknown whether the Bella Coolas visited the major sights during their stays in the various cities, such as the cathedrals of Cologne or Naumburg, or the ethnological museums in Leipzig, Dresden, or Berlin. Their reaction after viewing these buildings and the sculptures in which they surely must have been interested, or the collections, especially of the Northwest Coast, would have been of considerable interest, just as the reactions to what they may have told of their experiences after their return home to Bella Coola.

Illness seems to have been of infrequent occurence. Except for the one of their leader already mentioned - and probably more of a psychosomatic kind (see above) - only one can be documented at this point. On 10 June 1886 Adrian wrote to Hedwig from Cologne: "Nuskalusta [the Isk-ka-lusta of the contract] is very ill and has an abscess on his right leg which is swollen from the bone, and he has fever and is seriously ill." Five days later he reports: "The patient is somewhat better - but he cannot yet stand up and cannot be transported - if he only would recover sufficiently by 1 July so that he could come along, it costs much money again." And on 22 June from Aachen: "Nuskelusta is still lying in Cologne in the Panoptikum but is well enough so that we don't need a doctor anymore, it has already cost us far above 100 marks." After that, Isk-ka-lusta must have been well again, as Adrian mentions him no longer.

All in all the trip had its ups and downs, was certainly disappointing financially for Hagenbeck and Jacobsen, and an interesting experience for the Bella Coolas even though unfortunately we do not know the exact consequences on the further lives of the participants. For the Bella Coolas the trip lasted too long, however, was too exhausting, and too tedious. It cannot be ascertained how far the German public profited from the performances, or whether they did contribute to a better understanding of non-European - and especially of American Indian - peoples, but such results may reasonably be doubted. New experiences were primarily gathered by the interested scholars who for the first time were directly confronted with Northwest Coast Indian culture. Special performances were arranged for scientific organizations. One scholar in particular was thereby redirected in his research interests: Franz Boas who apparently received the idea or final impulse for his trip to the Northwest Coast which in turn laid the basis for his North American carreer.[38]

The collection

It has already been mentioned that an extensive ethnographic collection of Northwest Coast material, mostly collected by Fillip, but also partly by Adrian, and financed and owned by Hagenbeck, was part of the performances of the Bella Coolas. Indications for the number of objects shown range from 1,500 to 2,000, a variation perhaps caused by the fact that objects bought or ordered by Jacobsen on the Northwest Coast were arriving later and were added after the start of the German tour. Some newspaper reports deal extensively with this collection which should be made the subject of a separate investigation. Here it is mentioned only for the sake of completeness. It was pointed out above that the collection contained crest poles as well as masks, blankets and other objects used in the performances. This is also indicated by a remark of Hagenbeck in a letter to Adrian, dated 2 October 1885: "... under the condition that we retain about 200 or 300 objects necessarily needed until the end of our exhibition..." The sale of this collection became a great problem, also for Adrian. Initially, Hagenbeck had obviously rather exaggerated ideas regarding the price (apparently 28,000 marks) for which, however, it could not be sold. Leipzig and Vienna showed interest at first but the negotiations came to nothing primarily on account of the price asked. Leipzig moreover had just purchased the ethnographic portion of the dissolved Museum Goddefroy of Hamburg and thus had expended its budget. Finally, in October 1885, Leipzig

368

bought part of the collection (apparently a third of the items for 8,000 marks). Heger in Vienna wanted to buy 200 or 300 objects. He did receive an offer, but a direct sale could not be transacted. Several objects, however, marked "FCM, Hagenbeck" by Feest (1968:107-127) and received in exchange from the Field Museum in Chicago in 1894, most likely come from this collection whose remains were exhibited and offered for sale at the Chicago World's Fair of 1893. Still further remains later became the property of Umlauff Company in Hamburg and were ultimately sold to the museums im Lübeck and Cologne, but also to the ones in Hamburg and Freiburg/Breisgau. Another part consisting of 83 pieces was acquired after much contention in 1886 by the museum in Berlin for an unspecified amount (perhaps 3,000 marks). In addition, the museum in Oslo acquired items, as did several private persons, so that this (the second) Jacobsen collection from the Northwest Coast is now dispersed in all directions. To track it down would be a rewarding if difficult task.[39]

A curious incident may finally be indicative of the notions of the time. In the booklet by Schirp (1885) a whole paragraph on page 9 was blackened out as a result of censorship. What did this section contain? Fortunately, a bound copy from Adrian's private collection lacks the deletion and solves the mystery. The censored paragraph reads: "The children reach their marriageable age at 12 ot 13 years, respectively; among the boys the peculiar custom obtains that they are at this age fetched by a sister of the mother or the father or by another female relative who teaches them how to perform intercourse. In honor of this coming of age a big feast, the so-called Kouquale Feast is being held." Obviously, this was too offensive and was not supposed to be read. Or was anyone afraid that this custom might be imitated in Germany?

NOTES

1. This paper is based on records, letters, and other documents formerly owned by J. Adrian Jacobsen, and now in the collections of the Hamburgisches Museum für Völkerkunde.
2. Local and ethnic designations have been standardized throughout this paper especially in view of Jacobsen's wild and inconsistent orthography.
3. The Bella Coola are speakers of a Salishan language, whereas the Bellabella are a division of the Kwakiutl and thus Wakashan speakers.
4. A total of nine Bella Coolas signed the contract and went to Germany.
5. The contract surviving in the Jacobsen papers was signed by all nine of the Bella Coolas. It seems, however, that every member of the troupe had his own copy.
6. This may be the basis for a folk tradition apparently still current among the Kwakiutl in 1976/7, relating to a group of Kwakiutls who had gone to Germany and had all died there.
7. A third version was published by Kopas (1970:234-236). According to it, Fillip had hired the group directly in Bella Coola. This is unlikely as otherwise they would have taken their wives along. Adrian later on repeatedly regretted that the group did only consist of men. In contemporaneous *Völkerschauen* it was customary to display whole families.
8. According to Kopas (1970:259-260) Anglicized names were introduced to the Bella Coola only in 1896, long after their trip to Germany. Individual tribal members, such as Tom, must have had such names before.
9. Kopas (1970:200) gives his Indian name as Tactulus. By 1883 he was known as "Chief Tom". He is said to have been the first chief in Bella Coola who became a Christian (Kopas 1970:216-218).
10. It is uncertain whether this photograph shows Ham-chick, but a number of indications makes this identification likely. Thus, Ham-chick is said to have been the oldest participant. He is frequently called a "shaman." But the only photograph showing a "healing ceremony" (Fig. 10) is out of focus and does not allow a definite identification of the healer.
11. On 2 July 1885 Hagenbeck (in a letter to Jacobsen in Victoria) still had other plans: "I think we will start in Paris."
12. Only Hagenbeck's letters to Jacobsen are available, but from his replies Jacobsen's proposals can be deduced. In addition, Jacobsen himself wrote to different promoters as can be seen from their replies.
13. An offer made by Goteborg, 15 days per 200 crowns including advertisements, seemed too low to Hagenbeck; moreover, he had had bad experiences in Scandinavia with a troupe of Nubians.
14. I.e. in December. The Cathedral Fair ("Hamburger Dom") was and still is the major Christmas fair. At the time it was not yet being held in its present location, Heiligengeistfeld, but was divided among three

non-contiguous locations (Dammtorwall, Spielbudenplatz, Neuer [?] Pferdemarkt).

15. "Sagebiel's Halls" consisted of a number of rooms near Dammtorwall, some of which were among the largest such halls in Germany. During Cathedral Fair numerous events and performances in the field of light entertainment took place there.

16. It was in fact repeated over and over again.

17. "I think it will be a good thing if the guys build themselves a house and as closely as possible as in their home country" (Hagenbeck to Jacobsen, Berlin, 10 September 1885).

18. As it is unlikely that wood had been brought over from the Northwest Coast, the boards could hardly have been made of cedar (*Thuja*).

19. "We also have built here a small Indian house with the pole made in Hamburg" (Adrian Jacobsen to Hedwig Klopfer, Leipzig, 12 September 1885).

20. Bill of a Berlin carpenter of 1 March 1886 relating to the "erection of a victory column of the Bella Coola Indians."

21. "Special mention should be made of a big, carved and painted pictorial column of ancient origin, coming from Vancouver and representing a Kwakiutl Indian" (*Breslauer Zeitung*, 19 February 1886).

22. The photographs cannot have been made earlier than 19 January 1886. According to invoices, however, Jacobsen had been selling photographs made by E. Hattdorf of Hamburg-St. Pauli before that date. It is likely that these were general Northwest Coast photos rather than specifically relating to the Bella Coolas.

23. "We now have invited all schools and the only question is whether they will come - one school we have already had and tomorrow more will be coming - I ran around yesterday and today to invite the schools, which is not a pleasant job" (Adrian Jacobsen to Hedwig Klopfer, Chemnitz, 4 November 1885).

24. Such a case occurred in Berlin on 25 January 1885. Ya Coutlas was apparently about to kill Pooh-Pooh who had fallen down, and could only at pains be restrained by Adrian Jacobsen (*Staatsbürger-Zeitung*, 26 January 1886).

25. This is probably a mistake, as all the other papers and Adrian Jacobsen identify Pooh-Pooh as the *hamatsa*. Ham-chick, on the other hand, is commonly referred to as "shaman" or "medicine-man."

26. "'German women followed us around,' Billy Jones, one of the Indians said years later in Bella Coola. 'They wanted to marry us but the big German tyee says we could not stay in Germany. So we came back without our German girl.' ... 'But one Indian dancer, Alec Davis, rather than consorting with many women, associated himself with only one, and from her he learned to speak the German language, gaining an amazing fluency in it that he retained for the rest of his life. ... And a millionaire German

woman wanted Chief Tom Henry to marry her, but the chief said no. He had a wife back in Bella Coola and he was going back to her'" (Kopas 1970:236). Jacobsen was obliged by treaty to return the nine Bella Coolas to British Columbia, so he could not let it happen that one or more of them would have remained in Germany.

27. It is, of course, possible that these presumed recollections are actually based on the book by Kopas and the passages quoted above.

28. Jacobsen wanted to send the Bella Coolas back sooner, but apparently Hagenbeck had no funds to finance the trip back home. "We have to stand fast until 15 July so that we get the travel money together" (Adrian Jacobsen to Hedwig Klopfer, Aachen, 25 June 1886).

29. "Chief Tom of the troupe here on display, a few weeks ago had a letter written to his wife through Captain Jacobsen and had sent 40 dollars of the money earned here" (*Saale-Zeitung*, 18 November 1885).

30. A total of seven bills survive (they are missing for Huck-mulshe and Isk-ka-lusta). The sums range from 79 marks (Que-noh) to 212 marks (Kah-che-lis). The total of 1,075.50 marks (for the seven) was a considerable amount of money at the time.

31. Many of the pieces now in Lübeck, obtained from Umlauff, but ultimately from Jacobsen may belong to this group. This may explain Erna Gunther's remark when looking at this collection: "I never thought that Jacobsen collected such junk!"

32. There is a bill dated Breslau, 1 March 1886, for, i.a., "a gourd, a linden trunk, a wire mesh, and two skins," which probably had served for the fabrication or repair of objects.

33. The exception was certainly Leipzig where they had built their own house.

34. Unfortunately nothing is known about this method.

35. A bill dated Breslau, 1 March 1886, includes the item "For the Indians 19 days at lunch each one glass of beer = 171 glasses: M 25.65".

36. It seems that they occasionally gave private performances or participated in social events. It cannot be ascertained whether they received extra payment for such activities.

37. Director of the Zoological Garden.

38. On 25 January 1886 Boas had published an enthusiastic article on the dances of the Bella Coolas in the *Berliner Tageblatt*, as far as I know his first article dealing with the Northwest Coast. This essay has remained largely unknown (cp. also Boas 1886 a, b, c). Boas's relationship to Jacobsen is difficult to fathom out. But they were hardly friends. Both used the same interpreter, George Hunt, who may have been recommended to Boas by Jacobsen. Boas used many of the items collected in 1881-1883 by Jacobsen to illustrate "The Social Organization and the Secret Societies of the Kwakiutl Indians" (Boas 1897), but added new and more correct (?) designations. There are no letters from Boas to Jacobsen and the latter's

recollections of the Chicago World's Fair of 1893 do not mention Boas, even though both were present on the occasion.

39. To some extent this (second) collection has been confused with the first one of the 1881-1883 trip. Thus, Gunther's assertion (Jacobsen 1977:X) is wrong, namely, that the Berlin Museum let Jacobsen have a portion of the 1881-1883 collection and that this later ended up with Umlauff. The first collection virtually became completely part of the Berlin museum because the trip had been financed by it. Jacobsen collections in other museums (except those obtained by exchange from Berlin) all derive from the second collecting trip and were brought together for the better part (except some of the Nootka and Kwakiutl material) by Fillip Jacobsen.

REFERENCES CITED

Boas, Franz
1886a Mittheilungen über die Vilxula-Indianer. Original-Mittheilungen aus der Ethnologischen Abtheilung der Königlichen Museen, Berlin, 1:177-182. Berlin.
1886b Sprache der Bella-Coola-Indianer. Verhandlungen der Berliner Gesellschaft für Anthropologie, Ethnologie und Urgeschichte 1886:202-206. Berlin.
1886c The Language of the Bilhoola in British Columbia. Science, 1st series, 7:218.
1897 The Social Organization and the Secret Societies of the Kwakiutl Indians. Report of the U.S. National Museum for 1895:311-737. Washington.

Cronau, Rudolf
1892 Amerika. 2 vols. Leipzig: Abel & Müller.

Deckert, Emil
1904 Nordamerika. 2nd ed. Leipzig-Wien: Bibliographisches Institut.

Feest, Christian F.
1968 Indianer Nordamerikas. Wien: Museum für Völkerkunde.

Haberland, Wolfgang
1979 Donnervogel und Raubwal. Indianische Kunst der Nordwestküste Nordamerikas. Hamburg: Hamburgisches Museum für Völkerkunde - Christians Verlag.

Jacobsen, Johan Adrian
1977 Alaskan Voyage 1881-1883. An Expedition to the Northwest Coast of America. Translated by Erna Gunther. Chicago-London: The University of Chicago Press.

Kopas, Cliff
1970 Bella Coola. Vancouver: Mitchell Press Ltd.

Schirp, F. von
1885 Bella-Coola-Indianer von der Nordwest-Küste Nordamerikas. Berlin: Jacobsen & von Schirp.

Taylor, J. Garth
1981 An Eskimo abroad, 1880: His diary and death. Canadian Geographic 101(5):38-43. Ottawa.

Woldt, Adrian
1884 Captain Jacobsen's Reise an der Nordwestküste Amerikas 1881-1883. Leipzig: Max Spohr.

"REDSKINS AT THE ZOO":
SIOUX INDIANS IN BUDAPEST, 1886

Miklós Létay

Curiosity has always been aroused by things appearing to be unusual, that is, by things beyond the scope of one's own knowledge and experience. And this has been the foundation for a form of entertainment dating back to time immemorial: The display of peculiar people, animals, or objects. Among these constantly changing and for the most part shortlived displays, a type that became popular in many European countries in the 19th century was the public exhibition of members of exotic populations. This type of spectacle proved to be far more valuable than others in the genre, since the blank and dumb stares of audiences were animated by a supply of real information, though the ethnographic information was presented in a form very much akin to a circus production. The performances were related to, or rather happily coincided with, the increasing interest in ethnography at the time. This general conclusion can be specifically illustrated by looking at the details surrounding a performance of one such visiting ethnic group in Budapest.

The last decades of the 19th century presented Budapest audiences with not only Samoyed, Black African, and Bedouin groups, but also with North American Indians. It is believed that they arrived via Bohemia as part of a tour of Europe. They reached Budapest on 26 May 1886, and just as other ethnic groups, they set up their tents within the grounds of the Zoological Garden, on the site where the circus building stands today. Why there, of all places? The Zoological Garden had been founded in 1866 and until 1907 it was maintained by a stock company which received no financial support from the government. If the noble goal of proliferating knowledge of the natural sciences was to be attained, earning the income to be devoted to this cause was a key issue. Management tried to provide and even increase this income by attracting and entertaining audiences not only with the display of animals but by presenting other programs of interest in what we might call temporary exhibitions. As a part of this project, "it undertook as one of its tasks to organize ethnographic displays from time to time. Within this project, it was to bring here larger or smaller groups of several families of the most peculiar types of peoples from all over the world and present them to audiences in their original habitat, with their own stock, tents, and tools."

This is why the Indians settled in the Zoo, pitching their canvas tents decorated with "primitive pictorial symbols" and "scarlet embellishments" on the poles. Despite this very inexpert description, we can be certain that the audiences were seeing tipis, the habitations of the North American Plains Indians. These high, conical structures had many advantageous features: They could be pitched or taken down in very little time; they were capable of

ÁLLATKERT.

Holnap vasárnap, május-hó 30-án

először a

Sioux-Indiánok

és pedig az első előadás 11 és 12 óra között
fog megtartatni.   483
Belépti dij mint rendesen 30 kr.

Fig. 1. Newspapers advertisement for the show: "Zoological Garden. Tomorrow, Sunday, on the
30th of May for the first time Sioux Indians and the first of these performances will be
held between 11 and 12 o'clock."

accomodating as many as a dozen people; fires could be set within them. They
must have been of particularly good service during this tour. Indirectly, these
tipis verified the fact (which few doubted anyway) that the group of about 15
men, women, children, and elders belonged to the Dakota or "Sioux" tribe.

Led by R.C. Dawe, their Berlin impresario, they visited the offices of all the
larger Budapest newspapers on 28 May 1886, partly to advertise themselves,
and partly to present invitations. On the following day, 29 May at 5:00 p.m.
they held a special performance for the press accompanied by the impresario's
soft-voiced German language explanation of the more important rituals staged.
The performance ended at 7 o'clock in the evening. And based on what they
had seen, the journalists described the Indians and their production as follows:
"The men are tall and strong." To the European audience they appeared a bit
disproportionate since their muscular bodies stood upon short legs, a feature
supposedly deriving from their former equestrian, nomadic way of life. "They
are characterized by prominent foreheads, piercing eyes, strong chins, and
crudely formed features. Their faces do not speak of overt intelligence, but
determination and stamina rest upon them." They wore neither mustaches nor
beards but "they all paint themselves although they should be satisfied with
their copper skins which are colorful enough as it is," the *Pesti Napló* wrote
critically. "Even here they use red paint which is just as gaudy as the red

376

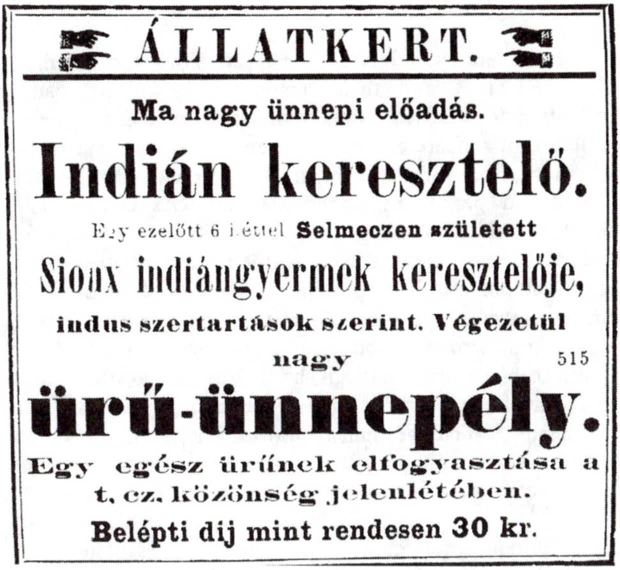

ÁLLATKERT.

Ma nagy ünnepi előadás.

Indián keresztelő.

Egy ezelőtt 6 héttel **Selmeczen született**

Sioux indiángyermek keresztelője,

indus szertartások szerint. Végezetül

nagy 515

ürű-ünnepély.

Egy egész ürűnek elfogyasztása a t. cz. közönség jelenlétében.

Belépti dij mint rendesen 30 kr.

Fig. 2. "Zoological Garden. Today, big ceremonious performance. Indian christening.Christening of a Sioux Indian child born six weeks ago in Selmecz according to Indian custom. Finally a great sheep ceremony. An entire sheep will be consumed in the presence of the honorable audience. Entrance free, as usual 30 kr."

feathers which they wear upon their heads in combination with white ones."

The most striking ornament of the Indian male "is his crown of feathers about a foot in height, which trails down way beyond the ground in two rows in the back, to drag behind him."

As far as their dress was concerned, they wore the traditional shirts and leggings of the Plains Indians. Most of their garments were of leather but a few were of colored fabric, indicating the growing influence of White civilization.

The women in the Indian group were unusually short. "They do not decorate their hair with anything and paint only their faces." The women's garments were of thin leather and, according to some, resembled the Turkish *shaloar* (robe), while according to others it was more like the Vlach (Romanian) dress, the difference being that they also wore "some capelike garment" on the upper part of their bodies, referring either to the typical dress-yokes or to shawls draped around the shoulders.

Both sexes wore "sandal-like fringed footwear," that is, tasseled mocassins. Another common feature was that the garment of both men and women was decorated with motifs embroidered in beads. The entourage of the group included "15 wild-bred prairie horses." However, critics cast doubts on their general qualifications as advertised, remarking that the animals moved a bit heavily.

In the area surrounded by a board fence, the Sioux Indians first presented "the manner in which they and their families take to the road, how they transform their tents into vehicles, with comfortable places for their wives and children." The interesting feature of the scene was the "vehicle" mentioned which was in fact a horse-drawn travois. The second part of the program consisted of a mounted parade of armed warriors. "As comic and in fact as pathetic as they look while rambling afoot, the picture is reversed on horseback. The principal feature causing this is their mastery over their bareback steeds." "One and another of them presents a picture of aesthetic beauty with his stately form and flying feathers." Then the men showed how they could handle their bows and arrows. "One was particularly master of the weapon, striking home with each arrow although he hardly aimed them at all, simply guiding them with his index finger." Then came "a less successful presentation, the throwing of lassos, which we might also call a lariat, in which our own horsemen are far more expert." Finally, they gave a presentation of how the Indians attack and scalp a family of White settlers sitting around the evening campfire.

Between the different productions, the Indians presented their "national dances." The musical accompaniment came from the rhythmic sound of rattles tied beneath the knees of the men and the monotone drumming of one of the older members of the group. A source of particular joy for the audience was that on one occasion "the dance was accompanied by loud howling, similar to the howl of a dog or jackal, a dance in which the feet were lifted in a way similar to the Hungarian czardas with rapid foot movement. They bend forward repeatedly as though seeking an invisible enemy, attentively anchor their faces towards the earth and wave their horrible weapons to the left and right." At other times the dance seemed to be "but waddling to a monotonous drumming," in which the Indians "simper about in one place, at most shaking their elbows a bit to the music."

The undeniably astute impresario of the Sioux group not only brought the performers and their equipment, such as the horses, to Budapest, but also a collection of pictures and ethnographic objects which he presented in an exhibition next to the site of the performance. Genre pictures, ethnographic sketches, drawings of Indians including eight portraits of the famous chiefs of the second half of the 19th century helped to bring the North American continent and its aborigines closer and at the same time made the performances themselves more comprehensible. The nearly 200 paintings, charcoal drawings and graphic works were the work of Rudolf Cronau who had spent three years (1880-1883) in the United States as illustrator for two German journals, *Illustrierte Zeitung* und *Gartenlaube*. A taste of a vanishing way of life was presented by the copper-handled tomahawks, moccassins, coats, bags, arrows, quivers, the stone headed clubs, feather headdresses, pipes, household utensils,

378

painted buffalo skins, and cradle boards. "Every single one of their wonderful objects is decorated with tiny beads. This type of bead is their most favored one, their women who prepare the dress and belts of their husbands only like to work with this type of bead." The journalists paid special attention to the "papoose sacks" one of which they were able to see in use since there was a baby of a few months with the group.

On 27 June 1886, towards the end of their sojourn in Budapest, the Sioux Indians held a naming ceremony, perhaps to attract the interest of the audience once again. "They presented the new-born infant, placed it on a buffalo skin and then the elders sat around it and for a time showed their joy over the tiny child. Then the oldest one lit a pipe, puffed on it once and passed on this smoking symbol of peace and friendship. Then the oldest Indian

Fig. 3. The picture of an Indian woman used by the Sunday Journal to illustrate the visiting Sioux group is in fact a copy of Paul Kane's portrait of Cunnawa-bum, a Cree half-breed, as published in Kane's *Wanderings of an Artist* (London 1859; probably here taken from the German edition, Leipzig 1862) as a frontispiece.

stood up and held a speech for his mates. At this point they dusted the tiny baby with some powder and all of them kissed it. Then the child's role was ended and it was returned to the tent."

The final performance was on 30 June, after which the Indians "who had met with such interest on the part of the Hungarian capital city" went on to Vienna, the next stop on their tour.

This is what happened during the only performance North American Indians were ever to give in Hungary. No matter what the concept or business interests behind the creation of this ethnographic group, their activities were a type of entertaining proliferation of information, and therefore might be considered predecessors to the folklore programs of today. The exhibition presented alongside the performance made the entire production not only more varied, but more informative as well, thus providing a good service to the cause of general culture.

REFERENCES CITED

Budapest Székesfővárosi Állatkert Utmutatója
1912   [Guide of the Zoo of Budapest.] Budapest.
Kállay, Bertalan
1903   A budapesti állatkert első 30 esztendejének története
[History of the first 30 years of the Zoo in Budapest]. Budapest.
Lappok Budapesten
1913   Budapest.

NEWSPAPERS

Budapest (daily) 1886
Budapest Hirlap (daily) 1886:
    A sziu indiánok Budapesten [Sioux Indians in Budapest], no. 148:3-4.
    Indián világ az állatkertben [Indian World at the Zoo], no. 149:1-2.
    Amerika legjobb lovasai (L. Madarassy) [America's Best Riders], no. 156:1.
Fővárosi Lapok (daily) 1886:
    Rézbőrüek az állatkertben [Redskins at the Zoo], no. 152:1108-1109.
Függetlenség (daily) 1886
Képes Családi Lapok (daily) 1886
Nemzet (daily) 1886
Ország-Világ (daily) 1886
Pesti Hirlap (daily) 1886:
    Sioux-indiánok [Sioux Indians], no. 148:4-5.
Vasárnapi Ujság (daily) 1886:
    Az állatkert uj vendégei [New guests of the Zoo], no. 23:370.
    Sioux-indiánok [Sioux Indians], no. 24:386-387.

ACROSS THE BIG WATER: AMERICAN INDIANS' PERCEPTIONS OF EUROPE AND EUROPEANS, 1887-1906

Rita G. Napier

"I started from my lodge two moons ago knowing nothing, and had I remained on the Indian Reservation, I should have been as a blind man. Now I can see a new dawn. The great houses which cross the mighty waters, the great villages which have no end where the pale faces swarm like insects in the summer sun... Our people will wonder at these things when we return to the Indian Reservation and tell them what we have seen."[1]

Thus observed Red Shirt, a Lakota band leader who traveled to Europe with Buffalo Bill in the Wild West on its first tour of Europe. Though the Indians, largely Sioux, were central figures in the show, no one has attempted to make Indians main characters in the story of the great tours of Europe. Their commentary on Europe largely has been ignored, and no one has attempted to examine their comments and insights within their own cultural context. Even when writers describe Indian participation, they use the observations of Euro-Americans of the time rather than the Indians' own views of themselves and their experience. In the pages of modern books they remain amusing curiosities. Yet the Indians had much to say about Europe, which they viewed from a distinct and unique perspective that deserves to be understood. Their observations arose from their most basic cultural values and reflect a distinctive Indian point of view.

Most of the Indians who joined the Wild West were right off the reservation, though as time passed and new tours were organized, a few had been educated in White boarding schools. Some, like Lone Bear, were nearly permanent members of the show and, of those, some went on to careers in show business.

The promoters of the Wild West organized three hugely successful tours of Europe, 1887-88; 1889-92; 1902-1906 (Russell 1960, 1970; Walsh and Salsbury 1928; Sell and Weybright 1955; Burke 1893, 1974). Buffalo Bill Cody was the star of the show, which was carefully managed by Nate Salsbury and rhetorically promoted by John M. Burke. From the first blood-tingling, hair-raising moment when the entire troupe burst forth from an ambuscade of rocks to the thrilling attack on a settler's cabin, the Indians were a prominent feature of the show. As Buffalo Bill himself put it: "My Indians are the principal feature of this show, and they are the one people I will not allow to be misused or neglected" (Standing Bear 1975:261). The show, however, was not just the performance. The outfit created a great camp wherever it went,

Fig. 1. "Red Shirt - The Fighting Chief of the Sioux Nation." Photo taken in London by Elliott & Fry in 1887 on the occasion of Red Shirt's presence with Buffalo Bill's Wild West. Photo courtesy Museum für Völkerkunde, Wien.

preferably outdoors, to illustrate the way of life of Western American people, and the Indian camp was a major part of it. Visitors could tour the camp and watch the Indian families at work and at play in the traditional manner. At Earl's Court in England in 1887, for example, "in the center of the vast arena - which already reminds one of the interior of the Colosseum - are placed rocks and fir trees, backed by a panorama of Rocky Mountain scenery 500 foot long. Here Buffalo Bill (the Hon. J. Cody) [sic] and 200 Indians, cowboys, and scouts will illustrate the wild sports of the Far West, assisted by no less than 250 animals, including many buffalos."[2] Great loads of earth and trees and rocks were freighted in to create this scene.

The promoters projected the show as "The Drama of Civilization." The image presented in the drama for Europeans was "a transferred picture of savage life" replete with "a grand village of BLANKET INDIANS, noted chiefs, distinguished warriors, squaws, papooses, teepees, lodges..."[3] Presented in this way to Europe, the Indian and the Wild West were irresistible. Since this was the "true" drama of civilization, the cowboys always won and the Indians, savages, always lost. Black Elk, a Lakota who toured in Europe from 1887 to 1889 commented: "I liked the part of the show we made, but *not* the part the

Wasichu made" (Neihardt 1972:184; emphasis mine).

The motives of the Indians for joining the Wild West show and touring in Europe were diverse. Apparently the largest number of Indians in the tours were Sioux and often of a band. On the 1887 tour men like Black Elk and Red Shirt were adults who had lived through the great wars, defeat, and reservating. Some may have been attracted by the decent wages Buffalo Bill paid that could be sent home or used to purchase luxuries - even necessities - no reservation Indian could afford. Kills Enemy Alone indicated this was his reason: "I came over here to see if I can make some money,"[4] her wrote. Some sent much of the money home to help their families. No doubt many were attracted by adventure, pure and simple. Certainly they had great freedom in the company to come and go as they pleased. Others saw in exhibiting the life they knew a way of partially continuing the old while avoiding the fate of forced acculturation as farmers on the reservation. One of the more bizarre causes for joining the show grew out of the Ghost Dance and the conflict at Wounded Knee, 1890-91. The army placed one hundred Sioux prisoners in Buffalo Bill's custody to become actors in the show on the 1891-92 tour of Europe.

Black Elk as a Lakota holy man had a unique and poignant reason for traveling with the show. He had established himself as a leader amongst his people, but he felt keenly the great responsibility given him in his vision to keep his people whole. He chose to go with the show as a quest after a cure for the death of his people. "The nation's hoop was broken, and there was no center any longer for the flowering tree. The people were in despair." Black Elk, too, was in despair as he observed the broken unity of his people and "everybody for himself and with little rules of his own" instead of the one, right way of life that made the culture flourish. And so when Pahuska (Long Hair, Buffalo Bill) came in 1887 to recruit a band of Oglalas, "They told us this show would go across the big water to strange lands and I thought I ought to go, because I might learn some secret of the Wasichu that would help my people somehow" (Neihardt 1972:184).

In later European tours some of the participants were products of boarding schools. Luther Standing Bear, for example, a Brule Sioux, had attended Carlisle, and had worked at a variety of non-Indian occupations. He says he decided to join the show in 1902 on a dare to show he could succeed at that too. His wife, who was half Sioux and half White, and who toured with the show, was elated with the idea of traveling in Europe.

Every ocean voyage was a trial for the Indians. They expressed great fear of crossing "the big water" and experienced terror in rough seas and continuous sea sickness - not unlike the Whites. Black Elk described the fear convincingly:

"They put us on a very big fire-boat, so big that when I first saw it, I could hardly believe it; and when it sent forth a voice, I was frightened... Afterwhile I could see nothing but water, water, water... I thought we must

385

drop off where the water ended; or maybe we might have to stop where the sky came down to the water...

"We were all in despair now and many were feeling so sick that they began to sing their death-songs" (Neihardt 1972:185).

Black Elk determined to die like a Lakota.

"When evening came, a big wind was roaring and the water thundered... Our women were crying and even some of the men cried, because it was terrible and they could do nothing... Afterwhile the Wasichus came and gave us things to tie around us so that we could float. I did not want to float. Instead, I dressed for death, putting on my best clothes that I wore in the show, and then I sang my death song... because if it was the end of our lives and we could do nothing, we wanted to die brave... so that our spirit relatives would not be ashamed of us" (Neihardt 1972:186).

Some, like Red Shirt, believed that if they crossed the ocean they would waste away, and he kept checking his flesh each day to see if he was losing any. This fear of crossing the ocean - a fear shared by many of the Whites yesterday and today as they fly across - was shared by most of the Indians on all the voyages.

Everywhere in Europe the Indian people were tourists as well as entertainers. As one reporter related for his readers in 1887, "some of Buffalo Bill's Red Indians are 'doing' the sights of London. They have paid several visits to popular resorts, and despite their proverbial stoicism, they are as much attracted by the curiosities on view as the public are pleased by the ornate appearance of the visitors."[5] Wherever they traveled, the Indians enjoyed sights like the Tower of London, the Vatican, or the Gallery of Machines in Paris.

However, they were tourists with a distinctly non-Western perspective on the sights they saw. For the majority of these experiences we have no first hand accounts from Indian people, but we can glean considerable information from the reports on their behavior, especially when that behavior is seen from the perspective of their own culture. In particular one can see their well-bred politeness, which the British sometimes mistook for haughtiness, their pleasure at being honored, and the spiritual vision that colored perception.

On some occasions, Indians were taken into public by Buffalo Bill to get publicity for his show, but the Indians were given considerable freedom to explore on their own - a freedom that sometimes resulted in their being left on their own and lost in a strange country. "There is," noted one reporter, "apparently, no restraint imposed on the movements of either Indians or cross-breeds. The untutored children of the prairie stalk about in their gorgeously coloured blankets, and seem quite indifferent to the sensation they

386

are causing."[6] On the 1902 tour the British would occasionally see a blanket-clad figure in a pub.

In 1887 the Indians saw several plays, at one of which Red Shirt was given the place of honor in the Royal box, attention he clearly enjoyed. Social recognition was much more highly valued by these Indian people than economic profit, and public prestige was significant indeed. The Indians enjoyed other pleasures of the theater as well for "it was something of a novelty in the classic Lyceum to see Indian chiefs in the full panoply of war-paint, holding the scalp-fringed banner in one hand and eating sugar plums with the other."[7]

They rode along Piccadilly in a large carriage - to see and be seen - to the astonishment of onlookers. "Their feathered head-dress broke up agreeably the top-hatted monotony of all other strollers..." Red Shirt made a speech in Lakota at the Savage Club, and after observing the members practicing "savage" customs, offered to send them an historical peace pipe. He also noted the similarity between their collected trophies and the Indian practice of keeping scalps and captured weapons. He thanked them for the invitation and for receiving him "with the warm hand of friendship." Some of the troupe, apparently those who had been missionized, went to the Congregational Chapel in West Kensington where they sang "Nearer My God To Thee" in their own tongue. The Indians were so impressed by the Tower of London, they asked to return.[8] In Paris in 1889 Indian tourists visited the Eiffel Tower, while Chief Rocky Bear and his braves explored the crater of Mt. Vesuvius and saw Venice in a gondola.

A central event during the first tour was Queen Victoria's Golden Jubilee. The Queen requested two command performances, the first a private showing at Earl's Court, the second at Windsor Castle on 20 June, the day before the event that climaxed the Jubilee. Black Elk left us an intriguing eye-witness account of the Jubilee from an Indian perspective. When Queen Victoria went to the first command performance of the Wild West Show on 12 May, Black Elk said "One day we were told that Majesty was coming. I did not know what that was at first, but I learned afterward. It was Grandmother England...." (Neihardt 1972:187). Black Elk was chosen to dance for the Queen

"because I was young and limber then and could dance many ways. We stood right in front of Grandmother England. She was little but fat and we liked her because she was good to us. After we had danced, she spoke to us. She said something like this: 'I am sixty-seven years old. All over the world I have seen all kinds of people; but to-day I have seen the best-looking people I know. If you *belonged* to me, I would not let them take you in a show like this...' She shook hands with all of us. Her hand was very little and soft" (Neihardt 1972:187; emphasis mine).

For the second command performance, the Indians were transported in gold-trimmed coaches and taken to Windsor where they performed with the rest of the troupe, but they were also tourist-observers of the event. In Black Elk's eyes

"we went to see the Grandmother. They put us in some of those shining wagons and took us to a very beautiful place where there was a very big house with sharp, pointed towers on it. There were many seats built high in a circle, and these were just full of Wasichus who were all pounding their heels and yelling: 'Jubilee! Jubilee! Jubilee!' I never heard what this meant" (Neihardt 1972:188).

Black Elk's description of Queen Victoria's entry to the Jubilee celebration is especially worth noting for both its perception and detail:

"They put us together in a certain place at the bottom of the seats. First there appeared a beautiful black wagon with two black horses, and it went all around the show place. I heard that Grandmother's grandson, a little boy, was in that wagon. Next came a beautiful black wagon with four gray horses. On each of the two right hand horses there was a rider, and a man walked, holding the front left hand horse. I heard that some of Grandmother's relatives were in this wagon. Next came eight buckskin horses, two by two, pulling a shining black wagon. There was a rider on each right-hand horse and a man walked, holding the front left hand horse. There were soldiers, with bayonets, facing outward all around this wagon. Now all the people in the seats were roaring and yelling 'Jubilee!' and 'Victoria!' Then we saw Grandmother England again. She was sitting in the back of the wagon and two women sat in the front, facing her. Her dress was all shining and so were the horses. She looked like a fire coming" (Neihardt 1972:188-89).

Buffalo Bill presented Red Shirt to the Queen, and he spoke to her in a fashion worthy of any fine diplomat. "It pleased all their hearts that she came to them as a mother and not with all her warriors about her." Queen Victoria's kindness pleased them all "and every one of his young men resolved that she should be their great mother."[9] Indeed, the Indian people sat up all night talking about her.

Although he did not comprehend the nature of "majesty" or "jubilee" from his own cultural context, the drama of the moment roused Black Elk and the other Indian people. On both occasions that they met Queen Victoria, the Indians expressed appreciation. At Windsor Castle they showed their respect and admiration in Plains Indian style. "We sent up a great cry," Black Elk said, "and our women made the tremolo." There was poetry in Black Elk's description of Queen Victoria's entrance in golden wagon as "like a fire coming"; but his political assessment was naive. He was a man questing for salvation for his defeated and disunified people, and so he was gratified by her friendliness as a European leader. "We liked Grandmother England because we could see that she was a fine woman, and she was good to us. Maybe if she had been our Grandmother, it would have been better for our people" (Neihardt 1972:189). Perceptive as he was, Black Elk misses the impact of that potent phrase in her remarks to the Indians, quoted earlier: "If you belonged to me..." He was not aware, of course, that Queen Victoria and the other personages who welcomed them with such courtesy and friendliness probably did so because they were part of a great public spectacle. Nor could he know that Queen Victoria, herself, at that very moment, presided over an empire in which the native people in places like Africa and India wer treated very much like the colonized Indians in the United States whose fate he bemoaned.

Luther Standing Bear was a Sioux who went on the last European tour, 1902-1906, and who, unlike most of the Indians in the Wild West Show, was a boarding school graduate. He approached the tour quite differently as a tourist. He had read widely about Europe and had developed a perspective that came less out of Sioux culture than out of Western society. His comments contrast basically with those of Black Elk and Red Shirt who saw the world in fundamentally different ways. Standing Bear recalled:

"I was sorry to leave this city, because I had been given a chance to see many wonderful sights and visit many interesting places. I recall that one day I visited the house where all the toys were kept with which Queen Victoria had played as a child, and I was shown where all her jewelry was on display. I also visited Westminster Abbey, one of the most beautiful churches in the world, and a very historic spot. The King's palace was also a place of great interest. So I, for one, was sorry when the show came to an end in London, and we had to leave the beautiful Olympia Theater" (Standing Bear 1975:259).

Indians commented on the friendliness of Europeans toward them wherever they went. There were, of course, gaping onlookers who saw them as curiosities. Indeed, newspapers often commented in stereotypic terms about their gaudy savagery. Black Elk and Red Shirt experienced the friendliness of royalty and aristocrats, as indicated above. Standing Bear gave a surprising picture of the contact with more ordinary people and the Indians' appreciation of it.

"The English people were very good to us. They would invite the Indians to their homes and give them plenty to eat. One lady in particular stands out in my memory. She was of middle age, and she always came twice a week to see the Indians. She always carried a pocketbook made of wire - one of the kind the white people call a 'mesh-bag.' You could look right through and see what was in it. In this pocketbook she always carried gold pieces. She would take out men or women - sometimes an entire family - and treat them until her pocketbook was empty. The Indians soon 'got wise' to this particular woman, and thought it a great treat to go out with her, because, if they happened to see a pin or a ring that sparkled and took their fancy, she would always buy it for them" (Standing Bear 1975:258-59).

Black Elk found special friendship in Paris. He went to England with the first tour but missed the departure of the show from Manchester and was stranded, traveling in Europe with another show, Mexican Joe's, for $1 a day. Mexican Joe's traveled around Europe from France to Germany and probably Italy. "There was a Wasichu girl who came to the show very often. She liked me and took me home to see her father and mother. They liked me, too, and were good to me. I could not talk their language. I made signs, and the girl learned a few Lakota words" (Neihardt 1972:190-91).

While with Mexican Joe, Black Elk became ill. When the show returned to Paris it was 1889, and he was so desperately homesick and physically ill he could not perform. His friends in Paris took him home and nursed him back to health. While staying with them he went into a trance and traveled home in a vision. He remained in the trance, "dead" for three days, and his friends were preparing to purchase a coffin in which to bury him when he came out of the trance. Fortunately Pahuska was in Paris again on his second tour of Europe. "... he was glad to see me. He had all his people give me three cheers. Then he asked me if I wanted to be in the show or if I wanted to go home. I told him I was sick to go home." Cody fed him, paid his way home, had him escorted to the boat for the ocean voyage, and gave him $90 (Neihardt 1972:190-91).

Homesickness was not unusual for these European travelers for whom kinship ties were central to their lives. However, all were not as fortunate as Black Elk. Homesickness, illness, and being stranded caused great distress. Of the seventy-two healthy young men that Cody and Salsbury recruited from Pine Ridge for the second tour, according to Carolyn Foreman, five died and seven others were sent home with shattered health. These figures seem to reflect the deadliest part of the tour, the stop in Barcelona, Spain, in December 1889. An epidemic gripped the city and the combination of influenza, cholera, and typhoid struck the Wild West particularly hard. Annie Oakley was desperately ill, and the popular announcer for the show, Frank Richmond, died. Even harder hit were the Indians. Estimates of the numbers who died and were buried in a desolate, windswept cemetery in Barcelona vary from four to ten (Foreman 1943:199-210; Burke 1974:192).

An Indian in one tour, White Horse, related a tale of cruelty and starvation. The *New York Herald* reported that "for months past the warriors have been straggling back in groups of three and five, sick and disgusted with their treatment while abroad. Fully two-thirds of the original band have returned to the country." However, an investigation by the consular staff in Berlin revealed no mistreatment in Cody's show. The Bureau of Indian Affairs briefly stopped the recruitment of Indians for shows, and Cody and Burke returned with all the Indians to refute the charges. All the Indians who have left written records have testified uniformly to the good treatment they received in Wild Bill's show. Numerous wild west shows, medicine shows, and circuses used Indian people as performers, and they may have accounted for much of the problem (Burke 1974:198; Foreman 1943:199-210; Russell 1970:37).

Some of the Indians' cultural experiences in Europe elicited responses that reflected the values and assumptions of the tribal world from which they came and the attempts to understand a different world through them.

On the 1887 tour of Great Britain, the Indians saw "Faust" at the Lyceum with the well-known actress Miss Ellen Terry. The Indians, who did not believe in a hell, were unimpressed by the fantastic scenes of Hades and, as their interpreter reported laconically, "took it for what it was worth" as a white man's vision. However in his reaction to Faust and to his experience of a service at Westminster Abbey, Red Shirt revealed a central aspect of the cultural lens through which he was seeing the world of England. To him the play was "like a great dream." At Westminster Abbey, Red Shirt felt that he received a vision. Clearly he was seeking, in his own way, to comprehend this new world. Though the reporters denigrated his reflections on this quest and wrote about it condescendingly, he tried to convey his perceptions to them honestly. He told them that "the Great Spirit speaks to me sometimes since I have been here."[10] To a Lakota like Red Shirt or Black Elk, knowledge, wisdom, understanding were received through visions. Though they might realistically and pragmatically observe life in London, essential understanding came through the spirit world. Knowing this, our comprehension of his experiences at Westminster Abbey and the theater gain a new dimension.

"The white man lodges for the great Spirit, whose pinnacles reach the sky, and which have stood for more seasons than the red man reckon, all strike me with a terrible wonder, and the Great Spirit speaks to me sometimes since I have been here. When I was in the Great Spirit lodge where the kings are buried (Westminster Abbey), I laid may face upon my hands. The words of the preacher I did not know but they sounded like the soft winds through a leafy forest and my eyelids were heavy. Then I heard soft music and sweet voices, and a great cloud came down towards me, and when it nearly reached me, it opened and I saw in a blaze of light the girls with wings and they beckoned me. And I was so certain that what I saw was true that I called out to my young men who were with me 'Come and see what this is,' and the young men replied, 'You have been dreaming.' But what I saw was true, for when I looked round the great lodge afterwards I saw on the walls the same girls with wings as I saw in my dreams. Our people will wonder at these things when we return to the Indian Reservation and tell them what we have seen."[11]

Some reported this interview without comment, while others implied the man went to sleep in the service as some men will do, but none of the reporters explored or indicated they understood this perception of experience in England through visions as a natural but profound expression of Plains Indian culture.

The demeanor of Red Shirt and the other Indians was a topic of great interest to the press. Reporters saw the Indians either through a lens created by romantic literature such as that produced by James Fenimore Cooper or Capt. Mayne Reid or by the stereotype of savage. One reporter described the "imperturbable self possession" of Red Shirt while another saw him as "being as solemn, as philosophical, and as dignified in his demeanor as the Last of the Mohicans himself." Others saw this self-control and dignity differently. One thought "they seem to regard their white admirers as belonging to a inferior race, and seldom waste a glance upon them."[12] Finally, some, unable to see beyond exteriors, saw them as just savages: "These dusky Indians, with their unearthy streaks of colour on the faces, and their weird, monotonous, and hollow cries as they ride past, fine as many of the faces are, yet remind us of the earlier forms of savage man whence we have evolved..."[13]

These stereotypic images prevented such observers from deriving new insight into the nature of Indian life. Seen in a larger sense, however, this dignified and taciturn demeanor reflected the essential character of human relationships from the point of view of Plains people. This character can be seen in those instances where Indian people were called upon to act as representatives of their people to European people. The best examples of this were when Red Shirt and others were called upon to meet and converse with royalty, aristocrats, or major political figures, to comment on European institutions such as parliaments, or the Vatican, or Westminster Abbey, or on cultural activities. Such a public and diplomatic role was not new to any Indian who had achieved some stature in his own tribe, for eloquence in speaking, tact in political discussion, and ability relating to representatives of other political bodies were well-developed skills.

Red Shirt, for example, became the focus of much attention. The aristocracy of England visited in his tent in the Indian camp at Earl's Court. Political figures asked his opinions and used contact with him to get publicity. Newspapers used his conversations with the great Liberal Gladstone as the take-off point for comment on political issues in Great Britain. The *Leeds Mercury* indicated the extent of this attention on May 7 when it said:

"Red Shirt, the Sioux Chief, is being lionised in a manner that might turn the heads of untutored savages less grave and serious-minded, but he accepts the honour of visits from the distinguished with imperturbable self-possession. He has had the satisfaction of an interview with Mr. Gladstone, and now the Prince of Wales has chatted with him and drawn him into a lively vein of conversation. This will inevitably lead to Red Shirt being courted extensively by London fashion, and perhaps he may figure at parties and receptions as a sensational personage in society, putting a few scalps in his belt to show how fierce and brave he was in tomahawking days."

The Indians expressed little awe in reaction to royalty though they were presented to Queen Victoria, King Edward VII, the Kaiser of Germany, and Pope Leo XIII. One might have expected a very negative response since Plains Indians found the idea of great authority to be obnoxious. Had the behavior of the royalty that the Indians came in contact with been haughty or condescending, the reaction might have been quite different. In most Plains tribes, certainly the Sioux, power was dispersed as widely as possible and leaders had no real authority. Consequently they placed great emphasis on a sense of self-worth and of responsible individual behavior. Leaders led by example, persuasion, and personal influence based on individual achievement and characteristics like generosity, kindness, self-control, wisdom. The Indians' reactions to royalty and to other personages who sought them out reflects these beliefs (Neihardt 1970, 1972; Hassrick 1964:3-61; Walker 1982:14-71). However, in those areas where Indians were critical of European society, particularly on the maldistribution of wealth, the Indians who left records appear not to have associated the royalty and politicans who lionized them with the governance of societies that produced such poor.

On subsequent tours the Indians on the tour met royalty, but the response of Indians like Standing Bear appears to have been somewhat different. Standing Bear in 1902 was asked by Col. Cody to dance directly in front of the king. He observed that King Edward VII's party came "all very elegantly dressed, the gentlemen in full dress, with silk hats, and the ladies in very low-necked dresses with long trains" (Standing Bear 1975:255). How very different a perception from that of Black Elk's of Queen Victoria. As Standing Bear, who was in charge of the Indians, described the performance:

"Everything worked splendidly. When it came time for the Indians to come in with their village in the center of the arena, we started the dance in which I was to appear before the King of England. I had a beautiful lance, and as the dance proceeded I worked over toward the King's box. There I shook the lance in his face and danced my very prettiest, you may be sure. The King had been very dignified thus far and had not even smiled. But when I got down to doing my fancy steps and gave a few Sioux yells, he had to smile in spite of himself. I saw that I had made a hit with him and was very happy."

Later the King went back to meet the troupe as he had done in 1887.
Standing Bear said, "We shook hands, although neither of us said a word. But
I had the honor of being introduced to King Edward the Seventh, the monarch
of Great Britain" (Standing Bear 1975:255-56).

Red Shirt was the focus of considerable attention in the 1887 season from
members of the House of Commons, William Ewart Gladstone, the Prince of
Wales, and Queen Victoria. In his responses to them he demonstrated his
excellent training as a Sioux and as a Plains Indian in diplomacy. Gladstone,
the great English Liberal politician, visited the Wild West show, as anybody
who was anybody was doing, late in April, before the opening in London. He
was introduced to Red Shirt as the leader of the Indian contingent and chatted
lightly with him, inquiring urbanely of him how he found the weather in
England and if he could see the resemblance, based on kinship, between the
English and their American cousins. At first Red Shirt seemed reticent and
short with Gladstone. One reporter wrote:

> "Red Shirt, possibly jealous of a chief greater than himself, took in Mr.
> Gladstone's measurements with a glance, drew his blanket closely about him,
> and exhibited a stolid reserve when questioned. Presently, however, in
> response to his interpreter, he answered more freely. Mr. Gladstone asked
> him what he thought of the English climate, [and he] said that he had not
> much to complain of in that respect so far.
> "'Well', said Gladstone, 'Do you see those similarities between Englishmen
> and Americans which might be expected to exist between kinsmen and
> brothers?' This time Red Shirt answered without loss of a moment that he
> didn't 'know so much about them being kinsmen and brothers' - a reply
> which created a burst of laughter, but... the Indian chief... never a muscle
> in his face relaxed, and he stood like a marble statue."[14]

Several slighty different versions of this encounter appeared with the
reporters, sometimes making Red Shirt's response appear to mean that he
didn't know anything about English-United States relations and sometimes to
mean that he replied sarcastically that he couldn't see resemblance or good
relationship between them. We get a better sense of what happened from Red
Shirt himself.

In his version he observed Gladstone, the man, and as a Sioux, saw that he
was without the symbols of great stature. However, as they talked, his
speaking ability, a trait greatly admired and needed in tribal culture and
intertribal relations, convinced Red Shirt that he was speaking with a great
man.

"When I saw the great White Chief I thought he was a great man. When I heard him speak then I felt sure he was a great man. But the White Chief is not as the big men of our tribes. He wore no plumes and no decorations. He had none of his young men (warriors) with him, and only that I heard him talk he would have been to me as other white men. But my brother (Mr. Gladstone) came to see me in my wigwam as a friend, and I was glad to see the great White Chief, for though my tongue was tied in his presence my heart was full of friendship. After he went away they told me that half of this great nation of white men have adopted him as their chief. Thus I am right, for if he were not both good and wise, so many young men of his nation would never have taken him for their leader."[15]

Further the *Times* reported him as replying diplomatically that his experience of the climate was insufficient to judge and that he had little knowledge of United States-British relations.

As a result of Gladstone's visit, numerous members of Parliament visited Red Shirt at the Indian village in the American Exhibition. "'Red Shirt,' whose intelligence is of a very high order, is a shrewd observer, and his good sense has been demonstrated again and again in his replies to the questions put to him,"[16] a newspaper reported. Shortly thereafter the Prince and Princess of Wales came for a special performance on 5 May. They watched a private performance and "The Prince, carried away by the excitement, rose from his seat. leaned over the front of the box, and remained standing during the greater portion of the performance, which lasted over an hour and a half."[17] On meeting them Red Shirt again acquitted himself well. In response to the Princess' greeting he said "tell the Great Chief's wife it makes my heart glad to hear her words of welcome." When the Prince gave Red Shirt the contents of his cigarette case, a somewhat condescending gesture, Red Shirt responded as a Sioux by generously distributing the cigarettes to all his followers. Red Shirt clearly rose to occasions of this sort in a poised, graceful and thoroughly Lakota diplomatic manner. To the Prince he said "it made his heart glad that one so high above other men men should visit him. Though his skin was red and the pale-faced chief's was white, their hearts were one."[18] As he spoke he repeatedly placed his hand over his heart to show his sincerity.

In a visit to the House of Commons Red Shirt showed the same composure and tact though he was a bit more outspoken. He sat through "a dreary debate" with "grave patience," a practice no doubt learned in Lakota councils where such patience was a requisite courtesy. When asked what he thought of the operation of Parliament, "he said he did not think much of it, laws being passed much more quickly in his country than in this."[19] Of course Red Shirt was a leader in a nation much smaller than that of England where great decisions could be and were made in councils where leaders discussed issues until they reached a consensus.

395

One can see a similar perception of Europe from a Lakota point of view in the attitude of Rocky Bear, the Sioux spokesman on the second tour of Europe, 1889-1892. French reporters paid to Rocky Bear some of the same kind of attention that Red Shirt received earlier in England. The Wild West went first to Paris and set up camp at Parc du Neuilly. Salsbury, Burke, and Cody timed the show to coincide with the Universal Exposition and to garner large, ready-made audiences.

As in London, Indian people were free to explore Paris on their own. A reporter from *Le Petit Journal*, who had discovered that Rocky Bear, while strolling about Paris, had witnessed part of a political meeting, interviewed him. He found Rocky Bear lounging with four other Indians around the central fire of a tent in traditional fashion, companionably smoking and conversing. It seems that Rocky Bear and Salsbury had been walking about Paris when the Indian was attracted by the noise coming out of a ground floor school room window. He saw a room with about 2000 people in it all of whom were smoking pipes. One was climbing on a table "making grand gestures," another looked on desperately at the proceedings, while a fourth was rapping on the table with a baton. All 2000 people seemed to be shouting at the same time from all sides.[20]

Rocky Bear said to Salsbury: "What is it they want? One would think it was a whole troupe of birds in the same tree all singing at once." Salsbury replied that they were gathered to decide the choice of a deputy to parliament - a chief. When asked what he thought of the process Rocky Bear responded by comparing the process of decisionmaking in his own band to that of the French. Since the reporter seems to have added his own interpretive twist to the way he stated Rocky Bear's answer, it is difficult to know if all the attitudes that were expressed were Rocky Bear's. Yet the essential message comes through clearly. In a similar situation, we, said Rocky Bear, seat ourselves around the family circle. We pass the pipe from hand to hand, and each in turn gives his opinion. An Indian would not speak before another person had finished. On the other hand, in the French political meeting he saw, "you smoke all at the same time, you speak all at the same time, and you understand anyhow."[21]

In the case of both Rocky Bear and Red Shirt, their ability to speak aptly about what they saw in Europe, to assess activities in the House of Commons or in a French election for deputy, and in particular, the perspective from which they viewed Europe all reflect the Lakota approach to political life. The upbringing of a young Lakota stressed the qualities we see so clearly in the behavior of Indian people like Red Shirt or Rocky Bear. Although stereotypes of Plains Indians emphasize bloodthirstiness and war, the characteristics the Lakota encouraged most were self-control, generosity, tact, wisdom, and responsibility toward the poor or helpless as well as courage and the skills required for a warrior. Those who achieved such character the Sioux respected and accorded the highest honor, to be *wichasha yatapika*. These were "men whom all praise," that is, men about whom no bad things could be said. They embodied the ideal characteristics. It was these men who were the role models for the young. Proper behavior as well as public recognition of it were major aspects of achieving that goal.

There were abundant opportunities to practice such behavior. Lakota leaders usually had extensive experience in councils and in intertribal diplomacy where they were expected to exhibit these characteristics. A good leader maintained self control if offended. He listened carefully and politely to others in council, and, after a suitable period of time had passed, offered his own opinion without interruption. Long periods of silence between speakers were a required courtesy, and one showed in this way that they weighed another's words thoughtfully. It demonstrated respect. Polite, non-aggressive behavior was the norm in formal settings like band or tribal councils as well as in diplomatic councils between tribes. On numerous occasions, then, a young Lakota had the opportunity to observe and practice the requisite behavior. Red Shirt, Rocky Bear, Black Elk, and others showed in their quiet demeanor, their stately bearing, their politeness, their ability to converse with great personages that they were well-trained Lakota (Hassrick 1964:32-61,296-339; Walker 1982:14-71). No wonder, then, that Rocky Bear seemed so amazed by the behavior of Frenchmen at a political meeting.

One of the most extraordinary experiences of the tours occurred when the Wild West went to Rome in 1890. Monsignor O'Connell of the American College in Rome, supported by Archbishop Corrigan of New York, arranged for the troupe to have an audience with Pope Leo XIII on March the third. Historians have tended to play up the farcical elements of the encounter and have seen the Indians behavior as superstitious and primitive or as amusingly curious. These interpretations indicate a lack of knowledge about the religious beliefs or values of the Indians themselves. Since vision and the relationship to the spirits were primary aspects of Plains Indians life, a proposed visit to the man believed by millions of Christians to be God's vicar on earth was a grand occasion. Though the concept of a person who interceded between God and people was a foreign one to Lakota thinking, the idea that such a man had received the power of God was bound to be an attractive one to Indian people. John Burke, the manager of the show, was a Catholic, and he determined to insure that the Indians would engage in the proper dignified behavior. In particular he seemed afraid the Indians would give "war whoops" when they saw the Pope or fling themselves into some pagan rite. The Indians, of course, saw such greetings when the men cried out and the woman gave the tremolo, as they did for Queen Victoria, as showing the greatest respect. As Nate Salsbury, Cody's partner in the show, observed:

"For a week before this day, John Burke who is a devout Catholic had worked on the Indians to impress them with the solemnity of the occasion we were about to assist in celebrating. He impressed them with the idea that they were going to see the Representative of God on Earth, and to those of them who had been under Catholic instruction at the Reservation, the coming event was of great interest" (Salsbury 1955:212).

The scene was a study in extraordinary contrasts. The Pope entered carried on the Papal Throne through the Sistine Chapel. "The sunlight fell upon the lines of glittering steel, nodding plumes, golden chairs, shimmering robes of silk, and all the blazing emblems of pontifical power and glory," said one onlooker (Burke 1893:244). He passed along a corridor lined by "a host of savages in war-paint, feathers, and blankets, carrying tomahawks and knives... Rocky Bear led the Sioux warriors, who brought up the rear. They were painted in every color that Indian imagination could devise. Every man carried something with which to make big medicine in the presence of the great medicine man sent by the great spirit" (Burke 1893:244).

As the Pope passed the Indians "Rocky Bear knelt and made the sign of the cross. The pontiff leaned affectionately toward the rude groups and blessed them. He seemed to be touched by the sight" (Burke 1893:244).

As the troupe was leaving they demonstrated that cultural curiosity and condecension works both ways. Salsbury signaled the Wild West to withdraw from the Sistine Chapel. The Indians came face to face with the Swiss Guard and found themselves as amused by their costumes as Europeans were of those of the Indians. Salsbury related that "Indians rarely express their amusement at anything by laughter, but when they caught sight of the variegated colors that make up the uniforms of the Swiss guards their faces took on a broad grin, which deepened into guttural shouts of laughter when told that the men who wore uniforms were soldiers on the pay of His Holiness" (Salsbury 1955:213).

The Indians were very intrigued with the Vatican. "... they were incredulous that so many people could be housed up in one place, and wanted to go exploring on their own account, and when restrained, they said they did not think much of God's Representative if his house was too good for anybody to go into. They compared the hospitality of their teepees with the etiquette of the Papal Court to the advantage of the savage" (Salsbury 1955:213). To Plains Indians, the worst thing one could call a man was stingy, and hospitality was mandatory.

We do not know if the Indians were as "touched" by the blessing of the Pope as he was by the sight of them, but his failure to provide proper hospitality had no doubt shaken their confidence somewhat. An event at the camp when they returned served to remove all belief in his powers. An Indian who had been left at the camp because he was not feeling well had died while the others visited the Pope. Salsbury observed that

"The death of this man had a peculiar effect on the Indians' minds, for they immediately called a council among themselves, and sending for Burke demanded to know why the Representative of God had not protected their comrade while they were away from him, and if he had so much power on earth why he had not exerted himself to shield their comrade from death in their absence" (Salsbury 1955:213).

Burke labored to restore the Indians belief in papal power, but to no avail. The Indians told him "that god should send another man to represent him if he expected the Indians to believe anything the missionaries might tell them in the future" (Salsbury 1955:213).

Power was a central preoccupation of the people in Plains Indian societies, but their definiton of it differed dramatically from that of the followers of the Pope. Little was more significant in an individual's or a tribe's life. Without power a person was insignificant; with power he or she could do almost anything. Most important of all, seeking power was seeking "the eyes to see and the strength to understand" that a Lakota might be like the Great Spirit, Wakan Tanka. This power, this understanding, this oneness with everything else was sought through dreams or visions because, according to Black Elk, "sometimes dreams are wiser than waking" (Neihardt 1982:8). For Plains Indians this was an individual undertaking which involved direct contact with the spirit world rather than reaching God through the intercession of a man like the Pope (Brown 1972; Neihardt 1970, 1972; Hassrick 1964:245-310; Walker 1982:65-147).

People sought this power to heal, to succeed in warfare or hunting, to undergo a great ordeal, to attract buffalo to the hunters, or to insure that the whole people as a group would flourish. Seeking power was seeking rapport with a universe that was filled with power so that one could become one with it. Black Elk in his vision sought to focus the powers of the four quarters of the universe into himself that he might have the understanding to make his people strong and the strength to make them flourish (Neihardt 1982:17-40).

Obtaining the trust of power was a great and serious responsibility. Plains people held those who had a vision and received power and understanding in high esteem. They expected such people to use their power for the good of others. The Sioux saw the Sun Dance, where a number of men sought visions, as a quest for mutual benefit for a better life for all the people.

In this context, the Indians' rejection of the Pope was a logical conclusion based on their own concepts about the nature of power and the responsible use of it. From their point of view he either had no great power because he let their comrade die, or he was not a proper representative of God because he refused to use the power he had to aid another.

The discriminating view the Indians had of Europe and Europeans emerged directly from their tribal cultures. Indians, not unlike observers from other non-Western cultures, had to make sense of this dissimilar world in their own terms. The result was a perspective on Europe that is engaging, perceptive, and distinct. Who could forget the image of Queen Victoria as little and fat, with small, soft hands, arriving in a Jubilee carriage "like a fire coming." Or the rejection of the Pope because he failed to use his powers in a practical, generous, and humane way. Indians who toured with the Wild West could enjoy the best bitter in a London pub, mingle with royalty in a dignified and courteous fashion, and yet retain their own values as the basis for their "vision" of life.

NOTES

1. *The Sheffield Leader* (England), 5 May 1887.
2. *Morning Post* (location missing), 12 April 1887, Cody Scrapbooks, Vol. 1, Western History Department, Denver Public Library, Denver, Colorado (hereafter cited as W.H.C.-D.P.L.).
3. Cody, Portfolio F1-11, W.H.C.-D.P.L.
4. Kills Enemy Alone to Little Whirlwind, 1889, Ms. 31, John L. Champe Collection, Manuscript Division, Nebraska State Historical Society, Lincoln, Nebraska.
5. *Newcastle* (England) *Daily Chronicle*, 4 April 1887.
6. *Newcastle* (England) *Daily Chronicle*, 4 April 1887.
7. *Era*, 23 April 1887, Cody Scrapbooks, Vol. I, W.H.C.-D.P.L.
8. *Huddersfield Daily Chronicle*, n.d., Cody Scrapbooks, microfilm edition, reel 4, W.H.C.-D.P.L.; Pall Mall Gazette, April 26, 1887.
9. *Derby Mercury*, n.d., Cody Scrapbooks, microfilm edition, reel no. 4.
10. *Era*, 23 April 1887, Cody Scrapbooks, Vol. 1, W.H.C.-D.P.L.; *Daily Post* (location illegible), 6 May 1887, ibid.
11. *Daily Post* (location illegible, 8 May 1887, Cody Scrapbooks, Vol. 1, W.H.C.-D.P.L.
12. *Leeds Mercury*, 7 May 1887, Cody Scrapbooks, Vol. 1, W.H.C.-D.P.L.; *Observer* (no location given), 24 April 1887, ibid.; clipping, no date, no name, ibid., p. 41.
13. *Sunday Chronicle* (no location), 17 October 1887, Cody Scrapbooks, Vol. 1, W.H.C.-D.P.L.
14. *Daily Telegraph* (no location), 29 April 1887, Cody Scropbooks, vol. 1, W.H.C.-D.P.L.
15. *The Times* (London), 29 April 1887.
16. *Plymouth News*, 5 May 1887.
17. *Daily Chronicle* (no location), 6 May 1887, Cody Scrapbooks, Vol. 1, W.H.C.-D.P.L.
18. *Morning Post*, 5 May 1887, ibid.
19. *Leeds Mercury*, Cody Scrapbooks, microfilm edition, reel no. 4, W.H.C.-D.P.L.
20. *Le Petit Journal* (Paris), 7 October 1889.
21. *Le Petit Journal* (Paris), 7 October 1889.

REFERENCES CITED

Manuscripts
Cody, Wyoming. Buffalo Bill Historical Center. William F. Cody Scrapbooks.
Denver, Colorado. Denver Public Library, Western History Collection. William F. Cody Collection. Nate Salsbury Scrapbooks.
Lincoln, Nebraska. Nebraska State Historical Society. Manuscript Division. John L. Champe Collection.
U.S., Department of Interior, Bureau of Indian Affairs. Annual Reports of the Commission of Indian Affairs, 1887-1906.

Secondary Sources
Burke, J.M.
    1893   Buffalo Bill from Prairie to Palace. Chicago: Rand McNally.
    1974   Buffalo Bill, the Noblest Whiteskin. New York: Capricorn Books.
Brown, J. E.
    1972   The Sacred Pipe. New York: Penguin Books.
Demallie, R.J.
    1984   The Sixth Grandfather. Lincoln: University of Nebraska Press
Foreman, C.
    1943   Indians Abroad, 1493-1938. Norman: University of Oklahoma Press.
Hassrick, R. B.
    1964   The Sioux. Norman: University of Oklahoma Press.
Linderman, F.
    1974   Pretty Shield, Medicine Woman of the Crow. Lincoln: University of Nebraska Press.
Neihardt, J. G.
    1970   When the Tree Flowered. Lincoln: University of Nebraska Press.
    1972   Black Elk Speaks. New York: Pocket Books.
Russell, D.
    1960   The Lives and Legends of Buffalo Bill. Norman: University of Oklahoma Press.
    1970   The Wild West; a History of the Wild West Shows. Fort Worth: Amon Carter Museum of Western Art.
Salsbury, N.
    1955   At the Vatican. Colorado Magazine of History.
Sell, H. B., and V. Weybright
    1955   Buffalo Bill and the Wild West. New York: Oxford University Press.
Standing Bear, L.
    1974   My People the Sioux. Lincoln: University of Nebraska Press.
Walsh, R. J., and M.S. Salsbury
    1928   The Making of Buffalo Bill. Indianapolis: Bobbs-Merrill.
Walker, J. R.
    1982   Lakota Society. R.J. DeMallie (ed.). Lincoln: University of Nebraska Press.

"THOSE RED-BRICK FACES":
EUROPEAN PRESS REACTIONS TO THE
INDIANS OF BUFFALO BILL'S WILD WEST SHOW

Daniele Fiorentino

In the spring of 1887 the Wild West Show of Buffalo Bill arrived for the first time in Europe. That year the American show performed only in the United Kingdom to come two years later to France for the World's Fair, and later on to Spain, Italy, Austria, Germany, and some other central and northern European countries.

Buffalo Bill's show met with the European audiences' favor. Thousands of Europeans went to the arenas where Colonel Cody and his troupe reenacted some of the most exciting events of the American West. Europeans were anxious to see a show which was expected to be as exciting as the books of James Fenimore Cooper and the Western novels by European writers such as Gustave Aimard in France and Karl May in Germany, that had had so much success among European readers. The Indians traveling with the show received special attention by European audiences. Many Europeans had a chance to see Native Americans for the first time.

The European press fueled this great excitement. Newspapers had special reporters sent to the places of arrival of the American troupe, and to the arenas where the show was being enacted. Journalists reported not only about the performances of the riders and snipers of the circus, but also, and one could say mainly, about the Indians, their appearance, their life-style, their culture. Some reporters toured the encampments, set next to the arenas, where the Indians pitched their tipis. They wrote about the Indians' life-style in the attempt of reviving in the readers' minds the literary scenes of the Old West. But journalists also echoed the widespread popular concepts concerning the indigenous populations of North America in the effort of pleasing their readers' expectations. Popular stereotypes mixed with the "scientific" interpretation in the articles dealing with the Indians.

Direct contact with the men of the Great American Plains provoked different reactions among reporters, who were also influenced by the readings of the American West's novels and by the then dominant stereotypes of the American Indian. If the French and English newspapermen appeared to be better informed than the Italian and the German ones, they nevertheless approached the Indians with certain biases typical of the European attitude toward the American Indian.

Journalists were influenced by the myth of the noble savage and by the Romantic vision of the Indian as a dying race; but they were also affected by the negative stereotypes generated by colonists' narratives and by the then flourishing doctrines of racial superiority. The journalists' attitude in approach-

403

ing the Indians proved to be contradictory.

They saw the Indians during the show as noble warriors bent by the adverse destiny which had made them the last representatives of a disappearing race. But they spoke of the Indians as savages and beast-like people once they approached them out of the show. In both these reactions it is possible to detect the influence of the most widespread stereotypes concerning the Indians in nineteenth century Europe. The Eurocentric attitude usually overwhelmed any other sentiment. When confronted directly with the Indian life-style reporters often concluded that these men were savages with "impressive red-brick faces," who go around "almost naked, ... eating raw meat."

Contact did not much to change European beliefs concerning the Indians. The Indians remained "savages," even though they were savages to be taken care of. The paternal attitude of the "civilized" European toward his "uncivilized" brethren remained. The European image of the Native American formed on the reports of travelers and colonists, on the speculations of scientists and philosophers and on the popular dime-novels of the West was always present in the writings of European newspapers' reporters.

The Enlightenment had represented the Indian as a noble savage. So had Romanticism. But these two currents of thought used this image as a means to criticize their own social system. The savage was nothing but the abstract ideal these thinkers had of man. The Indian was to the representatives of Enlightenment and Romanticism the exact opposite of the most degraded representatives of European society. It is not by chance that by the end of the eighteenth century European literature transformed the noble savage "... from a man of reason and good sense into a man of emotion and sensibility" (Berkhofer 1979:78). That is from the ideal of the Enlightenment to that of Romanticism.

It was Romanticism that favored the development of the image of a race rapidly passing away when confronted with civilization (Honour 1976:316-17; Berkhofer 1979:88). This image was widespread in the United States as well, and was very alive at the time the Wild West toured Europe (Dippie 1982:201-25). The Enlightenment's and Romanticism's views of the Indian relied however on the concept of the Indian as belonging to nature. Rousseau, Voltaire and Diderot found in the Indian all the positive aspects of man in his state of nature, as opposed to the civilized man of European societies. Another attitude developed in Europe toward the end of the eighteenth century. It was the "scientific" belief of the innate inferiority of the American race. Jean Louis Leclerc Buffon and Cornelius de Pauw were the two scientists who layed the foundations of this theory (Gerbi 1955:57- 59).

Hegel promptly revived these beliefs, without any proof to support his statements. Joseph de Maistre, instead, brought the condescending approach toward the Indian to its height. To de Maistre, the Indian was the example of the degeneration of the human species. The Indian represented "... no doubt a type subsequent to... civilized man..." (Gerbi 1955:434). The Native American was a unique specimen, the basic prototype of the savage (Gerbi 1955:435).

By the middle of the nineteenth century another factor came into play. American writers of the West became widely famous, so as to be imitated by European writers. Following the success of James Fenimore Cooper, Gabriel Ferry and Gustave Aimard in France, Mayne Reid in England, and Karl May in Germany poured on European readers an incredible number of novels on the American West (Honour 1976:315; Berkhofer 1979:101). These novels had their good and bad Indians, and mythicized the West. It is interesting to notice, however, that the good Indians, being a minority, were usually those who had adopted European life-styles or who had at least resolved themselves to cooperate with the backwoodsman, who impersonated the Romantic ideal of the courageous pioneer. Influenced by these writings and still with the vivid images of Indians as portrayed by painters like Francisco Goya, Karl Bodmer, and Eugène Delacroix, who had depicted Indians with some romantic traits, European journalists got ready to welcome to Europe the Native Americans traveling with the Wild West. Their encounter with these people coming from the new continent confirmed many of the stereotypes be they positive or negative ones.

The first appearance of the Wild West Show in Europe was for the American Exhibition in London, in the spring of 1887. Many British journalists stationed at Earl's Court, in West Brompton, where the show was being played. They had a chance to observe the London crowd's excitement for the American show as well as Queen Victoria's Court participating in the event (Sell and Weybright 1955:157-161). The year 1887 was also Queen Victoria's Golden Jubilee and the Wild West made special performances for the Royal Family. Mr. William E. Gladstone as well went to Earl's Court where he met Red Shirt, a Sioux who took part in the show. When commenting upon the meetings between the Royal Family and the Indians, and about that between Gladstone and Red Shirt, English newspapers took a chance to describe in vivid colors the physical appearance and the attitudes of the American Indians.

The romantic, paternalistic approach to the Indian showed its persistence on these occasions as when: "The Princess took great interest in the papooses, staying several minutes to chat with a little fellow of two or three years, who was wrapped in a yellow blanket, and had his body painted in most gorgeous colors..." (*Daily News* (London) May 6, 1887).

The paint used by the Indians on their bodies and their dark skin, not to speak about their nudity, was what mostly impressed English reporters. The reporter of the *Daily News* at Earl's Court wrote:

"Some of them (of the Indians) had little else about them except paint; but the yellow, or blue, or black and blue pigments took the edge off an effect which might otherwise have shocked the anti-nudists of modern times"

(*Daily News* (London) May 10, 1887).

The marvel of seeing men painted in different colors and almost naked, was mitigated by the humor used to speak about them. Italian newspapers remarked the same thing noticing that fortunately the ladies believed the Indians to wear some kind of skin-colored overalls, otherwise great scandal would have ensued (*Il Messaggero* (Rome) February 22, 1890; *Il Corriere di Napoli* January 28-29, 1890).

Colors and physical appearance of the Indians were also among the main aspects of French newspapers' reports. When the company arrived in Le Havre in 1889 to move to Paris for the World's Fair, some journalists of the most popular Parisian newspapers rowed a whole morning to meet the ship with its colorful American cargo. The correspondent of *Le Petit Journal* wrote to Paris that he eventually had a chance to see the Indians only at sunset, but this was enough to recognize "... the red-brick faces of men and women, who were wrapped in the most colorful blankets" (*Le Petit Journal* (Paris) May 14, 1889).

French journalists actually showed a strong interest in the Indians. They considered them the real attraction of the whole company. These reporters believed the presence of Indian encampments close to the arena to be a great chance to study the habits of a different culture (*Le Petit Journal* (Paris) May 13, 1889; *Le Temps* (Paris) May 20, 1889). To another journalist it was not a circus but "... something more; it is ethnographic art, something like a live and bigger picture of the *Tour du Monde en 80 Jours*" (*Le Petit Journal* (Paris) May 20, 1889), as if Jules Verne had had a chance to actually see the people his hero Phineas Fogg had met on his incredible trip. But the comparison fits after all. As Verne had used his imagination to write a popular book so had the European audiences in order to figure what the real life of an Indian encampment was like.

French reporters showed mixed feelings when describing the Indians seen in the encampments. Their descriptions, although inspired by the stereotyped Romantic image of the Indian, often included condescending comments on the Native Americans' naive nature:

"... we took great pleasure in walking in the park where the Red-Skins had set their tents. A sympathetic and curious approach had already taken place between the Parisian Pale-Faces and those tall men, with red-brick faces, awful expressions, hooked noses and proud eyes, whom you will really please if you give them a set of cheap mirrors or any other kind of object made of glass" (*Le Petit Journal* (Paris) May 20, 1889).

The Indian was considered an immature human being ready to accept any knick-knackery he was presented with.[1]

The same impressions were reported by the Italian newspapers. The contradiction between the Indians' physical appearance and their acting seemed evident also to Italian journalists. When the Indians showed their faces, a Florentine reporter could see at last their "... copper-golden-cocoa faces" (*La Nazione* (Florence) March 12, 1890).

"They (the Indians) are tall, with thin bodies, quick and agile" - wrote another Italian journalist - "they have long hair which is divided on their forehead like that of women. But let us tell the truth, they are overall rather ugly with good and proud eyes; sad eyes of a dying race" (*Il Messaggero* (Rome) February 22, 1890).

The stereotype of the Indian as a dying race was then widespread in Europe. The Indians were "savages" condemned to die when confronted with civilization. Nothing could be more romantic and heart-breaking than the resigned stare of a man who knows he is going to die. This was the keynote repeatedly struck by Europan journalists showing sympathy for the Indians. Many English and French reporters asked themselves as to what the future of the Native Americans was. The answer was always the same: The Indians were condemned to disappear under the blows of White civilization. The positive image of the Indians was thus focused on his decadence as a warrior and as an independent human being.[2]

According to the reporters the Indian had accepted his fate. He now relied on the United States government for help. This, of course, favored an even more positive image of the Native American in the eyes of European audiences. In this sense Red Shirt's interviews with English newspapers proved to be very useful to those journalists who wanted to celebrate the faded glory of the Indian. When asked about the future of the Indian Red Shirt answered:

"The red man is changing every season. The Indian of the next generation will not be the Indian of the last. Our buffaloes are nearly all gone, the deer have entirely vanished, and the white man takes more and more of our land. But the U.S. government is good. True it has taken away our land, and the white men have eaten up our deer and our buffalo, but the Government now give [sic] us food that we may not starve. They are educating our children, and teaching them to farm and to use farming implements. Our children will learn the white man's civilization and to live like him" (*Daily Telegraph* (London) May 6, 1887 - Cody Scrapbooks, vol. 1).

Red Shirt represented a good Indian who accepted his defeat and was ready to receive help from a government that represented the stronghold of European civilization in the Americas. The French *L'Illustration* took advantage of the interest in the American Indians' plight to attack U.S. Indian policy, especially the colonization of Oklahoma, which was by then being carried out (*L'Illustra-*

tion (Paris) June 15, 1889).

The European press' good feelings toward Native Americans went so far as to make some reporters write that Buffalo Bill's troupe mistreated the Indians traveling with it. In Germany, and especially in Hamburg, some newspapers wrote that the Indians were ill treated and underfed (O'Connor 1972:198). As many a journalist wrote, these people were practically forced to travel with Buffalo Bill's Wild West Show, since the U.S. government had ceded them to the show, these Indians being prisoners of war of the United States. The treatment did not appear to be so oppressive, but discrimination within the troupe existed. As a matter of fact, the Indians left Paris by train in a third class coach. The rest of the showmen traveled second class on the same train while Colonel Cody and his friends had made reservations in a first class wagon (*Le Petit Journal* (Paris) November 6, 1889). Indians never resided in a hotel. They always pitched their tents near the arenas where the show took place, their encampments being part of the show.

The conviction that these Indians were the last representatives of a dying race and the witnessing of these discriminatory attitudes moved some German journalists to accuse Buffalo Bill of mistreatments. It must be noted that German newspapers had up to then almost ignored the presence of the Indians but in the show. German journalists had been more concerned with identifying in the various performances of the Indians the brave deeds of Karl May's heroes than observing the actual performances of the Native Americans (*Frankfurter Allgemeine* October 4-9, 1890; *Gießener Anzeiger* October 10, 1890). The reaction of Hamburg's newspapers to the conditions of the Indians shook the great success the circus had had on its previous stops around the country; especially those in Berlin and Munich, where King Ludwig III of Bavaria met the Wild West's troupe. By winter 1890, because of all the rumors concerning the Indians who worked in the show, all Native Americans were sent home (O'Connor 1972:199).

The Italian press did not show the same kind of interest in the future of the Indians. It just recognized the Indians' fate, and used the image of a dying race as a means to present these people as good and worthy of all sympathy.[3]

As soon as the European reporters came into close contact with the Indians in the encampments or during the Show, condescension superseded empathy. Many Italian newsmen were actually disillusioned at the sight of the Indians and this can be accounted as a factor in their more detached attitude as compared to English and French newspapers.

The Wild West Show moved to Italy in the winter of 1890 where it began playing in Naples. Between February and April 1890 the company performed in many Italian cities, from Naples and Rome up to Verona and Milan. By that time the Italian press had already spoken repeatedly about the show, provoking great expectations in the audiences of all cities. In 1887 and 1889 Italian newspapers' correspondents from London and Paris had written about the Wild West in positive terms (*Il Corriere Della Sera* (Milan) April 4-5, 1890). After the show had left Paris and had toured the south of France, it went to Spain where it experienced a decided failure. When it moved from Barcelona to Naples the company was just recovering from the many unexpected misfortunes, especially from the death of many Indians belonging to the troupe.

The Italians thus met a worn-out company which was in the process of restructuring itself and that waited for a great success in Italy and Germany in order to reestablish its fame on the old continent. The Wild West Show actually met with success in Italy, but the Italian press was not so happy with it. The major Italian newspaper *Il Corriere della Sera* could not explain all the excitement the show had caused in London, Paris, and even in Rome. Not all the English newspapers, however, proved to be as excited as *Il Corriere della Sera* reported. The Birmingham *Gazette*'s correspondent criticized the show since it did not fit the idea people had of the American Indian:

"The Indian war-cry," he wrote, "is a decided failure. It is apparently a shrill and feeble screech, and not at all the blood-curdling yell that Fenimore Cooper and other writers have led us to believe..."[4]

The Italian journalists echoed this statement when writing about the first appearance of the Indians in Milan. The Indians, wrote a reporter, wore colorful materials and feathers, carried arms and made "... a savage scream, since all of them yelled, or we could even say they mewed" (*Il Corriere della Sera* (Milan) April 4-5, 1890).

Indians were often referred to as savages. They were a fierce people, their voices those of savages. When they sat on the benches around the Roman arena, they appeared to a Roman journalist as chickens in the hen-house (*Il Messaggero* (Rome) February 20, 1890). According to a Florentine journalist the Indians slept all together in a tent, went around almost naked with their paint on. They ate raw meat and their meals were three or four times those of a European (*La Nazione* (Florence) March 13, 1890). When the troupe left Paris, a journalist had a chance to see the "distribution" of meals to the Indians:

"Afterwards a railway employee passed by their [the Indians'] coaches carrying a box full of slices of raw meat; suddenly the box was empty; one could think he was in a zoo during the wild beasts' meal time" (*Le Petit Journal* (Paris) November 6, 1889).

Such descriptions recall the most trite stereotypes of the savage in European imagination. The Indians were, in fact, often depicted as warlike people whose main occupation was going on the war-path against other Indians or most likely against White Men.

Another Italian correspondent narrating about Indian wars wrote that:

"If Indians were so aggressive among themselves, they were not less aggressive toward White Men, against whom they have had for centuries a sentiment of hatred. Something that most likely will never disappear until the last Indian will have died" (*L'Arena* (Verona) April 4, 1890 - Cody Scrapbooks, vol. 1).

The belief in Indian cruelty was reinforced by the show's performances. The show claimed to represent "The Drama of Civilization," a drama which always portrayed the Indians as the savage aggressors who were eventually defeated by Buffalo Bill and other good cowboys. It is not surprising, after all, that journalists depicted the Indian warriors in the show as fierce and dangerous men.

"Their [the Indians'] picturesque look is the most truculent. They ride their horses without saddle, and they are naked as their animals... These things [Indian robes] are nothing but ornaments calculated to scare the enemy" (*Le Temps* (Paris) May 20, 1889).

The influence popular beliefs concerning the Indians and novels on the American West had on the European press is evident. Many journalists did not deny such influence, they actually expected to see in real life what their imagination had seen in the novels of Cooper or Reid. Although disillusioned at times, European journalists recalled in their articles the deeds of Western novels' heroes. They found that one could not help recalling personages like those of *The Last of the Mohicans*, people like Firewater, Laughing Water, and the dark Huron Warrior (O'Connor 1972:173). Watching the battle scenes, the buffalo hunts and the other "picturesque" performances of the show was like reading one of those illustrated books by Mayne Reid, wrote a Roman journalist. When the "Persian Monarch," the ship rented by the company to cross the ocean in 1889, landed in Le Havre the correspondent of *Le Figaro* wrote to Paris that he had seen

"... Sioux Indians, the tribes of the Cutois, Arapahoe, Brulay, Cheyennes and Comanches, who came with their wild horses, their buffaloes, their prairie-dogs and rein-deers, to give us a real sense of that Indian world we had a chance to know up to now only through the stories of Gustave Aimard and Fenimore Cooper" (*Le Figaro* (Paris) May 12, 1890).

European journalists switched from sympathetic attitudes toward the Indians to hostile ones. A certain degree of contradiction can always be detected in their writings; but this was caused after all by the European perception of the

Indian at the time. The Indian was according to Romantic ideals a man condemned to disappear. He was thus good and positive. But he was also the fierce warrior of the prairies depicted in the novels. He was the savage, naturally inferior to the White Man as held by de Pauw, or socially degenerated as stated by de Maistre.

All these stereotypes were present in the European press commenting upon the Wild West Show. The chance offered to journalists to contact the Indians directly did not solve these contradictions. European newspapers and magazines had accepted the views widespread in nineteenth century Europe, and they could not help sticking to them. It could not be otherwise. What European journalists saw of the American West and of Indian life was nothing but a distortion and reinterpretation of that life. It was something that could probably be easily assimilated to the Western dime novels then popular.

NOTES

1. The journalists' astonishment at the "immature" attitudes of the Indians probably did not please the press-agent of the company who in his advertising campaign had always fostered another image of the Indian. This was the epic image of a fierce warrior who was still able to love, with no space for sentimentality. The Indian the show intended to present was a proud, taciturn man. Overall the journalists seem to have relied more on their personal knowledge of the Indians rather than on press-agencies' information.

   It is interesting to notice that while at the time of the later tours, at the beginning of the twentieth century, some reports coincided in the description of the show, using the same adjectives and at times entire paragraphs; during the shows of the end of the nineteenth century, this seldom happened. The only thing that was exactly reproduced in different newspapers was Red Shirt's interview in England: *Standard* (London), May 6, 1887; *Daily News* (London) May 10, 1887; *Le Figaro* (Paris) May 12, 1889; *La Nazione* (Florence) March 12, 1890.

2. The idea of the Indian as a dying race was probably introduced by the advertising campaign of the show, but there is no proof for this. Journalists never mentioned, for example, John Burke, the press agent of the Wild West, although he wrote in his book *Buffalo Bill* that he gave interviews to Italian newspapers. In Italy there is no trace, whatsoever, of these interviews.

3. An Italian journalist commented:
   "The Indian tribes are rapidly decreasing in number. Civilization is not good for these children of the Prairies, born and raised in complete freedom. We can say that as soon as they inhale it, they die from it" (*L'Arena* (Verona) April 4, 1890 - Cody Scrapbooks, vol. 1).

4. The correspondent of the *Gazette* went on writing:
   "... I fear, too, that the 'war dance' as performed at Aston has not made a great impression on the popular mind. It is a tame - one might say almost a childish - jig, without rhythm or measure, and thus another hallucination of our boyhood is disposed of" (Quoted in Russell 1960:338).

REFERENCES CITED

Berkhofer, Robert F.
    1979   The White Man's Indian. Images of the American Indian from Columbus to the Present. New York: Knopf.
Cody Scrapbooks, Volume 1. Western History Department. Denver Public Library. Denver, Colorado.
Cody, William F.
    1917   Life And Adventures of Buffalo Bill. Chicago: John Stanton & Co.
    1928   An Autobiography of Buffalo Bill. New York: Cosmopolitan Books.
Dippie, Brian W.
    1982   The Vanishing American: White Attitudes and U.S. Indian Policy. Middletown: Wesleyan University Press.
Dudley, Edward, and Maximilian E. Novak (eds.)
    1972   The Wild Man Within: An Image in Western Thought from the Renaissance to Romanticism. Pittsburgh: University of Pittsburg Press.
Gerbi, Antonello
    1955   La Disputa del Nuovo Mondo: Storia di una Polemica, 1750-1900. Milano: Ricciardi.
Griffin, Charles E.
    1908   Four Years in Europe with Buffalo Bill. Iowa: Stage Publishing Co.
Honour, Hugh
    1976   The European Vision of America (A Special Exhibition to honor the Bicentennial of the United States). Cleveland: The Cleveland Museum of Art.
O'Connor, Richard (Pseud. John Burke)
    1972   Buffalo Bill: The Noblest Whiteskin. New York: Putnam.
Russell, Don
    1960   The Lives and Legends of Buffalo Bill. Norman: University of Oklahoma Press.
Sell, Henry B., and Victor Weybright
    1955   Buffalo Bill and the Wild West. New York: Oxford University Press.

NEWSPAPERS, MAGAZINES

Arranged by country and in alphabetical order.

Daily News (London) May 5-June 30, 1887.
Times (London) May 5-June 30, 1887.

Le Figaro (Paris) April 2-May 12, 1889.
Le Matin (Paris) May 2, 3, 1889.
Le Petit Journal (Paris) May 13-October 7, 1889.
Le Temps (Paris) May 20, 21, 1889.
L'Illustration (Paris) May 11, 25-June 8, 15, 22, 1889.

Il Corriere della Sera (Milan) April 1-May 26, 1890.
Il Corriere di Napoli January 28-29, 1890.
Il Messaggero (Rome) February 27-March 9, 1890.
La Nazione (Florence) March 12, 13, 14, 16, 1890.

Frankfurter Allgemeine October 1-10, 1890.
Giessener Anzeiger October 4, 10, 1890.

NATIVE AMERICANS IN COLUMBUS'S HOME LAND: A SHOW WITHIN THE SHOW

Naila Clerici

At the dawn of the movie industry, Buffalo Bill and his "wild" Indians came to Europe to present, live and on stage, what Europeans would see repeated on the screen many times during the course of the 20th century.[1]

According to the organizers, the Buffalo Bill Wild West Show was highly educational (Buffalo Bill 1906:1); it showed real life in the open spaces of the western plains and the eternal fight between the Whites and the Indians; it was a living drama of the history of the West in the second half of the 19th century. The white Americans performed as skillful riders and fighters - as they would later in the movies - and became "the cowboys." The Native Americans mainly demonstrated the customs and dances of the Plains tribes, and these tribes came to represent all "the Indians" for a century.[2] Buffalo Bill was a living legend in the U.S., a superstar who had also had a meaningful role in the history and in the tradition of the country. After his European tours, he was also considered "an emblem of peace and friendship to all the world" (Walsh 1928:267). The American people needed to glorify their recent past and to justify their subjugation of the Indian tribes in the name of progress and "manifest destiny." To do so, they needed to represent it visually in simplified moral categories of good and evil. As in a medieval mystery play, the Wild West Show answered this need and clarified the nature of the fights against the Indians:

"The bullet is a kind of pioneer of civilization. Although its mission is often deadly, it is useful and necessary. Without the bullet, America would not be a great, free, united and powerful country" (Buffalo Bill 1906:41).

In the Wild West Show, Buffalo Bill is the symbol of the white Anglo-Saxon, blonde and good looking, and always the hero:

"Cody, the intrepid pioneer, who led civilisation through barbarian populations and who, thanks to his courage, made the star of the Empire shine on the western trails" (Buffalo Bill 1906:24).

The Indians are not always savages, but they are always very colorfully different. In the dynamics of the action Buffalo Bill is the winner, just as the economic interests of the industrial section of the U.S. were the winner in the reality of that time. When the railroads crossed the continent there was no place left for the Plains tribes nor for their way of life economically based on large extensions of territory for migrating and hunting. The interest of white

415

society became the interest of civilization (Buffalo Bill 1906:9). The Wild West represented, through the frontier men, the American people as whole, and it rendered their conquest patriotic. In Europe, of course, it did not have the same patriotic meaning. Italians and other Europeans could not identify themselves with the American frontier, but their attitude toward people outside the European model of civilization was the same. European countries, too, had colonial plans, and Italy was in the process of conquering Somalia and Abyssinia. While Italian magazines showed a sympathetic view toward the "savages" in the middle third of the 19th century, they became more Euro-centric at the close of the century when Italy developed clear expansionist aims toward Africa and claimed the right to extend a protectorate over the native populations of "underdeveloped" countries.[3] So it was convenient for the Italian public to agree to what was written in the Wild West Show program regarding the Indian wars, for "the conquered country has become worthy of modern institutions" (Buffalo Bill 1906:9).

Ethnocentric Italian journalists judged the Indians as barbaric and primitive. They saw Indian manners and customs as strange as those of other exotic peoples. The curiosity of readers was excited by articles about Indians, Zulus, Chinese, and Turkomans in *Il Giornale Illustrato dei Viaggi e delle Avventure di Terra e di Mare* [The Illustrated Magazine of Travel and of Adventures on Land and Sea] (Solimano 1983). Theories of Social Darwinism about the struggle for survival and the natural selection of the species influenced Italian thinking. There was no doubt about the superiority of White culture and its leadership role in the world. Italians, too, accepted the "White Man's burden" to educate the peoples of other continents in the ways of civilization. And if the Native peoples did not accept this forced acculturation, they were condemned to disappear as a separate and inferior race (Surdich 1982:182).[4] Given Italy's growing economic interest in countries to be exploited in the African continent, it was easy for Italian readers to understand the economic interest the U.S. had toward the western part of North America. To subdue the Indian or the African race, and to conquer and exploit the territories of the tribes could bring great profits. In Italy, as in America, this sort of naked truth needed myth and legend to make it moral (Burke 1976).

So in Italy Buffalo Bill came to represent the law, and the Indians were the bloodthirsty savages. Serial booklets about Buffalo Bill's adventures comparable to the American dime novels were published in Italy weekly from 1890 on. In these short stories, Buffalo Bill was transformed into an Italian hero with black burly hair and a mustache. The settlements in the Great Plains are referred to as "colonies," the same term used in Italy for the overseas African territories.[5] "We are not bloodthirsty Indians, but Whites who are here for self defense, here out of necessity."[6]

This is said to justify the action of the army in one of these novels. Progress had to go on: there was no less doubt of that in the old than in the new continent. The iconography of the time tends to show the Indians in scenes of violence. We find drawings of Indians scalping and attacking stage coaches with horrifying details in *Il Giornale Illustrato dei Viaggi*[7] and in *L'Illustrazione Popolare* [Popular Illustrations], and also Indians who burn a prisoner alive.[8] In *Il Giro del Mondo* [A Trip around the World], Indians undertake torture.[9] Passages from diaries of travellers and explorers were also published. The readers of the time could imagine themselves among "Gli Indiani del Pacifico" [The Indians of the Pacific][10] or participate in "Escursioni tra le Tribù Indiane dei Bacini della Colombia e dell'Alto Missouri per il Signor G. Catlin" [Excursions among the Indian tribes of the Colombian basin and the Upper Missouri by Mr. G. Catlin][11] and appreciate the illustrations inspired by Catlin's paintings.

Despite a high rate of illiteracy - according to the 1861 census, 78 percent of the Italian population could not read and write (Barile 1977) - the information found a wide oral dissemination (Castronovo et al. 1979).

Through the illustrated magazines, Italian readers derived not only their knowledge of the adventures and curiosities related to the Natives of the American continent but also of their physical appearance.

In fact, some of the drawings show specific events or actions using techniques that in later decades would become typical of comic books. Some are simple portraits showing the racial peculiarities and the traditional costumes of the Indians.

The stories, like the drawings, are often uncritical and superficial. Their object was to amaze and to arouse the reader's curiosity by emphasizing the exotic in "Indian culture" (always represented as one single culture). Only a few aspects of Indian culture were stressed, while the whole context in which those habits originated was ignored. This helped to create some of the Indian stereotypes that remain popular in Italy today: the torturing of prisoners, the raping of women, and the scalping of the defeated (cf.Surdich 1982:181).

In the Italian dime novels some Indians were good, but even they retained habits typical of their savage breed. The good Indians are Buffalo Bill's friends in the novels and therefore completely subdued by his wisdom and his strong personality: "*Lupo Selvaggio* [Wild Wolf] was completely devoted to him. Everything Buffalo Bill asked he would do with pleasure." But in this series - whose general title is *Buffalo Bill, the Wild West Hero* - the Indians are mainly of the savage kind: bloodthirsty, damned, barbaric, cruel, brigand, bandit, disgusting; they are red demons, Sioux thieves, seditious redskins, given to raid, to murder and, of course, to scalp. "We will decorate our belts with the scalps of slaughtered palefaces and we will fill our wigwams with their young women and girls," says *Scudeo Bravo* (Brave Shield) in a dime-novel "made in Italy."[12]

As the Indians were so dangerous and treacherous, going West to meet the Natives meant "adventure." What Italian readers knew of the recent history of

417

the U.S. came more from such fiction than from serious historical studies.

The westward expansion of the U.S. finds little space in Italian newspapers (Ciliento 1983). A few military engagements and Presidential addresses were mentioned in the first half of the 19th century.

The Indians who came with Buffalo Bill were not the first to visit Italy in that century. Three "savages" of the Osage tribe had been introduced to King Carlo Felice and to Carlo Alberto of the Savoia family in 1828.[13]

Some articles supporting the Indian cause appeared in the late 1840's, and the same pro-Indian attitude was generally shown in the following decades. An article published in *La Gazzetta di Genova* in 1850 demonstrates this sympathetic attitude, starting from the title: "Due Piaghe degli Stati Uniti del North [sic] America" [Two open sores of the U.S.A.]. The open sores are slavery and the vicious war conducted against the Indians. The author analyzes the relationship between the Anglo-American and the Indian cultural systems, prizes the dignity and the moral code of the Native people, and ends up criticizing the U.S. for its contribution to the disappearence of these "natural" people.[14] Another article of 1851 sympathizes with the Chippewas in describing their threatened removal from their territories on Lake Superior.[15] More often the opinion of the Italian press is that the Indians must Americanize or disappear. Often American public authorities are criticized, especially during the Grant presidency (1869-77) (Ciliento 1983:56). *La Gazzetta di Genova*[16] and *L'Eco d'Italia*[17] praise Cochise in 1871. Italian readers were also informed about the Modoc war, Custer's Last Stand and about the Nez Perce war, even if very briefly (Ciliento 1983:56).

The prevailing opinion was that the Blue Coats - *tuniche azzurre* or *giacche blue* - as the American soldiers were called in Italy, beat the Cheyennes and Utes only because of their superiority in number and equipment.[18]

The first tour of Buffalo Bill and his show in 1890 increased interest in events related to the West. The papers reported news about Oklahoma statehood, the murder of Sitting Bull, and the last "insurrection" of the Sioux in 1890 (Ciliento 1983:57). The commentator of the *Caffaro* - a Genoa daily - stated that the Sioux were right to revolt because they had suffered from hunger and bad treatment.[19]

There are no specific newspaper reports about the minor role that Buffalo Bill had played in the events related to the Ghost Dance movement among the Sioux,[20] but in his Italian program for the 1906 tour, Buffalo Bill boasts of his role in subduing the Ghost Dancers. Some of the Indians involved in the Ghost Dance movement were even taken to Europe with the show (Buffalo Bill 1906:74). Buffalo Bill's show also had the aim, according to the 1906 Italian program, of "giving the younger generation the opportunity to see various peoples in their national costumes before they disappear to live on only in history books and paintings" (Buffalo Bill 1906:1).

A vanishing race, according to the theories of Social Darwinism, Indians

418

were often considered culturally interesting. Various books with a scientific approach mentioning "ethnographic curiosities" and dealing with topics such as "love among the savages," poetry, language, geography, and literature were translated into Italian during the course of the 19th century (Grossi 1888a, b, 1890, Ambrosi 1877, Moleti 1896, Venturali 1885, De Riseis 1899, Peruzzi 1898, Vancouver 1884, Faucon 1879).

La Gazzetta di Genova reviewed *A Synopsis of Indian tribes of Nord* [sic] *America* by Gallatin in 1853.[21] But the most popular books, published for children, were certainly the ones written by Salgari (1896,1900,1905,1908,1909, 1910a,b) and the translations of Cooper (1859,1878,1879,1886-1887,1901a,b,1907) and Irving (1837,1874,1876). A journalist of *Il Messaggero* referred to the books by the English writer Mayne Reid as if they were known in Italy in 1906.[22]

When Indians arrived with Buffalo Bill's show they were known to the Italian public not merely as exotic human beings, but as a race with well-defined cultural and physical traits, even if the common people had little idea of the cultural and geographic diversity of the various tribes. The Indians were not the stars of the show. In fact. Italian newspapers seldom comment on their performances, and then mainly about their ability to ride and fight.

The main attraction of Buffalo Bill's show was Buffalo Bill himself. There was also a deep interest in the horses and their performances, as horses were still extensively used in Italy at the time. Not accustomed to seeing many foreigners, Italian journalists commented on the physical appearance of the Indians, their colorful outfits, and noted they were often almost naked, and covered with body paintings.[23]

Il Messaggero announced the arrival of the show in the following way:

"In the cast we see the Indians and their Chiefs, American cowboys, authentic Redskins, the tribes of Cutt Off [sic], Cheyennes, and Boy Chiefs [sic], little chiefs of the Sioux country."[24]

There is more interest in the Indians as living representatives of a different race than for their roles in the historical scenes that made up the Wild West Show. The press accepted as natural the Indians' role as the losers throughout the show: "...their eyes are good and proud, they have the gentleness of a dying race."[25] And the White heroes, whom Buffalo Bill so well represented, were the winners. All the episodes in the 1906 program are oriented in this way except for the battle of the Little Big Horn, in which even though the army is overwhelmed, Custer and his men are given the heroic roles in the performance (Buffalo Bill 1906:42). Italian journalists wrote more about the Indians' daily activities in the camp than about their stage performances, probably to show that the Indians really lived as described in the books.[26] The journalist of *Il Messaggero* described his entrance into the Indian camp in Rome where he found tipis, bows and arrows, bridles, horses, and buffaloes. He

Fig. 1. Buffalo Bill's troup in front of St. Peter's Church in the Vatican.

saw the squaws cooking and working:

"The illusion was complete. I seemed to be in the middle of a Redskins encampment... in the wide Texas prairies."[27]

Buffalo Bill often sent the Indians out into *piazzas* to mingle with the crowds as a way of advertising the show. The Indians were seen everywhere: walking around Italian towns, shopping, or resting in cafés. The *New York Herald* referred to the attractive effect the Indians created in Venice and the curiosity they aroused in many Italian towns.[28] In the Italian press they were often described as ridiculous. (A Rome paper said that the Indians, sitting on benches and wrapped in their blankets, looked like chickens).

The people of the Wild West Show, including the Indians, came to Europe to show the life and the history of the western part of the U.S. They were proud to teach Europeans about their traditions and their culture. What the show represented dated back only few decades and its performers showed great admiration for the ancient remains they found in Italy. Buffalo Bill and the Indians liked to follow the paths of ancient history and had hoped to perform in Rome's Colosseum, which was impossible. They did perform in the ancient Roman Arena of Verona, where Burke, the general manager of the show, became lyric and declaimed: "Hoary antiquity and bounding youth kissed each

420

Fig. 2. Tipis of Buffalo Bill's Wild West in the Colosseum, Rome.

other under the sunny Italian skies" (Walsh 1928:278). They also visited the ruins of Herculaneum and Pompeii (Burke 1976:238). Photographs of Buffalo Bill and his "wild Indians" wearing war bonnets in a *gondola* or inside the Colosseum testify to this desire to be immortalized among the glorious ruins of the past (Burke 1976:239). Vesuvius, according to some Italian journalists, was considered by the Indians a sacred representation of nature. In Naples the Indians "did their war dances in the shadow of the mountain Vesuvius", performing a special dance in honour of the volcano (Yost 1979:224). In Naples they even decided not to use their painted sets, thinking that the natural beauty was enough. The Indians also performed a war dance in the Colosseum, honoring the proud Roman gladiators (Walsh 1928:278). On the whole they seem to have been more fascinated by Italy's natural beauty and its historical ruins than by its people. The only person they were greatly impressed by was the Pope. They met Leo XIII in Rome on the occasion of his eleventh anniversary as pontiff. Buffalo Bill and his troupe were invited to the Pope's public audience at the Vatican (Croft-Cooke 1952:194). This audience turned out to be a show within a show, which, Burke (1976:239) tells us, gave reciprocal pleasure. The Pope and his train gave a "dazzling fête" for the Indians and the cowboys:

421

"The grandeur of the spectacle, the heavenly music, the entrancing singing, and impressive adjuncts produced a most profound impression on the astonished children of the prairie" (Burke 1976:239).

The reporter of *The New York Herald* noticed

"the brilliant uniforms of the Swiss guards, Palatine guards, papal gendarmes, and private chamberlains. The sunlight fell upon the lines of glittering steel, nodding plumes, golden chains, shimmering robes of silk, and all the blazing emblems of pontifical power and glory" (Burke 1976:244).

The Pope and the Roman aristocracy looked curiously at the colorful people of the troupe: Buffalo Bill came first, then

"Rocky Bear led the Sioux warriors... They were painted in every color that Indian imagination could devise. Every man carried something with which to make big medicine in the presence of the great medicine man sent by the Great Spirit. Rocky Bear rolled his eyes and folded his hands on his breast as he stepped on tip-toe through the glowing sea of color. His braves furtively eyed the halberds and two-handed swords of the Swiss guards" (Burke 1976:245).

The Indians were astonished by the personality of the great "medicine man." When the Pope appeared

"in the *sedia gestatoria* carried above the heads of his guards, preceded by the knights of Malta and a procession of Cardinals and archbishops, the cowboys bowed, and so did the Indians. Rocky Bear knelt and made the sign of the cross. The pontiff leaned affectionaly toward the rude groups and blessed them. He seemed to be touched by the sight..." (Burke 1976:245).

Buffalo Bill was given a leading role even in religious matters; he was said to be a Catholic by *Il Messaggero* and to have converted some of the Indians.[29] In fact, only a few Indians had been converted in their reservations, and Buffalo Bill belonged to another Christian denomination (Croft-Cooke 1952:194). While Buffalo Bill was often interviewed, there is no evidence that any of the Indians were. An Italian journalist asked Buffalo Bill how many Indians he had killed; Buffalo Bill replied: "If you want a definite answer, you can say simply that I never killed an Indian except when my life was in danger" (Sell and Weybright 1955:185).

Nobody seemed to want to know why a hundred Indians had agreed to come so far and whether they were happy with their roles in the show. No clear

Indian personality emerged in the Italian press. Only once did an Indian "make" news: an Indian who played the role of Sitting Bull, fed up with being a loser on all occasions, quit the Wild West show in La Spezia and got drunk to cheer up.[30]

We do not know if the Indians saw the statue in honor of Columbus in Genoa. The message one finds in no Italian newspaper was delivered by the Indians in Barcelona in front of another Columbus statue: "It was a damned bad day when he discovered America" (Walsh 1928:278).

NOTES

1. Buffalo Bill's Wild West toured Italy twice in 1890 and in 1906.
2. Both Indian men and women were part of the show; they included Sioux, Cheyennes, and Arapahos (Buffalo Bill 1906:1).
3. The Italian kingdom showed interest in Abyssinia and Somalia especially from 1887 onwards when Francesco Crispi was head of the government.
4. See also the following articles in *Il Caffaro*: "Pelli Rosse" (22 April 1889), "Gli Ultimi Pelli Rosse" (5 December 1890), "L'Insurrezione dei Pelli Rosse" (9 December 1890).
5. The translation of these booklets was first published by Casa Editrice Americana of Milan, a branch of the New York publisher, and then by Casa Editrice Nerbini of Florence.
6. "La Pista di un Traditore," *Buffalo Bill l'Eroe del Wild West* 46 (7 January 1923):7.
7. See the following issues of *Il Giornale Illustrato dei Viaggi e delle Avventure di Terra e di Mare*: 12 (1878), 19 (1879), 81 (1880), 513 (1888), 581 (1889), 610 (1890), 141 (1899), 270 (1901), 421 (1904), 470 (1905), 548 (1906), 753 (1910).
8. *L'Illustrazione Popolare* VII/7 (15 June 1873), IX/21 (22 March 1874), X/20 (13 September 1874), XVI/14 (2 February 1879), XXX/43 (22 October 1893).
9. *Il Giro del Mondo* 3 (1869).
10. *Universo Illustrato* 1869:161-163.
11. *Il Giro del Mondo* 3(1869).
12. See "La Pista di un Traditore," *Buffalo Bill l'Eroe del Wild West* 46.
13. *Gazzetta di Genova*, 24 September 1828.
14. *Gazzetta di Genova*, 10 October 1850.
15. *Gazzetta di Genova*, 19 September 1851.
16. *Gazzetta di Genova*, 29 July 1871.
17. *L'Eco d'Italia*, 20 July 1871.
18. *Corriere Mercantile*, 16,18,27 January 1871.
19. *Il Caffaro*, 23 January 1891.

20. Colonel Cody understood that the uprising of the Sioux could become a national matter, so he went back to the U.S. thinking it would be good publicity. He received a telegram from General Miles requesting him to go to Chicago. (The fact that he was called in this emergency situation gives an idea of his image in American public opinion.) Miles asked the former scout to proceed instantly to Sitting Bull's camp and to convince the old Indian leader to come into Standing Rock Agency. In fact, the whites of that area of South Dakota were fearful of the uprising and believed Sitting Bull was at the core of the trouble. Cody, sure that if he could reach Sitting Bull in time he would listen to him, left at once on his mission. But others, chiefly Standing Rock agent James McLaughlin, felt this was the wrong action and went over Miles's head to President Harrison to have Cody recalled. The result was the assassination of Sitting Bull during an attempted arrest by Indian police (Cf. Yost 1979:224-226; Croft-Cooke and Meadmore 1952:196-197).

21. *Gazzetta di Genova*, 2-3 September 1853.

22. *Il Messaggero*, 21 March 1890.

23. *Il Messaggero*, 22 March 1890.

24. *Il Messaggero*, 18 March 1890.

25. *Il Messaggero*, 20 March 1890.

26. *Il Messaggero*, 21 March 1890.

27. *Il Messaggero*, 20 March 1890.

28. *New York Herald*, 16 April 1890, in Burke 1976:243.

29. *Il Messaggero*, 20 March 1890.

30. *Corriere della Spezia*, 18 March 1906.

REFERENCES CITED

Ambrosi, Francesco
   1877   I Selvaggi Antichi e Moderni Considerati nei loro Rapporti ca la
           Civiltà e la Religione.
Barile, L.
   1977   Per una storia dell'Editoria Popolare: le Riviste Illustrate Sonzogno.
           Esperienze Letterarie II:97.
Buffalo Bill
   1906   Buffalo Bill's Wild West and Congress of Rough Riders of the World.
           [Official Italian Program.]
Burke, John M.
   1976   Buffalo Bill. Milano.
Castronovo, V., L.Giacheri Fossati, N.Tranfaglia
   1979   La Stampa Italiana nell'età liberale. Bari.
Ciliento, Bruno
   1983   Gli Indiani sulla Stampa Genovese, 1802-1891. I Cerchi del Mondo -
           Proposte di Lettura (Genova):53-59.
Cooper, James Fenimore
   1859   Ochio di Falco. Milano
   1878   L'Ultimo dei Mohicani, Milano.
   1879   I Pionieri. Milano.
   1886-7 La Prateria. Milano.
   1901a   Il Cacciatore di Fiere. Torino.
   1901b   L'Esploratore di Sentieri. Torino.
   1907   Racconti Straordinari. Torino.
Crofte-Cooke, Rupert, and W.S.Meadmore
   1952   Buffalo Bill: The Legend, the Man of Action, the Showman, London.
De Riseis, Giovanni
   1899   Dagli Stati Uniti alle Indie: Paesaggi e Ricordi.
Faucon, Emma
   1879   Tre anni nelle Indie Occidentali presso gli Aricara.
Grossi, Vincenzo
   1888a   Fra i Pelli-rosse d'America: curiosità etnografiche.
   1888b   L'Amore fra i Selvaggi.
   1890   Lingue, Letteratura e Tradizioni Popolari degli Indigeni d'America.
Irving, Washington
   1837   Viaggi per le Praterie Occidentali degli Stati Uniti. Milano.
   1874   The Life and Voyages of Christopher Columbus with copious notes.
           Genova.
   1876   Storia e Viaggi di Cristoforo Colombo. Milano.
Moleti, Girolamo Ragusa
   1896   La Poesia dei Selvaggi.

Peruzzi, A.
    1898   Tra gli Indiani del Rio Vermejio.
Salgari, Emilio
    1896   Il Re della Prateria: Avventure. Firenze.
    1900   Avventure tra i Pellirosse. Torino.
    1905   La Sovrana del Campo d'Oro: Romanzo d'Avventure. Genova.
    1908   Sulle Frontiere del Far-West: Avventure. Firenze.
    1909   La Scotennatrice: Avventure. Firenze.
    1910a   Le selve Ardenti: Avventure. Firenze.
    1910b   Storie Rosse. Firenze.
Sell, Henry Blackman, and Victor Weybright
    1955   Buffalo Bill and the Wild West. New York.
Solimano, Sandra
    1983   Viaggio nel "Paese dei Pelli-Rosse" in due Riviste Italiane fra Otto
           e Novecento. I Cerchi del Mondo - Proposte di Lettura (Genova),
           107-109.
Surdich, Francesco
    1982   Aspetti ed Immagini delle Culture Extraeuropee nelle Prime Riviste
           Illustrate Italiane. Saggi di Storia del Giornalismo in Memoria di
           Leonida Balestreri (Genova), 177-186.
Vancouver, Giorgio
    1884   Fra gli Indiani d'America: Viaggi.
Venturali, Marcellino
    1885   Gli Uomini Fossili e gli Uomini Selvaggi.
Walsh, Richard John
    1928   The Making of Buffalo Bill: A Study in Heroics. Indianapolis.
Yost, Nellie Irene
    1979   Buffalo Bill, his family, friends, fame, failures, and fortune. Chicago.

THE BAD SPEAKERS AND THE LONG BRAIDS:
References to Foreign Enemies in Lakota Song Texts

R.D. Theisz

The warrior ethic of the Lakota[1] persists to this day.

The achieving of honor in battle in pre-reservation days had been focused on *toka* ('enemy') tribes - the Pawnee, Crow, Arikara, Shoshone, Ute, Cree, and Chippewa - and later, on military or civilian non-Indian enemies. With the advent of the reservation era in the late 1800's the references to historic tribal enemies gradually receded though they were still maintained by the older generation. During this most transitional period of Lakota history, the quest for war honors, paradoxically, led Lakota warriors to serve in the U.S. military, their former adversary. Young Indian men now sought to escape the monotony of reservation life, especially as it emasculated Lakota manhood, via the meaningful, socially rewarded excitement of warfare in the United States military. Only the anguish over the purpose and morality of the Vietnam conflict eventually tarnished, in Lakota eyes, the glory of fighting for one's family, community, and nations.

From early childhood, young boys had been historically instilled with the requisite attitude and skills for battle. Young girls in turn, learned early the obligation of honoring their menfolk for this most glorious avocation. Thus, the games of childhood served as preparation for the demands and hardship of war. Oral tradition, visual art, music and ceremony led the way in assuring that the *lakol wicoha'an*" ('Lakota heritage') was virtually synonymous with the warrior life.

After the confinement to the reservations, the twenty-four hours possibility of enemy attack - with the possibility of respite only in deep winter when travel was dangerous and difficult - gave way to sporadic and limited periods of war activity. Yet, the social dynamic of distinguishing oneself in battle remained very high in the hierarchy of male Lakota values. The opportunities were simply more limited than before and had to be sought more frequently in foreign wars.

Accordingly, the complex of generally six *akicita okolakiciye* or 'warrior societies' (Hassrick 1977, Bad Heart Bull and Blish 1967) gradually waned in functionality and experienced an accompanying loss of membership so that today the only warrior society songs still remembered by the older singers are those of the *'cante t'inza'* (Strong Hearts) and *'tokala'* (Kit Fox) societies. In our day, many of the functions of these societies have been consolidated under the role of the American Legion, an United States military service veterans' group.

The focus on Lakota soldier/veterans songs demonstrates the persistence of the warrior ethic but also its evolution. The Lakota warrior tradition maintained

427

Fig. 1. Honoring tribal and government flags at the beginning of celebration. Photo by K.Tsuji, 1981.

Fig. 2. Four dancers counting coup on a feather. Photo by K.Tsuji, 1981.

itself through the Omaha Society, which the Lakota patterned after the Omaha/Ponca tribes' traditions of honoring the valiant warrior (Howard 1951). Although it, too, underwent considerable secularization, a significant number of Omaha Dance songs to this day are considered "traditional songs" with words commemorating the bravery and sacrifice of the veteran, the scout, the daring warrior, and the deceased soldier.[2]

From my own field experience[3] and the published sources available to me,[4] the history of these traditional war songs experienced two great periods of composition and revival, respectively. The first is that between 1917-1945. As William Powers (1970) notes, many of the traditional war songs can be traced to World War I. Thus the first major conflict in which Lakota men possibly participated as U.S. soldiers, the Spanish-American War of 1898, seems not to have recognizably affected the stock of traditional war songs in circulation. At least, I have found not references to the *spaiola* ('Spanish') either in the literature nor in many conversations with older singers.

World War I, then, has resulted in the composition and popularization of many songs honoring the soldiers' efforts against foreign enemies. Powers (1980:219) stresses the view that this increased activity is less a sign of patriotism and more the welcoming of an opportunity to practice past cultural institutions. The formulaic, terse text of pre-World War I songs celebrating the victories over tribal enemies or the U.S. cavalry (*mila hanska*, 'long knives' or 'Americans') are now adjusted to the new international context. Frances Densmore (1918)[5] has recorded many samples of essentially this former period centering on intertribal warfare:

Mato-onziz'ca he heyin na iyaye.
Kangi wica'ša owale kte lo heyin na iyaye he.
Tanke lowanpi kin onspe iciciya yo.
Bobtail Bear [man's name] said this and went anway, never to return.
"Crow Indians I will seek," he said and went away never to return. "Older Sister, the songs [in honor of warriors who return victorious] you must learn" (Densmore 1918:368).
or
Psaloka kin natan ahiyelo;
Blotan hunka unyan napapi yelo.
The Crow Indians came attacking;
their leader was left behind (Densmore 1918:398).
or
Kola nayahonpi huwo.
Tašunke ko awakuwe.
Friend, do you hear?
Their [the enemy's] horses also I am bringing home (Densmore 1918:397).

Since these songs were recorded prior to 1915, they are not yet affected by World War I, but interestingly, as stated above, there are also no references to the Spanish-American War.

When the involvement in a foreign war finally begins to affect Lakota song texts, the melodies continue to follow the general descending contour pattern of Lakota songs as well as the formulaic treatment of war experiences and scenes. The major changes, to my mind, are first, the discontinuation of the mention of horses as the prize of war and the symbol of attack and victory, and second, the substitution of foreign enemies for tribal ones.

It is significant that of the enemies the Lakota might have faced in World War I only the reference to Germans (*iya sica*) is found in song texts. Thus Austro-Hungarian, Turkish, and Bulgarian references are absent. The designation *iya sica* refers to *iya* ('mouth,' 'speech') and *sica* ('bad,' 'funny'). Thus Lakotas refer to Germans as "the bad speakers" or "those who talk funny." The following texts contain typical mention of Germans who, in time, become the generic enemy.

Tehatan natan pelo (4 times).
Iyasica ki ceya napa pelo.
Lakota hokšila tehantan natan pelo.
Iyašica ki ceya napa pelo.
They are charging from afar (4 times).
The Germans retreat crying.
The Lakota boys they are charging from afar.
The Germans retreat crying.

Lakota hokšila iyažica tamakoce ki
Ota iyacu ca ekta win wicaceya pelo.
Lakota boy, the Germans whose many lands you have taken
are crying like woman there.
Lakota boy, you have taken many of the German lands,
so they are crying like women there.[6]

Tunkašila cemakiya ca iyašica ki
Wakasote nan makoce ko wakiye.
Grandfather beseeched me [to help him] so I destroyed the German and also took his land.

Iyašica ki taku maya ye laka
Nankehehca wiyutata nanya jinye.
It seems you, a German, consider me a relation,
so at least you are waving [a sign of surrender?].

Iyašica wan tawicun wasaskiye k'un,
Owah'an cunkecaye he silela nunke.
A German loved his wife,
but you have done an evil thing [probably a sexual taunt].

Iyašica ki owe wancinyanka he.
Wahtehni t'a! Toke le ke eyaš niciciye ka.
German, I have been watching your tracks.
Worthless one! I would have followed you wherever you would have gone![7]

Wayankiye kola iyašica natan hiye
Wayanki yelo. Kola iyašica makoce wan
Tehila ca unya napewa yelo.
Friends, observe this: I saw the German enemy come charging.
Friends, the German loved his land,
but I made him retreat and turn back.[8]

These sample songs demonstrate the standard type of reference to the German enemy for the period of both World Wars. The addition of another major enemy during World War II resulted in references to the Japanese as *pecokan hanska* translated as 'long braids' (*pecokan,* 'braid,' *hanska,* 'long'). The reference by my informants is to the braid or scalplock from the back of the head by the Japanese but also other Asian people whom the Lakota perceive similarly to have *kisonla* ('braids'). References to the third World War II U.S. enemy, the Italians (*si hanska,* 'long feet') are not recorded via song texts.

A number of thematic motifs deserve to be pointed out as they occur in many more songs than just those included in my analysis. Frequent references are made to the enemy or the Lakota "charging," "attacking," "withstanding a charge," and being in "the thick of the battle." The enemy is frequently "made to cry," "to retreat," "to give up his land," or "to run away." The courage of the Lakota generally results in the rout of the enemy or the death of the brave Lakota warrior. Considerable mention is made of *Tunkašila,* the President, asking the *Lakota hokšila,* the Sioux boys (warriors), for their help which they then successfully provide. The enemy may be referred to as *kola* (friend) or *wahtesni ki* (worthless one) but most often simply by using stereotypical physical attributes as a national designation. At times, the enemy city/capital or country may be used instead such as Berlin, Tokyo, Korea, Vietnam. In that case the preposition *ta* (*at, to, on*) may be added as a suffix.

Tehan natan pelo (5 times).
Lakota hokšila hena hecun pelo.
Kowakata Tokyo eyapi ki onapobiapelo.
Tehan natan pelo (2 times).

Lakota hokšila hena hecun pelo.
They are charging from afar (5 times).
The Lakota have done this.
A place called Tokyo they are bombing.
They are charging from afar (2 times).
The Lakota have done this.[8]

Okute natan pelo (4 times).
Koreata okute natan pelo.
Lakota hokšila cannumpa yuha
Okute natan pelo. Koreata okute natan pelo.
They shoot as they charge (4 times).
In Korea they shoot as they charge.
The Lakotas have the Sacred Pipe.
In Korea they shoot as they charge.[8]

The years 1917 to 1945 may thus be viewed as a period of great vitality, in the realm of war songs especially. Almost all references to the enemy, however, are restricted to Germans and Japanese. By the late 1950's and early 1960's, a waning of interest in these songs occurred as social intertribal dance songs became more popular, particularly with the small crop of younger singers.

During the 1970's a twofold renewal occurred. First, the growing number of singers began to appreciate the identity potential of traditional[9] singing in public. Second, traditional songs of various kinds - excepting social dances of the couples and round dance type (Rabbit, Owl, Kahomni) - showed a clear renewal of interest and popularity. Nevertheless, the original composition of Lakota traditional songs which speak of the warrior context and often a foreign enemy, is practically nonexistent at present. As a result, when this type of song is to be rendered, singers resort to the time-honored stock of warrior/soldier songs.

Many occasions to honor veterans or to use war-related songs occur, it is clear. In 1980, for example, I witnessed a World War II veteran on the Standing Rock Sioux Reservation who publicly, during a pow-wow, burned a German flag of the National Socialism period. Before doing so, he told of his exploits during the European campaign and especially in capturing this flag. Though not sharing his reason for burning the flag at this time, he requested a set of songs from the singing groups present which referred to the *iya sica* (Germans) and also included his "Indian name," a ceremonial name usually awarded during childhood. As the songs were rendered, the flag was spread on the grass in the center of the arena. Veterans danced around it and took turns ritually counting coup on the flag. Some women also took part. Then it was set ablaze accompanied by shouts and the high tremolo used by women to accentuate their enthusiastic approval or encouragement. The event concluded

432

with a series of give-away donations by those related to the central participant or those able to recount their past honors.

Although contemporary song groups are not creating new texts which include references to past European foes or even the more recent armed clashes of the United States in which Lakotas have taken part, they are nevertheless actively composing song texts. Their current output, however, is concerned with social comment subjects, particularly the affirmation of traditional Lakota ways, the exhortations to be strong in the face of difficult situations, and the joy of gathering to celebrate the essence of being Lakota.

The time-honored, war-oriented songs are thus taking on a somewhat nostalgic flavor as well as the function of asserting the identity of being Lakota. Rather than lamenting this shift, if a subjective point may be proposed, we need to recognize these changes in the sociopolitical and cultural experience of contemporary Lakota. In the final analysis, if a new United States military conflict should involve a lengthy and patriotically enthusiastic response by Lakota young people, I am convinced that the foreign enemy will once again appear in songs as the object of taunt, derision, and challenge much in the same manner as before.[10]

NOTES

1. The term refers to the western or Teton division of the Oceti Sakowin (Seven Council Fires) comprising the people referred to as the Sioux.
2. The encouragement of dramatic Omaha dances, billed as "war dances" in the Buffalo Bill Cody Wild West Show, is well documented by Mark G.Thiel, "The Omaha Dance in Oglala and Sicangu Sioux History, 1883-1923" (unpublished manuscript, 1983).
3. This is based on twenty-five years of observing and participating as a member of a traditional Lakota singing roup.
4. See the bibliography in Black Bear and Theisz (1976) for a somewhat dated list of sources.
5. Although these songs and others in Densmore (1918) were recorded primarily on the Standing Rock Reservation, they are typical of other Lakota divisions.
6. These two are Veterans songs from Black Bear and Theisz (1976:48-49).
7. These four songs are Waktegli or Victory songs.
8. Unpublished text.
9. The term "traditional" has by this time come to mean most songs that have Lakota words in them. Those songs with vocables only are therefore usually not considered traditional.
10. I feel compelled, in conclusion, to express my gratitude to Severt Young Bear, Francis Menard, Philip Wright, Calvin Jumping Bull, and George Squirrel Coat. Their comraderie and insights have revealed not only the Lakota warrior ethic but the Lakota soul.

REFERENCES CITED

Bad Heart Bull, Amos, and Helen H. Blish
    1967   A Pictographic History of the Oglala Sioux. Lincoln: University of Nebraska Press.

Black Bear, Ben, Sr., and R.D.Theisz
    1976   Songs and Dances of the Lakota. Rosebud, SD: Sinte Gleska College.

Densmore, Frances
    1918   Teton Sioux Music. Bureau of American Ethnology, Bulletin 61. Washington, DC: GPO (Reprinted 1972, New York: Da Capo Press).

Hassrick, Royal B.
    1977   The Sioux. Life and Customs of a Warrior Society. Norman: University of Oklahoma Press.

Howard, James H.
    1951   Notes on the Dakota Grass Dance. Southwestern Journal of Anthropology 7(1):82-85.

Powers, William K.
    1970   Contemporary Oglala Music and Dance: Pan-Indianism vs. Pan-Tetonism. In: Ethel Nurge (ed.), The Modern Sioux (Lincoln: University of Nebraska Press), 268-290.

    1980   Plains Indian Music and Dance. In: W.Raymond Wood and Margot Liberty (eds.), Anthropology of the Great Plains (Lincoln: University of Nebraska Press), 212-229.

THE REDMAN'S APPEAL FOR JUSTICE:
DESKAHEH AND THE LEAGUE OF NATIONS

Joëlle Rostkowski

The Archives of the League of Nations are a source of exclusive information on the diplomatic mission of Deskaheh,[1] the Cayuga chief, who in 1923 traveled to Geneva, where he stayed more than one year, hoping that the League would examine his people's case and declare the Six Nations an independent state.

Deskaheh, a member of the Sour Springs Longhouse, spokesman of the Six Nations of the Grand River Land, near Brantford, Ontario, claimed that he represented a sovereign state, recognized as a separate nation by the Haldimand Treaty of 1784. In the aftermath of the first world war, increasing tensions had opposed the Council of hereditary chiefs of the Grand River to the Canadian authorities, and Deskaheh was convinced that the best way to settle the matter was to bring it to the attention of the League. The controversial question of Iroquois sovereignty was then bound to remain confined to a confrontation between Canada and the Six Nations, the U.S. not being a member of the League.

While Deskaheh was bringing the cause of Iroquois nationalism to Geneva, the Dominion of Canada was anxious to benefit from its membership in the League to establish its status as a sovereign power internationally, "a status which before 1919 had in no sense existed" (Veach 1975:10). As a young country Canada sought to play upon its favorable image to develop its reputation in the international field. Deskaheh's appeal, which denounced infringements by the Canadian authorities of rights conferred upon the Six Nations by Great Britain in the eighteenth century, could only prove embarrassing for the Dominion.

Deskaheh was known for his negotiating ability and oratorical skills, and in Geneva, where he inspired much sympathy and respect as a patient and unflappable spokesman, he managed to secure the assistance of humanitarian societies and support groups and was encouraged by several Member Governments. Although he did not succeed in being heard by the League, his mission is still remembered on both sides of the Atlantic and is often referred to in respectful though rather vague terms in diplomatic circles.

Documents of major importance have been kept in the Archives, including Deskaheh's memorandum, entitled "The Redman's Appeal for Justice" (dated 6 August 1923), the official reply of the Canadian Government to Deskaheh's claims (dated 27 December 1923) and the Report of Colonel Andrew T. Thompson, Commissioner of the Canadian Government "to investigate and inquire into the Affairs of the Six Nations," dated November 1923 but communicated to the League at the end of 1924. The Archives also include the extensive correspondence of the League Secretariat with the various governments which were

435

involved or took an interest in Deskaheh's case. A perusal of that file leads to an assessment of Deskaheh's strategy and explains the variety of reactions to his claims. The correspondence is also revealing of the role of the League Secretariat and accounts not only for the official diplomatic response but also for the negotiations that went on behind the scenes at the time of Deskaheh's visit.

Comparatively, the whole file sheds an interesting light on current debates on Indian issues in the United Nations. Moreover, the impact and implications of Deskaheh's case illustrate the evolution of Canadian Indian policy in that period of transition. It is apparent from the file that the Canadian Government, although first hardly willing to acknowledge Deskaheh's attempt to be heard on the international scene, became increasingly impatient with his action in Geneva. Colonel Andrew T. Thompson, appointed to investigate the political and social state of the Grand River Land, firmly recommended in his report the establishment of an elected council to replace the traditional government and its troublesome and prestigious leader. The reform took effect in September 1924 and Deskaheh found himself unwelcome on his return to his native land. Putting aside the controversy about the respective value of traditional and elected governments and focussing rather on the ups and downs of Deskaheh's diplomatic action, it appears, on the basis of the historical documents of the League of Nations, that his mission attracted attention to the Indian cause and almost broke through the procedural intricacies of the organization. However, Deskaheh's action also speeded up the process of assimilation and enfranchisement that had been initiated on the Grand River Land in the wake of the first world war. His "Appeal for Justice" marks the end of an era.

Deskaheh's strategy and the "Spirit of Geneva"

When he arrived in Geneva in September 1923, Chief Deskaheh was confident that the appeal of the Six Nations (which he defined as the first League of Nations) could be heard on the international scene. Actually, during the years following the first world war, the "Spirit of Geneva," i.e. the ideology which inspired the defenders of a new international order, the emergence of new states and the commitment of the League to the protection of "small nations," reinforced Deskaheh's expectations. When he realized that his cause was lost, after more than a year of unsuccessful negotiations, his disillusionment had left him a broken man. He died less than a year after his return to America.

Looking back, it seems that his failure to be heard determined the course of further contacts between Indians and international organizations. From then on, although Indians kept referring to themselves as "Peoples" or "Nations," they would be classified as "ethnic minorities" in the diplomatic field, until new developments in UN procedures during the seventies led to the examination of Indian issues under the specific designation of "Indigenous Populations."

436

Fig.1.   Deskaheh (Levi General) in Geneva, 1923/4. Archives, BPU, Geneva University Library, Geneva.

Deskaheh's strategy has remained unique in so far as it was based primarily on his own individual efforts and charisma. With the assistance of the Six Nations' counsel, George P. Decker, he tried to bring his people's case before the League on a purely tribal basis, but the title of his memorandum: "The Redman's Appeal for Justice" was a general reference to the Indian cause. The action relied on historical alliances and treaties, in particular the Haldimand Treaty of 1784, whereby King George III conveyed to the Iroquois loyalists who had fought on the side of the British Crown during the American Revolutionary War a tract of land along the Grand River on the Canadian side of Lake Erie, as compensation for the loss of their possessions in the United States.

    As a preliminary step, Deskaheh appealed to the British Government, recalling past alliances and agreements. In 1921, he traveled to England to discuss the status and rights of the Six Nations, but failed to obtain British support in the conflict that opposed the Council of Chiefs to the Dominion.

The role of the Netherlands

At the end of 1922, Deskaheh and his lawyer went to see the Dutch *chargé d'affaires* in Washington to inform him that the Six Nations of the Grand River Land had decided

> "to appeal for justice to the Queen of the Netherlands, in view of the fact that they had had pleasant relations with the Dutch settlers in the Hudson Valley in the seventeenth century" (Veach 1975:32).

Deskaheh asked the Dutch representative to transmit the Six Nations' appeal to the Hague, hoping it could then be forwarded to the League. The fact that the Dutch authorities complied with his request was to initiate his action within the League.

Deskaheh's appeal to the Queen of the Netherlands went back to the first contacts of the Hau-de-no-sau-nee with the Dutch settlers and to the Haldimand Treaty in the following terms:

> "We are an organized and self-governing people who, on the coming of the Dutch to the valley of the Hudson in North America, entered into treaties with them and faithfully observed our promise of friendship. The British, who came later, in turn recognized us as a confederacy of independent States and established friendly relations with us solemnized by treaty, from the time when your Government of that day yielded its settlments to the British, down to the time of revolution of the British Colonies... we entered into an alliance in arms with them against the Colonies who had revolted. At the same time we were given the express promise of the British Crown to compensate us for all losses we might suffer in consequence of that alliance. Having been driven from our home-lands in that war with the revolting Colonies, King George III, in fulfillment of his promise, invited us to accept a home beyond the limits of the New United States, on the banks of the Grand River... We, through our great Chief, Joseph Brant, accepted this offer of the King, confirmed by his Governor General of Canada, Sir Frederick Haldimand, whereby the Grand River lands were bestowed upon us and our posterity for ever, under the express condition that we should enjoy them for ever as the separate people we had ever been and with the assurance of the British protection renewed" (League of Nations, Doc.No.28-075).

The petition of the Six Nations was sent to the League under the personal

438

recommendation of the Dutch Minister for Foreign Affairs, H.A. Van Karnebeeck, former President of the League Assembly, who declared himself impressed by the confidence shown by the Six Nations. Van Karnebeeck was careful to stress that, while complying with the request of Deskaheh, the Dutch authorities refrained from expressing any opinion in the dispute. Yet his decision was to trigger a diplomatic incident which opposed the Netherlands and the Dominion of Canada in a behind-the-scenes confrontation, and eventually involved the discreet intervention of the League Secretariat.

As far as international procedures were concerned, Deskaheh's approach was correct. His case could only be examined by the League - either its Council or its Assembly - at the request of a Member State. The fact that the Dutch authorities had shown an interest in his appeal and transmitted it to the Secretariat could have been a direct route to formal sponsoring of his case. But Deskaheh had probably underestimated the pressures that can be exercised, within the framework of international organizations, to protect Member States. The League was to demonstrate that it was, first and foremost, an exclusive and protective "club of Nations."

The reaction of the Canadian Government to the communication of Deskaheh's appeal was quick to follow. In its reply, dated 25 May 1923, the Canadian Government unequivocally denounced the Dutch initiative and implied that it would not tolerate any further action from the League with regard to the Six Nations; Sir Joseph Pope, Under-Secretary of State for Foreign Affairs, expressed his government's protest as follows:

"The Canadian Government has learned of this action of the Netherlands' Government with considerable surprise, and I am to express its confident hope that the Council will decide that the matter thus brought to its notice is one with which the League of Nations is not concerned. It finds it extremely difficult to understand how the Netherlands' Government, without knowledge (as it confesses) of the accuracy of the statements made... and without enquiry so far... considers itself warranted in intervening in a matter which it cannot too strongly be insisted is solely [domestic]... the claim that the Six Nations are an organized and self-governing people so as to form a political unit apart from Canada is to anyone acquainted with the actual conditions an absurd one... such action it believes finding no warrant in any provision of the Covenant, and being further calculated to embarrass this Government in the due administration of its domestic laws" (League of Nations, Doc.No.29185).

After Canada's indignant response, the Netherlands' Government quickly retorted, emphasizing that it had no other intention than to forward to its proper address the documents it had received. As for the Secretariat, anxious to relieve the tensions, it began to exert additional pressure in order to put an end to Deskaheh's claims. Its course of action is clearly defined in a letter sent on behalf of J. Avenol (at the time Acting Secretary-General) to a representative of the Dutch Government:

> "Avenol... has asked me to reply to your note on the Six Nations' question. He quite agrees that what must be done is 'enterrer' the matter. The question is how to do it... to Avenol, there appears to be two courses open: (1) The Dutch Government should inform us, officially, that they no longer wish the documents they sent us laid before the Council. (2) The alternative course is to distribute this correspondence to the ten Members of the Council 'for information.' There is no doubt that their communication for information would have no reaction... the question would be completely buried and never likely to be resuscitated" (League of Nations, Doc.No.29549).

As provided in alternative two, defined by Avenol, the petition of the Six Nations was communicated to the ten Members of the League Council in August 1923. At that point, the Netherlands having withdrawn from the scene, the Secretariat was under the impression that the Six Nations had exhausted all the possible sources of support. Great Britain had formally protested what it described as the "uncalled for interference" of the Netherlands in the internal affairs of Canada, and the League's senior officials appeared firmly determined to discourage any further action. But shortly after his arrival in Geneva, Deskaheh managed to resuscitate the matter.

Deskaheh's action in Geneva

When Deskaheh arrived in Geneva in September 1923, he still had high expectations and put together a rather effective plan of action. The familiarity with international procedures has been the key to the success or failure of Indian representation in the diplomatic field and, in that respect, Deskaheh's action is no exception. International civil servants have to play by the rules of the game and Deskaheh's patience and dogged determination might finally have led - if not to international recognition for the Six Nations - at least to a discussion of their case by the Assembly or the Council of the League, and to an assessment of the substance of their complaints.

Deskaheh came to Geneva with a detailed memorandum: "The Redman's Appeal for Justice," written under the assumption that the Six Nations would be accepted as a Member of the League. On the basis of the Covenant, and after consultation with the Information Section of the Organization, Deskaheh and his lawyer had reached the conclusion that the Six Nations' appeal should not be based upon Article 1 of the Covenant, which dealt with membership and the terms of acceptance of new Members, but rather on Article 17, which contained provisions regarding disputes between Members and States which were not yet Members. Article 17 read as follows:

"In the event of a dispute between a Member of the League and between States not Members of the League, the State or States not Members of the League shall be invited to accept the obligations of membership in the League of Nations."

It is worth noting that Deskaheh was applying for acceptance in the "family of Nations" not only to obtain international recognition for the Six Nations but also to arrange for international arbitration of the legal, political, and financial dispute on the reservation. He insisted on the fact that the idea of an arbitration of three proposed by the Canadian authorities in December 1922 had been abandoned, due to a lack of agreement on the selection of the Members.

The memorandum, originally addressed to the "Honourable Sir James Eric Drummond," Secretary-General of the League, was defined as prepared

"under the authority of the undersigned [Deskaheh] and the sole deputy by choice of the Council composed of forty-two chiefs, of the Six Nations of the Iroquois ... [to] bring to the notice of the League of Nations that a dispute and disturbance of peace has arisen between the State of the Six Nations of the Iroquois on the one hand and the British Empire and Canada, being Members of the League, on the other."

The core of the text, which included historical reference to the League of the Iroquois, the Haldemand Treaty, and the various treaties between the Six Nations and the Dutch, the French and the British, stressed that the Six Nations had "at all times enjoyed recognition by the Imperial Government of Great Britain of their right to independence in home rule and to protection therein by the British Crown - the Six Nations on their part having faithfully discharged the obligations of their alliance on all occasions of the need of Great Britain, under the Covenant chain of friendship between them including the occasion of the late world war." However, the memorandum also insisted upon "the Six Nations' cessions of certain parts of their Grand River domain for purpose of sale to British subjects," the latter "retaining, by consent of the Six Nations, the stipulated sales moneys for the cessions, but in express trust for the use of the Six Nations." In addition, it pointed out that the Imperial Government had eventually "of its sole accord" handed over those funds to the Dominion Government." The complaint with regard to that financial arrangement was stated as follows: "Large sums of the Six Nations' fund held by the Dominion Government have been misappropriated and wasted without consent of the Six Nations." The financial aspect of the dispute

441

between the Dominion Government and the Six Nations' Council was a significant element and reinforced Canada's defensive reaction to Deskaheh's appeal.

The appeal formulated in the memorandum rested on four major claims:

1. The Enfranchisement Act of 1919 was "imposing or purporting to improve Dominion rule upon neighbouring Redmen."

2. The Dominion Government was said to be enforcing upon the Six Nations certain penal laws of Canada "under protest of the duly constituted Council" and to have invaded the Six Nations' domain in December 1922, establishing and maintaining an armed force on their territory.

3. It was stated that large sums of the Six Nations' Fund had been misappropriated and wasted without consent of the Six Nations.

4. The Dominion Government was alleged to have been using those funds during the last two years to incite rebellion within the Six Nations, to furnish occasion "for setting up of a new Government... tribal in form but devised by the Dominion Government and intended to rest upon Canadian authorities."

The four champions of Deskaheh's appeal

Deskaheh communicated his memorandum to the Secretary-General of the League, hoping he could be convinced to intervene in his favor. The Secretary-General declined on technical grounds to conform to his appeal and reminded him that the only possible course of action was to secure the support of a Member State who could formally request that the Six Nations' question be put on the agenda of the League. Deskaheh then embarked upon a personal campaign in order to convey his message throughout the international community. His memorandum was widely distributed and he managed to obtain the commitment he required from four Member States, namely Estonia, Ireland, Panama, and Persia. With the backing of that unusual combination of countries, Deskaheh could again hope to break through the procedural intricacies of the Organization.

A few days before the end of the Fourth Assembly, on 27 September 1923, the four champions of the Six Nations' cause addressed a letter to the President of the Assembly, in which they declared that "considering the universal interest attached to the preservation of the ancient race of the red-skin Indians" (League of Nations, Doc.No.31340), they suggested that the Six Nations' appeal be put on the agenda of the Assembly. They also proposed to refer to the Permanent Court of International Justice in order to determine whether the dispute between the Government of Canada and the Iroquois might properly come before the League for adjudication under Article 17 of the Covenant.

The President of the Assembly's response was also based upon procedural grounds. He pointed out that an Assembly resolution was required before any

442

such request could be made. As the fourth Assembly was coming to an end, it was too late to contemplate any further action at that stage.

In spite of that negative reply, the support of four Member States put a thumb's worth of extra pressure on the Canadian authorities. After their forceful rebuff of the Dutch initiative, they had good reason to hope that Deskaheh's appeal would be forgotten. Yet the Canadian delegates, upon their return from their Geneva mission, frankly acknowledged the seriousness of what could become a truly embarrassing issue for Canada on the international scene; one of them wrote to the Department of Indian Affairs that they had

"some little trouble with the Six Nations' Indians question in Geneva and [that] at one time it looked as though it would really be brought up before the Assembly" (Veach 1975:96).

He suggested that a detailed reply be prepared and sent to the League.

The Persian prince and the Indian cause

Meanwhile, Prince Arfa-ed-Dowleh, the Persian representative to the League of Nations, took the lead of the group of countries committed to the defense of the Indian cause. On 27 December 1923, he addressed a telegram to the President of the Assembly, asking him to transmit to the Council the request that he had submitted jointly with Estonia, Ireland, and Panama at the September session. In his reply, the President asked Prince Arfa whether he could address him a letter indicating more precisely whether he wished to place the Six Nations' case before the next session of the League Council, to be held in March 1924. The Prince's telegram was communicated to the Council Members. In a letter sent on 8 January 1924, the Persian representative confirmed his request and stressed that the four supporters of the Iroquois cause wanted to give a small nation an opportunity of being heard. The President's response (24 January 1924) demanded a more formal commitment from the Persian government. This unusual and lengthy procedure seemed to imply that the first Persian delegate had not indicated his government's position clearly enough or that he might be exceeding his authority. Actually the League's senior officials seem to have tried to procrastinate while the Canadian authorities were urged to send a detailed response to Deskaheh's claims as quickly as possible.

One of the clearest assessments of the situation was formulated by Sir Herbert B.Ames, Financial Director of the League, who wrote to the Canadian Prime Minister, W.L. Mackenzie King, in December 1923 in order to stress the implications and the limits of Deskaheh's action in the following terms:

"Should the Persian Government insist that this question be placed on the agenda for the March meeting of the Council, the Secretary-General has no alternative but to conform with its request. This does not necessarily mean that the Council will decide to have the question referred to the [International] Court [of Justice], nor indeed that it will consider itself competent to deal with the matter at all. But if the rules of application are complied with by Persia, I think it will be impossible to avoid some deliberation by the Council... During the Assembly, a picturesque delegation of Iroquois Indians with their Chief, Deskaheh, were here in Geneva addressing meetings and interviewing delegates. They aroused a certain amount of sympathy among people who heard their side only. Since the Assembly, I understand that they have been following up this initiative by visiting several European countries. The recent action of the Persian delegate is the result of this campaign... As yet, there has been no serious presentation of the Canadian reply. I think that really it will be necessary to pay some attention to this, lest our apparent indifference be misinterpreted and thus our excellent reputation over here suffer somewhat" (League of Nations, Doc.No.32700).

On 3 February 1924, Prince Arfa addressed himself directly to the Council President, Hjalmar Branting of Sweden who had also received a communication from Deskaheh in mid-January, asking for his support. The response to the League Secretariat, sent on behalf of Branting by the Swedish Foreign Ministry demonstrates that the Swedish diplomat was hesitating about which course to take:

"Mr Branting thinks it would on the one hand be rather inopportune for the Swedish Government to ask for the case to be examined; on the other hand he thinks it rather hard if the poor Indian cannot be even heard" (League of Nations, Doc.No.33556).

Instructions from Sir Eric Drummond, the Secretary-General, were to put an end to Branting's doubts. The Secretary-General had "decided on the highly unusual procedure of challenging whether Prince Arfa was speaking for his Government in officially raising the Six Nations question" (Veach 1975:96).

Accordingly, Branting informed the Persian representative that nothing could be done until he could communicate a formal and direct confirmation from his government. On 23 February 1924, Joseph Pope, the Canadian Under-Secretary for external affairs sent his government's official reply to Deskaheh's memorandum, which was distributed to all the League Members in March 1924. The Council session was held without any other reference to Deskaheh's case.

444

From fame to disillusionment

The March 1924 session of the Council seems to have been the turning point of Deskaheh's action in the international scene. He had come close to reaching some of his objectives, but the partial success of his strategy reinforced the opposition to his cause within the League. What had first been viewed as a hopeless appeal by many diplomats had become a controversial issue in the Organization.

As a result of the publicity campaign conducted by a number of support groups, Deskaheh's visibility had been growing in Geneva and in several European cities. He had become a familiar figure in Switzerland and his case was usually received with a great deal of sympathy. Throughout his stay, he was one of the most celebrated "diplomats" in Geneva. His dignity and restraint seem to have fascinated his European public and many observers expressed genuine admiration for a man who related his story with such simplicity and sincerity. An Irish correspondent of the *Freeman's Journal* described him enthusiastically as

"a good-looking, broad-shouldered man... wearing ordinary dark clothes... and presenting every appearance of a well-to-do Canadian farmer with the one exception of his beautiful mocassins... his beautifully-shaped but stern mouth, firm chin and heavy jawbones are those of the born fighter, the strong man who knows his strength and believes in it, whilst his shining eyes speak of enthusiasm and idealism" (Akwesasne Notes 1978:23).

Not surprisingly, he was expected to conform to the ideal of the typical Indian chief and he often accepted to appear in full regalia to please his audience. On the contrary, when he was not perceived as a picturesque or exotic stereotype, he seems to have disappointed his potential supporters. For example, a Geneva cartoonist admitted to being "desolate to find him wearing a neat brown business suit and at his side no mocassined brave but a... vulturous paleface lawyer" (Veach 1975:95). A Hungarian journalist, thrilled to see "his first American Indian," after drawing a sketch of the Chief, deplored that he did not have "the typical Indian profile, the nose not the aquiline nose [he] had expected" (Akwesasne Notes 1978:23).

In the early twenties the "spirit of Geneva" had inspired or encouraged the development and establishment of many associations or humanitarian organizations whose activities were related to the mission of the League of Nations. Many of them provided the background that Deskaheh needed to organize a coherent publicity campaign. One association, however, remained firmly isolated from that general current of support. From the very beginning of the negotiations the League of Nations Union, which had been set up as a pressure group lobbying for the creation of the League, considered Deskaheh's appeal as a lost

445

cause. The Union's position was expressed clearly in an article published in the monthly issue of its magazine, *Headway*, in the following terms:

"The League's task today is with the future, not with the past. The Six Tribes today enjoy a considerable amount of autonomy within their limited reserve. They appear to have parted with a good deal of their land by voluntary sale, but they are not immune from the criminal and other laws of Canada, and they manifestly cannot claim the status of an independent sovereign state and approach the League of Nations as such. Whether they have a just grievance against the Canadian Government is a matter to be examined on its merits, but it is not a question the League can be expected to discuss" (*Headway* VI(8):143).

The group that was probably the most supportive of the Six Nation's appeal was an international association for the defence of Indigenous Peoples, the B.I.D.I. (*Bureau international pour la défense des Indigènes*), set up in Geneva. It was certainly the best organized and the most influential of the support groups. Its founder and determined spokesman, René Claparède, who had also supported the cause of the Montenegro, was relentlessly promoting the defense of indigenous peoples throughout the world, in particular in colonial Africa. He played a major role in the setting up, in 1923, of a committee for the defense of the rights of the Six Nations, called "Commission des Iroquois," which became a link between the local supporters, the municipal authorities, and the senior officials of the League. Its membership included eminent lawyers and respected scholars. The personal reputation and connections of Claparède and Junod (the Secretary-General of the B.I.D.I.), who were both influential figures in Geneva, conferred some weight to their action which otherwise might have been ignored or denounced within the League. They built up a network of support, organized fund-raising, and publicized Deskaheh's cause. They also provided him with the legal and linguistic support that he needed and put him in touch with a Swiss lawyer who prepared a statement of the case of the Six Nations in French. Claparède himself wrote an extensive analysis of the Six Nations' appeal.

The B.I.D.I. followed closely the evolution of Deskaheh's case within the League and, in September 1923, the "Commission des Iroquois" transmitted to the Secretariat a resolution adopted by their association in support of the Six Nations, which was officially acknowledged by the League (League of Nations, Doc.No.31197). Eventually the Director of the Legal Section of the Secretariat accepted to meet with Junod to inform him of the technical intricacies of the League's procedures, and "neither encouraged nor discouraged any further action" but advised him on the best avenues to support Deskaheh's case (League of Nations, Minutes, 7 February 1924).

The Archives of the Claparède Foundation, which are kept in Geneva, together with the Archives of the League, are useful complements to the latter. Besides the correspondence between the B.I.D.I. and the League, the Claparède file also includes a number of references that add a more personal touch to the ups and downs of Deskaheh's visit. They mention in particular his fading health, a bad case of bronchitis having hampered his action and weakened his spirit from the spring of 1924. A number of letters are very revealing of the diplomatic climate and of the personal reactions to Deskaheh's presence in Geneva. For instance they allude to the fact that Lord Cecil, one of the founding fathers of the League, kept refusing to address Deskaheh and once curtly instructed him to speak to his secretary. Such personal notes illustrate the official position of the British towards what they will keep considering as a "frivolous and impertinent complaint."

The Claparède file is also rich in information on the activities of other groups which became involved in Deskaheh's case and whose activities and modes of action herald the role that the Non-Governmental Organizations (NGOs) currently play within the United Nations system. Letters from the *Ligue française des droits de l'homme*, located in Paris, and from the Law Reform Association and the Anti-slavery Society, both based in London, indicate a rather wide geographical distribution of the support groups throughout Europe, although their interest by no means implied an unrestricted encouragement. A letter from J.R. Okleshaw Johnson, from the Law Reform Association, for example, rather dryly informed Deskaheh of the position of a number of well known British lawyers and politicians with regard to the Iroquois in the following terms:

"I must advise you that it can scarcely be expected that you can look to Lord Palmoor for any real sympathy in your case as he is first of all a lawyer specializing in Church of England law, which moreover is the Protestant and orthodox religion of the British Empire. The same remark also applies to Lord Cecil, who is looked upon by the world as the British pioneer of the League of Nations. He is a parliamentary lawyer of great experience, but as a kinsman of the reigning sovereigns of the Empire, he is bound to be unsympathetic with a people who are characterized by the Canadians as 'savages'."

The correspondence between the B.I.D.I. and the Anti-slavery Society (now an NGO within the UN) is all the more revealing since the two organizations were not in full agreement on every aspect of Deskaheh's case. It seems that, whereas the B.I.D.I. fully supported the Iroquois cause and firmly believed that it had a chance of being heard, the Anti-slavery Society was more doubtful that a positive solution could be reached. On 18 December 1923, Travers Buxton, Secretary of the Anti-slavery Society, wrote to Claparède to tell him that "the Chief seems to have set his mind on getting help from the League of

Nations, which, I am afraid, is a quite hopeless course." Later, in March 1924, after having offered his organization's support he declared: "Mr. Stoker, who is a Member of our Committee and has been helping Deskaheh as a sort of informal Counsel, hopes that he may be able to bring Deskaheh's matter before someone at the Colonial Office ... Deskaheh seems to have hoped that the new Government might reverse Mr. Churchill's decision that the matter was one for the Dominion Government but this is a matter of settled policy." In May 1924, commenting on the Canadian reply to Deskaheh's claims, Travers Buxton wrote to Claparède:

"It does not deny Deskaheh's right to represent the Six Nations Indians, but it makes no mention of the offer which the Government made to the Indians in December 1922, of an arbitration of three."

The Anti-slavery Society had then called attention to some of the most interesting aspects of that reply, which actually differed from that of the Canadian Commissioner, A.J. Thompson, whose report, communicated a few month later, challenged the representativity of the traditional Council.

The Canadian reply

The "Statement Respecting the Six Nations' Appeal to the League of Nations," which was distributed to the League Members during the Council session of March 1924, utterly repudiated Deskaheh's claim of sovereignty. The Canadian reply was based on the following arguments:

- "The Six Nations are not a State within the purview of meaning of Article 17 of the Covenant of the League of Nations... and are therefore not competent to apply for or receive membership in the League."
- "The Six Nations are not now, and have not been for centuries, a recognized or self-governing people but are subjects of the British Crown residing within the dominion of Canada".
- To contradict the claim referring to the independent status of the Six Nations, the Dominion was quoting an "Order of His Excellency in Council," approved on 13 November 1890 and confirmed by a subsequent order dated 27 November 1921, stipulating that "while the Government fully recognized and appreciates the loyalty of their forefathers and the continued loyalty of the present generation of the Six Nations Indians, it cannot sanction or hold as valid the claim... to special exemption from the effects of the law of the land, nor to that community being recognized as other than subjects of Her Majesty the Queen."
- The Canadian Government emphasized that the Enfranchisement provisions of

the Indian Act (sections 107-111) define a legislative machinery whereby Indians who so desired and who are duly qualified, may acquire Canadian citizenship. It was stressed that such a legislation was enacted to stimulate progress among the Indians and afford them an opportunity for self-government.

The spirit of compromise

During the months following the distribution of the Canadian reply the Iroquois cause inspired negotiations that went far beyond the discussion of their own case. Two months later, on 10 May, the Persian Government was telling its representative in the League "that the Government [did] not wish to interfere in the matter and that no further negotiations [were] to be made on the subject" (Veach 1975:98).

Discussions between Great Britain, Estonia, and Panama led to the conclusion that they would also abstain from any further action. All the tentative moves in support of the Six Nations were abandoned in view of strong opposition from Britain and Canada. On the other hand, the Iroquois appear to have been a pawn in a confrontation which opposed Canada to three of the champions of Deskaheh's case over the possible amendment of Article 10 of the Covenant. Article 10 provided that "the Members of the League undertake to respect and preserve as against external aggression the territorial integrity and existing political independence of all Members of the League." It was considered by many of the Nations that felt vulnerable in the face of potential threats from stronger States as a vital provision of the collective security system of the League. On the contrary, Canada viewed Article 10 as an unnecessary commitment that might imply involvement in conflicts on far away lands. As was very well demonstrated by R. Veach in his book on Canada and the League of Nations, the joint appeal in favor of the Six Nations was submitted to the Assembly only two days after Estonia, Panama, and Persia had opposed Canada's efforts to obtain an interpretative resolution on Article 10. As Veach pointed out:

"So far as Canada was concerned the frequent assertions by its delegates of a superior moral position must have served as an irritant and for Canada to be forced on the defensive on the same sort of minorities question as was plaguing so many other League Members, must have seemed fair enough. In addition Canada's insistent attempts through four Assemblies to get major changes in the collective security aspects of the League, through tampering with Article 10 - changes which were clearly not palatable to many League Members - must have been a further irritant. Certainly the Persian, Panamanian, and Estonian delegates' disagreement with Canada over Article 10 and their simultaneous interest in the Six Nations' grievances can be assumed to be related... But if a combination of sympathy with the Indians and irritation with Canada probably produced the initially favourable attitude on the part of several States to the Six Nations' appeal, instead of a virtually non-existent legal basis, those attitudes quickly evaporated when trouble resulted for the States themselves" (Veach 1975:99).

The time of vanishing hopes

For Deskaheh the summer of 1924 marked the beginning of the end. As his supporters within the League vanished, the lobbying groups continued to publicise his cause among the general public. However, from then on, the gap widened between popular support and increasing diplomatic indifference. When Deskaheh and his lawyer hired the Salle Centrale in Geneva in a last effort to promote their appeal, they received an enthusiastic response from the general public, although it was reported that no League official had attended the meeting. The Canadian Government had announced an election which would determine whether the traditional government of the Six Nations was to be dissolved and everybody refrained from any action within the League.

Deskaheh clearly sensed that his cause was lost. In November 1924 he wrote to the editor of a Swiss journal "it is the heart broken that I am against the most cruel indifference... My appeal to the Society of Nations has not been heard..." (Akwesasne Notes 1978:24).

It is also in November that the League Secretariat received from Ottawa two major documents, the Report of Commissioner Thompson and a letter announcing the change of government on the Grand River Land.

The end of the road

Andrew Thompson's report was a general survey of the social and political state of the Grand River Land but it was also an official challenge of Deskaheh's representativity. According to Thompson, the Six Nations had been trying to establish their sovereignty unduly under the influence of what he called the "separatist party," which he denounced as increasingly influential within the traditional Council of Chiefs.

An "usurpation of power"

Thompson's argument was formulated as follows:

"For some considerable time past there has been a strong agitation to have the Six Nations constituted as a separate and sovereign people. Those

450

supporting this course allege that, by wording of certain early treaties, the Six Nations are not subject but allies of the British Crown... The separatist party, if I may say so, is exceptionally strong in the Council of Chiefs, actually it is completely dominant there... I am fully convinced that the present Council has undoubtedly been guilty of a serious usurpation of power, with regard to the Government of Canada on the one hand, and the Six Nations Indians on the other..."

But it is worth noting that there is one point on which he is in agreement with Deskaheh's Memorandum, namely the claim referring to the misappropriation of funds. At the end of his report he confirms that "from the year 1834 to the year 1842, both inclusive, almost $160.000 of the Six Nations' Fund were invested in the stock of the Grand River Navigation Company, quite without the approval of the Indians and without consultation with them," an investment, which was "a total loss." Thompson further states that

"ever since it became so the Indians have been constantly seeking reparation. In answer to the appeals made, the Canadian Government took the stand that, therefore, responsibility could not rest upon it. The Six Nations Indians then forwarded, through the Government of Canada, an appeal to the British Government; the British Government replied that this was a matter for the Government of Canada and disclaimed all liability. The fact remains that the trust funds have been lost and that the Indians have been denied redress by the Governments to which they have appealed."

In his conclusion Thompson declares that: "This question undoubtedly constitutes a real grievance and should finally be dealt with in some way. It is a constant irritation to the Indians and, as one of them put it, shakes their confidence in British justice."

A "new elected Council"

But the League obviously never had to dwell on the merits of this case. Together with the Commissioner's Report an official letter dated 27 November 1924 complemented its conclusions in the following terms:

"It might be stated that the recommandation of the Commissioner in regard to the elective system of the Six Nations has already been put into effect and that on the 17 September 1924 an Order in Council was passed applying the election provisions of Part 2 of the Indian Act. An election was held on the 21 October 1924 and the new elected Council is now in office having replaced the former hereditary body. It is believed that this change to a more modern political system will have a good influence on the reserve and

act as a stimulant to progress and advancement among the Six Nations"
(League of Nations, Doc.No.40899).

Before the end of 1924 Deskaheh had left Geneva. His health had been deteriorating over the last few months and his failure to be heard, after coming close to achieving some of his objectives had weakened him both mentally and physically. An exile from Canada and from the land he represented on the international scene, he was to die among the Iroquois of western New York from an attack of pleurisy and pneumonia, in June 1925.

Whatever judgment may be passed on a man who can be considered as a symbol of the past, or as a herald of the future, he remains a powerful historical figure whose charisma seems to have exceeded his real power. The Archives of the League establish that - strictly from the procedural point of view and as far as his strategy on the international scene was concerned - he carried out his mission skillfully. The fact that his very achievements seem to have caused his downfall only illustrates the risks and limitations of such diplomatic endeavors.

Deskaheh died desperate to think that he had failed, but it set his mind at rest to think that his mission would not be forgotten. As he himself stated in his last speech in March 1925, "it has gone into the records where your children can find it when I may be dead."

NOTE

1. Deska(h)e(h) [teskáhe̅'] is a hereditary Cayuga chief's title of the Iroquois Confederacy. The actual name of the person bearing this title in the early 1920s was Levi General.

REFERENCES CITED

Akwesasne Notes
   1978   A Basic Call to Consciousness. Mohawk Nation via Rooseveltown
Claparède Foundation
   1923-24 Archives. Palais des Nations, Geneva. BPU Geneva University
   Library.
Carmer, Carl
   1949   Dark Trees to the Wind: A Cycle of York States Years. New York:
   William Sloane Associates.
Fenton, William N.
   1950   Review Note: C. Carmer, Dark Trees to the Wind. U.S. Quarterly
   Book List 6:87. Washington
Grinde, Donald A.
   1977   The Iroquois and the Founding of the American Nations. San
   Francisco: Indian Historian Press.
League of Nations
   1919   Covenant of the League of Nations. Original text, April 28.
   1923-24 Archives. Palais des Nations, Geneva.
   File n° 28075: The Six Nations and the League of Nations
   - The Indian Act, 1906. Doc. n° 57551.
   - The Redman's Appeal For Justice, the Position of the Six Nations that
   they Constitute an Independent State, Chief Deskaheh, Speaker for the Six
   Nations Council, August 6, 1923. Doc. n° 30626.
   - Statement Respecting the Six Nations Appeal to the League of Nations.
   Department of Indian Affairs, Canada, December 27, 1923 - Doc. n° 34286.
   - Report of Colonel Andrew T. Thompson, Commissioner of the Canadian
   Government to investigate and inquire into the Affairs of the Six Nations,
   November 22, 1923. Doc. n° 40899.
   - Documents n° 28075, 29185, 29549, 30035, 30296, 30626, 31197, 31340,
   31608, 33556, 33687, 34286, 40899.
Naville, René
   1973   Amerindiens et anciennes cultures précolombiennes. Contributions
   suisses aux sciences américanistes: "En 1923, pour faire valoir les droits
   d'un peuple indien, un Iroquois chez les Genevois." Genève: Perret-Gentil.
Veach, Richard
   1975   Canada and the League of Nations. Toronto: University of Toronto
   Press.
Wilson, Edmund
   1959   Apologies to the Iroquois. New York: Vintage Books.

MUTUAL FASCINATION: INDIANS IN DRESDEN AND LEIPZIG[1]

Rudolf Conrad

In April and October of 1983 the Indian hobbyists of the German Democratic Republic had their first opportunity of a personal encounter with a North American Indian representing himself as a traditional medicine man of the Miniconjou and Brulé Lakota: Archie Fire Lame Deer. During his two visits of about one week each to the tipi campground near Triptis (Thuringia), a varying number of Indian hobbyists were present. Archie Fire Lame Deer expressed the wish to meet Indian hobbyists and get information about their activities and over and over again he experienced the deep wish of many of them to become acquainted more thoroughly with Indian mentality and religion in order to better understand the Indians' way of life, their culture, history, and present political efforts. As I was sleeping in the same tipi as Archie, participated in most discussions, and attempted to record the event, I can report on this encounter exclusively on the basis of personal experience, without having to rely on hearsay.

We were impressed by his explanations of Indian traditions which obviously seemed to have been modified since the days of J.R.Walker by serious contemplation of the influences of modern life, a fact noticable in the fine Leipzig edition of his father's book (Fire and Erdoes 1983).

We were deeply touched by being able to take part with him in the sweat lodge and pipe ceremonies, by hearing his songs, and by seeing him pray with the sacred pipe of the Lame Deer family. We also found him to be a fine singer and a keeper of Sioux songs and we spoke a great deal about music. I told him about my particular interest in this subject, since as a member of the Leipzig Gewandhaus orchestra I also look upon myself as a traditional musician.

More than once, Archie expressed his pleasure to be here and to see tipis and excellent bead and quill work. This he regarded as a stimulus for his own people to resume some of their old traditions. He especially tried to make us comprehend the inseparable connection between these material things and the Indian way of "walking in balance with the earth."

Most of the hobbyist groups are interested in a distinct ethnic unit of a certain historical period and by studying the available sources as well as by recreating their crafts they try as closely as possible to approach an understanding of this culture. Karl May is clearly of no importance in such a context.

During a public lecture at the Leipzig "Klub der Intelligenz" (Club of Intelligence), Archie Fire Lame Deer was asked for his opinion about Karl May. After the audience had ceased laughing at the question, his answer seemed at first surprising: "Regardless of how things are set about and how people think, I would tend more to thank Karl May for writing about Indians, for he has

455

kept alive the thought of Indians in the minds of all European people... I wish we had had him in America at the turn of the century... In the system that we live in children are not taught about Indians. They are only taught about George Washington, the 'Father of America'..." This answer stresses the phenomenal degree of popularity of American Indians in Germany and confronts the fact that the German image of Indians in the absence of sufficient first-hand impressions is often based on non-authentic material, with the lack of a closely comparable amount of such an interest in the United States.

How to account for the different attitude? Without being able to fully detail the process of intellectual history leading to this difference, it must at least be outlined here. It characterizes the situation of Indian visitors to Germany, that finding themselves as a rule admired and cherished, they in turn become deeply impressed. In this way, the resulting process may be described as one of mutual fascination.

Knowledge and impressions about Native Americans were predominantely transmitted by literary sources. F.Sixel's analysis of the Indian image in Germany during the first 50 years after the discovery of America, takes off from the highly developed state of German book printing: "In the age of discoveries, Germany thus could boast of one of the most highly developed and the time most progressive publishing networks in Europe, thoroughly enabling it to play a leading role in the publication of Americana." This is seen as "the best example for compensation, in this respect of limited contact with the actual discoveries, by the potential of the printers." It appears noteworthy that "especially the frequency with which a conception of the Indian (whether true or false) was brought to the attention of the German reader has to be seen as significant for the interest and image-shaping power of authors and consumers of this literature." The statements "that the quantitative relationship between phantasy and objective fact varies, of course, according to the distance of the author to life in the New World," as well as that "the contemporaneous German was easily seduced to find in the Indians one of the figments of his imagination finally come true" - these statements may be considered valid well into the 20th century (Sixel 1966:53,54,79,211,212). Besides the curiosity inherent in such publications, these facts were major causes of a development, always accentuated by the spirit of the respective period.

Many good travel accounts were published in Germany, usually in translation. The age of Enlightenment, on the other hand, used the idea of the Noble Savage for its own purposes and shaped the Indian image according to a specifically European standard which looked at all problems from a considerable distance and whose ideal partiality was not compromised by regards for reality. Much of this is also still true today.

In view of the excessive growth of phantasy in later periods, it takes some effort to realize the amount of valuable ethnographic contents of the works published by the universally inquiring mind during the age of circumnavigations.

Interested Germans had therefore access to substantial information, even though its complexity hardly met the public inclination for stereotypes.

The rising popularity of Indian novels in Germany since about 1826 was seen by H.Plischke (1951:33) as a result of the enthusiasm for the young United States as a model of freedom and democracy and with a certain weariness about life in Europe: "The longing for the promises of the New World was increasing in Germany during the time of Metternich and the political disappointment resulting from it, and led to the desire to learn about America." This was followed by the publication of the collected works of Washington Irving and, above all J.F.Cooper, but also by large-scale translations of other writers. Embedded into romantic landscapes and partly historical contexts was a new ideal partiality for the Indians, which in Germany fell on fertile soil.

A week before his early death and already seriously ill, Franz Schubert, for example, wrote on 12 November 1828 in a short letter to a friend:

"Therefore be so kind to come to my help with reading matter in this desparate situation. Of Cooper I have read: The Last of the Mohicans, The Spy, The Pilot, and the Pioneers. In case you might have something else by him, I beseech you to deposit such for me with Madame von Bogner in the coffeehouse. My brother, the epitome of conscientiousness, will bring it to me most conscientiously. Or maybe something else. Your friend Schubert" (Dahms 1918:292).

Plischke describes the development beginning with authors like Charles Sealsfield, Friedrich Gerstäcker, or others who at least had been themselves to America and leading up to "all kinds of writing minds" motivated by the general success of the Indian novel. Ultimately, hardly any bounds seemed to exist for phantasy in the field of Indian fiction.

Until the period of romanticism, the purpose of "instructive entertainment" characterized the treatment of Indian subject matter. The enormous rise of the ethnographic novel led to a split between "entertaining" fiction and the much more slender branch of "instructive" literature of a popular scientific kind which lost much of its shaping influence on the general public through the popularity of the novels. Besides such travel accounts as that of George Catlin (German edition, 1848) or of Maximilian Prinz zu Wied, Waitz's armchair study *Die Indianer Nordamerica's* (Leipzig 1865) should be mentioned. Toward the end of the 19th century, the growth of fanciful writing increased. Traveling Indian shows with artistic or folkloristic programs did not place in doubt the Indian imagery of these writings. The authentic impressions of those shows were less calculated to stimulate critical comparison with the literature than to confirm the imagination of the German viewer, that is, "to find in the Indians one of the figments of his imagination finally come true."

Beginning in 1876 and based in Dresden, Karl May began his carreer as a writer for journals and of dime novels, leading up to those novels written until the turn of the century, which may be seen as the ultimate peak of the popular and fanciful ethnographic novel in German. "The products were a testimony to his elaborate imagination and considerable sympathetic understanding. The exotic novels did not contain anything based on observation and experience. They were rather shaped by the study of literature" (Plischke 1951:114).

The final ennoblement of May's Indian image is reached in his figure of Winnetou, and even the "evil Indian" as a rule is portrayed as the prey of White villains. In his *Geographische Predigten*, Karl May describes

"the site of that desparate fight in which the Indian lets fly his last arrow against the exponent of a bloodthirsty and reckless 'civilization.'... At the beginning of the 19th century the 'Redskin' was still master of the vast plains... But then came the 'Paleface,' the White man, drove the 'Red brother' from his own hunting grounds and through disease, 'firewater' and shotguns dealt out death and destruction in the ranks of the strong and trusting sons of the wilderness... What and how the Indian was not supposed to be, that and so did he become through his Christian brother who carried the scripture of love on his lips and the murderous weapon in his fist, depriving mankind and universal history of a rich number of inestimable potentials for development... but traditions will weave their golden gleam around the vanished warrior of the savanna, and the memory of the mortal sin committed against the brother will continue to live in the song of the poet"

- published in 1876, the year of the battle of the Little Big Horn (May 1916:46ff., cp.493).

Under the motto "Empor ins Reich des Edelmenschen" (Upwards to the empire of the noble man), Karl May formulated some high ethical-philosophical objectives of his Indian novels. His publisher Dr.E.A. Schmid added his opinion "that Karl May in 1909 foresaw with the prophetic look of the poet future upheavals in the life of the peoples when writing *Winnetous Erben* in which he predicted a new population in America, which would be regarded as especially valuable through the participation of a reflorescent Indian race" (May 1916:524). For the German reader, Karl May's Indian novels established a deeply effective romantic-emotional tie to the American Indian.

The sheer size of the editions of his works must have made his contribution to the German Indian image the most lasting. To this must be added an effectual public dispute about the value and credibility of his works, a separate publishing house only bent on increasing his fame and sales, a yearbook published by the Karl May Society, Karl May plays in the rocky scenery of the open air arena near Rathen, and not the least the magnificent ethnographic

458

Karl May Museum in Radebeul, a powerful magnet for huge crowds whose numbers have increased once again during the present Karl May renaissance in the German Democratic Republic.

The discussions about May clearly helped efforts to publish authentic material on Indians. The potential problems in achieving this end are demonstrated by the book *Wir Indianer* (1929) written by Edgar von Schmidt-Pauli for Big Chief White Horse Eagle, a rather dubious character who for some time traveled through Germany and who visited Dresden, too. Also published were the works of Charles Eastman, Grey Owl, or Chief Buffalo Child Long Lance's book. These very successful works are indeed more realistic than pure fiction, despite the fact that the identity of the two latter authors was not exactly what they or their publishers claimed them to be. In the preface to Buffalo Child Long Lance's book, Hans Rudolf Rieder, the translator and editor, gives the following pertinent opinion:

"The Indian is closer to the German than to any other European. This may be due to our stronger leaning for that which is close to nature. Negroes, Eskimos, peoples of the Pacific do not possess the human qualities to arouse our friendship and inclination. The Indian, however, is model and brother for us during our boyhood; among the dreams and longings of those years he remains one of our most cherished recollections. In this book, a real Indian steps forward in front of us. It is not a novel and no fanciful fiction... If some things look different from the way we had known them so far from our 'Indian books' we should recognize that reality is always more rich and valuable than the creations of phantasy... And our boys should learn to play their Indian war-games in a proper manner... Perhaps this book will help to bring the Indian ever closer to us, because we still have much to gain from him" (Langspeer 1929:1,2).

The aspect of propagating "the truth about the Indians" becomes clear. This campaign which continued into the recent past, tries to decry the Indian stereotypes without exposing their authentic contents and the process of their genesis. The widespread great love for Indians has also stimulated important scholarly activities. The best but not the only example is indubitably Curt Unckel-Nimuendajú who did field-work in Brazil and even took an Indian name (Menchén 1979). As an emigrant from Nazi Germany, Julius Lips did field work among the Naskapi and Ojibwa, wrote one of the best juvenile books about Indians (*Tents in the Wilderness*), and returned after the war to Leipzig, where after his death his wife continued to popularize scholarly research (Lips 1965).

The example of research on North American Indian music shows that this branch of ethnomusicology was initiated in Germany, even though it soon shifted almost entirely to America. The high standard of comparative musicology in mid-19th century Germany triggered systematic investigations of non-

European musical cultures and also attracted students from America. J.C.Fillmore, for example, studied in Leipzig before becoming active in the field of Indian music and playing an important role in educating a generation of American musicologists and ethnomusicologists.

From 1874, Theodore Baker also took up his studies of music and musicology in Leipzig. During term break he was encouraged to visit both the Seneca Indians and the Indian Training School in Carlisle, Pennsylvania, where he transcribed Indian melodies by ear. This was the basis for his dissertation *Über die Musik der nordamerikanischen Wilden* (On the Music of the North American Savages), published in 1882 by Breitkopf & Härtel. It marks the beginning of scholarly literature on North American Indian music.

A visit of several days in 1885 of Captain Jacobsen's Bella Coola troupe with the Geographic Society of Halle provided C.Stumpf with the opportunity to write "the first monograph in the field of modern comparative musicology" (Nettl 1957:1140; cp.Haberland, this volume). German interest in Indians was primarily literary in nature. As valuable places of research and education, the large ethnographic museums in Leipzig and Dresden were at the disposal of interested persons. Actual encounters with Indians remained the exception but if in fact they happened, they incited the enthusiasm to an extraordinary degree. Before discussing the major period of the presence of Indian groups in Germany, two other occasions may be mentioned in passing which caused Native Americans to visit Europe.

The activities of the Moravian missionaries of Herrnhut among North American Indians have been described in detail by Loskiel (1789) and Heckewelder (1819). They came to an end at the beginning of the 20th century, but the work among Eskimos continues until today. This was an important source of ethnographic information in the Lusatian-Saxonian region and made Herrnhut a point of call for some visitors from the New World.

"Soon it was not an uncommon sight to find former Negro slaves, Eskimos and representatives of other heathen congregations sitting among the German brothers and sisters." Regarding the Eskimo visitors of the 18th century "records from those days make it apparent that the Greenlanders were carrying with them not only their original costumes which they wore during performances and other events, but also implements characteristic for their way of life" (Israel 1965:45, quoting Bayreuther). Two graves of these visitors dating from 1748 can still be seen in Herrnhut. During the mid-19th century children of Greenland missionaries would disembark from the train in Bautzen, dressed in the fashion of the Eskimos with whom they had grown up, being on their way to Niesky where they would attend school with other children having come under similar circumstances from Tibet, Surinam, or South Africa.

These visits were mainly of an internal ecclesiastic character. The ethnographic museum of the town of Herrnhut, however, now a branch of the ethnographic museum in Dresden, works for the public and sometimes still receives an ethnographic object found in a corner of a Herrnhut house as a reminder of the former missionary work.

The World Wars should not be forgotten as events in which Indian soldiers took part. F.Densmore recorded Indian songs relating to World War I and Germany. About the Arapaho she reported that "... they had a victory dance for the soldiers, in which two women carried German helmets aloft on lances, as scalps were carried in the old days" (Densmore 1936:50; see also Theisz, this volume). German enthusiasm for Indians never seems to have abated because of such isolated indications of lacking reciprocity.

After World War II, the Cherokee Silkirtis Nichols remained in Germany, took the popular name of Buffalo Child Long Lance and became an attraction in the scene surrounding the new headquarters of the Karl May publishers in Bamberg and the new festival plays in Bad Segeberg. Several times he has also been to the German Democratic Republic, primarily to Dresden. The paper *Trommel* published his picture and reported:

"AN INDIAN IN BERLIN... Buffalo-Child-Long-Lance, chief of the Cherokee, rode on a horse furnished him for the occasion through Lippehner Strasse and through Friedrichshain... speaks in the GDR about his tribe and visits the ethnographic museum in Radebeul" (Trommel 1968:2).

Together with the hobbyist group "Old Manitou Radebeul" he rehearsed an Indian war dance which was performed publicly without himself participating. So much for an example of a non-traditional Indian closely linked to the Karl May scene.

The great period of traveling Indian shows which lasted until about 1930 is characterized by a shift of accents on the Indian image. Bearing in mind the visits of Eskimos and Bella Coolas, the first Native North Americans travelling in Germany must have offered insights into cultural variety. The archives of the ethnographic museum in Leipzig also contain drawings and photos made of Iroquois and Chippewa Indians produced on the occasion of such visits (Dräger 1975:195f.). A.Lehmann has treated "Völkerschauen" (displays of peoples) and some of their forerunners, primarily in Leipzig. The first group of 15 Oglala Lakota made their appearance in 1886 under the leadership of Frank Harvey and were billed as including some that had fought Custer in 1876 (see also Létay, this volume). In connection with the "Wild-America"-show of Dr.W.F.Carver, he emphasized that "it was the time during which the struggle for freedom of the Indians was nearing its sad end" (Lehmann 1955:37). Plains Indians in general and the Sioux in particular indeed do not seem to have become the focus of the Indian image until during and after these events.

As the quotations from Karl May have already shown, news about the last Indian wars met with much sympathy in Germany. Authentic representatives of the concerned tribes must have experienced this attitude even more so, first of

461

all the Lakota who now represented the vast majority of Indians in the traveling shows.

The first Indians of Buffalo Bill's Wild West in America were dressed-up Whites, the first genuine Indians of the show were Pawnees. From the same tribe, Indian scouts had been enlisted during the Indian wars in which Buffalo Bill had participated in person. Only in 1877 it is reported that "Bill left early in the fall for Red Cloud Agency where for the first time he engaged reservation Indians for one of his shows. 'Real Indians' had been advertised previously, and perhaps some had been employed, but more frequently they had been red men of the type of Captain Jack's Hoodlums" (Russell 1960:258).

Buffalo Bill owed his popularity to his huge and spectacular show and to an enormous number of dime novels published in his name, whose contents he soon was unable to control any longer and which made him a legend in his own lifetime. The show was a medley of historical pageant, rodeo, and display of animals and people. Its attraction derived from a certain authenticity caused by the high proportion of participants actually coming from the live Far West, including prominent Indians. Shortly after the virtual extermination of the species, his group of buffalo seemed a sensation by itself. During its second stay in Europe, the show traveled across Germany in 1890, including stops in Dresden and Leipzig. 72 Indians, for the most part Sioux, came along with Buffalo Bill, "and as Europeans had a great curiosity about the red men they were treated with much consideration. A few remained in Europe" (Russell 1960:351; cp. the papers of Napier and Fiorentino, this volume). A.Lehmann writes: "It was really a sensation... There was general agreement that the promises of the advertisments were surpassed by the facts" (Lehmann 1955:38).

In Frankfurt, a young Viennese left his horticultural apprenticeship and for a while joined the show as a stable-boy. Later on he was successful as a performer and traveled throughout the world, above all North America, with prominent circuses: Frank Tobis - better known under his alias Patty Frank. His extensive North American Indian ethnographic collection (plus specimens from Karl May's estate) formed the original basis of the Museum in Radebeul noted above. Until the time of his death in 1959, this great friend of the Indians remained in charge of the museum and wrote books about Indians. Regarding the museum, Russell (1960:353) says: "One of its prides is a painting of Custer's last fight by Elk Eber, who obtained his information from a Sioux woman, eyewitness of the fight, who left Buffalo Bill's Wild West to be married in Germany."

The Indians of the tour of 1890 returned to Pine Ridge at the end of the season. "About fifty of them were employed as Indian police and in a company of scouts sent to Fort Robinson for duty under Lieutenant Taylor."

Apparently, Buffalo Bill again did not visit any place twice when he returned to Germany in 1891 and 1906. Without doubt, a great demand remained for an equivalent event. This was turned to account by a circus from Dresden:

462

Sarrasani (see especially Günther 1984).

Since 1901, Hans Stosch-Sarrasani had built an impressive company whose outstanding artistic achievements were given utmost effect by unconventional ideas, and which made best use of modern advertising. As a man of practical life, he was always keen on professional competence. Until about 1932, seven issues of *Sarrasani* were published, documenting the work of this circus and expressing the intentions of Stosch-Sarrasani:

"What Bayreuth is for the lover of operas, Sarrasani is for the enthusiast of the circus... Sarrasani means public education, Sarrasani is to revel in aesthetic beauty. A true, heartfelt enjoyment of art, accessible to even the least of the widest audience... Sarrasani's ambition was striving for higher goals. The arena was to teach from real life, to be an enumeration, an opalescent survey or everything the world is offering in terms of remarkable animals and artful people... Object-lessons in natural history, but never dry, always full of heartbeat and life!... He had negotiated with the American government and so had succeeded to be the first company to bring genuine Sioux Indians to Europe. He surrounded himself with caravans of Indians, Chinese, Japanese, negroes from the Sudan, Arabs, Moroccans, Boers, and Eskimos; in his city prevailed a profusion of languages rivaling that of Babylon" (Sarrasani n.d.,6:1; 1:1,4,6).

Sarrasani's attempts to give a certain image to his company was, of course, accompanied by polemics against everything questioning his claim to exclusiveness, even though he adopted and imitated some of his competitors' ideas. He was certainly not the first one to present Sioux Indians in Europe. In the years before World War I, the model of peoples' displays was fully developed and since Buffalo Bill's Wild West some years had already passed.

"The Americans who had then moved across Europe, sucking in the golden money, were no models, were almost repelling. With their system of three stages they bluffed the German need for quality and beauty. As soon as the bluff is over, the American department store system, the method of wholesale junk is rejected by the Germans... The old Colonel Cody, himself a fighter in the last Indian wars, had formed around himself a body guard of subjugated redskins, they followed him to Europe and they disappeared with him. In his horse operas they had remained almost unnoticed" (Sarrasani n.d.,1:2; 2:20).

Especially the last remark is rather presumptuous, but it remains a matter of fact that Sarrasani's 22 Indians had a deeper effect on the German public especially in Dresden, than Buffalo Bill's 72 (and 100, respectively). This is less true for the program itself, since the Wild West in the arena, the staged

463

captures of mail coaches, the gauchos, cowboys, and rodeos must have rather been imitations, and reference to their superior quality can at best have been of a polemical nature. The effect of the activities by Sarrasani's Indians outside the proper performances, however, must have been enormous.

"Indians can ultimately be made with rouge and dyed feathers... But we, we didn't want that. We wanted to have them for real and in person."

Despite this remark, Sarrasani did not hesitate to supplement his cast with disguised natives of Dresden. The stereotypic characterization of Indians helped to perpetrate the fraud: "The redskins were calm and quiet, always taciturn and introvert, but never apathic" (Sarrasani n.d.,2:20,23). These pseudo-Indians were the founders of the first Indian hobbyist group in Radebeul, whose notable artistic achievements including marksmanship, knife-throwing, or lasso twirling remain to this day and are reminiscent of its prototype.

The development of such activities in and around Leipzig may have been furthered by the local folk tradition of the "Tauchscher" which relates to the Wild West and may no longer be observed today. The term stands in short for "Tauchischer Jahrmarkt" (Fair of Taucha), a public celebration of Leipzig held on the second Monday in September, including a parade with illuminated lanterns and exotic mummery for the children: In its heyday, it became an institutionalized mass phenomenon expressive of the enthusiasm for Indians. G.Wustmann (1895:544ff.) reports in the late 19th century:

"Many have painted their faces and don a fanciful dress. Here a band comes disguised as 'Indians' with feather crown and feather skirt, bow and arrows in their hand... then there are matches, parades, fights, escapes and pursuits with wild war cries - in short, it is indeed a strange sight which has to be seen to be understood... *Tauchischer Jahrmarkt* happens only one day of the year... Thirty years ago, nobody in Leipzig would have thought of dressing up as an Indian for the *Tauchische Jahrmarkt*. This playing of Indians and Bedouins is a modern addition whose source is easy to see: It is the ethnological displays, the dragged-about caravans of all kinds of peoples, which no700day virtually chase one another during the summer in the big cities, and are being gazed at by big and little children."

Even before founding his own circus, Hans Stosch-Sarrasani had made an acquaintance in America:

"Mister Zack Miller, first of three brothers, truly American types, although they were never able to hide the good German name Müller... they created a 'show.' It was the 101 Ranch-Show. And so it happened. The Millers had whole Indian tribes as their guests on their tracts of land. They settled in areas which still had not been opened up, they roved across the prairies, through the impenetrable woods of the back country. The Millers were not in the mood to go along with the fashion of supplanting the Indians and of pushing them deeper into misery. They had the whim to make friends with them and let them subsist somehow. Some of the German romantic spirit was still at their disposition, a little bit of hero worship based on reminiscences of Leatherstocking Tales as they are inoculated to the youth in our country. The Millers were also the first ones campaigning for the official protection of Indians by the government... The friendship between the Millers and the Indians became a hard and fast one. The Millers were able to count on the allegiance of their Indians. Their Indians became the basis of their traveling show" (Sarrasani n.d.,2:20,21).

Contacts were renewed, and in the beginning of 1912 Zack Miller came from Bliss, Oklahoma, to Dresden with a film showing the Indians and the rodeo of the 101 Ranch-Show. Only one obstacle remained in the way of the project of a German Indian show:

"Twenty-two of his national relics President Roosevelt was supposed to surrender and indeed he wanted to make sure that they would be returned to him. Hans Stosch-Sarrasani had to make a deposit in Washington of 10,000 gold marks per head for the 22 Indians. Moreover, in a contract he had to give the strictest guarantees: Travel and board for the Indians from their settlements to Dresden and back again, sufficient daily allowances, wages like for a heroic tenor for every Indian. And as a clincher: If one of the people would pass away far from home, even his body was not to be lost to the United States. He was to be embalmed in Germany according to Indian ritual and accompanied back by a guard consisting of four Indians to America's sacred soil, to the hunting grounds of the prairies where the great and gentle spirit Manitou would be able to receive the copper-red corpse into his care. Never has a private person concluded a more severe treaty with a government than Hans Stosch-Sarrasani did then with the Indian commissioner in Washington under securities supplied by Zack Miller. But the goal had been attained - and our Indian experiences began" (Sarrasani n.d.,2:23; but see Günther 1984:67-68).

It should be mentioned here that on the occasion of a performance with Pawnee Indians from Indian Territory in Washington in 1879, Buffalo Bill had likewise been informed "that his employment of Indians was of concern to the Indian Bureau. He went to Carl Schurz, Secretary of the Interior, and was told that Commissioner of Indian Affairs E.A.Hayt held that the native actors were wards of the government, absent from their reservations without leave" (Russell 1960:262). It took a certain gift of persuasion to get finally and under

465

certain conditions the official permission for hiring Indians.

The stipulations of Sarrasani's contract caused some problems in the course of the more than two years the first group of Sioux Indians worked for Sarrasani. K.A.Vollrath reports: "In February 1912,[2] Two-Two (which means two times two, thus four), the chief of the Sioux solemnly stepped down from the ocean steamer in Bremerhaven, surrounded by his warriors, a ruler... Full of majesty and stonefaced he walked through the lane formed by amazed people, with dignified gesture he lit himself a cigarette and sat down in the restaurant car of the special train. Around him, the Sioux and their squaws were grouped. Romanticism was travelling alive and tangibly through the German country and arrived in Dresden.

"In those times, we had occasionally welcomed potentates from all around the world... but Two-Two eclipsed all these events. Dresden was cleared out down to the last room, the factories afforded themselves the luxury to rest for one morning. Two-Two and his feather-bedecked following mounted the impatiently stirring horses and gallopped from the main railroad station through the venerable street of August the Strong. The people - a hundred thousand - cheered, the children wept for joy and for sympathy, and we, we were proud of these our guests, proud as never before in the existence of the Sarrasani show. And a faint smile of comfort started to gleam on the grave faces of the Indians. The ceremony of introduction, of greeting was solemn and sustained... Thereafter the redskins took up quarters in the *bel-etage* above the suite of our stables. Half of the people of Dresden were standing beneath the windows of the Indian apartments. Until deep into the night they listened to the melancholic songs resounding from the open windows. Blonde girls stood below wrapped up in their thoughts and sentimentally adored the heroes of the prairie. So it remained for a full month...

"The Sioux Indians were always surrounded by heart-stirring idyl. Only now and then a thunderstorm struck our Indian idyl. The redskins have a national poison: firewater. Whoever of them moistens his mind with firewater is bewitched by the devils... Not the gunfire, but the firewater has exterminated the Indian people, the sweet poison had nearly succeeded in emasculating a whole continent. And only during our age when the loss of the last Indian remnants was about to be feared, the law has created draconic punishments for those who either supply the Indians with alcohol or who drink alcohol with them... And on this basis all of our contracts with the government in Washington had to be concluded: That we should vouch for it under threat of penalty that the Indians would stay away from alcohol.

"All went well for a while until catastrophe suddenly broke loose. It did not happen by our fault, but by the assistance of the female admirers of the Indians. Charmed by their love, they had hoped to find access to the granite-hard hearts of their red heroes by way of the neck of a liquor bottle. Together they could not come, the female citizens of Dresden in their hero-worship and the redskins living on the first floor without a key to the house. But the Indians are still children of nature, they know how to help themselves in natural ways. While the moon was shining romantically, they let fishing lines hang from their windows down to the sidewalk, and instead of bouncing fish one could see liquor bottles dangling from them, which were then retrieved from the dark of Dresden-Neustadt to the abundance of light in the Indians' quarters.

"Two-Two, the venerable old chief, who had once fought against the palefaces was powerless against the cunning attacks of the ladies. He lost his authority over the warriors as soon as the secret sip began to bustle in their stomach and started to set their brains on fire. The bout turned into catastrophe. Knives flashed, wild yelling penetrated to the very marrow of a whole district of the city, and alarmed the night patrols of the police. Two-Two remained calm: With stone-like majesty he shrugged his shoulders. Until our cowboys intervened. They had a strong hand to massage the senseless redskins, with penetrating determination they had singled out the ring-leaders and locked them up in empty cages reserved for predators, each one in his own grate-bar villa, and had turned on the stand-pipes and took hold of the hoses... And we sent a telegram to Oklahoma: 'Send us a new chief who also inspires the fire spirits with respect.' Two-Two was shaken and frowned.

"Three weeks later the new chief arrived... Sternly vowing, he asserted that he was the only medicine man holding power over the alcohol devil of his red brothers... Towards dusk he had vanished, he had taken a crooked path to those abodes where wine is usually served by tender hands. Next morning he appeared, a staggering and tottering colossus led by two plump women who delivered him stammering to their tribe. Two-Two nodded his head in approval. The new chief was instantly invisible... to take the steamer back home - at his own cost. Two-Two had taken the scepter again, he has resided in our show for two years.

"Then it happened in the year 1914 that the tree of his life began to wither... Then, one day - it was in Dortmund - he finally lay down and made the request not to be disturbed... Even in the last night of his adventurous life the great chief Two-Two has smoked more than eighty cigarettes, then he asked that the consul of the United States be fetched. The closest consul resided in Elberfeld, and we sent a car by night and brought him in. To him Two-Two disclosed his last will: He disposed of his riches and surprisingly made the request to be buried in Dresden. Because this city had become second home to him" (Sarrasani n.d.,2:23-27). Two-Two died that very night. The following document was drawn up: "We, the undersigned relations of the deceased Indian chief Two-Two hereby certify that the dead during his life has often had the desire not to be embalmed and sent to America and be buried there. He has often wanted to be buried on a Catholic churchyard and it was his wish to be buried on the Catholic churchyard in Dresden because there is the home of the *Sarrasani-Schau*. The undersigned widow, son, daughter, and son-in-law declare that they have the same wish and request that the funeral take place on the Catholic churchyard in Dresden. Essen, 28 July 1914" (Günther 1977:111).

Three days later a funeral service was held. Afterwards the coffin was sent by rail to Dresden but because of the beginning mobilization it took a few days to get there. World War I was beginning. The grave still exists in Dresden. This description may best express the effect of the German Indian enthusiasm on the Indians themselves and confirm the need to explain the origin of this enthusiasm. Two-Two's troupe returned to the United States.

In 1925,[3] another group of Sioux came with Chief Black Horn, and in 1928 the third with Chief Big Snake. Black Horn may be seen on several photographs:

"Black Horn, sovereign prince of the Sioux, 97 years old... In Frankfurt-on-the-Main he celebrated his 50th anniversary as a chief and was presented on this occasion with gifts of honor by the city of Frankfurt... And with him and his warriors, romanticism was again moving through Germany... The Sioux had joined the Sarrasani show as it was crossing America... Dresden stood once more in the sign of the tomahawk... The Dresden tribe again formed a lane by the tens of thousands... The cavalcade was led by Hans Stosch-Sarrasani... donning a historic cowboy costume, and with his dapple fullblooded horse prancing, he sat on his silver sparkling saddle once owned by Emperor Maximilian of Mexico. He accompanied his allied Indian sovereign on his visit to the mayor of Dresden. Trumpets led the way. Across the August bridge, they brayed around the Saxonian Assembly... Dr. Blüher, the mayor of Dresden, welcomed the ruler of the Sioux in the state room of City Hall" (Sarrasani n.d.,2:27,29; 6:21).

Spectacular scenes such as this one carried the public relations effort of the Sarrasani company: The Indians in a canoe during the flooding of the Elbe, on horseback in the city during the morning workout, in small open Hanomag cars on sightseeing tours, Indians on pilgrimage in the monastery of Einsiedeln... Additional information on the Indians of the latest tour is also supplied:

"The Indians traveling this year with the Sarrasani show were fetched by Mr. Shoultz, a cowboy, and his wife directly for the show from their tribal seats in Pine Ridge in the state of South Dakota... They disembarked in Hamburg and representatives of the local university greeted them as welcome objects for ethnographic research... At the department of phonetics of the university of Hamburg songs of the Indians were recorded."

Letters of acknowledgement of the department of geography and the ethnographic museum are quoted. The continued claim of promoting the dif-

Fig. 1. "Hans Stosch-Sarrasani was joined by Black Horn, Chief of the Sioux, obliged to him by old friendship, together with a guard of his warriors and their wives.After a short rest in London, they accompanied the Sarrasani show to Europe" (Sarrasani n.d.,1:11).

fusion of geographic and ethnographic knowledge is supported by the publication in *Sarrasani* of pertinent articles and illustrations mostly unrelated to the activities of the company. Photos with Indians in front of studio microphones are captioned:

"People perform music - under this motto the Westgerman Broadcasting stations arranged for their listeners an educating evening during the late engagement of Circus Sarrasani in Cologne, featuring their exotic nations" (Sarrasani n.d.,6:21; 4:4-6; 7:23).

Several photos document the interaction of the two major forces contributing to German enthusiasm for Indians: "Sarrasani's Indians consecrate their death songs to Karl May. Sarrasani with the American consul general Haeberle and Chief Big Snake in Karl May's mausoleum. Sarrasani and some of his Indians visit Karl May's widow" (Sarrasani n.d.,4:9,10).

The reciprocity of both otherwise autonomous components ought to be regarded as the key for the culmination of German enthusiasm for Indians. Karl May died in 1912, the year when the first group of Sarrasani's Sioux

469

Fig. 2. "Big Chief White Horse Eagle with his white wife about to leave the Karl-May-Museum in Radebeul, which he visited 18 June 1929.In the doorway the American consul G.P.Waller, Dresden, on the right Mrs.Klara May, led by Patty Frank, the inhabitant of the log cabin" (old photographic postcard).

Indians came to Dresden. The time of vicious attacks against him was over, his fame prevailed. In 1928, in the midst of the heyday of Sarrasani's Indian shows, the Karl-May Museum was opened. The events supplemented one another, the result was outstanding. "There is deep symbolism in the fact that the Sioux Indians of Circus Sarrasani when visiting Dresden performed death songs and laid down flowers at Karl May's grave," L.Gurlitt wrote on the occasion of Big Snake's visit to the cemetery on 17 January 1928. "This act contained the recognition that Karl May second to none had perceived the tragic fate of the dying people and has erected an honorable memorial in its memory... Therefore I cannot look without affection at the picture of the Sioux Indian giving his testimonial in his native tongue in front of Karl May's grave" (Sarrasani n.d.,4:9,10).

Sarrasani's circus was destroyed with the city of Dresden on 13 February 1945. The museum in Radebeul was preserved, just as something else - the interest and love for the American Indians.

470

NOTES

1. Cordial thanks for suggestions and valuable support are due to Dr.L.Dräger and Mr.R.Krusche of the Museum für Völkerkunde in Leipzig. For references and research material, I am also grateful to Messrs. J.Hüttner, Dresden, S.Jahn and D.Kretzschmar, Leipzig.
2. Corrected to 14 March 1913 by Günther (1984:69).
3. Or 1926 (Günther 1984:72).

REFERENCES CITED

Dahms, Walter
1918   Schubert. Stuttgart-Berlin-Leipzig.
Densmore, Frances
1936   Cheyenne and Arapaho Music. Southwest Museum Papers 10. Los Angeles.
Dräger, Lothar
1975   Federhauben bei Indianern des östlichen Nordamerika. Jahrbuch des Museums für Völkerkunde Leipzig 30:191-204. Berlin.
Fire, John (Lame Deer), and Richard Erdoes
1982   Tahca Ushte. Medizinmann der Sioux. Leipzig.
Günther, Ernst
1977   33 Zirkusgeschichten. Berlin.
1984   Sarrasani wie er wirklich war. Berlin.
Heckewelder, J.G.E.
1819   An account of the history, manners and customs of the Indian nations who once inhabited Pennsylvania and the neighboring states. Philadelphia.
Israel, Heinz
1965   Grönland-Eskimo auf europäischen Gemälden aus dem 18. Jahrhundert. Abhandlungen und Berichte des Staatlichen Museums für Völkerkunde Dresden 25:35-78. Berlin.
Langspeer, Häuptling Büffelkind
1929   Langspeer. Eine Selbstdarstellung des letzten Indianers. Leipzig.
Lehmann, Alfred
1955   Zeitgenössische Bilder der ersten Völkerschauen. In: Von fremden Völkern und Kulturen. Hans Plischke zum 65. Geburtstag. Düsseldorf.
Lips, Eva
1965   Zwischen Lehrstuhl und Indianerzelt. Aus dem Leben und Werk von Julius Lips. Berlin.
1974   Nicht nur in der Prärie... Leipzig.
Loskiel, G.H.
1789   Geschichte der Mission der evangelischen Brüder unter den Indianern in Nordamerika. Barby.
May, Karl
1916   Ich. Aus Karl Mays Nachlass. E.A.Schmid, ed. Radebeul.
Menchén, Georg
1979   Nimuendajú. Bruder der Indianer. Leipzig.
Nettl, Bruno
1957   Indianer Nordamerikas. In: Die Musik in Geschichte und Gegenwart, vol.VI. Kassel-Basel.

Plischke, Hans
  1951   Von Cooper bis Karl May. Eine Geschichte des völkerkundlichen
          Reise- und Abenteuerromans. Düsseldorf.
Russel, Don
  1960   The Lives and Legends of Buffalo Bill. Norman.
Sarrasani
  n.d.   Heft 1-7. Dresden.
Sixel, Friedrich Wilhelm
  1966   Die deutsche Vorstellung vom Indianer in der ersten Hälfte des 16.
          Jahrhunderts. Annali Lateranensi 30:9-230.
Stumpf, C.
  1886   Lieder der Bellakula-Indianer. Vierteljahresschrift für Musik-
          wissenschaft 2:405-426.
Trommel
  1968   (issue of) 2./3.August. Berlin.
Wustmann, Gustav
  1895   Quellen zur Geschichte Leipzigs, Band 2. Leipzig.

LIFE AMONG THE "HUNKPAPAS":
A CASE STUDY IN GERMAN INDIAN LORE

Peter Bolz

A high-pitched rhythmic song accompanies the deep sound of a drum. Masked figures appear: one covered with a bearskin, another hidden beneath the hide of a mountain lion, and a third under the guise of a wolf. Two other figures in buffalo-robes bend forward and slowly step toward the middle of the dancing area in cadence with the drum. Mountain lion, wolf, and bear follow. Then the hunters arrive on the scene. The first is decked out in a traditional Blackfoot costume with a tall feathered bonnet and richly decorated leather garments. He carries a lance. The second hunter, armed with bow and arrows, is simply clad in loincloth, moccasins, and a fur cap. He sports a shield over his left arm. They both dance around the circle in search of game and espy the two buffalos. After a brief chase, they overtake and "kill" them with their hunting implements. But before they can rejoice over their success, they are threatened by the wolf and the mountain lion. The latter makes wild lunges at the second hunter who is barely able to ward these off. In the end, however, the hunter is the victor and the wolf too has bitten the dust. And then the bear attacks. Although pressed from both sides, he can't be brought down and even manages to mortally wound one of the hunters. At last, a precise spear-thrust by the Blackfoot finishes him off. The dancing area is littered with bodies as the women make their appearance. Some of them are wearing leather dresses decorated with beadworks, others don garments made of colorful fabrics. Two of them immediately set upon the buffalos and begin to skin them. Another delivers a death-blow to the gasping wolf as the wife of the dying hunter commences to wail plaintively. Three of the women finally carry off the "dead" Indian and the remainder follow with the dragging carcasses. End of scene and the public applauds.

The drama described above did not originate from a Hollywood movie or a Karl May novel, but was performed live by the Hunkpapa Indian Club on their grounds in the near vicinity of Frankfurt. The occasion was their Open Day in August 1, 1981. The *Indianerklub Hunkpapa e.V.*, an officially registered association, holds an Open Day once a year. Their purpose in doing so is twofold: to inform the general public of their activities on the one hand, and to raise funds through the sale of food and beverages, or payments for participation in games such as horseshoe-throwing, on the other.

The main attractions on such an Open Day are performances in lassoing, knife-throwing, and whip-cracking, when some of the members can show off their particular talents. A country band provides for musical entertainment. The performances by the cowboys, trappers, or Mexican vaqueros belonging to the club take place on that section of the grounds where a fort has been built,

Fig. 1. Tipis in the *Ginnheimer Wäldchen*, the "hunting grounds" of the Hunkpapa Club.Photo: Peter Bolz.

Fig. 2. Singers and drummers are performing as a prelude to the hunting dance.Photo: Peter Bolz.

complete with saloon, trading post, sheriff's office, and "boot hill." A little farther off stands the Indian camp, in which there is less evidence of hectic activity. The most important structure is the "Indian lodge," constructed of wood and resembling a Mandan earthlodge in form and furnishings. Inside, Indian costumes, tools, weapons, etc., made by the members themselves, are placed on display. Next to it, several canvas tipis have been set up that correspond to those used by 19th century Plains Indians in size and shape. There is an open area at the center on which the "Hunkpapas" hold their dances or other performances. For each Open Day, a special dance or an important scene out of Plains Indian life is staged. The hunter's dance described above, for example, was performed during my first visit to such an occasion in 1981. On other occasions, the "Hunkpapas" performed eagle, war, scalp, and other dances, or demonstrated the peaceful way in which goods were usually exchanged with fur traders. One of the averred goals behind such an Open Day, is to correct the popular cliché of the bloodthirsty savage promoted among the general public by the mass media. The chairman of the association, Michael Schubert, stated as follows: "So much nonsense has been spread about Indians, from scalping to the heroic Winnnetou image, that we find it important to give an account of the normal and not at all warlike Indians" (*Frankfurter Rundschau*, 16 August 1982).

According to the articles of the association, the "Hunkpapas" are an "ethnological club for the tradition and culture of the North American Indians" (*Frankfurter Nachrichten*, 23 June 1983). Members try to meet these rather high standards by placing great value on authenticity. Customs and traditions are to be copied as exactly as possible. Basic information is obtained either from scholary publications, especially those describing Indian material culture, or visits to museums. Although a subgroup of the Teton-Sioux or Lakota was chosen as namesake, the "Indian" members of the club do not limit themselves to representations of the Sioux alone. It is clear, however, that priority is given to Plains cultures, and thus, despite ethnological pretensions, the cliché of the Plains Indian as the Indian par excellence is sustained. Not even the Apache, brought so close to us by Karl May, are represented in this club (as is the case in most other clubs as well).

What about the ethnological pretensions of this club? This question will remain a source of contention not only between ethnologists and club members, but among the latter as well.

According to a report in the *Frankfurter Rundschau* of 16 August 1982, the Hunkpapa Club is an association "striving to preserve Indian customs, songs, and dances." This could lead to the interpretation that North American Indians have discarded their traditions and that these have only been preserved thanks to the efforts of the "Hunkpapas" and other "Indian" clubs. In a letter to the editor published by the *Frankfurter Rundschau* (28 August 1982), I pointed out that the Sioux certainly did not need a Hunkpapa Club on their reservations in

South and North Dakota in order to preserve their traditions. These dressed up Germans would appear as ridiculous to the Indians as a group of Japanese in Bavarian costumes would to us. As a result, a lively discussion flared up between the "Hunkpapas" and myself over their ethnological pretensions. As a consequence, I was invited to participate in a "regular" club meeting, far removed from the hustle and bustle that inevitably accompanies Open Day.

At first the "Hunkpapas" denied any aspirations to preserve Indian customs, songs, and dances as reported in the *Frankfurter Rundschau*, claiming that this was a statement formulated by the reporter and not by them. Again and again, they stressed the point that their activities are simply a hobby, just like those practiced by millions of others, from stamp-collecting to sky-diving. Thus they were primarily doing something for their own benefit, rather than pretending to instruct the Indians in any way. On this level, we were finally able to communicate. They explained to me, that it was not only of importance for them to faithfully reproduce the garments and jewelry of Indians, but also to gain an understanding of the Indian way of life, especially its close relationship to nature. Aside from regular meetings for the purpose of sharing experiences, the club members also spend much of their free time - sometimes their entire vacation - on the grounds in order to live for days or weeks in tipis together with their families, whereby they voluntarily renounce most comforts of civilization. Indian hospitality is also stressed (as I found out myself) and it is obviously fun to prepare Indian recipes over an open fire. Undoubtedly, a bit of camp-fire romanticism is also involved when one sits in front of the glowing embers way past midnight, wrapped in warm "Indian" blankets, listening to "Indian" songs, drinking German beer, and telling German jokes.

Some critics go so far as to denounce the "typical German clubbiness" going on there, claiming that the Open Day is little more than a bluff: "Terms like ethnology and Indian customs are being used although no one really knows what they mean" (Horst Feser, a former member of the club, in the *Frankfurter Nachrichten*, 31 August 1978). It seems, therefore, that there is some discrepancy between the way the club presents itself to the outside and what it can actually accomplish. But the activities of the Hunkpapa Club involving the outside public are not limited to the Open Day. They also include what could remotely be called "community oriented" events. The "Hunkpapas" perform at inaugurations of playgrounds, set up their tipis when a public open-air swimming pool is opened, or make their club-grounds available for the handicapped, sports associations, or kindergartens. The "Hunkpapas" were also represented at the *Frankfurter Ferienspiele* (plays for schoolchildren during holidays) in 1981:

"Together with an expert educationalist from the *Frankfurter Jugendamt* [youth welfare office in Frankfurt] and a number of students from various pedagogical fields, they introduced the children to Indian life-styles and

Fig. 3. The hunting dance: Killing one of the "buffaloes." Photo: Peter Bolz.

Fig. 4. Indians and trappers trading in front of the "Dakota Trading Post." Photo: Peter Bolz.

479

told them of their customs and characteristics... The hatchet remained buried on that day. Children arriving with pistols and rifles had to surrender their weapons if they wanted to play along. So there were no warwhoops or gunfire to be heard, nor did any bloodthirsty scalping scenes occur... Instead of Western nostalgia there were authentic Indian jewelry, eagle feathers, amulets, and medicine bags. Each child received a name and a corresponding symbol for his medicine bag" *(Frankfurter Rundschau,* 18 July 1981).

A more recent community oriented activity was the participation in a parade for the benefit of the *Aktion Sorgenkind* (an organization helping problem-children), in which the "Hunkpapas" marched through the wet streets of Frankfurt between a brass band and a group of cyclists on a rainy day in August, 1983. Aside from these community oriented activities that primarily involve entertainment as well as instruction on Indian matters, the club-grounds are sometimes also rented out to recording or advertising agencies desiring Western backgrounds for their products.

It is interesting to note, that the activities of the Hunkpapa Club always attract the attention of the mass media, be it on Open Day or during their participation in public events. This is true not only for local newspapers, but for American publications like *The Family* (edition of July 7, 1967) as well. The association is especially proud of such press coverage, which they will pin up on a board along with a short chronological account of their history on Open Day, in order to document their lively past.

The "Chronicle of the Hunkpapa Indian Club" begins as follows: "The association was founded in 1934 under the name *Indianerclub Frankfurt West* (Indian Club Frankfurt West) - a group of Western fans met regularly in private in order to exchange ideas on the subject and make traditional costumes."

Unfortunately, nothing is said concerning the motivation behind the founding of such an association, so that it would be appropriate here to give some thought to the possible background of German enthusiasm for Indians.

In 1887, "Buffalo Bill's Wild West" started off its first European tour in London as the main attraction of the "American Exhibition" commemorating Queen Victoria's fiftieth year as regent (Russell 1960:323). Ninety-seven Indians, most of them Sioux from North and South Dakota, accompanied Buffalo Bill's show. "His Indians were actually real Indians, but he only presented the most exotic of them - usually mounted Sioux with savagely painted faces and splendidly feathered war bonnets" (O'Neil 1981:64). Since the tour to England had been so successful, Buffalo Bill organized another European tour in 1889 which began in Paris. The show moved to southern France, Spain and Italy before it finally reached Germany in 1890. The first stop was

Munich, followed by Vienna, Dresden, Leipzig, Magdeburg, Braunschweig, Hannover, Berlin, Hamburg, Bremen, Cologne, Düsseldorf, Koblenz, Frankfurt, and Stuttgart. After spending the winter in Alsace-Lorraine, the show went on the road again in 1891 beginning with Karlsruhe. From there it continued on again to Baden-Baden, Mannheim, Darmstadt, Mainz, Wiesbaden, Cologne, Dortmund, Duisburg, Krefeld, Aachen, and from there on to Belgium and England (Russell 1960:353; 1970:40; Rennert 1976:27). Wherever Buffalo Bill appeared with his show, it was in triumph. Long before opening, his show was advertised on large posters and in newspaper ads, so that huge crowds gathered at the train-stations to witness its arrival. A Dortmund newspaper 13 of May 1891, describes the arrival as follows:

"Hundreds of people have gathered to watch the strange spectacle. This jumble of Indians, horses, and buffalos that finally fell into formation and slowly marched towards the Fredenbaum [festival grounds in Dortmund] was quite a sight indeed. First came the buffalos, surrounded by mounted drivers, and then the Indians on their horses, trailed by a strange vehicle, obviously a former stage-coach from the Wild West pulled by four mules. Especially the Indians attracted attention with their copper-colored faces that were sometimes painted, their fantastically bright-colored costumes, and their strange headdresses" (quoted in Klotzbach 1982:37).

Buffalo Bill apparently caused a "Wild West fever" to break out in Germany. Another reporter from Dortmund described the emotions, desires, and yearnings that were kindled by the show:

"What would we have given in our own childhood days, when we pored over Ferry's 'Coureur de Bois' with glowing cheeks, to witness the romantic Indian figures in reality. Now that we have settled with our childhood dreams, comes this Colonel Cody, called Buffalo Bill, and floods us with all that we once so desired. Therefore, the rule of the day for anyone who wants to return to his childhood days or make his children happy is: Onward to the Fredenbaum! This show is truly an experience" (quoted in Klotzbach 1982:38).

Along with dramatic scenes from Buffalo Bill's adventurous life, Annie Oakley's marksmanship, and cowboy stunts, the public got to see Indian attacks on wagon trains, stage-coaches, and bordertowns. Ethnological aspects were also provided. The various groups of Arapaho, Cheyenne, and Sioux Indians set up a camp in which horseraces were held as well as dances and other customs of daily Indian life demonstrated. A German program for "Buffalo Bill's Wild West" of 1890, emphasizes that the performances have nothing to do with regular circus acts. Instead, the events were acted out exactly "as they had occured and been recorded in history" (Rennert 1976:7). That is to say, that a special value was placed on authenticity in this show, and what could be more authentic than real buffalos, real cowboys, and real Indians.

At a time when people still did not get to view the wide world each evening through television, this mass concentration of figures coming from a far away land and bygone days must have made am impression that can hardly be comprehended today. The after-effects, however, can still be traced up to the present. The characteres appearing in the works of Karl May and other authors were mere products of the imagination and either so noble or so evil that their deeds could hardly be identified with nor were worth striving after. With Buffalo Bill it was another matter. Here real live people appeared before the public to offer at least a glimpse of their true life experiences as well as exotic costumes. Garments, feathered headdresses, dances, camp life, etc. were concrete things for Germans, which they could copy and through which they could transform fantasies that had been stimulated by literature into active deeds.

Other authors who have studied the after-effect of the Wild West also trace the development of Wild West clubs in Germany back to Buffalo Bill: "Large crowds of Germans thronged to Buffalo Bill's shows - and they didn't lose their enthusiasm for the Wild West after the troupe had departed again. For years they had kept track of the fantasy deeds of Old Shatterhand, the frontier hero of German author Karl May. Now they founded associations in order to act out their frontier fantasies. Wild West clubs were born in almost every German city" (O'Neil 1981:78).

But not only Buffalo Bill brought Indians to Germany. He had a number of emulators such as Pawnee Bill, the Miller Brothers' 101 Ranch, and 40 or 50 others who, nevertheless, were never able to match his popularity. Today, Buffalo Bill is considered to be the creator of the West that continues to exist in the imagination of Americans and the rest of the world. "His show distilled a handful of sparkling symbols out of the faraway and vast American frontier, which became indestructible standard metaphors for practically all those who worked Wild West themes into art or entertainment after him" (O'Neil 1981:87).

At the same time, another type of show was developed that laid claim to some degree of scholarly authenticity. During the Trans-Mississippi Exposition of 1898 in Omaha, the first "Great Indian Congress" was convened in which over 500 Indians from 36 tribes throughout the United States (most of them from the Plains) participated. This "Ethnological Congress of Red Men" was to help White visitors gain an understanding of the customs and rites of the various tribes (Rieske 1974:9). Under the direction of Colonel Frederic T.Cummins, this ethnological show toured Europe, including Germany, between 1907 and 1912 as "Colonel Cummins's Wild West and Indian Congress" (Russell 1960:383).

482

Carl Hagenbeck, who founded the Stellingen Zoological Garden near Hamburg in 1907, not only displayed animals, but human beings as well. His *Völkerschaustellungen* (exhibitions of peoples) were also ethnologically oriented. In the summer of 1910 he had an entire Indian agency set up at his zoo in which a group of Sioux Indians under Chief Spotted Weasel could be observed by the visitors. The exhibition included a program that was similar to Buffalo Bill's, with Indian attacks on a log cabin and a stage-coach, horse stealing, etc. (Maler-Sieber 1978: 22-24).

In 1912, circus director Sarrasani didn't want to inaugurate his "Circus-Theater" in Dresden without the inclusion of exotic Indians and contracted a group of 22 Sioux from the Pine Ridge reservation. This group's journey from Bremerhaven to Dresden led by their chief Edward Two-Two became a triumphal procession.

"All train-stations were clogged with people. Newspaper reports had long foretold what kind of visitors were due from the United States. Entire school classes lined up along the railway embankments and the grown-ups were just as excited. It seemed as if Karl May had produced his life's work just to prepare the people for this very moment" (Sievers 1973:172; Sommer 1971; cp.Conrad's paper, this volume).

Considering this massive appearance of Sioux Indians in Germany between 1890 and 1914, it is small wonder that their culture is better known to us than any other. These proud warriors in their feathered war bonnets were simply "the Indians," and all those who made a hobby out of their enthusiasm for Indians used these impressive figures as models. It mattered not how much Karl May may have written about the noble Apache and their chief Winnetou, their image remained pale in the face of such heroic figures from the northern Great Plains that could be seen live in Germany.

In my opinion, the connections are too obvious to leave room for any doubt that the emergence of the Indian hobbyism in Germany is directly related to the appearance of Sioux and other Plains Indians prior to World War I. They continue to be shining examples for all Indian hobbyists, and this will probably be the case for some time to come.

It is certainly not a coincidence that Charles A. Eastman's book "Indian Boyhood" was translated into German and published in 1912 under the title *Ohijesa, Jugenderinnerungen eines Sioux-Indianers*, right in the midst of this early wave of enthusiasm. Not a novel but a non-fictive work, written by an Indian author, *Ohijesa* describes the free and unrestrained life style of the Sioux prior to the advent of Europeans. Not sensational scenes from the warpath, but daily episodes of Indian life are described here such as the family, games, sports, hunting, celebrations, dances, old myths, and the life in the woods and in the winter-camp. The book must have appealed to the general public at that time as the fourth German edition was printed only one year after its initial publication. Together with the journals of Maximilian Prinz zu Wied (1839-41) and George Catlin (1851), Eastman's book probably became a standard text for members of the newly founded Indian clubs. That the enthusiasm for Indians persisted after the end of World War I is evident in the fact that a number of other "authentic" books about Indians were translated into German during the 20's and 30's: Eastman's *Winona* (1920), J.W. Schultz's accounts of his life among the Blackfoot (1922 and 1925), *Häuptling Büffelkind Langspeer erzählt sein Leben* (1929) by Buffalo Child Long Lance (Sylvester Long), *Standhafter Bär* (Luther Standing Bear): *Mein Volk, die Sioux* (1930). The tales by Archibald Belaney alias Grey Owl, an Englishman, about his life in the Canadian woods were published in Germany under his Germanized "Indian" name *Wäscha-kwonnesin*. His most successful book was *Männer der Grenze* (Men of the last frontier). Also to be mentioned are the novels by Fritz Steuben dealing on a historical basis with Tecumseh.

One of the oldest Wild West Clubs in Germany is the *Cowboy-Club München Süd*, which was founded in 1913. On these early associations O'Neil (1981:78) writes: "As the members were more interested in the daily life of the West than in the bloody deeds of gunslingers, they studied the history of the West, collected books and artefacts, and each one adopted the name and identity of some personality from the West. The 'Indians' attempted to master ceremonial songs and dances, while the 'Cowboys' concentrated on riding feats and stunts with the lasso - all this in preparation for the local Wild West shows put on by the eager associations." This may also apply to the Indian Club Frankfurt West founded in 1934, although not one of the members from that time remains alive to provide us with concrete information.

World War II brought most of the club activities to a standstill, so that it became necessary to re-establish the Frankfurt Indian club again in 1954. A few years prior to this, several other Indian clubs had reorganized as well, so that supra-regional meetings could be held. Since 1951, several nation-wide bulletins have been published, such as *Der Indianerfreund* (Friend of the Indian), organ of the *Internationaler Club der Indianerfreunde* (International Club of Indian Friends), which was already dissolved by 1953, however. Many other organizations were founded that put out newsletters like *Rauchzeichen* (Smoke Signals), *Dakota-Scout, Fährte* (Trail), and others, most of which were of short duration. An exception was the *Interessengemeinschaft für Indianerkunde* (Association for Indian Studies) which until 1971 published the magazine *Kalumet*. Out of this organization developed the *Deutsch-Indianischer Kreis* (German American Indian Group) which publishes the most important German Indian magazine today, *Amedian*. The activities of the German Indian clubs during the 50's and 60's were so lively, that their membership continually grew. This became especially evident with the increasing number of participants during the annual supra-regional council at Pentecost.

484

The actual birth date of the Hunkpapa Club in Frankfurt was in 1961, when it was officially registered under the name *Indianerclub Hunkpapa*. With this, it became possible to procure appropriate grounds on which buildings could be erected. The first ranch house was constructed in a gardening area in Frankfurt-Preungesheim. The following statement concerning the activities of the club can be read in the association's short chronicle: "The hobbyists of the Hunkpapa-Ranch are involved with the Western-hobby, especially with the study of customs and rites of Indians and of the trappers and mountain men living in Indian territory." But the ranch in Preungesheim was shortlived. Because the club-grounds were needed for the construction of a road, the ranch had to be torn down in 1966 and the association was forced to look for an alternative.

Only after a number of bureaucratic problems had finally been cleared up, did the city of Frankfurt allow them the use of their present grounds. The property involved is 30,000 square meters of meadow in the so-called *Ginnheimer Wäldchen*, a small piece of woodland in the western part of Frankfurt, near the Nidda, one of the larger tributaries of the Main. The first task that had to be undertaken by the members was to prepare the grounds for the installation of water and sewage pipes and electrical facilities. Months were spent digging pits and a well, until they finally could get started on the saloon. The latter was basically finished by 1968. Next a stable was erected for the horses and, at last, in 1970 the grounds that had been named "Dakota Trading Post" could be inaugurated. The festivities on this day remain one of the fondest memories in the history of the association. Among the guests were not only representatives from the city of Frankfurt, but also a U.S. general and a representative from the American consulate. The press gave a detailed report on the occasion. Aside from a saloon, the "Dakota Trading Post" also includes sleeping barracks, a sheriff's office, and eight large tipis for the "Indians." The ranch had been constructed as a veritable fort with palisades, towers, and even two old cannons. The grounds were completed on a later date with the inclusion of the Indian lodge, a barn, and a corral.

At this time the club counted 54 active and 12 passive members, according to a newspaper report (*Frankfurter Allgemeine Zeitung*, 9 June 1970). But already by then, the number of members was decreasing, as the chairman of the club mentioned in an interview that it once counted 120 (*Frankfurter Rundschau*, 5 June 1970).

The main event in the history of the association was when it hosted the annual Pentecost meeting of the council for all of the Western and Indian clubs in Germany in 1972. In cooperation with the Wyoming Club and the Hammer Ranch, the "Hunkpapas" had sent out invitations for all to come to Frankfurt-Ginnheim and some 1,100 made their way over. Aside from the German clubs with Munich, Berlin, Frankfurt, and Pirmasens as the most numerous, there were also representatives present from Switzerland, Belgium, France, Holland, England, and the U.S.A. In addition to the usual campfire activities a lively exchange of ideas and experiences as well as trade for costume materials goes on during such a council meeting. At the same time competitive events are carried out and historical scenes enacted. In 1972, the signing of the treaty between the Hunkpapa leader Sitting Bull and U.S. General Terry was the historical occasion chosen to be acted out in the *Ginnheimer Wäldchen* near Frankfurt (*Frankfurter Rundschau*, 23 May 1972).

Today there are only 26 active members left in the Hunkpapa Club. Since their activities always include the entire family, however, the "tribe" sometimes numbers up to 40 hobby Indians. A certain fluctuation in membership is still apparent. It is not surprising that such a hobby, with its emphasis on authenticity, will lead to some differences in opinion. The hobby Indians live in the 20th century and all of them have regular jobs so that they are continually forced to make certain compromises between the authentic and the technically and financially efficient and possible. While the "Hunkpapas" make use of a historical model, they still allow each individual member a certain leeway in his productions, depending largely upon the availability of funds and the proper materials. That is to say, they will use historical patterns as models but not limit themselves to strict reproductions so as to leave some room for individual creativity.

On the other hand there are the "perfectionists" among the hobbyists, who will use drawings and paintings by Karl Bodmer as reference and try to reproduce the articles depicted there as accurately as possible. Their products are actual replicas, consciously made as an effort to bring elements of a past culture back to life again. In 1983, the Deutsches Ledermuseum in Offenbach set up the first extensive display of such products under the title *Weiße Indianer* (White Indians). These can be easily differentiated from original museum pieces because they show no signs of use or wear. The garments of the "Hunkpapas," however, are used in all meetings for all purposes. They are not treated like display pieces but like everyday clothing, making traces of wear and tear inevitable.

Because of these essential differences among Indian hobbyists, it often occurs that one or the other will quit an association or that several former members will form a new one. The latest case was the foundation of the *Kitoki e.V.* ("kitoki" supposedly means 'prairie chicken') by two former "Hunkpapas," which enrolled ten new members by 1983. The reasons for this split had more to do with the "typical German clubbiness" mentioned above than questions of material detail. This clubbiness will frustrate much of the motivation and ideals brought along initially and therefore be a matter of dissension for many a member.

The foremost goal of the club is, according to what some of the members told me, the preparations for the annual great council at Pentecost. In 1981

486

another such council took place near Frankfurt, organized by the Indian and Cowboy Club Wyoming. As there were over 2,000 participants expected, the club had to rent a gliding site on the Vogelsberg north of Frankfurt as an alternative to their smaller club- grounds.

"It started off with a colorful Indian powwow and reached a climax with the rodeo, in which artistic stunts were performed with bull-whips, knives, axes, guns, and lassoes for prizes... Camp activities, trading, meeting old friends, dances at the Indian camp, cooking over an open fire, lively doings in the saloon and among the traders, all spiced with the smell of burning wood and horses, underscored with a myriad of sounds - all this gave a unique touch of 'freedom and adventure' to the great gathering of the last of the Western-romantics in our modern plastic-world as could only happen during such a council... The aura of the historical figures impersonated by those people showed clearly that, contrary to general opinion, the Western hobby is much more than a masquerade, it is an earthy philosophy of life" (Fleischer 1981:16-18).

In the midst of a large crowd of sympathizers and totally away from the problems of daily life, it is probably much easier to identify oneself with that person which one portrays as being "Hunkpapa." All participants do their best to live according to the part they play for those three days. This is also manifest in the strict traditional separation of activity among the sexes. While the men function solely as hunters and warriors, the women are occupied with the housework or handicrafts, such as adorning garments with beadwork or porcupine quill. Not one single "Hunkpapa" male would ever let himself down to perform any female task at this time, even if he had decorated before his own costume the same way at home. Within the hierarchy of the sexes, there is a further structure of leadership to which each member has to conform. This is expressed most clearly by the presence of men's societies like the Dog Soldiers, who exercise a kind of police power. This means that the hobby-Indians not only try to emulate the past life of the Plains Indians superficially, but also get involved with the foreign culture emotionally. Aside from material objects, they also try to adopt the values and the philosophy of the Indian. Obviously not every Indian hobbyist is successful at this, but they do their best. In this sense, they are not so different from other alternative groups here in Germany, which also try to adopt Indian values, especially in matters of ecology. But in contrast to members of the *Müslikultur*, ecology-freaks, and others looking for an alternative way of life, the hobby-Indians only turn their back to the reality of our consumer and plastic world from time to time. They limit their alternative activities to weekends and spare time without losing sight of reality or questioning their material safety. In other words, they do not aspire to leave our society, and want nothing else but to remain hobby Indians instead.

Above all else, the "Hunkpapas" in Frankfurt are currently facing local political problems, as their grounds in the *Ginnheimer Wäldchen* are needed for other purposes. This time it is the *Bundesgartenschau* (National Botanical Show), planned for 1989 by the city of Frankfurt, that threatens the existence of the Indian club. According to the official plans, the area upon which the ranch of the "Hunkpapas" is located will be turned into a parking lot. If these plans are actually carried out, it would mean that the Indian club would have to leave its grounds once again because of further construction projects by the city of Frankfurt.

In this sense it should be easy for the Frankfurt "Hunkpapas" of the 20th century to identify with the real Hunkpapas of the 19th century, as the "land theft" by the bureaucrats in Frankfurt shows remarkable parallels to some common practices in America back then.

NOTE

I am indebted to the members of the Hunkpapa Club for their informations given me at various occasions, especially to Michael Schubert, chairman of the association, who read the first draft of this article and gave me his o.k. for its publication.

REFERENCES CITED

Catlin, George
1851   Die Indianer und die während eines achtjährigen Aufenthaltes unter den wildesten ihrer Stämme erlebten Abenteuer und Schicksale. (First German edition 1851. New edition: Berlin: Continent, 1924.)

Eastman, Charles A.
1912   Ohijesa. Jugenderinnerungen eines Sioux-Indianers. Hamburg: Agentur des Rauhen Hauses. (New edition: Frankfurt: Insel, 1976.)
1920   Winona. Indianergeschichten aus alter Zeit. Hamburg: Agentur des Rauhen Hauses. (New edition: Frankfurt: Insel, 1977.)

Fleischer, Ulrich
1981   Far West made in Germany: Impressionen vom 31. Indian Council in Nidda bei Frankfurt. Country und Western 6 (Nov.-Dec. 1981):16-19.

Frankfurter Allgemeine Zeitung
1970   Frankfurter Allgemeine Zeitung. Frankfurt.

Frankfurter Nachrichten
1978-83 Frankfurter Nachrichten. Frankfurt.

Frankfurter Rundschau
1970-72, 1981-82 Frankfurter Rundschau. Frankfurt.

Klotzbach, Kurt
1982   Als Buffalo Bill in Deutschland ritt. Magazin für Amerikanistik 2/1982:34-41.

Langspeer, Büffelkind
1929   Häuptling Büffelkind Langspeer erzählt sein Leben. Munich: Paul List. (New edition: Munich: Paul List, 1958.)

Maler-Sieber, Gisela
1978   Völkerkunde die uns angeht. Gütersloh: Bertelsmann.

Maximilian Prinz zu Wied
1839-41 Reise in das innere Nord-America in den Jahren 1832 bis 1834. Two vols. Koblenz: J.Hoelscher. Reprint: Frankfurt, 1970.

O'Neil, Paul
1981   Das Ende und die Legende. Time-Life Bücher "Der Wilde Westen".

Rennert, Jack
1976   Buffalo Bill's Wild West. 100 Plakate. Berlin: Rembrandt.

Rieske, Bill and Verla
1974   Historic Indian Portraits. 1898 peace jubilee collection. Salt Lake City: Historic Indian Publishers.

Russell, Don
1960   The Lives and Legends of Buffalo Bill. Norman: University of Oklahoma Press.
1970   The Wild West, or a History of the Wild West Shows. Fort Worth: Amon Carter Museum of Western Art.

Schultz, James Willard
1922   Natahki und ich. Hamburg: Ernte-Verlag. (Reprint: Cologne: German-American Pioneer Society, 1974.)
1925   In Natahkis Zelt. Mein Leben als Indianer. Hamburg: Ernte-Verlag. (Reprint: Cologne: German-American Pioneer Society, 1974.)

Sievers, Leo
1973   Ein Preuße namens Sarrasani. [2nd part:] Als die Indianer Deutschland eroberten. Stern no. 43 (18.10.1973):165-173.

Sommer, Manfred
1971   Edward Two-Two. Ein Indianer ruht in Dresden. Kalumet 20 (4):29-31.

Standhafter Bär
1930   Mein Volk, die Sioux. Stuttgart: Strecker und Schröder.

Wäscha-kwonnesin
n.d.   (ca.1932) Männer der Grenze. Grau-Eule erzählt. Stuttgart: Franckh'sche Verlagshandlung.

Weiße Indianer
1983   Weiße Indianer. Kreationen in Leder nach dem Vorbild der Indianer vom oberen Missouri-Gebiet um 1830. Offenbach: Deutsches Ledermuseum.

NORTH AMERICAN INDIANS IN ITALIAN (1950 - 1981): A BIBLIOGRAPHY OF BOOKS

Fedora Giordano

The story of modern Italian interest in North American Indian cultures can be traced back to the middle of the 19th century when a bookstore in Milan opened a New York branch and thus made available through mail order the first publications of the Smithsonian Institution, the Reports of the Commissioner of Indian Affairs, and Schoolcraft's *Personal Memoirs* and *Historical and Statistical Information Respecting the History, Conditions and Prospects of the Indian Tribes* (Scuderi 1983). By 1886 Vincenze Grossi was reading a paper on the languages, literatures, and traditions of the indigenous populations of America ("Lingue, letteratura e tradizioni popolari degli Indigeni d'America," Genova 1890) at the Turin International Congress of Americanists, Ferdinando Borsari was writing a book on American Indian literature (*La letteratura degl'indigeni americani*, Napoli 1888) and a conspicuous number of American Indian songs were included by Girolamo Ragusa Moleti in his anthology of primitive poetry (*Poesie dei popoli selvaggi o poco civili*, Torino & Palermo 1891). Scholarly studies have continued to appear since then in scientific periodicals, while the general reader was left, until the 1940s, with the stereotypes offered by Western movies, cartoons, and popular fiction (cp.Mazzavilla 1983, Lapolla 1983, Solimano 1983). Even an encyclopaedia of world mythology offered in 1942 only a short general outline of the myths of Africa, Oceania, and the Americas (Giacomo Prampolini, *La mitologia nella vita dei popoli*, Milano, 2 vols.), while enough space was given to the American Indians only by Renato Biasutti in his encyclopaedia of geography and physical anthropology (*Razze e popoli della terra*, 1941).

The 1950's mark the transition of American Indian studies in Italy from discussions in scholarly cirles to consumption by the general reader.

Religion was the first aspect offered to the public, through the Indian songs included in Eckart von Sydow's anthology of primitive poetry (1951), the myths collected by Raffaele Pettazzoni in his encyclopaedia (1953), and the studies in shamanism by Mircea Eliade (1953). In 1956 appeared the first of the many editions of Hamilton's *Cry of the Thunderbird*, more songs were translated by Aldo Celli in his anthology concerned both with religious and aesthetic issues (1959). The late fifties saw the first studies on Mesoamerican Indians (Vaillant 1957, Bernal 1958, Séjourné 1959, Krickeberg 1959), preparing the public to the great exhibition of Precolumbian arts of Mexico and Central America in 1960 (Cerulli 1960). In the same year were published the *Popol Vuh* (Recinos 1960), and the studies by Trimborn and Caso, followed by an anthology of Aztec poems (Liberatore and Hernandez-Campos 1961) with a good introduction. An interest in Mesoamerican Indians was thus established and continued

491

during the sixties and seventies with a steady if not overwhelming flow of books (a total of 25 in the period considered).

By 1968, when *Black Elk Speaks* was respectfully reviewed in all major newspapers, the cultivated reader had quite a good choice of publications. Historical information was to be found in the paperback edition of Nölle's handbook (1962), in the pictorial history by La Farge (1961), in De Voto's *Course of Empire* (1963), or in Miller's book on Custer (1966). Some anthropological information was available in Benedict's *Patterns of Culture* (1960), Lowie's *Indians of the Plains* (1961), Radin's *Trickster* (1965), while Vittorio Lanternari offered a social study of the peyote cult, the Ghost Dance and the religion of Handsome Lake in his book on the religions of the oppressed (1960). Claude Lévi-Strauss's studies on the Tewa (1963) and on Northwest Coast art (1965) were available to all interested in structuralism, while the psychologist could study the initiation rituals of California and Plains Indians with Erik Erikson (1966). Those interested in the role of the informant in the anthropologist's work could chose between Theodora Kroeber's *Ishi* (1963) and Casagrande's choice of portraits by Lowie, Carpenter, Kluckhohn, Adair, and Sturtevant (1966).

The organization of the American Indian Movement and the taking of Alcatraz were reported by the Italian press, and in 1969 Zolla presented his students at the University of Genoa as well as the cultivated public with his story of the "Trail of Tears" which began with the images of the Indians in literature and ended with the literature by native authors. Zolla's interest in shamanism was continued in the publication of his journal *Conoscenza religiosa* (Religious Knowledge, 1969), the edition of *The Hako* (Fletcher 1970) and resulted in the publication of *The Sacred Pipe*, and of the biographies of Sun Chief (Talayesva 1969), Wooden Leg (Marquis 1970), and Crazy Horse (Sandoz 1971).

Among the eight books published in 1970 were Benjamin Whorf's studies on the Hopi - a remarkable publishers' event if one considers that Boas's "Introduction" to the *Handbook of American Indian Languages* came out nine years later - and Lewis H. Morgan's *Ancient Society* partly based on his study of the Iroquois. But the reviewers turned out to be more interested in Carlos Castaneda's *Teachings of Don Juan* which was followed (as in the rest of the world) by an increased interest in hallucinogens and shamanism (Benitez 1972) and fitted in perfectly with the ideals of the less politically involved area of the Italian counterculture. Castaneda's volumes of what has turned out to be good anthropological fiction (a *genre* akin to science fiction) have all been translated into Italian, one of them, *Tales of Power* (tr. 1975) with an introductory essay by Furio Jesi, a scholar of mythology (cp. Zolla 1983). Peter Farb's history of civilization as exemplified by the American Indians appeared in 1972 together with Vine Deloria, Jr.'s *Custer Died for Your Sins* and Dee Brown's *Bury My Heart at Wounded Knee*. And while the taking of Wounded

492

Knee was daily reported on by the press in all major newspapers through the spring of 1973, the Italian reader could also check (with Leslie Fiedler) the *Return of the Vanishing American*. Jaime de Angulo - the Spanish expatriate who is incredibly more popular in Italy than in the United States - could also give his own version of Californian myths to the charmed readers of *Indian Tales* (1973), who agreed with Ezra Pound that he was "the American Ovid" (cp. Giordano 1982). Since 1973 individual members or delegations from Indian nations have come to Italy on official visits. Adam Nordwall (Lucky Eagle) of the Chippewa came in September 1973 on a "discovery" mission, and the press drew the public attention to the Indian legal cases against the American Government. In February 1974 Shining Star and Flying Owl of the Wampanoag were received by Pope Paul VI. The publication of *The Way* (Witt and Steiner 1974) offered a survey of Native American traditions and contemporary issues. A number of books debated the role of the ethnologist in the progress of imperialism and his responsibility in the genocide of traditional societies (Lanternari 1974, Romano 1976, Cerulli 1977), or offered the Indians' side of the story (León-Portilla 1974 for the Aztec, Inca, and Maya, De La Fuente 1974 and Rizzi 1978 on the battle of Little Big Horn, Schwarz 1980 gives a chronicle of the period 1854-1915). From 1976 to 1981 the yearly number of publications on American Indian studies had ranged from a minimum of six to nine books per year, this last figure reached in 1978, 1979, and 1981). The topics covered extend from contemporary issues taken from *Akwesasne Notes* by members of INCOMINDIOS (Hansen 1977, Ranucci 1978, Bouchet 1979) to history (Jacquin 1977, Washburn 1981; Monti 1981 checks all the historical information for the lover of western movies), to the analysis of religious rituals (Sebag 1976, Monaco 1977, Marchiori 1980, Scarduelli 1980) to social anthropology (Signorini 1979, Pompa 1981, Meek 1981), with Italian contributions numbering 14 out of 46 books published.

Perhaps the most relevant aspect of Italian publications in this period is the constant presence of literature by Native American authors. The oral tradition in Jerome Rothenberg's version presented with a good introduction by Franco Meli (1977) has become a bestseller both among poetry readers and people interested in American Indian studies. *Winter in the Blood* by James Welch was first translated in 1978, *House Made of Dawn* by N.Scott Momaday followed in 1979 and was awarded the Mondello literary prize. Leslie Silko's *Ceremony* translated in 1981 concludes this survey of 118 books, while La Salamandra publishers in Milan promise a new series wholly by Native authors of which Leslie Silko's *Storyteller* (1983) was the first to appear. Among recent additions to what is now a consolidated aspect of Italian culture are *Shamanic Voices* by Joan Halifax (Milano, Adelphi, 1983), a book from the *Indian Story of the Conquest of Mexico* by Bernardino de Sahagun (Palermo, Sellerio, 1983), and Bierhorst's *The Red Swan* (Milano, Longanesi, 1984).

REFERENCES CITED
(see also the Bibliography below)

Giordano, Fedora
    1982   Jaime de Angulo. In: Novecento americano, vol.1. Roma: Lucarini.
Lapolla, Franco
    1983   L'immagine dell'Indiano nel cinema americano. Paper read at the 1st Congress on Historical Anthropology (Rome, 17-20 October 1983).
Mazzavilla, Silvano
    1983   Ombre rosse del fumetto italiano. Paper read at the 1st Congress on Historical Anthropology (Rome, 17-20 October 1983).
Scuderi, Gilberto
    1983   Indiani d'America nelle riviste milanesi della Restaurazione e del Risorgimento. Archivio trimestrale I(ix).
Solimano, Sandra (ed.)
    1983   I Cerchi del Mondo. Genova: Comune di Genova.
Zolla, Elémire
    1983   A vindication of Carlos Castaneda, In: "Labrys" 8.

BIBLIOGRAPHY OF BOOKS

At the time of this writing, both the Italian Union Catalog and the National Library circulation of books are unfortunately updated only to 1981. It is with great regret that the latest publications have been excluded due to the impossibility of giving a complete list.

Angulo, Jaime de
  1973   Racconti indiani (Indian Tales, 1953), tr. Romano Mastromattei, intr. Carl Carmer. Milano, Adelphi.
  1978   Indiani in tuta (Indians in Overalls, 1950), tr. Anna M. Musso Colli. Milano, Adelphi.
Arnold, Paul
  1980   Il libro dei morti Maya (Le livre des morts Maya, 1978), tr. Luciano Burei. Roma, Edizioni Mediterranee.
Bancroft-Hunt, Norman
  1979   Popoli del totem (People of the Totem, 1979), tr. Ornella Scaglia, ed. Franco Meli, Novara, Istituto Geografico De Agostini.
Barrett, Stephen M. (ed.)
  1971   Geronimo (Geronimo, His Own Story, 1906), tr. Elena Bona, intr. F.W. Turner III. Milano, Longanesi.
Benedict, Ruth
  1960   Modelli di cultura (Patterns of Culture, 1934), tr. Elena Spagnol. Milano, Feltrinelli.
Benitez, Fernando
  1972   Peyoteros (En la tierra magica del peyote, 1968), tr. Marcello Ravoni, Gianni Guadalupi. Milano, Il Saggiatore.
Bernal, Ignacio
  1958   Pitture precolombiane del Messico, pref. Jacques Soustelle. Milano, Silvana Editoriale, UNESCO.
  1971   L'arte precolombiana dell'America centrale (with P. Gendrop). Firenze, Sansoni.
Boas, Franz
  1979   Introduzione alle lingue indiane d'America (Introduction to the Handbook of American Indian Languages, 1911), ed. Giorgio R. Cardona. Torino, Boringhieri.
  1981   L'arte primitiva (Primitive Art, 1927), tr. Alessandra e Barbara Fiore, intr. Giorgio R. Cardona, Barbara Fiore. Torino, Boringhieri.
Bouchet, Bruno (ed.)
  1979   Wovoka. La proposta rivoluzionaria dei nativi americani (from Akwesasne Notes), tr. Giorgio Berretti, Pietro Crespi, Giannozzo Pucci. L.E.F., Firenze.

Brown, A. Dee
    1972   Seppellite il mio cuore a Wounded Knee (Bury My Heart at Wounded Knee, 1970), tr. Furio Belfiore. Milano, Mondadori.
    1981   Attorno al fuoco (Teepee Tales of the American Indian, 1979), tr. Chiara Salmaggi. Milano, Mondadori.

Brown, Joseph Epes (ed.)
    1970   La sacra pipa (The Sacred Pipe, 1953), tr. Donatella Tippett. Andalò. Torino, Borla.

Burland, Cottie, and Werner Forman
    1976   Aztechi (Aztecs, 1975), tr. M. Elisabetta Trovato, ed. Gianni Vianello. Novara, Istituto Geografico De Agostini.

Casagrande, Joseph
    1966   La ricerca antropologica (In the Company of Man, 1960), tr. Luciana Pecchioli. Torino, Einaudi.

Caso, Alfonso
    1961   Il popolo del sole (El pueblo del sol 1953), tr. Dario Puccini, ill. Miguel Covarrubias. Milano, Il Saggiatore.

Castaneda, Carlos
    1970   A scuola dallo stregone (The Teachings of Don Juan, 1968), tr. Francesco Cardelli. Roma, Astrolabio.
    1972   Una realtà separate (A Separate Reality, 1971), tr. Francesco Cardelli. Roma, Astrolabio.
    1973   Viaggio a Ixtlan (Journey to Ixtlan, 1972), tr. Francesco Cardelli. Roma, Astrolabio.
    1975   L'isola del Tonal (Tales of Power, 1974), ed., pref. Furio Jesi. Milano, Rizzoli.
    1978   Il secondo anello del potere (The second Ring of Power, 1977), tr. Pier Francesco Paolini. Milano, Rizzoli.

Celli, Aldo (ed.)
    1959   Canti indiani del Nord America. Firenze, Sansoni.

Cerulli, Ernesta
    1960   (ed.) Mostra d'arte precolombiana del Messico e dell'America centrale, pref. S.K. Lothrop, G. Kutscher. Roma, Ars nova.
    1973   Le alte culture dell'America precolombiana e loro condizione attuale. Genova, Tilgher.
    1977   Tradizione e etnocidio. I due poli della ricerca antropologica oggi. Torino, UTET.

Chiaia, Vittorio
    1962   I pueblos, villaggi indiani del Sud Ovest Americano. Bari, Dedalo.

Claiborne, Robert
    1980   I primi americani (The First Americans). Time-Life, Curcio.

Coe, Michael D.
1964   Il Messico fino alla conquista spagnola (Mexico), tr. Beatrice Boffito
        Serra. Milano, Il Saggiatore.
Corsini, Gianfranco
1974   Storia degli Indiani d'America. Messina, D'Anna.
Davies, Nigel
1975   Gli aztechi (The Aztecs, 1973), tr. Pina Sergi. Roma, Editori Riuniti.
De La Fuente, Maria
1974   Toro seduto e il genocidio dei Pellerossa. Roma, Cremonese.
Deloria, Vine, Jr.
1972   Custer è morto per i vostri peccati (Custer Died for your Sins,
        1969), tr. Alfonso Russo. Milano, Jaca Book.
De Voto, Bernard
1963   La corsa all'impero (The Course of Empire, 1952), tr. Ornella
        Gamalero. Bologna, Il Mulino.
Disselhoff, Hans-Dietrich, and Sigvald Linné
1961   Antica America (Alt-Amerika, 1960), tr. Maria Attardo Magrini.
        Milano, Saggiatore.
Dockstader, Frederick J.
1961   Arte indiana in America (Indian Art in America, 1961), tr. Ida Bona.
        Milano, Silvana Editoriale.
Drimmer, Frederick (ed.)
1973   Mocassini bianchi (Scalps and Tomahawks). Milano, Longanesi.
Dyk, Walter
1978   Navaho: una vita selvaggia (Son of Old Man Hat, 1974), tr.   Carlo
        Danna, pref. Edward Sapir. Milano, Rusconi.
Eastman, Charles Alexander (Ohiyesa)
1979   Ragazzo indiano (Indian Boyhood, 1902), tr. Maria Pavan Carraro.
        Milano, Mursia.
Eliade, Mircea
1953   Lo sciamanesimo (Le chamanisme, 1951), tr. Giulio C. Evola. Torino,
        Bocca.
Erikson, Erik
1966   Infanzia e società (Childhood and Society, 1963), tr. Luigi Antonello
        Armando. Roma, Armando.
Farb, Peter
1972   L'ascesa dell'uomo alla civiltà com'è dimostrata dagli Indiani del
        Nordamerica dall'epoca primitiva all'avvento della società industriale
        (Man's Rise to Civilization..., 1968), tr. Marco M. Sigiani. Milano,
        Mondadori.
Ferrero, Ernesto
1980   Cervo Bianco. Milano, Mondadori.

Fiedler, Leslie
1973   Il ritorno del Pellerossa (The Return of the Vanishing Amer-
        ican,1968), tr. Luigi Brioschi. Milano, Rizzoli.
Fletcher, Alice
1970   Il rito Hako. Una cerimonia della tribù dei Pawnee (The Hako,
        1904), tr. Elena Potsios, pref. Elémire Zolla. Firenze, La Nuova
        Italia.
Gliozzi, Giuliano (ed.)
1971   La scoperta dei selvaggi. Milano, Principato.
Hagen, Victor Wolfgang von
1963   Antichi imperi del sole delle Americhe (The Ancient Sun Kingdoms
        of the Americas, 1962), tr. Ettore Capriolo. Milano, Mondadori.
1975   Alla ricerca dei Maya (Search for the Maya, 1973), tr. Lydia
        Magliano. Milano, Rizzoli.
Halifax, Joan
1982   Voci sciamaniche (Shamanic voices, 1979), tr. Riccardo   Piccoli.
        Milano, Rizzoli.
Hamilton, Charles (ed.)
1956   Sul sentiero di guerra (Cry of the Thunderbird, 1950), tr. Adriana
        Dall'Orto. Milano, Feltrinelli.
Hansen, Diana (ed.)
1977   Indiani d'America (from Akwesasne Notes, 1972-75), tr. and ed.
        Diana Hansen, Lucio Ranucci, pref. Dario Paccino. Roma, Savelli.
Hyde, George E. (ed.)
1981   La mia gente Cheyenne (Life of George Bent, written from his
        letters, 1968), tr. B. Maria Bertoni Mauri, Alberto Viotti. Milano,
        Mursia.
Jacquin, Philippe
1977   Storia degli Indiani d'America (Histoire des Indiens d'Amérique,
        1976), tr. Franco Moccia. Milano, Mondadori.
Krickeberg, Walter
1959   Civiltà dell'antico Messico (Altmexikanische Kulturen, 1956), tr.
        Tullio de Mauro. Editrice Le Maschere.
Krickeberg, Walter, with Hermann Trimborn, Werner Müller, Otto Zerries
1966   Religioni dell'America precolombiana (Die Religionen des Alten
        Amerika, 1961), tr. Claudia Diversi Caprino. Milano, Il Saggiatore.
Kroeber, Theodora
1963   Il selvaggio in vetrina (Ishi in Two Worlds, 1961), tr. Maria
        Gallone, pref. Lewis Gannett. Milano, Rizzoli.
La Farge, Oliver
1961   Il mondo degli Indiani (A Pictorial History of the American Indian,
        1956, abridged), tr. Piero Pieroni. Milano, Mondadori.

Landucci, Sergio
1972   I filosofi e i selvaggi 1570-1780. Bari, Laterza.

Lanternari, Vittorio
1960   Movimenti religiosi di libertà e di salvezza dei popoli oppressi. Milano, Feltrinelli.
1974   Antropologia e imperialismo. Torino, Einaudi.

Laurencich Minelli, Laura
1979   Religione mesoamericana. Bologna, Esculapio.

Lanarda, Antonio
1979   L'esperienza della diversità 1580-1780. Torino, Loescher.

León-Portilla, Miguel
1974   Il rovescio della conquista. Testimonianze azteche, maya e inca (El reverso de la conquista), tr. Giorgio Segre, Giuliana e Gabriella Lapasini. Milano, Adelphi.

Lévi-Strauss, Claude
1964   Il pensiero selvaggio (La pensée sauvage, 1962), tr. Paolo Caruso. Milano, Il Saggiatore.
1966   Antropologia struttrale (Antropologie structurale, 1958). Milano, Il Saggiatore.

Liberatore, Ugo, and Jorge Hernandez-Campos (eds.)
1961   Canti aztechi. Parma, Guanda.

Lindermann, Frank B. (ed.)
1976   Molti trofei (Plenty-Coups, Chief of the Crows, 1974), tr. Annamarcella Falco Tedeschi, it. ed. Giorgio Spina. Milano, Rusconi.

Lowie, Robert Harry
1961   Gli Indiani delle pianure (Indians of the Plains, 1954), tr. Roberto Bosi. Milano, Il Saggiatore.

Maggi, Emilio
1964   Costumi sessuali amerindi. Milano, Zibetti.

Marchiori, Mario
1980   Stick Dance. Festa dei morti degli Indiani Koyukon d'Alaska. Genova, Mondini e Siccardi.

Marek, Kurt (C.W. Ceram)
1972   Il primo americano (Der erste Amerikaner, 1971), tr. Giuseppina Panzieri Saija. Torino, Einaudi.

Marquis, Thomas B. (ed.)
1970   Gambe di legno (Wooden Leg, a warrior who fought Custer, 1962), tr. Donatella Tippett Andalò. Milano, Rusconi.

Mazzoleni, Gilberto
1979   I buffoni sacri d'America. Roma, Bulzoni.

Meek, Ronald L.
1981   Il cattivo selvaggio (Social Science and the Ignoble Savage, 1976), pref. Salvatore Veca. Milano, Il Saggiatore.

Meli, Franco (ed.)
1977   Canti e narrazioni degli Indiani d'America (Jerome Rothenberg, Technicians of the Sacred, 1968; Shaking the Pumpkin, 1972). Milano, Guanda.
Merrick Mullet, George Crawford
1981   Le storie della donna ragno (Spider Woman Stories, 1979), tr. Sandra Busatta, pref. Fred Eggan, Suzanne Mullet. Milano, La Salamandra.
Miller, David Humphreys
1966   La fine del generale Custer (Custer's Fall, 1957), tr. Vittorio Di Giuro. Milano, Rizzoli.
Momaday, Nathan Scott
1979   Casa fatta d'alba (House Made of Dawn, 1966), tr. Franco Meli, L. Willis, ed. Franco Meli. Milano, Guanda.
Monaco, Emanuela
1977   Persona e impersonazione. L'uso rituale delle maschere presso gli Zuni. Roma, Bulzoni.
Monti, Mario
1981   Passarono di qui. Duecento anni della vita e delle guerre degli Indiani del Nord America con i capi Tori Seduto, Cavallo Pazzo, Capo Giuseppe e tutti gli altri. Milano, Bompiani.
Morgan, Lewis Henry
1970   La società antica (Ancient Society, 1877), tr. Alessandro Casiccia, Lucio Trevisan, pref. Mario De Stefanis. Milano, Feltrinelli.
Neihardt, John G. (ed.)
1968   Alce Nero parla (Black Elk Speaks, 1932), tr. Rodolfo Wilcock. Milano, Adelphi.
Nölle, Wilfried
1962   Gli Indiani del Nord America (Die Indianer Nordamerikas, 1959), tr. Fiorenza Paggi. Firenze, Sansoni.
Pettazzoni, Raffaele
1953   Miti e leggende, vol. III: America settentrionale. Torino, UTET.
Pompa, Cristina (ed.)
1981   L'America rifondata. Roma, La Goliardica.
Prescott, William H.
1970   La conquista del Messico (History of the Conquest of Mexico), pref. William Charvat, Michael Kraus. Torino, Einaudi.
1978   Il mondo degli aztechi (Le monde des Aztèques), tr. Lisa Clark. Milano, Euroclub.
Quattrocchi, Angelo
1976   Wounded Knee. Gli Indiani alla riscossa. Milano, Celuc libri.
Radin, Paul, C.Gustav Jung, Károly Kérènyi
1965   Il briccone divino (Der göttliche Schelm, 1941), tr. Nemi Dalmasso, Daniele Silvano. Milano, Bompiani.

Ranucci, Lucio
1978   Il lungo inganno. Roma, Savelli.
Recinos, Adrian (ed.)
1960   Popol Vuh (Popol Vuh), tr. Lore Terracini. Torino, Einaudi.
Ribaldone, Agostina (ed.)
1970   Il discorso sugli Indiani d'America di Samuel Farmar Jarvis (A
        Discourse on the Religion of the Indian Tribes of North America,
        1820), pref. Elémire Zolla. Università di Genova, Istituto di Lingue,
        Magistero.
Rizzi, Leo
1978   Hoka hey! L'ultima guerra indiana. Milano, Syntesis.
Rocchi, Carla
1980   Arte dell'America precolombiana. Roma, Kappa.
Romano, Ruggiero (ed.)
1976   America indiana. Torino, Einaudi.
Salsedo Savelli, Carla
1977   Civiltà dell'America settentrionale. Bologna, Patron.
Sandoz, Mari
1971   Cavallo pazzo. Lo strano uomo degli Oglala (Crazy Horse, 1968), tr.
        Donatella Tippett Andalò. Milano, Rusconi.
Scarduelli, Pietro
1980   Gli Aztechi e il sacrificio umano. Torino, Loescher.
Schneider, Richard S.
1976   Manuale del pellerossa (Crafts of North American Indians, 1972), tr.
        Virginio Sala. Milano, Longanesi.
Schwarz, Angelo
1980   1854-1915: cronaca fotografica del genocidio delle nazioni indiane
        d'America. Ivrea, Priuli e Verlucca.
Sebag, Lucien
1976   L'invenzione del mondo presso gli Indiani Pueblo (L'invention du
        monde chez les Indiens Pueblos, 1974), pref. Claude Lévi-Strauss,
        ed. Maria Solimini. Bari, Dedalo.
1979   Mitologia e realtà sociale (L'invention du monde..II), ed. Maria
        Solimini. Bari, Dedalo.
Séjourné, Laurette
1959   Quetzalcoatl, il serpente piumato (Burning Water, 1956), tr. Cornélie
        Brancaccio di Caprino.
Seppilli, Anita
1979   La memoria e L'assenza. Tradizione orale e scrittura nell'America dei
        Conquistadores. Bologna, Cappelli.
Signorini, Italo
1979   Gente di laguna. Ideologia e istituzioni sociali dei Huave di San
        Mateo del Mar. Milano.

Silko, Leslie Marmon
1981   Cerimonia (Ceremony, 1977), ed. Paola Ludovici. Milano, Editori
        Riuniti.
Snow, Dean
1977   Canti degli Indiani d'America (The American Indians, 1976), tr. Silvio
        Zavatti. Roma, Newton Compton.
Soustelle, Jacques
1965   Vita quotidiana degli Aztechi (La vie quotidienne des Aztèques,
        1955), tr. Paola Argan. Milano, Il Saggiatore.
Stammel, Heinz Josef
1978   Indiani. Leggenda e realtà (Indianer), tr. Paola Barberis. Torino, SEI.
Steiner, Stan
1978   Uomo bianco, scomparirai (The Vanishing White Man, 1976), tr.
        Corrado Pellegrini. Milano, Jaca Book.
Sydow, Eckart von (ed.)
1951   Poesia dei popoli primitivi (Dichtungen der Naturvölker), tr. Roberto
        Bazlen. Bologna e Parma, Guanda.
Talayesva, Don C.
1969   Capo Sole (Sun Chief, 1942), tr. Luigi Pellissari, pref. Claude
        Lévi-Strauss, ed. Leo Simmons.
Tentori, Tullio
1961   La pittura precolombiana. Milano, S.E.L.
1968   Scritti americanistici. Roma, Edizioni Ricerche.
Thevenin, René, and Paul Coze
1960   Storia e costumi dei Pellirosse (Moeurs et histoire des Indiens
        Peaux-Rouges, 1928), tr. Giorgio Galli. Milano, Schwarz.
Trimborn, Herman
1960   Le civiltà precolombiane (Das alte Amerika), tr. Guido Gentili e
        Tullio Tentori. Roma, Primato.
Vaillant, George C.
1957   La civiltà azteca (Aztecs of Mexico, 1944). Torino, Einaudi.
Washburn, Wilcomb
1981   Gli Indiani d'America (The Indian in America, 1975), tr. Paola
        Ludovici, Roger Meservey. Roma, Editori Riuniti.
Welch, James
1978   Inverno nel sangue (Winter in the Blood, 1974), tr. P. Ludovici,
        Giorgio Mariani, ed. Paola Ludovici. Roma, Savelli.
Westphal, Wilfried
1980   I Maya. Antichi e moderni schiavi (Die Maya, 1977), tr. Adriano
        Caiani, Aldo Runfola. Milano, SugarCo.
Whorf, Benjamin Lee
1970   Linguaggio, pensiero, realtà (Language, Thought and Reality, 1956),
        ed. John B. Carroll, tr. Francesco Ciafaloni. Torino, Boringhieri.

Wilson, Edmund
  1962   Dovuto agli Irochesi (Apologies to the Iroquois, 1960), tr. Marisa
          Bulgheroni, pref. John Mitchell. Milano, Il Saggiatore.
Witt, Shirley, and Stan Steiner
  1974   The Way. Scritti e racconti degli Indiani americani (1972), tr. Ileana
          Gervasini, Corrado Pellegrini. Milano, Jaca Book.
Zolla, Elémire
  1969   I letterati e lo sciamano. Milano, Bompiani.

"A FIFTH GOSPEL, ALMOST"
CHIEF SEATTLE'S SPEECH(ES):
AMERICAN ORIGINS AND EUROPEAN RECEPTION

Rudolf Kaiser

I

All those who have watched the development of ecological thinking in Europe over the last years, will realize that - more than any other group of people - American Indians are seen and presented as models of an ecological attitude, sometimes even as born conservationists, or as patron-saints of a close relationship between man and his natural environment. One of the reasons for this very special and very topical reputation of American Indians seems to reside in the enormous publicity of a text which is regarded and widely quoted as a manifesto of ecological feeling and thinking: a speech - sometimes also referred to as a letter - by Chief Seattle. While American Indians are seen by some people as ecologists by birth, Chief Seattle is hailed as the prophet of an ecological sentiment, which is said to be lacking in western industrialized nations.

Here are some random examples of the wide publicity which Chief Seattle's speech has gained in Europe:

In August 1978 a youth organization of Catholic students in the Federal Republic of Germany published a booklet about ecological problems. The title of the booklet is *Seattle* (Anonymous 1978). This booklet contains not only the text of Chief Seattle's speech, but also a somewhat similar speech by one Chief Tulavil from an island in the South Pacific Ocean. In addition to these two texts there are commentaries, notes, songs, and cartoons, all of them referring to the issue of ecology. At the same time the booklet serves as the guide to a musical, which is also called *Seattle*. Finally there is also a record, which goes with the musical and the booklet. The title of that record (for all those who do not yet know) is - *Seattle*.

Another example: At the end of a very committed, informative, and depressing German book about the exploitation and destruction of the earth, the author, Eugen Drewermann, wants to dismiss his reader with a glimpse of hope and a view of the right attitute of man towards nature: He finishes his book with the full text of Chief Seattle's speech (Drewermann 1982:160-165).

A third example: The inderdenominational Women's World Day of Prayer in 1981 had as its theme: "The Earth is the Lord's." The texts and prayers for the service had been prepared by American Indian women of Christian faith, representing Indian tribes from throughout the United States. The reason why Indian women had been asked to do this is given in the introduction to the prayers with the following words:

"Their special reverence for nature and their feeling of kinship with all creatures of the earth, sky, and water enable them to teach us how to live justly, respectfully, and in harmony with our world and each other" (Anonymous 1981:2).

One of the texts of the prayers is taken from the famous speech by Red Jacket, another text is taken from Chief Seattle's speech.

Yet another example: Many schools and other educational institutions in Europe teach courses on ecological issues. In these courses they often make use of a film which in German-speaking countries is available under the title of *Söhne der Erde* (Sons of the Earth) and which can be borrowed or purchased from a film center in Switzerland.[1] As the film was made in the United States it is probably also available in other languages. The text of the full film consists of nothing but the speech of Chief Seattle. (We shall see at a later stage that this film played an important part in the genesis of the speech.) The pictures try to illustrate and underline this text by showing the white man's destruction of the environment and contrasting it with pictures of a beautifully unpolluted countryside.

More examples:

During the 87th *Deutscher Katholikentag* (Congress of German Catholics) in Düsseldorf in 1982 a short song was repeatedly and enthusiastically sung, whose text repeats over and over again just one sentence from Chief Seattle's speech: "Jeder Teil dieser Erde ist meinem Volk heilig" (Every part of this earth is sacred to my people).

The periodical of a German order of missionaries published the full text of Chief Seattle's speech together with photographs of unspoiled nature in its edition of March 1983 (Anonymous 1983:33-37).

The Swiss singer René Bardet has produced a record which is entirely devoted to words and themes from Chief Seattle's speech, so that almost the complete text of the speech is reproduced in twelve songs. The cover, moreover, informs the reader/listener at great length about the singer's ideas and impressions of Chief Seattle's speech.[2]

Finally: Different German publishers have published booklets containing a German translation of Chief Seattle's speech. All of these booklets add illustrations of polluted and unpolluted nature to go with the text (e.g., Kaiser and Kaiser 1984, Weigert et al. 1980, Seattle 1982, Pförtner 1976).

These examples of Chief Seattle's publicity in Europe could give the impression that only Germany or German-speaking countries are at present following the trail of the Indian chief. This impression would be wrong, although it seems that Seattle's speech is more frequently referred to and utilized for discussions of ecological issues in German-speaking countries than in some other West European countries. The most comprehensive adaptation of

Seattle's ideas nevertheless comes from England:

The "United Society for the Propagation of the Gospel" in London has produced a multimedia teaching aid under the title: *Testimony - Chief Seattle.* This unit comprises a tape, a filmstrip and a script, all of them devoted to Seattle's speech. Together with these items goes a resource pack of no less than some 100 pages, which tries not only to present all the available information about Chief Seattle, his time, his tribe, and his language - but also to give parents, teachers, and leaders of youth groups suggestions about ways of dealing with the speech, e.g., using it for games as well as theological discussions, or comparing Seattle's words with texts from the Old Testament and with the central Christian prayer of "Our Father."

It is also in this resource pack that this address by Seattle receives the highest consecration imaginable in a Christian society: It is set on an - almost - equal footing with the four Gospels of the New Testament and called "a fifth Gospel, almost."[3]

A Dutch translation of Seattle's speech in typescript is being circulated and disseminated by - among others - the "Volkenkundige Boekhandel" named "The Trading Post" in Bennebroek, The Netherlands. Moreover, the Dutch text of the speech is included in a booklet, which was put together by the "Aktie Strohalm en den Ecologische Uitgeverij" and which is propagated and sold by the NANAI (= Nederlandse Aktiegroep Noord-Amerikaanse Indianen) in Rotterdam.[4]

In Sweden Seattle's speech was first published in two different Swedish translations in 1976 and 1977 and used in a third translation by a Swedish pop group in one of their records.[5] On the other hand it was an Englishman living in Sweden, Carl Ross, who underwent the task of putting the authenticity of the text to the test. More about this at a later stage.

Many, many more examples of an adaption and use of Seattle's speech for environmental purposes in other European countries (e.g., Italy, Portugal, Denmark) can easily be found. There is probably hardly a country in Western Europe where Seattle's speech has not been published in a translation and hailed as a document of an exemplary ecological sentiment. It is precisely this great number of publications which makes it impossible to mention them all.

Two final examples will show that Seattle's speech has not only been influential in books, brochures, on records, in films etc., but that it has also had its impact on radio programmes in Europe.

These two examples were taken from German radio programs, both of them concentrating on ecological problems and both of them intended for young listeners:

(1) In April 1979 the North German Broadcasting Corporation (Norddeutscher Rundfunk) in its programs for schools had a transmission about the destruction of the environment. In this program Seattle's speech was quoted in a German translation and contrasted with reports of present-day pollution in German

cities, rivers, and forests.[6]

(2) In October 1982 the West German Broadcasting Corporation (Westdeutscher Rundfunk) had a program about a project carried out by boys and girls in a German school. The pupils had read Seattle's speech and under the impression of this speech they discussed their own traditional understanding of the environment and their attitude towards nature. In the course of this project they found out that Seattle's attitude towards nature was of the greatest significance for them in their present-day ecological situation.[7]

In view of this immense publicity of Seattle's speech in Europe, the words of a young Swiss lady can probably be seen as representative for what many young people in Europe feel; in a letter to me she wrote that for her Seattle's speech has become "the embodiment of all 'environmental ideas'."[8]

As this paper is basically concerned with the European, not the American, reception of Seattle's speech, I want to present only a short glimpse of the American scene: The speech is also very popular in the United States. Dale Jones, the Northwest representative of "Friends of the Earth" in the city of Seattle writes in a letter referring to Seattle's speech, which he and some other publications call a "letter":

"I first saw the letter in September 1972 in a now out of business Native American tabloid newspaper. ... I clipped the article and mailed it to a few friends. Soon thereafter the letter appeared in *Environmental Action* and has subsequently appeared in a number of publications around the world" (Jones 1983).

One of these publications apparently was the April 1974 issue of *Passages*, a magazine of Northwest Orient Airlines, and after that the text spread like wildfire in the United States and was published in innumerable ways and places. Therefore it is "well known and widely hailed as a masterpiece of Indian oratory, speaking to our present-day concerns" (Holm 1983). The *Seattle Times* occasionally publishes the full version of the speech and the Sierra Club, a conservation organization, reprints it from time to time.

Nevertheless I was in for a surprise when I asked students of the Acoma-Laguna-High School on the Laguna Reservation about their associations with the name "Seattle." These young Pueblo Indians knew "Seattle" only as the name of an American city, but not as the name of an Indian chief! This experience seems to confirm the view that the situation in America appears very similar to the one in Europe: The text of the speech is famous in ecologically interested circles. But Chief Seattle as a historical person does not seem to be as well known as his words - not even among young Indians.

II

When we read or hear or see these numerous European utilizations and applications of Seattle's speech - and if we look and watch and listen carefully - something surprising strikes us: There are obvious differences between some of these various texts of the speech, all of which are ascribed to that American Indian, Chief Seattle - sometimes differences only in phrasing and wording, sometimes also in content. Moreover, these differences cannot be laid down to different translations of one identical text because in one case the difference amounts to the opposition between the sentence "Your god is not our god" versus the sentence "Our god is the same god." In this way we find all the shades from identical phrasing and thinking on the one hand to downright opposite phrasing and thinking on the other hand. (Further on we shall take a closer look at these differences.)

This discovery seems to lead us to one of the following conclusions:

(a) The different versions of the text refer to different speeches by Seattle;

(b) different versions of one speech are in existence.

In other words: The authenticity of the speech is in doubt.

So the questions are: What is the source material like - what does the basic research tell us - how authentic are these text?

There is no question that Chief Seattle was a historical person. He lived from about 1786 to 1866 and was a chief of the Suquamish and the Duwamish Indians on the Pacific northwest coast of what is now the United States. His native name, though, was not Seattle but Seeathl, a name which was debased by whites to its present spelling and pronunciation. Neither is there any doubt that Chief Seattle was present at the well-known Point Elliott Treaty negotiations of 1855 which signed away a good deal of Indian land to White settlement. Seattle was the first Indian chief to sign that treaty and on that occasion gave two short speeches which are well preserved to this day among the documents of the treaty proceedings in the National Archives in Washington, DC. Seattle was converted to Catholicism around 1830 and never fought in a war against white people. Since around 1860 the largest city of the state of Washington has borne his name.

Unfortunately we tread on less safe ground when we approach the question of the authenticity of his famous speech. The two short speeches just mentioned, which are preserved in the United States National Archives, bear no resemblance to what is publicized as "Seattle's speech" in America and Europe these days. The tone and subject matter of both those speeches are definitely at variance with the speech popularized in recent publications.[9] Yet, in spite of several searches by the staff of the National Archives, no further record of a speech or letter by Chief Seattle was found in the National Archives.[10]

In fact we can state that the oldest document of the speech which has become so famous in our time dates from the year 1887. On 29 October of that year the *Seattle Sunday Star*, a local newspaper in the region, that went out of print a few years later, published an article by a H. A. Smith. The article goes under the heading *Early Reminiscences No. 10* and bears the title: *Scraps from a diary - Chief Seattle - a gentleman by instinct - his native eloquence etc. etc.*" In this article this H. A. Smith - who is usually called Dr. Henry Smith, because he was a physician - begins with a very favorable description of the outer appearance and behavior of Chief Seattle, of his bearing and delivery of the speech as well as of his impact on the people around him. Then he carries on: "When Governor Stevens first arrived in Seattle and told the natives he had been appointed commissioner of Indian affairs for Washington Territory, they gave him a demonstrative reception in front of Dr. Maynard's office, near the water front on Main Street." After the governor had been introduced by Dr. Maynard and had given an explanation of his mission there,

> "Chief Seattle arose with all the dignity of a senator, who carries the responsibilities of a great nation on his shoulders. Placing one hand on the Governor's head and slowly pointing heavenward with the index finger of the other, he commenced his memorable address in solemn and impressive tones. 'Yonder sky, that has wept tears of compassion upon our fathers for centuries untold, ...'"

After recording Seattle's speech Dr. Smith concludes his article with the following remarks:

> "Other speakers followed, but I took no notes. Governor Stevens' reply was brief. He merely promised to meet them in general council on some future occasion to discuss the proposed treaty. Chief Seattle's promise to adhere to the treaty, should one be ratified, was observed to the letter, for he was ever the unswerving and faithful friend of the white man.
> "The above is but a fragment of his speech, and lacks all the charm lent by the grace and earnestness of the sable old orator, and the occasion."

I have quoted the introductory and the concluding remarks of Dr. Smith at some length, because there are some important points in it which we have to keep in mind if we want to blaze a trail through the thicket of differing opinions and misleading hints:

(a) According to Dr. Smith this address by Seattle was not given on the occasion of the signing of the Point Elliott Treaty, but at a reception for the new Commissioner of Indian Affairs for Washington Territory, Governor Stevens, and the location was "in front of Dr. Maynard's office" on Main Street. This means at the same time that this speech was not made in January 1855, when the Treaty of Point Elliott was signed, but in November

510

or December 1853 or in the year 1854, for it was in November 1853 that Stevens arrived in the new Washington Territory as Governor and Commissioner of Indians Affairs. The most likely date for the address seems to be December 1854, when Stevens returned from a trip to the East.

(b) The second point which we ought to remember is Dr. Smith's remark: "The above is but a fragment of his speech, and lacks all the charm ...". This means that Dr. Smith does not claim to have recorded Seattle's speech word for word and in full.

(c) On the other hand, Dr. Smith obviously took notes of Seattle's speech, which is indicated both by the heading "Scraps from a diary" and by the concluding remark "Other speakers followed, but I took no notes." By pointing out that he took no notes of the other speakers, Dr. Smith implies that he did take notes of Seattle's speech.

There is, moreover, another document confirming that Dr. Smith on his deathbed told one Mr. Vivian M. Carkeek "that he had made extended notes of the address at the time it was given and from those notes he reconstructed the entire address" (Rich 1970:45). In the last part of this sentence ("reconstructed the entire address") Dr. Smith seems to run counter to and contradict his own statement which he makes towards the end of his original newspaper publication in 1887: "The above is but a fragment of his speech."

A solution of this seeming contradiction may be that with the phrase "the entire address" Dr. Smith did not refer to Seattle's actual address but to his own newspaper rendition of that address. - However that may be, Dr. Smith's notes have been lost - and unless somebody should happen to find them, almost a hundred years after that publication, we shall never know what the notes in Dr. Smith's diary said and how closely he stuck to them when he wrote that newspaper article 33 years after the occasion.

There is, moreover, the question whether Seattle gave the speech in English or in his native language, and, if so, whether Dr. Smith understood this native language. William Arrowsmith, who himself made a "translation" of Dr. Smith's Seattle - address, says that "Seattle's English was minimal" and that he purportedly delivered his speech "in his native Duwamish" (Arrowsmith 1978a). All the authors who have written about Seattle seem to agree that he did not speak, let alone write, English. - About Dr. Smith's mastery of Seattle's language W. C. Vanderwerth says that Dr. Smith "mastered the Duwamish language in about two years," but that Seattle's speech "was delivered through an interpreter" (Vanderwerth 1971:117). John M. Rich says that Seattle "conveyed his thoughts in the dignified, picturesque, Indian language" (Rich 1970:48). But neither Vanderwerth nor Rich give the source of this information. Nevertheless we can take it for granted that Seattle did not deliver his speech in English, but that he used his native Indian language, Southern Puget Sound Salish or Lushotseed. As was the custom on such occasions, the speech was then translated by interpreters, first probably into the so-called Chinook Jargon, which consisted of elements from European and Indian languages and was used as an interlanguage at that time in the area, and then into English.

Whether Dr. Smith took his notes of Seattle's native Lushotseed or of the translation on the spot, must remain open.

When all is said and done, this point is not actually very relevant, because Dr. Smith does not even claim to give a full record of Seattle's speech in the original phrasing.

Putting together our findings so far we can say:

(1) Two short speeches by Seattle recorded in the National Archives in Washington DC, bear no resemblance to the text of the speech popularized under Seattle's name.

(2) The first published version of the now famous speech was presented to the public by a Dr. Smith in 1887, more than 30 years after the Chief is said to have delivered it. Although this text is different from most of the publicized versions of today, it is similar enough to indicate a relationship.

(3) The selection of the material and the formulation of the text is possibly as much Dr. Smith's as Seattle's. There is no way of determining the degree of authenticity of this text, as Dr. Smith's notebook has not been found.

(4) We can, however, take it for granted that there is at least a core, a nucleus of authentic thinking and - possibly - language in the text, as Dr. Smith was able to base his version of the speech on "extended notes" in that diary which he took on the occasion of the delivery of the speech. "I incline to think that much of Smith's version was authentic" (Arrowsmith 1978a) and "the speech in Smith's version evidently followed the original closely" (Arrowsmith 1975:25n12).

It seems that during the following years not many people took notice of Dr. Smith's publication of Seattle's speech. Apart from a full reprint of the text in the *History of Seattle* by Frederic James Grant (1891:432ff) there is hardly a reference to the speech prior to the early thirties of this century. In 1931 Clarence B. Bagley published an article in the *Washington Historical Quarterly* under the title of "Chief Seattle and Angeline." In this article the author reprints the complete text of Chief Seattle's speech - with some variations - from Dr. Smith's publication in the *Seattle Sunday Star*.

The most striking variation is probably that he adds three short sentences to the speech; Dr. Smith had ended Seattle's address with the words:

"The white man will never be alone. Let him be just and deal kindly with my people, for the dead are not altogether powerless."

Bagley adds:

"Dead - did I say? There is no death. Only a change of worlds" (Bagley 1931:255).[11]

This wilful handling of the text seems to have had two important effects:

(a) The addition was accepted by the public. Most later publications of the address have it.
(b) It may have opened up the way for a very free and wilful handling of the original text by other editors.

Only one year later, in 1932, John M. Rich published a booklet with the title *Chief Seattle's Unanswered Challenge* (Rich 1970). This booklet does not only contain Dr. Smith's version of Chief Seattle's speech from the *Seattle Sunday Star* - again with some variations and Bagley's addition to the text - but also the story of how the text was discovered by John M. Rich, what the occasion of Seattle's address was and some very flattering remarks about the impact of the speech on the author, John M. Rich. Moreover the booklet tries to confirm the authenticity of the text by producing a letter from a law office in Seattle. This letter was quoted above, because it endorsed the view that Dr. Smith reconstructed Seattle's address from extended notes, which he had taken while the speech was being given. The book by John M. Rich containing Seattle's speech was reprinted several times, without arousing too much attention. - Occasional excerpts of Seattle's speech, mostly adopting Bagley's modifications of the text, appeared in the 1960's, e.g. in Jones (1965:99). Interest in Seattle's words seemed to be growing again.

But it is only in the late sixties and early seventies of this century that the scene suddenly changes. It seems that by that time a greater awareness had developed for problems which Seattle had touched on in his speech. In 1969 an American poet and writer, William Arrowsmith, published the "Speech of Chief Seattle" (Arrowsmith 1969).

The reader will quickly see that not so much the content as the wording and phrasing of this text is different from that published by Dr. Smith.

Only a few year later, between 1972 and 1974, yet another text appeared under the title: "The Decidedly Unforked Message of Chief Seattle" (Seattle 1974) and, in order to make matters even more complicated, at the World Fair in Spokane (Washington State) 1974, in the U.S. pavilion, a *Speech by Chief Seattle* was displayed, which again seemed different in style and wording.

What had happened? Had new speeches by Seattle been discovered which had been unknown to the world until then?

Not at all! Although all these "Speeches", "Addresses," "Messages," or even "Letters" of Chief Seattle differ from each other - sometimes more, sometimes less - they are yet similar enough to indicate that they all used one text as a base. William Arrowsmith, moreover, expressly states at the end of his "Speech of Chief Seattle" that the text is "Translated from the Victorian English of Dr. Henry Smith of Seattle, published in the *Seattle Star* on October 29, 1877."[12] - And the text "The Decidedly Unforked Message of Chief Seattle" of 1974 notes in a preliminary remark: "An adaptation of his [= Chief Seattle's] remarks, based on an English translation by William Arrowsmith." - Finally, the text from the 1974 Expo at Spokane displays on close reading a very great similarity with this "Decidedly Unforked Message."

We can see that, although all three versions of Chief Seattle's speech differ more or less in their contents and in their language, none of them claims a new or direct line of descent from the old Chief, which might have escaped the public's attention so far. On the contrary: All of them - directly or indirectly - refer to, and are therefore dependent on, that text of Seattle's speech which was published by Dr. Smith in the *Seattle Sunday Star* in 1887. Dr. Smith's version (which therefore we should fittingly call Version No. 1 from now on) is the only true ancestor of all those later legitimate - or illegitimate - children and children's children. It is the source of the text by William Arrowsmith (Version No. 2), of the "Decidedly Unforked Message of Chief Seattle" (Version No. 3) and of the text from the Expo at Spokane (Version No. 4).

III

When we compare these four versions with each other and then look at the texts of the speech which roam around Europe and America, a striking recognition emerges: In those texts which find highest acclaim nowadays and are most widely publicized there is little of version No. 1 and little of version No. 2. By far most of the texts *en vogue* here and now are either excerpts or relatively complete renderings of version No. 3. This applies also to a so-called "Letter" by Chief Seattle to President Pierce in Washington: This letter appeared in America and in Europe in the mid-seventies along with version No. 3 and 4, and is virtually identical with other circulating texts of Seattle's speech No. 3 (and partly No. 4).

So the letter does by no means represent a separate version - which could be No. 5 - but it is just one type of version No. 3. By the way: No trace of the original of such a letter could be found in the National Archives in Washington (cp. note 10) nor in the Seattle Public Library.

Starting with a comparison of versions No. 1 and 2 we find that throughout the texts the two authors follow the same ideas in the same order so that the subject matter and the content of the two texts are very much the same, almost identical. One of the recurring aspects of the texts is the 19th century Manifest Destiny ideology from a seemingly Indian point of view. Moreover, both texts display a good number of metaphors and similes. But it is in the use

514

of vocabulary where they differ markedly: Version No. 1 uses very elevated, literary, and sometimes even archaic language while the author of version No. 2 writes simpler sentences and uses more modern and down-to-earth language.

The following examples may serve to demonstrate this:

Version No. 1 (Dr. Smith)

"My words are like the stars, that never set."
"No bright star hovers about the horizon."
"I will not mourn over our untimely decay, nor reproach my pale-face brothers with hastening it, for we, too, may have been somewhat to blame."
"Our religion is the tradition of our ancestors."
"We will ponder your proposition."

Version No. 2 (William Arrowsmith)

"My words are like the stars. They do not set."
"No bright star shines on the horizon."
"But I will not mourn the passing by of my people. Nor do I blame our white brothers for causing it. We too were perhaps partly to blame."
"Our religion is the way of our forefathers."
"We will consider your offer."

These examples may be sufficient to show that the difference between versions No. 1 and 2 is above all a difference of language, not a difference of ideas. Version No. 2 is, according to its author, William Arrowsmith, a translation "from the Victorian English of Dr. Henry Smith" (Arrowsmith 1969).

We enter into a markedly different kind of relationship if we now take version No. 3 into consideration and compare it with version No. 1 and 2. Whereas the step from No. 1 to No. 2 had brought a change of language but not of content, the step from No. 2 to No. 3 brings not only a change of language but also of subject matter and content. Moreover this change of content takes several directions: One is the attitude of the speaker towards the white man; for, whereas No. 1 displays a positive and friendly feeling towards the white man (it calls the President of the U.S.A. "our great and good father" and later on continues: "I will not ... reproach my pale-face brothers"), the text of No. 3 shows a much unfriendlier and sometimes resentful attitude towards whites:

"... the white man may come with guns and take our land."
"We know that the white man does not understand our ways."
"Continue to contaminate your bed and you will one night suffocate in your own waste."

515

But this change of attitude towards the white man in version No. 3 is by far outdone by the change of attitude towards nature. Whereas in versions No. 1 and 2 considerations of the natural environment play only a secondary role, the text of version No. 3 concentrates almost entirely on environmental issues, and it puts forward the great dangers that arise out of the white man's irresponsible dealings with the natural world. So it is only in version No. 3 that the text adopts a definite ecological slant and that Chief Seattle becomes an ecologist. Here are some of these new environmental phrases and sentences:

"How can you buy or sell the sky, the warmth of the land? The idea is strange to us... The rivers are our brother, they quench our thirst. The rivers carry our canoes, and feed our children... The air is precious to the red man, for all things share the same breath - the beast, the tree, the man, they all share the same breath."
"This we know. The earth does not belong to man. Man belongs to the earth. This we know. All things are connected like the blood which unites one family. All things are connected.
"Whatever befalls the earth, befalls the sons of the earth. Man did not weave the web of life; he is merely a strand in it. Whatever he does to the web, he does to himself..."

These differences of attitude towards the white man and towards the natural environment in version No. 3 are even topped by a difference in attitudes towards God. Compare the following quotations:

Version No. 1

"Your God loves your people and hates mine; ... he has forsaken his red children; ... The white man's God cannot love his red children..."

Version No. 3

"Our God is the same God. ... He is the God of man, and His compassion is equal for the red man and the white."

We see: Version No. 3 does not only bring changes of attitudes into the world of versions No. 1 and 2 - it even develops a downright opposite view of God.

Finally we should not fail to mention a number of historical errors in version No. 3, i.e. remarks which Seattle could never have made in 1854. We read, e.g., the following sentence in this text:

516

"I have seen a thousand rotten buffaloes on the prairie, left by the white man who shot them from a passing train."

There are several errors in this one sentence:

(1) When Seattle made his speech in 1854, there were not trains running across the prairie in America. It was more than 10 years later that the first transcontinental railway was built.

(2) The appalling and senseless killing of buffaloes by white people occurred mainly in the second half of the 19th century - above all between 1860 and 1890 - and not in its first half, so that Seattle could not have seen it and referred to it in 1854.

(3) For all we know, in all his life Seattle never left the area in the northwest corner of the United States and on the Pacific Ocean where he was born. One more reason why he cannot have seen "a thousand rotting buffaloes on the prairie."

There are other minor errors in the text, e.g., references to birds and trees that are not native to the area where Seattle lived. They all constitute additional confirmation that Seattle did not compose the text which we know as version No. 3 of his speech. It seems that the author of this version mainly adopted from the first and second versions the idea that "the Great Chief in Washington sends word that he wishes to buy our land." This is, therefore, and fittingly, the very starting line of No. 3. After that the text soon deviates from the thought pattern of the former versions and develops its own concept of white people, of God and - above all - of the essential significance of an unspoiled natural environment. In other words: Seattle's speech is used as a peg on which to hang one's own story.

Little need be said about version No. 4. The author of this text obviously used the third version which he shortened and simplified in its range but which he enlarged by means of style and rhetoric. We find many repetitions, alliterations, enumerations, and even fragmentary sentences in this text. It is largely a concise and poetic rendering of the third version and was exhibited in the U.S. pavilion at the 1974 World Fair in Spokane/Washington. It is wholly ecological and nature-related in its outlook, it has therefore concentrated on the environmental passages of the third version - and it is very impressive through its poetic language. But it has, to my knowledge, never been published in a book. Its influence should, therefore, only be considered in close connection with that of version No. 3.

A comparison of the four versions has produced the following results:

(a) William Arrowsmith's text - version No. 2 - varies mainly in language from the Dr. Smith text, while in content it clearly follows that version No.

1. Arrowsmith himself calls his version a "translation" of the Seattle speech, by which he means "the removal of the dense patina of 19th century literary diction and syntax" (Arrowsmith 1978a).

(b) Version No. 3 differs markedly from No. 1 and No. 2 in language and in content, but at the same time it is obvious that the writer of No. 3 knew No. 1 and No. 2 and used them as a base. What is most strikingly new in No. 3 is that it is profusely ecological. It is only here that Seattle becomes a modern ecologist. Therefore: Although some lines of versions No. 1 and 2 have been used verbatim, the greatest part of this text is new material with a new slant.

(c) Version No. 4 is very close to No. 3 in content and in language, it is basically a shortened, poetic adaptation of No. 3.

IV

In view of the fact that versions No. 3 and 4 are very similar to each other, but markedly different from versions No. 1 and 2 in content and form - and in view of the fact that the authors of Nos. 1 and 2 are known to us - the question arises: Who wrote Nos. 3 and 4? Whose authorship can they claim? And remembering that No. 4 is a somewhat modified replica of No. 3 - and keeping in mind that version No. 3 is the source of most speeches in Europe (and America) that are attributed to Chief Seattle - the problem actually boils down to the question: Where, when, and - above all - by whom was the text of version No. 3 produced?

In 1975 a journalist in the city of Seattle by the name of Janice Krenmayr delved into the question of the authenticity of No. 3 and published an article in the *Seattle Times Magazine*. The title of the article was "'The Earth is our Mother' - Who Really Said that?" In this article Janice Krenmayr tries to uncover the origin of the so-called "Letter" by Chief Seattle to President Pierce in Washington. (As we have seen before, this letter is virtually identical with what we have called the third version of Chief Seattle's speech.) Janice Krenmayr writes about her search for the source of the text: "It [the text] first came to notice as an except in *Wildlife Omnibus*, a newsletter published by the National Wildlife Federation, November 15, 1973. ... A request was dispatched to the Wildlife Federation for a copy of the entire letter. The editor replied, it had been 'picked up' from *Environmental Action Magazine*, November 11, 1972. *Environmental Action* indicated, its source was the Seattle Office of 'Friends of the Earth'... we queried the latter organization. It disclaimed any knowledge of the authenticity and suggested we contact the Seattle Public Library. But that we had done in the beginning. The letter was not on record" (Krenmayr 1975). Such experiences of futility and frustration seemed to await all those who tried to reveal the secret of the authorship of version No. 3. It was like poking into a bale of cotton: it gives 'way' but no 'answers' - or like turning a big loop and returning to one's point of departure without results. I turned several of those loops myself.

In this frustrating situation help came from "Friends of the Earth" in the City of Seattle, from Carl A. Ross in Herrljunga/Sweden, from William Arrowsmith - and from the man who wrote No. 3 (!!).

The Northwest representative of "Friends of the Earth" in Seattle, Dale Jones, writes in a letter:

"I first saw the letter [speech version No. 3] in September 1972 in a now out of business Native American tabloid newspaper... I clipped the article and mailed it to a few friends. Soon thereafter, the letter appeared in *Environmental Action* [11 November 1972] and has subsequently appeared in a number of publications around the world" (Jones 1983; one of the "number of publications" was Seattle 1974).

William Arrowsmith, author of version No. 2, in a number of letters, goes further back to the roots of the creation of text No. 3:

"In the early seventies a colleague at Texas, Ted Perry, ... asked me if I would let him use the speech in my rendering as the basis of a filmscript. I said yes, provided I could approve the results. Perry wrote a script - largely 'ecological' in its emphasis, and freely adding new materials *ad libitum*. (... he had no intention of redoing Seattle and then claiming the results were historically genuine; he was doing a script 'after' Seattle's speech...) Perry tried to insist to his producer for the film (The Southern Baptist Convention) that the speech was not in any sense a translation. But they overrode his decision... Hence they talked glibly about a 'letter' to President Pierce. ...

"In the course of their work, the Baptists added still more 'material' to the speech. The bulk of *their* additions is the (Baptist) religiosity of *their* Seattle... Ted Perry broke with his producer and the Baptists over their high-handed procedures" (Arrowsmith 1978a, 1983).

"I feel quite certain that *all* 'ecological' texts and reprints of the Seattle speech derive ultimately from Ted Perry's script. ... the Perry script is profusely 'ecological' - unmistakably, Perry's 'contribution' to the original" (Arrowsmith 1978b).

This sounds like a complete and knowledgeable report of how version No. 3 come into existence.

It is confirmed in a highly informative article by Carl Ross (1979) and in a letter by Bonita Sparrow of the Radio and Television Commission, Southern Baptist Convention:

"Ted Perry used brief portions of the speech [by Seattle] in his film script for *Home*, a film on ecology produced by the Southern Baptist Radio and Television Commission in the early 1970's... the film... won several industry awards for excellence...

"I do not know if Ted Perry's version of the script was altered or modified in any way but I doubt that it was..." (Sparrow 1983).

Finally here is Ted Perry's, i.e. the author's own point of view in this matter:

"Some time in 1969 or 1970 the Southern Baptists proposed to me the making of several films, one of them on the subject of pollution. While I was beginning to work on the script I heard Professor Arrowsmith read the Chief Seattle speech at some kind of rally; Earth Day, I think it was called. In any case, it was a large gathering devoted to environmental issues. Subsequently, I asked Professor Arrowsmith (he and I were both teaching at the University of Texas) if I might use the idea as the basis for the script; he graciously said yes... So I wrote a speech which was a fiction. I would guess that there were several sentences which were paraphrases of sentences in Professor Arrowsmith's translation but the rest was mine. In passing the script along to the Baptists, I always made it clear that the work was mine. And they, of course, knew the script was original; they would surely not have paid me, as they did, for a speech which I merely retyped.

"In presenting them with a script, however, I made the mistake of using Chief Seattle's name in the body of the text. I don't remember why this was done; my guess is that it was just a mistake on my part. In writing a fictional speech I should have used a fictional name. In any case, when next I saw the script it was the narration for a film entitled *Home* aired on ABC or NBC-TV in 1972, I believe. I was surprised when the telecast was over, because there was no 'written by' credit on the film. I was more than surprised; I was angry. So I called up the producer and he told me that he thought the text might seem more authentic if there were no 'written by' credit given. Surprise. I cancelled my contract with the Baptists to do another script for them..." (Perry 1983).

"I ... certainly would never have allowed anyone to believe that it was anything but a fictitious item written by me" (Perry 1978).

So here we are: This so-called speech by Seattle, which we called version No. 3, and which has by now conquered the imagination of millions of people in many countries all over the world - this text was in its main parts written in the winter of 1970/71 as a filmscript for the Southern Baptist Convention by Ted Perry, at that time teaching at the University of Texas. He used as his opening lines brief portions from Seattle's speech - versions No. 1 and 2 - but then composed his own ecological text. In their film the Southern Baptists neglected to give credit to Ted Perry for his part in the filmscript, but gave credit to Seattle for what he in fact had never said nor written.

The essence of our findings then is that of the different versions of Chief Seattle's speech only version No. 1 can claim a certain authenticity, as Dr. Smith, the author of that version, obviously was present and took "extended" notes when Chief Seattle made his speech in 1854. The later versions of 1969, 1970 and 1974 consist of translations or adaptions of that first version or constitute new creations.

This seems to be the end of a detective story. - But it cannot be the end of the whole story. For we cannot be content with calling the text "a fake," "spurious," "fictitious," "bogus," "not authentic," "fraudulent," "a pollution of the past" (all these terms have been used by people who were in the know or who doubted the authenticity of the text), but we must ask ourselves: How could the text (version No. 3), whose claim to Seattle's authorship must largely be called unjustified, how could it spread as it did - first in America, then in Europe? How could it captivate the imagination of hundreds of thousands of people and strongly influence their thinking and possibly also their actions? How could this text tempt Monsignore Bruce Kent, the National Chaplain of Pax Christi in Britain, to his remark: "It's a whole religious concept... I think it's really a fifth gospel, almost..." (cp. note 3).

Trying to answer these questions we cannot but largely depend on presumption.

Nevertheless I shall venture an answer:

(1) The text seems to give expression to thoughts and feelings which are on many people's minds these days, which find nourishment in publications of the Club of Rome about an end to industrial growth, and which have led to social and political groupings with which many young people identify themselves wholeheartedly: It is the complex of ideas which circle round the term "ecology" and which include sentiments, fears and hopes expressed in terms like "exploitation of nature," "destruction of the environment," "pollution," "conservation of natural resources," "anti-nuclear movement," "alternative ways of life," and many others. These issues seem to be on the way towards becoming one - if not *the* - major issue of people and nations around the turn of the millenium, at least in the Western world. The text of version No. 3 seems to have given language and expression to this emotionally charged problem-situation, and in this way to have pushed it forward on its way. "If it wasn't written it should have been".[13]

(2) The imagery, the symbolism, the phrasing, and the wording of the text seem to be in perfect unison with its purpose and its message on the one hand and with the wishes, the concerns, and the expectations of many people on the other hand. I think it would be difficult for all of us to arm ourselves against the impact of phrases like these: "Every part of this earth is sacred to my people... we are part of the earth and it is part of us. The perfumed flowers

are our sisters, the deer, the horse, the great eagle, these are our brothers. The rocky crests, the juices in the meadows, the bodyheat of the pony, and men, all belong to the same family... The rivers are our brothers, they quench our thirst... and you must henceforth give the rivers the kindness you would give any brother... the ashes of our fathers are sacred. Their graves are holy ground, and so these hills, these trees, this portion of the earth is consecrated to us. The air is precious to the red man, for all things share the same breath - the beast, the tree, the man, they all share the same breath... you must remember that the air is precious to us. The air shares its spirit with all the life it supports. The wind that gave our grandfather his first breath so receives his last sigh. And the wind must also give our children the spirit of life... All things are connected... Whatever befalls the earth, befalls the sons of the earth. If men spit upon the ground, they spit upon themselves. This we know. The earth does not belong to man; man belongs to the earth. This we know. All things are connected like the blood which unites one family. All things are connected... When the last red man has vanished from this earth and his memory is only the shadow of a cloud moving across the prairie, these shores and forests will still hold the spirits of my people. For they love this earth as a new born loves its mother's heartbeat. So if we sell you our land, love it as we have loved it. Care for it as we have cared for it... We may be brothers after all." Even if we did not know the name of the person who wrote this, many of us would probably admit that whoever wrote these words: They constitute an impressive piece of writing. And it is easy to see that such words may well function rather as a mythical or religious statement than as a historical document.

(3) Lastly, these words seem to touch on an idea and a feeling which has so far largely been banned from our occidental, Christian, Western culture. It is the idea that the worldly and the spiritual, the mundane and the beyond, the profane and the sacred are not wholly separate from each other, as we are used to thinking - but that these seeming opposites are actually very closely connected in this world and that therefore everything in this world without any exception is seen as sacred in its nature and its character. This idea that each and every thing and creature in this world is spiritual and sacred, may well prove to be the salient point of this text - salient for a society which has always neatly separated the temporal and the spiritual and in this way has tried to justify man's claim that all the non-sacred world is at his disposal.

We may well acknowledge such qualities of this text and appreciate it as an impressive ecological text in its own right. But we must at the same time repudiate its claim to the authorship of Chief Seattle (and William Arrowsmith). This text does not represent the mind of the old Chief, but the mind of a sensitive Euro-American, worried about our ecological situation and the general dualism in our culture. Not the text of the speech is, therefore, spurious, but the headline which names Chief Seattle as the author.

NOTES

1. *Söhne der Erde* - Erzählung nach einer Rede des Dwamish-Oberhauptes Seathl. The film is available at Zoom-Filmverleih, Saatwiesenstr. 22, CH-8600 Dübendorf (Switzerland).
2. René Bardet, Poesie und Musik, *Vielleicht weil ich ein Wilder bin...*; Worte des indianischen Häuptlings Seattle an den amerikanischen Präsidenten im Jahre 1855. Zweitausendeins-Versand, Ferdinand-Porsche-Str. 37-39, D-6000 Frankfurt 61 (Fed. Rep. of Germany).
3. "A Fifth Gospel" - An interview with Bruce Kent. Resource Pack of *Testimony - Chief Seattle*, TCS 94/95; United Society for the Propagation of the Gospel, London. Monsignore Bruce Kent is quoted as saying about this text of Seattle's address: "I think it is a whole religious concept of the value of people, of animals, of land, of our transitory nature. I think it is really a fifth Gospel, almost - of what life is all about." At a later stage: "The significance of Seattle is terrific! The response to Seattle... I'd no idea when I got it into the Catholic Herald originally. It was reprinted as a piece, and they had hundreds and hundreds of requests for back copies of that edition. Then we got it reprinted in a little red booklet, three or four thousand of these, (I've forgotten how many). And they have all gone now. From all over the world - from the Ocean Islands to Finland and Yugoslavia - from all over the world someone has written, and this massage has gone out somehow, and people have accepted it. The World Council of Churches has spread the book too, they reprinted it. And so it has absolutely caught on" (p. 98).
4. In a leaflet, handed out by *NANAI*, Seattle's speech is characterized with the following words: "In de onvergetelijke toespraak van Chief Seattle die hij in 1854 uitsprak, klinkt de verbondenheid en afhankelijkheid van de Indiaan met de aarde en met alles wat erop leeft, door. Seattle's woorden zijn nog steeds aktueel en zeker van toepassing op de 'Blanke man' van deze tijd."
5. The publication of 1976 was in the January edition of the periodical *Miljö och framtid* 1976/1, the publication of 1977 in the June edition of the Magazin *Pax* 1977/6. The pop group "Nationalteatern Nynningen" used it in their record "Vi kommer att leva igen". Cf. Ross (1979:3).
6. "Wie die Zerstörung der Umwelt begann: Die Rede des Indianerhäuptlings Seattle"; Norddeutscher Rundfunk, 1. Programm, Schulfunk, 23 April 1979.
7. "Die Erde ist unsere Mutter - Indianer wandeln das Naturverständnis deutscher Schüler," Westdeutscher Rundfunk, 3. Programm, 24 October 1982.
8. Quotation from a letter, written by Beate Weyrich to me, dated 10 March 1983: "Die Rede des Häuptlings Seattle ist für mich zum Inbegriff aller 'Umweltgedanken' geworden."
9. According to the original manuscript of the record of the Point Elliott

Treaty negotiations (National Archives, Washington, DC), Governor Stevens made a somewhat long speech at the treaty negotiations on Monday, 22 January 1855, and then added: "Does anyone object to what I have said? Does my venerable friend Seattle object? I want Seattle to give his will to me and to his people."

According to the original manuscript Seattle answered: "I look upon you as my father. I and the rest regard you as such. All of the Indians have the same good feeling towards you and will send it on paper to the Great Father. All of them, men, old men, women and children rejoice that he has sent you to take care of them. My mind is like yours. I don't want to say more. My heart is very good towards Dr. Maynard (a physician who was present) I want always to get medicine from him."

Later in the treaty proceedings - it is 23 January 1855 - the document states: "Seattle then on behalf of himself and the other Chiefs brought a white flag and presented it saying: "Now by this we make friends and put away all bad feelings if we ever had any. We are the friends of the Americans. All the Indians are of the same mind. We look upon you as our father. We will never change our minds, but since you have been to see us we will be always the same. Now, now do you send this paper of our hearts to the Great Chief. That is all I have to say."

Indeed, this is all he *did* say according to the original manuscript of the Point Elliott Treaty proceedings! Apart from these two short speeches - and apart from the one long speech which is dealt with in this paper - only two other short speeches by Seattle are recorded: a fragment of a speech recorded by the interpreter B.F. Shaw in 1850 and a lament by Seattle in May 1858 that the Treaty of Point Elliott had not been ratified by the U.S.Senate, leaving the Indian tribes in poverty and poor health (Krenmayr 1975:4).

10. "We have made several searches of the records of the Department of the Interior and of the War Department in the National Archives Building, but have not found the speech or the letter ascribed to Seattle." Quotation from a letter, written by the General Services Administration, National Archives and Records Service, Washington, DC 20408, to me, dated 19 August 1983. Neither does the Library of Congress or the Seattle Public Library have any record of such a letter.

11. It must, at this moment, remain open whether Bagley added these sentences on his own account or whether he adopted them from some other publication of the address, possibly even from John M. Rich's publication (1970) although Rich's booklet was published a year later (1932)!

12. There are two mistakes in this remark by William Arrowsmith: The paper of the first publication was not the *Seattle Star*, but the *Seattle Sunday Star*, and the year was not 1877 but 1887. These mistakes have been copied over and over again in later publication of the text.

13. J. Lindholm in *Outdoor America*, December 1975.

REFERENCES CITED

Anonymous
    1978   Seattle. Köln 1978: Katholische Studierende Jugend.
    1981   Women's World Day of Prayer, Order of Service, 6 March 1981.
    1983   Michaelskalender. Nettetal: Steyler Presse-Vertrieb.
Arrowsmith, William
    1969   Speech of Chief Seattle, January 9th, 1855. Arion, A Journal of Humanities and the Classics, 8(4):461-464. Austin.
    1975   Speech of Chief Seattle. The American Poetry Review 1975.
    1978a   Letter to Carl Ross, 20 January 1978.
    1978b   Letter to Carl Ross, 21 March 1978.
    1983   Letter to Rudolf Kaiser, 9 September 1983.
Bagley, Clarence B.
    1931   Chief Seattle and Angeline. Washington Historical Quarterly 22:243-275.
Drewermann, Eugen
    1982   Der tödliche Fortschritt - Von der Zerstörung der Erde und des Menschen im Erbe des Christentums. Regensburg.
Grant, Frederic James
    1891   History of Seattle. New York.
Holm, Bill
    1983   Letter to Rudolf Kaiser, 7 April 1983.
Jones, Dale
    1983   Letter to Rudolf Kaiser, 8 July 1983.
Jones, L.T.
    1965   Aboriginal American Oratory. Los Angeles: Southwest Museum.
Kaiser, Rudolf, and Michaela Kaiser
    1984   Diese Erde ist uns heilig. Münster: Edition Blaschzok.
Krenmayr, Janice
    1975   "'The Earth is our Mother' - Who Really Said that." The Seattle Times Magazine, Sunday, 5 January 1975.
Perry, Ted
    1978   Letter to Carl Ross, 19 May 1978.
    1983   Letter to Rudolf Kaiser, 11 November 1983.
Pförtner, Karl (ed.)
    1976   Seattles Brief an den weißen Häuptling. Weißenburg 1976: Kanalpresse.
Rich, John M.
    1970   Chief Seattle's Unanswered Challenge. Fairfield, WA (1st ed., 1932).
Ross, Carl
    1979   What Did Chief Seattle Say? Paper sent to Dale Jones, "Friends of the Earth," Seattle, WA, dated 23 April 1979.

Seattle

  1974   The Decidedly Unforked Message of Chief Seattle. Passages,
          Magazine of Northwest Orient Airlines. April 1974.

  1982   Wir sind ein Teil der Erde. Olten und Freiburg i.Br.: Walter.

Sparrow, Bonita

  1983   Letter from Bonita Sparrow, Radio and Television Commission of the
          Southern Baptist Convention, to Rudolf Kaiser, 14 November 1983.

Vanderwerth, W.C.

  1971   Indian Oratory. Norman, OK: University of Oklahoma Press.

Weigert/Musall/Werth

  1980   Mutter Erde, Bruder Himmel. Gelnhausen: Burckhardthaus - Laetare
          Verlag.

"THEY LIVED TOGETHER WITH THEIR DOGS AND HORSES": "INDIAN COPY" IN WEST GERMAN NEWSPAPERS 1968-1982

Aribert Schroeder

The analysis below was based on West German newspaper articles received from 28 editorial offices out of 100 contacted. Their addresses had been taken from a list.[1] Principles of selection were the type of newspaper, its estimated circulation, and its multiplicator function for other newspapers. Among the editorial offices answering my request for "Indian copy" were national daily papers like the *Frankfurter Allgemeine*, which sent the largest number of Indian-related articles by far, the *Süddeutsche Zeitung*, *Die Welt*, and the "tabloid" paper *Bild*. Regional daily newspapers from all parts of the Federal Republic of Germany were represented too; so were the national weekly papers by *Die Zeit*. Due to an insufficient number of articles received for earlier periods, the analysis given below was limited to the years 1968 until 1982.

In the news articles a great variety of themes was covered. Their respective focus already differs considerably depending on whether news was reported from the United States or European countries. Whereas news copy received from the United States is mainly concerned with Indian activists' demonstrations in the late sixties and early seventies, Federal Government Indian policies and Native American activities developed in the courts and international organizations, like the United Nations for example, become main themes in the middle seventies. International activities of Indians were also covered if they extended to, or evolved from, Europe. More prominently, however, figure articles on Native Americans touring various West European countries. They range from members of dance groups and trade delegations to representatives of Native American interest groups who enjoy no legal status in the United States, like Hopi "traditionalists" or the "Iroquois League," for example. In addition, self-styled Native American "spokesmen" were occasionally given attention too. A few news articles deal with Native Americans living in West Germany as students, musicians, or American soldiers.[2] West Germans themselves became news items whenever they developed Indian-related activities in clubs or support groups, e.g., the Indian sections of *Survival International* (BZ Jul. 22, 1981).

The feature articles printed in West German newspapers include a considerable number of news features written by American journalists, German foreign correspondents representing news agencies as well as individual newspapers, and West German "experts" on Indian issues, like journalists, having shown a special interest in Native American issues, authors, or travelers.[3] In addition, features were written about historical, anthropological, and ethnological themes and, on a personal basis, about travels in "Indian country."

527

Table: News Agencies Employed in Key Events
(Only sources named were counted)

	Alcatraz Island (1968)/1969-1971	BIA"raid" 1972	Wounded Knee 1973	Longest Walk 1978
AFP			2	
AFP/ddp		2	6	
AFP/ddp/dpa			1	
AP	2	1	58	5
AP/AFP			1	
AP/dpa			5	
AP/epd			2	
AP/Reuter			2	
ddp		1		3
dpa	13	7	30	7
dpa/AP			5	
dpa/UPI		1	10	
Eigenbericht/dpa			1	
epd			1	
Reuter			3	
Reuter/dpa			2	
sad			1	
UPI			1	
wp			1	

A group of its own can be formed of "Indian literature," i.e. English and German language publications on Native Americans. They were discussed in individual or summary reviews, or briefly commented upon in reading lists attached to background articles. On the American side, authors like Dee Brown, Vine Deloria,Jr., Charles A. Eastman, Ruth Beebe Hill, Alvin M. Josephy,Jr., Oliver La Farge, Wilcomb E. Washburn, and Edmund Wilson were mentioned among others, and, on the West German side, Claus Biegert, Thomas Jeier, René König, H.J. Stammel, Christopher S. Hagen,[4] and Lieselotte Unger. The larger part of these reviews, it seems, was composed in expert ways. The reviewer of Ruth Beebe Hill's *Hanta Yo*, however, basing himself on a characterization given in the "Introduction" where the book is called "a two-thousand-page documented novel," hardly enlightens his readers when he labels it "documented fiction" (HeA May 14, 1980).

Among the three letters to the editor discovered, two were written by West Germans and one by a Native American living in West Germany. Whereas the first German letter writer defends the Indians against a caption in which an analogy was attempted between past ways of Indian fighting in battle and those of the Vietkong, the second writer draws a parallel between the treatment given to Indians by Whites in the United States and the one given to "gipsies" in Germany in the past.[5] The Native American expresses agreement with the positions taken by American Indian Movement (AIM) activists at Wounded Knee.[6]

The number of opinion articles concerning Indian-related news events is rather small. In 1971, for example, an editor comments on the disappearance of the term "Apache" from a German dictionary. Basing himself on the meaning of this term in French, he points out that the jungle conception lies at its bottom. He also warns against Indian clichés (FA Aug. 20). The events of Wounded Knee provoked several "op articles." In most of them attention is drawn to the detrimental effects of White-held clichés and myths concerning Indians. The Native Americans' .claim of "self-determination" and "cultural autonomy" is occasionally supported (e.g., in SZ Mar. 9, 1973). Severe attacks on white American policies or attitudes adopted by individuals toward Indians, are the exception rather than the rule.

In the 1968-1982 period the following major Indian-related events in North America and West Europe were covered: In the United States, the occupation of Alcatraz Island in San Francisco Bay, California (Nov. 19, 1969-Jul. 14, 1971; 12/22[7]); the attempts to take over Forts Lawton and Lewis, Washington (Mar. 1970; 4/7), the former missile firing positions at Richmond, California (Jun. 1971; 2/2), and Belmont in Chicago, Illinois (Jul. 1971; 2/2); and the abandoned National Coast Guard station near Milwaukee, Wisconsin (Aug. 1971; 2/2); the occupation of the Bureau of Indian Affairs (BIA) building in Washington, D.C. (Nov. 2-Nov. 9, 1972; 7/20); the occupation and siege of the hamlet of Wounded Knee on the Pine Ridge Reservation, South Dakota (Feb. 27-May 8, 1973;

20/185), including the aftermath of this event, such as the trial of Dennis Banks and Russell Means (Jan. 1974; 2/2), the Senate subcommittee hearing concerning the Wounded Knee massacre of December 29, 1890, and the reactions of the United States Army to it (Dec. 1975-Spring 1976; 6/6), and the gun fight between FBI agents and members of the American Indian Movement (AIM) (Jun. 1975; 5/5), for example; the occupation of a monastery building near Gresham, Wisconsin, by Menominee activists (Jan. 1-Feb. 1975; 4/5); the "Longest Walk" demonstration (Feb. 11-Jul. 30, 1978; 15/21).

Legal events, like Native American land claims and their settlement in and out of court, or Indian-related civil rights issues, were reported as well, e.g., the promise and return of Blue Lake to the Tiwa Indians of Taos pueblo, New Mexico (Dec. 1970; 2/4); the land claims and their settlement of the Passamaquoddy and Penobscot of Maine in the years 1974 till 1977 and 1978 (19/19); film actor Marlon Brando's land donation effected in Agura, California, in favor of the Survival of American Indians Association (Jan. 1975, May 1980; 6/6); the settlement of the Seminole claim regarding Florida (Jan. 1976; 3/3); the Wampanoag claim concerning the city of Mashpee on Cape Cod, Massachusetts (1977; 4/4); the Sioux claims concerning the Black Hills (from 1977 until 1981; 12/17). The civil rights case *Martinez v. Santa Clara Pueblo* was written up once only in May 1977. The exploitation of mineral resources on Indian reservations, including the attempt of Native Americans to organize themselves for protection of their rights as the Council of Energy Resources Tribes (CERT), and the conflicts with "traditionalist" Indians arising from this exploitation were increasingly given attention from 1971 onward (6/6). Outside the United Stated, the "World Assembly of First Nations" in Regina, Saskatchewan, Canada (Jul. 1981) was covered.

Of European Indian-related events, the "International Non-Governmental Organizations Conference on Discrimination against Indigenous Populations" in Geneva, Switzerland, sponsored by the United Nations, (Sept. 20-23, 1977; 16/23), the Fourth Russell Tribunal on "The Rights of the Indians of the Americas" in Rotterdam, The Netherlands (Nov. 24-30, 1980; 2/2), and the second NGO Geneva conference on "Indigenous Peoples and the Land" (Sept. 13-18, 1981; 3/3) had the journalists' special interest.

A large number of news articles written for West German newspapers was based on "copy" received from several news agencies. Whereas *United Press International* (UPI) and, less frequently, *UPI* and *Deutsche Presseagentur* (dpa) were given credit for the photographs published in most cases, most of the "news copy" was provided by *Associated Press* (AP). It is followed by *Deutscher Depeschendienst* (ddp), *Deutsche Presseagentur* (dpa), *Agence France Press* (AFP), and *Reuters*. Special news agencies owned by religious bodies, like *Evangelischer Pressedienst* (epd), or newspaper chains, like *Springer Auslandsdienst* (SAD), make up the remainder.

West German news editors, it seems, implemented a number of strategies

530

aimed at obtaining a high degree of objectivity in reporting the news. Editors, for example, frequently drew on several news agencies for the same news item. Thus, West German news agencies were not only named together with American ones, which could be expected, but also in combination with British and French ones, when it was probably felt that American sources had to be supplemented, or when they were not available. In addition, editors also recurred to "Eigenberichte," i.e. reports coming in from the individual newspapers' own journalists in the field. The strategies mentioned so far show most clearly in the news articles written about the events of Wounded Knee.[8]

The ways in which United States-based West German foreign correspondents were employed seem significant too. Perhaps for reasons of obtaining "copy" directly from "location" without any mediators, German foreign correspondents were called upon to report directly from Washington,DC, New York City, or San Francisco. They were even sent elsewhere in some instances, like the German correspondent who is known to have reported to his news agency from Wounded Knee,[9] which might account for the strong second position of *dpa* among the sources employed. In the instance of the United Nations-sponsored Geneva conference of 1981, it seems that a German Washington-based correspondent was invited to present the United States government's position on the issues raised there.[10] In addition to this, American journalists provided background articles too, like David Anderson for example, whose article on "the new Indians" and the occupation of Alcatraz Island was brought by two West German newspapers (MM Dec. 30, HeA Dec. 31, 1969).

Indicative of efforts made in the direction of balanced reporting, too, are a special writing technique employed by the journalists and policies concerning the practice of news editing. Quite a number of West German journalists, for example, in composing their news articles used personal quotes. This technique, which is common practice in American journalism, allows for presentation of views opposed to one another. Due to it, spokesmen for the Federal Government and various Native American groupings, but also individuals, like white farmers or businessmen, were given an opportunity to present their own side regarding a specific event.

At the same time, however, ideological propaganda coming from these sources found its way into West German newspapers. During the occupation of the hamlet of Wounded Knee, for example, Federal Government spokesmen promoted collocations like "rebel Indians" ('rebellische Indianer'), "insurgent Sioux" ('aufrührerische Sioux'), or "Indian War" ('Indianerkrieg'), for example, whereas AIM activists suggested analogies between their actual situation in the hamlet and the Vietnam War by mentioning the Demilitarized Zone (DMZ) and My Lai, or by styling themselves as "warriors" who were ready to die for their cause.[12] It must be doubted, however, that all of the German journalists analyzed here and even less many of their readers disposed of the background knowledge required for an understanding of the ideological implication of these terms.

German news editors themselves contributed to balanced reporting in that they "edited out" a number of passages, justly I think, which they considered interpretation rather than presentation of news items, or which in their eyes might have bent the scales in favor of one of the parties involved in the event. Thus, when a German foreign correspondent reported on claims pushed by Maine and Massachusetts Indians in the Courts several editors threw out a paragraph in which stereotyped allusion was made to the Indians' historic ways of fighting with tomahawks and Bowie knives(!). Another news editor eliminated a reference made regarding the effect of the claim on the real estate market.[13]

Only two news articles among the materials subjected to analysis in this paper may be characterized as having been "slanted" against Native Americans. One of these articles has this impact in an indirect way only because in it, somewhat uncritically, the results of archaeological findings near Port Clinton, Ohio, were used for an attack against the myth of Indians enjoying better health before the arrival of Whites (HeA Jul. 29, 1968). The other article was based on a UPI release concerning a protest by Indian activists that was directed against the exhibition of bones of their ancestors at a Los Angeles museum. In rewriting the release, the West German news editor employed sterotyped German terms and collocations against the activists in order to ridicule them. Thus mention was made of "Manitou's sons," a "palavering" "chief," who was a "squaw," and even the fictional Karl May figures "Winnetou" and "Old Shatterhand" were brought in. The editor concludes his article with the German version of an Indian "grunt": "Uff, uff, uff" (HeA Jan. 14, 1971).

A large number of feature articles was received from West German foreign correspondents working in the United States. Despite certain cognitive deficits regarding Native Americans, which German correspondents sometimes tried to reduce by drawing on American journalists as sources, they, by and large, demonstrated a high degree of independent thinking with regard to the "Indian problem," I believe.

The major Indian activist demonstrations were all commented upon, and analyzed, from a wide perspective. The takeover of Alcatraz Island, for example, was put in the context of an "Indian Renaissance" brought about by the "New Indian" (FNP Dec. 2; SchwZ Dec. 5, 1969), or a "Red Power" movement. In addition, comparison was made between the Red and Black Power movements (HAZ Dec. 31; W Mar. 23, 1970). Several contributors apparently based themselves on an article written by Vine Deloria, Jr.,[14] but so did David Anderson.[15]

The occupation of the BIA building in Washington, DC, was featured in an article, in which the "Trail of Broken Treaties" demonstration - which culminated in the takeover of the BIA - is contrasted with the "death march" of the Cherokees, the "Trail of Tears." The legal status of (recognized) tribes as "quasi-sovereign" nations and "urban Indians" are briefly mentioned, but the problems relating to them not explained to the readers (HAZ Dec. 19, 1972).

Another correspondent establishes a link between the "Trail of Broken Treaties" demonstration and the cancellation of Indian treaty-making power in 1871 on one hand, and various Federal reservation policies on the other, giving special emphasis to the "termination policy" of the Eisenhower administration, and the reversal of this policy during the Nixon administration (SchwZ Dec. 8, 1972).

Wounded Knee background articles mirror a variety of views which are not necessarily pro-Government or pro-activist in tenor. Perhaps stimulated by American newspaper articles written in a similar vein, one correspondent voices his criticism of AIM, for example, by pointing out that disagreement existed among the Indian activists themselves, as well as with other Native Americans, regarding the usefulness of the contemporary tribal administrative structure, as it has developed on the basis of the Indian Reorganization Act (IRA) of 1934. But he also criticizes the White-controlled public media for their role in the events at Wounded Knee (FAZ Apr. 16, 1973). Taking the songs of Cree popular folksinger Buffy Sainte-Marie for a starting point, a New York-based German foreign correspondent draws his background tableau of Wounded Knee by distinguishing between well-to-do and poor reservation Indians, and by applying this distinction to urban Indians too. He also discusses various stages of assimilation of Native Americans before he arrives at the conclusion that the Indians' "cry for selfdetermination" and "social equality" should not be overheard (HAB Mar. 17, 1973). Another German correspondent, however, writing from Washington, develops analogies between the events at Wounded Knee and the Vietnam War, as far as official Federal Government Indian policies are concerned, as if he had been cued by AIM spokesmen (HAZ Mar. 13, 1973). Several writers of background articles include historical materials, on the Wounded Knee massacre of 1890, for example, in order to provide a wider perspective (e.g., HeA Mar. 24, 1973). One German Washington foreign correspondent digs deep indeed when, in the first part of his feature, he relates the story of Ishi, the last Yahi, and his contacts with anthropologists T.T. Waterman and A.L. Kroeber, focusing on the Yahi's views of Whites at the same time. He then discusses the assimilationist approach taken by BIA officials toward this Indian and analyzes White "misunderstandings" of Indians. Emphasis is laid at this point on the "metaphysical non-comprehension" of the Indians' animistic world view. Clichés about Indians are also briefly mentioned. Moving on to Pan-Indianism and Wounded Knee, the correspondent then argues that the Indian activists' actions should be understood mainly as a reaction to Federal Government Indian policies. In his eyes, despite many changes in these policies, the "egalitarian ideology of the American social experiment" has always been at their bottom. The Indians, therefore, have been subject to continued attempts of depriving them what makes them different in a "religious," "mystical," or "metaphysical" sense (SZ Aug. 11/12, 1973).

In feature articles, attempts of correcting German stereotyped views of Indians were made so frequently that this approach, in a way, may be said to have become a cliché in its own right in West German "Indian copy." That many German-held stereotypes about Indians are due to the fiction produced by Karl May and James Fenimore Cooper, is pointed out to the readers with nearly unfailing regularity. At the same time, however, quite a few of these feature writers demonstrate by their preference for certain words, e.g., their frequent use of the term "redskins," that perhaps they ought to have studied this issue more deeply.

A variety of other features informed West German newspaper readers about Native Americans. Travel reports, for example, rank very high in number and quality. Most of them are concerned with the Southwest of the United States and include expert information borrowed from history, archaeology, and ethnology. The number of impressionistic articles among them is rather small. Several feature articles exclusively deal with research in progress in archaeology and ethnology. Features were also written about Native American art and artifacts, and Indian-related works by American and West German artists.[16] Expositions on Native Americans organized in West Germany and auctions of Indian medals and artifacts were given attention too.[17]

The errors discovered in the "Indian copy" analyzed here, it seems to me, sufficiently prove that a certain degree of ignorance about Native American history existed among American and German journalists. Legal aspects concerning Indian-White relations before and after 1871, for example, were often disregarded. So one can hardly be surprised to note that Indian treaties were frequently called "Acts"[18] and a variety of dates given to them.[19] Not always was a distinction made between "recognized" and "non-recognized" Indian tribes. Little known were contemporary (self-)administrative structures, as the indiscriminate use of "chief" ('Häuptling') in American and German "Indian copy" demonstrates. Unacknowledged, i.e. "traditional," Native American leaders as well as acknowledged leaders, whose authority derives from the Indian Reorganization Act (IRA) of 1934, were often labeled "Häuptling," which does not carry the negative and derogatory connotations of American English "chief" however. Due to this, distinction was not made in many West German news and feature articles between these two types of leaders. The chairman of the tribal council of the Pine Ridge Reservation, Richard Wilson, for example, was commonly called a "chief." But so was the traditionalist Oglala Sioux Frank Fools Crow who had the support of AIM. Only in a few instances was translational equivalence attempted by means of "Oberhäuptling" ('First Chief') or "Stammeshäuptling" ('Tribal Chief'), and even less common was the correct translation of "chairman of the tribal council" ('Vorsitzender des Stammesrates').[20] When an agreement between U.S. Government representatives on one hand and Sioux AIM members and traditional chiefs on the other was signed at Wounded Knee early in May 1973, an *AP* release referred to the latter as "members of a council of elders of the Ogallala Sioux tribe" (MP May 8, 1973).

The following errors may be due to superficial research on the part of American and German journalists, to casual transmission of copy via news agencies, or to faulty translations. As some reporters failed to see a connection between Sitting Bull's violent death at Standing Rock in 1890 and the Wounded Knee Massacre of the same year, they transferred the scene of the assassination to Pine Ridge (e.g., B Mar. 29; FAZ Mar. 3, 1973). The Indian profile on the first United Stated 5-cent coin is not attributed to Iron Tail, but to John Big Bear, supposedly a descendant of Sitting Bull's.[21] Walking Buffalo was introduced as a "Sioux" and "First Chief" (AZ Oct. 10, 1968). Paul Jones was still named as chairman of the Navajo tribal council when this position had already been filled by Peter MacDonald (NN Nov. 6/7, 1971).[22] The Oglala Sioux medicine man Leonard Crow Dog, a traditionalist and AIM activist, became "Crow Doc" in one newspaper and "War Dog," which was also translated into German, in another one (NN Mar. 6; BrZ Mar. 10, 1973). AIM was rendered as "AJM" once (BrZ Mar. 16, 1973). Oscar Bear Runner's name almost invariably appeared as "Oscar Running Bear" ('Laufender Bär').[23] Dates, names, and details concerning the various Indian activist demonstrations, like the three attempts to take over Alcatraz Island, for example, were frequently mixed up (e.g., FA Nov. 12, SchwZ Dec. 5, 1969).

German translators had problems of their own with American proper names and classificatory terms. The metaphor "Rolling Hills," for example, was taken for a place name but fortunately left untranslated (BrZ Mar. 14, 1973). "Wounded Knee" is rendered as "Flußkrümmung" in one instance and as "Gewundene Flußbiegung" ('Winding River Bend') in another one (RN Mar. 2; HAZ Mar. 13, 1973). These errors may be due to the German title of Dee Brown's *Bury My Heart at Wounded Knee*.[24] A particular problem for translators were apparently terms like "Native Americans," "American Indians," "Indian Americans," "Red Indians," etc. whose ideological implications were altogether lost in translation. "Geborene Amerikaner," it seems to me, is a German version of 'Native Americans.' The same may be true for "eingeborene Amerikaner," which however could also be the equivalent collocation of 'Indigenous Americans.'[25] "Indo-Amerikaner" seems to be a clear case of 'Indian Americans' (StN Nov. 8, 1972). Even those writers who may be assumed to have known about these implications either employed "Ureinwohner," i.e. 'aborigines,' 'natives,' or "Eingeborene," i.e. 'natives.'[26]

Indian "photo copy" was not frequently used in the West German newspapers articles analyzed here, and one can hardly be surprised that, in accordance with common editorial practice, more pictures were inserted in feature than in news articles. In addition to photographs, this "copy" includes film frames and reproductions of paintings, aquatints, drawings, etc. Pictures were printed mostly to attract the readers' attention to Indian-related articles and, less frequently, to provide additional information. Editors therfore often selected from the picture materials available to them details, e.g., Native Americans in costumes or scenes depicting "Indian life," which in their eyes were "typical" of Indians. They also brought historical and contemporary materials which visualize White-held stereotypes about Indians, and had recourse to certain types of pictures regularly because they had taken on a symbolic value of their own.

Judging by the number of close-up or full-size photographs found among the Indian "photo copy," Native Americans in traditional costumes, wearing eagle feather bonnets or other Indian headgear, and having their hair braided, presenting themselves in non-Indian or Indian settings like pueblos or in front of hogans, tipis, or totem poles, must have been considered very typical. The two aspects to be considered here are, it seems, that Native American representatives of all kinds of groupings, as well as individuals put on traditional costumes, sometimes surrounding themselves with Indian paraphernalia like peace pipes, drums, and even tipis, in order to have themselves identified as Indians, or to give emphasis to the "Indianness" of certain events. Picture editors, on the other hand, would look for such "copy" to supplement news or feature articles. When no current materials of this kind were available, they would draw on their archive materials, and not hesitate to use historical photographs or reproductions of paintings etc., and avail themselves even of film frames, i.e. materials documenting the film makers' fantasies about Native Americans. One can hardly be surprised therefore that quite a few of the picture materials employed by West German editors, apart from showing Indian motifs, have no thematic links with the articles to which they were attached.

One set of photographs taken of Native Americans in full costume that was printed in West German newspapers concerns individuals or groups who came to West Germany or other European countries as visitors, promotors, or demonstrators. The picture of Walking Buffalo, taken during his visit to Bonn in December 1959, for example, shows him in complete costume wearing an eagle feather bonnet. Together with the photograph of a Blackfoot chief, who is depicted in traditional dress teaching a white child how to shoot an arrow, it appears in a background article on the Navajo(!) (AZ Oct. 10, 1968). A photograph showing two Indian chiefs accompanied by a group of dancers, all of them in full costumes, was included in a background article on the first United Nations-sponsored NGO International Conference in Geneva (KStA Oct. 13, 1977). A detail taken from this picture, i.e. a close-up of the two Indian chiefs, was used again by the editor of another newspaper for an article on the "First World Conference" at Regina, Saskatchewan, Canada (!) (BZ Jul. 31/Aug.1, 1982). Other photographs published in connection with articles dedicated to the above conference are focused on braided Indian activists in traditional costumes, some of them wearing feathers in their hair and carrying drums and other paraphernalia. The caption to one of the photographs, which was brought in two regional newspapers, reads:

(1) "North American redskins adorned with feathers move into the Geneva United Nations palace to the beat of drums."
(HAB Sept. 21, 1977)

The snapshot published in a third regional newspaper also bears a caption drawing attention to the Indians' colorful costumes, their chants of mourning, and their beating of drums (HeA Sept. 21, 1977). Poet Joseph Brant Maracle, representing the "Iroquois Federation" during his visit to West Germany, is depicted in a regional paper in 1978 (BZ Mar. 17). For promotional purposes, groups of Canadian Indians including their chiefs had donned their costumes for photographers in 1979 (HeA Mar. 15; May 7, 1979), showing them in Geneva and Bonn.

Photographs printed in connection with "Indian copy" concerning the United States display traditionalists, i.e. chiefs and others, and, increasingly in the late sixties and in the seventies, Indian activists who were dressed in traditional costumes, wore their hair in braids, or at least sported items of garment or ornaments considered "Indian." Thus, in a photograph of 1968, feather-capped chief Burning Forest is seen offering his button, "Chief Burning Forest for President," for sale (HeA, Jan. 12). In another one Cherokee Chief Red Bird is shown in his eagle feather bonnet holding a second one in his hands (HeA Mar. 6, 1969). As the caption reveals, he had already made feather bonnets for several United States Presidents and prepared the bonnet then finished as a gift for President Nixon. In a ceremony conducted during the occupation of Alcatraz Island, a Sioux chief by name of "Vergeßlicher Bär" ('Forgetful Bear') was photographed wearing an eagle-feather bonnet and an otherwise nearly full array. In the respective caption, attention is drawn to his sun glasses standing in contrast to the costume, but not to his "conservative"-style trousers (W Jun. 6, 1970). In a snapshot taken of actress Jane Fonda and a group of Indian activists at a demonstration in Seattle, Washington, in 1970, a few Indians among the activists are seen wearing blankets over their otherwise "civilian" clothes (FAZ Mar. 18, 1970).

During the occupation of the hamlet of Wounded Knee in 1973, traditionalist Indians were fronted together with the activists' leaders. Due to the semantic problem already explained above,[27] and the photographs published about these Indians, this strategy could hardly be recognized by German readers. Traditionalist Frank Fools Crow's picture, for example, was brought twice only in close-ups showing him in his braids, but without his impressive eagle-feather bonnet (MP May 8, AA May 10, 1973). Medicine man Leonard Crow Dog appears just twice in photographs. In a close-up of his, Crow Dog's long braids vividly contrast with his sports shirt, and in the other picture he is seen standing near peace pipes ceremoniously arranged by himself on a buffalo skull, being dressed in fashionable "White man's" clothes (NN Mar. 3; BrZ Mar. 12, 1973). The detail of the skull was displayed alone and printed in another regional newspaper (HeA Mar. 3, 1973). Russell Means, whose picture was frequently brought in West German newspapers, appears in one photograph together with Dennis Banks, both of them smoking a peace pipe. Their braids, and a black beret (!) covering the head of Banks, are well visible (SchwZ Mar. 12, 1973). Neither Banks's nor Means's name, however, is given in the respective caption. Banks apparently exchanged his beret for a silver-studded headband soon afterwards (cf. MP Mar. 27, 1973). During their trial in St. Paul, Minnesota, both AIM leaders appeared as "braided long hairs" (HAZ Jan. 10, 1974). In a photograph printed in 1977, finally, both of them can be admired as fashionably dressed men, who discreetly sport their braids, AIM symbols, single plumes, and other "Indian" ornaments (HeA May 17, 1980).

A photograph of Walking Buffalo - this time he appears in full array in an "Indian" setting among tipis - is part of a background article on Indian-White relations, including the changes resulting from the events of Wounded Knee (SZ Aug. 11/12, 1973). In the caption, Walking Buffalo is simply called "an American medicine man." Two close-up photographs featuring Indian chiefs wearing eagle-feather bonnets and a frame showing film actor Pierre Brice as the fictional Apache chief Winnetou (!) in full size, were printed in a background article on Prairie Indians (NOZ Aug. 14, 1976). In the caption, one of the chiefs is identified as "Walking Buffalo, chief of the Stony-Indians [sic!]," and the other one as "John Big Bear" whose profile is said to have adorned the first American five-cent coin(!).[28]

In 1977, a photograph was inserted in an article concerning legal steps taken by the Sioux about land lost to White settlers (HAB Sept. 10). A group of costumed Indians can be seen in it, their faces turned in the direction of a single Indian, probably Archie Fire Lame Deer, who to his business suit, the coat having been taken off, is just wearing an eagle-feather bonnet. The group was posing in imitation of the flag-raising ceremony conducted on Iwo Jima in World War II (!), with one Indian holding up the United States flag above them in the appropriate way. The reader is told in the caption that by driving a U.S. flag into the ground, these Indian activists were giving emphasis to Native American demands for a return of land illegally taken from them. He is not informed, however, that the setting of the picture was Alcatraz Island. As several details given in it are out of tune with the seventies, it seems probable that this photograph was taken during the first attempt made by Indian activists to take over the island in 1964. Indian costumes and an eagle-feather bonnet as conspicuous details were apparently reason enough for the West German editor in charge to employ this kind of archive material. Among the pictures published about the "Longest Walk" demonstration only one close-up photograph features two traditionalist Indian chiefs with Iroquois head-dresses (RP Jul. 21, 1978).

West German picture editors also drew on historical photographs and portraits created by artists for their "typical" materials. Thus the enlarged portrait photograph of Kiowa Chief Two Hatchet, taken by Edward S. Curtis, I believe, was added to a small article on "The Longest Walk" demonstration together with a group photograph featuring Marlon Brando and a number of Indian activists (HeA Jul. 18, 1978). Two months later the same regional newspaper printed a picture showing an Indian family in their travel gear ready for departure from Fort Keogh, Montana (HeA Sept. 7, 1978). Geronimo, the Chiricahua Apache, is depicted in two photographs. Once he is seen posing martially in his traditional Apache dress. When this picture appears as a detail, a poster, in the photograph taken of an "Indian classroom," attention is specially drawn to him in the caption (HeA Oct. 16, 1971). For a feature article on Indian reservations, Geronimo serves as a contrast figure because his picture showing him dressed in the "White man's" clothes (!) was placed above that of a former Navajo tribal chairman. This is confirmed by the caption which reads:

(2) "*Geronimo*, a chief of the Mimbreno Apaches (above), was the unreconciled enemy of Whites. *Paul Jones* (below) has a civil name and a civilian profession: he is chairman of the Navajo tribal council: a chief [dressed] in a suit made to measure."[29]
(NN Nov. 6/7, 1971)

Indians in full costume riding mustangs are not often shown in the West German newspapers analyzed. However, a picture of this kind can be studied in an article on the "Red Power" movement and the Council of Energy Resource Tribes (CERT). It bears the following caption:

(3) "Like the Indians of the cinema and the picture book: proud, in war ornaments, and on the back of a mustang."
(NOZ Oct. 20, 1979)

The same photograph was brought again, together with three other ones, in a feature article on the "Red Power" movement, CERT, and AIM (HAZ Jan. 12/13, 1980). In the caption for it and for two portraits of Indian chiefs, the rider is identified as "chief Tota of the Crow." The names of the other Indians are given as "chief Janus Ryder of the Stones [sic!]"[30] and "chief Barker of the Cheyenne." The fourth photograph shows members of a traditionalist Indian delegation during their visit in West Germany in 1978. A frame taken from an Indian movie made by Native Americans displays an adolescent on the back of his mustang. This print belongs to an article on the "Third Festival of North American Indians" (BZ Jul. 1, 1978).

More clearly than in the case of the portraits of Geronimo, Sitting Bull's photographs, apart from showing a traditional Indian "chief," were given special functions by West German picture and news editors. The portrait of this famous Hunkpapa Sioux medicine man was printed seven times in the period analyzed. With a few exceptions, he was spoken of as the victor of the Battle on the Little Big Horn of 1876. War Chief Crazy Horse was seldom mentioned in connection with the battle. Sitting Bull's and General Custer's close-ups were published together in a background article of 1973 on historic Wounded Knee, 1890 (HeA Mar. 24). They were supplemented by an Indian drawing of the battle between the Indians and General Crook, and the photographs taken of the frozen body of Sioux chief Big Foot and of a ghost dancer. Sitting Bull's enlarged close-up is part of an article on Indian activism and the possibility of a "White backlash." It bears the following caption:

(4) "The descendants of Chief Sitting Bull fear the political backlash as a possible answer of White U.S. citizens to the emancipation efforts of Native Americans."
(RP Mar. 25, 1978)

His photograph also appears in an article on a U.S. Appeals Court decision regarding the Black Hills (BrZ Jun. 15, 1979). Another regional newspaper, reporting on the same event, used the photographs of President Grant and General Custer, but no materials on the Sioux (HAZ Jun. 15). Sitting Bull's portrait, however, together with that of General Custer and an etching of the Battle of the Little Big Horn, was featured again in a background article on an U.S. Supreme Court decision concerning the Black Hills (HAB Jul. 2, 1980). Two other regional newspapers covering the same news event employed Sitting Bull's portrait to remind of the "victor" of the battle against General Custer (RN Jul. 2, HAZ Jul. 3, 1980). In a long feature article, including speeches made by Chief Seattle in 1855, and attorneys Russel Barsh and Mario Gonzales in West Germany in 1981, the photographs of Sitting Bull and Standing Elk were contrasted with a third one showing Oglala Sioux Larry Red Shirt and Mario Gonzales during their visit in Freiburg. The respective caption includes a remark in which a link is established between those fighting for the rights of Native Americans then and now (BZ Jul. 31/Aug. 1, 1982). It hardly seems difficult to understand that in the eyes of West German editors Sitting Bull's portrait symbolizes Native Americans generally and the Sioux tribes more specifically. But he also represents a determined fighter for Indians rights.

Costumed Indian chiefs in "Indian setting," I think, must have appealed to picture editors too. A background article on the "Red Power" movement, for example, carries two photographs. One shows "Shoshone Chief" Frank Randall together with his grandchild in front of a shack, and the other one a "Navajo grandmother spinning her thread" (HAZ Dec. 31, 1970). Another regional newspaper editor was hardly more consistent when he selected the following three photographs for the same article, a Navajo family posing in front of their hogan, Navajos working in a factory on the Navajo Reservation, and Lower Brule Sioux representing their tribe at an industrial fair in Chicago (MM Oct. 6, 1970).

In addition to providing Indians in full array, sometimes even in "Indian" settings, prints of aquatints, etchings, and paintings, etc. were also used by West German editors for stereotyping of Native Americans, and some of them even gave warning against clichés in the captions formulated for them. Several of these works of art are by Swiss painter Carl Bodmer who accompanied Maximilian Prince of Wied on his journey to the Indians of the Upper Missouri in the years 1832 - 1834. In a caption to the picture showing the interior of a Mandan lodge - together with a photograph of Oscar Bear Runner (see below) it was featured in a travel report in 1975 - allusion was made, for example to the "primitive Indian" stereotype despite the concomitant attempt to relate Indian life of the past to present-day Indian nationalism in a more positive way:

(5) *"They Lived Together with their Dogs and Horses.* Increasingly, the Indians have taken up early customs and rites again. In their growing nationalism of today, they recognize their ancestors' way of life with pride, which they had been ashamed of for several decades. Until the settlement of America by Whites, the Indians lived in wigwams and roughly hewn huts together with their dogs and horses."
(StN Aug. 7, 1975)

Two other Bodmer reproductions were added to an article about a press conference given by a pan-Indian delegation in Bonn, West Germany, in 1977 (AZ Oct. 8). In the caption attention is drawn to the clichés of the "romantic Indian" and the "Indian doing the war dance." A weekly paper published two full-size Bodmer portraits as parts of a feature article concerning the legal position of Native Americans in the United States (Z Nov. 11, 1977). The picture of a Mandan hero, who is seen in a belligerent pose recalling the "warrior" stereotype, adorns an article on the problem of dating human remains discovered at La Jolla near San Diego, California. This view is already confirmed in the first part of the caption which reads:

(6) "The Indians, first friends [and] then determined enemies of the settlers from overseas, have been regarded so far as people without prehistory...."
(NW Jul. 18, 1979)

The stereotype of the "savage Indian fighter"[31] was brought up in a feature article on the "Red Power" movement at the time of the occupation of the BIA building in Washington, DC, by means of the reproduction of a painting showing the surprise attack of French units from Fort Duquesne and Indians on General Braddock's British troops in 1755. The print was brought side by

541

side with a photograph taken of Indian activists being orderly seated in a room of the BIA building. A large-sized boxed insert, "Zum Thema" ('Concerning the theme'), includes an engraving displaying Kiowa Chief White Bear and his warriors in negotiation with General Custer and his soldiers. The caption to the first two pictures runs:

(7) "[An] uprising at the Bureau of Indian Affairs, [a] surprise attack on General Braddock's troops in the forest near Fort Duquesne - the pictures of 1972 (above left) and 1755 (above) are equally characteristic of the history of a continent that was conquered from the outside. ..."
(StN Dec. 8, 1972)

Among the photographs taken of Indian activist-created news events that found their way into West German newspapers, examples can be discovered in which Indian activists posed for their photographers in stereotyped ways. But there also exist pictures that were exploited for negative stereotyping of activists. In order to be seen as "warriors," for example, the Indian demonstrators borrowed "White American" as well as "Indian" models. A person posing with a gun held crosswise before the chest and one finger being put to its trigger, has been an American militant protest gesture of long standing, I believe. The best Indian activist specimen of this kind is Oscar Bear Runner's half-close photograph taken of him at Wounded Knee. It was printed five times in West German newspapers in 1973, and used again for a travel report in 1975 and a background article on Sioux land claims in 1977.[32] Activists on guard duty posing for journalists in trenches (!) or other defense positions, on roofs of buildings, or in front of entrances, and even on horseback, were popular "photo copy" for West German editors too. The picture showing an Indian guard and his "squaw," both riding horses, was carried by four newspapers. One of its captions reads:

(8) "Sioux warriors [!]: determined to go to extremes."
(HeA Mar. 14, 1973)

Several of the photographs mentioned were used again in later years.[33]
Though photographs that had served the purpose of negatively stereotyping Indian activists in American newspapers were published in West German papers too, only one example among the three discovered was exploited in this way. It deals with the occupation of the BIA building in 1972. A picture showing disorder and destruction caused by activists in a room, is captioned:

(9) "*Like Vandals* the Indians ravaged the Washington offices which they had occupied a week ago and evacuated only after they had been given the promise that a special commission would look into their complaints against

542

[federal] government policies."
(StN Nov. 11, 1972)

A photograph employed by American journalists to recall the "Indian clown" stereotype,[34] which displays two Indian activists riding on a small tractor, one of them holding a gun over his head, was printed twice. In one instance, the caption reads: "On a tractor with gun and tomahawk" (SAZ Apr. 21, 1973), and in the second one: "Despite the blockade, the situation is not deadly serious" (StN Apr. 20). Another picture focusing on a white man who slew a bull calf for the Indian activists - it had been used to demonstrate a better-than-thou attitude[35] - was printed in two regional newspapers with captions reporting on the general food situation only (HAB Mar. 17, SchwZ Mar. 20, 1973).

Symbols which Indian activists employed for reasons of self-expression and/or provocation can be identified in West German Indian "photo copy," but were hardly ever pointed out to the readers. A tipi, for example, was put up during most of the protest demonstrations, probably to mark news events as "Indian." Pictures showing one were printed in articles about the Forts Lewis and Lawton demonstrations, in this instance, the same photograph was published in three different newspapers;[36] the protest activities at a former missile firing position near Richmond - the tipi bears the inscription "[Indians of] All Tribes" - (MP Jan. 16, 1971); and the occupation of Wounded Knee - a tipi is shown here in the state of being dismantled in order to be put up again in a "Demilitarized Zone" (DMZ), as the caption explains (NN Mar. 6, 1973). Together with an article on the "Longest Walk" demonstration, a picture was published in a regional paper displaying a tipi with a tourist tent and a military tent on either side (!), all of them pitched in a park near the Capitol which can be recognized in the background (AA Mar. 1, 1978). Its caption gives 1971 as the year in which it was taken. In that year, another German newspaper had already featured this picture in an article on the "Red Power" movement (HeA May 8, 1971). It seems probable though that this snapshot was taken at an earlier date, perhaps the "Poor People's March" in 1968. Other symbols, like the sign designed for the "Longest Walk," for example (MP Jul. 21, 1978, cf. also FAZ Jun. 20), can be interpreted in the light of models offered by "maintream" society for similar events.

Details in the photographs printed, which Indian activists had intended as provocations, or which American journalists wanted to be seen in this way, were not given attention in the captions or articles in West German newspapers. The photograph of the jubilant Indian activist waving his Kalashnikov rifle above his head, for example, was printed once only, and its Russian (i.e. "Communist"!) origin[37] not pointed out (MP Mar. 10, cf. also MP Mar. 9, 1973). A U.S. flag is worn as a gown by a "BIA" Indian activist (HeA Nov. 4, StN Dec. 9, HAZ Dec. 19, 1972) and by a "Wounded Knee" militant (SaZ Apr. 21, 1973). A U.S. flag being raised upside down and even torn appears in several photographs taken of the hamlet (e.g., NN Mar. 6, 1973). But no attention was drawn to these details.

In combination with photographs, but more often individually, headlines served the function of making "Indian copy" attractive to West German newspaper readers. Editors therefore employed a number of classificatory terms, proper names, composite terms, and designations of Indian paraphernalia repeatedly because they may have thought them appealing. The term "Red Man" has had a long tradition of denoting Native Americans in American English, British English, and German. In the newspaper articles discussed here, however, the singular and plural forms of "Red Man" were used sparingly only. The editors' intention seems to have been a double one, to point out that a certain event was an "Indian" one, and that Native American *men* were responsible for it. Thus the two headlines discovered about the occupation of Alcatraz Island read:

(10) "Red Men on the war path"
(NW Dec. 12, 1969)
(11) "The Red Man lost a fortress [!]"
(StN Jun. 15, 1971)

A sympathetic attitude, it seems, is signaled in the following examples taken from a background article and a book review of 1980:

(12) "The Red Man plucks up courage again"
(HAZ Jan. 12, 1980)
(13) "The soul of the Red Man"
(HeA May 14, 1980)

The contrast conception of "Red Man," the "White Man," appears in a heading attached to the reprint of a speech made by Chief Seattle only (FAZ Dec. 20, 1980). The term "Redskins" being of English or French origin, is frequently used in American English "journalese" with a humourous intention. Among West German journalists, however, it seems to be popular as a synonym for "Indians." With a few exceptions, the term was not employed pejoratively, and sometimes even inverted commas were put in for reasons of having such an interpretation excluded. In a background article on the BIA raid, its synonymous use can hardly be overlooked:

(14) "The Redskins want to catch up with the Whites"
(HaZ Dec. 19, 1972)

In headlines on the occupation of Wounded Knee, "Redskins" appears twice and always as a synonym for "Indians."[38] The same is true for the four examples

544

found for 1977.[39] In one of them, however, a humourous note is struck:

(15) "The Redskins are out to get their White brothers' hide"
(AA Nov. 1, 1977)

Three additional specimens could be counted for 1978, and one for 1981.[40]

Several classificatory terms brought in West German newspaper headlines are translations of American journalistic slants, whose impact was perhaps lost on most German readers. "Rebel Indians," for example, in American English associates Indians with the "Confederate rebels" of the American Civil War - which the Cherokee fought on the side of the "Southern rebels." In German translation this term appears in a Wounded Knee headline as "rebellische Indianer" (MP Mar. 3, 1973). "Aufständische Indianer" ('insurgent Indians') links the Wounded Knee activists to international guerilla movements (SchwZ Mar. 3, 1973). The collocation "rote Rebellen" ('red rebels'), finally appears to be a double-edged slant because it is equally suggestive of communism and rebellion (MP Jun. 14, 1970).

Two proper names and their respective collocations are rather common as synonymous terms for Indians in West German newspaper headlines. Thus Sitting Bull's name was used for denoting the Sioux generally as well as the Native Americans:

(16) "Belated justice: 100 millions for Sitting Bull's red brother"
(BrZ Jun. 15, 1979)
(17) "Sitting Bull's heirs try to blow up the ghetto misery prescribed for them"
(SchwZ Mar. 17, 1973)

"Winnetou," the name of a fictional Apache chief created by German writer Karl May also served as a synonym for "Indians." Examples could be traced for 1970 (3), 1973 (1), 1977 (2), 1978 (1), and 1982 (1).[41]

Of the composite terms employed in headlines, "Indian war" and "war path" merit special attention. The former, it seems, was an imitation of American models (cf. FNP Nov. 4, 1972). Headline examples could be provided for the Wounded Knee event only, in which it occurred thirteen times, however.[42] The "war path" expression, often used in combination with the term "Redskins," enjoyed great popularity among West German headline writers. Three specimens of this kind refer to the Alcatraz event of 1969[43] (cf. no. 10). An example of 1972 concerns a land dispute between the Navajo and the Hopi:

(18) "Indians driven on the war path because of drought"
(PNP Apr. 29, 1972).

In Wounded Knee headlines, the composite term can be found five times.[44] It appears three times in 1977 and once in 1978 in headlines concerning native American land claims in different states.[45] Whereas the examples discussed so far fall into a pattern saying that Indians "go" on the "war path" or "are" on it, "still" or "again," a significantly modified pattern occurs in 1977, in which Indian activist strategies are contrasted with each other:

(19) "The Indians switch from the war path to the legal path" [i.e. take the course of law]
(KStA Oct. 13, 1977)

The same contrast is developed in headlines to a background article received from a German Washington correspondent (HAZ Jan. 21/22; StN Sept. 24, 1978).

Indian paraphernalia like drums, peace pipes, or tomahawks were employed in a literal as well as metaphorical sense in the headlines analyzed. The "Trail of Broken Treaties" drum, for example, which was beaten in the BIA building and at Wounded Knee, must be thought of in the following examples:

(20) "The sound of war drums comes from the BIA"
(AA Nov. 6, 1972)
(21) "The beat of the drums and the peace pipe: the Sioux are celebrating"
(HeA Mar. 12, 1973)

A personal experience lies at the bottom of a headline formulated for a travel report in 1980 (FAZ Jan. 10, 1980). A metaphorical use, however, seems probable in the headline:

(22) "War drums at the White House"
(HeA Nov. 6, 1972)

The "peace pipe" was used in both ways too. Thus five examples to be taken literally refer to the Wounded Knee events in which peace pipe ceremonies were conducted.[46] In another headline a high degree of Indian assimilation to Whites is suggested by means of the literal meaning:

(23) "The peace pipe is suspended peacefully above the dishwasher"
(RP Mar. 25, 1978)

A metaphorical, and slighty pejorative, example is given in:

(24) "The calumet was smoking on the Wounded Knee"
(W Apr. 7, 1973)

A metaphorical meaning, was also intended in a headline concerning the United Nations-sponsored NGO conference in Geneva (MM Sept. 26, 1977). "Tomahawk," in German, is used synonymously with "Kriegsbeil" (translated from "hatchet") which in reverse translation means "war hatchet." Due to this, West German editors used both forms in adaptations of the colonial Indian metaphor of "burying" or "raising the hatchet."[47] The pattern derived from the headlines discovered gives emphasis either to the beginning or the end of Indian news events. In headlines of 1969 the "war hatchet" was dug up twice,[48] only one of the cases directly concerning Alcatraz Island. In connection with the "BIA raid" one editor had the Indian activists bury the "war hatchet" (StN Nov. 9, 1972). The Wounded Knee events of 1973 gave rise to five headlines including the "war hatchet."[49] Further specimens could be provided for the years 1977 (2), 1978 (1), and 1980 (1).[50] Untranslated forms of "tomahawk" were equally used during the period analyzed. In the following version, the reader's attention was ironically drawn to actress Jane Fonda's involvement in the Forts Lewis and Lawton demonstrations:

(29) "'Barbarella' dug up [the] tomahawk"
(MP Mar. 11, 1970)

Further "tomahawk"-headlines were formulated in 1972 (StN Dec. 9) and 1975 (BZ Febr. 5). The "tomahawk" also served West German headline writers to contrast Indian activist militant with non-violent strategies (see above, ex. no. 19):

(29) "The law instead of the tomahawk"
(HaAb Sept. 10, 1977)
(27) "The tomahawks were left back home"
(NOZ Sept. 22, 1977)

Other Indian paraphernalia, like the wigwam (cf. MP Apr. 7, 1973), were used too infrequently to merit attention here.

Any evaluation made on the basis of the materials gathered for this analysis, I believe, ought to acknowledge the great variety of "Indian copy" found in West German newspapers as an asset. This variety may be seen as a response to the readers' wide interest in Indian themes. Positive cognizance should also be taken of the effort made by a great number of editors to present news events and features, on the basis of the "copy" available to them, as objectively as possible. Less satisfactory is, it seems to me, that in order to attract the readers' attention Indian "photy copy" and headlines were employed in ways that may be called stereotyped, and even worse, which include stereotypes of Indians. Also on the negative side, regrettably, a considerable cognitive deficit on the part of West German journalists, including United

States-based foreign correspondents, independent contributors, and editors, concerning (contemporary) Native American history, anthropology, and ethnology would have to be pointed out. Most of those concerned would perhaps agree that Native Americans deserve better.

ABBREVIATIONS

AA   Augsburger Allgemeine
AZ   Allgemeine Zeitung
B   Bild
BZ   Badische Zeitung
BrZ Braunschweiger Zeitung
DZ   Deutsche Zeitung/Christ und Welt
FA   Frankfurter Allgemeine
FNP Frankfurter Neue Presse
FR   Frankfurter Rundschau
HaAB Hamburger Abendblatt
HaMP Hamburger Morgenpost
HAZ Hannoversche Allgemeine Zeitung
HeA Hessische Allgemeine
KStA Kölner Stadtanzeiger
NOZ Neue Osnabrücker Zeitung
MM   Mannheimer Morgen
NN   Nürnberger Nachrichten
NW   Neue Westfälische
PNP Passauer Neue Presse
RN   Ruhr-Nachrichten
RP   Rheinische Post
RZ   Rhein-Zeitung
SaZ Saarbrücker Zeitung
SZ   Süddeutsche Zeitung
SchwZ Schwäbische Zeitung
StN Stuttgarter Nachrichten
W   Die Welt
WaS Welt am Sonntag
Z   Die Zeit

NOTES

1. *Presse- und Medienhandbuch - Stamm 1982 - Leitfaden durch Presse und Werbung.* 35th edition. Essen 1982.
2. Cf. HeA Mar. 22, 1973, DZ May 25, 1979, HeA Apr. 6. 1982.
3. E.g. Peter Baumann, author of *Reise zum Sonnentanz-Indianer zwischen gestern und morgen*, Berlin 1970: Safari-Verlag; Claus Biegert, journalist, member of Survival International and author of *Seit 200 Jahren ohne Verfassung*, Reinbek 1976: Rowohlt Taschenbuchverlag; Richard S. Kelly, editor of an Indian newsletter in West Germany; Jürgen Offenbach, journalist. Cf. HAZ Apr. 7/8, SchwZ Mar. 17, 1973; FR Jul. 1, 1976, SZ Nov. 22/23, Sept. 19, 1981; StN Oct. 3, 1970; StN Aug. 7, 1975.
4. This name is a pseudonym for H. J. Stammel. (Thanks to Christian Feest).
5. FA Nov. 1, 1969, Mar. 19. 1980.
6. HeA Mar. 21, 1973.
7. The first figure gives the number of newspapers, the second the number of articles published.
8. See the table below.
9. Harper's, June 1973, p. 53; *The New York Times*, Mar. 4, 1973.
10. Cf. BZ Oct. 8, NN Oct. 8, 1977.
11. Cf. NN Mar. 1, SchwZ Mar. 3, NOZ Mar. 2, 1973.
12. Cf. NN Mar. 1, HeA Mar. 14, MP Mar. 14, 1973.
13. BZ, SchwZ, StN Mar. 8, NN Mar. 9, 1977.
14. Vine Deloria, Jr., "The War Between The Redskins and the Feds," *The New York Times Magazine*, Dec. 7, 1969.
15. HeA Dec. 31, MM Dec. 30, 1969.
16. E.g., FA May 25, 1968, Aug. 21, 1969, Febr. 10, 1973, Apr. 5 1975; HeA Jun. 3, 1972, StN Aug. 17, 1976.
17. FA Jul. 29, Oct. 26, 1968, HeA Dec. 2, 1975, KStA May 6, 1976.
18. E.g., B Nov. 11, 1969, FA Nov. 9, 1970.
19. E.g., AA Jul. 2, AZ Jul. 12, 1980.
20. E.g., NN Mar. 5, 7; BZ,FA Mar. 12; MP Mar. 28; MM Apr. 3; HeA Apr. 12, 1973.
21. NOZ Aug. 14, 1976. (Thanks to Christian Feest).
22. Cf. Virgil J. Vogel, *This Country Was Ours*, New York (repr.) 1974: Harper & Row, p. 319.
23. E.g., BrZ Mar. 7, 1973, NN Oct. 8, 1977.
24. It is: *Begrabt mein Herz an der Biegung des Flusses.* (Thanks to Christian Feest).
25. Cf. Heinz Messinger and Werner Rüdenberg, *Langenscheidts Handwörterbuch*, ren. and enl. ed., Berlin etc. 1977: Langenscheidt, vol. I, p. 324.
26. E.g., Claus Biegert in SZ Nov. 22/23, 1980; Sept. 19, 1981.
27. See page 534

28. Cf. note 21.
29. Cf. note 22.
30. He is meant to be a Stoney Indian, rather than a Rolling Stone.
31. For this and other stereotypes cf. Robert F. Berkhofer, *The White Man's Indian*, New York 1979: Vintage Books; The Council on Interracial Books for Children (ed.), *Chronicles of American Indian Protest*, Greenwich 1971: Fawcett Publications; Stan Steiner, *The New Indians*, New York 1968: Dell Publishing Co.
32. RN, MP Mar. 6, BrZ, NN Mar. 7, HAZ Apr. 7/8, 1973; StN Aug. 7, 1975; NN Oct. 8, 1977.
33. 1976: HAZ Feb. 2, FR Jul. 1; 1977: HaAB Jan. 1, SZ May 4.
34. See above note 31.
35. Harper's June, 1973, pp. 46ff.
36. B, HeA Mar. 10, WaS Mar. 15, 1970.
37. Cf. *Washington Post*, Mar. 10, 1973.
38. AA, NOZ Mar. 2, 1973.
39. StN Mar. 8, Mar. 30, Sept. 3; AA Nov. 1, 1977.
40. AA Mar. 1, BZ Jul. 1, SZ Jul. 19, 1978; W Jun. 6, 1981.
41. HeA Sept. 11, MM Oct. 6, HAZ Dec. 31, 1970; SaZ Apr. 21, 1973; HaAB, SchwZ Sept. 21, 1977; DZ Jan. 27, 1978; HeA Apr. 6, 1982.
42. MP Mar. 5;FA Mar. 7;BZ Mar. 10;MM, SchwZ Mar. 12; HeA Mar. 19,28; BrZ Apr. 4; HaMP, StN Apr. 7; RZ Apr. 7/8, MP Apr. 27, 1973.
43. NW Dec. 12; HeA, MM Dec. 30, 1969.
44. MP, SchwZ Mar. 1; AA, RN Mar. 2; StN Mar. 5, 1973.
45. SchwZ, StN Mar. 8, KStA Oct. 13, 1977; HaAB Jul.17, 1978.
46. HAZ Mar. 12; BZ Apr. 4, MP Apr. 7, NN Apr. 7/8.
47. Cf. Christian F. Feest, "Tomahawk und Keule im östlichen Nordamerika," *Archiv für Völkerkunde* 19 (Wien 1964/65), pp. 39ff.
48. NN Aug. 28, SchwZ Dec. 5, 1969.
49. SchwZ, HeA Mar. 1, RN Mar. 2, FA Mar. 10, HeA Apr. 7, 1973.
50. NN, SchwZ Mar. 8, 1977; StN Jan. 9, 1978; NOZ Oct. 20, 1979; HeA May 17, 1980.

WHO IS AFRAID OF AIM?

Bernd C. Peyer

The American Indian Movement (AIM) has attracted more public attention than any other Indian political organization of the past and present. For many, the AIM "Warrior" personifies all living Indians and is thereby in danger of being transformed into yet another stereotype. While students in German schools and universities have shown a pronounced interest in and sympathy for AIM, the established academics teaching them have tended to ignore it. Presently, most of the sparse information on AIM available in the German language was recorded and disseminated by students and journalists. Academics, however, seldom make use of this type of information because of the presumed lack of professional qualifications and/or the political inclinations of the informants. By avoiding a scholarly confrontation with the subject, academics have inadvertently promoted the mystification of AIM in Germany. Considering that the activities of this Indian organization now span a period of sixteen years (July 1968 to July 1984), it seems to merit serious academic consideration. This article endeavors to present some suggestions to this effect.

The affinity between German students and AIM has its roots in the "Studentenbewegung" of the 60's und 70's, at a time in which similar social movements were occurring elsewhere in Europe and North America. One important characteristic of the "Studentenbewegung" was the manifestation of a feeling of solidarity with Third World liberation movements and the struggle of oppressed ethnic minorities, e.g., the Civil Rights Movement in the U.S. Subgroups specifically concerned with Indians already began to appear in the early 60's (Wagner 1971), but it was the surge of AIM with its spectacular activities like "The Trail of Broken Treaties" in 1972 and the occupation of Wounded Knee in 1973 that transformed the contemporary Indian into a primitivistic symbol of resistance against the system, in this case U.S. capitalism. Images of Geronimo and Sitting Bull were posted up alongside of Ché Guevara's, and the AIM "Warrior" became their immediate reincarnation.

Simultaneously, AIM leaders were also developing a policy of international diplomacy. Together with others, they organized a conference in 1974 on the Standing Rock Reservation in South Dakota and founded the International Indian Treaty Council (IITC). The main function of the IITC has been to focus international attention on Indian problems as a means to bring outside pressure to bear upon the U.S. government. Clyde Bellecourt, one of AIM's principal leaders, toured Europe that same year, following an invitation by the World Council of Churches. In 1975, AIM leaders Dennis Banks and Vernon Bellecourt authorized the first representative office in West Berlin and soon after AIM Support Groups began to crop up all over Germany. The IITC was given consultant status as a Non-Governmental Organization (NGO) in the United

551

Nations in 1977 and sent representatives to the "International NGO Conference on Discrimination Against Indigenous Populations in the Americas," conducted in Geneva that year, and the "International NGO Conference on Indigenous Peoples and the Land," also held in Geneva in 1981 (see IITC 1977 and 1981). The IITC was present at the 1980 "4th International Russell-Tribunal" in Rotterdam and numerous of its representatives, most of them AIM members, traveled all over Europe on various other occasions (Council on Interracial Books for Children 1980).

The two major organizations in German speaking areas that have been involved with AIM are the Gesellschaft für Bedrohte Völker, the German/Austrian equivalent of Survival International established in 1969, and the International Committe for the Indians of the Americas (Incomindios), founded 1974 in Switzerland. The former publishes a magazine with current international news on ethnic minorities and tribal peoples titled *Pogrom*, of which two issues (50/51, October 1977 and 89/90, June-July 1982) deal specifically with North and South American Indians and give a good deal of space to AIM representatives' opinions. The latter publishes *Incomindios*, a pamphlet containing similar information with abundant reference to AIM activities.

Another important German magazine is *Rundbrief. Indianer und Stammeskulturen Heute* (formerly *Rundbrief. Indianer Heute*), which was published under different editors from the early 70's until 1982. Many other smaller publications, which have appeared sporadically and are usually limited to certain university campuses, could be listed, such as the *Danai Notes* brought out by the Deutsche Arbeitsgruppe für Nordamerikanische Indianer. Sometimes organizations not directly concerned with Indians will also publish information on the subject, as in *Grüner Zweig* (18, 1973 and 22, 1974), an ecological magazine put out by the Grüne Kraft.

The only other magazine on contemporary Indian events of importance in Germany is *Amedian*, published by the German American Indian Group/ Deutsch-Indianischer Kreis since 1972. As this organization professes to maintain itself politically neutral, its coverage of AIM activity and more controversial issues (e.g., sterilization) has been too minimal to make it relevant in that particular context.

Besides the Gesellschaft für Bedrohte Völker and Incomindios, there are numerous other organizations that cooperate directly with AIM, usually referred to as AIM Support Groups. Because they vary in size and sometimes disappear as quickly as they are formed, it is difficult to keep track of them. Support Groups are generally founded by students, but they must first obtain official sanction from AIM leaders before they can begin operations. One of the most stable and effective of these is the AIM Support Group Hamburg, which edited a pamphlet titled *Indianer im Widerstand* in 1977. In answer to popular demand, a second updated edition under the same title was published in 1980 by the affiliated AIM *Unterstützungsgruppe* Neumünster. These publications, which are openly pro-AIM in orientation, contain brief sketches of historical Indian-White confrontations, interviews with AIM leaders on all sorts of Indian issues, and summaries of AIM activism. Much of the information is gleaned from *Akwesasne Notes*, undoubtedly the major source of news for all of the publications mentioned above.

The main function of AIM Support Groups and similar German organizations, aside from raising money, is to inform the general public on current Indian events. Several either directly or indirectly involved individuals have also published monographs on contemporary Indians that have reached a wide circulation. These include Carl-Ludwig Reichert's *Red Power* (1974), Claus Biegert's *Seit 200 Jahren ohne Verfassung* (1976) and *Indianerschulen* (1979), and Mathias R. Schmidt's *Wenn wir gehen - geht die Welt* (1980). Each author follows an established pattern of assembling various data on Indian problems supported by numerous interviews with key figures, not infrequently AIM leaders. Other curious publications include *Kapitalismus und Indianer in den USA* by Manfred Wibich and Urs Winter (1976), which limits the entire subject of Indian resistance to a doctrine of class struggle, and *Gegen Ende der Reise* (Brandes *et al.* 1983), containing several critical reflections on personal involvement in the German Indian scene. Further publications by these authors appear in the form of newspaper articles, translations, and educational materials. Claus Biegert, the most prolific and widely read, has also put together radio and television broadcasts. As a general rule, the publishers of the magazines and authors of the monographs mentioned above pretend neither to be politically neutral nor strictly objective in their work. Claus Biegert (1976) classifies his own writing as "engagierte Dokumentation" (committed documentation) and consciously rejects traditional ethnographic or sociological methods of approach. "Committed" in this case means that the author refuses to regard the Indian "Problem" apart from his own critical views on modern society and feels the responsibility to try and do something about it in deeds as well as words. While such a position inevitably forces the author to take definite sides, it does not necessarily mean the resulting work is mere propaganda, as is too often assumed with writings categorized simply as "leftist." Thus, despite the open sympathy for AIM, there is also evidence of disagreement with some of its actions. Recent confrontations between AIM and traditionalists over Yellow Thunder Camp, an AIM occupied section of land protesting the illegal seizure of the Black Hills, as well as the offensive comportment of a few IITC representatives during the Russell-Tribunal have produced negative reactions among some supporters (Domnick 1978). Evidently AIM has forfeited some of its initial popularity with German students, partially because of its own incongruities and because the "Studentenbewegung" has disbanded in political disillusionment. In the wake of a current fixation on religious experiences, Indian spirituality is being rediscovered. The AIM "Warrior" now competes with the "Medicine Man" as Germany's favorite Indian.

553

Although the "committed" publications often contain one-sided or oversimplified information, the reader at least knows the author's position and should be able to make use of it accordingly, especially if alternative reference works were also available. Unfortunately, however, this is not the case. Anthropologists restrict themselves to traditional ethnography and are only too willing to leave the study of contemporary Indians to other disciplines. As a result, scholarly well founded books on modern Indian affairs are scarce in Germany. Notable exceptions are René König's *Indianer - wohin?* (1973) and *Navajo Report* (1980), Christian Feest's *Das Rote Amerika* (1976), and Schulze-Thulin's *Weg ohne Mokassins* (1976). As these authors cover a wide range of subjects, it is understandable that they only deal with Indian political activism on the periphery, if at all. Feest (1976:332-378) and Schulze-Thulin (1976:252-276) at least devote their closing chapters to the upsurge of AIM with the occupation of the BIA Headquarters and the siege at Wounded Knee. The latter suggests that time is still needed in order to tell whether AIM will have a positive effect on Indian-White relations or not. But the long silence seems to imply some other reasons behind the academic reluctance to deal with AIM aside from the more obvious difficulties of establishing personal contacts or obtaining reliable uptodate information. If anthropologists have inclined to be sceptical of "committed" authors, the latter have been equally critical of the former's apparent conservativism and occasionally made derogatory statements to this effect. It could very well be that the relationship between AIM and politically involved students has led more conservative academics to judge the organization in response to their very own fear of "radicalism." In a symbolic way, AIM may just pose a threat to the proverbial ivory tower.

One way in which to approach AIM, is to clear up some of the obvious misconceptions surrounding it. When it comes to Indians, Germans have a persistent tradition of romantic naturalism which has always given precedence to the "Noble Savage" image over its bloodthirsty counterpart. In contrast to the U.S., where AIM has met with a lot of negative criticism and slander, the German reception of this organization has generally been unreflectedly positive.

To begin with, AIM is neither the first nor the "only Indian controlled organization since the days of Crazy Horse and Geronimo" as its leaders like to claim (AIM 1982). Writers on the subject of Indian political development usually pick the American Indian Conference held at Chicago in 1961 as a point of departure (Josephy 1972; Steiner 1968). Jack Forbes (1972) has pointed out, however, that there is little "new" in the history of Indian resistance since Opechancanough's rebellion in 1622. Pan-Indian strategies were formulated by leaders like King Philip, Pontiac, and Tecumseh. Modern tactics of political lobbying and mobilization of the press were practiced to perfection by representatives of the Five Civilized Tribes in the attempt to prevent removal during the Jackson administration. Only the focus on pan-Indian (national) policies has augmented steadily in relation to tribal (regional) concerns.

554

The first national Indian organization was the Society of American Indians (SAI), which promoted Indian civil rights from 1911 to 1920 (Hertzberg 1971). One of the most important organizations of the present, the National Congress of American Indians (NCAI), was founded in 1944 and the more militant National Indian Youth Council (NIYC), which gave rise to the notion of "Red Power," was established in 1961. Even the spectacular activism of AIM was foreshadowed by the occupation of Alcatraz Island in 1969, organized by the shortlived United Native Americans (UNA) centered in the Bay Area (Michels 1972). It should also be remembered that AIM was only one of several organizations involved in the "Trail of Broken Treaties" such as the National Indian Brotherhood, Native American Rights Fund, National Indian Youth Council, National Council on Indian Work, National Indian Leadership Training, and American Indian Commission on Alcohol and Drug Abuse. Since then, hundreds of organizations have appeared throughout the U.S. and Canada dealing with all kinds of national and regional Indian issues.

Although AIM is not unique, it continues to be one of the more permanent and effective Indian political organizations in North America. Its distinctive characteristic is the scope of its international relations. Indian delegations have been visiting Europe for centuries and Indian activists of the 60's, such as the legendary Clyde Warrior and Mad Bear Anderson, also went on diplomatic missions. But it was AIM with its IITC that really brought Indian politics into the realm of world affairs. AIM representatives have traveled extensively, in socialist countries as well, and established connections with various Third World organizations. Recently, the AIM National General Council has decided to inaugurate teaching Spanish as a second language in the AIM Survival Schools in order to facilitate communication with the Indian peoples of Central and South America. Thus, as far as calling international attention to the Indian situation and mobilizing support is concerned, AIM has been quite effective.

Secondly, AIM does not officially claim to represent all Indians, even though some of its actions and public statements seem to imply this. It is quite obvious, for example, that AIM does not even enjoy majority support in Sioux territory, which is considered to be one of its strongholds (Grobsmith 1981:107-108). In more conservative areas, such as Pueblo Indian territory, AIM has never been able to establish a base. The peak of its popularity among Indians probably occurred during the Wounded Knee drama in 1973 and then began to diminish in the violent years that followed (Burnette and Koster 1974:256; Mathiessen 1983:427). More recently, AIM has also lost much of its standing with formerly sympathetic traditionalists, a fact that bears heavily on its "grass roots" aspirations. The ambivalent feelings among these traditionalists are clearly expressed by Frank Fools Crow: "But we Indians are so poor, so frustrated, and we have been so bound up in our cicumstances that we feel we have little to lose. Even the questionable attention collected by AIM has given a much-needed boost to the Indian's dignity and self-esteem. The traditionalists do not like violent tactics, so we do not support AIM anymore. But they have accomplished things our passive methods did not accomplish" (Mails 1979:216; quoted in Mathiessen 1983:427).

The overevaluation of AIM's spectacular tactics, in either a positive or negative sense, is usually perpetrated by non-Indians. Directly after the occupation of the BIA headquarters in 1972, the FBI classified AIM as an extremist organization and the conservative press began a relentless campaign of slander labeling it as a communist funded guerrilla operation led by savage criminals. Although all of this defamation was never acknowledged by most Europeans, the abundant reports of the activities that sometimes involved violence inevitably furthered its reputation as a militant organization.

The official record of AIM's activities (AIM 1982) contains an impressive number of occupations, demonstrations, and confrontations up until 1978, but these nevertheless only constitute a part of the total picture. Many programs to prevent drug and alcohol abuse, provide free legal counsel, expose discrimination, and correct misconceptions were also initiated. AIM has been a source of regeneration for numerous young Indians whose only other alternative would have been addiction or crime. This type of constructive involvement is especially evident in the development of Survival Schools (sometimes referred to as Survival Groups), which are exemplary for Indian initiative in the sector of education (Biegert 1979; Schierle 1981). "Quiet" activity of this sort obviously will not attract the attention of mass media and unless AIM carries out more events like the Longest Walk in 1978, a cross-country protest march from Alcatraz Island to Washington, DC, many will come to the assumption that it has ceased to exist altogether.

A certain degree of militance is essential for the self-understanding of the AIM "Warrior." "A warrior should be the first one to go hungry or the last one to eat. He should be the first one to give away his mocassins and the last one to get new ones. That type of feeling among Indian people is what a warrior society is all about. He is ready to defend his family in time of war - to hold off any enemy - and is perfectly willing to sacrifice himself to the good of his people. That's what a warrior society is to Indian people, and that's what we envision ourselves as, what we idealistically try to be" (Akwesasne Notes 1974:61-62). A list of AIM casualties since 1973 (see AIM Support Group Hamburg 1977) is a tragic indication that there is in fact a "war" going on and AIM's "warrior society" is not just a nostalgic revitalization of a 19th century Plains Indian institution. Much more violence has been perpetrated on members of AIM than the other way around. The very fact that AIM militance has been an effective means of attracting public attention to Indian problems actually says more about the role of violence in our own society than it does about AIM.

The popular warning that militant activity will eventually result in backlash and strain the positive relationship between Indians and the federal government since the Johnson administration sounds hollow in view of the facts. Backlash can occur as long as Indians still own a scrap of land of any value. The history of federal Indian policy leaves little room for doubt in this, no matter how willing to assimilate peacefully an Indian tribe has been. The fate of the Five Civilized Tribes before and after removal to Indian Territory (present day Oklahoma) is one case in many. Backlash warnings sound paternalistic and reflect too much confidence in the good will of public administrators on the one hand, and underplay the results of Indian political activism in all of its ramifications on the other. Those tribes that offered the most militant resistance to Euro-Americans, such as the Sioux and the Apache, have also gained the most in terms of sympathy and respect all over the world.

Thirdly, AIM is often thought to be solely an urban organization. Probably following the example set by the Black Panthers, AIM did emerge in Minneapolis-St. Paul as an "Indian Patrol" to protect urban Indians from police brutality, but most of the initial founders had been brought up on one of the Ojibwa reservations in Minnesota and not in a city. The division of the Indian population according to residence in urban or reservation areas is highly misleading as there is a steady flux between both. In other words, urban and reservation experience is common for Indians who belong to tribes with a land base. While the special problems confronting Indians in the cities are an additional incentive to form pan-Indian organizations, this does not mean that an urban based operation will exclude reservation areas. Although AIM was founded in response to specific Indian needs in the city, it quickly incorporated the reservation into its political strategy. "At times, you will hear politicians or critics say that the American Indian Movement is an urban Indian group, which is totally false. At one time it was true, but it almost immediately changed. Because along with getting deeply involved in the spiritual direction of our people, they soon realized that the very people that are in the cities suffering were the same people that are on the reservation suffering" (Akwesasne Notes 1974:61).

Like the NCAI and the NIYC, AIM draws people from many different Indian communities with various degrees of "acculturation." Even if the organization's ideology emphasizes a sort of universal Indianness, the individual member continues to have tribal affiliations and kinship ties. Participation in one does not contradict the other.

The Plains tribes have played a central role in the development of Pan-Indianism and it is thus not surprising that AIM should turn to Sioux traditions, notably the Sun Dance, for spiritual orientation. AIM's option for the Sioux version of this increasingly popular ceremony is due not only to the relatively high quota of recruitment from this tribe, but also to the particular emphasis on physical suffering involved in the piercing sacrifice, which corresponds to its own "Warrior" ideals. Apparently introduced by Russell Means in 1972, it became common practice for AIM members, regardless of tribal affiliations, to

557

pledge themselves for four dances. In 1976, the AIM Sun Dance also spread to California, where it is conducted every year on the grounds at D-Q University.

Ironically, however, AIM's involvement with the Sioux Sun Dance has recently become a source of factionalism within that tribe. A number of Sioux people feel that AIM may have misused this highly sacred ceremony as an initiation rite and consequently stay away from the annual event in South Dakota altogether or start up alternative dances (Bolz 1983). The rift between AIM and non-AIM Sun Dancers is also evident at D-Q University, but the very precarious situation of this educational institution, which is currently in danger of being shut down by the federal government, has prevented serious conflicts so far.

In all, AIM's self-understanding is made up of a mixture of tribal and pan-Indian elements and its field of action includes both urban and reservation areas. The Dakota AIM, for instance, operates primarily in and around the Sioux reservations while the West Coast Group is located in the Bay Area. There are well over 70 AIM Chapters in major cities and a number of reservations all over the U.S. Some of the more important recent AIM activities have revolved around reservation issues, such as the establishment of Big Mountain Camp to protest the forced relocation of Indians resulting from the so called Navajo-Hopi Land Conflict, and the previously mentioned Yellow Thunder Camp in South Dakota.

Lastly, AIM has been identified much too closely with a few key individuals. Contrary to popular notion, AIM is not the creation of a couple of "founding fathers," who have come to personify Indian resistance altogether. The initial conference in 1968 was attended by some 200 previously active Indians and collectively they decided to form a new organization called Concerned Indians of America. Realizing that an abbreviation of this name (CIA) would produce an involuntary association with a certain governmental agency, they quickly changed it to American Indian Movement. "AIM was a spontaneous event evolving out of a mass meeting," says Dennis Banks, credited with being one of the original founders (Interview, 31 July 1982).

Mass media immediately focussed upon the more verbal and charismatic AIM representatives such as Banks and the Bellecourt brothers while other equally important figures like Eddi Benton Banai or George Mitchell hardly attracted attention, either because of their own self-restraint or because they simply did not fit the stereotype as well. Dennis Banks and Russell Means - the latter did not join AIM until 1970 - are probably the most often cited and photographed Indians of the 20th century. This kind of popularity, which in many cases approaches the level of a personality cult, inevitably endowed certain individuals with more power within the organization and thus helped to create a kind of hierarchy that did not conform to the original charter.

The power struggle between AIM leaders soon became a major source of disruption, which finally resulted in uneasy and sometimes rival factions such as the West Coast Group under Banks and Bill Wahpepah and the Dakota AIM under the Means clan. The clash of personalities intensified shortly after the surge of AIM in the mass media as an instigator of spectacular events. George Mitchell, who had been instrumental in formulating the original AIM charter, quit the organization after the occupation of the BIA headquarters, supposedly out of disgust with the behavior of some of the leaders (see Burnette and Koster 1974:215). The situation came to a climax in 1973, when the co-chairman, Carter Camp, shot at and severely wounded Clyde Bellecourt. This kind of internal rivalry ultimately cost AIM a lot of its initial sympathy among Indians.

The concentration of power has also made it easier for the FBI, which had declared total war on AIM following the brutal and controversial killing of two agents at the Pine Ridge Reservation in 1975, to interfere with its activities. AIM leaders were constantly either in court and jail, or forced to go underground. Dennis Banks, for example, was politically isolated in California between 1976 and 1983, where he was granted sanction from charges pressed by South Dakota since 1975 for assault and riot. With the election of a new governor, Banks fled to the Onondaga in New York for fear of being extradited to South Dakota, where threats had been made against his life.

Apparently Euro-Americans, and Indians for that matter, have a need to personify the course of history with mythic leaders. If these leaders should ever turn out to be anything less than what they are put up to be, it is quite likely that their failure will reflect negatively upon whatever it is they may represent. The fact that Dennis Banks, Russell Means, or any of the other AIM leaders are human and consequently do not always behave like the mythical Indian leaders of the past are reputedly to have done, has also led to disillusionment with the organization they have come to personify all over the world. Much of the criticism I have heard directed at AIM actually involved one of the leaders personally rather than the organization itself.

As Mathiessen (1983:75) correctly points out, AIM should be understood as a movement rather than an organization. It was originally conceived as a number of independently operating Chapters with representation in a National General Council to coordinate joint activities whenever necessary. The relatively loose bureaucratic structure was intended as a self-protective measure, making the assessment of members at any given time difficult. As little more is required of an Indian wanting to join other than a demonstration of good will, AIM has inevitably attracted opportunists who have done their share of damage to its reputation. Not a few of these have been paid infiltrators, as in the case of Bill Durham, a close confidant of Dennis Banks, who was publicly revealed as an FBI agent.

Like any other political organization, AIM depends entirely upon the voluntary participation of regular members. Its various programs are carried out by hundreds of individuals whose names will never appear in print. These make up the American Indian Movement and not, as is too aften assumed, a few charismatic public figures.

AIM needs to be studied in terms of the long history of Indian resistance and as a product thereof. The main problem it will present to the perspective scholar, aside from the misconceptions already discussed, is its amorphous structure. The West Coast Group is actually a different organization from the Dakota AIM, although there are rules binding both together. In the same way that Indian people differ from each other, so will AIM Chapters vary according to membership and location. It might be more sensible, therefore, to analyse a particular Chapter rather than trying to draw conclusions about the organization as a whole. Another obvious problem, which has already been pointed out elsewhere (Cohen 1976), will be the personal responsibility of the scholar in handling his/her information, as AIM continues to be subject to repression from the U.S. government and some private American interest groups.

Although AIM has lost much of its impetus since 1973, it continues to be an important political force in Indian affairs. This persistence, which stands in marked contrast to the fate of other organizations often compared to it, such as the Black Panthers and the Brown Berets, indicates that there is more involved here than "militance." In January 1982, AIM representatives held a meeting in San Francisco to reaffirm the goals and policies established in 1968. Western education, co-opted Indians, Christian Churches, the U.S. government together with multi-national corporations, and the Indian Health Service were reinstated as the "Enemies of American Indian People" and it was decided to continue the effort to expose them as such. Further topics of discussion were legal and treaty rights, employment, housing, welfare, education, and cultural heritage. Special emphasis was given to the continuation of AIM's international work through its representative offices abroad and the IITC (AIM 1982). The real significance behind this highly optimistic conference, however, lies in the fact that AIM leaders have apparently managed to give precedence to the organization's future over their personal disagreements. It was the first time in years that they could be coerced to make a public show of solidarity.

As long as the interest in North American Indians persists, it is unlikely that AIM will ever fade out completely in Germany. Most of the traditionalists who are currently being invited over in the wake of the new spiritual trend are sympathetic towards AIM and hold similar views. The people involved in AIM Support Groups and those seeking to understand Indian religions are often one and the same or at least cooperate with each other. In 1983, when the plans for a Sun Dance at the "1st European Medicine Wheel Gathering and Spiritual Camp" in the Black Forest (one of several dubious "spiritual" orgies to be conducted in Europe recently) were made public, letters of protest from AIM, together with loud complaints from traditionalists in South Dakota, caused quite a bit of discomfort among a few of the organizers, who finally decided to drop the issue. Ultimately, of course, the degree of AIM's popularity will depend upon its future activities.

A fair number of articles on AIM have been published in the U.S. (e.g., Bigony 1979; Bonney 1977; Cohen 1973 and 1976; Ortiz 1980; Pittmann 1973; Talbert 1976; Talbot 1979), most of which deal with the occupation of Wounded Knee. More inclusive are Rex Weyler's *Blood of the Land* (1982), dealing with the events leading up to the establishment of Yellow Thunder Camp, and Peter Mathiessen's *In the Spirit of Crazy Horse* (1983), focussing on the Leonard Peltier case - the AIM leader convicted of the killing of the two FBI agents mentioned previously - but also including a detailed summary of AIM's history. Again, both monographs fit the "committed documentation" category, so that a major academic contribution on the subject is still pending. Finally, AIM has recently published its own history in the form of a photographic documentary narrated by Dennis Banks (Banks 1983).

So who is afraid of AIM? I would venture to say those who insist on fabricating imaginary Indians in order to suit their primitivistic ideals or those who can't shake off the archaic dust that sometimes clings to academia. The former might be afraid of the traumatic recognition that Indians are just humans after all, and the latter of the possibility of becoming obsolete. Most of us, I am afraid, are not completely free of either.

REFERENCES CITED

AIM
  1982   AIM. Papers from the "AIM Non-alignment Summit Meeting" in San Francisco, Sept. 13 - 16. Partially translated in Pogrom 13(89/90): 56-57.

AIM Support Group Hamburg
  1977   Indianer im Widerstand. Hamburg: AIM Support Group Hamburg.

AIM Unterstützungsgruppe Neumünster
  1980   Indianer im Widerstand II. Neumünster: AIM Unterstützungsgruppe Neumünster.

Banks, Dennis
  1983   The American Indian Movement 1968-1982. Aptos, CA: Aptos Press.

Biegert, Claus
  1976   Seit 200 Jahren ohne Verfassung. Reinbek: rororo Verlag.
  1979   Indianerschulen: Als Indianer überleben - von Indianer lernen. Survival Schools. Reinbek: rororo Verlag.

Bigony, Beatrice
  1979   Attempting to Close the Sacred Circle: The Endeavor of the American Indian Movement. Central Issues in Anthropology 1(2):41-62.

Bolz, Peter
  1983   Oglala-Sioux. In: Klaus E. Müller (ed.), Menschenbilder früher Gesellschaften (Frankfurt/New York: Campus Verlag), 422-449.

Bonney, Rachel A.
  1977   The Role of AIM Leaders in Indian Nationalism. American Indian Quarterly 3(3):204-223.

Brandes, Volkhard et al.
  1983   Gegen Ende der Reise: Auf der Suche nach der Indianischen Botschaft. Frankfurt: extrabuch Verlag.

Burnette, Robert, and John Koster
  1974   The Road to Wounded Knee. New York: Bantam Books.

Cohen, Fay
  1973   The Indian Patrol in Minneapolis: Social Control and Social Change in an Urban Context. Law and Society Review 7:779-787. (Also the title to her unpublished dissertation, Univ. of Minnesota, 1973.)
  1976   The American Indian Movement and the Anthropologist: Issues and Implications of Consent. In: M. Rynkiewich and J. Spradley (eds.), Ethics and Anthropology (New York: John Wiley and Sons), 81-92.

Council on Interracial Books for Children
  1980   Die Wunden der Freiheit. Reinbeck: rororo. (Translation of "Chronicles of American Indian Protest," 1971, with additional data on Indians in Europe.)

562

Dewing, Rolland (ed.)
1987   The FBI Files on the American Indian Movement and Wounded
         Knee. 26 reels of microfilm.
         Frederick, MD: University Publications of America.
Domnick, Renate
1982   Wer spricht für das Volk?. Rundbrief Indianer und Stammeskulturen
         Heute 40:21-26.
Feest, Christian F.
1976   Das Rote Amerika. Wien: Europa Verlag.
Forbes, Jack D.
1972   "The New Indian Resistance?" Akwesasne Notes 4(3):20-22.
Grobsmith, Elisabeth S.
1981   Lakota of the Rosebud. Case Studies in Cultural Anthropology. New
         York: Holt, Rinehart and Winston.
International Indian Treaty Council
1977   The Geneva Conference. Special issue of Treaty Council News 1(7).
1981   International NGO Conference on Indigenous Peoples and the Land.
         Minneapolis: Haymarket Press.
Josephy, Alvin Jr.
1971   Red Power. New York: McGraw-Hill Book Co.
König, René
1973   Indianer - wohin? Opladen: Westdeutscher Verlag.
1980   Navajo Report 1970-1980: Von der Kolonie zur Nation. Neustadt:
         Arca Verlag. Revised edition, Berlin: Dietrich Reimer Verlag, 1983.
Mails, Thomas F.
1979   Fools Crow. New York: Doubleday.
Mathiessen, Peter
1983   In the Spirit of Crazy Horse. New York: Viking Press.
Michels, Peter M.
1972   Aufstand in den Ghettos. Frankfurt: Fischer Verlag.
Ortiz, Roxanne D.
1980   Wounded Knee 1890 to Wounded Knee 1973: A Study in United
         States Colonialism. Journal of Ethnic Studies 8(2):1-15.
Pittmann, John
1973   Wounded Knee and the Indian Future. Political Affairs 52(7):66-74.
Reichert, Carl-Ludwig
1974   Red Power: Indianisches Sein und Bewußtsein Heute. München: R.
         Piper & Co. Verlag.
Schierle, Sonja
1981   Funktion einer Survival School für städtische Indianer. Arbeiten aus
         dem Seminar für Völkerkunde der Johann Wolfgang Goethe Universi-
         tät, Frankfurt. Wiesbaden: Franz Steiner Verlag.

Schmidt, Mathias R.
  1980   Wenn wir gehen - geht die Welt. Lampertheim: Kübler Verlag KG.
Schulze-Thulin, Axel
  1976   Weg ohne Mokassins: Die Indianer Nordamerikas Heute. Düsseldorf:
          Droste Verlag.
Steiner, Stan
  1968   The New Indians. New York: Dell.
Talbert, Carol
  1976   The Resurgence of Ethnicity Among American Indians: Some
          Comments on the Occupation of Wounded Knee. In: F. Henry (ed.),
          Ethnicity in the Americas (The Hague - Paris: Mouton Publishers),
          365-383.
Talbot, Steve
  1979   The Meaning of Wounded Knee, 1973: Indian Self-Government and
          the Role of Anthropology. In: G. Huizer and B. Mannheim (eds.),
          The Politics of Anthropology (The Hague - Paris: Mouton Pub-
          lishers), 227-258.
Wagner, Waltraud
  1971   Kampagne gegen die Kohlkultur. Universität Bochum: Studienverlag.
Weyler, Rex
  1982   Blood of the Land: The Government Corporate War Against the
          American Indian Movement. New York: Everest House Publishers.
Wibich, Manfred, and Urs Winter
  1976   Kapitalismus und Indianer in den USA. Frankfurt: Verlag Marxisti-
          sche Blätter.

EUROPE'S ROLE IN DISPLACING NATIVE CANADIANS

Russel Lawrence Barsh

The development of unsurrendered native lands in the Americas, resulting in the destruction of subsistence resources and population displacements, tends to be viewed as an American responsibility. European industry is a major participant, however, even in the United States and Canada. European participation includes direct control of land-development projects, ownership of minority interests in American firms, relocation of manufacturing operations in the Americas to take advantage of proximity to raw materials and energy, and investment in international financial institutions such as the World Bank that provide the capital for exploring and developing remote areas. Europeans depend on unsurrendered native lands in the Americas for much of their supply of metal ores and wood products. The development of indigenous territories also reduces prices by increasing world supplies.

It has always been so, of course. The New World supplied Europe's precious metals in the 16th century, its lumber and furs in the 18th century, and much of its wheat and fiber in the 19th century. The abundance and low cost of American exports reflected colonists' ability to acquire undeveloped land from the original inhabitants at low cost through violence or the threat of violence. Profits from North American trade produced the capital concentrations needed to finance Europe's rapid mechanical industrialization. Until it, too, industrialized, in the 1850s, the United States was chiefly an exporter of raw materials (Table 1), supplying European factories and feeding Europe's factory labor. The United States has now gained control of more than 95 per cent of its contiguous territorial area from the natives, exhausting most of its non-renewable resources and becoming a net importer of raw materials. Other nations in the Americas continue to depend economically on the gradual dispossession of native groups and the exportation of minerals, fuel and timber.

Canada is a case in point. Manufacturing technology is well established in southern Ontario and Quebec, but most of the rest of the country is thinly populated and either agricultural or undeveloped. Although more than half of Canada lies above 60° north latitude, as late as 1940 only one per cent of Euro-Canadians lived there. Until the 1950's, when U.S. firms looked to the Arctic to replace dwindling domestic supplies of petroleum and iron, "the North" remained chiefly an indigenous hunting domain. Apart from the northeastern part of Quebec, acquired from the Crees under the 1976 James Bay-Northern Quebec Agreement (Whyte 1982), none of this vast northern region has been sold or surrendered by the native inhabitants. Canada recently recognized four native aggregations for negotiating northern land settlements: the Dene Nation, Inuit Tapirisat, Committee of Original Peoples Entitlement (COPE) and Council of Yukon Indians (CYI) (Cole 1982; Legge 1981; MacGregor

1981; Souchette 1982).[1]

Among Western industrial nations, Canada is second only to Australia in its overall economic reliance on exports of raw materials. Primary products such as ores and raw lumber accounted for 46 per cent of all Canadian exports in 1978, compared with 72 per cent for Australia and 31 per cent for the United States (Gross 1983:43). Forest products supplied 12 per cent of Canada's manufacturing employment and 28 per cent of the value of its 1980 exports, while mining added 1 1/2 per cent to Canadian employment and 14 per cent of the value of 1980 exports (World Bank 1983:463; Wilkinson 1980:20,81,83,100). A substantial share of the metals (Table 2) and forest products (Table 3) shipped from Canada are destined for Western Europe. Western European nations depend on Canada for much of their iron and zinc (Table 4), and wood pulp for containers and building materials (Table 5). Canada leads world production of zinc and nickel, and is the West's largest supplier of iron (Table 6).

Foreign investment has played a critical role in the development of Canadian industry. Canadian mineral exports have trebled, both in value and as a per cent of GNP, since the 1920's as a result of U.S. investment in eastern Arctic iron in the 1950's, U.S. development of Saskatchewan's potash in the 1960's, and Western European and Japanese exploration of western Arctic coal, copper, and zinc in the 1970's (Wilkinson 1980:84). Foreign investment in Canada peaked at $4 billion in 1970-1974, but has fallen somewhat due to nationalization ("Canadianization") of much of the petrochemical industry, which is now about 35 per cent Canadian-owned (Byleveld 1982:42). According to one estimate, about 58 per cent of Canada's metal-mining assets, 68 per cent of its petroleum facilities, and 40 per cent of its forestry industry are foreign-owned or controlled (Wilkinson 1980:93,100). Canadian government statistics are somewhat more conservative (Table 7). Foreign investment in forestry is heaviest in the southern and eastern parts of the country where most native lands purportedly were purchased under 19th and 20th-century treaties. Foreign investment in mining is greatest in the North, however, where native rights have not yet been settled (Tables 8-10, map, appendix).

Half of Canada's iron and lead and one-third of its zinc currently come from the North (Table 6), and exploration of this unsurrendered region is intensifying. In 1980 Canada's Department of Energy, Mines and Resources evaluated twelve promising but underdeveloped mineral regions, including three in the western Arctic - Baker Lake on the west shore of Hudson Bay (uranium), the Great Slave Lake in central N.W.T. (base and precious metals), and the southern Yukon (base metals). Besides the obvious physical constraints of mining these northern areas such as severe cold, isolation, and rugged terrain, the Department complained that "native interests, including land claims and a demand that native benefit from employment opportunities, could complicate development plans" (DEMR 1980:9):

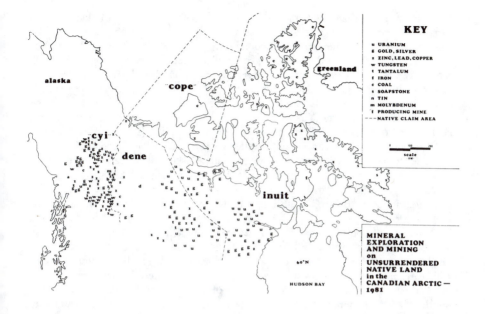

"Problems stemming from the development of the Pine Point Mine (in the North West Territory), such as destruction of traplines by line cutting crews, poisoning of streams by unchecked leakage from tailings ponds and a poor record in training and employment of natives may make some of the native people hostile to mineral development."

Native rights and environmental concerns inevitably intersect, the Department observed (DEMR 1980:6):

"The Indian, Inuit and Métis populations demand compensation for loss of exclusive access to their ancestral hunting, trapping and fishing lands. They also wish to retain exclusive access to certain portions, to have exclusive use of wildlife resources and to ensure that air and water quality and the fragile northern ecosystems are protected. Until these issues are resolved, mineral development proposals in the Territories will almost certainly be opposed by native groups."

The environmental effects of northern mining on subsistence resources have not yet been ascertained fully. Most operations are open-pit and require roads, railways, or pipelines to link them with mills and ice- free ports. There have

567

been some indications that the Alyeska oil pipeline diverted Alaskan caribou migrations and led to a severe decline in herds' size (Strong 1977:48). The Cullaton Lake gold mine jointly operated by Consolidated Durham Mines and O'Brien Gold Mines, and Sissons Lake uranium field discovered by Urangesellschaft (F.R.G.), are near caribou migration routes in the North West Territory (DEMR 1980:12). Oil spills and contamination from mill tailings are another continuing concern. Cyprus Anvil's Grum lead-zinc mine, located in a predominatly native area of the Yukon, will produce mercury - rich concentrates that could jeopardize local wildlife and human water supplies (DEMR 1980:13; Gray 1981). Mining leases and land settlements reduce the geographical area available to subsistence hunters - enough, in Alaska and James Bay, to make survival on hunting alone impossible (Berger 1977:177; Whyte 1982).

Arctic potential for hydroelectric power and forestry may soon overtake its value for minerals. Brinco, a subsidiary of Rio Tinto Zinc (U.K.), completed one of the world's largest hydroelectric power stations at Churchill Falls, Labrador, in 1974. Now operated by the Government of Quebec, Churchill Falls can generate 6,630 megawatts and supplies subsidized power to the Montreal area. Similar projects are feasible on major river systems in the western Arctic. Although most of Canada's high-yield forests are located in southern Quebec and British Columbia, about 14 per cent of the country's forest potential lies "north of 60°" (Bonnor 1982). Some Newfoundland forests are already under development by Bowater-Mersey (U.K.), and a subisidary of ITT-Rayonier (U.S.) leased 26,000 square miles of Labrador in 1971. Because of the slow growth rate of northern forests, silviculture may never be profitable, encouraging low-cost "mining" of trees, i.e., clearcutting without replanting.

Firms active in Canada's north also tend to be involved in displacing indigenous populations elsewhere. Of the 20 U.S. multinational corporations with mining interests in the north, 18 have mining subsidiaries in Brazil, 11 in Australia, and 7 in South Africa and Namibia (Dun & Bradstreet 1983). Of the 6 Canadian multinationals mining the north, 6 are active in Brazil, 3 in Australia, and 2 in South Africa/Namibia. And of the 10 Western European firms with northern mining interests, 4 operate mining ventures in Brazil, 7 in Australia, and 5 in South Africa. In addition, two major South African companies - the Anglo-American Corporation of South Africa and its affiliate, DeBeers - have substantial interests in both Canada and Australia (appendix).

A recent World Bank policy study underscored the "considerable loss of life," involuntary resettlement, and poor health suffered by tribal populations swept aside by development projects in Amazonia, Central America, and tropical Asia (Goodland 1982:17,20-24). Negative effects of industrialization are also sociocultural (Goodland 1982:25):

"(P)eople in a hunting and gathering society are trained to be independent and opportunistic, and to use initiative. These qualities become disadvantage

568

when such people are forced to offer themselves as dependent and obedient wage or debt-bondage laborers."

World Bank projects throughout South America have displaced native populations, but henceforth will require assurances of compliance with international human-rights norms - including respect for native land tenure and cultural autonomy (Goodland 1982:1,12,27):

"It is not the Bank's policy to prevent the development of areas presently occupied by tribal people. However, the Bank will assist projects within areas used or occupied by such people only if it is satisfied that best efforts have been made to obtain the voluntary, full, and conscionable agreement of the tribal people."[2]

Unfortunately, the Bank supplies less than one-tenth of the development financing in these countries. Most comes from individual industrial nations and commercial banks.

Brazil is the largest South American nation, with the largest claims to unsurrendered native lands. It is also the western hemisphere's largest debtor, with an external debt in 1980 of nearly $38 billion, of which more than 90 per cent was owed to the United States, France, the Federal Republic of Germany, and Japan (OECD 1983:44; World Bank 1982:111). This staggering investment sustains and, for the repayment of loans and interest requires the aggressive development of the country's interior. In 1980 primary products accounted for about two-thirds of Brazil's exports, led by coffee (13.8 per cent), sugar (6.8 per cent), and minerals (8.6 per cent) (World Bank 1982:111; United Nations Statistical Office 1983:974). Two thirds was shipped to the OECD - chiefly the U.S. (17.4 per cent), Federal Republic of Germany (6.6 per cent), Netherlands (5.7 per cent), and Japan (6.1 per cent) (United Nations Statistical Office 1983:964).

In Canada and the United States (at least), mining firms themselves have now recognized the practical importance of settling native claims because of what Goodland (1982:10) tactfully calls "the vulnerability of projects." Native groups in Alaska demanded a land settlement for decades before the discovery of petroleum at Prudhoe Bay - and the threat of native legal action or sabotage against the pipeline corridor - gave the situation sufficient urgency to force Congress to act (Arnold 1978:86-144). Likewise, the Canadian mining industry has taken much of the credit for the James Bay-Northern Quebec Agreement (Ciaccia 1977). Obviously the physical security and stability of projects depends on good relations with neighboring native populations. The incentive to avoid conflict is greatest among local managers and their employees, less for absent corporate headquarters, and least, perhaps, for the host government's rear-echelon administrators.

569

The point here is that the displacement of indigenous peoples is never a domestic affair. It is nearly always the result of international economic forces hosted, but rarely controlled by national governments. Developed countries are the principal beneficiaries of new supplies of raw materials, without which they cannot maintain a high standard of living through employment in trade and manufacturing. Western Europeans have condemned violations of native peoples' rights in the Americas, notably in the remarks of the Danish, Norwegian and Dutch governments at recent meetings of the United Nations Commission on Human Rights. They have taken no action to disinvest from multinational mining firms, however, or to boycott their products. It is particularly noteworthy that the British, French and Italian governments themselves own mining projects in the unsurrendered Arctic (Table 8; appendix). In this regard, the European invasion of America cannot yet be dismissed to history. It continues.

NOTES

1. Since this article was written, Canada has approved a settlement with COPE that follows the same broad outlines as the James Bay-Northern Quebec Agreement. This still leaves the majority of Arctic lands in dispute.
2. At a meeting of the International Labour Office, Geneva, in September 1986 attended by the author, a World Bank representative repudiated the Goodland study and said it had never been adopted as Bank policy. See I.L.O. Doc. Nr. APPL/MER/107/1986/D.7, 134.

APPENDIX

OWNERSHIP STRUCTURE OF FIRMS ACTIVE IN NORTHERN CANADIAN MINING
By Country of Parent/Control

Canadian Parents

Alberta Government (50.0)——————————ALBERTA ENERGY
Edward & Peter Bronfman Group (0.0A)
  Edper Equities (42.0)
    BRASCAN (50.1)————————————————WESTERN MINES

Brascan (14.0)——————————————┐
The Black Group (0.0A)   │
  Western Dominion Investment (52.7)   │
    Ravelston Corp. (58.8)   │
      Hollinger Argus (7.4)———————————MATTAGAMI REFINING
Hollinger Argus (66.9)   NORANDA MINES
Hanna Mining (20.0)   (33.1) PLACER CEGO
  Labrador Mining & Exploration (3.0)——   (41.2) KERR-ADDISON
Fenswick Holdings (36.3)   │
Noranda Mines (36.3)   │
  Zinor Holdings (23.6)———————————————┘
Canada Government (100.0)————————————PETRO-CANADA
                                          ELDORADO NUCLEAIRE

Canada Government (48.7)
  Canada Development Corp. (34.3)————————TEXASGULF

Canadian Pacific (54.0)
  COMINCO (69.1)————————————————————PINE POINT MINES

Hiram Walker Consumer's Home (100.0)
  Home Oil (85.6)————————————————————SCURRY RAINBOW OIL

Inco (100.0)————————————————————————CANADIAN NICKEL
                                          INCO METALS
Leitch Transport (11.5)————————————————DOFASCO

Manoil (99.9)————————————————————————EXPLORAM

Osler Wills Bidde (12.9)
  Minaco Equipment (62.9)————————————TINTINA MINES

571

Saskatchewan Government (100.0)——————SASKATCHEWAN MINING

Security Trading (13.9)
  Mineral Resources Int'l (53.6)———┐
Torcal Investments (32.7)——————————┤
Canada Government (18.0)———————————├—NANISIVIK MINES
Metallgesellschaft (11.2)——————————┤
Royal Dutch/Shell (11.2)———————————┘
Vancouver Stock Exchange Service (12.8)—PRISM RESOURCES

United States Parents

Arco (100.0)————————————————————ANACONDA
Baker Int'l (100.0)——————————————MILCHEM
Bendix (19.4)—————————————————————ASARCO
The Buckley Group (0.0A)
  Catawba Corp. (50.8)———————————BOREALIS EXPLORATIONS
CRA (100.0)———————————————————————TERRA RESOURCES
Cyprus Mines (62.8)————————————————CYPRUS ANVIL
E.I. DuPont (74.9)————————————————DUPONT OF CANADA
Exxon (69.5)
  Imperial Oil (100.0)————————————ESSO RESOURCES
General Electric (100.0)——————————UTAH MINES
Gulf Oil (60.2)———————————————————GULF CANADA
IU Int'l (100.0)——————————————————ECHO BAY MINES
Marathon Oil (100.0)——————————————PAN OCEAN OIL
Occidental Petroleum (16.0)———————CANADIAN OCCIDENTAL
Reynolds Metals (22.6)————————————┐
Canflo Mines (16.8)——————————————┴LYNX CANADA EXPLORATIONS
Standard Oil California (100.0)———CHEVRON CANADA
Standard Oil California (20.0)
  AMAX (64.7)———————————————————┐
Dome Petroleum (39.5)   ├—CANADA TUNGSTEN
  Dome Mines (20.1)——————————————┘
Standard Oil Indiana (100.0)——————AMOCO
Sun Co. (98.1)————————————————————SUNCOR
Superior Oil (100.0)
  Canadian Superior (1.2A)
    McIntyre Mines (36.9)
      Falconbridge Nickel Mines (48.4)———UNITED KENO HILL MINES
      Falconbridge Nickel Mines (19.2)———GIANT YELLOWKNIFE MINES
Union Carbide (51.0)——————————————UNION CARBIDE
Union Oil of California (86.3)————UNION OIL OF CANADA

572

U.S. Steel (100.0)————————————ESSEX MINERALS
Vangus Resources (52.2)————————
The Desmarais Group (0.0A)
 Paul Desmarais &S.A. (69.4)
  Power Corp. of Canada (37.2)   ——SULPETRO
   Consolidated Bathurst (7.4)————
Donbarn Investments (39.4)
HCI Holdings (5.0)————————

European Parents

Alianz Versicherungs-
Aktiengesellschaft (25.0)
Daimler-Benz (25.0)
Deutsche Bank (25.0)
Siemens (25.0)
 METALLGESELLSCHAFT (33.3)————————URANGESELLSCHAFT

Compagnie Generale des
Matieres Nucleaires (COGEMA)(98.8)————SERU NUCLEAR CANADA

Italy Government (100.0)
 Ente Nazionale Idrocarburi (100.0)———— AGIP CANADA
 Instituto per la Recostruzione
  Industriale (92.5)———————————— FINSIDER (SOCIETA FINANZIARIA
                                       SIDERUGICA)

Phoenix Assurance (15.7)
Guardian Royal Exchange Ass. (12.2)
Norwich Union Fire Insurance (15.0)
Commercial Union Assurance (8.2)
Prudential Assurance (6.2)
 RIO TINTO ZINC (80.0)
  Thornwood Investments (24.0)—————— BRINCO

Uranerzbergbau (97.0)————————————URANERZ EXPLORATIONS &
MINING

U.K. Government (100.0)————————————BRITISH STEEL
 Bank of England (21.5)
  British Petroleum (65.6)
   BP Canada (100.0)——————————— BP MINERALS

Anglo-American Corp. South Africa (22.5)
  Anglo-American Corp. Canada (41.2)
   Hudson Bay Mining & Smelting (37.5)
Cabot Corp. (37.5) ————————————————— TANTALUM MINING CORP.
CANADA
Manitoba Government (25.0) ———————————

Anglo-American Corp. South Africa (22.5)
  Anglo-American Corp. Canada (3.0)
Anglo-American Corp. South Africa (17.0)   DIAPROS
  DeBeers Consolidated Mines (60.6) —————————

Power Reactor of Japan (100.0) ———————————— PNC EXPLORATION

SOURCE: Statistics Canada 1981.

Not shown - Canadian operating companies wholly-owned by parents with same name.
"A" indicates control via interlocking directorates rather than direct ownership.

Table 1.

EXPORTS FROM BRITISH NORTH AMERICA IN 1770
Value in Pounds Sterling by Commodity and Destination

	Britain& Ireland	Other Europe	West Indies& Africa	Total Value	Percent
Metals, minerals, ores[1]	128.4	.2	4.1	132.7	3.9
Wood products, lumber[2]	62.6	5.8	92.3	160.7	4.7
Skins and furs	149.2	-	-	149.2	4.3
Animal fats and oils	82.9	6.0	31.7	120.7	3.5
Pitch and tar	26.6	-	1.3	27.9	.8
Meat, fish, livestock[4]	32.0	245.8	227.4	567.7	16.5
Grains and beans[5]	237.3	401.7	393.5	1032.5	30.0
Vegetable dyes and fibres[6]	166.7	-	-	166.8	4.9
Tobacco	905.0	-	1.7	906.6	26.4
Rum	.5	2.8	18.5	21.8	.6
Total value	1871.3	691.9	870.6	3437.7	
Percent of total value	*54.4*	*20.1*	*25.3*		

[1]*Chiefly iron (51%).*
[2]*Including hoops, staves, and turpentine.*
[3]*Chiefly whale oil (70%). Includes candles.*
[4]*Chiefly dried fish (66%). Includes butter and cheese.*
[5]*Chiefly bread and flour (49%) and rice (34%).*
[6]*Chiefly indigo (79%).*

Source: Bureau of the Census 1960:761, Table Z76.

Table 2.

DESTINATIONS OF CANADIAN EXPORTS OF COAL AND METAL ORES - 1979
Exports to Each Destination as Percent of Total Exports

	IRON	LEAD	ZINC	COPPER	URANIUM	NICKEL	COAL
United States	57.8	8.0	18.3	1.6	91.7	15.3	.1
Western Europe	36.2	18.8	51.0	12.0	8.3	82.0	7.4
Eastern Europe*	.5	9.7	1.9	4.0	-	-	-
South America	-	-	-	-	-	2.7	4.7
Africa	-	-	.7	-	-	-	-
Asia**	5.7	63.5	33.1	77.6	-	.8	87.3
Total value (millions US$)	1156	94	200	416	324	280	625

*Chiefly U.S.S.R.
**Chiefly Japan.
SOURCE: United Nations Statistical Office 1981.

Table 3.

DESTINATIONS OF CANADIAN EXPORTS OF FOREST RESOURCES - 1979
Exports to Each Destination as Percent of Total Exports

	LUMBER	PULP	COMBINED
United States	72.1	54.4	64.4
Western Europe	11.9	28.0	18.9
Eastern Europe	.1	.2	.1
South America	.3	1.1	.6
Africa	.5	.5	.5
Asia*	13.3	13.7	13.5
Australia	1.9	.9	1.4
Total value (millions US$)	3439	2645	6084

*Chiefly Japan.
SOURCE: United Nations Statistical Office 1981.

Table 4.

WESTERN EUROPEAN DEPENDENCE ON CANADIAN METAL ORES
AND CONCENTRATES - 1979
Imports from Canada as Percent of Total Imports

	IRON	LEAD	ZINC	COPPER	TUNG-STEN	MOLYB-DENUM
Belgium	5.2	-	26.6	39.8	-	32.3
France	7.2	2.5	26.0	-	2.7	22.7
Germany (FRG)	13.6	15.2	37.6	5.5	7.4	7.0
Netherlands	22.3	-	36.9	-	-	-
Italy	15.8	26.0	26.7	-	69.4	6.7
United Kingdom	40.9	14.3	11.8	-	-	-
Denmark	-	-	-	-	-	-
Sweden	-	-	-	-	10.6	3.7
Norway	-	-	-	-	-	-
Austria	22.7	-	-	-	5.4	-
Spain	22.3	-	6.7	19.0	-	4.0
Portugal	13.9	-	-	-	-	-

SOURCE: United Nations Statistical Office 1981.

Table 5.

WESTERN EUROPEAN DEPENDENCE ON CANADIAN FORESTS - 1979
Imports from Canada as Percent of Total Imports

	LUMBER	PULP	COMBINED
Belgium	7.6	20.2	10.7
France	6.4	19.3	11.7
Germany (FRG)	4.1	18.8	9.7
Ireland	13.2	9.4	12.8
Italy	3.0	20.3	8.5
Netherlands	3.9	16.6	7.2
United Kingdom	16.3	18.1	17.0
Austria	1.0	8.8	3.2
Finland	1.7	3.1	4.0
Portugal	-	10.5	3.6
Switzerland	1.0	4.9	3.2
Greece	.8	5.3	1.7
Spain	.9	16.0	5.2

*SOURCE: United Nations Statistical Office 1981. Not shown if Canadian
imports (combined) equalled 1 per cent of less of total imports.*

Table 6.
CANADIAN PRODUCTION OF METAL ORES 1980
By Region and Share of World Production

	Percent Produced in:		Total Metric Tons	Share of World Production		
	Labrador	NWT-Yukon	(1000s)	Per cent	Rank	
iron	53.0	-	31,283	6.2	6	(a)
lead	1.6	46.6	274	7.8	4	(b)
zinc	4.5	29.3	895	15.9	1	
copper	0.8	1.5	708	8.9	5	(c)
uranium	-	-	7	16.3	2	(d)
nickel	-	-	195	26.6	1	

(a) After U.S.S.R., Australia, Brazil, U.S. China.
(b) After U.S., U.S.S.R., Australia.
(c) After U.S., U.S.S.R., Chile, Zambia.
(d) After U.S.
Source: United Nations Statistical Office 1983: Tables 109-122; DEMR 1982.

Table 7.

FOREIGN CONTROL OF CANANDIAN MINING AND FORESTRY 1978-1981
Per Cent of Total Capital Expenditures by Region and Country of Control

	----------Forestry----------			---------- Mining---------		
	U.S.	Other Foreign	All Foreign	U.S.	Other Foreign	All Foreign
Atlantic	-	-	42.0	48.6	6.5	55.1
Quebec	-	-	54.0	62.7	6.0	67.7
Ontario	-	-	49.8	16.7	11.9	28.6
Prairies	-	-	70.6	36.4	10.8	47.2
B.C.	21.6	5.1	26.7	20.9	22.5	43.4
N.W.T.-Yukon	0	0	0	65.6	6.4	72.0
CANADA	23.2	5.4	28.6	34.0	11.3	45.3 All minerals
				30.7	15.3	46.0 Metals only

SOURCE: Statistics Canada 1979: Table 4; Statistics Canada 1983: Table 4.

All figures for 1981 except Quebec and Ontario (1979), Atlantic and Prairies forestry (1979), and N.W.T.-Yukon mining (1978). Unavailable data indicated by (-).

578

Table 8.

OWNERSHIP OF NORTHEAST ARTIC IRON PRODUCERS
Percent Control of Each Operating Company, by Parent and Country

	IRON - ORE CO.	WABUSH	QUEBEC- CARTIER	SIDBEC
UNITED STATES				
United States Steel	-	-	100.0	12.2
Hanna Mining	27.4	-	-	-
Bethlehem Steel	20.3	-	-	-
National Steel	19.0	-	-	-
Armco	6.1	-	-	-
Republic Steel	6.3	-	-	-
LTV (Youngstown Sheet and Tube)	6.3	15.6	-	-
Wheeling-Pittsburg Steel	4.9	10.2	-	-
Inland Steel	-	10.2	-	-
Interlake	-	10.2	-	-
Moore-McCormack	-	5.2	-	-
Total, U.S. Parents	*90.6*	*51.4*	*100.0*	*12.2*
CANADA				
Government of Quebec	-	-	-	46.1
Hollinger Argus[1]	9.4	-	-	-
Stelco	-	25.6	-	-
Dofasco	-	16.4	-	-
Total, Canadian Parents	*9.4*	*42.0*	*-*	*46.1*
UNITED KINGDOM				
British Steel[2]	-	-	-	41.7
ITALY				
Finsider	-	6.6	-	-
Total, European Parents	*-*	*6.6*	*-*	*41.7*

[1]*Controlled   (93%) by Dominion Stores.*
[2]*Wholly owned by the Government of the United Kingdom.*

Sources: Financial Post 1983; Boucher 1981.

579

Table 9.

DESTINATIONS OF IRON ORES, PELLETS AND CONCENTRATE FROM THE NORTHEASTERN ARCTIC
Shipments to Each Destination as Percent of Total Shipments, by Producer and Product

		CANADA	U.S.	EEC	JAPAN	OTHER	TOTAL TONS (1000s)
IRON ORE CO. CANADA	ore	-	83.6	16.4	-	-	4124
	pellets	10.3	70.6	15.4	-	3.8	15380
	concentrate	-	1.2	46.5	52.3	-	8363
WABUSH MINES	pellets	45.2	50.5	4.3	-	-	5539
QUEBEC-CARTIER	concentrate	-	22.1	67.7	2.4	7.9	14809
SIDBEC-NORMINES	concentrate	33.7	13.1	52.6	-	.7	4089
ALL PRODUCERS	ore	-	83.6	16.4	-	-	4124
	pellets	20.3	64.3	12.6	-	2.7	21227
	concentrate	5.0	14.3	58.9	17.3	4.4	27261

SOURCE: Boucher 1981. Not shown separately - Sidbec-Normines shipments of pellets (less than 100,000 tons).
"EEC" = European Economic Community.

Table 10.

EXPLORATION AND MINING COMPANIES IN THE NORTHWEST TERRITORY AND YUKON 1981-1982
By Mineral Group and Country of Control

	COUNTRY OF CONTROL[1]								MINORITY INTERESTS							
	CAN	US	UK	FRG	FR	IT	SAF	JPN	US	UK	FRG	FR	NLD	SWZ	LUX	JPN
Gold, silver	12	17	1	-	-	1	1	-	10	-	-	2	1	1	1	-
Lead, zinc, copper	16	16	2	-	1	1	1	-	13	1	1	2	1	6	1	-
Tungsten	2	6	-	-	1	-	1	-	3	-	-	-	1	-	1	-
Molybdenum	2	-	-	-	-	1	1	-	2	-	-	-	-	-	-	-
Tin	-	3	-	-	-	-	-	-	-	-	-	-	-	-	-	-
Barium	1	4	-	-	-	-	1	-	2	1	-	-	-	-	1	-
Tantalum	1	-	-	-	-	-	1	-	2	-	-	-	1	-	-	-
Uranium	10	9	1	2	1	1	1	1	8	-	-	1	3	1	1	-
Coal	2	2	-	-	-	-	-	-	-	-	-	-	-	-	-	-
Diamonds	-	-	-	-	-	-	1	-	-	1	-	-	-	-	-	-
Asbestos	2	-	-	-	-	-	-	-	1	1	-	-	-	-	-	1

Sources: DINA 1981; DINA 1982: Financial Post 1983.

[1]*Abbreviations used: (FR)ance, (IT)aly, (LUX)embourg, NLD = Netherlands, SWZ = Switzerland, FRG = Federal Republic of Germany, SAF = South Africa, JPN = Japan.*

581

REFERENCES CITED

Arnold, R.D.
1978   Alaska Native Claims. 2d ed. Anchorage: Alaska Native Foundation.

Berger, T.R.
1977   Northern Frontier, Northern Homeland. Report of the MacKenzie Valley Pipeline Inquiry. Toronto: Lorimer & Co.

Bonnor, G.M.
1982   Canada's Forest Inventory 1981. Ottawa: Canadian Forestry Service, Department of the Environment.

Boucher, M.A.
1981   Canadian Iron Ore Industry Statistics 1979-1980. Mineral Policy Sector Internal Report MRI81/11. Ottawa: Department of Energy, Mines and Resources.

Bureau of the Census (United States)
1960   Historical Statistics of the United States, Colonial Times to 1957. Washington, D.C.

Byleveld, H.C.
1982   Foreign Investment in Canada: What's the Score? Canadian Business Review 9(Summer):38-42.

Ciaccia, J.
1977   The Settlement of Native Claims. Alberta Law Review 15:556- 562.

Clark, A.
1981   Resource Assessment of Northern Lands Federal Government Activities. Mineral Policy Sector Internal Report MRI81/12. Ottawa: Department of Energy, Mines and Resources.

Cole, L.
1982   A Settlement for the Yukon. Macleans 95 (27 December):27.

Department of Energy, Mines and Recources (DEMR)
1980   Some Common Regional Constraints to Mine Development. Mineral Policy Sector Internal Report MRI80/18. Ottawa.
1982   Regional Mineral Report 1980. Mineral Policy Sector Internal Report MRI82/1. Ottawa.

Department of Indian and Northern Affairs (DINA)
1981   Mines and Mineral Activities 1981 (Northern Affairs Program). Ottawa.
1982   Mines and Mineral Activities 1982 (Northern Affairs Program). Ottawa.

Dun & Bradstreet
1983   Who Owns Whom 1983. London: Dun & Bradstreet.

Financial Post (Canada)
1983   Financial Post Survey of Mines and Energy Resources 1983. Toronto: MacLean-Hunter.

Goodland, R
    1982   Tribal Peoples and Economic Development: Human Ecological
            Considerations. New York: World Bank.

Gray, M.
    1981   Red faces in Alice Arm. Macleans 94 (8 June):26.

Gross, A.C.
    1983   Canada's Global Competitiveness - Once More With Feeling And With
            Statistics. Business Quarterly 48(Fall):39-49.

Legge, G.
    1981   Growing sense of northern déjà vu. Macleans 94 (4 May):40.

MacGregor, R.
    1981   This land is whose land. Macleans 94 (1 June):49-52.

Organization for Economic Co-Operation and Development (OECD)
    1983   Geographical Distribution of Financial Flows to Developing Countries
            1978/1981. Paris.

Souchette, S.
    1982   Pride and politics over land claims. Macleans 95 (13 Septem-
            ber):18-19.

Statistics Canada
    1979   Domestic and Foreign Control of Forestry, Mining and Manufacturing
            Capital Expenditures in Canada 1977-1979. Ottawa.
    1983   Capital Expenditures of Domestic and Foreign Controlled Establish-
            ments in Manufacturing, Mining and Forestry 1983. Ottawa.
    1981   Inter-corporate Ownership 1980. Ottawa.

Stopford, J.M.
    1982   The World Directory of Multinational Enterprises 1982-83. Detroit:
            Gale Research.

Strong, B.S.
    1977   Alaska Pipeline: Social and Economic Impact on Native People.
            ESCOM Report N. AI-O1. Ottawa: Department of Indian and
            Northern Affairs.

Untited Nations Statistical Office
    1981   1979 World Trade Annual. New York: Walker & Co.
    1983   1981 Statistical Yearbook. New York.

Whyte, K.
    1982   Aboriginal Rights: The Native American's Struggle for Survival.
            Human Organization 41(2):178-182.

Wilkinson, B.W.
    1980   Canada in the Changing World Economy. Montreal: Howe Research
            Institute.

World Bank (International Bank for Reconstruction and Development)
    1982   World Development Report 1982. London: Oxford University Press.
    1983   World Tables. 1. Economic Data. Baltimore: Johns Hopkins University.

"WAS ANYBODY MORE OF AN INDIAN THAN KARL MARX?" THE *INDIANI METROPOLITANI* AND THE 1977 MOVEMENT

Giorgio Mariani

It is difficult, and perhaps even somewhat embarrassing, to write about the *Indiani Metropolitani* (Metropolitan Indians) when we consider that one of the main objectives of the group was to defy current political and cultural categories. Thus, to begin by labeling the *Indiani Metropolitani* as a political group - which in some sense they certainly were - might be misleading, especially in light of the *Indiani's* rejection of all forms of traditional politics. It is in fact no accident that they generally referred to politics as "politika," with a "k" instead of a "c," following the fashion of calling imperialist America, "Amerika." For the *Indiani*, politics remained always a vicious word. In order to make things a little clearer, I shall begin by providing some indispensable background information concerning the so-called "1977 Movement" in which the *Indiani Metropolitani* flourished. This social and political movement, formed mainly by students, unemployed, and young people, shook Italy between February and October 1977, before the advent of terrorism radically changed the Italian political scenario. Since I wish to focus on the *Indiani Metropolitani* I shall not be able to spend too much time and space on the causes of the 1977 revolt, and on its political impact and consequences. What follows, then, is not meant to be a thorough description of the 1977 social uprising, but simply a schematic presentation of some major issues relevant to our main subject.

On February 1, 1977, a group of right-wing extremists attacked some students who were meeting in the Department of Literature and Philosophy - department with a strong leftist reputation - on the University of Rome campus. During the attack a philosophy student was seriously wounded in the head by a revolver bullet, and remained in critical condition for several days before eventually recovering. This incident was the spark that set fire to the prairie. On the following day a rally of thousands of students, protesting Fascist violence, clashed with the police not far from the campus. Two students were wounded by bullets fired by plainclothes policemen. Enraged, the student demonstration moved on to the university and occupied the building of the Department of Literature and Philosophy. In the following days the whole university was occupied and all classes suspended. In a short time, under the students' control, the University of Rome became a sort of "liberated" zone where not only college students, but also the unemployed, feminists, "freaks," and young people from various oppressed social strata had a chance to meet, debate their social as well as personal problems, and devise plans which could help them to improve their situation.

The social causes of this sudden revolt were many. Perhaps the most important one was to be found in the new social status of Italian college students in the late 70's. In Italy, as in many other countries in the Western world, college population had continued to grow steadily during the 60's and early 70's. This was especially true of the University of Rome which counted in 1977 something like 180,000 students, although only 30 or 40% of them were actually taking courses and making some regular progress towards their degrees. This latter fact is hardly surprising if we think of how difficult it had become (and, of course, the situation is not much different today) for college graduates to get those jobs for which they were qualified. Students graduating in the humanities were facing a particularly difficult situation since any kind of brain work, let alone stable teaching positions at either high school or college level, appeared to be a chimera. Feelings of frustration towards the job market situation were heightened by other social problems. Unable to find means to support themselves, many students were forced to continue living off their parents' money, and in their parents' houses, even after graduation. The 1977 revolt was also a rebellion against this quite discouraging social condition which was particularly serious in cities like Rome and Bologna. In fact, it was in these two cities that the students' protest was stronger, often culminating in violent clashes between students and the police.[1]

At another level - and, in my view, an important one - the revolt was also fueled by bitter political disillusionment following the June 1976 general elections in Italy. The organizations of the Italian "New Left"[2] - of which many of the students who led the 1977 revolt had formerly been members - had seen in those elections an unprecedented opportunity for traditional leftist parties - the Communist (P.C.I.) and Socialist (P.S.I) party - to overcome moderate and conservative forces led by the Christian Democrats (D.C.), and thus form a "popular," leftist government paving the way to a socialist revolution. Therefore, the different small organizations of the New Left decided to build together an electoral alliance under the name of "Proletarian Democracy" (D.P.) in the hope of winning about 3% of the total vote, and of pushing towards radical social changes a possibly moderate leftist government.[3] One must note, however, that neither the Communist nor the Socialist party called for a popular front, judging that the Italian situation - for both internal and international reasons - was not ready for such a drastic political change. At any rate, the outcome of the elections was rather different from the one the New Leftists had hoped for. Although leftist parties gathered more votes than ever in the history of Italian politics, they remained below 51%. At the same time, D.P. received only a small 1.5% and, more importantly, the Christian Democrats scored a strong 39% which left them by far the strongest party. In short, a leftist government remained a dream, while New Left leaders were puzzled and incapable of formulating adequate political strategies for their groups. Moreover, after the elections, traditional leftist parties were more often than not cooperating with conservatives instead of building a strong opposition against the government. The 1977 revolt was doubtlessly also a consequence of the crisis of both "traditional" and "new" leftist tactics, and of the bitter disappointment spreading among New Left militants who felt that their organizations, not unlike the Socialist and Communist parties, were run by bureaucrats incapable, or perhaps unwilling, to understand the real problems of the masses.

As I mentioned earlier, the 1977 uprising began in Rome and, except for Bologna, no other Italian city saw a movement as strong and as frenetic as the Roman movement. In these two cities the movement found for a while new and original ways to express itself, mixing aggressiveness and rage against the establishment with an ironic unmasking of the latter's blindness and contradictions. One must add immediately, however, that this exciting, if confused, atmosphere, lasted only a few weeks. In a short time the hard-core militants of *autonomia operaia* (worker's autonomy) - a group considered even by new left organizations as extremist - decided that repeated clashes with police forces would have made the whole movement stronger and more radical. Never losing the opportunity to turn a rally into urban guerrilla. *Autonomia operaia* managed, along with police repression, to deprive the 1977 movement of its most original and valuable qualities. In a few months thousands of people decided to give up political involvement and - to use a phrase popular in those days - "went back home" even more frustrated about their social problems than when the revolt had begun. Yet what happened during the first weeks is worth some close consideration. Trying to reject traditional forms of political organization - considered not to be really democratic - people in the movement also called into question the belief that "politics" should be exclusively concerned with large social, "public" issues, whereas "personal" problems had to be dealt with by each person individually. Appropriating a famous slogan of the young Italian feminist movement "il privato è politica" (the private is political) - 1977 militants declared that they did not want to fight any longer for a mythical Revolution scheduled for a distant future. Instead, they wished to change their own lives *now*, improving their social condition without waiting for the working class to decide when the times were ripe for a major upset of the bourgeois order. Although generally the movement considered itself a leftist movement, and Marxist or pseudo-Marxist ideologies played an important role in it, traditional leftist culture had little to offer to young people often labelled by P.C.I., P.S.I. and trade-union leaders "provokers" or even "Fascists"! It is no surprise, then, that the movement made several attempts to create new ways of thinking about politics, and especially a new language to talk about social issues. One such attempt led to the birth of the *Indiani Metropolitani*.

It is impossible to say exactly when the *Indiani* were born, or who brought the group together. However, we may trace briefly how the idea of exploiting the image of the Indian originated. During the last months of 1976, in Milan as well as in other large Italian cities, some young people formed new political groups called *Circoli del Proletariato Giovanile* (Young Proletarians' Circles). The Young Proletarians were perhaps the first to criticize severely all forms of politics, including leftist and new leftist ones. Thus they often turned their attention to counter culture more than to Marxism, as may be seen in a popular leaflet written by "The Subterraneans," a group of Roman high school students that eventually joined the *Indiani Metropolitani*. "Howl" - this is the title of the leaflet - is an overt attempt to echo some famous lines from Allen Ginsberg's 1956 poem,

> "I saw the best minds of my generation suffocated by fancy coats scarfs and pointed shoes
> Vomiting feigned rage in W.C. ears of poor beasts looking for a diploma
> Putting numbered toilet paper in the ballot boxes of polychrome power
> Playing in front of their schools songs of alienating pseudorevolutionary alienation
> Copying translations in front of gates and burying themselves afterwards in prison-classrooms
> Learning by heart Plotinus Euripides and Spinoza and buying during the break half-million lire pizzas and brioches and going back home
> With their heart at rest riding their blued gray motorcycles.
> Let's take out from the subterraneans of our consciousness
> FREEDOM AND CREATIVITY"
> (La Nostra Assemblea 1977:79-80).[4]

The Young Proletarians, however, did not find in counterculture the kind of symbol they were looking for. Some of them, therefore, decided to play "Western games" and to adopt Indian names, while others preferred a provoking, nonsense language which would irritate politicians from all sides. By the end of 1976, *Circoli* with names like "Apache," "Felce e Mirtillo," "Il Panettone," were to be found in all major cities (La Nostra Assemblea 1977:51).[5] The *Circoli* were then the first to think about the Indians, to use an "Indian" language, and to decorate their faces with "war paint."

However, it was only in Rome, during February and March 1977, that the *Indiani Metropolitani* became a large and significant group, attracting also considerable mass media attention. With painted faces, colorful headbands and rubber tomahawks, the *Indiani Metropolitani* were certainly the most "folkloristic" members of the whole movement. Their presence during demonstrations was enough to transform "serious" political rallies into happenings with songs and round dances. Beating on their drums, the *Indiani* sang a chant never heard before during leftist demonstrations: "eah eah eah eah eah eh-eh!" New slogans were also heard for the first time: The traditional "Fascisti, padroni

588

/Per voi non c'è domani /Stanno arrivando i nuovi partigiani" (Fascists, capitalists /For you there's no tomorrow /The new partisans are coming) became "Fascisti, padroni /Per voi non c'è domani /Siamo gli Indiani Metropolitani" (Fascists, capitalists /For you there's no tomorrow /We are the *Indiani Metropolitani*). An even more popular slogan by the *Indiani* was "Geronimo, Cochise, Red Cloud /Are all pissed off and strike back."[6] At the same time, on the walls of the university one could read graffiti like "10, 100, 1000 Little Big Horns," and "Hangman Custer." In brief, the *Indiani* were looking back at the old Indian warriors of the nineteenth century as forerunners of their own struggle for complete freedom, and no longer at the much nearer past of the Italian partisans who had fought against the Fascist dictatorship. Even from such a limited example, one may see that young people were tired of many leftist commonplaces and rituals, and they were looking for something new and "other," for an alternative language different from the one of official politics. The *Indiani Metropolitani* were perhaps the first to embody this desire for renewal shared by most of the movement, although, in their search for something original, they turned back to the dreams of their adolescence, to the Wild West as portrayed in countless Western movies and comics. As young boys and girls, of course, they had identified with the good cowboys fighting the bad Indians; as adults, they simply turned everything upside down by calling the good bad, and vice versa.

The Indian to whom the *Indiani Metropolitani* referred in their slogans and writings was essentially the stereotypical nineteenth century archenemy of the whites, although he may be best described as a combination of the two stereotypes of the Indian as Dangerous Savage, and as Noble Savage. The *Indiani*, though identifying the Indians as victims of European and American colonialism, never seemed to care too much about the "real" Indians of the past, or about the struggles of contemporary Native Americans, of which they did not even seem to know the existence.[7] They were by and large satisfied with exploiting the conventional image of the Indian in what they considered a revolutionary way. This attitude of exalting as genuinely revolutionary everything normally considered evil by society - an attitude defined by Franco Rella as an "idealization of the negative" - was widesspread in the 1977 movement. Rella has traced the origin of this "myth of the Other" in the work of French intellectuals, notably Felix Guattari and Gilles Deleuze, and, to a limited extent, also Jacques Lacan and Michel Foucault (Rella 1978). Deleuze and Guattari, especially in books like *L'Anti-Oedipe* and *Rizoma* - works which circulated among the movement - idealize the "other" of society as a harbinger of revolution. Tramps, freaks, punks, and madmen are considered as being *automatically* bearers of alternative values which society cannot tolerate. Drawing a simple conclusion from such assumptions, many in the movement ended up believing that "the evil expelled by society must necessarily be our own good, our own value" (Rella 1978:13). Yet, no matter how much one may wish to turn this "evil" into a "new value," one is still using definitions taken from the very language of power rejected in the first place, thus reinforcing, rather than undermining, such language. To a large extent, the *Indiani* provide a virtual textbook explanation of this theoretical deadlock. They idealized the Indian as a pure "other" of Western civilization; yet, the Indian thus idealized was still the Indian as perceived and depicted by Western civilization itself. This contradiction can be effectively illustrated by quoting in its entirety a poster written by the *Indiani* sometime in February 1977. The poster was handwritten and divided into two parts by a drawing of an Indian with a tomahawk, smoking his calumet.

"We shall never bury our hatchet again!
AUGH! The season of the great rains is coming to an end; the colors of nature are reappearing, wiping out sadness and boredom, the cold and fear of our bodies.
More than once the People of the Human Beings have, during the winter, called together all their tribes in order to seek joy and happiness, love and light, warmth and fantasy.
We have danced around the fire of our fantasy for a long time; we have danced around the totem of our lucid madness for a long time; then, the People of the Human Beings were scattered... the Blue-coats crowed over their victory, thinking we had been defeated for good, and pushed us, with their thundering sticks, into our reservations.
BUT THE PEOPLE OF THE HUMAN BEINGS ARE ALIVE! THEIR STRENGTH AND THEIR CREATIVITY WERE NEVER EXTINGUISHED!! THE GREAT SPIRIT OF FANTASY HAS BURST ONCE AGAIN INTO OUR VIBRATIONS!!
Augh! Last Wednesday the new moon illuminated our faces with new war colors, our minds exploded in thousands and thousands of colors of woe, happiness, love... It is time for all the tribes of the Human Beings to get together around the big totem to sing with more joy and more strength our songs of war and revel... it is time for the People of the Human Beings to go down the valleys and get back everything that the Blue-coats have denied us...
OUT OF THE RESERVATIONS!! LET'S STRIKE UP OUR WAR CRY.
OUR TOM TOMS WILL SOUND LOUDER AND LOUDER TO CALL TOGETHER ALL THE CREATIVE GROUPS OF THE MOVEMENT....
Monday, at 4 p.m. - Room 6, Dept. of Literature, in order to organize the Carnival of the People of the Human Beings and destroy the Blue-coats with the colors of our FANTASY....
AUGH!
(La Nostra Assemblea 1977:103).

590

The *Indiani* write in language typical of average Western movies. They grunt "AUGH," invoke the "Great Spirit" (of fantasy), and call the policemen "Blue-coats" and their guns "thundering sticks." The *Indiani Metropolitani* seem undistrubed by the fact that this kind of language is, essentially, the racist language put in the mouth of Indians by Whites. Thus, the "myth of the Indian" created by the *Indiani Metropolitani* ends up, paradoxically, endorsing, rather than criticizing or exposing, current stereotypes about Native Americans. Even those sections of the poster devoted to "vibrations" and "fantasy" are just stale attempts to create a late twentieth century Noble Savage.

Yet it is fair to note that this is only one side of the coin. Although the language used by the *Indiani* may be irritating, one should add that it was often effectively employed to talk about political issues in ironic, even ludicrous, ways. The following excerpts, from a "letter" sent by the *Indiani* to Cossiga - at the time the Italian Home Secretary - provide a good example of this strategy:

"Dear Secretary,
with deep satisfaction we were able to watch, thanks to the magic-box, your Teutonic pale face, and to listen to your hissing forked tongue and your metallic voice spitting venom against the People of the Human Beings.
'These people should know that we will not tolerate their efforts to transform the university into a den of Metropolitan Indians, freaks, and hippies. We are ready to employ what they call the forces of repression and what I call the forces of order and democracy.'
With these words you declared war on us....
You would like to push us back into those reservations you have prepared for us, into the ghettos of oppression and desperation....
Your Blue-coats, dressed up like extra-terrestrials, have pushed us out of the university, thus thinking they could break up our dreams, our hopes of changing the world and ourselves....
But with your tin brains, capable only of devising famine, repression, violence, special laws, and death, you haven't realized that you cannot destroy us because our rage and our fantasy are stronger than your desire for revenge.
We shall take the university back....
As long as the grass shall grow and the sun shall warm our bodies and the water wet us and the wind blow through our hair
WE SHALL NEVER BURY OUR HATCHET AGAIN!!!"
(La Nostra Assemblea 1977:140-141).

The *Indiani* are still calling themselves "the People of the Human Beings" and display a faked wonder in front of "White" technology - "magic box," of course, stands for television. The last sentence of the letter, along with the second-rate romanticism of the whole piece, shows that its authors have probably read Dee Brown's *Bury My Heart at Wounded Knee* or *Black Elk Speaks*, and are trying to echo them. However, we see no attempt whatsoever to criticize stereotypes and clichés about the Indians. Following an old and lasting European tradition which goes back at least to Lahontan's *Dialogues Curieux* (1705), the *Indiani Metropolitani* used the Indian simply as a mask through which they could attack Western society. Even the parallel proposed in the letter between urban ghettos and Indian reservations cannot be taken too seriously. In spite of all this, one must admit that, adopting an "Indian" point of view, the *Indiani Metropolitani* were able to draw sarcastic pictures of complex political problems, forcing people to look at them in a new light.

More importantly, one of the most dramatic problems of the 1977 movement was that of finding a language capable of justifying a revolt often defined by the majority of traditional leftist authorities in very unfavorable terms. Generally speaking, for the two traditional leftist parties - and especially for the P.C.I. -, for the trade-unions, and even for some among the New Left, the movement was at best a desperate and irrational rebellion of young lumpenproletarians and petit-bourgeois students, and at worst a direct attack against the primacy of the working class itself. Massimo d'Alema, at the time secretary of the Communist Party Youth Council, declared once that, "gli indiani, più che metropolitani, sono democristiani" (the Indians, rather than being Metropolitan, are Christian Democratic), claiming that the movement - harshly critical of the P.C.I. and of the trade-unions' policy of cooperation with industrialists for common action against economic depression - was objectively helping conservative forces in a "conspiracy" against unionized working class (La Nostra Assemblea 1977:141).

This is not the place to comment on such intricate and thorny problems. All I wish to argue is that, for a movement of students and unemployed that could neither call itself a workers' movement, nor claim to share some of the same objectives of the trade-unions (as it had happened during the 1968 uprising), the Indian became a convenient symbol of all those people who were forced to live within society without sharing its goals and benefitting from it. Since conventional Marxist jargon seemed to lack the right terms to describe the condition and aspirations of many young people. some of them resorted to an "Indian" language. Thus, the 1876 Little Big Horn battle came to replace the Paris Commune or the Russian revolution as an early example of revolutionary struggle, while General Custer was regarded as a prototype of American imperialism. But while some among the *Indiani* were indeed eager to attack all forms of Western thought, including Marxism, many were also taking pains to keep the group within the boundaries of the New Left. Since the *Indiani* were always a very informal group, lacking any kind of centralized structure, it is quite hard to discuss their politics. However, it may be argued that, following

592

the first weeks of the 1977 revolt, when it became more urgent to define strategies for political action, three different positions emerged among the *Indiani*. For some, the *Indiani Metropolitani* had to keep alive their link with genuine Marxist traditions. For others, the *Indiani* had to remain radically different from leftist organizations, emphasizing instead their anarchist and countercultural trends. Finally, for some others, the *Indiani* were to emphasize their aggressiveness and warlike attitudes, doing away with "folklore" and with pacifist ideologies. Of course, to each one of these positions corresponds a different image of the Indian.[8]

The first group was not content simply to place the *Indiani* within the tradition of revolutionary Marxism, and even claimed that the *Indiani Metropolitani* represented an important return to a genuine Marxist spirit. This idea is advanced in a letter published in the leftist daily newspaper *Lotta Continua* and signed by "Beccofino." "Beccofino" - a nickname for a shrewd philosophy student - argued that the *Indiani's* revolt against the world of politics had been first called for by Karl Marx himself. In his letter, aptly entitled "Was anybody more of an Indian than Karl Marx?", he writes:

"It seems to me paradoxical that we, people of the reservations, should introduce Marxist criticism in the political debate of the movement.... Let me quote the famous Karl Marx. Here's what good old Karl writes, 'Aren't all revolts exploding, with no exceptions, in a desperate isolation from community? Isn't this isolation necessary to each revolt? But the community from which the worker is isolated is very much different from the political community. The community from which his work separates him is life itself, physical and spiritual life, human morality, human pleasure, human essence. Human essence is the true human community. Just as the desperate isolation from it is incomparably more universal, unbearable, threatening, contradictory than the isolation from political community, so the overcoming of such isolation, and even a partial revolt against it, is more infinite, as the more infinite is human life compared to political life. Thus social revolt may be as much limited as you wish, but it carries within itself a universal spirit; political revolt may be as much universal as you wish but, hidden behind its colossal forms, it conceals a narrow spirit....' Was Karl Marx an Indian? And, more importantly, are the *Indiani Metropolitani* the best interpreters of the Marxist gospel?"[9]

"Beccofino" goes on to argue that he is not so much interested in establishing whether the *Indiani* are the only pure Marxists or not, but rather in noting that those who attack them for being either too moderate ("worker's autonomy" groups) or too extremist (conservatives and traditional leftists alike) are both trying to force the movement into the "narrow spirit" and the narrow views of conventional politics. On the contrary, the *Indiani* are Marxist in that

593

they embody the "universal spirit" of social revolt. The Indian, therefore, is used in the letter as a symbol of those who aspire to be reconciled with their own selves and the surrounding world. "Indians" are all the people who refuse alienation and struggle to stay "human" - those who look forward to that society where, in Marx's own words, "the free development of each is the condition for the free development of all."[10] "Indian" becomes thus a code word for a particular political position within the 1977 movement.

A second group among the *Indiani* seemed more anxious to identify the Indian with the "other" of Western culture. Though continuing to talk a great deal about communism, these *Indiani* were clearly more indebted to counterculture, beat literature, and ecologism than to Marxism. Using the Indian as a symbol of the utterly free individual, of the anarchist living without ties and worries, this group was largely responsible for the so-called "Indian platform" presented by the *Indiani Metropolitani* during the national assembly of the movement on February 26. Among other things, the platform called for "complete liberalization of marijuana, hashish, L.S.D.," for a "square kilometer of green for each citizen," and for "freedom for all animals imprisoned in cages and private houses" (La Nostra Assemblea 1977:146). Describing the movement as "a flux of vibrations," some among these countercultural Indians also started the publication of an irregular, "wow-dada" magazine called *OASK*, which lasted for a few months.

A final group was made up of those *Indiani* who sympathized with the strategy of "autonomia operaia" - a strategy attacked by "Beccofino" as being just another embodiment of an ultimately bourgeois ideology. Lamenting that the *Indiani Metropolitani* were prone to intellectual abstractions and had rapidly become "folkloristic," this group eventually gave up the name *Indiani Metropolitani* and formed a new "tribe": the *Indiani dei Pascoli Alti* (Indians of the High Pastures). The group chose as its motto "true hatchet," in juxtaposition to the purely symbolical rubber hatchets of the *Indiani Metropolitani*. The *Indiani dei Pascoli Alti* looked at the Indian as a subversive warrior par excellence, breaking off with the too peaceful *Indiani Metropolitani* whom they considered ready to sign separate "peace treaties" with the enemy.

Internal divisions, along with a general weakening of the whole movement, brought the *Indiani* to an end. By the last months of 1977, when the Red Brigades and other terrorist groups came violently on the scene, the *Indiani Metropolitani*, as well as the other "creative" groups of the movement, had disappeared. The hope of reconciling politics with private life, keeping alive the "universal spirit" of social revolt, had thus been frustrated. Looking at the 1977 revolt today, no one can fail to see its several shortcomings and the naive beliefs of a movement that seemed to ask no less than the birth of a utopian society in a few months time. Yet we cannot choose to ignore the social causes of a revolt which would be definitely wrong to discard as a "conspiracy." At the same time, I think, young people in the movement could

594

hardly be criticized for having protested that unionized working class could not be seen as the only legitimate bearer of the new values of a socialist future.

But our concern is with how the *Indiani* exploited the image of the Indian. More than a decade ago, Vine Deloria wrote that Whites are generally incapable of seeing Indians; instead, they see *through* them.

"The American public feels most comfortable with the mythical Indians of stereotype-land.... These Indians are fierce, they wear feathers and grunt.... To be an Indian in modern American society is in a very real sense to be unreal and ahistorical" (Deloria 1969:10).

Deloria's critique could also be applied to the *Indiani Metropolitani*, who thought that Indians should wear colorful feathers, grunt "augh," and be always fierce and ready to fight. The *Indiani* showed some elementary knowledge of Indian history (Custer, the Little Big Horn, and a few other events often portrayed in Western movies), but they seemed to regard Indians largely as "unreal and ahistorical" figures. The ultimate irony of a group that cherished irony as one of the best weapons against bourgeois ideology, is that, in the name of revolution, the *Indiani Metropolitani* resorted to reactionary stereotypes, or to blatant distortions of the Indian world. One should only think of the efforts made by some *Indiani* to depict Indians as anarchists in front of how much Indian societies were - and are - formed on status and social prestige.[11] Similarly, the enthusiasm for "freedom and creativity" made the *Indiani* prefer trite romantic notions about primitive peoples to everything Lévi-Strauss and structuralist anthropology have taught us about the rationality, as well as the rigidity, of tribal cultures.

It is worth noting, that, in their political exploitation of the Indian, the *Indiani Metropolitani* had some renowned forerunners. The Illuminists and the French *philosophes* from Rousseau to Diderot often used the image of the free savage to support their political battle in favor of bourgeois rights (see Gliozzi 1971). Unconsciously following that example, the *Indiani* used the image of the Indian to articulate their unorthodox views about leftist politics. Especially in view of their revolutionary aims, one can hardly forgive the *Indiani* their naive acceptance of a stereotyped portrait of the Indian. The *Indiani* would probably defend themselves by answering that they never meant to endorse colonialist commonplaces, nor indeed to talk about "real" Indians. They simply wished to use the Indian world as a metaphor for describing the alienating conditions in which many young people live today. Up to a certain point, a parallel between the oppression experienced by many "young proletarians" in the great cities of the Western hemisphere, and the oppression experienced by urban Indians in the United States, may have been a legitimate one. But ignoring the contemporary life conditions of Native Americans, and referring to them only as mythical figures from a fairy tale past, the *Indiani Metropolitani* unwittingly accepted too many stereotypes and clichés. Although their original intention might have been to expose the myth of the American frontier and the Wild West, the *Indiani* were not able to change the rules of the game. Once again, America showed itself capable of providing people with a myth which had built into itself its own critique, its own negation. Maybe this is why in the Western world - even for leftists - it is hard to get rid of American mythologies. But this is a problem which goes far beyond the case of the *Indiani Metropolitani*.

NOTES

1. The most interesting works on the 1977 movement include Autori Molti Compagni 1977, La Nostra Assemblea 1977, Collettive Primo Maggio 1978, Lerner et al. 1978. Among the journals that have devoted entire issues to the 1977 movement in Rome one should mention at least *L'Altra Roma* 11-12 (March/April 1977), and *Quaderni Comunisti* 3 (May 1977). For a strictly theoretical and philosophical discussion of some political issues raised by the 1977 movement see also *Aut-Aut* 161 (September/October 1977).
2. To avoid confusion, one has to keep in mind that the Italian New Left comes from a Marxist tradition and bears little resemblance to the American New Left.
3. It is perhaps noteworthy that in spite of the severe crisis of the Italian New Left, at the time of this writing (1984) D.P. is still alive and holds seven seats in the Italian parliament and one seat in the European parliament.
4. My translation. I have omitted one untranslatable line.
5. The names "Felce e Mirtillo" and "Il Panettone" require a few words of explanation. The first - literally "Firn and Bilberry" - implies a word-play on the Italian "Falce e Martello" - "Sickle and Hammer." The second is the name of a Milanese Christmas cake.
6. Here and elsewhere the translations are mine.
7. A fine article on this and related issues is Ludovici (1977). The *Indiani Metropolitani*, however, were instrumental in bringing about a renewed interest in the American Indians; many books on Indians have been published in Italy since 1977 (cp. Giordano, this volume). On some early reactions to the *Indiani Metropolitani* see Ludovici and Mariani (1977).
8. One should not think of these groups within the *Indiani* as being rigidly separated. Often people fluctuated between two groups, or felt they did not belong to any one of them.
9. *Lotta Continua*, 29 April 1977. Also reprinted in *Quaderni Comunisti* 3 (May 1977), 93-94. The long Marx quotation is from "Glosse," in the Italian edition of Marx's complete works, vol.III, p.220.
10. The phrase is from *The Communist Manifesto*.
11. Deloria (1969:229) makes the same point in relation to the hippies' "tribalizing attempts."

REFERENCES CITED

Autori Molti Compagni
  1977   Bologna 1977... Fatti Nostri... Verona: Bertani.
Collettivo Primo Maggio
  1978   La Tribù delle Talpe. Milano: Feltrinelli.
Deloria, Vine Jr.
  1969   Custer Died for Your Sins. New York: Avon Books.
Gliozzi, Giuliano
  1971   La Scoperta dei Selvaggi. Milano: Pricipato.
La Nostra Assemblea
  1977   Le Radice di una Rivolta. Milano: Feltrinelli.
Lerner, Gad, Luigi Manconi, Marino Sinibaldi
  1978   Uno Strano Movimento di Strani Studenti. Milano: Feltrinelli.
Ludovici, Paola
  1977   Chi sono gli Indiani Metropolitani. I Giorni Cantati 10 (April-May
           1977):46-47.
Ludovici, Paola, and Giorgio Mariani
  1977   Gli Indiani Usa: dal folklore alla lotta contro l'imperialismo
           americano. Quotidiano dei Lavoratori 19 (August 1977):3.
Rella Franco
  1978   Il Mito dell'Altro. Milano: Feltrinelli.

THE "POLISH MOVEMENT OF
FRIENDS OF THE AMERICAN INDIANS"

Ewa Nowicka

About ten years ago the "Polish Movement of Friends of the American Indians" arose in Poland and has since tended to gain permanency and to grow. This paper will present data on this phenomenon and aims to formulating hypotheses on its origin and to proving their validity.

Because of the lack of a formal organization and of any doctrinal documents such as programs, manifestos, etc., a systematic presentation of the movement in question is not an easy talk. The following data are based on various materials that are neither full nor satisfactory. As members of the Movement spend a considerable amount of time engaging in conversations, discussions, and social contacts, the basic sources of this paper are on one hand written and recorded statements, and on the other hand observations of behavior. Among the behavioral aspects are, e.g., the way the Movement's annual rallies are held, the mutual relations of the members of the Movement among themselves and with other persons, their reading, and their kind of emotions.

Another problem with such an overall description of the Movement is the high level of personal differentiation and individualization among the members. Individualism could even be regarded as an important point of their program or rather a consciously accepted life-orientation.

The Movement, *Polski Ruch Przyjaciół Indian* (hereinafter abbreviated: PRPI), is obviously not a mass phenomenon. It embraces several hundred young people of both sexes living in various regions of Poland. Apart from the Warsaw group, the most active chapters are those in small towns. The "core" of the PRPI consists of no more than 150 persons, though it is difficult to give the exact number. Apart from the "core" of the PRPI, there is a much larger and at the same time much more fluctuating group of "ordinary" members (as they might be called), and the still larger group of sympathizers - people who maintain friendly but rather sporadic relations with "the core" and with the "ordinary" members of the Movement. Altogether there are no more than one thousand Friends of the American Indians, people who consider themselves members of the Movement.

The average age of members is about twenty years, and the range is between seventeen and twenty-five. The majority of them is male. Former members of the "core" usually become "ordinary" members after getting married, and move to the ranks of sympathizers when they have children of their own. The struggles with everyday life represent the basic obstacle in the continuation of activities in the Movement.

Most often, members of PRPI are high-school, college, or university students, clerks, rarely also workers or young peasants. Their age to a high dregree determines their social status: The fact that members of the urban and rural working class mature earlier socially seems to be the main factor responsible for the lesser interest in the Movement among the more down-to-earth youths of these social classes. On the other hand, the interest in the Movement appears to be stronger in small towns rather than in the big cities. For the young people in those and in isolates towns, the PRPI supposedly becomes the symbol of an important exotic and world cause.

Polish society at large is almost totally unaware of the Movement: PRPI is almost invisible to the public. Though it is of small size and does not have a large appeal, in a way the Movement is an important phenomenon in the lives of the young generation of contemporary Poles. As an element on the cultural and social scene, it is one of the expressions of young Poles' aspirations, dreams, values, and ideological solutions.

The PRPI consists of small, informal groups, which are in more or less permanent contact or at least know about each other. Piotruś and a few other boys fulfil the role of messengers or go-betweens. Members of the Movement visit and write letters to each other. The doctrine of PRPI is neither clearly structured, nor codified, nor coherent. It manifests itself in the interests and preoccupations of its members. One can, however, observe a process of crystallization of their ideology, as it was reflected in the debates about the name of the Movement and the organization of sections in the Movement. At the very beginning, its slighty more than a hundred members were not interested in giving themselves a name. Some of them used the name "Polish Movement for American Indians," others chose "The Movement of the People of Nature" (or just "People of Nature"). It was only at the rally of 1981 that the name "Polish Movement of Friends of the American Indians" was accepted by the majority of the participants. Some believed that the name was not important at all and not necessary, but others insisted that it should be chosen and should express the essence of the Movement's program. The name finally decided upon is now commonly used, even though all three former names afford a reasonable insight into the general differentiation of the interests and activities of its members.

During the 1983 rally, five separate sections were organized: 1. Protection of Nature, 2. Socio-Political Section, 3. Folklore, 4. Research, 5. Translation and Publication. Thus the three basic lines of activities and interests were formally channelled by being named, articulated, and separated. Ultimately these different tendencies are inseparable, but in individuals one type of activity or the other usually dominates. The three trends which will be discussed below are:

(1) an interest in nature, the environment; this is very close to the ecological movement, and to the ideology of Green parties elsewhere;

(2) activities in support for the political and social rights of contemporary American Indians;

(3) propagation of sound information on the history, cultures, and present

600

condition of the American Indians.

The members of PRPI, who are interested in the Indians as the people of nature, have come to their current preoccupation from two different directions: There are those whose interest in nature and the ecological movement has led them to the life-ways and philosophies of the American Indian, which seemed to provide ready-made formulas for the solution of their problems; others have moved from a romantic fascination with American Indian life to the concepts of protection of the natural environment, and to the struggle against the disastrous effects of industrial civilization. In the latter case, the interest in nature is secondary; it results from an interest in the history and the life of American Indians. Twenty-three year-old Tadeusz, one of the older PRPI members, claims priority for the Indian movement: "Now ecological clubs are being founded in Kraków and in Olsztyn, but the Movement for Nature under the auspices of Indian ideas has developed much earlier." This ecological priority is stressed by the fact that many members of PRPI have chosen occupations that bring them into close contact with nature: forestry, horticulture, or agriculture. There are also a few eccentrics who actually try to live in isolation from industrial civilization.

One of the most popular ideas among the members of PRPI is the opinion that Western civilization, produced by the White people, leads to man's self-destruction. The culture of American Indians, on the other hand, offers true humanistic values, authentic spiritual goods, and indicates a possible way to save the world from total annihilation. Tadeusz says explicitly: "I'm sure that the ideas from there [i.e. from American Indians] will point out the way to the future." And:

"When I look at the progress of the ecological movement, I am surprised that the scholars speak about nature exactly in the same way the Indians have done. There is an Indian text that originated very long ago. It says that the earth does not belong to man but on the contrary that man belongs to the earth. And, what happens to the earth, will happen to man. Man has not woven the web of life; he is only a thread in this web. Through destroying this web of life, he destroys himself."[1]

All members of PRPI that I have met are very sensitive to the beauty of nature. They love to spend their free time in the fields and particularly in the forests. Annual summer rallies are held in places especially chosen for the beauty of their surroundings: lakes, forests, mountains, or picturesque meadows. During these rallies the participants pay special attention to the cleanliness and the protection of the natural environment. They offer free help to local rangers and thus gain their confidence.

The nature-protection motive is usually linked to the motive of solidarity with the contemporary aspirations and struggles of the American Indians. The linking factor is that Indians are being viewed as the people of nature, living in an ideal harmony with their natural environment. One of the younger members of PRPI says:

"I believe sincerely that the support for the cause of the Indians is indeed the support for the cause of all people. And if the Indians are defeated, mankind will also have lost."

Polish Friends of American Indians maintain relatively permanent contact with several Indian organizations, periodicals, and even with specific individuals. The major difficulty arises from the fact that the majority of PRPI members does not know any English at all or at least well enough to read Indian newspapers or to write letters. This is why some of them work as translators for the others, but this procedure slows down the frequency of contact by letters. In spite of this PRPI regularly receives *Akwesasne Notes* and other Indian periodicals. Through these channels they keep in touch with the present problems of American Indian communities in particular places, yet their knowledge is far from being full or profound. Because of the nature of these contacts, the information PRPI members get is incomplete and limited.

The activities that PRPI members call "socio-political" include active support for the Indians, e.g., writing and sending of petitions protesting the abuse of legally guaranteed Indian rights, or sending letters and parcels to Indian prisoners. Due to the shortage of food and clothing in Poland itself, the sending of such parcels has recently been blocked by postal regulations. The PRPI plans a Long March on behalf of American Indians, but due to police regulations there is no chance for it in the near or distant future. Thus, support has to remain rather in the sphere of good will and symbolic gestures.

Lately the PRPI has kept in touch with other European groups and associations interested in American Indians: Particularly close are the ties with West German and Russian counterparts. Such contacts could give rise to new forms of activities.

Many members of PRPI consider the diffusion of correct and substantial information on Indians in Polish society the principal goal of the Movement. One of the older members of PRPI explains this point: "No nation (except White people) did such harm to another nation by falsifying its history and culture." The PRPI people believe that Polish society should learn the truth about American Indians, about their tragic history and often no less tragic present-day problems. They stress that the image of American Indians in our society is formed by Western movies and bad literature. In order to propagate true knowledge, they have to read about Indian life and history. For this reason the Warsaw chapter has organized a section devoted to scholarly research on American Indians. The people interested in this section are mostly university students. Witek, a 19-year old philosophy student, and his friends (students and future students) have organized a scholarly conference on this subject matter in March 1984. Translation of fragments from the Indian press and from the professional anthropological and historical literature are to play an important role in the process of self-education, and later on also in propaganda.

The so-called "folklore" section is interested in gathering information on American Indian art, material culture, religion, and philosophy. They sew their own Indian costumes, and learn Indian songs and dances. During the annual summer rallies participants smoke the pipe, dance and sing in an Indian way, and live in a kind of tipi made of textile. There is obviously an element of play involved, but it is treated seriously and with true sentiments. Some of the local PRPI chapters name themselves after Indian tribes such as Ottawa or Dakota. Genuine identification is mixed here with the children's game of Cowboys and Indians. The costumes and the behavior of the participants of the rallies often results in mockery and ridicule of local people and of tourists who happen to come across such assemblies.

All statements of PRPI members are permeated by a poetic and romantic aura. They use a language full of metaphors, often naive and cheap, but always full of true and authentic involvement. Yet, this type of speech is not always easy to interpret and rather vague. The following passage from a statement of 18-year old Agnieszka is probably a fair illustration of this style:

"Indians will not perish as long as nature exists, as long as the luxuriant grass of the prairies is billowy thanks to the wind, as long as animals are in the forests..."

A mystic trend, connected with a preoccupation with herbs, prophecies, oracles, and magic is to be found in PRPI. This, however, is not the dominant tendency.

Much more important is an element of self-improvement in the Movement. All members stress their indebtedness to the Indians. They claim that their lives (in fact, only their minds) have changed radically under the influence of Indian philosophy. Indian life has opened their eyes to a new and authentic perspective. Jacek, one of the younger members, put it thus:

"Thanks to the American Indian Movement philosophy I began to understand the world - the world in the spirit of Crazy Horse, Sitting Bull, Crow Dog, and Russell Means. Thanks to the Indians I have found my place in life. I feel well."

Another young member of the Movement states:

"Indians taught me how to walk a path of beauty, truth, and honesty. They taught me how to love nature and live in friendship and harmony with the world. They taught me perseverance in difficult situations of life. Thanks to them I am simply better. I have never been disappointed in them," Romek, a 22-year old worker, explains how Indian philosophy helped him to live trough the obligatory military service.

All the PRPI members I know air their strong feeling that their commitment to the Indian cause has been an important step in their lives. Anna, a 21-year old student, says:

"Among these people who call themselves Friends of Indians, I have undergone my spiritual transformation. Thanks to Indian philosophy, which contains profound ideas that cannot be expressed in simple words, I have obtained strength and confidence. Indians are my spiritual teachers. Words are unable to express the treasure I have received from them. Words cannot express what the heart feels that is full of love for my red brothers."

The members of PRPI unanimously stress that one of the most important motivations of their continued association with the Movement is the satisfaction of being together in a friendly group of people sharing the same thoughts and feelings. Nineteen-year-old Magda, a high school student, says that her first contact with the Movement occured at the annual rally of 1983: "The rally was a wonderful experience of cordial relations, of close and profound friendship." Thus it is symptomatic that PRPI members often marry amongst themselves and that long lasting friendship are the rule.

An important person in the process of integration of the Movement was and in a way still is Stefania Antoniewicz, better known as *Indiahska Babcia* (Indian Grandma). She died on 13 December 1982, at the age of 85. I remember her as a little, slender old woman with great personal charm and rhetoric talent. There was a mysterious spiritual power in the small body of the Indian Grandma. People connected with the Movement often met in her apartment, which she shared with her large family: her grandson, his wife and daughter, her granddaughter, her husband and daughter. Indian Grandma could not speak any English and could hardly read English language literature (as she had received her education at a time when French was taught as the major foreign language). Her knowledge about American Indians was equal to that of the average member of the Movement: very detailed and fragmentary at the same time. She knew how to talk in a poetic and beautiful way about the Indians. Her identification with the problems of the Indians was truly amazing. "When they had taken the Black Hills from *us*...," she once said. Her spiritual identification was reflected in her correspondence with Indian prisoners. In her lifetime, Indian Grandma was a "living voice" of the Indian people for PRPI members. Now that she is dead, she has become a symbol consolidating the

Movement. PRPI members plan to donate a commemorative plaque to be placed on her grave in a Warsaw cemetery. The Indian Grandma once said about the origins of her interests in Indians:

"In fact, my interest in the American Indian awoke at the same time that the American Indian Movement came into being. But spiritually, I've always lived according to Indian values, ever since my childhood. Indian values are dear to me: these were the earth, the plants, the animals, and the stars."

She was already over seventy years old when her interest in the Indians "became formal." At that time she started to write letters to several Indian organizations and received answers. From *Akwesasne Notes* she took the list of prisoners to whom she began sending letters. Yellow Hand was one of the most faithful pen-pals of Indian Grandma.

Yet another source of inspiration for Indian Grandma were the books of Carlos Castaneda. She was completely taken by "the other way of knowledge," different from the European (or rather Greek) tradition. In this way of thinking she found the true reality.

Contacts with Indian Grandma gave PRPI members the feeling of having real contact with Indians, their values, problems, and traditions. She was the spiritual leader of the Movement, albeit completely informal and mysteriously powerful. Tadeusz jokingly remarked that when he wanted to explain the nature of Indian Grandma's personality to his friends in Olsztyn, he used to say: "Grandma hovers five centimeters above her bed." He thought that there was no other way to describe her. Grandma contributed the basic general ideas to the Movement. She thought that the most important element of everybody's life should be love, and consistency in the implementation of one's decisions. From one of her American friends she once received a handful of the soil of Wounded Knee, which she kept under her bed, thus literally sleeping on it.

An explanation for the origin of PRPI must go beyond the observation that most Polish children and youths go through the stage of standard readings on American Indians: James Fenimore Cooper, Karl May, as well as Polish authors such as Arkady Fiedler, Alfred Szklarski, Nora Szczepanska, Wiesław Wernic. But not every young person develops this early fascination into a more serious interest in the history and particularly in the contemporary situation of American Indians. The first manifestation of the Movement began in the early 1970s. One of the stimuli were the well known and publicized events surrounding the occupation of Alcatraz and of Wounded Knee. At the same time, this was a period of ascendancy for counter-culture, protest, and youth ideology in Poland. In spite of their weakness in Poland, these ideologies represented values identical to those appearing earlier on in the United States and in Western Europe. When the ethnic minorities and particularly the American

Indians became elements of the political scene, problems of Native Americans assumed the role of principal ideological themes. The voice of the new American Indian Movement, Red Power in other words, reached Poland and added a new emotional feature to the traditional image of American Indians promoted by earlier and mostly fictional literature among children and teen-agers.

The sense of friendship in the group, as mentioned above, is yet another element in the origin of PRPI. All PRPI members who participated in the first rally of 1977, which was then organized by the Polish Scouts Organization, remember this first meeting as a source of a wonderful feeling of being together with like-minded people, and of no longer being alone in identifying with certain values. This community spirit is still present in PRPI and for many participants acts as an important source of motivation for the activities of the Movement.

Three factors, then, seem to have importantly contributed to the process of formation of PRPI:
(1) The image of the American Indian as determined by juvenile fiction;
(2) The ideas and events of the youth protest movements;
(3) The need of belonging and of close interpersonal contacts.

As Polish junvenile fiction dealing with Indians is but little known outside its country of origin, it may be worthwhile to take a short look at some of its peculiarities. Features such as romanticism, the apology of good and noble characters versus evil and mean creatures, and admiration of nature and the close relationship between people and nature, as well as a fondness for an adventurous yet honest life - all of these may be counted among the shared features of Polish and non-Polish literature of this kind. In these few common characteristics we may also easily identify several important elements of PRPI ideology.

One of the peculiarities of the Polish books on Native Americans is the presence of heroes of Polish origin or nationality. While this is paralleled in other national literatures, for readers in Poland the presence of a specifically Polish brand of Indian fiction made all the difference. In it the Polish romantic value set as represented by Polish national heroes is smoothly combined with the usual value syndrome as outlined above. Accordingly, this Polish national hero complex paved the way for an easier assimilation of values associated with American Indians into the minds of Polish youths.

The most popular book among young Poles undoubtedly is *Tomek na wojenney ściezce* (Tomek on the war path) by Alfred Szklarski. Its hero is a sixteen-year-old Polish boy visiting the United States. Tomek is tall, strong, intelligent, honest, rightful, and sensitive to human suffering - a young man of integrity and courage. Having read a lot of books, he knows all about Indians and has a high regard for them. He understands and excuses the Indians' distrust and hatred towards the Whites. Due to his noble conduct, he himself gains their respect and friendship. Being a Pole, he can understand Indians even better: he points out that his country remains under the Russian yoke (the action of the book is set at the beginning of the 20th century), so he knows from personal experience the fate of people denied its freedom. American authorities treat Indians in a similar way the Czarist rule treats Polish patriots. The lot of the Seminole tribe is comparable, according to Tomek's account, to the lot of the Polish political emigrants who are practically banned from returning to their own country. Thanks to these political similarities he has a much better rapport with the Indians than white Americans have. He always tries to explain to his Indian friends that he is not an American and that his far-away people knows the meaning of foreign rule and persecution.

Another Polish character in the book is the boatswain Nowicki, a colorful personality and Tomek's tutor. He is much less sophisticated than Tomek; but he is a strong and big young man, simple and good-natured, brave and honest. His opinions about Indians are frequently simplistic and stereotyped, thus requiring to be corrected by the much more knowledgable Tomek. Yet his bravery and courage saves him from the hands of hostile Indians. Being tied to the post awaiting his tortures and ultimately the end of his life, he sings an old Polish patriotic song expressing the determination to fight and praising the value of courage: "Albeit the storm is roaring around us, Let us hold our heads high..." The Indians are awed by such brave conduct and the boatswain is saved.

Szklarski describes the Ghost Dance as a revolutionary movement and compares it to the Polish national insurrections against foreign rule. This is in agreement with the sentiments of Karl May's hero, Old Shatterhand, that "Indians are friends of their friends, and enemies of their enemies."

While the majority of Indians are good and noble people, there are also bad Indians: Those who are not loyal to other tribes and who reject their traditional ways and are effectively servants of the Whites. But these bad Indians are only just as bad as the bad Whites. There are good and bad people in every nation or race, Tomek concludes. Unconditional friendship and loyalty are the prominent feature of Indian conduct. Serious friendship is often expressed in acts of bravery and self-sacrifice.

The wild Indians still living off the reservation represent the highest level of moral values, as they have not yet been corrupted by contacts with Whites and their civilization. The influence of Whites kills the healthy spirit of the traditional Indian community. The situation of political submission makes the people less pround and self-confident. The groups that had not yet accepted reservation status are compared with the Poles who organized insurrections and would never agree to foreign rule.

This element, in a sense, recurs in the opinions of PRPI members. They stress that they are neither members of any official organization, nor accept the principal elements defining the political situation of contemporary Poland.

There are, however, traditional Indian customs that are repulsive to the Polish characters in Szklarski's book, especially the bloodthirsty habit of killing their captives. Tomek ultimately succeeds in persuading his Indian friends to stop that custom. He teaches them to avoid bloodshed whenever possible and points to the example of two Polish national heroes (Pawel Strzelecki and Tadeusz Kościuszko) who stood up for the defense of prisoners of war.

Indians are always described as the people of nature, living in a close contact with their natural environment. They know how to use the natural resources, they are knowledgable about the habits of animals and the values of plants. They live in full harmony with nature. This is one of the central elements of PRPI doctrine, and it is certainly based on this type of literature. For most of the PRPI members this literature is the primary and basic source of their knowledge about Indians, and undoubtedly it shapes their attitudes towards European civilization, nature, and moral duties.

NOTE

1. Reference is, of course, to the most recent version of the Seattle Speech. Cp. Rudolf Kaiser's paper in this volume (Editor's note).

INDIANS AND EUROPE?
EDITOR'S POSTSCRIPT

Christian F. Feest

A simple explanation for the reasons of the special relationship between Europeans and the native populations of North America is that no such relationship exists. Under closer scrutiny it becomes apparent that all that interested and still interests Europeans is "Indians," a wholly fictional population inhabiting the Old World mind rather than the New World land. (Similar observations apply, of course, to the largely derivative notions of white Americans; cp. Berkhofer 1978.)

Images

Since the time of first contact, Europeans perceived the New People of the New World in terms of older traditions and experiences, submitting their new experiences to what might be called a process of intellectual domestication. A favorite approach was the application of the ancient rule by which distance in time and space is translated into difference in kind, and there is little wonder that the inhabitants of the now extended margins of the populated earth (as seen from Europe) were perceived as either being only marginally human, or "most gentle, louing, and faithfull, void of all guile, and treason, and such as liued after the manner of the golden age" (Quinn 1955:108) - or both. This was probably the easiest way to say that they were different, and there may be evidence to support the view that Native Americans perceived their first European guests in similarly generalized and antithetical terms.

For European visitors to North America, the power of expectation was such that they even saw phenomena which plainly never existed. Unipeds - humanoid monsters with only one leg - were "seen" both by the Viking explorers of Vinland and by Jacques Cartier more than five centuries later (Morison 1971:56). The gigantic stature of peoples in marginal locations could be observed in the case of the Susquehannock as seen by the early Jamestown colonists (Barbour 1969:343, 354, 408), as it had already been in the 16th century in the case of the Patagonians (Lestringant, this volume). Cynocephali or dog-headed natives were illustrated from South America (Colin, this volume), but they were also shown as inhabitants of North America by le Testu in 1555 (Cumming, Skelton, Quinn 1971: Fig.99).

The moral correlate of these physical deviations, in fact the ultimate negation of humanity, was considered to be cannibalism, both actually reported from the New World and imputed across the board where it could not be observed, as in the case of the Inuit (Sturtevant and Quinn, this volume; cp. Lestringant, this volume). The association of North American Indians with cannibalism was preserved into the 20th century and occurs even in the context of "noble savagism," adding a little spice to all the dull nobility (cp. Ferrero 1980:66).

"Indian" images were first shaped in 16th century Europe and did relate to the area south of the Rio Grande. The examples just given of identical approaches to native populations of North and South America show that these earliest stereotypes cannot be dismissed as irrelevant for North America. While in some cases the same generalized preconceptions were applied independently, in other instances the North American imagery was firmly built upon South American precedent. (In connection with clearly documented iconographic transfers, W.C. Sturtevant has elsewhere referred to this phenomenon as the "Tupinambization" of North American Indians.)

"Settling with the Indians" (Kupperman 1980) in the course of the actual European colonization of North America widened the horizons of observation, but attempts to recognize the shared human features in the neighboring native populations were shortlived due to the unwillingness of most of them to accept the fate of becoming subjects of those who derived a right to conquest from their alleged "superiority." Another reason working against a realistic approach was the tremendous range of different native cultures and languages encountered in America. As reasonable generalizations were almost impossible, stereotypes remained common.

It was in the 18th century that Indians began to be featured in European fiction on a larger scale (cp. Chinard 1934, Bissell 1925), and fiction was as what many of the earlier accounts should perhaps have been regarded anyway. But rather than ultimately exposing the images to public view as undisguised fiction, the new literary prominence (first French, then English, ultimately German - only much later in other languages) actually helped to contribute to the credibility of the characterizations. The prominence of literature in the proliferation of stereotypes was certainly aided by the comparable lack of well-written non-fiction in the face of public interest. The success of a few books that dealt extensively with native peoples of North America is illustrated by Jonathan Carver's "Travels" (see Williams, this volume) or John Dunn Hunter's "Memoirs" (1823) - both of which either contain fictional features or have at least been suspected of incorporating them. By the time journalism began to devote attention to Native American matters, the temptation to use established and recognizable images instead of differentiated realism was too strong to be overcome (cp. Schroeder, this volume). The perennial juxtaposition of Indians noble and savage provided enough tension to supply all the necessary ingredients Charles Dickens needed in twenty-one years to deal with American Indians (Orestano, this volume), and it even kept whole nations happy for a century or so (Borsányi, Rusinowa, this volume).

With increasing European exploration of the Pacific islands in the 18th century, the "Indian" image proved itself to be independent of the narrow confines of geography and was freely transferred from the continent to the islands. In a poem inspired by Captain Cook's voyages, the minor German village poet Schmidt (of Werneuchen) first describes the dreamy-eyed admiration felt by a European reader for the inhabitants of the Friendly Isles who are seen as sleeping peacefully and in eternal bliss in their "wigwams" after having devoured a hearty meal of bear's meat, ostrich eggs, and coconuts while using their patoo-patoos to chase away the cheatful traders; this striking image is contrasted with the self-confessed wretchedness of native life on the islands, defined by a continual state of war, by scalping and cannibalism, by a prevalence of fish for food, and by the naked rock for a bed (Schmidt 1981:179-182). Both of these opposing and competing images, merely embellished by some of the specific cultural features used to define "Indianness," may be seen alive and well in the poem.

Two centuries after South American images had been transplanted to the northern hemisphere, the North American Indian image had become dominant. Botocudos displayed in London in 1822 were dressed both in Plains Indian and Hawaiian costumes to protect them against the London weather (King, this volume). Even George Catlin's South American Indians bear an obvious resemblance to their North American colleagues (but then most of Catlin's Indians look alike, and in addition Catlin's South American trip appears to be mostly imaginary).

At the same time, the rapidly advancing frontier helped to shift the focus of European interest from the East to the trans-Mississippi West. New, but compatible visual imagery was supplied by Karl Bodmer and George Catlin, and found its widest distribution in third- and fourth-generation derivatives. The several waves of German immigration to the United States helped to keep alive the concern of those remaining behind for the new circumstances of their family, friends, and former compatriots, and the same is true of other countries affected by emigration to America (cp. Rusinowa, this volume). French attempts to gain a foothold in Mexico caused French writers to forget about the Hurons and make the Comanche and Apache their new stock heroes and villains, respectively. Karl May, the most influential of the 19th century German makers of Indian images, had learned his lesson when he had edited one of the several German translations of Gabriel Ferry's *Coureur de bois*. While the whole setting must have attracted May as it did many other German readers, he seems to have drawn his own conclusions from the fact that Ferry was French: If the arch-enemy of the German people was siding with the Comanche against the Apache, the latter necessarily had to be the Germans' potential allies. Winnetou, the "red gentleman" and slightly effeminate Indian chief and companion of the German first-person hero of May's novels, thus had to be an Apache. (More recently, a reform-minded member of the Socialist Party of Austria published an appeal for "more Comanches" in his party - if the Apache were friends of May, the petit bourgeois, the Comanches had to be the

611

socialists.)

A considerable amount of creative thought has been spent on the question of whether there were any differences in the attitudes of European colonial powers towards the native populations of North America (e.g., Peckham and Gibson 1969). That some such differences did exist can hardly be doubted, yet they may have been of less importance than the diversity of attitudes existing within the respective colonial societies, such as between missionaries, traders, and administrators. National differences in imagery were probably slight. It does not matter that the Hungarians were more interested in the Indians' horsemanship, or the French in making love to Indian maidens - in fact, these details relate to stereotypes about the European observers rather than the Indians. If nations who had themselves become colonial powers should be a little more prejudiced than those who had to do without the benefit of overseas possessions, this is hardly surprising. Most peoples actually perceived themselves in their respective literatures as the potentially better colonialists (e.g., Nowicka, this volume; also the unabashed anti-Americanism of the *Sarrasani* booklets in Conrad, this volume).

German claims for a special relationship with Indians may be correct to the extent that the "Indian" image was shaped significantly in Germany since the 16th century (Conrad, this volume), and that indeed the Germanic tribes as described by Tacitus once had been the "Indians" of the Romans. If a special relationship was perceived by German audiences, however, it was perhaps not so much true because of superior information or shared, parallel history. In an analysis of Karl May's treatment of Indians (in which the difference between imagery and reality is totally neglected), Lisa Barthel-Winkler, who during the Nazi period would write (under the pen name Barwin) novels in which the heroism of Indian leaders was explained by their assumed Viking ancestry, concluded: "In Winnetou Karl May delineates the Indian drama. It is also the German drama. Winnetou is the noble man of his race - he knows about the purity of the blood, the longing, and the hope of his brothers, but they have to founder because they are worn down by discord... This is Indian, this is also German. Who has grasped the meaning of the Indian drama has also grasped the meaning of the German drama" (Barthel-Winkler 1924:34). But it is not an analogy between the groups, it is identity: "The Beautiful Day [the lone Indian heroine of May's Indian novels] is - a German! Indian in her looks, her character, her fate - but her mind is German, is the poet's own, often almost womanlike tender, affectionate mind" (Winkler 1918:367).

Reports about Lakotas who wanted to be buried in Germany notwithstanding, the references to Germans in Lakota war songs indicate that the sentiments may not have been mutual (Theisz, this volume). During World War II, it is said that many Germans felt betrayed by their emotional allies when learning that Native Americans were serving in the U.S. Army to fight Germany.

Growing American influence in Western Europe since World War II, also known as "American cultural imperialism," has undoubtedly helped to level remaining differences in the way Indians are being perceived. American attempts to influence the contents of European textbooks were quite successful, and on a less official level of cultural politics the dissemination of Western movies and other popular culture accounts of American history proved to be equally effective. Despite all of these efforts, there remains a noticeable anti-American background to the European preoccupation with Indians. These sentiments apparently go back to the conservative shock about the American Revolution, and the biased view of American institutions and values, that Billington (1981) was displeased to note in 19th century European literature, is clearly carried by conservativism. It is ironic that the contemporary heirs of this time-hallowed Noble Indian/Ugly American-syndrome should mostly inhabit the left (red) side of the political spectrum.

Identification of possibly existing regional variables in European Indian visual imagery is hampered by a lack of sound and comparable data. In pre-photographic times, for example, it seems as if there was a difference in the frequency of pictorial representations of Indians, with English and Spanish material being quite rare, especially when compared to the works of French, Dutch, and German artists.

Similarly, 20th century comics with Indian subject matter have an erratic pattern of distribution in Europe and may be seen as an example of potential differences in the perception and diffusion of images (cp., e.g., Pompa 1983, Musso 1983, Malcorps 1982). More detailed studies of differences in which books are translated into which languages (cp. Giordano, this volume), or of contemporary newspaper coverage (cp. Schroeder, this volume) may also supply useful evidence.

If the "Indian" image in Europe has not remained static over time, the implication is not that perceptions of Native Americans have become different. A younger generation with strong ties to the peace movement has replaced the traditional Indian warrior stereotype with the new-fangled one of the peaceful Hopi - only the old-fashioned peace pipe has survived the change of emphasis. The 1887 version of Chief Seattle's speech, a product of American manifest-destiny thinking, never really caught on in Europe; the new ecological version, however, has made him Saint Seattle for Green Party sympathizers and the World Wildlife Fund (cp. Kaiser, this volume), and even a potential forerunner of Women's Lib (M. Kaiser 1984). Times are gone when Indians stood for macho values; today the "matriarchal" Indians - often epitomized by the Iroquois, sometimes by the Hopi - increasingly lead the way. In some respects, the cultural diversity of Native American societies, that was linked to the rise of the stereotypes, has also made it easier for the image to adapt.

Visitors

Given the spurious nature of the imagery, there was an understandable

613

desire on the part of critical Europeans to be finally faced with some facts. Short of taking the risk involved in going to the New World, observing live specimens of the American native race in Europe was the most obvious way to see for oneself. The history of Indian visits to Europe and European reactions to them still remains to be written (undocumented Foreman 1943 and a few partial summaries, such as Dickason 1984:205-229, notwithstanding). The following notes are primarily aimed at supplying some comparative context for the cases discussed in the present volume.

The practice of presenting native peoples as evidence for some "discovery" was established by Columbus himself who was able to present to the King of Spain six survivors out of ten "Indians" taken on board in the course of the first voyage. By 1501, at the latest, North American Indians had been brought to Lisbon and London (Quinn 1981:12-13). The likelihood that any of these visitors made their trans-Atlantic trip voluntarily is small. The detailed documentation of the circumstances under which Frobisher acquired his "new prey" three quarters of a century later (Sturtevant and Quinn, this volume) is at best evidence for a "special relationship" of a most peculiar kind between Europeans and Native Americans. Apart from the quasi-documentary purpose of these early kidnappings, the 16th century in particular saw a series of slave raids along the Atlantic coast of eastern North America as a result of which native people were brought to Europe. The same susceptibility to European diseases, which was causing large-scale depopulation in the New World was also leading to a higher mortality rate of those brought to the Old World and contributed to the quickly declining importance of Native American enslavement. Although involuntary trips to Europe remained far from uncommon in later periods (cp. the transportation of native prisoners of war to France - Dickason 1984:221-224), they became a distinct minority in the long run.

To say that the earliest captives brought to Europe were simply taken there as evidence is to oversimplify the matter. They were likewise to arouse the curiosity of the people back home, and to promote their enthusiasm for the colonial ventures. They were seen as sources of information on what was then still their country. Their likenesses were added to books of costumes and to allegorical representations of the luckily now four continents (by comparison, the idea of a fifth or even sixth continent never caught the imagination of Europe to the same extent; note also, that for most Europeans America is one continent rather than two). Those who could be brought to make themselves understood were interviewed in the hope of gaining new knowledge (e.g., Manteo and Wanchese in 1584 - Quinn 1955:127) or at least a confirmation of old prejudices (Sturtevant and Quinn, this volume).

On a less intellectual level, they were regarded as a source of entertainment and displayed for their physical abnormity - including tattooing and artificial head deformation - or the strangeness of their habits. Two Creek "princes," whose names recorded by contemporaneous newspaper accounts confirm their high status, were displayed in the 1720's by Captain John Pight, an Indian trader, militia officer, and all-purpose rascal from Charleston, primarily because of their extensive tattoos; they wore scarlet coats which they would flash open upon payment of the admission price to reveal the permanent images of suns, snakes, dragons, and various hieroglyphics (Sicul 1719-1731, 3:441; *Wienerisches Diarium*, 20 May 1722:[4r]). Others were made to perform scenes from their savage lives, juggle with rubber balls and logs as the Aztecs brought to Spain in 1528, paddle their kayaks as most of the Eskimos brought to Europe (Sturtevant and Quinn, Idiens, Wright, this volume), drill fire, throw their spears or shoot with their bows and arrows. Hadlock's Inuit (one genuine, one fake) performed a "marriage ceremony" (Wright, this volume). The Micmac of the 19th century were still telling the story about one of their own who had been taken to France shortly after first contact with Europeans, who was made to demonstrate his hunting skills in front of the King and his retinue: after having killed the deer in an enclosure surrounded by the spectators he not only butchered the animal and cooked the meat, but - at least according to the Micmac story - also ate it and finally defecated in front of the noble audience to complete the cycle and to register his disgust (Rand 1894:279).

Whereas these performances sometimes took a competitive turn and natives were pitched against the local boatsmen or runners (ultimately leading up to the development of professional sports in the 19th century, in which American Indian athletes like Deerfoot, the Seneca runner who also performed in England, played a minor role - Cumming 1981:61-62), the more common development was to stress the educational aspects of such displays. In the *Völkerschau*-type of exhibition characteristic of the 19th century, efforts were made to bring to life for Europeans the actual lifeways of peoples, by bringing whole families who would dwell in replicas of their native habitations and behave as aboriginal as possible. Whole classes of school-children were brought in for special performances as part of their geography courses, and anthropologists found it convenient to conduct field-work right out of their arm-chairs; in this connection, American troupes, such as Buffalo Bill's, were often considered less educational and more show-oriented than those promoted by Europeans (cp. Wright, King, Mulvey, Letay, Napier, Fiorentino, Clerici, Conrad, but especially Haberland, this volume). For the native performers in these productions, participation increasingly meant an opportunity for gainful employment, for their employers more often than not an opportunity to rip off both their employees and the public (see Hamell, Wright, this volume).

Rather than serve the education of the European public, some Native Americans were brought to Europe to receive themselves a European education. This was true of Don Luis, a native from the Chesapeake Bay area, who was brought to Spain in 1566 and was educated in the hope that he would later lead a group of missionaries to his home country (Lewis and Loomie 1953), as well as of others who were trained to become interpreters. Since the early 17th century, French missionaries would send children to France to be reared in the true civilization and later to become models for their savage brothers and sisters - at a time when boarding schools for Indians were not yet available (Dickason 1984:217-221). Even the English in Virginia, who were much less given to the idea of formal education for the Indians, sometimes argued that taking native servants to England would qualify their masters to collect funds reserved for Indian education (Kingsbury 1906-1935, 1:589; 2:532; McIlwaine 1924:477-478). The impulse at least to convert visiting natives remained strong throughout the 19th century. Bible societies and the local clergy tried their luck even with those who had come to Europe as show people (cp. Mulvey, this volume; Calloway 1979:310-312).

Beyond these very unspecific educational attempts, some possibilities for the specialized instruction of Native Americans remain to be noted. Several natives attended Roman Catholic seminaries in Rome to become priests, the most famous of them being William Blackbird, the Ottawa, whose mysterious murder in Italy aroused widespread interest (McKenney and Hall 1836-1844, 2:234-235; Blackbird 1887:35-44). In recent years, efforts have been made to offer Native American students an education in Austrian forestry training schools. The two Oglalas from Pine Ridge Reservation, who came over for a summer course in 1986, had to find that fiction had long ago overtaken fact: Almost a hundred years earlier Karl May had described in his novel *Winnetou* how the son of the Navajo chief by his German wife had been sent to the forestry school in Dresden.

The desire for information about the newly "discovered" people was not limited to Europeans. Native Americans were likewise curious to know more about the land whence the White men had hailed. In 1608, for example, Powhatan agreed to an exchange of hostages with the English, giving to Captain Newport "Namontacke his trusty servant, one of a shrewd subtill capacity" "to goe with him to England...,ye cause I assure me was to know our strength and countries condition" (Barbour 1969:392,199). Independent of the native leader's request for information, Namontack was made to appear as Powhatan's son, an Indian prince, by the Virginia Company in London. The Venetian ambassador was led to believe that Namontack was to negotiate "some agreement about that navigation," whereas his Spanish colleague was amused to note that "they have coached him that if he sees the King he is not to take off his hat... for I hold it for surer that he must be a very ordinary person" (Barbour 1969:163). Namontack was unable to report back to Powhatan. On his way back home he was killed by another Virginia Algonquian on the Bermudas. This may have been the reason why Powhatan sent another councilor, Uttamato-makin, when Pocahontas came to England in 1616, with instructions "to number the people here, and informe him well what wee were and our state. Arriuing at Plimoth, according to his directions, he got a long sticke, whereon by notches hee did thinke to haue kept the number of all the men hee could see, but he was quickly wearie of that taske" (Arber 1884:638,534). This story became an anecdote repeated by later visitors to Virginia when writing about Virginia's Indians. It is related to later similar accounts of tally-keeping by Native American visitors in Europe, including the Iowa Jim in Catlin's troupe (Mulvey, this volume).

Ever since Namontack's time numerous delegations of Native American politicians have come to Europe either goaded by the colonial authorities eager to convince their uncertain allies of the wealth and power of whichever Great White Father, or spurred by motives of their own, including simple curiosity or a desire for a redress of wrongs. Their list includes the famous Four Kings of Canada, the three Iroquois and one Mahican who became a smash hit in London society in 1710 (Bond 1952); Tomochichi, the Yamacraw chief, in 1734, and three Cherokee delegations in 1730, 1762, and 1764/5 (Timberlake 1948). As an example of the difficulties involved in drawing a line between visiting dignitaries and the desire of their European observers to have a good look, the case of the Cherokee chiefs of 1762 may be mentioned. Their landlord-despite the fact that "they are shy of Company, especially in a Crowd, by whom they avoid being seen as much as possible" - would admit visitors for money, who would then press "into the Indians dressing room, which gave them the highest disgust, these people having a particular aversion to being stared at while dressing or eating" (Timberlake 1948:134,141). Conversely, show Indians, like Red Shirt, would get into politicking once the occasion arose (cp. Napier, this volume).

After the American Revolution, at first only Canadian Indians continued to come to England for politics' sake - and they have continued to do so until the recent past, e.g., in connection with their protests over the first draft of the Canadian Constitution. Another reason for making the trip over the Atlantic arose after the creation of international organizations. such as the League of Nations (Rostkowski, this volume) and its successor, the United Nations, whose Geneva-based sub-organizations have become increasingly involved in attracting Native American spokespersons (Rostkowski 1984). Since the enormous publicity generated in Europe for contemporary Indian causes by the occupation of Wounded Knee in 1973, the American Indian Movement was not only able to establish itself as the sole and true representative of all Native Americans, but also to create a network of European support groups (Peyer, this volume) providing traveling Native American politicians with an organizational infrastructure. In the recent past, neo-traditionalist politicians have suceeded to break into AIM's former monopoly.

Other classes of Native American visitors have only sporadically made their appearances in Europe. In distinction from European soldiers and traders, few Indian warriors have come to Europe in the course of military conflicts before World War I. And although there was always some market for Native American products in the Old World, such items were rarely if ever sold directly by their producers. In connection with the human displays of the 19th century, however, the sale of drawings or carvings produced on the spot contributed to the visitors' income (cp. Wright, Haberland, this volume). Some European museums also have items in their collections ultimately purchased from native participants in such shows - not all of them as grisly as the pair of moccasins, formerly in the City Museum of Brunswick, which had belonged to an Indian of Buffalo Bill's troupe who had been run over by a train between Hanover and Brunswick - donated by the physician who had performed the autopsy.

Similarly, many more European artists (irrespective of the question of their styles and quality of their work) have sought contact with native peoples in America than vice versa. This fact is clearly related to the late integration of Native American arts into the Eurocentric domain of "Art." Oscar Howe, who came to Europe as a soldier, is sometimes described as having been one of the first to actively look at art (particularly the work of Picasso and other cubists) in Europe - a contention vehemently denied by Howe himself, who asserted that service in the army allowed him no time to go to museums, and that he wasn't interested in European modern art, anyway (Dockstader 1982:13).

The example of Oscar Howe indicates how often the normative power of images helps to shape the perception of reality: Howe simply had to be influenced by the cubists whose work he never saw in Europe. Similarly, the European public increasingly had certain expectations with regard to potential Native American visitors. Since the public's preconceived notions made the difference between success and failure, close approximation to the stereotype often decided who would be regarded as an Indian. As soon as the reality deviated measurably from the imagery, the reality was rejected as misleading (cp. Haberland, this volume). Distrust and disbelief were mutual in this respect. Very often, native people returning from Europe were thought to be liars when giving an account of their strange experiences: It happened as early as 1617 after the return of Uttamatomakin from England (Kingsbury 1906-1935, 3:73). Tribal politicians traveling to Europe these days are also sometimes not only suspected by their constituents of misappropriating funds but also of making up the better part of their reports.

The corollary of this mutual mistrust is that those whose appearance closely matched the imagery were and are always taken for real, even though they may be impostors. Not every case is as clear as that of William Augustus Bowles, a white American loyalist dressed as an Indian who managed to pass in 1791 in the upper crust of London's society as "commander-in-chief of the Creek and Cherokee nations" (Sturtevant 1979), or that of the second (or rather third) Mary Coonahnik, substituted by Captain Hadlock after the death of his genuine Eskimo woman and the suspicious behavior of the first impostor (Wright, this volume). In most cases, the fraud consisted more in the specific claims than in the basic assertion of Indianness. Sylvester Long, whose success in Europe was almost exclusively based on his book, *Long Lance*, although he did visit the Old World, would probably be regarded today as a Lumbee Indian - in his own day sticking to his actual ancestry would have made him a Black person, which is why he graduated from North Carolina Cherokee to Oklahoma Cherokee to Blackfoot Indian to Blackfoot Chief Buffalo Child Long Lance (Smith 1982). Whoever Big Chief White Horse Eagle really was, his "autobiography" as written by Edgar Schmidt-Pauli (1931) must be regarded as highly fictional. He found it profitable enough to travel Europe in the 1920's and 1930's adopting unsuspecting arm-chair anthropologists who (like the director of the ethnological museum in Vienna) also happened to be avid readers of Karl May's novels into his "tribe." Photographs show him sporting a feather bonnet, Navajo silver jewelry, and a button reading "Lions Club Pasadena," which must have been exotic enough for most Europeans.

These days, most of the doubtful characters in the Indian show business belong to the faculty of medicine. The selection that has reached Europe includes everyone from clever Native American business men with a keen eye for the weaknesses of the Old World, medical practitioners with, at best, vague claims to Indianness and no serious background in native medicine, to former medicine men who are trying to make up for their loss of clientele on the reservation (cp. Feest 1982, 1984). Their success is completely independent of their traditional knowledge as long as they can convince a public whose expectations have been deformed by the books of that latter-day Baron de Lahontan, Carlos Castaneda. Attempts have been made by various Native American organizations, sometimes themselves of dubious competence in the matter, to publish black-lists and warnings against "non-authorized" medicine men visiting Europe.

On closer look, some of the Indian spokespersons appearing in Europe lately may also have problems in establishing the legitimacy of their representation. None of them, however, could match the most flamboyant fake Indian politician to make his appearance in Europe: Edgardo Laplante a.k.a. Capo Cervo Bianco, coming to Italy in the wake of Deskaheh's mission to the League of Nations, claimed to be likewise on his way to Geneva to represent the Iroquois of up-state New York. While ostensibly waiting for his moneys to arrive from the United States, he not only managed to live off his believers' pockets, but also ravished an Austrian countess, and had an interview with Mussolini, before being taken to court and publicly defeathered.

There is only a narrow line of distinction between these fake visitors and the fictional visitors of European Indian literature. The Huron in Voltaire's *L'Ingénu* turns out to be a Frenchman after all, yet his unadulterated Huron straightforwardness wins him the hearts of the ladies and the fierce enmity of the government (Voltaire 1767).

Even more revealing is the account of Winnetou's visit to Dresden in the second volume of Karl May's *Satan und Ischariot*, written in 1894/5, not long after Buffalo Bill's troupe had been in Dresden. According to the novel, May (Old Shatterhand) is attending the weekly meeting of the local singing club, of which he is an honorary member, when two unannounced guests call at the door. One of them, "a strangely dark complexioned man..., with looks one could be afraid of," dressed in a dark suit, lifts his high-topped hat to expose his long, full hair "falling over his back like a cloak." Now even the sceptical singers need no further proof to accept the visitor as Winnetou. The Apache gentleman requests a performance of German music, and the choir is pleased to oblige. In the meantime Winnetou orders himself a beer, which "he likes to drink, but with moderation." Winnetou does not comment on the music, "but as I knew his personality, I knew quite well how deep an impression the German song had left on his soul." After coming home, May takes two peace pipes from the wall, and they smoke together while talking business. Unfortunately, Winnetou has to leave Dresden on the morning train, so nothing else is known about his reactions. Yet the message to the reader is clear enough. Someone who likes German songs and drinks beer with moderation must be a kindred soul.

A related document dealing with the encounter of the images and the image-maker is supplied by May's widow who published her recollections of the meeting between her husband and the Indians of Buffalo Bill's show. The Mays had gone to see the performance in Dresden (apparently in 1906) and upon Buffalo Bill's invitation, they visited behind the scenes before the show started. The writer, it must be remembered, by this time had never been to America, yet had claimed in writing to have performed all the incredible feats described in his novels (or "tales of travel") and to be able to speak and write "...the Indian languages of the Sioux, Apache, Comanche, Snakes, Utahs, Kiowas, next to the Ketchumany three South American dialects" (Wollschläger 1965:72). In Klara May's account, Karl was introduced to the Indians and immediately started to speak to them earnestly in a foreign, presumably indigenous language. After a while, Buffalo Bill interrupted the conversation which Klara had been unable to follow: "You are an idealist, my dear," he said, patting the writer's back, "the only valid law is that of the strong and clever!" (May 1918:203). To Klara it seemed as if the facial expression of the Indian(s) changed all of a sudden - "and hate seemed to flash in his beautiful dark eye."

Interaction

There can be no doubt that the Indians visiting Europe did have an impact on European attitudes about the native peoples of North America. It may be suspected, however, that it was mostly the illusion of reality conveyed by the visitors which helped to convince the public of the accuracy of its preconceived notions. In the absence of a sufficient body of Native American personal

620

documents that is unimpeachable in terms of its truly native perspective, the comparison of the Indians' views as reported on the occasion of different visits offers suggestive evidence for the pervasive nature of the stereotype (cp., e.g., the Indians' reaction to Europe in the case of the various groups accompanying George Catlin and Buffalo Bill in Mulvey's and Napier's papers, this volume). Notes taken by one of the Four Kings of Canada as published by an English journalist (and translated into German as observations of an East Indian prince in London) stand even more clearly in the literary tradition of exotic criticism of European society (Anonymous 1825). In addition to European projections, a certain amount of self-fulfilling prophecy may have been involved: being treated either as noble or as a savage could indeed have produced the predicted behavior. It is therefore hardly surprising to find the results of Native American-European contacts to be based almost exclusivly on notions existing in the minds of the Europeans.

A special relationship with "the Indians" was and is, in fact, claimed by several European nations for a number of related reasons. During the 17th century, English colonial propaganda tried to draw parallels between the ancestors of the English and the Native Virginians in their present wild and heathen state (cp. Feest 1967). But whereas this model only pointed at the Indians' potential to follow the English path to salvation, other models stressed the analogy of historical or existential experience as a basis for mutual understanding: It may be the belief in a genetic or linguistic relationship (such as in the case of the "Welsh Indians" as descended from Prince Madoc's crew), it may be the feeling of a shared pantheistic view of nature in the case of the Russians (Vaschenko, this volume), it may be the shared fate of a country divided, occupied, and deprived of self-determination in the case of the Poles (see Nowicka, this volume), it may be the shared struggle for national unity (or what was perceived to be such among the American Indians) also in the case of the Germans.

Fictional heroes in Euro-American literature whose superiority over others is ultimately derived from an ancestor sharing the author's nationality are paralleled by Euro-Indian authors claiming mixed-blood status themselves: Sat-Okh, the Shawnee-Pole (Vaschenko, this volume), or William Camus, the Iroquois-French (e.g., Camus 1978). The desire to become one with the "Indian" people is not only expressed in a brilliant short text by Franz Kafka, it is also manifestly present in the wish of European women to marry Indian men - a precondition for the rise of mixed-blood heroes, of course. Apart from a number of well-known cases, such as Luther Standing Bear marrying an Austrian countess, and both Oscar Howe and Scott Momaday marrying German women, a colleague at a museum in the Canadian Plains reports that every summer a significant number of German females come to ask for directions where to find an Indian to take for their husband.

Not so long ago, a couple in Germany was unable to convince the authori-

621

ties that it would be appropriate to name their baby girl "Winnetou" (they finally settled on "Louise"). Not only was there, however, precedent in German playwright Carl Zuckmayer who had succeeded in naming his daughter "Winnetou"; it might surprise outsiders that people would want to bestow the fictional Apache chief's name on female offspring at all. A partial explanation may be found in Arno Schmidt's (1963) convincing theory that the Old Shatterhand/Winnetou-relationship is nothing but a displacement of homoerotic drives.

The deeply felt identification of Europeans with "Indians" was obviously independent of the amount of actual and personal contact. Johann Georg Seume, an 18th century German poet and impressed British mercenary in the American Revolution sometimes stationed in Nova Scotia, would later refer to his "half-Huron personality" without ever having encountered any Hurons other than the noble Huron philosopher of Baron de Lahontan and his descendants (cp. Friedrichs 1984).

This sort of identification in turn provided the basis for all European attempts to emulate the "Indian" lifestyle. Given the nature of the underlying ideology, all such "Indian hobbyist" endeavors involve - at least in part - the living of fiction. This is not to deny that some roots of the hobbyist movement may be grounded on more solid facts; that 18th century British army officers stationed in North America, such as Sir John Caldwell or Guy Johnson would dress as Indians partly because they were in fact part Indian (Johnson). Caldwell certainly knew the native people of the Great Lakes region at close range, yet it is hard to interpret the portrait showing him in his Indian finery as an indication of an attempt to become a Native American. Though he probably just could have stayed with them, as others had done who were adopted into tribes and "turned native," Caldwell returned to England and died as an Englishman. The masquerade obviously served a more or less philosophical purpose, as a symbol of personal values selected from the vast supermarket of Native American cultures - yet different in intent from the masquerade of the American patriots of Boston Tea Party fame. Even a century before Caldwell, there were Englishmen who thought that dressing as Indians was the thing to do. William Byrd, the Virginian trader, in 1686 sent to John Clayton, an English clergyman who had recently visited Virginia, "an Indian habit for your boy, the best I could procure amongst our neighbour Indians" (Tinling 1977, 1:61). There were others in the 19th and 20th centuries in England and on the continent who would keep this tradition alive (cp. Taylor, Bolz, Conrad, this volume).

The fact that hobbyists are actually cultural transvestites is symbolically illustrated by the example of Clare Sheridan, Winston Churchill's cousin, who not only as an artist went to live on a reservation to produce portraits of Blood Indians, but also had photographs taken of herself dressed as an Indian *man* (B. Taylor 1984). It is supported by the observation that the top-notch

European hobbyist men produce high-quality American Indian crafts made in traditional native societies only by women - or transvestites.

Not all such transvestites are as successful as Archie Belaney, the Englishman who became Grey Owl, a figure even today widely regarded as the epitome of "the Indian" (cp. Vaschenko, this volume). A German review of his works published in 1936 stressed the fact that no white writer ever could hope to become so one with nature as Grey Owl did and that his call for a return to nature in the face of the ravages of World War I had found an unbelievably strong reception in Germany (a country, it may be remembered, that had just swept Hitler to power and was about to push the world into an even more devastating war) (Anonymous 1936). The traumatic war experience as a motivation to look for a counter-image to the real world in "Indianness" was not limited to Belaney. Especially the Vietnam War has led to the (re)discovery of an Indian identity by quite a few (Whites and) Native Americans, including some of the "Indian medicine men" touring Europe.

A history of the European Indian support group scene also remains to be written. One of its sources must clearly be seen in early and more broadly-based human rights movements (such as the Anti-Slavery Society or, more recently, Amnesty International). In its specific development relating to American Indians, however, it appears to be based on an identification quite similar to that of the hobbyists. This relationship is supported by observations on the number of political activists who as children very seriously played the Indian part in "Cowboys and Indians," and by a partial overlap in support group and hobbyist activities and publications (cp., e.g., Nowicka, this volume). There is a tendency by some support group people to look down upon the mere imitators of native life-ways as hopeless and socially irrelevant romantics. But many of the support activists, on the other hand, are hardly more realistic. In the course of making their interest in far-away people relevant in terms of their own culture and society, they necessarily run the danger of bending the facts to suit their needs.

In a way, the third branch developing out of the same root is European scholarly interest in the native populations of the Americas. Some "Indian specialists" in the academic field have grown out of the hobbyist movement or are active in support work. In any way, anthropologists are a possible source of information for either of the two other groups, although a certain amount of ritual anthropologist-beating has become fashionable in the wake of Vine Deloria's writings even by Europeans imitating Native Americans. But it is obvious that all academic approaches, no matter how innovative, are ultimately part of a European and not Native American tradition of looking at the world. Anthropology as propagated by Franz Boas explicitly makes use of the otherness of cultures that are studied by participant observation, and its practitioners are thus invited to identify with the people they study.

It is this otherness, which has also caused artists, musicians, or designers of fashion to look for interaction (more indirect than direct) with the indigenous peoples and cultures of North America (although admittedly this does not explain why it was American Indians and not Africans or Australians). The results of such interaction, however, exhibit a dramatic lack of specificity. The widespread Fascist fascination with the Indian is related to the widely accepted image of the Indian chief as a symbol of leadership and is aided by the notion of the pleasantly martial nature of the American savage. The American Indian Movement's (or some of its spokespersons') insistence on the importance of "being of one blood" and "Mother Earth" has struck familiar chords in various dubious nationalist groups all over Europe. At the same time, revisionist Marxist and anarchist fringe groups have equally found it possible to regard "Indian" societies as models. The feeling that nobody "was more of an Indian than Karl Marx" (Mariani, this volume) may not be shared by the members of the Polish Movement Friends of the American Indians (Nowicka, this volume), and yet Indians are cited as evidence in both cases.

What seems to characterize the European relationship to the "Indian" is the willingness to accept the expectation raised by the likewise European prediction that the Indian has a "message." People are willing to listen to the most absurd statements if validated by Indianness. On closer inspection, what to the European (and Euro-American) appears to be a counter-cultural battering ram derived from a brush with exotism (Rubin 1984), very often ultimately turns out to be a very much homegrown device embellished with the trappings of exotic stereotype. Non-European cultures may, after all, have derived a greater intellectual profit from the genuine multiculturalism resulting from their contacts with European civilization than vice versa - but this is already another question.

NOTE

Some of the specific materials on which parts of this paper are based were published since 1981 in the *American Indian Workshop Newsletter*, an informal publication edited by the present author. Thanks are due, once more, to all who contributed items or commentary to this publication which has meanwhile become part of the *European Review of Native American Studies*.

REFERENCES CITED

Anonymous
    1825   Die Inder Fürsten zu London. Archiv für Geschichte, Statistik, Literatur und Kunst 16:19-20. Wien.
    1936   Wäscha-kwonnesin, "Vater der Biber". Kosmos 33(5):171-174. Stuttgart.

Arber, Edward (ed.)
    1884   Captain John Smith Works 1608-1631. The English Scholar Library 16. Birmingham.

Barbour, Philip L.
    1969   The Jamestown Voyages Under the First Charter 1606-1609. 2 vols. Works issued by the Hakluyt Society, 2nd series, 136-137. Cambridge.

Bartel-Winkler, Lisa
    1924   Das Drama des sterbenden Volkes. Karl-May-Jahrbuch 7:338-343. Radebeul.

Berkhofer, Robert F., Jr.
    1978   The White Man's Indian. New York.

Billington, Ray Allen
    1981   Land of Savagery, Land of Promise. New York - London.

Bissell, Benjamin
    1925   The American Indian in English Literature of the Eighteenth Century. New York.

Blackbird, Andrew J.
    1887   History of the Ottawa and Chippewa Indians of Michigan; A Grammar of Their Language, and Personal and Family History of the Author. Ypsilanti.

Bond, Richmond P.
    1952   Queen Anne's American Kings. Oxford.

Calloway, Colin C.
    1979   The "Wild Indian Savages" in Leeds. Thoresby Society Miscellany 16(4):305-315.

Camus, William
    1978   Les Oiseaux de Feu et autres contes peaux-rouges. Folio Junior 44. Paris.

Chinard, Gilbert
    1934   L'Amérique et le rêve exotique. Paris.

Cumming, John
    1981   Runners and Walkers, a Nineteenth Century Sports Chronicle. Chicago.

Cumming, W.P., R.A. Skelton, and D.B. Quinn
    1971   The Discovery of North America. London.

Dickason, Olive Patricia
  1984   The Myth of the Savage and the Beginnings of French Colonialism in the Americas. Edmonton.
Dockstader, Frederick J.
  1982   Oscar Howe. A Retrospective Exhibition. Tulsa.
Feest, Christian F.
  1967   The Virginia Indian in Pictures, 1612-1624. The Smithsonian Journal of History 2(1):1-30. Washington.
  1982   Not Even Apples for the Austrians. American Indian Workshop Newsletter 10:1-2. Wien.
  1984   Black Elk Speaks. American Indian Workshop Newsletter 16:7-8. Wien.
Ferrero, Ernesto
  1980   Cervo Bianco. Romanzo. Milano.
Foreman, Carolyn T.
  1943   Indians Abroad: 1493-1938. Norman.
Friedrichs, Michael
  1984   "Meine halbhuronische Personalität": Seumes unfreiwilliger Kanada-Besuch 1782-83 und seine literarischen Folgen. Zeitschrift der Gesellschaft für Kanada-Studien 4(1):71-82. Neumünster.
Hunter, John Dunn
  1823   Memoirs of a Captivity among the Indians of North America. London.
Kaiser, Michaela
  1984   'Maybe we are brothers after all.' Bemerkungen zur Übersetzung. In: Rudolf Kaiser, Diese Erde ist uns heilig (Münster), 75-78.
Kingsbury, Susan Myra (ed.)
  1906-1935 The Records of the Virginia Company of London. 4 vols. Washington.
Kupperman, Karen O.
  1980   Settling with the Indians: The Meeting of English and Indian Cultures in America, 1580-1640. Totowa.
Lewis, Clifford M., and Albert J. Loomie
  1953   The Spanish Jesuit Mission in Virginia, 1570-1572. Chapel Hill.
McKenney, Thomas L., and James Hall
  1836-1844 History of the Indian Tribes of North America, with Biographical Sketches and Anecdotes of the Principal Chiefs. Philadelphia.
Malcorps, Johan
  1982   Van tomohawks en martenpalen: de Indiaan in het strip-verhaal. In: J. Van Vaerenbergh and A. Devos (eds.), Vanwege mijn rode huid (Infodok), 47-52.
May, Klara
  1918   Old Shatterhand and Buffalo Bill. Karl-May-Jahrbuch 1:201-205. Breslau.

Morison, Samuel Eliot
  1971   The European Discovery of America. The Northern Voyages A.D.500-1600. New York.
Musso, Franco
  1983   Indiani a fumetti. In: Sandra Solimano, I Cerchi del Mondo, Proposte di Lettura (Genova), 117-120.
Peckham, Howard, and Charles Gibson (eds.)
  1969   Attitudes of Colonial Powers Toward the American Indian. Salt Lake City.
Pompa, Cristina
  1983   L'immagine degli Indiani nel fumetto popolare italiano. In: Cultura Planetaria: Omologazione o Diversità? (Roma), 65-70.
Quinn, David Beers
  1955   The Roanoke Voyages, 1584-1590. Works issued by the Hakluyt Society, 2nd series, 104-105. London.
  1981   Sources for the Ethnography of Northeastern North America to 1611. National Museum of Man, Mercury Series, Canadian Ethnology Service, Paper 76. Ottawa.
Rand, Silas T.
  1894   Legends of the Micmacs. New York.
Rostkowski, Joëlle
  1984   The Struggle for Political Autonomy: U.S. Indians and the United Nations. In: Pieter Hovens (ed.), North American Indian Studies 2 (Göttingen), 86-98.
Rubin, William
  1984   Modernist Primitivism. In: William Rubin (ed.), "Primitivism" in 20th Century Art (New York), 1-81.
Schmidt, Arno
  1963   Sitara und der Weg dorthin. Karlsruhe.
Schmidt, Friedrich Wilhelm August
  1981   Einfalt und Natur. Berlin.
Schmidt-Pauli, Edgar von
  1931   We Indians. The Passion of a Great Race. Big Chief White Horse Eagle. London.
Sicul, Christoph Ernst
  1719-1731 Neo-Annalium Lipsiensium oder Des mit dem 1715ten Jahre Neuangehendes Leipziger Jahrbuchs Erste Probe ... 4 vols. Leipzig.
Smith, Donald B.
  1982   Long Lance. The True Story of an Impostor. Toronto.
Sturtevant, William C.
  1979   The Cherokee Frontier, the French Revolution, and William Augustus Bowles. In: Duane H. King (ed.), The Cherokee Indian Nation: A Troubled History (Knoxville), 61-91.

Taylor, Betty
    1984   Clare Sheridan (1885-1970). Hastings.
Timberlake, Henry
    1948   Lieut. Henry Timberlake's Memoirs 1756-1765. Marietta.
Tinling, Marion (ed.)
    1977   The Correspondence of the Three William Byrds of Westover,
            Virginia, 1684-1776. 2 vols. Charlottesville.
Voltaire
    1767   L'Ingénu. Genève.
Winkler, Lisa
    1918   Die Gestalten des Buches "Winnetou". Karl-May-Jahrbuch 2:366-383.
            Breslau.
Wollschläger, Hans
    1965   Karl May. Rowohlts Monographien 104. Reinbek.

INDEX OF NAMES

Prepared by Sylvia Kasprycki and Margit Krpata
with Christian F. Feest

642